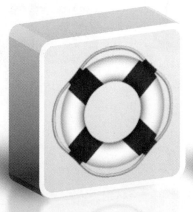

JAVA FOR EVERYONE

LATE OBJECTS

JAVA FOR EVERYONE

LATE OBJECTS

SECOND EDITION

Cay Horstmann

San Jose State University

WILEY

John Wiley & Sons, Inc.

VICE PRESIDENT AND EXECUTIVE PUBLISHER	Don Fowley
EXECUTIVE EDITOR	Beth Lang Golub
CONTENT MANAGER	Kevin Holm
SENIOR PRODUCTION EDITOR	John Curley
EXECUTIVE MARKETING MANAGER	Christopher Ruel
CREATIVE DIRECTOR	Harry Nolan
SENIOR DESIGNER	Madelyn Lesure
SENIOR PHOTO EDITOR	Lisa Gee
PRODUCT DESIGNER	Thomas Kulesa
CONTENT EDITOR	Wendy Ashenberg
EDITORIAL PROGRAM ASSISTANT	Elizabeth Mills
MEDIA SPECIALIST	Lisa Sabatini
PRODUCTION SERVICES	Cindy Johnson
COVER PHOTO	© TeeJe/Flickr/Getty Images

This book was set in Stempel Garamond by Publishing Services, and printed and bound by R.R. Donnelley & Sons Company. The cover was printed by R.R. Donnelley & Sons, Jefferson City.

This book is printed on acid-free paper. ∞

ISBN 978-1-118-06331-6 (Main Book)
ISBN 978-1-118-12941-8 (Binder-Ready Version)

Printed in the United States of America

10 9 8 7 6 5 4 3 2 1

PREFACE

This book is an introduction to Java and computer programming that focuses on the essentials—and on effective learning. The book is designed to serve a wide range of student interests and abilities and is suitable for a first course in programming for computer scientists, engineers, and students in other disciplines. No prior programming experience is required, and only a modest amount of high school algebra is needed. Here are the key features of this book:

Present fundamentals first.

The book takes a traditional route, first stressing control structures, methods, procedural decomposition, and arrays. Objects are used when appropriate in the early chapters. Students start designing and implementing their own classes in Chapter 8.

Guidance and worked examples help students succeed.

Beginning programmers often ask "How do I start? Now what do I do?" Of course, an activity as complex as programming cannot be reduced to cookbook-style instructions. However, step-by-step guidance is immensely helpful for building confidence and providing an outline for the task at hand. "Problem Solving" sections stress the importance of design and planning. "How To" guides help students with common programming tasks. Additional Worked Examples are available online.

Practice makes perfect.

Of course, programming students need to be able to implement nontrivial programs, but they first need to have the confidence that they can succeed. This book contains a substantial number of self-check questions at the end of each section. "Practice It" pointers suggest exercises to try after each section. And additional practice opportunities, including code completion questions, guided lab exercises, and skill-oriented multiple-choice questions are available online.

A visual approach motivates the reader and eases navigation.

Photographs present visual analogies that explain the nature and behavior of computer concepts. Step-by-step figures illustrate complex program operations. Syntax boxes and example tables present a variety of typical and special cases in a compact format. It is easy to get the "lay of the land" by browsing the visuals, before focusing on the textual material.

Visual features help the reader with navigation.

Focus on the essentials while being technically accurate.

An encyclopedic coverage is not helpful for a beginning programmer, but neither is the opposite— reducing the material to a list of simplistic bullet points. In this book, the essentials are presented in digestible chunks, with separate notes that go deeper into good practices or language features when the reader is ready for the additional information. You will not find artificial over-simplifications that give an illusion of knowledge.

New to This Edition

Problem Solving Strategies

This edition adds practical, step-by-step illustrations of techniques that can help students devise and evaluate solutions to programming problems. Introduced where they are most relevant, these strategies address barriers to success for many students. Strategies included are:

- Algorithm Design (with pseudocode)
- First Do It By Hand (doing sample calculations by hand)
- Flowcharts
- Test Cases
- Hand-Tracing
- Storyboards
- Reusable Methods
- Stepwise Refinement

- Adapting Algorithms
- Discovering Algorithms by Manipulating Physical Objects
- Tracing Objects (identifying state and behavior)
- Patterns for Object Data
- Thinking Recursively
- Estimating the Running Time of an Algorithm

Optional Science and Business Exercises

End-of-chapter exercises have been enhanced with problems from scientific and business domains. Designed to engage students, the exercises illustrate the value of programming in applied fields.

New and Reorganized Topics

All chapters were revised and enhanced to respond to user feedback and improve the flow of topics. Loop algorithms are now introduced explicitly in Chapter 4. Debugging is now introduced in a lengthy Video Example in Chapter 5. Additional array algorithms are presented in Chapter 6 and incorporated into the problem-solving sections. Input/output is moved up to Chapter 7, but the first two sections may be used to introduce simple text file processing sooner. New example tables, photos, and exercises appear throughout the book.

A Tour of the Book

Figure 1 shows the dependencies between the chapters and how topics are organized. The core material of the book is:

Chapter 1.   Introduction
Chapter 2.   Fundamental Data Types
Chapter 3.   Decisions
Chapter 4.   Loops
Chapter 5.   Methods
Chapter 6.   Arrays and Array Lists
Chapter 7.   Input/Output and Exception Handling

These chapters use a traditional approach. Objects are only used for input/output and string processing.

Three chapters cover object-oriented programming and design:

Chapter 8.   Objects and Classes
Chapter 9.   Inheritance
Chapter 12.   Object-Oriented Design ⊕ (on the Web)

Graphical user interfaces are presented in two chapters:

Chapter 10.   Graphical User Interfaces
Chapter 11.   Advanced User Interfaces ⊕ (on the Web)

The first of these chapters enables students to write programs with buttons, text components, and simple drawings. The second chapter covers layout management and additional user-interface components.

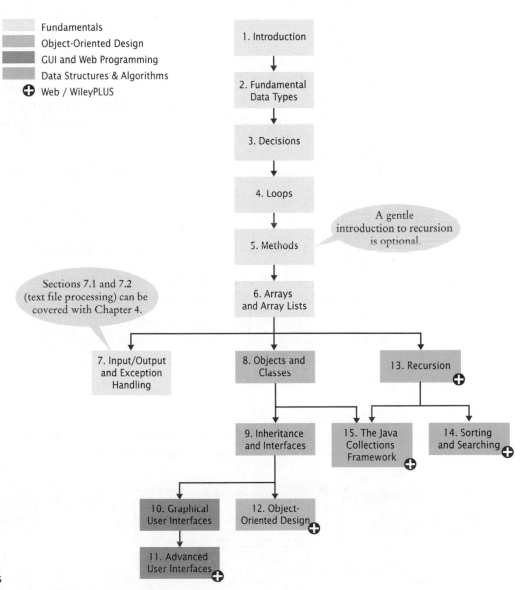

Figure 1
Chapter
Dependencies

To support a course that goes more deeply into algorithms and data structures, three additional chapters are available in electronic form on the Web and in WileyPLUS:

Chapter 13.   Recursion ✚
Chapter 14.   Sorting and Searching ✚
Chapter 15.   The Java Collections Framework ✚

Any chapters can be incorporated into a custom print version of this text; ask your Wiley sales representative for details.

Appendices   The first four appendices are in the book; the remainder on the Web.

A. The Basic Latin and Latin-1 Subsets of Unicode
B. Java Operator Summary
C. Java Reserved Word Summary
D. The Java Library
E. Java Syntax Summary
F. HTML Summary

G. Tool Summary
H. Javadoc Summary
I. Number Systems
J. Bit and Shift Operations
K. UML Summary
L. Java Language Coding Guidelines

Many instructors find it highly beneficial to require a consistent style for all assignments. If the style guide in Appendix L conflicts with instructor sentiment or local customs, however, it is available in electronic form so that it can be modified.

Web Resources

This book is complemented by a complete suite of online resources and a robust WileyPLUS course. Go to www.wiley.com/college/horstmann to visit the online companion sites, which include

- Source code for all examples in the book.
- Worked Examples that apply the problem-solving steps in the book to other realistic examples.
- Video Examples in which the author explains the steps he is taking and shows his work as he solves a programming problem.
- Lab exercises that apply chapter concepts (with solutions for instructors only).
- Lecture presentation slides (in PowerPoint format).
- Solutions to all review and programming exercises (for instructors only).
- A test bank that focuses on skills, not just terminology (for instructors only).

WileyPLUS

WileyPLUS is an online teaching and learning environment that integrates the digital textbook with instructor and student resources. See pages xv–xvi for details.

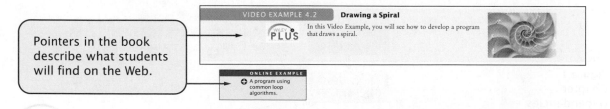

Pointers in the book describe what students will find on the Web.

VIDEO EXAMPLE 4.2   **Drawing a Spiral**

In this Video Example, you will see how to develop a program that draws a spiral.

ONLINE EXAMPLE
✚ A program using common loop algorithms.

A Walkthrough of the Learning Aids

The pedagogical elements in this book work together to focus on and reinforce key concepts and fundamental principles of programming, with additional tips and detail organized to support and deepen these fundamentals. In addition to traditional features, such as chapter objectives and a wealth of exercises, each chapter contains elements geared to today's visual learner.

Throughout each chapter, **margin notes** show where new concepts are introduced and provide an outline of key ideas.

Additional **online example code** provides complete programs for students to run and modify.

Annotated **syntax boxes** provide a quick, visual overview of new language constructs.

Annotations explain required components and point to more information on common errors or best practices associated with the syntax.

Analogies to everyday objects are used to explain the nature and behavior of concepts such as variables, data types, loops, and more.

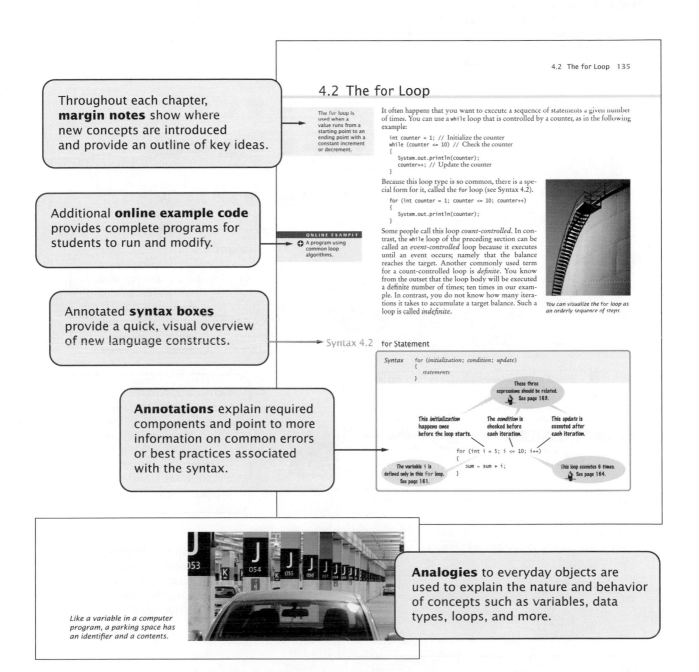

4.2 The for Loop 135

4.2 The for Loop

The for loop is used when a value runs from a starting point to an ending point with a constant increment or decrement.

It often happens that you want to execute a sequence of statements a given number of times. You can use a while loop that is controlled by a counter, as in the following example:

```
int counter = 1; // Initialize the counter
while (counter <= 10) // Check the counter
{
    System.out.println(counter);
    counter++; // Update the counter
}
```

Because this loop type is so common, there is a special form for it, called the for loop (see Syntax 4.2).

```
for (int counter = 1; counter <= 10; counter++)
{
    System.out.println(counter);
}
```

ONLINE EXAMPLE
A program using common loop algorithms.

Some people call this loop *count-controlled*. In contrast, the while loop of the preceding section can be called an *event-controlled* loop because it executes until an event occurs; namely that the balance reaches the target. Another commonly used term for a count-controlled loop is *definite*. You know from the outset that the loop body will be executed a definite number of times; ten times in our example. In contrast, you do not know how many iterations it takes to accumulate a target balance. Such a loop is called *indefinite*.

You can visualize the for loop as an orderly sequence of steps

Syntax 4.2   for Statement

Syntax   for (*initialization*; *condition*; *update*)
{
    statements
}

These three expressions should be related. See page 165.

This *initialization* happens once before the loop starts.

The *condition* is checked before each iteration.

This *update* is executed after each iteration.

```
for (int i = 5; i <= 10; i++)
{
    sum = sum + i;
}
```

The variable i is defined only in this for loop. See page 161.

This loop executes 6 times. See page 164.

Like a variable in a computer program, a parking space has an identifier and a contents.

Memorable photos reinforce analogies and help students remember the concepts.

A recipe for a fruit pie may say to use any kind of fruit. Here, "fruit" is an example of a parameter variable. Apples and cherries are examples of arguments.

Problem Solving sections teach techniques for generating ideas and evaluating proposed solutions, often using pencil and paper or other artifacts. These sections emphasize that most of the planning and problem solving that makes students successful happens away from the computer.

6.5   Problem Solving: Discovering Algorithms by Manipulating Physical Objects   277

Now how does that help us with our problem, switching the first and the second half of the array?

Let's put the first coin into place, by swapping it with the fifth coin. However, as Java programmers, we will say that we swap the coins in positions 0 and 4:

Next, we swap the coins in positions 1 and 5:

HOW TO 1.1   **Describing an Algorithm with Pseudocode**

This is the first of many "How To" sections in this book that give you step-by-step procedures for carrying out important tasks in developing computer programs.

Before you are ready to write a program in Java, you need to develop an algorithm—a method for arriving at a solution for a particular problem. Describe the algorithm in pseudocode: a sequence of precise steps formulated in English.

For example, consider this problem: You have the choice of buying two cars. One is more fuel efficient than the other, but also more expensive. You know the price and fuel efficiency (in miles per gallon, mpg) of both cars. You plan to keep the car for ten years. Assume a price of $4 per gallon of gas and usage of 15,000 miles per year. You will pay cash for the car and not worry about financing costs. Which car is the better deal?

Step 1   Determine the inputs and outputs.

In our sample problem, we have these inputs:
- **purchase price1** and **fuel efficiency1**, the price and fuel efficiency (in mpg) of the first car
- **purchase price2** and **fuel efficiency2**, the price and fuel efficiency of the second car

We simply want to know which car is the better buy. That is the desired output.

How To guides give step-by-step guidance for common programming tasks, emphasizing planning and testing. They answer the beginner's question, "Now what do I do?" and integrate key concepts into a problem-solving sequence.

WORKED EXAMPLE 1.1   **Writing an Algorithm for Tiling a Floor**

This Worked Example shows how to develop an algorithm for laying tile in an alternating pattern of colors.

Worked Examples and **Video Examples** apply the steps in the How To to a different example, showing how they can be used to plan, implement, and test a solution to another programming problem.

Table 1 Variable Declarations in Java	
Variable Name	Comment
int cans = 6;	Declares an integer variable and initializes it with 6.
int total = cans + bottles;	The initial value need not be a constant. (Of course, cans and bottles must have been previously declared.)
⊘ bottles = 1;	**Error:** The type is missing. This statement is not a declaration but an assignment of a new value to an existing variable—see Section 2.1.4.
⊘ int bottles = "10";	**Error:** You cannot initialize a number with a string.
int bottles;	Declares an integer variable without initializing it. This can be a cause for errors—see Common Error 2.1 on page 37.
int cans, bottles;	Declares two integer variables in a single statement. In this book, we will declare each variable in a separate statement.

Example tables support beginners with multiple, concrete examples. These tables point out common errors and present another quick reference to the section's topic.

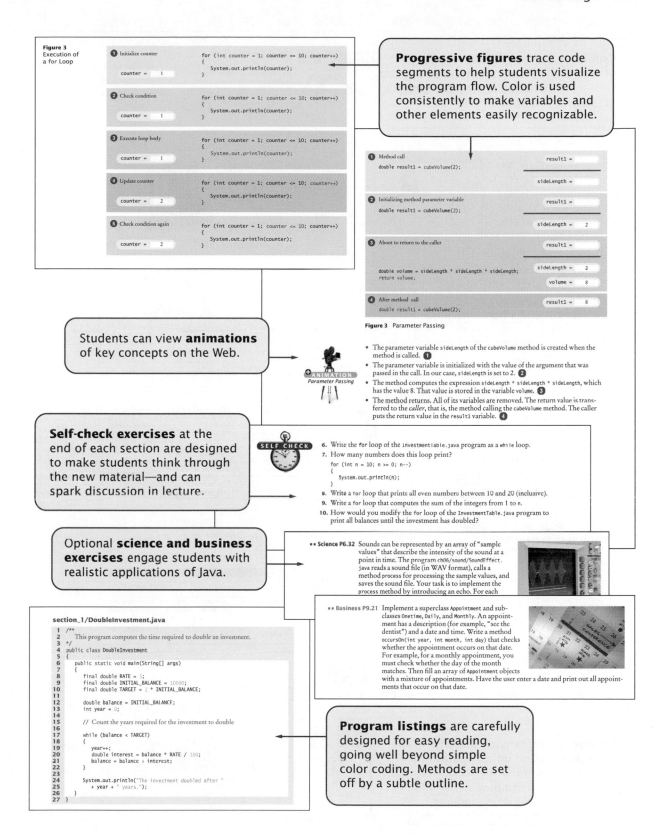

Figure 3
Execution of
a for Loop

❶ Initialize counter

```
for (int counter = 1; counter <= 10; counter++)
{
    System.out.println(counter);
}
```

counter = 1

❷ Check condition

```
for (int counter = 1; counter <= 10; counter++)
{
    System.out.println(counter);
}
```

counter = 1

❸ Execute loop body

```
for (int counter = 1; counter <= 10; counter++)
{
    System.out.println(counter);
}
```

counter = 1

❹ Update counter

```
for (int counter = 1; counter <= 10; counter++)
{
    System.out.println(counter);
}
```

counter = 2

❺ Check condition again

```
for (int counter = 1; counter <= 10; counter++)
{
    System.out.println(counter);
}
```

counter = 2

Progressive figures trace code segments to help students visualize the program flow. Color is used consistently to make variables and other elements easily recognizable.

❶ Method call

```
double result1 = cubeVolume(2);
```

result1 =

sideLength =

❷ Initializing method parameter variable

```
double result1 = cubeVolume(2);
```

result1 =

sideLength = 2

❸ About to return to the caller

```
double volume = sideLength * sideLength * sideLength;
return volume;
```

result1 =

sideLength = 2

volume = 8

❹ After method call

```
double result1 = cubeVolume(2);
```

result1 = 8

Figure 3 Parameter Passing

Students can view **animations** of key concepts on the Web.

ANIMATION
Parameter Passing

- The parameter variable sideLength of the cubeVolume method is created when the method is called. ❶
- The parameter variable is initialized with the value of the argument that was passed in the call. In our case, sideLength is set to 2. ❷
- The method computes the expression sideLength * sideLength * sideLength, which has the value 8. That value is stored in the variable volume. ❸
- The method returns. All of its variables are removed. The return value is transferred to the *caller*, that is, the method calling the cubeVolume method. The caller puts the return value in the result1 variable. ❹

Self-check exercises at the end of each section are designed to make students think through the new material—and can spark discussion in lecture.

SELF CHECK

6. Write the for loop of the InvestmentTable.java program as a while loop.
7. How many numbers does this loop print?
   ```
   for (int n = 10; n >= 0; n--)
   {
       System.out.println(n);
   }
   ```
8. Write a for loop that prints all even numbers between 10 and 20 (inclusive).
9. Write a for loop that computes the sum of the integers from 1 to n.
10. How would you modify the for loop of the InvestmentTable.java program to print all balances until the investment has doubled?

Optional **science and business exercises** engage students with realistic applications of Java.

•• Science P6.32 Sounds can be represented by an array of "sample values" that describe the intensity of the sound at a point in time. The program ch06/sound/SoundEffect.java reads a sound file (in WAV format), calls a method process for processing the sample values, and saves the sound file. Your task is to implement the process method by introducing an echo. For each

•• Business P9.21 Implement a superclass Appointment and subclasses Onetime, Daily, and Monthly. An appointment has a description (for example, "see the dentist") and a date and time. Write a method occursOn(int year, int month, int day) that checks whether the appointment occurs on that date. For example, for a monthly appointment, you must check whether the day of the month matches. Then fill an array of Appointment objects with a mixture of appointments. Have the user enter a date and print out all appointments that occur on that date.

section_1/DoubleInvestment.java

```
1  /**
2     This program computes the time required to double an investment.
3  */
4  public class DoubleInvestment
5  {
6     public static void main(String[] args)
7     {
8        final double RATE = 5;
9        final double INITIAL_BALANCE = 10000;
10       final double TARGET = 2 * INITIAL_BALANCE;
11
12       double balance = INITIAL_BALANCE;
13       int year = 0;
14
15       // Count the years required for the investment to double
16
17       while (balance < TARGET)
18       {
19          year++;
20          double interest = balance * RATE / 100;
21          balance = balance + interest;
22       }
23
24       System.out.println("The investment doubled after "
25          + year + " years.");
26    }
27 }
```

Program listings are carefully designed for easy reading, going well beyond simple color coding. Methods are set off by a subtle outline.

Common Errors describe the kinds of errors that students often make, with an explanation of why the errors occur, and what to do about them.

Common Error 6.4

Length and Size

Unfortunately, the Java syntax for determining the number of elements in an array, an array list, and a string is not at all consistent. It is a common error to confuse these. You just have to remember the correct syntax for every data type.

Data Type	Number of Elements
Array	a.length
Array list	a.size()
String	a.length()

Programming Tips explain good programming practices, and encourage students to be more productive with tips and techniques such as hand-tracing.

Programming Tip 3.5

Hand-Tracing

A very useful technique for understanding whether a program works correctly is called *hand-tracing*. You simulate the program's activity on a sheet of paper. You can use this method with pseudocode or Java code.

Get an index card, a cocktail napkin, or whatever sheet of paper is within reach. Make a column for each variable. Have the program code ready. Use a marker, such as a paper clip, to mark the current statement. In your mind, execute statements one at a time. Every time the value of a variable changes, cross out the old value and write the new value below the old one.

For example, let's trace the tax program with the data from the program run on page 102. In lines 15 and 16, tax1 and tax2 are initialized to 0.

Hand-tracing helps you understand whether a program works correctly.

```
 8  public static void main(String[] args)
 9  {
10     final double RATE1 = 0.10;
11     final double RATE2 = 0.25;
12     final double RATE1_SINGLE_LIMIT = 32000;
13     final double RATE1_MARRIED_LIMIT = 64000;
14
15     double tax1 = 0;
16     double tax2 = 0;
17
```

tax1	tax2	income	marital status
0	0		

In lines 22 and 25, income and maritalStatus are initialized by input statements.

```
20     Scanner in = new Scanner(System.in);
21     System.out.print("Please enter your income: ");
22     double income = in.nextDouble();
23
24     System.out.print("Please enter s for single, m for married: ");
25     String maritalStatus = in.next();
```

tax1	tax2	income	marital status
0	0	$0000	m

Special Topics present optional topics and provide additional explanation of others. New features of Java 7 are also covered in these notes.

Special Topic 7.2

● ONLINE EXAMPLE
A program that demonstrates how to use a file chooser.

File Dialog Boxes

In a program with a graphical user interface, you will want to use a file dialog box (such as the one shown in the figure below) whenever the users of your program need to pick a file. The JFileChooser class implements a file dialog box for the Swing user-interface toolkit.

The JFileChooser class has many options to fine-tune the display of the dialog box, but in its most basic form it is quite simple: Construct a file chooser object; then call the showOpenDialog or showSaveDialog method. Both methods show the same dialog box, but the button for selecting a file is labeled "Open" or "Save", depending on which method you call.

For better placement of the dialog box on the screen, you can specify the user-interface component over which to pop up the dialog box. If you don't care where the dialog box pops up, you can simply pass null. The showOpenDialog and showSaveDialog methods return either JFileChooser.APPROVE_OPTION, if the user has chosen a file, or JFileChooser.CANCEL_OPTION, if the user canceled the selection. If a file was chosen, then you call the getSelectedFile method to obtain a File object that describes the file. Here is a complete example:

```
JFileChooser chooser = new JFileChooser();
Scanner in = null;
if (chooser.showOpenDialog(null) == JFileChooser.APPROVE_OPTION)
{
    File selectedFile = chooser.getSelectedFile();
    in = new Scanner(selectedFile);
    . . .
}
```

Call with showOpenDialog method

Random Facts provide historical and social information on computing—for interest and to fulfill the "historical and social context" requirements of the ACM/IEEE curriculum guidelines.

Random Fact 4.1 The First Bug

According to legend, the first bug was found in the Mark II, a huge electromechanical computer at Harvard University. It really was caused by a bug—a moth was trapped in a relay switch. Actually, from the note that the operator left in the log book next to the moth (see the figure), it appears as if the term "bug" had already been in active use at the time.

The pioneering computer scientist Maurice Wilkes wrote, "Somehow, at the Moore School and afterwards, one had always assumed there would be no particular difficulty in getting programs right. I can remember the exact instant in time at which it dawned on me that a great part of my future life would be spent finding mistakes in my own programs."

The First Bug

WileyPLUS

WileyPLUS is an online environment that supports students and instructors. This book's WileyPLUS course can complement the printed text or replace it altogether.

For Students

Different learning styles, different levels of proficiency, different levels of preparation—each student is unique. WileyPLUS empowers all students to take advantage of their individual strengths.

Integrated, multi-media resources—including audio and visual exhibits and demonstration problems—encourage active learning and provide multiple study paths to fit each student's learning preferences.

- Worked Examples apply the problem-solving steps in the book to another realistic example.
- Video Examples present the author explaining the steps he is taking and showing his work as he solves a programming problem.
- Animations of key concepts allow students to replay dynamic explanations that instructors usually provide on a whiteboard.

Self-assessments are linked to relevant portions of the text. Students can take control of their own learning and practice until they master the material.

- Practice quizzes can reveal areas where students need to focus.
- "Learn by doing" lab exercises can be assigned for self-study or for use in the lab.
- "Code completion" questions enable students to practice programming skills by filling in small code snippets and getting immediate feedback.

For Instructors

WileyPLUS includes all of the instructor resources found on the companion site, and more.

WileyPLUS gives you tools for identifying those students who are falling behind, allowing you to intervene accordingly, without having to wait for them to come to office hours.

- Practice quizzes for pre-reading assessment, self-quizzing, or additional practice can be used as-is or modified for your course needs.
- Multi-step laboratory exercises can be used in lab or assigned for extra student practice.

WileyPLUS simplifies and automates student performance assessment, making assignments, and scoring student work.

- An extensive set of multiple-choice questions for quizzing and testing have been developed to focus on skills, not just terminology.
- "Code completion" questions can also be added to online quizzes.
- Solutions to all review and programming exercises are provided.

To order *Java for Everyone, 2e,* with its WileyPLUS course for your students, use ISBN 978-1-118-28614-2.

With WileyPLUS ...

Students can read the book online and take advantage of searching and cross-linking.

Instructors can assign drill-and-practice questions to check that students did their reading and grasp basic concepts.

Students can practice programming by filling in small code snippets and getting immediate feedback.

Students can play and replay dynamic explanations of concepts and program flow.

Students can watch and listen as the author solves a problem step-by-step.

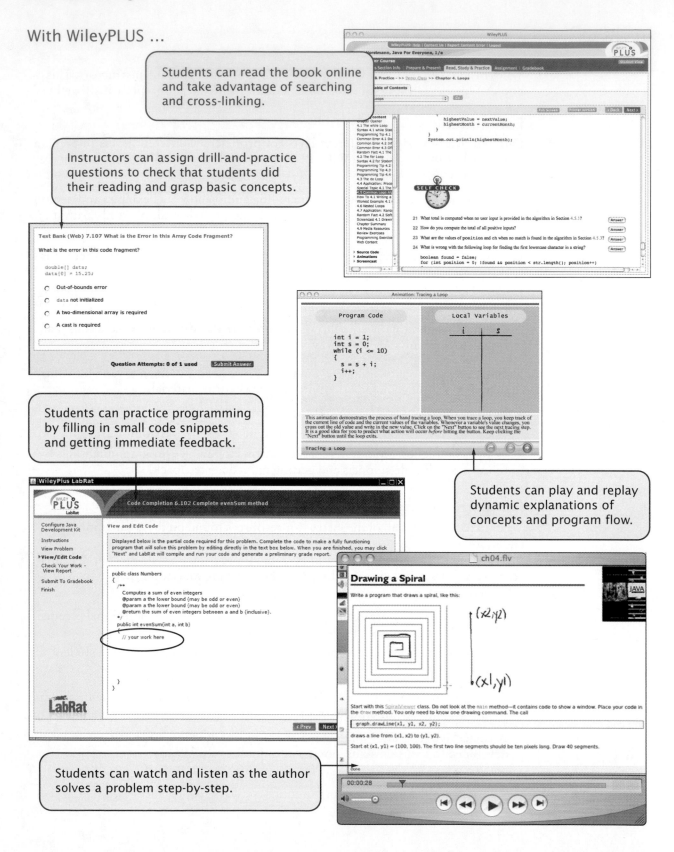

Acknowledgments

Many thanks to Beth Lang Golub, Don Fowley, Elizabeth Mills, Thomas Kulesa, Wendy Ashenberg, Lisa Gee, Andre Legaspi, Kevin Holm, and John Curley at John Wiley & Sons, and Vickie Piercey at Publishing Services for their help with this project. An especially deep acknowledgment and thanks goes to Cindy Johnson for her hard work, sound judgment, and amazing attention to detail.

I am grateful to Jose Cordova, *University of Louisiana, Monroe*, Amitava Karmaker, *University of Wisconsin, Stout*, Khaled Mansour, *Washtenaw Community College*, Patricia McDermott-Wells, *Florida International University*, Brent Seales, *University of Kentucky*, Donald Smith, *Columbia College*, and David Woolbright, *Columbus State University*, for their excellent work on the supplemental material. Thank you also to Jose-Arturo Mora-Soto, Jesica Rivero-Espinosa, and Julio-Angel Cano-Romero of the University of Madrid for their contribution of business exercises.

Many thanks to the individuals who provided feedback, reviewed the manuscript, made valuable suggestions, and brought errors and omissions to my attention. They include:

Lynn Aaron, *SUNY Rockland Community College*

Karen Arlien, *Bismarck State College*

Jay Asundi, *University of Texas, Dallas*

Eugene Backlin, *DePaul University*

William C. Barge, *Trine University*

Bruce J. Barton, *Suffolk County Community College*

Sanjiv K. Bhatia, *University of Missouri, St. Louis*

Anna Bieszczad, *California State University, Channel Islands*

Jackie Bird, *Northwestern University*

Eric Bishop, *Northland Pioneer College*

Paul Bladek, *Edmonds Community College*

Paul Logasa Bogen II, *Texas A&M University*

Irene Bruno, *George Mason University*

Paolo Bucci, *Ohio State University*

Joe Burgin, *College of Southern Maryland*

Robert P. Burton, *Brigham Young University*

Leonello Calabresi, *University of Maryland University College*

Martine Ceberio, *University of Texas, El Paso*

Uday Chakraborty, *University of Missouri, St. Louis*

Xuemin Chen, *Texas Southern University*

Haiyan Cheng, *Willamette University*

Chakib Chraibi, *Barry University*

Ta-Tao Chuang, *Gonzaga University*

Vincent Cicirello, *Richard Stockton College*

Mark Clement, *Brigham Young University*

Gerald Cohen, *St. Joseph's College*

Rebecca Crellin, *Community College of Allegheny County*

Leslie Damon, *Vermont Technical College*

Geoffrey D. Decker, *Northern Illinois University*

Khaled Deeb, *Barry University, School of Adult and Continuing Education*

Akshaye Dhawan, *Ursinus College*

Julius Dichter, *University of Bridgeport*

Mike Domaratzki, *University of Manitoba*

Philip Dorin, *Loyola Marymount University*

Anthony J. Dos Reis, *SUNY New Paltz*

Elizabeth Drake, *Santa Fe College*

Tom Duffy, *Norwalk Community College*

Michael Eckmann, *Skidmore College*

Sander Eller, *California State Polytechnic University, Pomona*

Amita Engineer, *Valencia Community College*

Dave Evans, *Pasadena Community College*

James Factor, *Alverno College*

Chris Fietkiewicz, *Case Western Reserve University*

Terrell Foty, *Portland Community College*

Valerie Frear, *Daytona State College*

Ryan Garlick, *University of North Texas*

Aaron Garrett, *Jacksonville State University*

Stephen Gilbert, *Orange Coast College*

Peter van der Goes, *Rose State College*

Billie Goldstein, *Temple University*

Michael Gourley, *University of Central Oklahoma*

Grigoriy Grinberg, *Montgomery College*

Linwu Gu, *Indiana University*

Bruce Haft, *Glendale Community College*

Nancy Harris, *James Madison University*

Allan M. Hart, *Minnesota State University, Mankato*

Ric Heishman, *George Mason University*

Guy Helmer, *Iowa State University*

Katherin Herbert, *Montclair State University*

Rodney Hoffman, *Occidental College*

May Hou, *Norfolk State University*

John Houlihan, *Loyola University*

Andree Jacobson, *University of New Mexico*

Eric Jiang, *University of San Diego*

Christopher M. Johnson, *Guilford College*

Jonathan Kapleau, *New Jersey Institute of Technology*

Amitava Karmaker, *University of Wisconsin, Stout*

Rajkumar Kempaiah, *College of Mount Saint Vincent*

Mugdha Khaladkar, *New Jersey Institute of Technology*

Julie King, *Sullivan University, Lexington*

Samuel Kohn, *Touro College*

April Kontostathis, *Ursinus College*

Ron Krawitz, *DeVry University*

Debbie Lamprecht, *Texas Tech University*

Jian Lin, *Eastern Connecticut State University*

Hunter Lloyd, *Montana State University*

Cheng Luo, *Coppin State University*

Kelvin Lwin, *University of California, Merced*

Frank Malinowski, *Dalton College*

John S. Mallozzi, *Iona College*

Kenneth Martin, *University of North Florida*

Deborah Mathews, *J. Sargeant Reynolds Community College*

Louis Mazzucco, *State University of New York at Cobleskill and Excelsior College*

Drew McDermott, *Yale University*

Hugh McGuire, *Grand Valley State University*

Michael L. Mick, *Purdue University, Calumet*

Jeanne Milostan, *University of California, Merced*

Sandeep Mitra, *SUNY Brockport*

Kenrick Mock, *University of Alaska Anchorage*

Namdar Mogharreban, *Southern Illinois University*

Shamsi Moussavi, *Massbay Community College*

Nannette Napier, *Georgia Gwinnett College*

Tony Tuan Nguyen, *De Anza College*

Michael Ondrasek, *Wright State University*

K. Palaniappan, *University of Missouri*

James Papademas, *Oakton Community College*

Gary Parker, *Connecticut College*

Jody Paul, *Metropolitan State College of Denver*

Mark Pendergast, *Florida Gulf Coast University*

James T. Pepe, *Bentley University*

Jeff Pittges, *Radford University*

Tom Plunkett, *Virginia Tech*

Linda L. Preece, *Southern Illinois University*

Vijay Ramachandran, *Colgate University*

Craig Reinhart, *California Lutheran University*

Jonathan Robinson, *Touro College*

Chaman Lal Sabharwal, *Missouri University of Science & Technology*

Namita Sarawagi, *Rhode Island College*

Ben Schafer, *University of Northern Iowa*

Walter Schilling, *Milwaukee School of Engineering*

Jeffrey Paul Scott, *Blackhawk Technical College*

Amon Seagull, *NOVA Southeastern University*

Linda Seiter, *John Carroll University*

Kevin Seppi, *Brigham Young University*

Ricky J. Sethi, *UCLA, USC ISI, and DeVry University*

Ali Shaykhian, *Florida Institute of Technology*

Lal Shimpi, *Saint Augustine's College*

Victor Shtern, *Boston University*

Rahul Simha, *George Washington University*

Jeff Six, *University of Delaware*

Donald W. Smith, *Columbia College*

Peter Spoerri, *Fairfield University*

David R. Stampf, *Suffolk County Community College*

Peter Stanchev, *Kettering University*

Stu Steiner, *Eastern Washington University*

Robert Strader, *Stephen F. Austin State University*

David Stucki, *Otterbein University*

Jeremy Suing, *University of Nebraska, Lincoln*

Dave Sullivan, *Boston University*

Vaidy Sunderam, *Emory University*

Hong Sung, *University of Central Oklahoma*

Monica Sweat, *Georgia Tech University*

Joseph Szurek, *University of Pittsburgh, Greensburg*

Jack Tan, *University of Wisconsin*

Cynthia Tanner, *West Virginia University*

Russell Tessier, *University of Massachusetts, Amherst*

Krishnaprasad Thirunarayan, *Wright State University*

Megan Thomas, *California State University, Stanislaus*

Timothy Urness, *Drake University*

Eliana Valenzuela-Andrade, *University of Puerto Rico at Arecibo*

Tammy VanDeGrift, *University of Portland*

Philip Ventura, *Broward College*

David R. Vineyard, *Kettering University*

Qi Wang, *Northwest Vista College*

Jonathan Weissman, *Finger Lakes Community College*

Reginald White, *Black Hawk Community College*

Ying Xie, *Kennesaw State University*

Arthur Yanushka, *Christian Brothers University*

Chen Ye, *University of Illinois, Chicago*

Wook-Sung Yoo, *Fairfield University*

Bahram Zartoshty, *California State University, Northridge*

Frank Zeng, *Indiana Wesleyan University*

Hairong Zhao, *Purdue University Calumet*

Stephen Zilora, *Rochester Institute of Technology*

A special thank you to our class testers for this edition:

Nancy Harris and the students of James Madison University

Mohammed Morovati and the students of College of DuPage

Chris Taylor and the students of Milwaukee School of Engineering

and the first edition:

Michael Ondrasek and the students of Wright State University

Irene Bruno and the students of George Mason University

Cihan Varol and the students of Sam Houston University

David Vineyard and the students of Kettering University

Cindy Tanner and the students of West Virginia University

Andrew Juraszek and the students of J. Sargeant Reynolds Community College

Daisy Sang and the students of California State Polytechnic University, Pomona

Dawn McKinney and the students of University of South Alabama

Nadimpalli Mahadev and the students of Fitchburg State College

Robert Burton and the students of Brigham Young University

Nancy Harris and the students of James Madison University

Tim Weale, Paolo Bucci, and the students of Ohio State University

CONTENTS

PREFACE **vii**
SPECIAL FEATURES **xxvi**

CHAPTER 1   INTRODUCTION   **1**

1.1   Computer Programs   **2**
1.2   The Anatomy of a Computer   **3**
1.3   The Java Programming Language   **5**
1.4   Becoming Familiar with Your Programming Environment   **8**
1.5   Analyzing Your First Program   **12**
1.6   Errors   **15**
1.7   Problem Solving: Algorithm Design   **16**

CHAPTER 2   FUNDAMENTAL DATA TYPES   **29**

2.1   Variables   **30**
2.2   Arithmetic   **41**
2.3   Input and Output   **48**
2.4   Problem Solving: First Do It By Hand   **57**
2.5   Strings   **59**

CHAPTER 3   DECISIONS   **81**

3.1   The if Statement   **82**
3.2   Comparing Numbers and Strings   **88**
3.3   Multiple Alternatives   **96**
3.4   Nested Branches   **100**
3.5   Problem Solving: Flowcharts   **105**
3.6   Problem Solving: Test Cases   **108**
3.7   Boolean Variables and Operators   **111**
3.8   Application: Input Validation   **116**

CHAPTER 4   LOOPS   **139**

4.1   The while Loop   **140**
4.2   Problem Solving: Hand-Tracing   **147**
4.3   The for Loop   **150**
4.4   The do Loop   **156**

4.5   Application: Processing Sentinel Values   **158**
4.6   Problem Solving: Storyboards   **162**
4.7   Common Loop Algorithms   **165**
4.8   Nested Loops   **172**
4.9   Application: Random Numbers and Simulations   **176**

CHAPTER 5   METHODS   **201**

5.1   Methods as Black Boxes   **202**
5.2   Implementing Methods   **204**
5.3   Parameter Passing   **207**
5.4   Return Values   **210**
5.5   Methods Without Return Values   **214**
5.6   Problem Solving: Reusable Methods   **215**
5.7   Problem Solving: Stepwise Refinement   **218**
5.8   Variable Scope   **225**
5.9   Recursive Methods (Optional)   **228**

CHAPTER 6   ARRAYS AND ARRAY LISTS   **249**

6.1   Arrays   **250**
6.2   The Enhanced for Loop   **257**
6.3   Common Array Algorithms   **258**
6.4   Using Arrays with Methods   **268**
6.5   Problem Solving: Adapting Algorithms   **272**
6.6   Problem Solving: Discovering Algorithms by Manipulating Physical Objects   **279**
6.7   Two-Dimensional Arrays   **282**
6.8   Array Lists   **289**

CHAPTER 7   INPUT/OUTPUT AND EXCEPTION HANDLING   **317**

7.1   Reading and Writing Text Files   **318**
7.2   Text Input and Output   **323**
7.3   Command Line Arguments   **330**
7.4   Exception Handling   **337**
7.5   Application: Handling Input Errors   **347**

CHAPTER 8   OBJECTS AND CLASSES   **361**

8.1   Object-Oriented Programming   **362**
8.2   Implementing a Simple Class   **364**

8.3 Specifying the Public Interface of a Class **367**
8.4 Designing the Data Representation **371**
8.5 Implementing Instance Methods **372**
8.6 Constructors **375**
8.7 Testing a Class **380**
8.8 Problem Solving: Tracing Objects **386**
8.9 Problem Solving: Patterns for Object Data **388**
8.10 Object References **395**
8.11 Static Variables and Methods **400**

CHAPTER 9 INHERITANCE AND INTERFACES **415**

9.1 Inheritance Hierarchies **416**
9.2 Implementing Subclasses **420**
9.3 Overriding Methods **424**
9.4 Polymorphism **430**
9.5 Object: The Cosmic Superclass **441**
9.6 Interface Types **448**

CHAPTER 10 GRAPHICAL USER INTERFACES **465**

10.1 Frame Windows **466**
10.2 Events and Event Handling **470**
10.3 Processing Text Input **481**
10.4 Creating Drawings **487**

CHAPTER 11 ADVANCED USER INTERFACES (WEB ONLY) ✚

11.1 Layout Management
11.2 Choices
11.3 Menus
11.4 Exploring the Swing Documentation
11.5 Using Timer Events for Animations
11.6 Mouse Events

CHAPTER 12 OBJECT-ORIENTED DESIGN (WEB ONLY) ✚

12.1 Classes and Their Responsibilities
12.2 Relationships Between Classes
12.3 Application: Printing an Invoice
12.4 Packages

✚ Available online in WileyPLUS and at www.wiley.com/college/horstmann.

CHAPTER 13   RECURSION   (WEB ONLY) ✚

13.1 Triangle Numbers Revisited
13.2 Problem Solving: Thinking Recursively
13.3 Recursive Helper Methods
13.4 The Efficiency of Recursion
13.5 Permutations
13.6 Mutual Recursion
13.7 Backtracking

CHAPTER 14   SORTING AND SEARCHING   (WEB ONLY) ✚

14.1 Selection Sort
14.2 Profiling the Selection Sort Algorithm
14.3 Analyzing the Performance of the Selection Sort Algorithm
14.4 Merge Sort
14.5 Analyzing the Merge Sort Algorithm
14.6 Searching
14.7 Problem Solving: Estimating the Running Time of an Algorithm
14.8 Sorting and Searching in the Java Library

CHAPTER 15   THE JAVA COLLECTIONS FRAMEWORK   (WEB ONLY) ✚

15.1 An Overview of the Collections Framework
15.2 Linked Lists
15.3 Sets
15.4 Maps
15.5 Stacks, Queues, and Priority Queues
15.6 Stack and Queue Applications

APPENDICES

APPENDIX A   THE BASIC LATIN AND LATIN-1 SUBSETS OF UNICODE   **507**
APPENDIX B   JAVA OPERATOR SUMMARY   **511**
APPENDIX C   JAVA RESERVED WORD SUMMARY   **513**
APPENDIX D   THE JAVA LIBRARY   **515**
APPENDIX E   JAVA SYNTAX SUMMARY   ✚
APPENDIX F   HTML SUMMARY   ✚
APPENDIX G   TOOL SUMMARY   ✚
APPENDIX H   JAVADOC SUMMARY   ✚

✚ Available online in WileyPLUS and at www.wiley.com/college/horstmann.

APPENDIX I   NUMBER SYSTEMS   ✪

APPENDIX J   BIT AND SHIFT OPERATIONS   ✪

APPENDIX K   UML SUMMARY   ✪

APPENDIX L   JAVA LANGUAGE CODING GUIDELINES   ✪

GLOSSARY   **547**

INDEX   **559**

CREDITS   **585**

ALPHABETICAL LIST OF SYNTAX BOXES

Arrays   251
Array Lists   290
Assignment   34

Cast   44
Catching Exceptions   341
Comparisons   89
Constant Declaration   35
Constructor with Superclass Initializer   430
Constructors   376

for Statement   152

if Statement   84
Input Statement   49
Instance Methods   373
Instance Variable Declaration   365
Interface Types   449

Java Program   13

Static Method Declaration   205
Subclass Declaration   422

The Enhanced for Loop   258
The finally Clause   344
The instanceof Operator   445
The throws Clause   343
Throwing an Exception   338
Two-Dimensional Array Declaration   283

while Statement   141

Variable Declaration   31

✪ Available online in WileyPLUS and at www.wiley.com/college/horstmann.

CHAPTER	Common Errors	How Tos and Worked Examples
1 Introduction	Omitting Semicolons — 14 Misspelling Words — 16	Describing an Algorithm with Pseudocode — 20 Compiling and Running a Program ⊕ Writing an Algorithm for Tiling a Floor ⊕ Dividing Household Expenses ⊕
2 Fundamental Data Types	Using Undeclared or Uninitialized Variables — 37 Overflow — 38 Roundoff Errors — 38 Unintended Integer Division — 46 Unbalanced Parentheses — 46	Using Integer Division ⊕ Carrying out Computations — 54 Computing the Cost of Stamps ⊕ Computing Travel Time ⊕ Computing Distances on Earth ⊕
3 Decisions	A Semicolon After the if Condition — 86 Exact Comparison of Floating-Point Numbers — 91 Using == to Compare Strings — 92 The Dangling else Problem — 104 Combining Multiple Relational Operators — 113 Confusing && and || Conditions — 114	Implementing an if Statement — 93 Extracting the Middle ⊕ Computing the Plural of an English Word ⊕ The Genetic Code ⊕
4 Loops	Don't Think "Are We There Yet?" — 144 Infinite Loops — 145 Off-by-One Errors — 145	Evaluating a Cell Phone Plan ⊕ Writing a Loop — 169 Credit Card Processing ⊕ Manipulating the Pixels in an Image ⊕ Drawing a Spiral ⊕

⊕ Available online in WileyPLUS and at www.wiley.com/college/horstmann.

Programming Tips

Special Topics

Random Facts

Backup Copies   11

Choose Descriptive Variable
  Names   38
Do Not Use Magic Numbers   39
Spaces in Expressions   47
Use the API Documentation   53

Brace Layout   86
Always Use Braces   86
Tabs   87
Avoid Duplication in Branches   88
Hand-Tracing   103
Make a Schedule and Make
  Time for Unexpected
  Problems   109

Use for Loops for Their
  Intended Purpose Only   155
Choose Loop Bounds That
  Match Your Task   155
Count Iterations   156

Numeric Types in Java   39
Big Numbers   40
Combining Assignment
  and Arithmetic   47
Instance Methods and
  Static Methods   64
Using Dialog Boxes for Input
  and Output   65

The Conditional Operator   87
Lexicographic Ordering
  of Strings   92
The switch Statement   99
Enumeration Types   105
Logging   110
Short-Circuit Evaluation
  of Boolean Operators   114
De Morgan's Law   115

The Loop-and-a-Half Problem
  and the break Statement   160
Redirection of Input
  and Output   161
Drawing Graphical Shapes   179

The ENIAC and the Dawn
  of Computing   5

The Pentium
  Floating-Point Bug   48
International Alphabets
  and Unicode   66

The Denver Airport
  Luggage Handling System   95
Artificial Intelligence   119

The First Bug   146
Software Piracy   182

➕ Available online in WileyPLUS and at www.wiley.com/college/horstmann.

CHAPTER	Common Errors	How Tos and Worked Examples
5 Methods	Trying to Modify Arguments 209 Missing Return Value 212	Implementing a Method 212 Generating Random Passwords ⊕ Calculating a Course Grade ⊕ Debugging ⊕ Thinking Recursively 231 Fully Justified Text ⊕
6 Arrays and Array Lists	Bounds Errors 255 Uninitialized Arrays 255 Underestimating the Size of a Data Set 267 Length and Size 299	Working with Arrays 275 Rolling the Dice ⊕ Removing Duplicates from an Array ⊕ A World Population Table ⊕ Game of Life ⊕
7 Input/Output and Exception Handling	Backslashes in File Names 321 Constructing a Scanner with a String 321	Computing a Document's Readability ⊕ Processing Text Files 333 Analyzing Baby Names ⊕ Detecting Accounting Fraud ⊕
8 Objects and Classes	Forgetting to Initialize Object References in a Constructor 378 Trying to Call a Constructor 379 Declaring a Constructor as void 379	Implementing a Class 382 Implementing a Bank Account Class ⊕ Paying Off a Loan ⊕ Modeling a Robot Escaping from a Maze ⊕

⊕ Available online in WileyPLUS and at www.wiley.com/college/horstmann.

Programming Tips	Special Topics	Random Facts

Programming Tips		Special Topics		Random Facts	
Method Comments	207			The Explosive Growth of Personal Computers	232
Do Not Modify Parameter Variables	209				
Keep Methods Short	223				
Tracing Methods	223				
Stubs	224				
Use Arrays for Sequences of Related Items	256	Sorting with the Java Library	267	An Early Internet Worm	256
Reading Exception Reports	274	Binary Search	267		
		Methods with a Variable Number of Parameters	272		
		Two-Dimensional Arrays with Variable Row Lengths	288		
		Multidimensional Arrays	289		
		The Diamond Syntax in Java 7	299		
Throw Early, Catch Late	345	Reading Web Pages	321	Encryption Algorithms	336
Do Not Squelch Exceptions	345	File Dialog Boxes	321	The Ariane Rocket Incident	347
Do Not Use catch and finally in the Same try Statement	346	Reading and Writing Binary Data	322		
		Regular Expressions	330		
		Automatic Resource Management in Java 7	346		
All Data Variables Should Be Private; Most Methods Should Be Public	374	The javadoc Utility	370	Electronic Voting Machines	394
		Overloading	380	Open Source and Free Software	402
		Calling One Constructor from Another	399		

➕ Available online in WileyPLUS and at www.wiley.com/college/horstmann.

CHAPTER	Common Errors	How Tos and Worked Examples
9 Inheritance and Interfaces	Replicating Instance Variables from the Superclass 423 Confusing Super- and Subclasses 424 Accidental Overloading 428 Forgetting to Use super When Invoking a Superclass Method 429 Don't Use Type Tests 446 Forgetting to Declare Implementing Methods as Public 453	Developing an Inheritance Hierarchy 436 Implementing an Employee Hierarchy for Payroll Processing ✚ Building a Discussion Board ✚ Drawing Geometric Shapes ✚
10 Graphical User Interfaces	Modifying Parameter Types in the Implementing Method 478 Forgetting to Attach a Listener 478 Forgetting to Repaint 496 By Default, Components Have Zero Width and Height 497	Drawing Graphical Shapes 497 Coding a Bar Chart Creator ✚ Solving Crossword Puzzles ✚
11 Advanced User Interfaces (WEB ONLY) ✚		Laying Out a User Interface ✚ Programming a Working Calculator ✚ Adding Mouse and Keyboard Support to the Bar Chart Creator ✚ Designing a Baby Naming Program ✚
12 Object-Oriented Design (WEB ONLY) ✚		Using CRC Cards and UML Diagrams in Program Design ✚ Simulating an Automatic Teller Machine ✚

✚ Available online in WileyPLUS and at www.wiley.com/college/horstmann.

Programming Tips	Special Topics	Random Facts

Use a Single Class for Variation in Values, Inheritance for Variation in Behavior 420	Calling the Superclass Constructor 429	
	Dynamic Method Lookup and the Implicit Parameter 433	
	Abstract Classes 434	
	Final Methods and Classes 435	
	Protected Access 436	
	Inheritance and the toString Method 446	
	Inheritance and the equals Method 447	
	Constants in Interfaces 453	
	Function Objects 454	
Don't Use a Frame as a Listener 478	Adding the main Method to the Frame Class 470	
	Local Inner Classes 479	
	Anonymous Inner Classes 480	
Use a GUI Builder ⊕	Keyboard Events ⊕	
	Event Adapters ⊕	
Make Parallel Arrays into Arrays of Objects ⊕	Attributes and Methods in UML Diagrams ⊕	
Consistency ⊕	Multiplicities ⊕	
	Aggregation, Association, and Composition ⊕	

⊕ Available online in WileyPLUS and at www.wiley.com/college/horstmann.

CHAPTER	Common Errors	How Tos and Worked Examples
13 Recursion (WEB ONLY) ✚	Infinite Recursion ✚	Finding Files ✚ Towers of Hanoi ✚
14 Sorting and Searching (WEB ONLY) ✚	The compareTo Method Can Return Any Integer, Not Just –1, 0, and 1 ✚	Enhancing the Insertion Sort Algorithm ✚
15 The Java Collections Framework (WEB ONLY) ✚		Choosing a Collection ✚ Word Frequency ✚ Simulating a Queue of Waiting Customers ✚ Building a Table of Contents ✚

✚ Available online in WileyPLUS and at www.wiley.com/college/horstmann.

Programming Tips	Special Topics	Random Facts
		The Limits of Computation ⊕
	Oh, Omega, and Theta ⊕	The First Programmer ⊕
	Insertion Sort ⊕	
	The Quicksort Algorithm ⊕	
	The Parameterized Comparable Interface ⊕	
	The Comparator Interface ⊕	
Use Interface References to Manipulate Data Structures ⊕		Standardization ⊕
		Reverse Polish Notation ⊕

⊕ Available online in WileyPLUS and at www.wiley.com/college/horstmann.

CHAPTER 1

INTRODUCTION

CHAPTER GOALS

To learn about computers
and programming

To compile and run your first Java program

To recognize compile-time and run-time errors

To describe an algorithm with pseudocode

CHAPTER CONTENTS

1.1 COMPUTER PROGRAMS 2

1.2 THE ANATOMY OF A COMPUTER 3

Random Fact 1.1: The ENIAC and the Dawn of
Computing 5

**1.3 THE JAVA PROGRAMMING
LANGUAGE** 5

**1.4 BECOMING FAMILIAR WITH YOUR
PROGRAMMING ENVIRONMENT** 8

Programming Tip 1.1: Backup Copies 11
Video Example 1.1: Compiling and Running
a Program ✚

**1.5 ANALYZING YOUR FIRST
PROGRAM** 12

Syntax 1.1: Java Program 13
Common Error 1.1: Omitting Semicolons 14

1.6 ERRORS 15
Common Error 1.2: Misspelling Words 16

**1.7 PROBLEM SOLVING:
ALGORITHM DESIGN** 16

How To 1.1: Describing an Algorithm with
Pseudocode 20
Worked Example 1.1: Writing an Algorithm for
Tiling a Floor ✚
Video Example 1.2: Dividing Household
Expenses ✚

Just as you gather tools, study a project, and make a plan for tackling it, in this chapter you will gather up the basics you need to start learning to program. After a brief introduction to computer hardware, software, and programming in general, you will learn how to write and run your first Java program. You will also learn how to diagnose and fix programming errors, and how to use pseudocode to describe an algorithm—a step-by-step description of how to solve a problem—as you plan your computer programs.

1.1 Computer Programs

Computers execute very basic instructions in rapid succession.

You have probably used a computer for work or fun. Many people use computers for everyday tasks such as electronic banking or writing a term paper. Computers are good for such tasks. They can handle repetitive chores, such as totaling up numbers or placing words on a page, without getting bored or exhausted.

The flexibility of a computer is quite an amazing phenomenon. The same machine can balance your checkbook, lay out your term paper, and play a game. In contrast, other machines carry out a much narrower range of tasks; a car drives and a toaster toasts. Computers can carry out a wide range of tasks because they execute different programs, each of which directs the computer to work on a specific task.

A computer program is a sequence of instructions and decisions.

The computer itself is a machine that stores data (numbers, words, pictures), interacts with devices (the monitor, the sound system, the printer), and executes programs. A **computer program** tells a computer, in minute detail, the sequence of steps that are needed to fulfill a task. The physical computer and peripheral devices are collectively called the **hardware**. The programs the computer executes are called the **software**.

Today's computer programs are so sophisticated that it is hard to believe that they are composed of extremely primitive instructions. A typical instruction may be one of the following:

- Put a red dot at a given screen position.
- Add up two numbers.
- If this value is negative, continue the program at a certain instruction.

The computer user has the illusion of smooth interaction because a program contains a huge number of such instructions, and because the computer can execute them at great speed.

Programming is the act of designing and implementing computer programs.

The act of designing and implementing computer programs is called **programming**. In this book, you will learn how to program a computer—that is, how to direct the computer to execute tasks.

To write a computer game with motion and sound effects or a word processor that supports fancy fonts and pictures is a complex task that requires a team of many highly-skilled programmers. Your first programming efforts will be more mundane. The concepts and skills you learn in this book form an important foundation, and you should not be disappointed if your first programs do not rival the sophisticated software that is familiar to you. Actually, you will find that there is an immense thrill even in simple programming tasks. It is an amazing experience to see the computer precisely and quickly carry out a task that would take you hours of drudgery, to make small changes in a program that lead to immediate improvements, and to see the computer become an extension of your mental powers.

SELF CHECK

1. What is required to play music on a computer?
2. Why is a CD player less flexible than a computer?
3. What does a computer user need to know about programming in order to play a video game?

1.2 The Anatomy of a Computer

To understand the programming process, you need to have a rudimentary understanding of the building blocks that make up a computer. We will look at a personal computer. Larger computers have faster, larger, or more powerful components, but they have fundamentally the same design.

At the heart of the computer lies the **central processing unit (CPU)** (see Figure 1). The inside wiring of the CPU is enormously complicated. For example, the Intel Core processor (a popular CPU for personal computers at the time of this writing) is composed of several hundred million structural elements, called *transistors*.

The CPU performs program control and data processing. That is, the CPU locates and executes the program instructions; it carries out arithmetic operations such as addition, subtraction, multiplication, and division; it fetches data from external memory or devices and places processed data into storage.

There are two kinds of storage. **Primary storage** is made from memory chips: electronic circuits that can store data, provided they are supplied with electric power. **Secondary storage**, usually a **hard disk** (see Figure 2), provides slower and less expensive storage that persists without electricity. A hard disk consists of rotating platters, which are coated with a magnetic material, and read/write heads, which can detect and change the magnetic flux on the platters.

The computer stores both data and programs. They are located in secondary storage and loaded into memory when the program starts. The program then updates the data in memory and writes the modified data back to secondary storage.

> The central processing unit (CPU) performs program control and data processing.

> Storage devices include memory and secondary storage.

Figure 1 Central Processing Unit

Figure 2 A Hard Disk

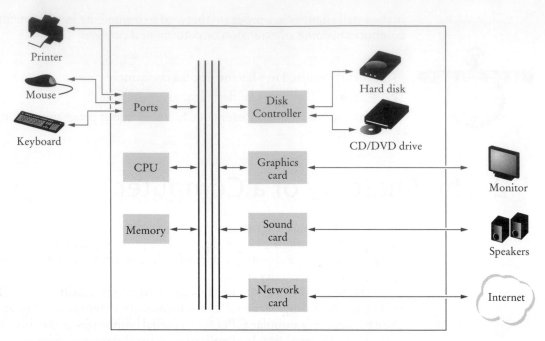

Figure 3 Schematic Design of a Personal Computer

To interact with a human user, a computer requires peripheral devices. The computer transmits information (called *output*) to the user through a display screen, speakers, and printers. The user can enter information (called *input*) for the computer by using a keyboard or a pointing device such as a mouse.

Some computers are self-contained units, whereas others are interconnected through **networks**. Through the network cabling, the computer can read data and programs from central storage locations or send data to other computers. To the user of a networked computer, it may not even be obvious which data reside on the computer itself and which are transmitted through the network.

Figure 3 gives a schematic overview of the architecture of a personal computer. Program instructions and data (such as text, numbers, audio, or video) are stored on the hard disk, on a compact disk (or DVD), or elsewhere on the network. When a program is started, it is brought into memory, where the CPU can read it. The CPU reads the program one instruction at a time. As directed by these instructions, the CPU reads data, modifies it, and writes it back to memory or the hard disk. Some program instructions will cause the CPU to place dots on the display screen or printer or to vibrate the speaker. As these actions happen many times over and at great speed, the human user will perceive images and sound. Some program instructions read user input from the keyboard or mouse. The program analyzes the nature of these inputs and then executes the next appropriate instruction.

SELF CHECK

4. Where is a program stored when it is not currently running?
5. Which part of the computer carries out arithmetic operations, such as addition and multiplication?

Practice It Now you can try these exercises at the end of the chapter: R1.2, R1.3.

Random Fact 1.1 The ENIAC and the Dawn of Computing

The ENIAC (electronic numerical integrator and computer) was the first usable electronic computer. It was designed by J. Presper Eckert and John Mauchly at the University of Pennsylvania and was completed in 1946—two years before transistors were invented. The computer was housed in a large room and consisted of many cabinets containing about 18,000 vacuum tubes (see Figure 4). Vacuum tubes burned out at the rate of several tubes per day. An attendant with a shopping cart full of tubes constantly made the rounds and replaced defective ones. The computer was programmed by connecting wires on panels. Each wiring configuration would set up the computer for a particular problem. To have the computer work on a different problem, the wires had to be replugged.

Work on the ENIAC was supported by the U.S. Navy, which was interested in computations of ballistic tables that would give the trajectory of a projectile, depending on the wind resistance, initial velocity, and atmospheric conditions. To compute the trajectories, one must find the numerical solutions of certain differential equations; hence the name "numerical integrator". Before machines like the ENIAC were developed, humans did this kind of work, and until the 1950s the word "computer" referred to these people. The ENIAC was later used for peaceful purposes, such as the tabulation of U.S. Census data.

Figure 4   The ENIAC

1.3 The Java Programming Language

In order to write a computer program, you need to provide a sequence of instructions that the CPU can execute. A computer program consists of a large number of simple CPU instructions, and it is tedious and error-prone to specify them one by one. For that reason, **high-level programming languages** have been created. In a high-level language, you specify the actions that your program should carry out. A **compiler** translates the high-level instructions into the more detailed instructions required by the CPU. Many different programming languages have been designed for different purposes.

In 1991, a group led by James Gosling and Patrick Naughton at Sun Microsystems designed a programming language, code-named "Green", for use in

James Gosling

consumer devices, such as intelligent television "set-top" boxes. The language was designed to be simple, secure, and usable for many different processor types. No customer was ever found for this technology.

Gosling recounts that in 1994 the team realized, "We could write a really cool browser. It was one of the few things in the client/server mainstream that needed some of the weird things we'd done: architecture neutral, real-time, reliable, secure." Java was introduced to an enthusiastic crowd at the SunWorld exhibition in 1995, together with a browser that ran **applets**—Java code that can be located anywhere on the Internet. Figure 5 shows a typical example of an applet.

Since then, Java has grown at a phenomenal rate. Programmers have embraced the language because it is easier to use than its closest rival, C++. In addition, Java has a rich **library** that makes it possible to write portable programs that can bypass proprietary operating systems—a feature that was eagerly sought by those who wanted to be independent of those proprietary systems and was bitterly fought by their vendors. A "micro edition" and an "enterprise edition" of the Java library allow Java programmers to target hardware ranging from smart cards and cell phones to the largest Internet servers.

Because Java was designed for the Internet, it has two attributes that make it very suitable for beginners: safety and portability.

The safety features of the Java language make it possible to run Java programs in a browser without fear that they might attack your computer. As an added benefit, these features also help you to learn the language faster. When you make an error that results in unsafe behavior, you receive an accurate error report.

The other benefit of Java is portability. The same Java program will run, without change, on Windows, UNIX, Linux, or Macintosh. In order to achieve portability, the Java compiler does not translate Java programs directly into CPU instructions. Instead, compiled Java programs contain instructions for the Java **virtual machine**,

Java was originally designed for programming consumer devices, but it was first successfully used to write Internet applets.

Java was designed to be safe and portable, benefiting both Internet users and students.

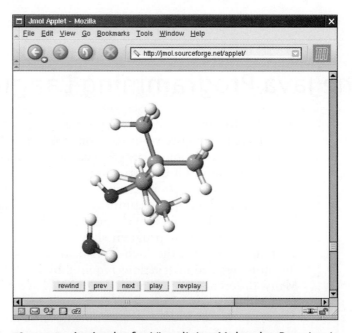

Figure 5   An Applet for Visualizing Molecules Running in a Browser Window (http://jmol.sourceforge.net/)

Java programs are distributed as instructions for a virtual machine, making them platform-independent.

a program that simulates a real CPU. Portability is another benefit for the beginning student. You do not have to learn how to write programs for different platforms.

At this time, Java is firmly established as one of the most important languages for general-purpose programming as well as for computer science instruction. However, although Java is a good language for beginners, it is not perfect, for three reasons.

Because Java was not specifically designed for students, no thought was given to making it really simple to write basic programs. A certain amount of technical machinery is necessary in Java to write even the simplest programs. This is not a problem for professional programmers, but it can be a nuisance for beginning students. As you learn how to program in Java, there will be times when you will be asked to be satisfied with a preliminary explanation and wait for more complete detail in a later chapter.

Java has been extended many times during its life—see Table 1. In this book, we assume that you have Java version 5 or later.

Java has a very large library. Focus on learning those parts of the library that you need for your programming projects.

Finally, you cannot hope to learn all of Java in one course. The Java language itself is relatively simple, but Java contains a vast set of *library packages* that are required to write useful programs. There are packages for graphics, user-interface design, cryptography, networking, sound, database storage, and many other purposes. Even expert Java programmers cannot hope to know the contents of all of the packages—they just use those that they need for particular projects.

Using this book, you should expect to learn a good deal about the Java language and about the most important packages. Keep in mind that the central goal of this book is not to make you memorize Java minutiae, but to teach you how to think about programming.

Table 1 Java Versions		
Version	Year	Important New Features
1.0	1996	
1.1	1997	Inner classes
1.2	1998	Swing, Collections framework
1.3	2000	Performance enhancements
1.4	2002	Assertions, XML support
5	2004	Generic classes, enhanced for loop, auto-boxing, enumerations, annotations
6	2006	Library improvements
7	2011	Small language changes and library improvements

SELF CHECK

6. What are the two most important benefits of the Java language?

7. How long does it take to learn the entire Java library?

Practice It   Now you can try this exercise at the end of the chapter: R1.5.

1.4 Becoming Familiar with Your Programming Environment

Set aside some time to become familiar with the programming environment that you will use for your class work.

Many students find that the tools they need as programmers are very different from the software with which they are familiar. You should spend some time making yourself familiar with your programming environment. Because computer systems vary widely, this book can only give an outline of the steps you need to follow. It is a good idea to participate in a hands-on lab, or to ask a knowledgeable friend to give you a tour.

Step 1 Start the Java development environment.

Computer systems differ greatly in this regard. On many computers there is an **integrated development environment** in which you can write and test your programs. On other computers you first launch an **editor**, a program that functions like a word processor, in which you can enter your Java instructions; you then open a *console window* and type commands to execute your program. You need to find out how to get started with your environment.

An editor is a program for entering and modifying text, such as a Java program.

Step 2 Write a simple program.

The traditional choice for the very first program in a new programming language is a program that displays a simple greeting: "Hello, World!". Let us follow that tradition. Here is the "Hello, World!" program in Java:

```java
public class HelloPrinter
{
   public static void main(String[] args)
   {
      System.out.println("Hello, World!");
   }
}
```

We will examine this program in the next section.

No matter which programming environment you use, you begin your activity by typing the program statements into an editor window.

Create a new file and call it HelloPrinter.java, using the steps that are appropriate for your environment. (If your environment requires that you supply a project name in addition to the file name, use the name hello for the project.) Enter the program instructions *exactly* as they are given above. Alternatively, locate the electronic copy in this book's companion code and paste it into your editor.

Figure 6 Running the HelloPrinter Program in a Console Window

Figure 7
Running the
`HelloPrinter`
Program in an
Integrated
Development
Environment

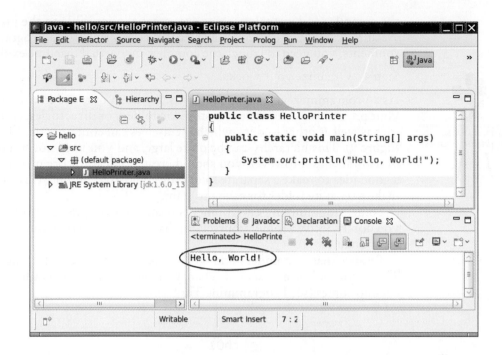

As you write this program, pay careful attention to the various symbols, and keep in mind that Java is **case sensitive**. You must enter upper- and lowercase letters exactly as they appear in the program listing. You cannot type `MAIN` or `PrintIn`. If you are not careful, you will run into problems—see Common Error 1.2 on page 16.

> Java is case sensitive.
> You must be careful
> about distinguishing
> between upper- and
> lowercase letters.

Step 3   Run the program.

The process for running a program depends greatly on your programming environment. You may have to click a button or enter some commands. When you run the test program, the message

```
Hello, World!
```

will appear somewhere on the screen (see Figures 6 and 7).

> The Java compiler
> translates source
> code into class files
> that contain
> instructions for the
> Java virtual machine.

In order to run your program, the Java compiler translates your **source code** (that is, the statements that you wrote) into *class files*. (A class file contains instructions for the Java virtual machine.) After the compiler has translated your program into virtual machine instructions, the virtual machine executes them. Figure 8 summarizes the process of creating and running a Java program. In some programming environments,

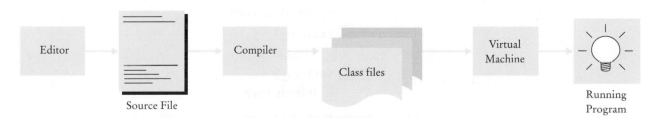

Figure 8   From Source Code to Running Program

ANIMATION
Compilation Process

the compiler and virtual machine are essentially invisible to the programmer—they are automatically executed whenever you ask to run a Java program. In other environments, you need to launch the compiler and virtual machine explicitly.

Step 4 Organize your work.

As a programmer, you write programs, try them out, and improve them. You store your programs in **files**. Files are stored in **folders** or **directories**. A folder can contain files as well as other folders, which themselves can contain more files and folders (see Figure 9). This hierarchy can be quite large, and you need not be concerned with all of its branches. However, you should create folders for organizing your work. It is a good idea to make a separate folder for your programming class. Inside that folder, make a separate folder for each program.

Some programming environments place your programs into a default location if you don't specify a folder yourself. In that case, you need to find out where those files are located.

Be sure that you understand where your files are located in the folder hierarchy. This information is essential when you submit files for grading, and for making backup copies (see Programming Tip 1.1).

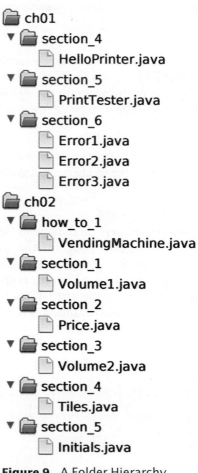

Figure 9 A Folder Hierarchy

8. Where is the `HelloPrinter.java` file stored on your computer?

9. What do you do to protect yourself from data loss when you work on programming projects?

Practice It Now you can try this exercise at the end of the chapter: R1.6.

Programming Tip 1.1

Backup Copies

You will spend many hours creating and improving Java programs. It is easy to delete a file by accident, and occasionally files are lost because of a computer malfunction. Retyping the contents of lost files is frustrating and time-consuming. It is therefore crucially important that you learn how to safeguard files and get in the habit of doing so *before* disaster strikes. Backing up files on a memory stick is an easy and convenient storage method for many people. Another increasingly popular form of backup is Internet file storage. Here are a few pointers to keep in mind:

- *Back up often.* Backing up a file takes only a few seconds, and you will hate yourself if you have to spend many hours recreating work that you could have saved easily. I recommend that you back up your work once every thirty minutes.

- *Rotate backups.* Use more than one directory for backups, and rotate them. That is, first back up onto the first directory. Then back up onto the second directory. Then use the third, and then go back to the first. That way you always have three recent backups. If your recent changes made matters worse, you can then go back to the older version.

> Develop a strategy for keeping backup copies of your work before disaster strikes.

- *Pay attention to the backup direction.* Backing up involves copying files from one place to another. It is important that you do this right—that is, copy from your work location to the backup location. If you do it the wrong way, you will overwrite a newer file with an older version.

- *Check your backups once in a while.* Double-check that your backups are where you think they are. There is nothing more frustrating than to find out that the backups are not there when you need them.

- *Relax, then restore.* When you lose a file and need to restore it from a backup, you are likely to be in an unhappy, nervous state. Take a deep breath and think through the recovery process before you start. It is not uncommon for an agitated computer user to wipe out the last backup when trying to restore a damaged file.

VIDEO EXAMPLE 1.1   **Compiling and Running a Program**

This Video Example shows how to compile and run a simple Java program.

1.5 Analyzing Your First Program

In this section, we will analyze the first Java program in detail. Here again is the source code:

section_5/HelloPrinter.java

```
1   public class HelloPrinter
2   {
3      public static void main(String[] args)
4      {
5         System.out.println("Hello, World!");
6      }
7   }
```

The line

```
public class HelloPrinter
```

indicates the declaration of a **class** called `HelloPrinter`.

> Classes are the fundamental building blocks of Java programs.

Every Java program consists of one or more classes. Classes are the fundamental building blocks of Java programs. You will have to wait until Chapter 8 for a full explanation of classes.

The word `public` denotes that the class is usable by the "public". You will later encounter `private` features.

In Java, every source file can contain at most one public class, and the name of the public class must match the name of the file containing the class. For example, the class `HelloPrinter` must be contained in a file named `HelloPrinter.java`.

The construction

```
public static void main(String[] args)
{
   . . .
}
```

> Every Java application contains a class with a main method. When the application starts, the instructions in the main method are executed.

declares a **method** called `main`. A method contains a collection of programming instructions that describe how to carry out a particular task. Every Java application must have a `main` method. Most Java programs contain other methods besides `main`, and you will see in Chapter 5 how to write other methods.

The term `static` is explained in more detail in Chapter 8, and the meaning of `String[] args` is covered in Chapter 7. At this time, simply consider

> Each class contains declarations of methods. Each method contains a sequence of instructions.

```
public class ClassName
{
   public static void main(String[] args)
   {
      . . .
   }
}
```

as a part of the "plumbing" that is required to create a Java program. Our first program has all instructions inside the `main` method of the class.

The `main` method contains one or more instructions called **statements**. Each statement ends in a semicolon (;). When a program runs, the statements in the `main` method are executed one by one.

Syntax 1.1   Java Program

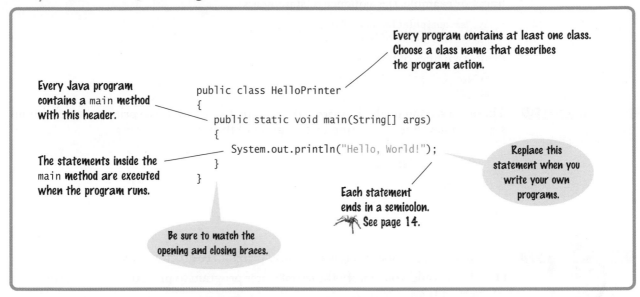

Every Java program contains a `main` **method** with this header.

Every program contains at least one class. Choose a class name that describes the program action.

The statements inside the `main` **method** are executed when the program runs.

Be sure to match the opening and closing braces.

Each statement ends in a semicolon. See page 14.

Replace this statement when you write your own programs.

```
public class HelloPrinter
{
    public static void main(String[] args)
    {
        System.out.println("Hello, World!");
    }
}
```

In our example program, the `main` method has a single statement:

```
System.out.println("Hello, World!");
```

This statement prints a line of text, namely "Hello, World!". In this statement, we *call* a method which, for reasons that we will not explain here, is specified by the rather long name `System.out.println`.

We do not have to implement this method—the programmers who wrote the Java library already did that for us. We simply want the method to perform its intended task, namely to print a value.

Whenever you call a method in Java, you need to specify

A method is called by specifying the method and its arguments.

1. The method you want to use (in this case, `System.out.println`).

2. Any values the method needs to carry out its task (in this case, `"Hello, World!"`). The technical term for such a value is an **argument**. Arguments are enclosed in parentheses. Multiple arguments are separated by commas.

A sequence of characters enclosed in quotation marks

```
"Hello, World!"
```

A string is a sequence of characters enclosed in quotation marks.

is called a **string**. You must enclose the contents of the string inside quotation marks so that the compiler knows you literally mean `"Hello, World!"`. There is a reason for this requirement. Suppose you need to print the word *main*. By enclosing it in quotation marks, `"main"`, the compiler knows you mean the sequence of characters m a i n, not the method named `main`. The rule is simply that you must enclose all text strings in quotation marks, so that the compiler considers them plain text and does not try to interpret them as program instructions.

You can also print numerical values. For example, the statement

```
System.out.println(3 + 4);
```

evaluates the expression 3 + 4 and displays the number 7.

The System.out.println method prints a string or a number and then starts a new line. For example, the sequence of statements

```
System.out.println("Hello");
System.out.println("World!");
```

prints two lines of text:

```
Hello
World!
```

ONLINE EXAMPLE

A program to demonstrate print commands.

There is a second method, System.out.print, that you can use to print an item without starting a new line. For example, the output of the two statements

```
System.out.print("00");
System.out.println(3 + 4);
```

is the single line

```
007
```

SELF CHECK

10. How do you modify the HelloPrinter program to greet you instead?

11. How would you modify the HelloPrinter program to print the word "Hello" vertically?

12. Would the program continue to work if you replaced line 5 with this statement?

    ```
    System.out.println(Hello);
    ```

13. What does the following set of statements print?

    ```
    System.out.print("My lucky number is");
    System.out.println(3 + 4 + 5);
    ```

14. What do the following statements print?

    ```
    System.out.println("Hello");
    System.out.println("");
    System.out.println("World");
    ```

Practice It   Now you can try these exercises at the end of the chapter: R1.7, R1.8, P1.5, P1.7.

Common Error 1.1

Omitting Semicolons

In Java every statement must end in a semicolon. Forgetting to type a semicolon is a common error. It confuses the compiler, because the compiler uses the semicolon to find where one statement ends and the next one starts. The compiler does not use line breaks or closing braces to recognize the end of statements. For example, the compiler considers

```
System.out.println("Hello")
System.out.println("World!");
```

a single statement, as if you had written

```
System.out.println("Hello") System.out.println("World!");
```

Then it doesn't understand that statement, because it does not expect the word System following the closing parenthesis after "Hello".

The remedy is simple. Scan every statement for a terminating semicolon, just as you would check that every English sentence ends in a period.

1.6 Errors

Experiment a little with the `HelloPrinter` program. What happens if you make a typing error such as

```
System.ou.println("Hello, World!");
System.out.println("Hello, Word!");
```

Programmers spend a fair amount of time fixing compile-time and run-time errors.

In the first case, the compiler will complain. It will say that it has no clue what you mean by ou. The exact wording of the error message is dependent on your development environment, but it might be something like "Cannot find symbol ou". This is a **compile-time error**. Something is wrong according to the rules of the language and the compiler finds it. For this reason, compile-time errors are often called *syntax errors*. When the compiler finds one or more errors, it refuses to translate the program into Java virtual machine instructions, and as a consequence you have no program that you can run. You must fix the error and compile again. In fact, the compiler is quite picky, and it is common to go through several rounds of fixing compile-time errors before compilation succeeds for the first time.

If the compiler finds an error, it will not simply stop and give up. It will try to report as many errors as it can find, so you can fix them all at once.

Sometimes, an error throws the compiler off track. Suppose, for example, you forget the quotation marks around a string: `System.out.println(Hello, World!)`. The compiler will not complain about the missing quotation marks. Instead, it will report "Cannot find symbol Hello". Unfortunately, the compiler is not very smart and it does not realize that you meant to use a string. It is up to you to realize that you need to enclose strings in quotation marks.

The error in the second line above is of a different kind. The program will compile and run, but its output will be wrong. It will print

```
Hello, Word!
```

This is a **run-time error**. The program is syntactically correct and does something, but it doesn't do what it is supposed to do. Because run-time errors are caused by logical flaws in the program, they are often called *logic errors*.

This particular run-time error did not include an error message. It simply produced the wrong output. Some kinds of run-time errors are so severe that they generate an **exception**: an error message from the Java virtual machine. For example, if your program includes the statement

```
System.out.println(1 / 0);
```

you will get a run-time error message "Division by zero".

During program development, errors are unavoidable. Once a program is longer than a few lines, it would require superhuman concentration to enter it correctly without slipping up once. You will find yourself omitting semicolons or quotation marks more often than you would like, but the compiler will track down these problems for you.

Run-time errors are more troublesome. The compiler will not find them—in fact, the compiler will cheerfully translate any program as long as its syntax is correct—

but the resulting program will do something wrong. It is the responsibility of the program author to test the program and find any run-time errors.

SELF CHECK

15. Suppose you omit the "" characters around Hello, World! from the HelloPrinter. java program. Is this a compile-time error or a run-time error?

16. Suppose you change println to printline in the HelloPrinter.java program. Is this a compile-time error or a run-time error?

17. Suppose you change main to hello in the HelloPrinter.java program. Is this a compile-time error or a run-time error?

18. When you used your computer, you may have experienced a program that "crashed" (quit spontaneously) or "hung" (failed to respond to your input). Is that behavior a compile-time error or a run-time error?

19. Why can't you test a program for run-time errors when it has compiler errors?

Practice It   Now you can try these exercises at the end of the chapter: R1.9, R1.10, R1.11.

Common Error 1.2

Misspelling Words

If you accidentally misspell a word, then strange things may happen, and it may not always be completely obvious from the error messages what went wrong. Here is a good example of how simple spelling errors can cause trouble:

```
public class HelloPrinter
{
    public static void Main(String[] args)
    {
        System.out.println("Hello, World!");
    }
}
```

This class declares a method called Main. The compiler will not consider this to be the same as the main method, because Main starts with an uppercase letter and the Java language is case sensitive. Upper- and lowercase letters are considered to be completely different from each other, and to the compiler Main is no better match for main than rain. The compiler will cheerfully compile your Main method, but when the Java virtual machine reads the compiled file, it will complain about the missing main method and refuse to run the program. Of course, the message "missing main method" should give you a clue where to look for the error.

If you get an error message that seems to indicate that the compiler or virtual machine is on the wrong track, it is a good idea to check for spelling and capitalization. If you misspell the name of a symbol (for example, ou instead of out), the compiler will produce a message such as "cannot find symbol ou". That error message is usually a good clue that you made a spelling error.

1.7 Problem Solving: Algorithm Design

You will soon learn how to program calculations and decision making in Java. But before we look at the mechanics of implementing computations in the next chapter, let's consider how you can describe the steps that are necessary for finding the solution for a problem.

You may have run across advertisements that encourage you to pay for a computerized service that matches you up with a love partner. Think how this might work. You fill out a form and send it in. Others do the same. The data are processed by a computer program. Is it reasonable to assume that the computer can perform the task of finding the best match for you? Suppose your younger brother, not the computer, had all the forms on his desk. What instructions could you give him? You can't say, "Find the best-looking person who likes inline skating and browsing the Internet". There is no objective standard for good looks, and your brother's opinion (or that of a computer program analyzing the digitized photo) will likely be different from yours. If you can't give written instructions for someone to solve the problem, there is no way the computer can magically find the right solution. The computer can only do what you tell it to do. It just does it faster, without getting bored or exhausted.

Finding the perfect partner is not a problem that a computer can solve.

For that reason, a computerized match-making service cannot guarantee to find the optimal match for you. Instead, you may be presented with a set of potential partners who share common interests with you. That is a task that a computer program can solve.

Now consider the following investment problem:

> You put $10,000 into a bank account that earns 5 percent interest per year. How many years does it take for the account balance to be double the original?

Could you solve this problem by hand? Sure, you could. You figure out the balance as follows:

year	interest	balance
0		10000
1	10000.00 x 0.05 = 500.00	10000.00 + 500.00 = 10500.00
2	10500.00 x 0.05 = 525.00	10500.00 + 525.00 = 11025.00
3	11025.00 x 0.05 = 551.25	11025.00 + 551.25 = 11576.25
4	11576.25 x 0.05 = 578.81	11576.25 + 578.81 = 12155.06

You keep going until the balance is at least $20,000. Then the last number in the year column is the answer.

Of course, carrying out this computation is intensely boring to you or your younger brother. But computers are very good at carrying out repetitive calculations quickly and flawlessly. What is important to the computer is a description of the steps for finding the solution. Each step must be clear and unambiguous, requiring no guesswork. Here is such a description:

Start with a year value of 0, a column for the interest, and a balance of $10,000.

year	interest	balance
0		10000

Repeat the following steps while the balance is less than $20,000
   Add 1 to the year value.
   Compute the interest as balance x 0.05 (i.e., 5 percent interest).
   Add the interest to the balance.

year	interest	balance
0		10000
1	500.00	10500.00
14	942.82	19799.32
(15)	989.96	20789.28

Report the final year value as the answer.

> Pseudocode is an informal description of a sequence of steps for solving a problem.

Of course, these steps are not yet in a language that a computer can understand, but you will soon learn how to formulate them in Java. This informal description is called **pseudocode**.

There are no strict requirements for pseudocode because it is read by human readers, not a computer program. Here are the kinds of pseudocode statements that we will use in this book:

- Use statements such as the following to describe how a value is set or changed:

  total cost = purchase price + operating cost
  Multiply the balance value by 1.05.
  Remove the first and last character from the word.

- You can describe decisions and repetitions as follows:

  If total cost 1 < total cost 2
  While the balance is less than $20,000
  For each picture in the sequence

  Use indentation to indicate which statements should be selected or repeated:

  For each car
     operating cost = 10 x annual fuel cost
     total cost = purchase price + operating cost

  Here, the indentation indicates that both statements should be executed for each car.

- Indicate results with statements such as:

  Choose car 1.
  Report the final year value as the answer.

The exact wording is not important. What is important is that pseudocode describes a sequence of steps that is

- Unambiguous
- Executable
- Terminating

An algorithm for solving a problem is a sequence of steps that is unambiguous, executable, and terminating.

The step sequence is *unambiguous* when there are precise instructions for what to do at each step and where to go next. There is no room for guesswork or personal opinion. A step is *executable* when it can be carried out in practice. Had we said to use the actual interest rate that will be charged in years to come, and not a fixed rate of 5 percent per year, that step would not have been executable, because there is no way for anyone to know what that interest rate will be. A sequence of steps is *terminating* if it will eventually come to an end. In our example, it requires a bit of thought to see that the sequence will not go on forever: With every step, the balance goes up by at least $500, so eventually it must reach $20,000.

An algorithm is a recipe for finding a solution.

A sequence of steps that is unambiguous, executable, and terminating is called an **algorithm**. We have found an algorithm to solve our investment problem, and thus we can find the solution by programming a computer. The existence of an algorithm is an essential prerequisite for programming a task. You need to first discover and describe an algorithm for the task that you want to solve before you start programming (see Figure 10).

Understand the problem

Develop and describe an algorithm

Test the algorithm with simple inputs

Translate the algorithm into Java

Compile and test your program

Figure 10   The Software Development Process

SELF CHECK

20. Suppose the interest rate was 20 percent. How long would it take for the investment to double?

21. Suppose your cell phone carrier charges you $29.95 for up to 300 minutes of calls, and $0.45 for each additional minute, plus 12.5 percent taxes and fees. Give an algorithm to compute the monthly charge from a given number of minutes.

22. Consider the following pseudocode for finding the most attractive photo from a sequence of photos:

> Pick the first photo and call it "the best so far".
> For each photo in the sequence
>   If it is more attractive than the "best so far"
>   Discard "the best so far".
>   Call this photo "the best so far".
> The photo called "the best so far" is the most attractive photo in the sequence.

Is this an algorithm that will find the most attractive photo?

23. Suppose each photo in Self Check 22 had a price tag. Give an algorithm for find-ing the most expensive photo.

24. Suppose you have a random sequence of black and white marbles and want to rearrange it so that the black and white marbles are grouped together. Consider this algorithm:

Repeat until sorted
   Locate the first black marble that is preceded by a white marble, and switch them.

What does the algorithm do with the sequence ○●○●●? Spell out the steps until the algorithm stops.

25. Suppose you have a random sequence of colored marbles. Consider this pseudo-code:

Repeat until sorted
   Locate the first marble that is preceded by a marble of a different color, and switch them.

Why is this not an algorithm?

Practice It   Now you can try these exercises at the end of the chapter: R1.15, R1.17, P1.4.

HOW TO 1.1   Describing an Algorithm with Pseudocode

This is the first of many "How To" sections in this book that give you step-by-step proce-dures for carrying out important tasks in developing computer programs.

Before you are ready to write a program in Java, you need to develop an algorithm—a method for arriving at a solution for a particular problem. Describe the algorithm in pseudo-code: a sequence of precise steps formulated in English.

For example, consider this problem: You have the choice of buying two cars. One is more fuel efficient than the other, but also more expensive. You know the price and fuel efficiency (in miles per gallon, mpg) of both cars. You plan to keep the car for ten years. Assume a price of $4 per gallon of gas and usage of 15,000 miles per year. You will pay cash for the car and not worry about financing costs. Which car is the better deal?

Step 1   Determine the inputs and outputs.

In our sample problem, we have these inputs:
- **purchase price1** and **fuel efficiency1**, the price and fuel efficiency (in mpg) of the first car
- **purchase price2** and **fuel efficiency2**, the price and fuel efficiency of the second car

We simply want to know which car is the better buy. That is the desired output.

Step 2   Break down the problem into smaller tasks.

For each car, we need to know the total cost of driving it. Let's do this computation separately for each car. Once we have the total cost for each car, we can decide which car is the better deal.

The total cost for each car is **purchase price + operating cost**.

We assume a constant usage and gas price for ten years, so the operating cost depends on the cost of driving the car for one year.

The operating cost is **10 x annual fuel cost**.
The annual fuel cost is **price per gallon x annual fuel consumed**.

The annual fuel consumed is **annual miles driven / fuel efficiency**. For example, if you drive the car for 15,000 miles and the fuel efficiency is 15 miles/gallon, the car consumes 1,000 gallons.

Step 3   Describe each subtask in pseudocode.

In your description, arrange the steps so that any intermediate values are computed before they are needed in other computations. For example, list the step

> **total cost = purchase price + operating cost**

after you have computed **operating cost**.

Here is the algorithm for deciding which car to buy:

> **For each car, compute the total cost as follows:**
>   **annual fuel consumed = annual miles driven / fuel efficiency**
>   **annual fuel cost = price per gallon x annual fuel consumed**
>   **operating cost = 10 x annual fuel cost**
>   **total cost = purchase price + operating cost**
> **If total cost1 < total cost2**
>   **Choose car1.**
> **Else**
>   **Choose car2.**

Step 4   Test your pseudocode by working a problem.

We will use these sample values:

> Car 1: $25,000, 50 miles/gallon
> Car 2: $20,000, 30 miles/gallon

Here is the calculation for the cost of the first car:

> **annual fuel consumed = annual miles driven / fuel efficiency = 15000 / 50 = 300**
> **annual fuel cost = price per gallon x annual fuel consumed = 4 x 300 = 1200**
> **operating cost = 10 x annual fuel cost = 10 x 1200 = 12000**
> **total cost = purchase price + operating cost = 25000 + 12000 = 37000**

Similarly, the total cost for the second car is $40,000. Therefore, the output of the algorithm is to choose car 1.

WORKED EXAMPLE 1.1    **Writing an Algorithm for Tiling a Floor**

This Worked Example shows how to develop an algorithm for laying tile in an alternating pattern of colors.

VIDEO EXAMPLE 1.2   **Dividing Household Expenses**

This Video Example shows how to develop an algorithm for dividing household expenses among roommates.

➕ Available online in WileyPLUS and at www.wiley.com/college/horstmann.

CHAPTER SUMMARY

Define "computer program" and programming.

- Computers execute very basic instructions in rapid succession.
- A computer program is a sequence of instructions and decisions.
- Programming is the act of designing and implementing computer programs.

Describe the components of a computer.

- The central processing unit (CPU) performs program control and data processing.
- Storage devices include memory and secondary storage.

Describe the process of translating high-level languages to machine code.

- Java was originally designed for programming consumer devices, but it was first successfully used to write Internet applets.
- Java was designed to be safe and portable, benefiting both Internet users and students.
- Java programs are distributed as instructions for a virtual machine, making them platform-independent.
- Java has a very large library. Focus on learning those parts of the library that you need for your programming projects.

Become familiar with your Java programming environment.

- Set aside some time to become familiar with the programming environment that you will use for your class work.
- An editor is a program for entering and modifying text, such as a Java program.
- Java is case sensitive. You must be careful about distinguishing between upper- and lowercase letters.
- The Java compiler translates source code into class files that contain instructions for the Java virtual machine.
- Develop a strategy for keeping backup copies of your work before disaster strikes.

Describe the building blocks of a simple program.

- Classes are the fundamental building blocks of Java programs.
- Every Java application contains a class with a main method. When the application starts, the instructions in the main method are executed.
- Each class contains declarations of methods. Each method contains a sequence of instructions.
- A method is called by specifying the method and its arguments.
- A string is a sequence of characters enclosed in quotation marks.

Classify program errors as compile-time and run-time errors.

- A compile-time error is a violation of the programming language rules that is detected by the compiler.
- A run-time error causes a program to take an action that the programmer did not intend.

Write pseudocode for simple algorithms.

- Pseudocode is an informal description of a sequence of steps for solving a problem.
- An algorithm for solving a problem is a sequence of steps that is unambiguous, executable, and terminating.

STANDARD LIBRARY ITEMS INTRODUCED IN THIS CHAPTER

```
java.io.PrintStream          java.lang.System
    print                        out
    println
```

REVIEW EXERCISES

■ **R1.1** Explain the difference between using a computer program and programming a computer.

■ **R1.2** Which parts of a computer can store program code? Which can store user data?

■ **R1.3** Which parts of a computer serve to give information to the user? Which parts take user input?

■■■ **R1.4** A toaster is a single-function device, but a computer can be programmed to carry out different tasks. Is your cell phone a single-function device, or is it a programmable computer? (Your answer will depend on your cell phone model.)

■ **R1.5** Explain two benefits of using Java over machine code.

■■ **R1.6** On your own computer or on a lab computer, find the exact location (folder or directory name) of

   a. The sample file `HelloPrinter.java`, which you wrote with the editor

   b. The Java program launcher `java.exe` or `java`

   c. The library file `rt.jar` that contains the run-time library

■■ **R1.7** What does this program print?

```java
public class Test
{
   public static void main(String[] args)
   {
      System.out.println("39 + 3");
      System.out.println(39 + 3);
   }
}
```

■ ■ **R1.8** What does this program print? Pay close attention to spaces.

```java
public class Test
{
    public static void main(String[] args)
    {
        System.out.print("Hello");
        System.out.println("World");
    }
}
```

■ ■ **R1.9** What is the compile-time error in this program?

```java
public class Test
{
    public static void main(String[] args)
    {
        System.out.println("Hello", "World!");
    }
}
```

■ ■ **R1.10** Write three versions of the `HelloPrinter.java` program that have different compile-time errors. Write a version that has a run-time error.

■ **R1.11** How do you discover syntax errors? How do you discover logic errors?

■ ■ **R1.12** Write an algorithm to settle the following question: A bank account starts out with $10,000. Interest is compounded monthly at 6 percent per year (0.5 percent per month). Every month, $500 is withdrawn to meet college expenses. After how many years is the account depleted?

■ ■ ■ **R1.13** Consider the question in Exercise R1.12. Suppose the numbers ($10,000, 6 percent, $500) were user selectable. Are there values for which the algorithm you developed would not terminate? If so, change the algorithm to make sure it always terminates.

■ ■ ■ **R1.14** In order to estimate the cost of painting a house, a painter needs to know the surface area of the exterior. Develop an algorithm for computing that value. Your inputs are the width, length, and height of the house, the number of windows and doors, and their dimensions. (Assume the windows and doors have a uniform size.)

■ ■ **R1.15** You want to decide whether you should drive your car to work or take the train. You know the one-way distance from your home to your place of work, and the fuel efficiency of your car (in miles per gallon). You also know the one-way price of a train ticket. You assume the cost of gas at $4 per gallon, and car maintenance at 5 cents per mile. Write an algorithm to decide which commute is cheaper.

■ ■ **R1.16** You want to find out which fraction of your car's use is for commuting to work, and which is for personal use. You know the one-way distance from your home to work. For a particular period, you recorded the beginning and ending mileage on the odometer and the number of work days. Write an algorithm to settle this question.

■ **R1.17** In How To 1.1, you made assumptions about the price of gas and annual usage to compare cars. Ideally, you would like to know which car is the better deal without making these assumptions. Why can't a computer program solve that problem?

■ ■ ■ **R1.18** The value of π can be computed according to the following formula:

$$\frac{\pi}{4} = 1 - \frac{1}{3} + \frac{1}{5} - \frac{1}{7} + \frac{1}{9} - \cdots$$

Write an algorithm to compute π. Because the formula is an infinite series and an algorithm must stop after a finite number of steps, you should stop when you have the result determined to six significant digits.

■■ R1.19 Suppose you put your younger brother in charge of backing up your work. Write a set of detailed instructions for carrying out his task. Explain how often he should do it, and what files he needs to copy from which folder to which location. Explain how he should verify that the backup was carried out correctly.

■ Business R1.20 Imagine that you and a number of friends go to a luxury restaurant, and when you ask for the bill you want to split the amount and the tip (15 percent) between all. Write pseudocode for calculating the amount of money that everyone has to pay. Your program should print the amount of the bill, the tip, the total cost, and the amount each person has to pay. It should also print how much of what each person pays is for the bill and for the tip.

PROGRAMMING EXERCISES

■ P1.1 Write a program that prints a greeting of your choice, perhaps in a language other than English.

■■ P1.2 Write a program that prints the sum of the first ten positive integers, $1 + 2 + \ldots + 10$.

■■ P1.3 Write a program that prints the product of the first ten positive integers, $1 \times 2 \times \ldots \times 10$. (Use * to indicate multiplication in Java.)

■■ P1.4 Write a program that prints the balance of an account after the first, second, and third year. The account has an initial balance of $1,000 and earns 5 percent interest per year.

■ P1.5 Write a program that displays your name inside a box on the screen, like this:

```
Dave
```

Do your best to approximate lines with characters such as | - +.

■■■ P1.6 Write a program that prints your name in large letters, such as

```
*    *   **   ****   ****   *   *
*    *  *  *  *   *  *   *   *  *
*****  *    * ****   ****    * *
*    * ******  *   *  *   *     *
*    * *    *  *   *  *   *     *
```

■■ P1.7 Write a program that prints a face similar to (but different from) the following:

```
   /////
  +"""""+
 (| o o |)
  |  ^  |
  | '-' |
  +-----+
```

■■ P1.8 Write a program that prints an imitation of a Piet Mondrian painting. (Search the Internet if you are not familiar with his paintings.) Use character sequences such as @@@ or ::: to indicate different colors, and use - and | to form lines.

•• P1.9 Write a program that prints a house that looks exactly like the following:

```
      +
     + +
    +   +
   +-----+
   | .-. |
   | | | |
   +-+-+-+
```

••• P1.10 Write a program that prints an animal speaking a greeting, similar to (but different from) the following:

```
 /\_/\      -----
( ' ' )  / Hello \'
(  -  ) <  Junior |
 | | |    \ Coder!/
(_|_)       -----
```

• P1.11 Write a program that prints three items, such as the names of your three best friends or favorite movies, on three separate lines.

• P1.12 Write a program that prints a poem of your choice. If you don't have a favorite poem, search the Internet for "Emily Dickinson" or "e e cummings".

•• P1.13 Write a program that prints the United States flag, using * and = characters.

•• P1.14 Type in and run the following program:

```java
import javax.swing.JOptionPane;

public class DialogViewer
{
   public static void main(String[] args)
   {
      JOptionPane.showMessageDialog(null, "Hello, World!");
   }
}
```

Then modify the program to show the message "Hello, *your name*!".

•• P1.15 Type in and run the following program:

```java
import javax.swing.JOptionPane;

public class DialogViewer
{
   public static void main(String[] args)
   {
      String name = JOptionPane.showInputDialog("What is your name?");
      System.out.println(name);
   }
}
```

Then modify the program to print "Hello, *name*!", displaying the name that the user typed in.

••• P1.16 Modify the program from Exercise P1.15 so that the dialog continues with the message "My name is Hal! What would you like me to do?" Discard the user's input and display a message such as

```
I'm sorry, Dave. I'm afraid I can't do that.
```

Replace Dave with the name that was provided by the user.

•• P1.17 Type in and run the following program:

```java
import java.net.URL;
import javax.swing.ImageIcon;
import javax.swing.JOptionPane;

public class Test
{
    public static void main(String[] args) throws Exception
    {
        URL imageLocation = new URL(
            "http://horstmann.com/java4everyone/duke.gif");
        JOptionPane.showMessageDialog(null, "Hello", "Title",
            JOptionPane.PLAIN_MESSAGE, new ImageIcon(imageLocation));
    }
}
```

Then modify it to show a different greeting and image.

• Business P1.18 Write a program that prints a two-column list of your friends' birthdays. In the first column, print the names of your best friends; in the second column, print their birthdays.

• Business P1.19 In the United States there is no federal sales tax, so every state may impose its own sales taxes. Look on the Internet for the sales tax charged in five U.S. states, then write a program that prints the tax rate for five states of your choice.

```
Sales Tax Rates
----------------
Alaska:     0%
Hawaii:     4%
. . .
```

• Business P1.20 To speak more than one language is a valuable skill in the labor market today. One of the basic skills is learning to greet people. Write a program that prints a two-column list with the greeting phrases shown in the following table; in the first column, print the phrase in English, in the second column, print the phrase in a language of your choice. If you don't speak any language other than English, use an online translator or ask a friend.

List of Phrases to Translate
Good morning.
It is a pleasure to meet you.
Please call me tomorrow.
Have a nice day!

ANSWERS TO SELF-CHECK QUESTIONS

1. A program that reads the data on the CD and sends output to the speakers and the screen.
2. A CD player can do one thing—play music CDs. It cannot execute programs.
3. Nothing.
4. In secondary storage, typically a hard disk.
5. The central processing unit.

6. Safety and portability.

7. No one person can learn the entire library—it is too large.

8. The answer varies among systems. A typical answer might be `/home/dave/cs1/hello/HelloPrinter.java` or `c:\Users\Dave\Workspace\hello\HelloPrinter.java`

9. You back up your files and folders.

10. Change `World` to your name (here, `Dave`):

```
System.out.println("Hello, Dave!");
```

11.
```
System.out.println("H");
System.out.println("e");
System.out.println("l");
System.out.println("l");
System.out.println("o");
```

12. No. The compiler would look for an item whose name is `Hello`. You need to enclose `Hello` in quotation marks:

```
System.out.println("Hello");
```

13. The printout is `My lucky number is12`. It would be a good idea to add a space after the `is`.

14.
```
Hello
a blank line
World
```

15. This is a compile-time error. The compiler will complain that it does not know the meanings of the words `Hello` and `World`.

16. This is a compile-time error. The compiler will complain that `System.out` does not have a method called `printline`.

17. This is a run-time error. It is perfectly legal to give the name `hello` to a method, so the compiler won't complain. But when the program is run, the virtual machine will look for a `main` method and won't find one.

18. It is a run-time error. After all, the program had been compiled in order for you to run it.

19. When a program has compiler errors, no class file is produced, and there is nothing to run.

20. 4 years:

```
0 10,000
1 12,000
2 14,400
3 17,280
4 20,736
```

21. Is the number of minutes at most 300?

  a. If so, the answer is $29.95 \times 1.125 = 33.70$.

  b. If not,

    1. Compute the difference: (number of minutes) − 300.

    2. Multiply that difference by 0.45.

    3. Add $29.95.

    4. Multiply the total by 1.125. That is the answer.

22. No. The step **If it is more attractive than the "best so far"** is not executable because there is no objective way of deciding which of two photos is more attractive.

23. **Pick the first photo and call it "the most expensive so far".**
For each photo in the sequence
  If it is more expensive than "the most expensive so far"
    Discard "the most expensive so far".
    Call this photo "the most expensive so far".
The photo called "the most expensive so far" is the most expensive photo in the sequence.

24. The first black marble that is preceded by a white one is marked in blue:

○●○●●

Switching the two yields

●○○●●

The next black marble to be switched is

●○○●●

yielding

●○●○●

The next steps are

●●○○●

●●○●○

●●●○○

Now the sequence is sorted.

25. The sequence doesn't terminate. Consider the input ○●○●○. The first two marbles keep getting switched.

FUNDAMENTAL DATA TYPES

LIGHT
742
201
435
770
54
753
114
618
24
454
815
787

DESTINATION
LOS ANGELES
LONDON
MADRID
PARIS
TOKYO
HONG KONG
MIAMI
NEW YORK
RIO DEJANEIRO
SYDNEY
BANGKOK
MILAN

GATE #
A23
C72
B34
A14
C89
G12

CHAPTER GOALS

To declare and initialize variables
and constants

To understand the properties and limitations of integers and floating-point numbers

To appreciate the importance of comments and good code layout

To write arithmetic expressions and assignment statements

To create programs that read and process inputs, and display the results

To learn how to use the Java `String` type

CHAPTER CONTENTS

2.1 VARIABLES 30

Syntax 2.1: Variable Declaration 31

Syntax 2.2: Assignment 34

Syntax 2.3: Constant Declaration 35

Common Error 2.1: Using Undeclared or Uninitialized Variables 37

Programming Tip 2.1: Choose Descriptive Variable Names 38

Common Error 2.2: Overflow 38

Common Error 2.3: Roundoff Errors 38

Programming Tip 2.2: Do Not Use Magic Numbers 39

Special Topic 2.1: Numeric Types in Java 39

Special Topic 2.2: Big Numbers 40

2.2 ARITHMETIC 41

Syntax 2.4: Cast 44

Common Error 2.4: Unintended Integer Division 46

Common Error 2.5: Unbalanced Parentheses 46

Programming Tip 2.3: Spaces in Expressions 47

Special Topic 2.3: Combining Assignment and Arithmetic 47

Video Example 2.1: Using Integer Division ✚

Random Fact 2.1: The Pentium Floating-Point Bug 48

2.3 INPUT AND OUTPUT 48

Syntax 2.5: Input Statement 49

Programming Tip 2.4: Use the API Documentation 53

How To 2.1: Carrying out Computations 54

Worked Example 2.1: Computing the Cost of Stamps ✚

2.4 PROBLEM SOLVING: FIRST DO IT BY HAND 57

Worked Example 2.2: Computing Travel Time ✚

2.5 STRINGS 59

Special Topic 2.4: Instance Methods and Static Methods 64

Special Topic 2.5: Using Dialog Boxes for Input and Output 65

Video Example 2.2: Computing Distances on Earth ✚

Random Fact 2.2: International Alphabets and Unicode 66

Numbers and character strings (such as the ones on this display board) are important data types in any Java program. In this chapter, you will learn how to work with numbers and text, and how to write simple programs that perform useful tasks with them.

2.1 Variables

When your program carries out computations, you will want to store values so that you can use them later. In a Java program, you use **variables** to store values. In this section, you will learn how to declare and use variables.

To illustrate the use of variables, we will develop a program that solves the following problem. Soft drinks are sold in cans and bottles. A store offers a six-pack of 12-ounce cans for the same price as a two-liter bottle. Which should you buy? (Twelve fluid ounces equal approximately 0.355 liters.)

In our program, we will declare variables for the number of cans per pack and for the volume of each can. Then we will compute the volume of a six-pack in liters and print out the answer.

What contains more soda? A six-pack of 12-ounce cans or a two-liter bottle?

2.1.1 Variable Declarations

The following statement declares a variable named cansPerPack:

```
int cansPerPack = 6;
```

A **variable** is a storage location in a computer program. Each variable has a name and holds a value.

> A variable is a storage location with a name.

A variable is similar to a parking space in a parking garage. The parking space has an identifier (such as "J 053"), and it can hold a vehicle. A variable has a name (such as cansPerPack), and it can hold a value (such as 6).

Like a variable in a computer program, a parking space has an identifier and a contents.

Syntax 2.1 Variable Declaration

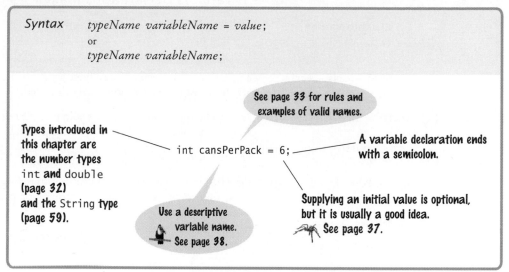

Syntax   *typeName*   *variableName* = *value*;
               or
               typeName   *variableName*;

See page 33 for rules and examples of valid names.

Types introduced in this chapter are the number types `int` **and** `double` **(page 32) and the** `String` **type (page 59).**

`int cansPerPack = 6;`

A variable declaration ends with a semicolon.

Use a descriptive variable name. See page 38.

Supplying an initial value is optional, but it is usually a good idea. See page 37.

When declaring a variable, you usually specify an initial value.

When declaring a variable, you usually want to **initialize** it. That is, you specify the value that should be stored in the variable. Consider again this variable declaration:

```
int cansPerPack = 6;
```

The variable `cansPerPack` is initialized with the value 6.

When declaring a variable, you also specify the type of its values.

Like a parking space that is restricted to a certain type of vehicle (such as a compact car, motorcycle, or electric vehicle), a variable in Java stores data of a specific **type**. Java supports quite a few data types: numbers, text strings, files, dates, and many others. You must specify the type whenever you declare a variable (see Syntax 2.1).

The `cansPerPack` variable is an **integer**, a whole number without a fractional part. In Java, this type is called `int`. (See the next section for more information about number types in Java.)

Note that the type comes before the variable name:

```
int cansPerPack = 6;
```

After you have declared and initialized a variable, you can use it. For example,

```
int cansPerPack = 6;
System.out.println(cansPerPack);
int cansPerCrate = 4 * cansPerPack;
```

Table 1 shows several examples of variable declarations.

Each parking space is suitable for a particular type of vehicle, just as each variable holds a value of a particular type.

Table 1 Variable Declarations in Java

Variable Name	Comment
`int cans = 6;`	Declares an integer variable and initializes it with 6.
`int total = cans + bottles;`	The initial value need not be a fixed value. (Of course, cans and bottles must have been previously declared.)
🚫 `bottles = 1;`	**Error:** The type is missing. This statement is not a declaration but an assignment of a new value to an existing variable—see Section 2.1.4.
🚫 `int volume = "2";`	**Error:** You cannot initialize a number with a string.
`int cansPerPack;`	Declares an integer variable without initializing it. This can be a cause for errors—see Common Error 2.1 on page 37.
`int dollars, cents;`	Declares two integer variables in a single statement. In this book, we will declare each variable in a separate statement.

2.1.2 Number Types

Use the int type for numbers that cannot have a fractional part.

In Java, there are several different types of numbers. You use the int type to denote a whole number without a fractional part. For example, there must be an integer number of cans in any pack of cans—you cannot have a fraction of a can.

When a fractional part is required (such as in the number 0.335), we use **floating-point numbers**. The most commonly used type for floating-point numbers in Java is called double. (If you want to know the reason, read Special Topic 2.1 on page 39.) Here is the declaration of a floating-point variable:

```
double canVolume = 0.335;
```

Table 2 Number Literals in Java

Number	Type	Comment
6	int	An integer has no fractional part.
–6	int	Integers can be negative.
0	int	Zero is an integer.
0.5	double	A number with a fractional part has type double.
1.0	double	An integer with a fractional part .0 has type double.
1E6	double	A number in exponential notation: 1×10^6 or 1000000. Numbers in exponential notation always have type double.
2.96E-2	double	Negative exponent: $2.96 \times 10^{-2} = 2.96 / 100 = 0.0296$
🚫 100,000		**Error:** Do not use a comma as a decimal separator.
🚫 3 1/2		**Error:** Do not use fractions; use decimal notation: 3.5

Use the double type for floating-point numbers.

When a value such as 6 or 0.335 occurs in a Java program, it is called a **number literal**. If a number literal has a decimal point, it is a floating-point number; otherwise, it is an integer. Table 2 shows how to write integer and floating-point literals in Java.

2.1.3 Variable Names

When you declare a variable, you should pick a name that explains its purpose. For example, it is better to use a descriptive name, such as canVolume, than a terse name, such as cv.

In Java, there are a few simple rules for variable names:

1. Variable names must start with a letter or the underscore (_) character, and the remaining characters must be letters, numbers, or underscores. (Technically, the $ symbol is allowed as well, but you should not use it—it is intended for names that are automatically generated by tools.)

2. You cannot use other symbols such as ? or %. Spaces are not permitted inside names either. You can use uppercase letters to denote word boundaries, as in cansPerPack. This naming convention is called *camel case* because the uppercase letters in the middle of the name look like the humps of a camel.)

3. Variable names are **case sensitive**, that is, canVolume and canvolume are different names.

4. You cannot use **reserved words** such as double or class as names; these words are reserved exclusively for their special Java meanings. (See Appendix C for a listing of all reserved words in Java.)

By convention, variable names should start with a lowercase letter.

It is a convention among Java programmers that variable names should start with a lowercase letter (such as canVolume) and class names should start with an uppercase letter (such as HelloPrinter). That way, it is easy to tell them apart.

Table 3 shows examples of legal and illegal variable names in Java.

Table 3 Variable Names in Java

Variable Name	Comment
canVolume1	Variable names consist of letters, numbers, and the underscore character.
x	In mathematics, you use short variable names such as x or y. This is legal in Java, but not very common, because it can make programs harder to understand (see Programming Tip 2.1 on page 38).
⚠ CanVolume	**Caution:** Variable names are case sensitive. This variable name is different from canVolume, and it violates the convention that variable names should start with a lowercase letter.
🚫 6pack	**Error:** Variable names cannot start with a number.
🚫 can volume	**Error:** Variable names cannot contain spaces.
🚫 double	**Error:** You cannot use a reserved word as a variable name.
🚫 ltr/fl.oz	**Error:** You cannot use symbols such as / or .

2.1.4 The Assignment Statement

An assignment statement stores a new value in a variable, replacing the previously stored value.

You use the **assignment statement** to place a new value into a variable. Here is an example:

```
cansPerPack = 8;
```

The left-hand side of an assignment statement consists of a variable. The right-hand side is an expression that has a value. That value is stored in the variable, overwriting its previous contents.

There is an important difference between a variable declaration and an assignment statement:

```
int cansPerPack = 6;          Variable declaration
...
cansPerPack = 8;              Assignment statement
```

ANIMATION
Variable Initialization and Assignment

The first statement is the declaration of `cansPerPack`. It is an instruction to create a new variable of type `int`, to give it the name `cansPerPack`, and to initialize it with 6. The second statement is an *assignment statement:* an instruction to replace the contents of the *existing* variable `cansPerPack` with another value.

The = sign doesn't mean that the left-hand side is *equal* to the right-hand side. The expression on the right is evaluated, and its value is placed into the variable on the left.

The assignment operator = does *not* denote mathematical equality.

Do not confuse this *assignment operation* with the = used in algebra to denote *equality*. The assignment operator is an instruction to do something—namely, place a value into a variable. The mathematical equality states that two values are equal.

For example, in Java, it is perfectly legal to write

```
totalVolume = totalVolume + 2;
```

It means to look up the value stored in the variable `totalVolume`, add 2 to it, and place the result back into `totalVolume`. (See Figure 1.) The net effect of executing this statement is to increment `totalVolume` by 2. For example, if `totalVolume` was 2.13 before execution of the statement, it is set to 4.13 afterwards. Of course, in mathematics it would make no sense to write that $x = x + 2$. No value can equal itself plus 2.

Syntax 2.2   Assignment

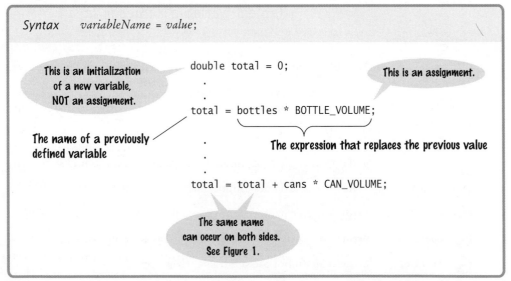

Syntax   *variableName* = *value*;

```
double total = 0;
.
.
total = bottles * BOTTLE_VOLUME;
.
.
.
total = total + cans * CAN_VOLUME;
```

This is an initialization of a new variable, NOT an assignment.

This is an assignment.

The name of a previously defined variable

The expression that replaces the previous value

The same name can occur on both sides. See Figure 1.

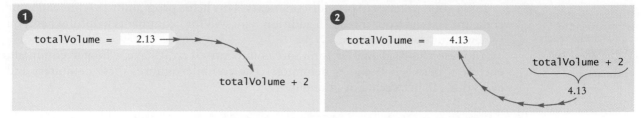

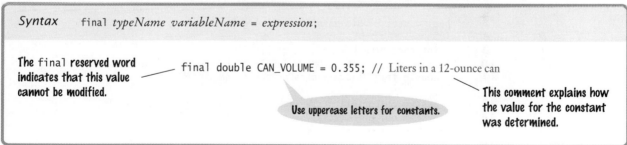

Figure 1 Executing the Assignment totalVolume = totalVolume + 2

2.1.5 Constants

You cannot change the value of a variable that is defined as final.

When a variable is defined with the reserved word final, its value can never change. Constants are commonly written using capital letters to distinguish them visually from regular variables:

```
final double BOTTLE_VOLUME = 2;
```

It is good programming style to use named constants in your program to explain the meanings of numeric values. For example, compare the statements

```
double totalVolume = bottles * 2;
```

and

```
double totalVolume = bottles * BOTTLE_VOLUME;
```

A programmer reading the first statement may not understand the significance of the number 2. The second statement, with a named constant, makes the computation much clearer.

Syntax 2.3 Constant Declaration

Syntax   final *typeName variableName* = *expression*;

The final **reserved word indicates that this value cannot be modified.**

```
final double CAN_VOLUME = 0.355; // Liters in a 12-ounce can
```

Use uppercase letters for constants.

This comment explains how the value for the constant was determined.

2.1.6 Comments

As your programs get more complex, you should add **comments**, explanations for human readers of your code. For example, here is a comment that explains the value used in a variable initialization:

```
final double CAN_VOLUME = 0.355; // Liters in a 12-ounce can
```

This comment explains the significance of the value 0.355 to a human reader. The compiler does not process comments at all. It ignores everything from a // delimiter to the end of the line.

Use comments to add explanations for humans who read your code. The compiler ignores comments.

It is a good practice to provide comments. This helps programmers who read your code understand your intent. In addition, you will find comments helpful when you review your own programs.

You use the `//` delimiter for short comments. If you have a longer comment, enclose it between `/*` and `*/` delimiters. The compiler ignores these delimiters and everything in between. For example,

```
/*
    There are approximately 0.335 liters in a 12-ounce can because one ounce
    equals 0.02957353 liter; see The International Systems of Units (SI) - Conversion
    Factors for General Use (NIST Special Publication 1038).
*/
```

Finally, start a comment that explains the purpose of a program with the `/**` delimiter instead of `/*`. Tools that analyze source files rely on that convention. For example,

```
/**
    This program computes the volume (in liters) of a six-pack of soda cans.
*/
```

The following program shows the use of variables, constants, and the assignment statement. The program displays the volume of a six-pack of cans and the total volume of the six-pack and a two-liter bottle. We use constants for the can and bottle volumes. The `totalVolume` variable is initialized with the volume of the cans. Using an assignment statement, we add the bottle volume. As you can see from the program output, the six-pack of cans contains over two liters of soda.

section_1/Volume1.java

```java
1  /**
2      This program computes the volume (in liters) of a six-pack of soda
3      cans and the total volume of a six-pack and a two-liter bottle.
4  */
5  public class Volume1
6  {
7     public static void main(String[] args)
8     {
9        int cansPerPack = 6;
10       final double CAN_VOLUME = 0.355; // Liters in a 12-ounce can
11       double totalVolume = cansPerPack * CAN_VOLUME;
12
13       System.out.print("A six-pack of 12-ounce cans contains ");
14       System.out.print(totalVolume);
15       System.out.println(" liters.");
16
17       final double BOTTLE_VOLUME = 2; // Two-liter bottle
18
19       totalVolume = totalVolume + BOTTLE_VOLUME;
20
21       System.out.print("A six-pack and a two-liter bottle contain ");
22       System.out.print(totalVolume);
23       System.out.println(" liters.");
24    }
25 }
```

Program Run

```
A six-pack of 12-ounce cans contains 2.13 liters.
A six-pack and a two-liter bottle contain 4.13 liters.
```

*Just as a television commentator explains the news,
you use comments in your program to explain its behavior.*

SELF CHECK

1. Declare a variable suitable for holding the number of bottles in a case.
2. What is wrong with the following variable declaration?

   `int ounces per liter = 28.35`
3. Declare and initialize two variables, `unitPrice` and `quantity`, to contain the unit price of a single bottle and the number of bottles purchased. Use reasonable initial values.
4. Use the variables declared in Self Check 3 to display the total purchase price.
5. Some drinks are sold in four-packs instead of six-packs. How would you change the `Volume1.java` program to compute the total volume?
6. What is wrong with this comment?

   `double canVolume = 0.355; /* Liters in a 12-ounce can //`
7. Suppose the type of the `cansPerPack` variable in `Volume1.java` was changed from `int` to `double`. What would be the effect on the program?
8. Why can't the variable `totalVolume` in the `Volume1.java` program be declared as `final`?
9. How would you explain assignment using the parking space analogy?

Practice It Now you can try these exercises at the end of the chapter: R2.1, R2.2, P2.1.

Common Error 2.1

Using Undeclared or Uninitialized Variables

You must declare a variable before you use it for the first time. For example, the following sequence of statements would not be legal:

```
double canVolume = 12 * literPerOunce; // ERROR: literPerOunce is not yet declared
double literPerOunce = 0.0296;
```

In your program, the statements are compiled in order. When the compiler reaches the first statement, it does not know that `literPerOunce` will be declared in the next line, and it reports an error. The remedy is to reorder the declarations so that each variable is declared before it is used.

A related error is to leave a variable uninitialized:

```java
int bottles;
int bottleVolume = bottles * 2; // ERROR: bottles is not yet initialized
```

The Java compiler will complain that you are using a variable that has not yet been given a value. The remedy is to assign a value to the variable before it is used.

Programming Tip 2.1

Choose Descriptive Variable Names

We could have saved ourselves a lot of typing by using shorter variable names, as in

```java
double cv = 0.355;
```

Compare this declaration with the one that we actually used, though. Which one is easier to read? There is no comparison. Just reading `canVolume` is a lot less trouble than reading `cv` and then *figuring out* it must mean "can volume".

In practical programming, this is particularly important when programs are written by more than one person. It may be obvious to *you* that cv stands for can volume and not current velocity, but will it be obvious to the person who needs to update your code years later? For that matter, will you remember yourself what cv means when you look at the code three months from now?

Common Error 2.2

Overflow

Because numbers are represented in the computer with a limited number of digits, they cannot represent arbitrary numbers.

The `int` type has a *limited range:* It can represent numbers up to a little more than two billion. For many applications, this is not a problem, but you cannot use an `int` to represent the world population.

If a computation yields a value that is outside the `int` range, the result *overflows*. No error is displayed. Instead, the result is truncated, yielding a useless value. For example,

```java
int fiftyMillion = 50000000;
System.out.println(100 * fiftyMillion); // Expected: 5000000000
```

displays 705032704.

In situations such as this, you can switch to `double` values. However, read Common Error 2.3 for more information about a related issue: roundoff errors.

Common Error 2.3

Roundoff Errors

Roundoff errors are a fact of life when calculating with floating-point numbers. You probably have encountered that phenomenon yourself with manual calculations. If you calculate 1/3 to two decimal places, you get 0.33. Multiplying again by 3, you obtain 0.99, not 1.00.

In the processor hardware, numbers are represented in the binary number system, using only digits 0 and 1. As with decimal numbers, you can get roundoff errors when binary digits are lost. They just may crop up at different places than you might expect.

Here is an example:

```java
double price = 4.35;
double quantity = 100;
double total = price * quantity; // Should be 100 * 4.35 = 435
System.out.println(total); // Prints 434.99999999999999
```

In the binary system, there is no exact representation for 4.35, just as there is no exact representation for 1/3 in the decimal system. The representation used by the computer is just a little less than 4.35, so 100 times that value is just a little less than 435.

You can deal with roundoff errors by rounding to the nearest integer (see Section 2.2.5) or by displaying a fixed number of digits after the decimal separator (see Section 2.3.2).

Programming Tip 2.2

Do Not Use Magic Numbers

A **magic number** is a numeric constant that appears in your code without explanation. For example,

```java
totalVolume = bottles * 2;
```

Why 2? Are bottles twice as voluminous as cans? No, the reason is that every bottle contains 2 liters. Use a named constant to make the code self-documenting:

```java
final double BOTTLE_VOLUME = 2;
totalVolume = bottles * BOTTLE_VOLUME;
```

There is another reason for using named constants. Suppose circumstances change, and the bottle volume is now 1.5 liters. If you used a named constant, you make a single change, and you are done. Otherwise, you have to look at every value of 2 in your program and ponder whether it meant a bottle volume, or something else. In a program that is more than a few pages long, that is incredibly tedious and error-prone.

Even the most reasonable cosmic constant is going to change one day. You think there are seven days per week? Your customers on Mars are going to be pretty unhappy about your silly prejudice. Make a constant

```java
final int DAYS_PER_WEEK = 7;
```

We prefer programs that are easy to understand over those that appear to work by magic.

Special Topic 2.1

Numeric Types in Java

In addition to the int and double types, Java has several other numeric types.

Java has two floating-point types. The float type uses half the storage of the double type that we use in this book, but it can only store about 7 decimal digits. (In the computer, numbers are represented in the binary number system, using digits 0 and 1.) Many years ago, when computers had far less memory than they have today, float was the standard type for floating-point computations, and programmers would indulge in the luxury of "double precision" only when they needed the additional digits. Today, the float type is rarely used.

By the way, these numbers are called "floating-point" because of their internal representation in the computer. Consider numbers 29600, 2.96, and 0.0296. They can be represented in a very similar way: namely, as a sequence of the significant digits—296—and an indication of the position of the decimal point. When the values are multiplied or divided by 10, only the position of the decimal point changes; it "floats". Computers use base 2, not base 10, but the principle is the same.

In addition to the int type, Java has integer types byte, short, and long. Their ranges are shown in Table 4. (Their strange-looking limits are related to powers of 2, another consequence of the fact that computers use binary numbers.)

Table 4 Java Number Types		
Type	Description	Size
int	The integer type, with range −2,147,483,648 (Integer.MIN_VALUE) ... 2,147,483,647 (Integer.MAX_VALUE, about 2.14 billion)	4 bytes
byte	The type describing a single byte consisting of 8 bits, with range −128 ... 127	1 byte
short	The short integer type, with range −32,768 ... 32,767	2 bytes
long	The long integer type, with about 19 decimal digits	8 bytes
double	The double-precision floating-point type, with about 15 decimal digits and a range of about $\pm 10^{308}$	8 bytes
float	The single-precision floating-point type, with about 7 decimal digits and a range of about $\pm 10^{38}$	4 bytes
char	The character type, representing code units in the Unicode encoding scheme (see Random Fact 2.2)	2 bytes

Special Topic 2.2

Big Numbers

If you want to compute with really large numbers, you can use big number objects. Big number objects are objects of the BigInteger and BigDecimal classes in the java.math package. Unlike the number types such as int or double, big number objects have essentially no limits on their size and precision. However, computations with big number objects are much slower than those that involve number types. Perhaps more importantly, you can't use the familiar arithmetic operators such as (+ - *) with them. Instead, you have to use methods called add, subtract, and multiply. Here is an example of how to create a BigInteger object and how to call the multiply method:

```
BigInteger oneHundred = new BigInteger("100");
BigInteger fiftyMillion = new BigInteger("50000000");
System.out.println(oneHundred.multiply(fiftyMillion)); // Prints 5000000000
```

The BigDecimal type carries out floating-point computations without roundoff errors. For example,

```
BigDecimal price = new BigDecimal("4.35");
BigDecimal quantity = new BigDecimal("100");
BigDecimal total = price.multiply(quantity);
System.out.println(total); // Prints 435.00
```

2.2 Arithmetic

In the following sections, you will learn how to carry out arithmetic calculations in Java.

2.2.1 Arithmetic Operators

Java supports the same four basic arithmetic operations as a calculator—addition, subtraction, multiplication, and division—but it uses different symbols for multiplication and division.

You must write a * b to denote multiplication. Unlike in mathematics, you cannot write a b, a · b, or a × b. Similarly, division is always indicated with a /, never a ÷ or a fraction bar.

For example, $\dfrac{a+b}{2}$ becomes (a + b) / 2.

The combination of variables, literals, operators, and/or method calls is called an **expression**. For example, (a + b) / 2 is an expression.

Parentheses are used just as in algebra: to indicate in which order the parts of the expression should be computed. For example, in the expression (a + b) / 2, the sum a + b is computed first, and then the sum is divided by 2. In contrast, in the expression

    a + b / 2

only b is divided by 2, and then the sum of a and b / 2 is formed. As in regular algebraic notation, multiplication and division have a *higher precedence* than addition and subtraction. For example, in the expression a + b / 2, the / is carried out first, even though the + operation occurs further to the left.

> Mixing integers and floating-point values in an arithmetic expression yields a floating-point value.

If you mix integer and floating-point values in an arithmetic expression, the result is a floating-point value. For example, 7 + 4.0 is the floating-point value 11.0.

2.2.2 Increment and Decrement

> The ++ operator adds 1 to a variable; the -- operator subtracts 1.

Changing a variable by adding or subtracting 1 is so common that there is a special shorthand for it. The ++ operator increments a variable—see Figure 2:

    counter++; // Adds 1 to the variable counter

Similarly, the -- operator decrements a variable:

    counter--; // Subtracts 1 from counter

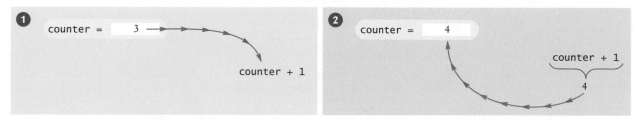

Figure 2 Incrementing a Variable

2.2.3 Integer Division and Remainder

Division works as you would expect, as long as at least one of the numbers involved is a floating-point number. That is,

```
7.0 / 4.0
7 / 4.0
7.0 / 4
```

all yield 1.75. However, if *both* numbers are integers, then the result of the division is always an integer, with the remainder discarded. That is,

```
7 / 4
```

evaluates to 1 because 7 divided by 4 is 1 with a remainder of 3 (which is discarded). This can be a source of subtle programming errors—see Common Error 2.4.

Integer division and the % operator yield the dollar and cent values of a piggybank full of pennies.

If you are interested in the remainder only, use the % operator:

```
7 % 4
```

is 3, the remainder of the integer division of 7 by 4. The % symbol has no analog in algebra. It was chosen because it looks similar to /, and the remainder operation is related to division. The operator is called **modulus**. (Some people call it *modulo* or *mod*.) It has no relationship with the percent operation that you find on some calculators.

Here is a typical use for the integer / and % operations. Suppose you have an amount of pennies in a piggybank:

```
int pennies = 1729;
```

You want to determine the value in dollars and cents. You obtain the dollars through an integer division by 100:

```
int dollars = pennies / 100;   // Sets dollars to 17
```

The integer division discards the remainder. To obtain the remainder, use the % operator:

```
int cents = pennies % 100;   // Sets cents to 29
```

See Table 5 for additional examples.

Table 5 Integer Division and Remainder

Expression (where n = 1729)	Value	Comment
n % 10	9	n % 10 is always the last digit of n.
n / 10	172	This is always n without the last digit.
n % 100	29	The last two digits of n.
n / 10.0	172.9	Because 10.0 is a floating-point number, the fractional part is not discarded.
–n % 10	–9	Because the first argument is negative, the remainder is also negative.
n % 2	1	n % 2 is 0 if n is even, 1 or –1 if n is odd.

2.2.4 Powers and Roots

The Java library declares many mathematical functions, such as `Math.sqrt` (square root) and `Math.pow` (raising to a power).

In Java, there are no symbols for powers and roots. To compute them, you must call methods. To take the square root of a number, you use the `Math.sqrt` method. For example, $\sqrt{x}$ is written as `Math.sqrt(x)`. To compute x^n, you write `Math.pow(x, n)`.

In algebra, you use fractions, exponents, and roots to arrange expressions in a compact two-dimensional form. In Java, you have to write all expressions in a linear arrangement. For example, the mathematical expression

$$b \times \left(1 + \frac{r}{100}\right)^n$$

becomes

```
b * Math.pow(1 + r / 100, n)
```

Figure 3 shows how to analyze such an expression. Table 6 shows additional mathematical methods.

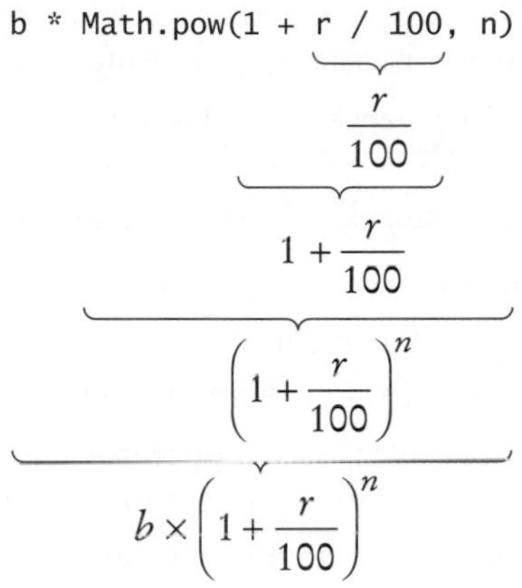

Figure 3
Analyzing an Expression

Table 6 Mathematical Methods

Method	Returns
`Math.sqrt(x)`	Square root of x (≥ 0)
`Math.pow(x, y)`	x^y ($x > 0$, or $x = 0$ and $y > 0$, or $x < 0$ and y is an integer)
`Math.sin(x)`	Sine of x (x in radians)
`Math.cos(x)`	Cosine of x
`Math.tan(x)`	Tangent of x
`Math.toRadians(x)`	Convert x degrees to radians (i.e., returns $x \cdot \pi/180$)
`Math.toDegrees(x)`	Convert x radians to degrees (i.e., returns $x \cdot 180/\pi$)
`Math.exp(x)`	e^x
`Math.log(x)`	Natural log ($\ln(x)$, $x > 0$)

Table 6 Mathematical Methods	
Method	Returns
`Math.log10(x)`	Decimal log ($\log_{10}(x)$, $x > 0$)
`Math.round(x)`	Closest integer to x (as a `long`)
`Math.abs(x)`	Absolute value $|x|$
`Math.max(x, y)`	The larger of x and y
`Math.min(x, y)`	The smaller of x and y

2.2.5 Converting Floating-Point Numbers to Integers

Occasionally, you have a value of type `double` that you need to convert to the type `int`. It is an error to assign a floating-point value to an integer:

```
double balance = total + tax;
int dollars = balance; // Error: Cannot assign double to int
```

The compiler disallows this assignment because it is potentially dangerous:

- The fractional part is lost.
- The magnitude may be too large. (The largest integer is about 2 billion, but a floating-point number can be much larger.)

You must use the **cast** operator `(int)` to convert a convert floating-point value to an integer. Write the cast operator before the expression that you want to convert:

You use a cast (*typeName*) to convert a value to a different type.

```
double balance = total + tax;
int dollars = (int) balance;
```

The cast `(int)` converts the floating-point value `balance` to an integer by discarding the fractional part. For example, if `balance` is 13.75, then `dollars` is set to 13.

When applying the cast operator to an arithmetic expression, you need to place the expression inside parentheses:

```
int dollars = (int) (total + tax);
```

Syntax 2.4   Cast

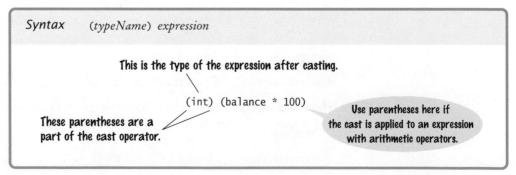

Syntax   (*typeName*) *expression*

This is the type of the expression after casting.

(int) (balance * 100)

These parentheses are a part of the cast operator.

Use parentheses here if the cast is applied to an expression with arithmetic operators.

ONLINE EXAMPLE

A program demonstrating casts, rounding, and the % operator.

Discarding the fractional part is not always appropriate. If you want to round a floating-point number to the nearest whole number, use the `Math.round` method. This method returns a `long` integer, because large floating-point numbers cannot be stored in an `int`.

```
long rounded = Math.round(balance);
```

If `balance` is 13.75, then `rounded` is set to 14.

If you know that the result can be stored in an `int` and does not require a `long`, you can use a cast:

```
int rounded = (int) Math.round(balance);
```

Table 7 Arithmetic Expressions

Mathematical Expression	Java Expression	Comments
$\dfrac{x + y}{2}$	`(x + y) / 2`	The parentheses are required; x + y / 2 computes $x + \frac{y}{2}$.
$\dfrac{xy}{2}$	`x * y / 2`	Parentheses are not required; operators with the same precedence are evaluated left to right.
$\left(1 + \dfrac{r}{100}\right)^n$	`Math.pow(1 + r / 100, n)`	Use `Math.pow(x, n)` to compute x^n.
$\sqrt{a^2 + b^2}$	`Math.sqrt(a * a + b * b)`	a * a is simpler than `Math.pow(a, 2)`.
$\dfrac{i + j + k}{3}$	`(i + j + k) / 3.0`	If i, j, and k are integers, using a denominator of 3.0 forces floating-point division.
π	`Math.PI`	`Math.PI` is a constant declared in the Math class.

SELF CHECK

10. A bank account earns interest once per year. In Java, how do you compute the interest earned in the first year? Assume variables `percent` and `balance` of type `double` have already been declared.

11. In Java, how do you compute the side length of a square whose area is stored in the variable `area`?

12. The volume of a sphere is given by

$$V = \frac{4}{3}\pi r^3$$

If the radius is given by a variable `radius` of type `double`, write a Java expression for the volume.

13. What is the value of `1729 / 10` and `1729 % 10`?

14. If `n` is a positive number, what is `(n / 10) % 10`?

Practice It Now you can try these exercises at the end of the chapter: R2.3, R2.5, P2.4, P2.25.

Unintended Integer Division

It is unfortunate that Java uses the same symbol, namely /, for both integer and floating-point division. These are really quite different operations. It is a common error to use integer division by accident. Consider this segment that computes the average of three integers.

```java
int score1 = 10;
int score2 = 4;
int score3 = 9;

double average = (score1 + score2 + score3) / 3; // Error
System.out.println("Average score: " + average); // Prints 7.0, not 7.666666666666667
```

What could be wrong with that? Of course, the average of score1, score2, and score3 is

$$\frac{score1 + score2 + score3}{3}$$

Here, however, the / does not mean division in the mathematical sense. It denotes integer division because both score1 + score2 + score3 and 3 are integers. Because the scores add up to 23, the average is computed to be 7, the result of the integer division of 23 by 3. That integer 7 is then moved into the floating-point variable average. The remedy is to make the numerator or denominator into a floating-point number:

```java
double total = score1 + score2 + score3;
double average = total / 3;
```

or

```java
double average = (score1 + score2 + score3) / 3.0;
```

Unbalanced Parentheses

Consider the expression

```
((a + b) * t / 2 * (1 - t)
```

What is wrong with it? Count the parentheses. There are three (and two). The parentheses are *unbalanced*. This kind of typing error is very common with complicated expressions. Now consider this expression.

```
(a + b) * t) / (2 * (1 - t)
```

This expression has three (and three), but it still is not correct. In the middle of the expression,

```
(a + b) * t) / (2 * (1 - t)
         ↑
```

there is only one (but two), which is an error. In the middle of an expression, the count of (must be greater than or equal to the count of), and at the end of the expression the two counts must be the same.

Here is a simple trick to make the counting easier without using pencil and paper. It is difficult for the brain to keep two counts simultaneously. Keep only one count when scanning the expression. Start with 1 at the first opening parenthesis, add 1 whenever you see an opening parenthesis, and subtract one whenever you see a closing parenthesis. Say the numbers aloud as you scan the

expression. If the count ever drops below zero, or is not zero at the end, the parentheses are unbalanced. For example, when scanning the previous expression, you would mutter

```
(a + b) * t) / (2 * (1 - t)
1     0   -1
```

and you would find the error.

Spaces in Expressions

It is easier to read

```
x1 = (-b + Math.sqrt(b * b - 4 * a * c)) / (2 * a);
```

than

```
x1=(-b+Math.sqrt(b*b-4*a*c))/(2*a);
```

Simply put spaces around all operators + - * / % =. However, don't put a space after a *unary* minus: a – used to negate a single quantity, such as -b. That way, it can be easily distinguished from a *binary* minus, as in a - b.

It is customary not to put a space after a method name. That is, write Math.sqrt(x) and not Math.sqrt (x).

Combining Assignment and Arithmetic

In Java, you can combine arithmetic and assignment. For example, the instruction

```
total += cans;
```

is a shortcut for

```
total = total + cans;
```

Similarly,

```
total *= 2;
```

is another way of writing

```
total = total * 2;
```

Many programmers find this a convenient shortcut. If you like it, go ahead and use it in your own code. For simplicity, we won't use it in this book, though.

Using Integer Division

A punch recipe calls for a given amount of orange soda. In this Video Example, you will see how to compute the required number of 12-ounce cans, using integer division.

✚ Available online in WileyPLUS and at www.wiley.com/college/horstmann.

Random Fact 2.1 The Pentium Floating-Point Bug

In 1994, Intel Corporation released what was then its most powerful processor, the Pentium. Unlike previous generations of its processors, it had a very fast floating-point unit. Intel's goal was to compete aggressively with the makers of higher-end processors for engineering workstations. The Pentium was a huge success immediately.

In the summer of 1994, Dr. Thomas Nicely of Lynchburg College in Virginia ran an extensive set of computations to analyze the sums of reciprocals of certain sequences of prime numbers. The results were not always what his theory predicted, even after he took into account the inevitable roundoff errors. Then Dr. Nicely noted that the same program did produce the correct results when running on the slower 486 processor that preceded the Pentium in Intel's lineup. This should not have happened. The optimal round-off behavior of floating-point calculations has been standardized by the Institute for Electrical and Electronic Engineers (IEEE) and Intel claimed to adhere to the IEEE standard in both the 486 and the Pentium processors. Upon further checking, Dr. Nicely discovered that indeed there was a very small set of numbers for which the product of two numbers was computed differently on the two processors. For example,

$$4{,}195{,}835 - \big((4{,}195{,}835/3{,}145{,}727) \times 3{,}145{,}727\big)$$

is mathematically equal to 0, and it did compute as 0 on a 486 processor. On his Pentium processor the result was 256.

As it turned out, Intel had independently discovered the bug in its testing and had started to produce chips that fixed it. The bug was caused by an error in a table that was used to speed up the floating-point multiplication algorithm of the processor. Intel determined that the problem was exceedingly rare. They claimed that under normal use, a typical consumer would only notice the problem once every 27,000 years. Unfortunately for Intel, Dr. Nicely had not been a normal user.

Now Intel had a real problem on its hands. It figured that the cost of replacing all Pentium processors that it had sold so far would cost a great deal of money. Intel already had more orders for the chip than it could produce, and it would be particularly galling to have to give out the scarce chips as free replacements instead of selling them. Intel's management decided to punt on the issue and initially offered to replace the processors only for those customers who could prove that their work required absolute precision in mathematical calculations. Naturally, that did not go over well with the hundreds of thousands of customers who had paid retail prices of $700 and more for a Pentium chip and did not want to live with the nagging feeling that perhaps, one day, their income tax program would produce a faulty return.

Ultimately, Intel caved in to public demand and replaced all defective chips, at a cost of about 475 million dollars.

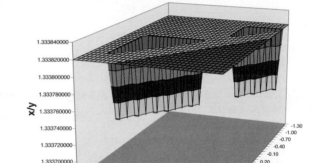

This graph shows a set of numbers for which the original Pentium processor obtained the wrong quotient.

2.3 Input and Output

In the following sections, you will see how to read user input and how to control the appearance of the output that your programs produce.

2.3.1 Reading Input

You can make your programs more flexible if you ask the program user for inputs rather than using fixed values. Consider, for example, a program that processes prices and quantities of soda containers. Prices and quantities are likely to fluctuate. The program user should provide them as inputs.

When a program asks for user input, it should first print a message that tells the user which input is expected. Such a message is called a **prompt**.

```java
System.out.print("Please enter the number of bottles: "); // Display prompt
```

Use the `print` method, not `println`, to display the prompt. You want the input to appear after the colon, not on the following line. Also remember to leave a space after the colon.

Because output is sent to `System.out`, you might think that you use `System.in` for input. Unfortunately, it isn't quite that simple. When Java was first designed, not much attention was given to reading keyboard input. It was assumed that all programmers would produce graphical user interfaces with text fields and menus. `System.in` was given a minimal set of features and must be combined with other classes to be useful.

To read keyboard input, you use a class called `Scanner`. You obtain a `Scanner` *object* by using the following statement:

```java
Scanner in = new Scanner(System.in);
```

You will learn more about objects and classes in Chapter 8. For now, simply include this statement whenever you want to read keyboard input.

A supermarket scanner reads bar codes. The Java Scanner reads numbers and text.

Java classes are grouped into packages. Use the import statement to use classes from packages.

When using the `Scanner` class, you need to carry out another step: import the class from its **package**. A package is a collection of classes with a related purpose. All classes in the Java library are contained in packages. The `System` class belongs to the package `java.lang`. The `Scanner` class belongs to the package `java.util`.

Only the classes in the `java.lang` package are automatically available in your programs. To use the `Scanner` class from the `java.util` package, place the following declaration at the top of your program file:

```java
import java.util.Scanner;
```

Once you have a scanner, you use its `nextInt` method to read an integer value:

```java
System.out.print("Please enter the number of bottles: ");
int bottles = in.nextInt();
```

Syntax 2.5 Input Statement

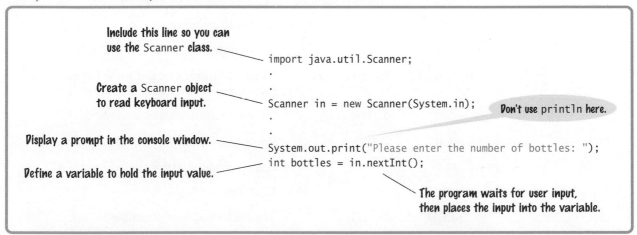

Include this line so you can use the Scanner class. ── `import java.util.Scanner;`

Create a Scanner object to read keyboard input. ── `Scanner in = new Scanner(System.in);` — Don't use `println` here.

Display a prompt in the console window. ── `System.out.print("Please enter the number of bottles: ");`

Define a variable to hold the input value. ── `int bottles = in.nextInt();`

The program waits for user input, then places the input into the variable.

Use the `Scanner` class to read keyboard input in a console window.

When the `nextInt` method is called, the program waits until the user types a number and presses the Enter key. After the user supplies the input, the number is placed into the `bottles` variable, and the program continues.

To read a floating-point number, use the `nextDouble` method instead:

```
System.out.print("Enter price: ");
double price = in.nextDouble();
```

2.3.2 Formatted Output

When you print the result of a computation, you often want to control its appearance. For example, when you print an amount in dollars and cents, you usually want it to be rounded to two significant digits. That is, you want the output to look like

```
Price per liter: 1.22
```

instead of

```
Price per liter: 1.215962441314554
```

Use the `printf` method to specify how values should be formatted.

The following command displays the price with two digits after the decimal point:

```
System.out.printf("%.2f", price);
```

You can also specify a *field width*:

```
System.out.printf("%10.2f", price);
```

The price is printed using ten characters: six spaces followed by the four characters `1.22`.

```
       1 . 2 2
```

The construct `%10.2f` is called a *format specifier:* it describes how a value should be formatted. The letter `f` at the end of the format specifier indicates that we are displaying a floating-point number. Use `d` for an integer and `s` for a string; see Table 8 for examples.

Table 8 Format Specifier Examples

Format String	Sample Output	Comments
`"%d"`	24	Use `d` with an integer.
`"%5d"`	24	Spaces are added so that the field width is 5.
`"Quantity:%5d"`	Quantity: 24	Characters inside a format string but outside a format specifier appear in the output.
`"%f"`	1.21997	Use `f` with a floating-point number.
`"%.2f"`	1.22	Prints two digits after the decimal point.
`"%7.2f"`	1.22	Spaces are added so that the field width is 7.
`"%s"`	Hello	Use `s` with a string.
`"%d %.2f"`	24 1.22	You can format multiple values at once.

You use the `printf` *method to line up your output in neat columns.*

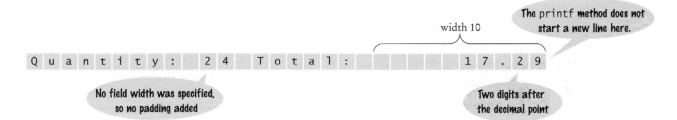

A format string contains format specifiers and literal characters. Any characters that are not format specifiers are printed verbatim. For example, the command

```
System.out.printf("Price per liter:%10.2f", price);
```

prints

```
Price per liter:      1.22
```

You can print multiple values with a single call to the `printf` method. Here is a typical example:

```
System.out.printf("Quantity: %d Total: %10.2f", quantity, total);
```

width 10

The `printf` method does not start a new line here.

```
Quantity:  24  Total:            17.29
```

No field width was specified, so no padding added

Two digits after the decimal point

The `printf` method, like the `print` method, does not start a new line after the output. If you want the next output to be on a separate line, you can call `System.out.println()`. Alternatively, Section 2.5.4 shows you how to add a newline character to the format string.

Our next example program will prompt for the price of a six-pack and the volume of each can, then print out the price per ounce. The program puts to work what you just learned about reading input and formatting output.

section_3/Volume2.java

```
1   import java.util.Scanner;
2
3   /**
4      This program prints the price per ounce for a six-pack of cans.
5   */
6   public class Volume2
7   {
8      public static void main(String[] args)
9      {
```

```
10      // Read price per pack
11
12        Scanner in = new Scanner(System.in);
13
14        System.out.print("Please enter the price for a six-pack: ");
15        double packPrice = in.nextDouble();
16
17      // Read can volume
18
19        System.out.print("Please enter the volume for each can (in ounces): ");
20        double canVolume = in.nextDouble();
21
22      // Compute pack volume
23
24        final double CANS_PER_PACK = 6;
25        double packVolume = canVolume * CANS_PER_PACK;
26
27      // Compute and print price per ounce
28
29        double pricePerOunce = packPrice / packVolume;
30
31        System.out.printf("Price per ounce: %8.2f", pricePerOunce);
32        System.out.println();
33    }
34 }
```

Program Run

```
Please enter the price for a six-pack: 2.95
Please enter the volume for each can (in ounces): 12
Price per ounce:     0.04
```

SELF CHECK

15. Write statements to prompt for and read the user's age using a Scanner variable named in.

16. What is wrong with the following statement sequence?

    ```
    System.out.print("Please enter the unit price: ");
    double unitPrice = in.nextDouble();
    int quantity = in.nextInt();
    ```

17. What is problematic about the following statement sequence?

    ```
    System.out.print("Please enter the unit price: ");
    double unitPrice = in.nextInt();
    ```

18. What is problematic about the following statement sequence?

    ```
    System.out.print("Please enter the number of cans");
    int cans = in.nextInt();
    ```

19. What is the output of the following statement sequence?

    ```
    int volume = 10;
    System.out.printf("The volume is %5d", volume);
    ```

20. Using the printf method, print the values of the integer variables bottles and cans so that the output looks like this:

    ```
    Bottles:       8
    Cans:         24
    ```

    The numbers to the right should line up. (You may assume that the numbers have at most 8 digits.)

Practice It Now you can try these exercises at the end of the chapter: R2.10, P2.6, P2.7.

Use the API Documentation

The classes and methods of the Java library are listed in the **API documentation**. The API is the "**application programming interface**". A programmer who uses the Java classes to put together a computer program (or *application*) is an *application programmer*. That's you. In contrast, the programmers who designed and implemented the library classes (such as Scanner) are *system programmers*.

> The API (Application Programming Interface) documentation lists the classes and methods of the Java library.

You can find the API documentation at `http://download.oracle.com/javase/7/docs/api`. The API documentation describes all classes in the Java library—there are thousands of them. Fortunately, only a few are of interest to the beginning programmer. To learn more about a class, click on its name in the left hand column. You can then find out the package to which the class belongs, and which methods it supports (see Figure 4). Click on the link of a method to get a detailed description.

Appendix D contains an abbreviated version of the API documentation.

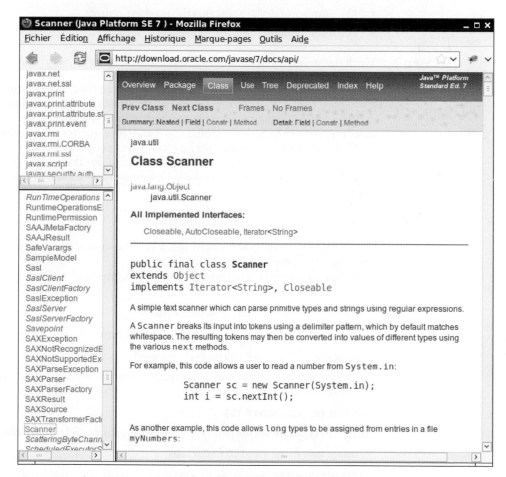

Figure 4 The API Documentation of the Standard Java Library

HOW TO 2.1

Carrying out Computations

Many programming problems require arithmetic computations. This How To shows you how to turn a problem statement into pseudocode and, ultimately, a Java program.

For example, suppose you are asked to write a program that simulates a vending machine. A customer selects an item for purchase and inserts a bill into the vending machine. The vending machine dispenses the purchased item and gives change. We will assume that all item prices are multiples of 25 cents, and the machine gives all change in dollar coins and quarters.

Your task is to compute how many coins of each type to return.

Step 1   Understand the problem: What are the inputs? What are the desired outputs?

In this problem, there are two inputs:
- The denomination of the bill that the customer inserts
- The price of the purchased item

There are two desired outputs:
- The number of dollar coins that the machine returns
- The number of quarters that the machine returns

Step 2   Work out examples by hand.

This is a very important step. If you can't compute a couple of solutions by hand, it's unlikely that you'll be able to write a program that automates the computation.

Let's assume that a customer purchased an item that cost $2.25 and inserted a $5 bill. The customer is due $2.75, or two dollar coins and three quarters, in change.

That is easy for you to see, but how can a Java program come to the same conclusion? The key is to work in pennies, not dollars. The change due the customer is 275 pennies. Dividing by 100 yields 2, the number of dollars. Dividing the remainder (75) by 25 yields 3, the number of quarters.

Step 3   Write pseudocode for computing the answers.

In the previous step, you worked out a specific instance of the problem. You now need to come up with a method that works in general.

Given an arbitrary item price and payment, how can you compute the coins due? First, compute the change due in pennies:

    change due = 100 x bill value - item price in pennies

To get the dollars, divide by 100 and discard the remainder:

    dollar coins = change due / 100 (without remainder)

The remaining change due can be computed in two ways. If you are familiar with the modulus operator, you can simply compute

    change due = change due % 100

Alternatively, subtract the penny value of the dollar coins from the change due:

    change due = change due - 100 x dollar coins

To get the quarters due, divide by 25:

    quarters = change due / 25

Step 4 Declare the variables and constants that you need, and specify their types.

Here, we have five variables:

- `billValue`
- `itemPrice`
- `changeDue`
- `dollarCoins`
- `quarters`

Should we introduce constants to explain 100 and 25 as `PENNIES_PER_DOLLAR` and `PENNIES_PER_QUARTER`? Doing so will make it easier to convert the program to international markets, so we will take this step.

It is very important that `changeDue` and `PENNIES_PER_DOLLAR` are of type `int` because the computation of `dollarCoins` uses integer division. Similarly, the other variables are integers.

Step 5 Turn the pseudocode into Java statements.

If you did a thorough job with the pseudocode, this step should be easy. Of course, you have to know how to express mathematical operations (such as powers or integer division) in Java.

```
changeDue = PENNIES_PER_DOLLAR * billValue - itemPrice;
dollarCoins = changeDue / PENNIES_PER_DOLLAR;
changeDue = changeDue % PENNIES_PER_DOLLAR;
quarters = changeDue / PENNIES_PER_QUARTER;
```

Step 6 Provide input and output.

Before starting the computation, we prompt the user for the bill value and item price:

```
System.out.print("Enter bill value (1 = $1 bill, 5 = $5 bill, etc.): ");
billValue = in.nextInt();
System.out.print("Enter item price in pennies: ");
itemPrice = in.nextInt();
```

When the computation is finished, we display the result. For extra credit, we use the `printf` method to make sure that the output lines up neatly.

```
System.out.printf("Dollar coins: %6d", dollarCoins);
System.out.printf("Quarters:     %6d", quarters);
```

Step 7 Provide a class with a `main` method.

Your computation needs to be placed into a class. Find an appropriate name for the class that describes the purpose of the computation. In our example, we will choose the name `Vending-Machine`.

Inside the class, supply a `main` method.

A vending machine takes bills and gives change in coins.

In the main method, you need to declare constants and variables (Step 4), carry out computations (Step 5), and provide input and output (Step 6). Clearly, you will want to first get the input, then do the computations, and finally show the output. Declare the constants at the beginning of the method, and declare each variable just before it is needed.

Here is the complete program, how_to_1/VendingMachine.java:

```java
import java.util.Scanner;

/**
    This program simulates a vending machine that gives change.
*/
public class VendingMachine
{
    public static void main(String[] args)
    {
        Scanner in = new Scanner(System.in);

        final int PENNIES_PER_DOLLAR = 100;
        final int PENNIES_PER_QUARTER = 25;

        System.out.print("Enter bill value (1 = $1 bill, 5 = $5 bill, etc.): ");
        int billValue = in.nextInt();
        System.out.print("Enter item price in pennies: ");
        int itemPrice = in.nextInt();

        // Compute change due

        int changeDue = PENNIES_PER_DOLLAR * billValue - itemPrice;
        int dollarCoins = changeDue / PENNIES_PER_DOLLAR;
        changeDue = changeDue % PENNIES_PER_DOLLAR;
        int quarters = changeDue / PENNIES_PER_QUARTER;

        // Print change due

        System.out.printf("Dollar coins: %6d", dollarCoins);
        System.out.println();
        System.out.printf("Quarters:     %6d", quarters);
        System.out.println();
    }
}
```

Program Run

```
Enter bill value (1 = $1 bill, 5 = $5 bill, etc.): 5
Enter item price in pennies: 225
Dollar coins:      2
Quarters:          3
```

WORKED EXAMPLE 2.1   **Computing the Cost of Stamps**

This Worked Example uses arithmetic functions to simulate a stamp vending machine.

⊕ Available online in WileyPLUS and at www.wiley.com/college/horstmann.

2.4 Problem Solving: First Do It By Hand

A very important step for developing an algorithm is to first carry out the computations *by hand*. If you can't compute a solution yourself, it's unlikely that you'll be able to write a program that automates the computation.

To illustrate the use of hand calculations, consider the following problem.

A row of black and white tiles needs to be placed along a wall. For aesthetic reasons, the architect has specified that the first and last tile shall be black.

Your task is to compute the number of tiles needed and the gap at each end, given the space available and the width of each tile.

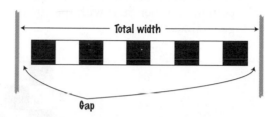

Pick concrete values for a typical situation to use in a hand calculation.

To make the problem more concrete, let's assume the following dimensions:

- Total width: 100 inches
- Tile width: 5 inches

The obvious solution would be to fill the space with 20 tiles, but that would not work—the last tile would be white.

Instead, look at the problem this way: The first tile must always be black, and then we add some number of white/black pairs:

The first tile takes up 5 inches, leaving 95 inches to be covered by pairs. Each pair is 10 inches wide. Therefore the number of pairs is 95 / 10 = 9.5. However, we need to discard the fractional part since we can't have fractions of tile pairs.

Therefore, we will use 9 tile pairs or 18 tiles, plus the initial black tile. Altogether, we require 19 tiles.

The tiles span 19 × 5 = 95 inches, leaving a total gap of 100 − 19 × 5 = 5 inches.

The gap should be evenly distributed at both ends. At each end, the gap is (100 − 19 × 5) / 2 = 2.5 inches.

This computation gives us enough information to devise an algorithm with arbitrary values for the total width and tile width.

ONLINE EXAMPLE

➕ A program that implements this algorithm.

> **number of pairs = integer part of (total width − tile width) / (2 x tile width)**
> **number of tiles = 1 + 2 x number of pairs**
> **gap at each end = (total width − number of tiles x tile width) / 2**

As you can see, doing a hand calculation gives enough insight into the problem that it becomes easy to develop an algorithm.

SELF CHECK

21. Translate the pseudocode for computing the number of tiles and the gap width into Java.

22. Suppose the architect specifies a pattern with black, gray, and white tiles, like this:

Again, the first and last tile should be black. How do you need to modify the algorithm?

23. A robot needs to tile a floor with alternating black and white tiles. Develop an algorithm that yields the color (0 for black, 1 for white), given the row and column number. Start with specific values for the row and column, and then generalize.

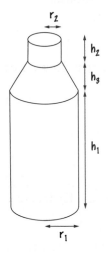

24. For a particular car, repair and maintenance costs in year 1 are estimated at $100; in year 10, at $1,500. Assuming that the repair cost increases by the same amount every year, develop pseudocode to compute the repair cost in year 3 and then generalize to year **n**.

25. The shape of a bottle is approximated by two cylinders of radius r_1 and r_2 and heights h_1 and h_2, joined by a cone section of height h_3.

Using the formulas for the volume of a cylinder, $V = \pi r^2 h$, and a cone section,

$$V = \pi \frac{\left(r_1^2 + r_1 r_2 + r_2^2\right)h}{3},$$

develop pseudocode to compute the volume of the bottle. Using an actual bottle with known volume as a sample, make a hand calculation of your pseudocode.

Practice It Now you can try these exercises at the end of the chapter: R2.15, R2.17, R2.18.

WORKED EXAMPLE 2.2   **Computing Travel Time**

In this Worked Example, we develop a hand calculation to compute the time that a robot requires to retrieve an item from rocky terrain.

⊕ Available online in WileyPLUS and at www.wiley.com/college/horstmann.

2.5 Strings

Strings are sequences of characters.

Many programs process text, not numbers. Text consists of **characters**: letters, numbers, punctuation, spaces, and so on. A **string** is a sequence of characters. For example, the string "Harry" is a sequence of five characters.

2.5.1 The String Type

You can declare variables that hold strings.

```
String name = "Harry";
```

We distinguish between string variables (such as the variable name declared above) and string **literals** (character sequences enclosed in quotes, such as "Harry"). A string variable is simply a variable that can hold a string, just as an integer variable can hold an integer. A string literal denotes a particular string, just as a number literal (such as 2) denotes a particular number.

The `length` method yields the number of characters in a string.

The number of characters in a string is called the *length* of the string. For example, the length of "Harry" is 5. You can compute the length of a string with the length method.

```
int n = name.length();
```

A string of length 0 is called the *empty string*. It contains no characters and is written as "".

2.5.2 Concatenation

Use the + operator to *concatenate* strings; that is, to put them together to yield a longer string.

Given two strings, such as "Harry" and "Morgan", you can **concatenate** them to one long string. The result consists of all characters in the first string, followed by all characters in the second string. In Java, you use the + operator to concatenate two strings.

For example,

```
String fName = "Harry";
String lName = "Morgan";
String name = fName + lName;
```

results in the string

```
"HarryMorgan"
```

What if you'd like the first and last name separated by a space? No problem:

```
String name = fName + " " + lName;
```

This statement concatenates three strings: fName, the string literal " ", and lName. The result is

```
"Harry Morgan"
```

When the expression to the left or the right of a + operator is a string, the other one is automatically forced to become a string as well, and both strings are concatenated.

For example, consider this code:

```
String jobTitle = "Agent";
int employeeId = 7;
String bond = jobTitle + employeeId;
```

Because jobTitle is a string, employeeId is converted from the integer 7 to the string "7". Then the two strings "Agent" and "7" are concatenated to form the string "Agent7".

This concatenation is very useful for reducing the number of System.out.print instructions. For example, you can combine

> Whenever one of the arguments of the + operator is a string, the other argument is converted to a string.

```
System.out.print("The total is ");
System.out.println(total);
```

to the single call

```
System.out.println("The total is " + total);
```

The concatenation "The total is " + total computes a single string that consists of the string "The total is ", followed by the string equivalent of the number total.

2.5.3 String Input

You can read a string from the console:

> Use the next method of the Scanner class to read a string containing a single word.

```
System.out.print("Please enter your name: ");
String name = in.next();
```

When a string is read with the next method, only one word is read. For example, suppose the user types

```
Harry Morgan
```

as the response to the prompt. This input consists of two words. The call in.next() yields the string "Harry". You can use another call to in.next() to read the second word.

2.5.4 Escape Sequences

To include a quotation mark in a literal string, precede it with a backslash (\), like this:

```
"He said \"Hello\""
```

The backslash is not included in the string. It indicates that the quotation mark that follows should be a part of the string and not mark the end of the string. The sequence \" is called an **escape sequence**.

To include a backslash in a string, use the escape sequence \\, like this:

```
"C:\\Temp\\Secret.txt"
```

Another common escape sequence is \n, which denotes a **newline** character. Printing a newline character causes the start of a new line on the display. For example, the statement

```
System.out.print("*\n**\n***\n");
```

prints the characters

```
*
**
***
```

on three separate lines.

You often want to add a newline character to the end of the format string when you use System.out.printf:

```
System.out.printf("Price: %10.2f\n", price);
```

2.5.5 Strings and Characters

Strings are sequences of Unicode characters (see Random Fact 2.2). In Java, a **character** is a value of the type char. Characters have numeric values. You can find the values of the characters that are used in Western European languages in Appendix A. For example, if you look up the value for the character 'H', you can see that is actually encoded as the number 72.

A string is a sequence of characters.

Character literals are delimited by single quotes, and you should not confuse them with strings.

- 'H' is a character, a value of type char.
- "H" is a string containing a single character, a value of type String.

The charAt method returns a char value from a string. The first string position is labeled 0, the second one 1, and so on.

H	a	r	r	y
0	1	2	3	4

String positions are counted starting with 0.

The position number of the last character (4 for the string "Harry") is always one less than the length of the string.

For example, the statement

```
String name = "Harry";
char start = name.charAt(0);
char last = name.charAt(4);
```

sets start to the value 'H' and last to the value 'y'.

2.5.6 Substrings

Use the substring method to extract a part of a string.

Once you have a string, you can extract substrings by using the substring method. The method call

```
str.substring(start, pastEnd)
```

returns a string that is made up of the characters in the string str, starting at position start, and containing all characters up to, but not including, the position pastEnd. Here is an example:

```
String greeting = "Hello, World!";
String sub = greeting.substring(0, 5); // sub is "Hello"
```

The substring operation makes a string that consists of the first five characters taken from the string greeting.

H	e	l	l	o	,		W	o	r	l	d	!
0	1	2	3	4	5	6	7	8	9	10	11	12

Let's figure out how to extract the substring "World". Count characters starting at 0, not 1. You find that W has position number 7. The first character that you don't want, !, is the character at position 12. Therefore, the appropriate substring command is

```java
String sub2 = greeting.substring(7, 12);
```

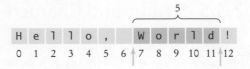

It is curious that you must specify the position of the first character that you do want and then the first character that you don't want. There is one advantage to this setup. You can easily compute the length of the substring: It is pastEnd - start. For example, the string "World" has length $12 - 7 = 5$.

If you omit the end position when calling the substring method, then all characters from the starting position to the end of the string are copied. For example,

```java
String tail = greeting.substring(7); // Copies all characters from position 7 on
```

sets tail to the string "World!".

Following is a simple program that puts these concepts to work. The program asks for your name and that of your significant other. It then prints out your initials.

The operation first.substring(0, 1) makes a string consisting of one character, taken from the start of first. The program does the same for the second. Then it concatenates the resulting one-character strings with the string literal "&" to get a string of length 3, the initials string. (See Figure 5.)

Initials are formed from the first letter of each name.

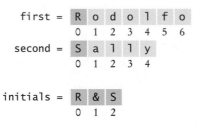

Figure 5 Building the initials String

section_5/Initials.java

```java
1   import java.util.Scanner;
2
3   /**
4      This program prints a pair of initials.
5   */
6   public class Initials
7   {
8      public static void main(String[] args)
9      {
10        Scanner in = new Scanner(System.in);
11
```

```
12          // Get the names of the couple
13
14          System.out.print("Enter your first name: ");
15          String first = in.next();
16          System.out.print("Enter your significant other's first name: ");
17          String second = in.next();
18
19          // Compute and display the inscription
20
21          String initials = first.substring(0, 1)
22             + "&" + second.substring(0, 1);
23          System.out.println(initials);
24       }
25 }
```

Program Run

```
Enter your first name: Rodolfo
Enter your significant other's first name: Sally
R&S
```

Table 9 String Operations

Statement	Result	Comment
string str = "Ja"; str = str + "va";	str is set to "Java"	When applied to strings, + denotes concatenation.
System.out.println("Please" + " enter your name: ");	Prints Please enter your name:	Use concatenation to break up strings that don't fit into one line.
team = 49 + "ers"	team is set to "49ers"	Because "ers" is a string, 49 is converted to a string.
String first = in.next(); String last = in.next(); (User input: Harry Morgan)	first contains "Harry" last contains "Morgan"	The next method places the next word into the string variable.
String greeting = "H & S"; int n = greeting.length();	n is set to 5	Each space counts as one character.
String str = "Sally"; char ch = str.charAt(1);	ch is set to 'a'	This is a char value, not a String. Note that the initial position is 0.
String str = "Sally"; String str2 = str.substring(1, 4);	str2 is set to "all"	Extracts the substring starting at position 1 and ending before position 4.
String str = "Sally"; String str2 = str.substring(1);	str2 is set to "ally"	If you omit the end position, all characters from the position until the end of the string are included.
String str = "Sally"; String str2 = str.substring(1, 2);	str2 is set to "a"	Extracts a String of length 1; contrast with str.charAt(1).
String last = str.substring(str.length() - 1);	last is set to the string containing the last character in str	The last character has position str.length() - 1.

26. What is the length of the string `"Java Program"`?

27. Consider this string variable.

```
String str = "Java Program";
```

Give a call to the `substring` method that returns the substring `"gram"`.

28. Use string concatenation to turn the string variable `str` from Self Check 27 into `"Java Programming"`.

29. What does the following statement sequence print?

```
String str = "Harry";
int n = str.length();
String mystery = str.substring(0, 1) + str.substring(n - 1, n);
System.out.println(mystery);
```

30. Give an input statement to read a name of the form "John Q. Public".

Practice It   Now you can try these exercises at the end of the chapter: R2.7, R2.11, P2.15, P2.23.

Special Topic 2.4

Instance Methods and Static Methods

In this chapter, you have learned how to read, process, and print numbers and strings. Many of these tasks involve various method calls. You may have noticed syntactical differences in these method calls. For example, to compute the square root of a number num, you call `Math.sqrt(num)`, but to compute the length of a string str, you call `str.length()`. This section explains the reasons behind these differences.

The Java language distinguishes between values of **primitive types** and **objects**. Numbers and characters, as well as the values `false` and `true` that you will see in Chapter 3, are primitive. All other values are objects. Examples of objects are

- a string such as `"Hello"`.
- a Scanner object obtained by calling `in = new Scanner(System.in)`.
- `System.in` and `System.out`.

In Java, each object belongs to a **class**. For example,

- All strings are objects of the `String` class.
- A scanner object belongs to the `Scanner` class.
- `System.out` is an object of the `PrintStream` class. (It is useful to know this so that you can look up the valid methods in the API documentation; see Programming Tip 2.4 on page 53.)

A class declares the methods that you can use with its objects. Here are examples of methods that are invoked on objects:

```
"Hello".substring(0, 1)
in.nextDouble()
System.out.println("Hello")
```

A method is invoked with the **dot notation**: the object is followed by the name of the method, and the method is followed by parameters enclosed in parentheses.

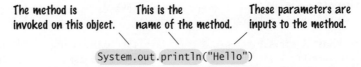

The method is invoked on this object.   This is the name of the method.   These parameters are inputs to the method.

```
System.out.println("Hello")
```

You cannot invoke methods on numbers. For example, the call `2.sqrt()` would be an error.

In Java, classes can declare methods that are *not* invoked on objects. Such methods are called **static methods**. (The term "static" is a historical holdover from the C and C++ programming languages. It has nothing to do with the usual meaning of the word.) For example, the Math class declares a static method sqrt. You call it by giving the name of the class and method, then the name of the numeric input: Math.sqrt(2).

The name of the class   The name of the static method

Math.sqrt(2)

In contrast, a method that is invoked on an object is called an **instance method**. As a rule of thumb, you use static methods when you manipulate numbers. You use instance methods when you process strings or perform input/output. You will learn more about the distinction between static and instance methods in Chapter 8.

Special Topic 2.5

Using Dialog Boxes for Input and Output

Most program users find the console window rather old-fashioned. The easiest alternative is to create a separate pop-up window for each input.

An Input Dialog Box

ONLINE EXAMPLE

⊕ A complete program that uses option panes for input and output.

Call the static showInputDialog method of the JOptionPane class, and supply the string that prompts the input from the user. For example,

```
String input = JOptionPane.showInputDialog("Enter price:");
```

That method returns a String object. Of course, often you need the input as a number. Use the Integer.parseInt and Double.parseDouble methods to convert the string to a number:

```
double price = Double.parseDouble(input);
```

You can also display output in a dialog box:

```
JOptionPane.showMessageDialog(null, "Price: " + price);
```

VIDEO EXAMPLE 2.2   **Computing Distances on Earth**

In this Video Example, you will see how to write a program that computes the distance between any two points on Earth.

⊕ Available online in WileyPLUS and at www.wiley.com/college/horstmann.

Random Fact 2.2 International Alphabets and Unicode

The English alphabet is pretty simple: upper- and lowercase *a* to *z*. Other European languages have accent marks and special characters. For example, German has three so-called *umlaut* characters, ä, ö, ü, and a *double-s* character ß. These are not optional frills; you couldn't write a page of German text without using these characters a few times. German keyboards have keys for these characters.

The German Keyboard Layout

Many countries don't use the Roman script at all. Russian, Greek, Hebrew,

Arabic, and Thai letters, to name just a few, have completely different shapes. To complicate matters, Hebrew and Arabic are typed from right to left. Each of these alphabets has about as many characters as the English alphabet.

Hebrew, Arabic, and English

The Chinese languages as well as Japanese and Korean use Chinese characters. Each character represents an idea or thing. Words are made up of one or more of these ideographic characters. Over 70,000 ideographs are known.

Starting in 1988, a consortium of hardware and software manufacturers developed a uniform encoding scheme

called **Unicode** that is capable of encoding text in essentially all written languages of the world. An early version of Unicode used 16 bits for each character. The Java char type corresponds to that encoding.

Today Unicode has grown to a 21-bit code, with definitions for over 100,000 characters. There are even plans to add codes for extinct languages, such as Egyptian hieroglyphics. Unfortunately, that means that a Java char value does not always correspond to a Unicode character. Some characters in languages such as Chinese or ancient Egyptian occupy two char values.

The Chinese Script

CHAPTER SUMMARY

Declare variables with appropriate names and types.

- A variable is a storage location with a name.
- When declaring a variable, you usually specify an initial value.
- When declaring a variable, you also specify the type of its values.
- Use the int type for numbers that cannot have a fractional part.
- Use the double type for floating-point numbers.
- By convention, variable names should start with a lowercase letter.
- An assignment statement stores a new value in a variable, replacing the previously stored value.
- The assignment operator = does *not* denote mathematical equality.

- You cannot change the value of a variable that is defined as `final`.
- Use comments to add explanations for humans who read your code. The compiler ignores comments.

Write arithmetic expressions in Java.

- Mixing integers and floating-point values in an arithmetic expression yields a floating-point value.
- The `++` operator adds 1 to a variable; the `--` operator subtracts 1.
- If both arguments of `/` are integers, the remainder is discarded.
- The `%` operator computes the remainder of an integer division.
- The Java library declares many mathematical functions, such as `Math.sqrt` (square root) and `Math.pow` (raising to a power).
- You use a cast (*typeName*) to convert a value to a different type.

Write programs that read user input and print formatted output.

- Java classes are grouped into packages. Use the `import` statement to use classes from packages.
- Use the `Scanner` class to read keyboard input in a console window.
- Use the `printf` method to specify how values should be formatted.
- The API (Application Programming Interface) documentation lists the classes and methods of the Java library.

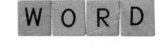

Carry out hand calculations when developing an algorithm.

- Pick concrete values for a typical situation to use in a hand calculation.

Write programs that process strings.

- Strings are sequences of characters.
- The `length` method yields the number of characters in a string.

- Use the `+` operator to *concatenate* strings; that is, to put them together to yield a longer string.
- Whenever one of the arguments of the `+` operator is a string, the other argument is converted to a string.
- Use the `next` method of the `Scanner` class to read a string containing a single word.
- String positions are counted starting with `0`.
- Use the `substring` method to extract a part of a string.

java.io.PrintStream	max	java.math.BigDecimal
printf	min	add
java.lang.Double	pow	multiply
parseDouble	round	subtract
java.lang.Integer	sin	java.math.BigInteger
MAX_VALUE	sqrt	add
MIN_VALUE	tan	multiply
parseInt	toDegrees	subtract
java.lang.Math	toRadians	java.util.Scanner
PI	java.lang.String	next
abs	charAt	nextDouble
cos	length	nextInt
exp	substring	javax.swing.JOptionPane
log	java.lang.System	showInputDialog
log10	in	showMessageDialog

REVIEW EXERCISES

■ R2.1 What is the value of mystery after this sequence of statements?

```
int mystery = 1;
mystery = 1 - 2 * mystery;
mystery = mystery + 1;
```

■ R2.2 What is wrong with the following sequence of statements?

```
int mystery = 1;
mystery = mystery + 1;
int mystery = 1 - 2 * mystery;
```

■■ R2.3 Write the following mathematical expressions in Java.

$$s = s_0 + v_0 t + \frac{1}{2} g t^2$$

$$G = 4\pi^2 \frac{a^3}{p^2(m_1 + m_2)}$$

$$FV = PV \cdot \left(1 + \frac{INT}{100}\right)^{YRS}$$

$$c = \sqrt{a^2 + b^2 - 2ab\cos\gamma}$$

■■ R2.4 Write the following Java expressions in mathematical notation.

   a. `dm = m * (Math.sqrt(1 + v / c) / Math.sqrt(1 - v / c) - 1);`

   b. `volume = Math.PI * r * r * h;`

   c. `volume = 4 * Math.PI * Math.pow(r, 3) / 3;`

   d. `z = Math.sqrt(x * x + y * y);`

■■ R2.5 What are the values of the following expressions? In each line, assume that

```
double x = 2.5;
double y = -1.5;
```

```
int m = 18;
int n = 4;
```

a. x + n * y - (x + n) * y

b. m / n + m % n

c. 5 * x - n / 5

d. 1 - (1 - (1 - (1 - (1 - n))))

e. Math.sqrt(Math.sqrt(n))

- **R2.6** What are the values of the following expressions, assuming that n is 17 and m is 18?

    a. n / 10 + n % 10

    b. n % 2 + m % 2

    c. (m + n) / 2

    d. (m + n) / 2.0

    e. (int) (0.5 * (m + n))

    f. (int) Math.round(0.5 * (m + n))

- - **R2.7** What are the values of the following expressions? In each line, assume that

    ```
    String s = "Hello";
    String t = "World";
    ```

    a. s.length() + t.length()

    b. s.substring(1, 2)

    c. s.substring(s.length() / 2, s.length())

    d. s + t

    e. t + s

- **R2.8** Find at least five *compile-time* errors in the following program.

    ```java
    public class HasErrors
    {
        public static void main();
        {
            System.out.print(Please enter two numbers:)
            x = in.readDouble;
            y = in.readDouble;
            System.out.printline("The sum is " + x + y);
        }
    }
    ```

- - **R2.9** Find three *run-time* errors in the following program.

    ```java
    public class HasErrors
    {
        public static void main(String[] args)
        {
            int x = 0;
            int y = 0;
            Scanner in = new Scanner("System.in");
            System.out.print("Please enter an integer:");
            x = in.readInt();
            System.out.print("Please enter another integer: ");
            x = in.readInt();
            System.out.println("The sum is " + x + y);
        }
    }
    ```

■ R2.10 Consider the following code segment.

```
double purchase = 19.93;
double payment = 20.00;
double change = payment - purchase;
System.out.println(change);
```

The code segment prints the change as 0.07000000000000028. Explain why. Give a recommendation to improve the code so that users will not be confused.

■ R2.11 Explain the differences between 2, 2.0, '2', "2", and "2.0".

■ R2.12 Explain what each of the following program segments computes.

   a. x = 2;
        y = x + x;
   b. s = "2";
        t = s + s;

■■ R2.13 Write pseudocode for a program that reads a word and then prints the first character, the last character, and the characters in the middle. For example, if the input is Harry, the program prints H y arr.

■■ R2.14 Write pseudocode for a program that reads a name (such as Harold James Morgan) and then prints a monogram consisting of the initial letters of the first, middle, and last name (such as HJM).

■■■ R2.15 Write pseudocode for a program that computes the first and last digit of a number. For example, if the input is 23456, the program should print 2 and 6. *Hint:* %, Math.log10.

■ R2.16 Modify the pseudocode for the program in How To 2.1 so that the program gives change in quarters, dimes, and nickels. You can assume that the price is a multiple of 5 cents. To develop your pseudocode, first work with a couple of specific values.

■■ R2.17 A cocktail shaker is composed of three cone sections.

Using realistic values for the radii and heights, compute the total volume, using the formula given in Self Check 25 for a cone section. Then develop an algorithm that works for arbitrary dimensions.

■■■ R2.18 You are cutting off a piece of pie like this, where *c* is the length of the straight part (called the chord length) and *h* is the height of the piece.

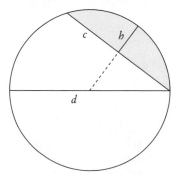

There is an approximate formula for the area: $A \approx \frac{2}{3}ch + \frac{h^3}{2c}$

However, *h* is not so easy to measure, whereas the diameter *d* of a pie is usually well-known. Calculate the area where the diameter of the pie is 12 inches and the chord length of the segment is 10 inches. Generalize to an algorithm that yields the area for any diameter and chord length.

■■ **R2.19** The following pseudocode describes how to obtain the name of a day, given the day number (0 = Sunday, 1 = Monday, and so on.)

> Declare a string called names containing "SunMonTueWedThuFriSat".
> Compute the starting position as 3 x the day number.
> Extract the substring of names at the starting position with length 3.

Check this pseudocode, using the day number 4. Draw a diagram of the string that is being computed, similar to Figure 5.

■■■ **R2.20** The following pseudocode describes how to swap two letters in a word.

> We are given a string str and two positions i and j. (i comes before j)
> Set first to the substring from the start of the string to the last position before i.
> Set middle to the substring from positions i + 1 to j - 1.
> Set last to the substring from position j + 1 to the end of the string.
> Concatenate the following five strings: first, the string containing just the character at position j,
>   middle, the string containing just the character at position i, and last.

Check this pseudocode, using the string "Gateway" and positions 2 and 4. Draw a diagram of the string that is being computed, similar to Figure 5.

■■ **R2.21** How do you get the first character of a string? The last character? How do you remove the first character? The last character?

■■■ **R2.22** Write a program that prints the values

```
3 * 1000 * 1000 * 1000
3.0 * 1000 * 1000 * 1000
```

Explain the results.

■ **R2.23** This chapter contains a number of recommendations regarding variables and constants that make programs easier to read and maintain. Briefly summarize these recommendations.

PROGRAMMING EXERCISES

■ **P2.1** Write a program that displays the dimensions of a letter-size (8.5 × 11 inches) sheet of paper in millimeters. There are 25.4 millimeters per inch. Use constants and comments in your program.

■ **P2.2** Write a program that computes and displays the perimeter of a letter-size (8.5 × 11 inches) sheet of paper and the length of its diagonal.

■ **P2.3** Write a program that reads a number and displays the square, cube, and fourth power. Use the Math.pow method only for the fourth power.

■■ **P2.4** Write a program that prompts the user for two integers and then prints

- The sum
- The difference

- The product
- The average
- The distance (absolute value of the difference)
- The maximum (the larger of the two)
- The minimum (the smaller of the two)

Hint: The max and min functions are declared in the Math class.

■■ **P2.5** Enhance the output of Exercise P2.4 so that the numbers are properly aligned:

```
Sum:            45
Difference:     -5
Product:        500
Average:        22.50
Distance:        5
Maximum:        25
Minimum:        20
```

■■ **P2.6** Write a program that prompts the user for a measurement in meters and then converts it to miles, feet, and inches.

■ **P2.7** Write a program that prompts the user for a radius and then prints

- The area and circumference of a circle with that radius
- The volume and surface area of a sphere with that radius

■■ **P2.8** Write a program that asks the user for the lengths of the sides of a rectangle. Then print

- The area and perimeter of the rectangle
- The length of the diagonal (use the Pythagorean theorem)

■ **P2.9** Improve the program discussed in How To 2.1 to allow input of quarters in addition to bills.

■■■ **P2.10** Write a program that helps a person decide whether to buy a hybrid car. Your program's inputs should be:

- The cost of a new car
- The estimated miles driven per year
- The estimated gas price
- The efficiency in miles per gallon
- The estimated resale value after 5 years

Compute the total cost of owning the car for five years. (For simplicity, we will not take the cost of financing into account.) Obtain realistic prices for a new and used hybrid and a comparable car from the Web. Run your program twice, using today's gas price and 15,000 miles per year. Include pseudocode and the program runs with your assignment.

■■ **P2.11** Write a program that asks the user to input

- The number of gallons of gas in the tank
- The fuel efficiency in miles per gallon
- The price of gas per gallon

Then print the cost per 100 miles and how far the car can go with the gas in the tank.

- **P2.12** *File names and extensions.* Write a program that prompts the user for the drive letter (C), the path (\Windows\System), the file name (Readme), and the extension (txt). Then print the complete file name C:\Windows\System\Readme.txt. (If you use UNIX or a Macintosh, skip the drive name and use / instead of \ to separate directories.)

- **P2.13** Write a program that reads a number between 1,000 and 999,999 from the user, where the user enters a comma in the input. Then print the number without a comma. Here is a sample dialog; the user input is in color:

  ```
  Please enter an integer between 1,000 and 999,999: 23,456
  23456
  ```

  Hint: Read the input as a string. Measure the length of the string. Suppose it contains *n* characters. Then extract substrings consisting of the first *n* – 4 characters and the last three characters.

- **P2.14** Write a program that reads a number between 1,000 and 999,999 from the user and prints it with a comma separating the thousands. Here is a sample dialog; the user input is in color:

  ```
  Please enter an integer between 1000 and 999999: 23456
  23,456
  ```

- **P2.15** *Printing a grid.* Write a program that prints the following grid to play tic-tac-toe.

  ```
  +--+--+--+
  |  |  |  |  |
  +--+--+--+
  |  |  |  |  |
  +--+--+--+
  |  |  |  |  |
  +--+--+--+
  ```

  Of course, you could simply write seven statements of the form

  ```
  System.out.println("+--+--+--+");
  ```

  You should do it the smart way, though. Declare string variables to hold two kinds of patterns: a comb-shaped pattern and the bottom line. Print the comb three times and the bottom line once.

- **P2.16** Write a program that reads in an integer and breaks it into a sequence of individual digits. For example, the input 16384 is displayed as

  ```
  1 6 3 8 4
  ```

  You may assume that the input has no more than five digits and is not negative.

- **P2.17** Write a program that reads two times in military format (0900, 1730) and prints the number of hours and minutes between the two times. Here is a sample run. User input is in color.

  ```
  Please enter the first time: 0900
  Please enter the second time: 1730
  8 hours 30 minutes
  ```

  Extra credit if you can deal with the case where the first time is later than the second:

  ```
  Please enter the first time: 1730
  Please enter the second time: 0900
  15 hours 30 minutes
  ```

■■■ **P2.18** *Writing large letters.* A large letter H can be produced like this:

```
*   *
*   *
*****
*   *
*   *
```

It can be declared as a string literal like this:

```
final string LETTER_H = "*   *\n*   *\n*****\n*   *\n*   *\n";
```

(The \n escape sequence denotes a "newline" character that causes subsequent characters to be printed on a new line.) Do the same for the letters E, L, and O. Then write the message

```
H
E
L
L
O
```

in large letters.

■■ **P2.19** Write a program that transforms numbers 1, 2, 3, …, 12 into the corresponding month names January, February, March, …, December. *Hint:* Make a very long string "January February March ...", in which you add spaces such that each month name has *the same length*. Then use substring to extract the month you want.

■■ **P2.20** Write a program that prints a Christmas tree:

```
    /\'
   /  \'
  /    \'
 /      \'
 --------
   "  "
   "  "
   "  "
```

Remember to use escape sequences.

■■ **P2.21** Easter Sunday is the first Sunday after the first full moon of spring. To compute the date, you can use this algorithm, invented by the mathematician Carl Friedrich Gauss in 1800:

1. Let y be the year (such as 1800 or 2001).
2. Divide y by 19 and call the remainder a. Ignore the quotient.
3. Divide y by 100 to get a quotient b and a remainder c.
4. Divide b by 4 to get a quotient d and a remainder e.
5. Divide 8 * b + 13 by 25 to get a quotient g. Ignore the remainder.
6. Divide 19 * a + b - d - g + 15 by 30 to get a remainder h. Ignore the quotient.
7. Divide c by 4 to get a quotient j and a remainder k.
8. Divide a + 11 * h by 319 to get a quotient m. Ignore the remainder.
9. Divide 2 * e + 2 * j - k - h + m + 32 by 7 to get a remainder r. Ignore the quotient.

10. Divide h - m + r + 90 by 25 to get a quotient n. Ignore the remainder.

11. Divide h - m + r + n + 19 by 32 to get a remainder p. Ignore the quotient.

Then Easter falls on day p of month n. For example, if y is 2001:

```
a = 6              h = 18             n = 4
b = 20, c = 1      j = 0, k = 1       p = 15
d = 5, e = 0       m = 0
g = 6              r = 6
```

Therefore, in 2001, Easter Sunday fell on April 15. Write a program that prompts the user for a year and prints out the month and day of Easter Sunday.

■■ Business P2.22 The following pseudocode describes how a bookstore computes the price of an order from the total price and the number of the books that were ordered.

> Read the total book price and the number of books.
> Compute the tax (7.5 percent of the total book price).
> Compute the shipping charge ($2 per book).
> The price of the order is the sum of the total book price, the tax, and the shipping charge.
> Print the price of the order.

Translate this pseudocode into a Java program.

■■ Business P2.23 The following pseudocode describes how to turn a string containing a ten-digit phone number (such as "4155551212") into a more readable string with parentheses and dashes, like this: "(415) 555-1212".

> Take the substring consisting of the first three characters and surround it with "(" and ") ". This is the area code.
> Concatenate the area code, the substring consisting of the next three characters, a hyphen, and the substring consisting of the last four characters. This is the formatted number.

Translate this pseudocode into a Java program that reads a telephone number into a string variable, computes the formatted number, and prints it.

■■ Business P2.24 The following pseudocode describes how to extract the dollars and cents from a price given as a floating-point value. For example, a price 2.95 yields values 2 and 95 for the dollars and cents.

> Assign the price to an integer variable dollars.
> Multiply the difference price - dollars by 100 and add 0.5.
> Assign the result to an integer variable cents.

Translate this pseudocode into a Java program. Read a price and print the dollars and cents. Test your program with inputs 2.95 and 4.35.

■■ Business P2.25 *Giving change.* Implement a program that directs a cashier how to give change. The program has two inputs: the amount due and the amount received from the customer. Display the dollars, quarters, dimes, nickels, and pennies that the customer should receive in return. In order to avoid roundoff errors, the program user should supply both amounts in pennies, for example 274 instead of 2.74.

■ Business P2.26 An online bank wants you to create a program that shows prospective customers how their deposits will grow. Your program should read the initial balance and the annual interest rate. Interest is compounded monthly. Print out the balances after the first three months. Here is a sample run:

```
Initial balance: 1000
Annual interest rate in percent: 6.0
After first month:    1005.00
After second month:   1010.03
After third month:    1015.08
```

■ Business P2.27 A video club wants to reward its best members with a discount based on the member's number of movie rentals and the number of new members referred by the member. The discount is in percent and is equal to the sum of the rentals and the referrals, but it cannot exceed 75 percent. (*Hint:* Math.min.) Write a program Discount-Calculator to calculate the value of the discount.

Here is a sample run:

```
Enter the number of movie rentals: 56
Enter the number of members referred to the video club: 3
The discount is equal to:    59.00 percent.
```

■ Science P2.28 Consider the following circuit.

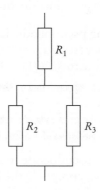

Write a program that reads the resistances of the three resistors and computes the total resistance, using Ohm's law.

■■ Science P2.29 The dew point temperature T_d can be calculated (approximately) from the relative humidity RH and the actual temperature T by

$$T_d = \frac{b \cdot f(T,RH)}{a - f(T,RH)}$$

$$f(T,RH) = \frac{a \cdot T}{b + T} + \ln(RH)$$

where $a = 17.27$ and $b = 237.7°$ C.

Write a program that reads the relative humidity (between 0 and 1) and the temperature (in degrees C) and prints the dew point value. Use the Java function log to compute the natural logarithm.

■■■ Science P2.30 The pipe clip temperature sensors shown here are robust sensors that can be clipped directly onto copper pipes to measure the temperature of the liquids in the pipes.

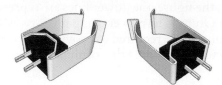

Each sensor contains a device called a *thermistor*. Thermistors are semiconductor devices that exhibit a temperature-dependent resistance described by:

$$R = R_0 \, e^{\beta\left(\frac{1}{T} - \frac{1}{T_0}\right)}$$

where R is the resistance (in Ω) at the temperature T (in $°K$), and R_0 is the resistance (in Ω) at the temperature T_0 (in $°K$). β is a constant that depends on the material used to make the thermistor. Thermistors are specified by providing values for R_0, T_0, and β.

The thermistors used to make the pipe clip temperature sensors have $R_0 = 1075 \, \Omega$ at $T_0 = 85 \, °C$, and $\beta = 3969 \, °K$. (Notice that β has units of $°K$. Recall that the temperature in $°K$ is obtained by adding 273 to the temperature in $°C$.) The liquid temperature, in $°C$, is determined from the resistance R, in Ω, using

$$T = \frac{\beta T_0}{T_0 \ln\left(\frac{R}{R_0}\right) + \beta} - 273$$

Write a Java program that prompts the user for the thermistor resistance R and prints a message giving the liquid temperature in $°C$.

■■■ Science P2.31 The circuit shown below illustrates some important aspects of the connection between a power company and one of its customers. The customer is represented by three parameters, V_t, P, and pf. V_t is the voltage accessed by plugging into a wall outlet. Customers depend on having a dependable value of V_t in order for their appliances to work properly. Accordingly, the power company regulates the value of V_t carefully. P describes the amount of power used by the customer and is the primary factor in determining the customer's electric bill. The power factor, pf, is less familiar. (The power factor is calculated as the cosine of an angle so that its value will always be between zero and one.) In this problem you will be asked to write a Java program to investigate the significance of the power factor.

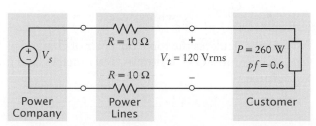

In the figure, the power lines are represented, somewhat simplistically, as resistances in Ohms. The power company is represented as an AC voltage source. The source voltage, V_s, required to provide the customer with power P at voltage V_t can be determined using the formula

$$V_s = \sqrt{\left(V_t + \frac{2RP}{V_t}\right)^2 + \left(\frac{2RP}{pf\,V_t}\right)^2 \left(1 - pf^2\right)}$$

(V_s has units of Vrms.) This formula indicates that the value of V_s depends on the value of pf. Write a Java program that prompts the user for a power factor value and then prints a message giving the corresponding value of V_s, using the values for P, R, and V_t shown in the figure above.

■■■ **Science P2.32** Consider the following tuning circuit connected to an antenna, where C is a variable capacitor whose capacitance ranges from C_{min} to C_{max}.

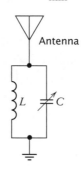

The tuning circuit selects the frequency $f = \dfrac{2\pi}{\sqrt{LC}}$. To design this circuit for a given frequency, take $C = \sqrt{C_{min}C_{max}}$ and calculate the required inductance L from f and C. Now the circuit can be tuned to any frequency in the range $f_{min} = \dfrac{2\pi}{\sqrt{LC_{max}}}$ to $f_{max} = \dfrac{2\pi}{\sqrt{LC_{min}}}$.

Write a Java program to design a tuning circuit for a given frequency, using a variable capacitor with given values for C_{min} and C_{max}. (A typical input is $f = 16.7$ MHz, $C_{min} = 14$ pF, and $C_{max} = 365$ pF.) The program should read in f (in Hz), C_{min} and C_{max} (in F), and print the required inductance value and the range of frequencies to which the circuit can be tuned by varying the capacitance.

■ **Science P2.33** According to the Coulomb force law, the electric force between two charged particles of charge Q_1 and Q_2 Coulombs, that are a distance r meters apart, is

$F = \dfrac{Q_1 Q_2}{4\pi\varepsilon r^2}$ Newtons, where $\varepsilon = 8.854 \times 10^{-12}$ Farads/meter. Write a program

that calculates the force on a pair of charged particles, based on the user input of Q_1 Coulombs, Q_2 Coulombs, and r meters, and then computes and displays the electric force.

ANSWERS TO SELF-CHECK QUESTIONS

1. One possible answer is

```
int bottlesPerCase = 8;
```

You may choose a different variable name or a different initialization value, but your variable should have type `int`.

2. There are three errors:
- You cannot have spaces in variable names.
- The variable type should be `double` because it holds a fractional value.
- There is a semicolon missing at the end of the statement.

3.
```
double unitPrice = 1.95;
int quantity = 2;
```

4.
```
System.out.print("Total price: ");
System.out.println(unitPrice * quantity);
```

5. Change the declaration of `cansPerPack` to

```
int cansPerPack = 4;
```

6. You need to use a `*/` delimiter to close a comment that begins with a `/*`:

```
double canVolume = 0.355;
   /* Liters in a 12 ounce can */
```

7. The program would compile, and it would display the same result. However, a person reading the program might find it confusing that fractional cans are being considered.

8. Its value is modified by the assignment statement.

9. Assignment would occur when one car is replaced by another in the parking space.

10. `double interest = balance * percent / 100;`

11. `double sideLength = Math.sqrt(area);`

12. `4 * PI * Math.pow(radius, 3) / 3`
or `(4.0 / 3) * PI * Math.pow(radius, 3)`,
but not `(4 / 3) * PI * Math.pow(radius, 3)`

13. 172 and 9

14. It is the second-to-last digit of n. For example, if n is 1729, then `n / 10` is 172, and `(n / 10) % 10` is 2.

15.
```
System.out.print("How old are you? ");
int age = in.nextInt();
```

16. There is no prompt that alerts the program user to enter the quantity.

17. The second statement calls `nextInt`, not `nextDouble`. If the user were to enter a price such as 1.95, the program would be terminated with an "input mismatch exception".

18. There is no colon and space at the end of the prompt. A dialog would look like this:

```
Please enter the number of cans6
```

19.
```
The total volume is     10
```

There are four spaces between `is` and 10. One space originates from the format string (the space between `s` and `%`), and three spaces are added before 10 to achieve a field width of 5.

20. Here is a simple solution:

```
System.out.printf("Bottles: %8d\n", bottles);
System.out.printf("Cans:    %8d\n", cans);
```

Note the spaces after `Cans:`. Alternatively, you can use format specifiers for the strings. You can even combine all output into a single statement:

```
System.out.printf("%-9s%8d\n%-9s%8d\n",
"Bottles: ", bottles, "Cans:", cans);
```

21.
```
int pairs = (totalWidth - tileWidth)
   / (2 * tileWidth);
int tiles = 1 + 2 * pairs;
double gap = (totalWidth -
   tiles * tileWidth) / 2.0;
```

Be sure that `pairs` is declared as an `int`.

22. Now there are groups of four tiles (gray/white/gray/black) following the initial black tile. Therefore, the algorithm is now

number of groups = integer part of (total width − tile width) / (4 x tile width)
number of tiles = 1 + 4 x number of groups

The formula for the gap is not changed.

23. Clearly, the answer depends only on whether the row and column numbers are even or odd, so let's first take the remainder after dividing by 2. Then we can enumerate all expected answers:

Row % 2	Column % 2	Color
0	0	0
0	1	1
1	0	1
1	1	0

In the first three entries of the table, the color is simply the sum of the remainders. In the fourth entry, the sum would be 2, but we want a zero. We can achieve that by taking another remainder operation:

color = ((row % 2) + (column % 2)) % 2

24. In nine years, the repair costs increased by $1,400. Therefore, the increase per year is $1,400 / 9 ≈ $156. The repair cost in year 3 would be $100 + 2 × $156 = $412. The repair cost in year n is $100 + n × $156. To avoid accumulation of roundoff errors, it is actually a good idea to use the original expression that yielded $156, that is,

Repair cost in year n = 100 + n x 1400 / 9

25. The pseudocode follows easily from the equations:

bottom volume = π x r_1^2 x h_1
top volume = π x r_2^2 x h_2
middle volume = π x (r_1^2 + r_1 x r_2 + r_2^2) x h_3 / 3
total volume = bottom volume + top volume + middle volume

Measuring a typical wine bottle yields $r_1 = 3.6$, $r_2 = 1.2$, $h_1 = 15$, $h_2 = 7$, $h_3 = 6$ (all in centimeters). Therefore,

bottom volume = 610.73

top volume = 31.67

middle volume = 135.72

total volume = 778.12

The actual volume is 750 ml, which is close enough to our computation to give confidence that it is correct.

26. The length is 12. The space counts as a character.

27. `str.substring(8, 12)` or `str.substring(8)`

28. `str = str + "ming";`

29. `Hy`

30.
```
String first = in.next();
String middle = in.next();
String last = in.next();
```

CHAPTER 3

DECISIONS

To implement decisions using if
statements

To compare integers, floating-point numbers, and strings

To write statements using the Boolean data type

To develop strategies for testing your programs

To validate user input

3.1 THE IF STATEMENT 82

Syntax 3.1: if Statement 84

Programming Tip 3.1: Brace Layout 86

Programming Tip 3.2: Always Use Braces 86

Common Error 3.1: A Semicolon After the
if Condition 86

Programming Tip 3.3: Tabs 87

Special Topic 3.1: The Conditional Operator 87

Programming Tip 3.4: Avoid
Duplication in Branches 88

**3.2 COMPARING NUMBERS
AND STRINGS** 88

Syntax 3.2: Comparisons 89

Common Error 3.2: Exact Comparison of
Floating-Point Numbers 91

Common Error 3.3: Using == to Compare Strings 92

Special Topic 3.2: Lexicographic Ordering
of Strings 92

How To 3.1: Implementing an if Statement 93

Worked Example 3.1: Extracting the Middle ⊕

Random Fact 3.1: The Denver Airport Luggage
Handling System 95

3.3 MULTIPLE ALTERNATIVES 96

Special Topic 3.3: The switch Statement 99

3.4 NESTED BRANCHES 100

Programming Tip 3.5: Hand-Tracing 103

Common Error 3.4: The Dangling else Problem 104

Special Topic 3.4: Enumeration Types 105

Video Example 3.1: Computing the Plural of an
English Word ⊕

3.5 PROBLEM SOLVING: FLOWCHARTS 105

3.6 PROBLEM SOLVING: TEST CASES 108

Programming Tip 3.6: Make a Schedule and Make
Time for Unexpected Problems 109

Special Topic 3.5: Logging 110

**3.7 BOOLEAN VARIABLES
AND OPERATORS** 111

Common Error 3.5: Combining Multiple
Relational Operators 113

Common Error 3.6: Confusing && and ||
Conditions 114

Special Topic 3.6: Short-Circuit Evaluation of
Boolean Operators 114

Special Topic 3.7: De Morgan's Law 115

3.8 APPLICATION: INPUT VALIDATION 116

Video Example 3.2: The Genetic Code ⊕

Random Fact 3.2: Artificial Intelligence 119

One of the essential features of computer programs is their ability to make decisions. Like a train that changes tracks depending on how the switches are set, a program can take different actions depending on inputs and other circumstances.

In this chapter, you will learn how to program simple and complex decisions. You will apply what you learn to the task of checking user input.

3.1 The if Statement

The if statement allows a program to carry out different actions depending on the nature of the data to be processed.

The if statement is used to implement a decision (see Syntax 3.1). When a condition is fulfilled, one set of statements is executed. Otherwise, another set of statements is executed.

Here is an example using the if statement: In many countries, the number 13 is considered unlucky. Rather than offending superstitious tenants, building owners sometimes skip the thirteenth floor; floor 12 is immediately followed by floor 14. Of course, floor 13 is not usually left empty or, as some conspiracy theorists believe, filled with secret offices and research labs. It is simply called floor 14. The computer that controls the building elevators needs to compensate for this foible and adjust all floor numbers above 13.

Let's simulate this process in Java. We will ask the user to type in the desired floor number and then compute the actual floor. When the input is above 13, then we need to decrement the input to obtain the actual floor. For example, if the user provides an input of 20, the program determines the actual floor as 19. Otherwise, we simply use the supplied floor number.

This elevator panel "skips" the thirteenth floor. The floor is not actually missing—the computer that controls the elevator adjusts the floor numbers above 13.

```java
int actualFloor;

if (floor > 13)
{
   actualFloor = floor - 1;
}
else
{
   actualFloor = floor;
}
```

The flowchart in Figure 1 shows the branching behavior.

In our example, each branch of the if statement contains a single statement. You can include as many statements in each branch as you like. Sometimes, it happens that

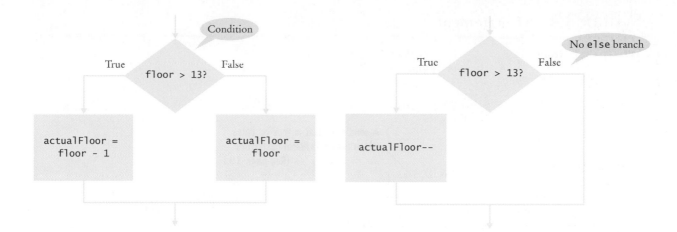

Figure 1
Flowchart for if Statement

Figure 2
Flowchart for if Statement with No else Branch

there is nothing to do in the else branch of the statement. In that case, you can omit it entirely, such as in this example:

```
int actualFloor = floor;

if (floor > 13)
{
   actualFloor--;
} // No else needed
```

See Figure 2 for the flowchart.

An if statement is like a fork in the road. Depending upon a decision, different parts of the program are executed.

Syntax 3.1 if Statement

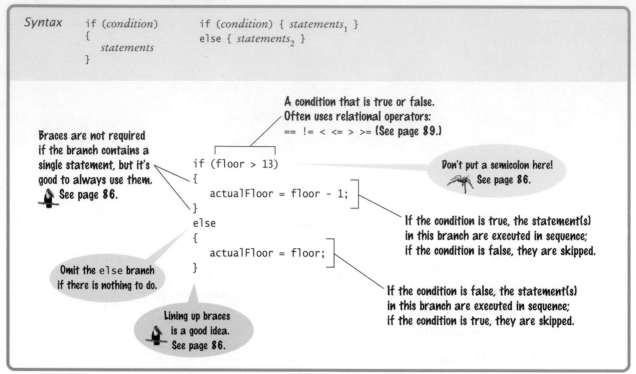

Syntax
```
if (condition)                if (condition) { statements₁ }
{                             else { statements₂ }
    statements
}
```

A condition that is true or false.
Often uses relational operators:
== != < <= > >= (See page 89.)

Braces are not required if the branch contains a single statement, but it's good to always use them. See page 86.

Don't put a semicolon here! See page 86.

```
if (floor > 13)
{
    actualFloor = floor - 1;
}
else
{
    actualFloor = floor;
}
```

If the condition is true, the statement(s) in this branch are executed in sequence; if the condition is false, they are skipped.

Omit the else branch if there is nothing to do.

If the condition is false, the statement(s) in this branch are executed in sequence; if the condition is true, they are skipped.

Lining up braces is a good idea. See page 86.

The following program puts the if statement to work. This program asks for the desired floor and then prints out the actual floor.

section_1/ElevatorSimulation.java

```java
1   import java.util.Scanner;
2
3   /**
4      This program simulates an elevator panel that skips the 13th floor.
5   */
6   public class ElevatorSimulation
7   {
8      public static void main(String[] args)
9      {
10        Scanner in = new Scanner(System.in);
11        System.out.print("Floor: ");
12        int floor = in.nextInt();
13
14        // Adjust floor if necessary
15
16        int actualFloor;
17        if (floor > 13)
18        {
19           actualFloor = floor - 1;
20        }
21        else
22        {
```

```
23              actualFloor = floor;
24          }
25
26          System.out.println("The elevator will travel to the actual floor "
27              + actualFloor);
28      }
29  }
```

Program Run

```
Floor: 20
The elevator will travel to the actual floor 19
```

SELF CHECK

1. In some Asian countries, the number 14 is considered unlucky. Some building owners play it safe and skip *both* the thirteenth and the fourteenth floor. How would you modify the sample program to handle such a building?

2. Consider the following if statement to compute a discounted price:

```
if (originalPrice > 100)
{
   discountedPrice = originalPrice - 20;
}
else
{
   discountedPrice = originalPrice - 10;
}
```

   What is the discounted price if the original price is 95? 100? 105?

3. Compare this if statement with the one in Self Check 2:

```
if (originalPrice < 100)
{
   discountedPrice = originalPrice - 10;
}
else
{
   discountedPrice = originalPrice - 20;
}
```

   Do the two statements always compute the same value? If not, when do the values differ?

4. Consider the following statements to compute a discounted price:

```
discountedPrice = originalPrice;
if (originalPrice > 100)
{
   discountedPrice = originalPrice - 10;
}
```

   What is the discounted price if the original price is 95? 100? 105?

5. The variables fuelAmount and fuelCapacity hold the actual amount of fuel and the size of the fuel tank of a vehicle. If less than 10 percent is remaining in the tank, a status light should show a red color; otherwise it shows a green color. Simulate this process by printing out either "red" or "green".

Practice It   Now you can try these exercises at the end of the chapter: R3.5, R3.6, P3.31.

Brace Layout

The compiler doesn't care where you place braces. In this book, we follow the simple rule of making { and } line up.

```
if (floor > 13)
{
    floor--;
}
```

This style makes it easy to spot matching braces. Some programmers put the opening brace on the same line as the if:

```
if (floor > 13) {
    floor--;
}
```

Properly lining up your code makes your programs easier to read.

This style makes it harder to match the braces, but it saves a line of code, allowing you to view more code on the screen without scrolling. There are passionate advocates of both styles.

It is important that you pick a layout style and stick with it consistently within a given programming project. Which style you choose may depend on your personal preference or a coding style guide that you need to follow.

Always Use Braces

When the body of an if statement consists of a single statement, you need not use braces. For example, the following is legal:

```
if (floor > 13)
    floor--;
```

However, it is a good idea to always include the braces:

```
if (floor > 13)
{
    floor--;
}
```

The braces make your code easier to read. They also make it easier for you to maintain the code because you won't have to worry about adding braces when you add statements inside an if statement.

A Semicolon After the if Condition

The following code fragment has an unfortunate error:

```
if (floor > 13) ; // ERROR
{
    floor--;
}
```

There should be no semicolon after the if condition. The compiler interprets this statement as follows: If floor is greater than 13, execute the statement that is denoted by a single semicolon, that is, the do-nothing statement. The statement enclosed in braces is no longer a part of the if statement. It is always executed. In other words, even if the value of floor is not above 13, it is decremented.

Programming Tip 3.3

Tabs

Block-structured code has the property that nested statements are indented by one or more levels:

```java
public class ElevatorSimulation
{
|  public static void main(String[] args)
|  {
|  |  int floor;
|  |  . . .
|  |  if (floor > 13)
|  |  {
|  |  |  floor--;
|  |  }
|  |  . . .
|  }
|  |  |  |
0  1  2  3    Indentation level
```

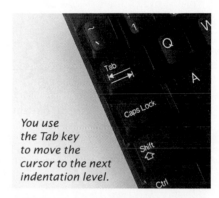

You use the Tab key to move the cursor to the next indentation level.

How do you move the cursor from the leftmost column to the appropriate indentation level? A perfectly reasonable strategy is to hit the space bar a sufficient number of times. With most editors, you can use the Tab key instead. A tab moves the cursor to the next indentation level. Some editors even have an option to fill in the tabs automatically.

While the Tab *key* is nice, some editors use *tab characters* for alignment, which is not so nice. Tab characters can lead to problems when you send your file to another person or a printer. There is no universal agreement on the width of a tab character, and some software will ignore tab characters altogether. It is therefore best to save your files with spaces instead of tabs. Most editors have a setting to automatically convert all tabs to spaces. Look at the documentation of your development environment to find out how to activate this useful setting.

Special Topic 3.1

The Conditional Operator

Java has a *conditional operator* of the form

condition ? *value*₁ : *value*₂

The value of that expression is either $value_1$ if the test passes or $value_2$ if it fails. For example, we can compute the actual floor number as

```java
actualFloor = floor > 13 ? floor - 1 : floor;
```

which is equivalent to

```java
if (floor > 13) { actualFloor = floor - 1; } else { actualFloor = floor; }
```

You can use the conditional operator anywhere that a value is expected, for example:

```java
System.out.println("Actual floor: " + (floor > 13 ? floor - 1 : floor));
```

We don't use the conditional operator in this book, but it is a convenient construct that you will find in many Java programs.

Avoid Duplication in Branches

Look to see whether you *duplicate code* in each branch. If so, move it out of the if statement. Here is an example of such duplication:

```java
if (floor > 13)
{
   actualFloor = floor - 1;
   System.out.println("Actual floor: " + actualFloor);
}
else
{
   actualFloor = floor;
   System.out.println("Actual floor: " + actualFloor);
}
```

The output statement is exactly the same in both branches. This is not an error—the program will run correctly. However, you can simplify the program by moving the duplicated statement, like this:

```java
if (floor > 13)
{
   actualFloor = floor - 1;
}
else
{
   actualFloor = floor;
}
System.out.println("Actual floor: " + actualFloor);
```

Removing duplication is particularly important when programs are maintained for a long time. When there are two sets of statements with the same effect, it can easily happen that a programmer modifies one set but not the other.

3.2 Comparing Numbers and Strings

Use relational operators
(< <= > >= == !=)
to compare numbers.

Every if statement contains a condition. In many cases, the condition involves comparing two values. For example, in the previous examples we tested floor > 13. The comparison > is called a **relational operator**. Java has six relational operators (see Table 1).

As you can see, only two Java relational operators (> and <) look as you would expect from the mathematical notation. Computer keyboards do not have keys for ≥, ≤, or ≠, but the >=, <=, and != operators are easy to remember because they look similar. The == operator is initially confusing to most newcomers to Java.

In Java, you use a relational operator to check whether one value is greater than another.

Table 1 Relational Operators		
Java	Math Notation	Description
>	>	Greater than
>=	≥	Greater than or equal
<	<	Less than
<=	≤	Less than or equal
==	=	Equal
!=	≠	Not equal

In Java, = already has a meaning, namely assignment. The == operator denotes equality testing:

```
floor = 13;  // Assign 13 to floor

if (floor == 13)   // Test whether floor equals 13
```

You must remember to use == inside tests and to use = outside tests.

Syntax 3.2   Comparisons

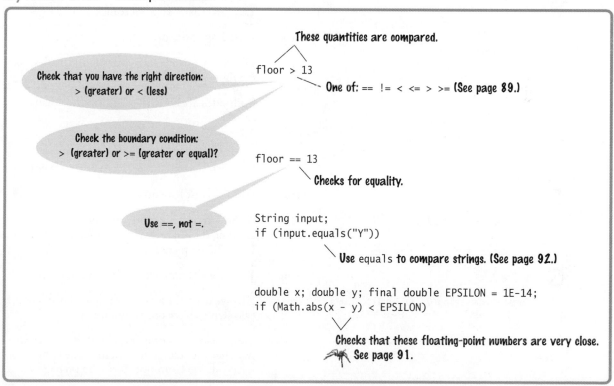

The relational operators in Table 1 have a lower precedence than the arithmetic operators. That means, you can write arithmetic expressions on either side of the relational operator without using parentheses. For example, in the expression

```
floor - 1 < 13
```

both sides (`floor - 1` and `13`) of the `<` operator are evaluated, and the results are compared. Appendix B shows a table of the Java operators and their precedence.

To test whether two strings are equal to each other, you must use the method called `equals`:

```
if (string1.equals(string2)) . . .
```

Do not use the `==` operator to compare strings. The comparison

```
if (string1 == string2) // Not useful
```

Do not use the `==` operator to compare strings. Use the `equals` method instead.

has an unrelated meaning. It tests whether the two strings are stored in the same location. You can have strings with identical contents stored in different locations, so this test never makes sense in actual programming; see Common Error 3.3 on page 92.

Table 2 summarizes how to compare values in Java.

Table 2 Relational Operator Examples

Expression	Value	Comment
`3 <= 4`	true	3 is less than 4; `<=` tests for "less than or equal".
🚫 `3 =< 4`	**Error**	The "less than or equal" operator is `<=`, not `=<`. The "less than" symbol comes first.
`3 > 4`	false	`>` is the opposite of `<=`.
`4 < 4`	false	The left-hand side must be strictly smaller than the right-hand side.
`4 <= 4`	true	Both sides are equal; `<=` tests for "less than or equal".
`3 == 5 - 2`	true	`==` tests for equality.
`3 != 5 - 1`	true	`!=` tests for inequality. It is true that 3 is not 5 – 1.
🚫 `3 = 6 / 2`	**Error**	Use `==` to test for equality.
`1.0 / 3.0 == 0.333333333`	false	Although the values are very close to one another, they are not exactly equal. See Common Error 3.2 on page 91.
🚫 `"10" > 5`	**Error**	You cannot compare a string to a number.
`"Tomato".substring(0, 3).equals("Tom")`	true	Always use the `equals` method to check whether two strings have the same contents.
`"Tomato".substring(0, 3) == ("Tom")`	false	Never use `==` to compare strings; it only checks whether the strings are stored in the same location. See Common Error 3.3 on page 92.

6. Which of the following conditions are true, provided a is 3 and b is 4?

    a. a + 1 <= b

    b. a + 1 >= b

    c. a + 1 != b

7. Give the opposite of the condition

    ```
    floor > 13
    ```

8. What is the error in this statement?

    ```
    if (scoreA = scoreB)
    {
        System.out.println("Tie");
    }
    ```

9. Supply a condition in this `if` statement to test whether the user entered a Y:

    ```
    System.out.println("Enter Y to quit.");
    String input = in.next();
    if (. . .)
    {
        System.out.println("Goodbye.");
    }
    ```

10. How do you test that a string `str` is the empty string?

Practice It   Now you can try these exercises at the end of the chapter: R3.4, R3.7, P3.18.

Common Error 3.2

Exact Comparison of Floating-Point Numbers

Floating-point numbers have only a limited precision, and calculations can introduce roundoff errors. You must take these
inevitable roundoffs into account when comparing floating-
point numbers. For example, the following code multiplies the
square root of 2 by itself. Ideally, we expect to get the answer 2:

```
double r = Math.sqrt(2.0);
if (r * r == 2.0)
{
    System.out.println("Math.sqrt(2.0) squared is 2.0");
}
else
{
    System.out.println("Math.sqrt(2.0) squared is not 2.0 but "
        + r * r);
}
```

*Take limited precision into
account when comparing
floating-point numbers.*

This program displays

```
Math.sqrt(2.0) squared is not 2.0 but 2.00000000000000044
```

It does not make sense in most circumstances to compare floating-point numbers exactly.
Instead, we should test whether they are *close enough*. That is, the magnitude of their difference should be less than some threshold. Mathematically, we would write that x and y are close
enough if

$$|x - y| < \varepsilon$$

for a very small number, ε. ε is the Greek letter epsilon, a letter used to denote a very small quantity. It is common to set ε to 10^{-14} when comparing `double` numbers:

```java
final double EPSILON = 1E-14;
double r = Math.sqrt(2.0);
if (Math.abs(r * r - 2.0) < EPSILON)
{
    System.out.println("Math.sqrt(2.0) squared is approximately 2.0");
}
```

Common Error 3.3

Using == to Compare Strings

If you write

```java
if (nickname == "Rob")
```

then the test succeeds only if the variable `nickname` refers to the exact same location as the string literal `"Rob"`. The test will pass if a string variable was initialized with the same string literal:

```java
String nickname = "Rob";
. . .
if (nickname == "Rob") // Test is true
```

However, if the string with the letters R o b has been assembled in some other way, then the test will fail:

```java
String name = "Robert";
String nickname = name.substring(0, 3);
. . .
if (nickname == "Rob") // Test is false
```

In this case, the `substring` method produces a string in a different memory location. Even though both strings have the same contents, the comparison fails.

You must remember never to use `==` to compare strings. Always use `equals` to check whether two strings have the same contents.

Special Topic 3.2

Lexicographic Ordering of Strings

If two strings are not identical to each other, you still may want to know the relationship between them. The `compareTo` method compares strings in "lexicographic" order. This ordering is very similar to the way in which words are sorted in a dictionary. If

```java
string1.compareTo(string2) < 0
```

then the string `string1` comes before the string `string2` in the dictionary. For example, this is the case if `string1` is `"Harry"`, and `string2` is `"Hello"`. If

```java
string1.compareTo(string2) > 0
```

then `string1` comes after `string2` in dictionary order.
Finally, if

```java
string1.compareTo(string2) == 0
```

then `string1` and `string2` are equal.

To see which of two terms comes first in the dictionary, consider the first letter in which they differ.

There are a few technical differences between the ordering in a dictionary and the lexicographic ordering in Java. In Java:

- All uppercase letters come before the lowercase letters. For example, "Z" comes before "a".
- The space character comes before all printable characters.
- Numbers come before letters.
- For the ordering of punctuation marks, see Appendix A.

When comparing two strings, you compare the first letters of each word, then the second letters, and so on, until one of the strings ends or you find the first letter pair that doesn't match.

If one of the strings ends, the longer string is considered the "larger" one. For example, compare "car" with "cart". The first three letters match, and we reach the end of the first string. Therefore "car" comes before "cart" in lexicographic ordering.

When you reach a mismatch, the string containing the "larger" character is considered "larger". For example, let's compare "cat" with "cart". The first two letters match. Because t comes after r, the string "cat" comes after "cart" in the lexicographic ordering.

> The compareTo method compares strings in lexicographic order.

c a r

c a r t

c a t

Letters match   r comes before t

Lexicographic Ordering

HOW TO 3.1   **Implementing an if Statement**

This How To walks you through the process of implementing an if statement. We will illustrate the steps with the following example problem:

The university bookstore has a Kilobyte Day sale every October 24, giving an 8 percent discount on all computer accessory purchases if the price is less than $128, and a 16 percent discount if the price is at least $128. Write a program that asks the cashier for the original price and then prints the discounted price.

Step 1   Decide upon the branching condition.

In our sample problem, the obvious choice for the condition is:

original price < 128?

That is just fine, and we will use that condition in our solution.

But you could equally well come up with a correct solution if you choose the opposite condition: Is the original price at least $128? You might choose this condition if you put yourself into the position of a shopper who wants to know when the bigger discount applies.

Sales discounts are often higher for expensive products. Use the if statement to implement such a decision.

Step 2   Give pseudocode for the work that needs to be done when the condition is true.

In this step, you list the action or actions that are taken in the "positive" branch. The details depend on your problem. You may want to print a message, compute values, or even exit the program.

In our example, we need to apply an 8 percent discount:

discounted price = 0.92 x original price

Step 3   Give pseudocode for the work (if any) that needs to be done when the condition is *not* true.

What do you want to do in the case that the condition of Step 1 is not satisfied? Sometimes, you want to do nothing at all. In that case, use an if statement without an else branch.

In our example, the condition tested whether the price was less than $128. If that condition is *not* true, the price is at least $128, so the higher discount of 16 percent applies to the sale:

discounted price = 0.84 x original price

Step 4   Double-check relational operators.

First, be sure that the test goes in the right *direction*. It is a common error to confuse > and <. Next, consider whether you should use the < operator or its close cousin, the <= operator.

What should happen if the original price is exactly $128? Reading the problem carefully, we find that the lower discount applies if the original price is *less than* $128, and the higher discount applies when it is *at least* $128. A price of $128 should therefore *not* fulfill our condition, and we must use <, not <=.

Step 5   Remove duplication.

Check which actions are common to both branches, and move them outside. (See Programming Tip 3.4 on page 88.)

In our example, we have two statements of the form

discounted price = ___ x original price

They only differ in the discount rate. It is best to just set the rate in the branches, and to do the computation afterwards:

If original price < 128
    discount rate = 0.92
Else
    discount rate = 0.84
discounted price = discount rate x original price

Step 6   Test both branches.

Formulate two test cases, one that fulfills the condition of the if statement, and one that does not. Ask yourself what should happen in each case. Then follow the pseudocode and act each of them out.

In our example, let us consider two scenarios for the original price: $100 and $200. We expect that the first price is discounted by $8, the second by $32.

When the original price is 100, then the condition 100 < 128 is true, and we get

discount rate = 0.92
discounted price = 0.92 x 100 = 92

When the original price is 200, then the condition 200 < 128 is false, and

discount rate = 0.84
discounted price = 0.84 x 200 = 168

In both cases, we get the expected answer.

Step 7   Assemble the if statement in Java.

Type the skeleton

```
if ()
{
```

```
}
else
{
}
```

and fill it in, as shown in Syntax 3.1 on page 84. Omit the `else` branch if it is not needed. In our example, the completed statement is

```
if (originalPrice < 128)
{
    discountRate = 0.92;
}
else
{
    discountRate = 0.84;
}
discountedPrice = discountRate * originalPrice;
```

ONLINE EXAMPLE

The complete program for calculating a discounted price.

WORKED EXAMPLE 3.1   **Extracting the Middle**

This Worked Example shows how to extract the middle character from a string, or the two middle characters if the length of the string is even.

c	r	a	t	e
0	1	2	3	4

Random Fact 3.1 The Denver Airport Luggage Handling System

Making decisions is an essential part of any computer program. Nowhere is this more obvious than in a computer system that helps sort luggage at an airport. After scanning the luggage identification codes, the system sorts the items and routes them to different conveyor belts. Human operators then place the items onto trucks. When the city of Denver built a huge airport to replace an outdated and congested facility, the luggage system contractor went a step further. The new system was designed to replace the human operators with robotic carts. Unfortunately, the system plainly did not work. It was plagued by mechanical problems, such as luggage falling onto the tracks and jamming carts. Equally frustrating were the software glitches. Carts would uselessly accumulate at some locations when they were needed elsewhere.

The airport had been scheduled to open in 1993, but without a functioning luggage system, the opening was delayed for over a year while the contractor tried to fix the problems. The contractor never succeeded, and ultimately a manual system was installed. The delay cost the city and airlines close to a billion dollars, and the contractor, once the leading luggage systems vendor in the United States, went bankrupt.

Clearly, it is very risky to build a large system based on a technology that has never been tried on a smaller scale. As robots and the software that controls them get better over time, they will take on a larger share of luggage handling in the future. But it is likely that this will happen in an incremental fashion.

The Denver airport originally had a fully automatic system for moving luggage, replacing human operators with robotic carts. Unfortunately, the system never worked and was dismantled before the airport was opened.

Available online in WileyPLUS and at www.wiley.com/college/horstmann.

3.3 Multiple Alternatives

Multiple if statements can be combined to evaluate complex decisions.

In Section 3.1, you saw how to program a two-way branch with an if statement. In many situations, there are more than two cases. In this section, you will see how to implement a decision with multiple alternatives.

For example, consider a program that displays the effect of an earthquake, as measured by the Richter scale (see Table 3).

The 1989 Loma Prieta earthquake that damaged the Bay Bridge in San Francisco and destroyed many buildings measured 7.1 on the Richter scale.

Table 3 Richter Scale	
Value	Effect
8	Most structures fall
7	Many buildings destroyed
6	Many buildings considerably damaged, some collapse
4.5	Damage to poorly constructed buildings

The Richter scale is a measurement of the strength of an earthquake. Every step in the scale, for example from 6.0 to 7.0, signifies a tenfold increase in the strength of the quake.

In this case, there are five branches: one each for the four descriptions of damage, and one for no destruction. Figure 3 shows the flowchart for this multiple-branch statement.

You use multiple if statements to implement multiple alternatives, like this:

ANIMATION
Multiple Alternatives

```
if (richter >= 8.0)
{
    System.out.println("Most structures fall");
}
else if (richter >= 7.0)
{
    System.out.println("Many buildings destroyed");
}
else if (richter >= 6.0)
{
    System.out.println("Many buildings considerably damaged, some collapse");
}
else if (richter >= 4.5)
{
    System.out.println("Damage to poorly constructed buildings");
}
else
{
    System.out.println("No destruction of buildings");
}
```

As soon as one of the four tests succeeds, the effect is displayed, and no further tests are attempted. If none of the four cases applies, the final else clause applies, and a default message is printed.

Figure 3
Multiple Alternatives

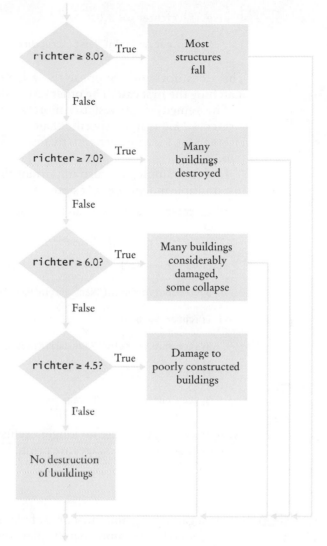

Here you must sort the conditions and test against the largest cutoff first. Suppose we reverse the order of tests:

```
if (richter >= 4.5) // Tests in wrong order
{
   System.out.println("Damage to poorly constructed buildings");
}
else if (richter >= 6.0)
{
   System.out.println("Many buildings considerably damaged, some collapse");
}
else if (richter >= 7.0)
{
   System.out.println("Many buildings destroyed");
```

```
    }
    else if (richter >= 8.0)
    {
        System.out.println("Most structures fall");
    }
```

This does not work. Suppose the value of richter is 7.1. That value is at least 4.5, matching the first case. The other tests will never be attempted.

The remedy is to test the more specific conditions first. Here, the condition richter >= 8.0 is more specific than the condition richter >= 7.0, and the condition richter >= 4.5 is more general (that is, fulfilled by more values) than either of the first two.

In this example, it is also important that we use an if/else if/else sequence, not just multiple independent if statements. Consider this sequence of independent tests.

```
    if (richter >= 8.0) // Didn't use else
    {
        System.out.println("Most structures fall");
    }
    if (richter >= 7.0)
    {
        System.out.println("Many buildings destroyed");
    }
    if (richter >= 6.0)
    {
        System.out.println("Many buildings considerably damaged, some collapse");
    }
    if (richter >= 4.5)
    {
        System.out.println("Damage to poorly constructed buildings");
    }
```

Now the alternatives are no longer exclusive. If richter is 7.1, then the last *three* tests all match, and three messages are printed.

> When using multiple if statements, test general conditions after more specific conditions.

ONLINE EXAMPLE

⊕ The complete program for printing earthquake descriptions.

SELF CHECK

11. In a game program, the scores of players A and B are stored in variables scoreA and scoreB. Assuming that the player with the larger score wins, write an if/else if/else sequence that prints out "A won", "B won", or "Game tied".

12. Write a conditional statement with three branches that sets s to 1 if x is positive, to −1 if x is negative, and to 0 if x is zero.

13. How could you achieve the task of Self Check 12 with only two branches?

14. Beginners sometimes write statements such as the following:

```
    if (price > 100)
    {
        discountedPrice = price - 20;
    }
    else if (price <= 100)
    {
        discountedPrice = price - 10;
    }
```

Explain how this code can be improved.

15. Suppose the user enters -1 into the earthquake program. What is printed?

16. Suppose we want to have the earthquake program check whether the user entered a negative number. What branch would you add to the if statement, and where?

Practice It Now you can try these exercises at the end of the chapter: R3.22, P3.9, P3.34.

Special Topic 3.3

The switch Statement

An if/else if/else sequence that compares a *value* against several alternatives can be implemented as a switch statement. For example,

```
int digit = . . .;
switch (digit)
{
   case 1: digitName = "one"; break;
   case 2: digitName = "two"; break;
   case 3: digitName = "three"; break;
   case 4: digitName = "four"; break;
   case 5: digitName = "five"; break;
   case 6: digitName = "six"; break;
   case 7: digitName = "seven"; break;
   case 8: digitName = "eight"; break;
   case 9: digitName = "nine"; break;
   default: digitName = ""; break;
}
```

The switch statement lets you choose from a fixed set of alternatives.

This is a shortcut for

```
int digit = . . .;
if (digit == 1) { digitName = "one"; }
else if (digit == 2) { digitName = "two"; }
else if (digit == 3) { digitName = "three"; }
else if (digit == 4) { digitName = "four"; }
else if (digit == 5) { digitName = "five"; }
else if (digit == 6) { digitName = "six"; }
else if (digit == 7) { digitName = "seven"; }
else if (digit == 8) { digitName = "eight"; }
else if (digit == 9) { digitName = "nine"; }
else { digitName = ""; }
```

It isn't much of a shortcut, but it has one advantage—it is obvious that all branches test the *same* value, namely digit.

The switch statement can be applied only in narrow circumstances. The values in the case clauses must be constants. They can be integers or characters. As of Java 7, strings are permitted as well. You cannot use a switch statement to branch on floating-point values.

Every branch of the switch should be terminated by a break instruction. If the break is missing, execution *falls through* to the next branch, and so on, until a break or the end of the switch is reached. In practice, this fall-through behavior is rarely useful, but it is a common cause of errors. If you accidentally forget a break statement, your program compiles but executes unwanted code. Many programmers consider the switch statement somewhat dangerous and prefer the if statement.

We leave it to you to use the switch statement for your own code or not. At any rate, you need to have a reading knowledge of switch in case you find it in other programmers' code.

3.4 Nested Branches

When a decision statement is contained inside the branch of another decision statement, the statements are *nested*.

It is often necessary to include an if statement inside another. Such an arrangement is called a *nested* set of statements.

Here is a typical example: In the United States, different tax rates are used depending on the taxpayer's marital status. There are different tax schedules for single and for married taxpayers. Married taxpayers add their income together and pay taxes on the total. Table 4 gives the tax rate computations, using a simplification of the schedules in effect for the 2008 tax year. A different tax rate applies to each "bracket". In this schedule, the income in the first bracket is taxed at 10 percent, and the income in the second bracket is taxed at 25 percent. The income limits for each bracket depend on the marital status.

Table 4 Federal Tax Rate Schedule		
If your status is Single and if the taxable income is	the tax is	of the amount over
at most $32,000	10%	$0
over $32,000	$3,200 + 25%	$32,000
If your status is Married and if the taxable income is	the tax is	of the amount over
at most $64,000	10%	$0
over $64,000	$6,400 + 25%	$64,000

Nested decisions are required for problems that have two levels of decision making.

Now compute the taxes due, given a marital status and an income figure. The key point is that there are two *levels* of decision making. First, you must branch on the marital status. Then, for each marital status, you must have another branch on income level.

The two-level decision process is reflected in two levels of if statements in the program at the end of this section. (See Figure 4 for a flowchart.) In theory, nesting can go deeper than two levels. A three-level decision process (first by state, then by marital status, then by income level) requires three nesting levels.

⊕ ANIMATION
Nested Branches

Computing income taxes requires multiple levels of decisions.

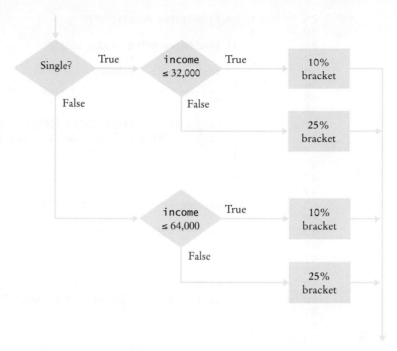

Figure 4 Income Tax Computation

section_4/TaxCalculator.java

```
 1  import java.util.Scanner;
 2
 3  /**
 4     This program computes income taxes, using a simplified tax schedule.
 5  */
 6  public class TaxCalculator
 7  {
 8     public static void main(String[] args)
 9     {
10        final double RATE1 = 0.10;
11        final double RATE2 = 0.25;
12        final double RATE1_SINGLE_LIMIT = 32000;
13        final double RATE1_MARRIED_LIMIT = 64000;
14
15        double tax1 = 0;
16        double tax2 = 0;
17
18        // Read income and marital status
19
20        Scanner in = new Scanner(System.in);
21        System.out.print("Please enter your income: ");
22        double income = in.nextDouble();
23
24        System.out.print("Please enter s for single, m for married: ");
25        String maritalStatus = in.next();
26
27        // Compute taxes due
28
```

```
29        if (maritalStatus.equals("s"))
30        {
31           if (income <= RATE1_SINGLE_LIMIT)
32           {
33              tax1 = RATE1 * income;
34           }
35           else
36           {
37              tax1 = RATE1 * RATE1_SINGLE_LIMIT;
38              tax2 = RATE2 * (income - RATE1_SINGLE_LIMIT);
39           }
40        }
41        else
42        {
43           if (income <= RATE1_MARRIED_LIMIT)
44           {
45              tax1 = RATE1 * income;
46           }
47           else
48           {
49              tax1 = RATE1 * RATE1_MARRIED_LIMIT;
50              tax2 = RATE2 * (income - RATE1_MARRIED_LIMIT);
51           }
52        }
53
54        double totalTax = tax1 + tax2;
55
56        System.out.println("The tax is $" + totalTax);
57     }
58  }
```

Program Run

```
Please enter your income: 80000
Please enter s for single, m for married: m
The tax is $10400
```

SELF CHECK

17. What is the amount of tax that a single taxpayer pays on an income of $32,000?

18. Would that amount change if the first nested if statement changed from

```
if (income <= RATE1_SINGLE_LIMIT)
```

to

```
if (income < RATE1_SINGLE_LIMIT)
```

19. Suppose Harry and Sally each make $40,000 per year. Would they save taxes if they married?

20. How would you modify the TaxCalculator.java program in order to check that the user entered a correct value for the marital status (i.e., s or m)?

21. Some people object to higher tax rates for higher incomes, claiming that you might end up with less money after taxes when you get a raise for working hard. What is the flaw in this argument?

Practice It Now you can try these exercises at the end of the chapter: R3.9, R3.21, P3.18, P3.21.

Programming Tip 3.5

Hand-Tracing

A very useful technique for understanding whether a program works correctly is called *hand-tracing*. You simulate the program's activity on a sheet of paper. You can use this method with pseudocode or Java code.

Get an index card, a cocktail napkin, or whatever sheet of paper is within reach. Make a column for each variable. Have the program code ready. Use a marker, such as a paper clip, to mark the current statement. In your mind, execute statements one at a time. Every time the value of a variable changes, cross out the old value and write the new value below the old one.

For example, let's trace the tax program with the data from the program run on page 102. In lines 15 and 16, tax1 and tax2 are initialized to 0.

Hand-tracing helps you understand whether a program works correctly.

```
 8  public static void main(String[] args)
 9  {
10     final double RATE1 = 0.10;
11     final double RATE2 = 0.25;
12     final double RATE1_SINGLE_LIMIT = 32000;
13     final double RATE1_MARRIED_LIMIT = 64000;
14
15     double tax1 = 0;
16     double tax2 = 0;
17
```

tax1	tax2	income	marital status
0	0		

In lines 22 and 25, income and maritalStatus are initialized by input statements.

```
20     Scanner in = new Scanner(System.in);
21     System.out.print("Please enter your income: ");
22     double income = in.nextDouble();
23
24     System.out.print("Please enter s for single, m for married: ");
25     String maritalStatus = in.next();
```

tax1	tax2	income	marital status
0	0	80000	m

Because maritalStatus is not "s", we move to the else branch of the outer if statement (line 41).

```
29     if (maritalStatus.equals("s"))
30     {
31        if (income <= RATE1_SINGLE_LIMIT)
32        {
33           tax1 = RATE1 * income;
34        }
35        else
36        {
37           tax1 = RATE1 * RATE1_SINGLE_LIMIT;
38           tax2 = RATE2 * (income - RATE1_SINGLE_LIMIT);
39        }
40     }
41     else
42     {
```

Because income is not <= 64000, we move to the else branch of the inner if statement (line 47).

```
43        if (income <= RATE1_MARRIED_LIMIT)
44        {
45           tax1 = RATE1 * income;
46        }
47        else
48        {
49           tax1 = RATE1 * RATE1_MARRIED_LIMIT;
50           tax2 = RATE2 * (income - RATE1_MARRIED_LIMIT);
51        }
```

The values of tax1 and tax2 are updated.

```
48      {
49          tax1 = RATE1 * RATE1_MARRIED_LIMIT;
50          tax2 = RATE2 * (income - RATE1_MARRIED_LIMIT);
51      }
52   }
53
```

tax1	tax2	income	marital status
0̸	0̸	80000	m
6400	4000		

Their sum totalTax is computed and printed.
Then the program ends.

```
54      double totalTax = tax1 + tax2;
55
56      System.out.println("The tax is $" + totalTax);
57   }
```

tax1	tax2	income	marital status	total tax
0̸	0̸	80000	m	
6400	4000			10400

Because the program trace shows the expected output ($10,400), it successfully demonstrated that this test case works correctly.

Common Error 3.4

The Dangling else Problem

When an if statement is nested inside another if statement, the following error may occur.

```
double shippingCharge = 5.00; // $5 inside continental U.S.
if (country.equals("USA"))
    if (state.equals("HI"))
        shippingCharge = 10.00; // Hawaii is more expensive
else // Pitfall!
    shippingCharge = 20.00; // As are foreign shipments
```

The indentation level seems to suggest that the else is grouped with the test country.equals("USA"). Unfortunately, that is not the case. The compiler ignores all indentation and matches the else with the preceding if. That is, the code is actually

```
double shippingCharge = 5.00; // $5 inside continental U.S.
if (country.equals("USA"))
    if (state.equals("HI"))
        shippingCharge = 10.00; // Hawaii is more expensive
    else // Pitfall!
        shippingCharge = 20.00; // As are foreign shipments
```

That isn't what you want. You want to group the else with the first if.

The ambiguous else is called a *dangling else*. You can avoid this pitfall if you always use braces, as recommended in Programming Tip 3.2 on page 86:

```
double shippingCharge = 5.00; // $5 inside continental U.S.
if (country.equals("USA"))
{
    if (state.equals("HI"))
    {
        shippingCharge = 10.00; // Hawaii is more expensive
    }
}
else
{
    shippingCharge = 20.00; // As are foreign shipments
}
```

Special Topic 3.4

Enumeration Types

In many programs, you use variables that can hold one of a finite number of values. For example, in the tax return class, the `maritalStatus` variable holds one of the values "s" or "m". If, due to some programming error, the `maritalStatus` variable is set to another value (such as "d" or "w"), then the programming logic may produce invalid results.

In a simple program, this is not really a problem. But as programs grow over time, and more cases are added (such as the "married filing separately" status), errors can slip in. Java version 5.0 introduces a remedy: **enumeration types**. An enumeration type has a finite set of values, for example

```
public enum FilingStatus { SINGLE, MARRIED, MARRIED_FILING_SEPARATELY }
```

You can have any number of values, but you must include them all in the `enum` declaration.

You can declare variables of the enumeration type:

```
FilingStatus status = FilingStatus.SINGLE;
```

If you try to assign a value that isn't a `FilingStatus`, such as 2 or "S", then the compiler reports an error.

Use the `==` operator to compare enumeration values, for example:

```
if (status == FilingStatus.SINGLE) . . .
```

Place the enum declaration inside the class that implements your program, such as

```
public class TaxReturn
{
    public enum FilingStatus { SINGLE, MARRIED, MARRIED_FILING_SEPARATELY }

    public static void main(String[] args)
    {
        . . .
    }
}
```

VIDEO EXAMPLE 3.1   **Computing the Plural of an English Word**

The plural of apple is apples, but the plural of cherry is cherries. In this Video Example, we develop an algorithm for computing the plural of an English word.

3.5 Problem Solving: Flowcharts

Flow charts are made up of elements for tasks, input/output, and decisions.

You have seen examples of flowcharts earlier in this chapter. A flowchart shows the structure of decisions and tasks that are required to solve a problem. When you have to solve a complex problem, it is a good idea to draw a flowchart to visualize the flow of control.

The basic flowchart elements are shown in Figure 5.

➕ Available online in WileyPLUS and at www.wiley.com/college/horstmann.

Figure 5
Flowchart Elements

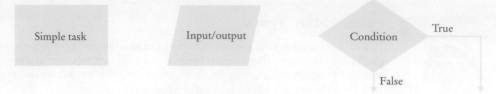

Each branch of a decision can contain tasks and further decisions.

The basic idea is simple enough. Link tasks and input/output boxes in the sequence in which they should be executed. Whenever you need to make a decision, draw a diamond with two outcomes (see Figure 6).

Each branch can contain a sequence of tasks and even additional decisions. If there are multiple choices for a value, lay them out as in Figure 7.

There is one issue that you need to be aware of when drawing flowcharts. Unconstrained branching and merging can lead to "spaghetti code", a messy network of possible pathways through a program.

Never point an arrow inside another branch.

There is a simple rule for avoiding spaghetti code: Never point an arrow *inside another branch*.

To understand the rule, consider this example: Shipping costs are $5 inside the United States, except that to Hawaii and Alaska they are $10. International shipping costs are also $10.

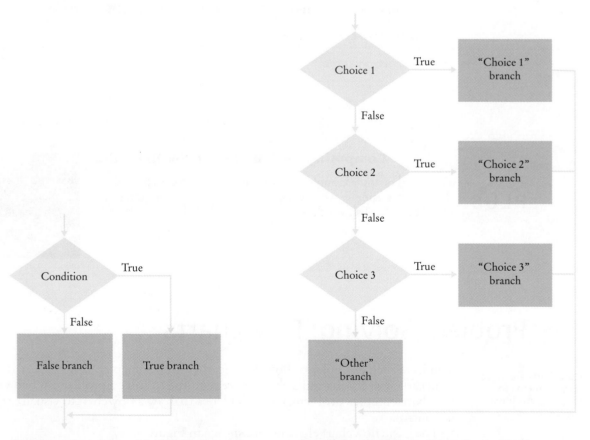

Figure 6 Flowchart with Two Outcomes

Figure 7 Flowchart with Multiple Choices

You might start out with a flowchart like the following:

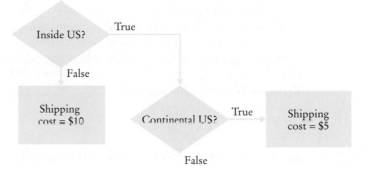

Now you may be tempted to reuse the "shipping cost = $10" task:

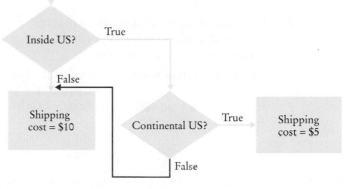

Don't do that! The red arrow points inside a different branch. Instead, add another task that sets the shipping cost to $10, like this:

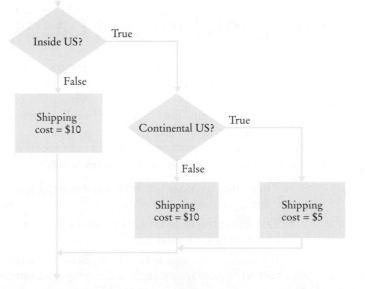

ONLINE EXAMPLE

A program to compute shipping costs.

Not only do you avoid spaghetti code, but it is also a better design. In the future it may well happen that the cost for international shipments is different from that to Alaska and Hawaii.

Flowcharts can be very useful for getting an intuitive understanding of the flow of an algorithm. However, they get large rather quickly when you add more details. At that point, it makes sense to switch from flowcharts to pseudocode.

Spaghetti code has so many pathways that it becomes impossible to understand.

SELF CHECK

22. Draw a flowchart for a program that reads a value temp and prints "Frozen" if it is less than zero.

23. What is wrong with the flowchart at right?

24. How do you fix the flowchart of Self Check 23?

25. Draw a flowchart for a program that reads a value x. If it is less than zero, print "Error". Otherwise, print its square root.

26. Draw a flowchart for a program that reads a value temp. If it is less than zero, print "Ice". If it is greater than 100, print "Steam". Otherwise, print "Liquid".

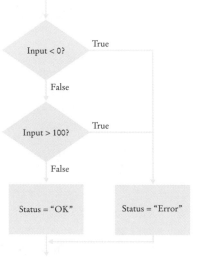

Practice It Now you can try these exercises at the end of the chapter: R3.12, R3.13, R3.14.

3.6 Problem Solving: Test Cases

Consider how to test the tax computation program from Section 3.4. Of course, you cannot try out all possible inputs of marital status and income level. Even if you could, there would be no point in trying them all. If the program correctly computes one or two tax amounts in a given bracket, then we have a good reason to believe that all amounts will be correct.

You want to aim for complete *coverage* of all decision points. Here is a plan for obtaining a comprehensive set of test cases:

Each branch of your program should be covered by a test case.

- There are two possibilities for the marital status and two tax brackets for each status, yielding four test cases.

- Test a handful of *boundary* conditions, such as an income that is at the boundary between two brackets, and a zero income.

- If you are responsible for error checking (which is discussed in Section 3.8), also test an invalid input, such as a negative income.

Make a list of the test cases and the expected outputs:

Test Case	Expected Output	Comment
30,000 s	3,000	10% bracket
72,000 s	13,200	3,200 + 25% of 40,000
50,000 m	5,000	10% bracket
104,000 m	16,400	6,400 + 25% of 40,000
32,000 s	3,200	boundary case
0	0	boundary case

When you develop a set of test cases, it is helpful to have a flowchart of your program (see Section 3.5). Check off each branch that has a test case. Include test cases for the boundary cases of each decision. For example, if a decision checks whether an input is less than 100, test with an input of 100.

It is a good idea to design test cases *before* starting to code. Working through the test cases gives you a better understanding of the algorithm that you are about to implement.

It is a good idea to design test cases before implementing a program.

SELF CHECK

27. Using Figure 1 on page 83 as a guide, follow the process described in Section 3.6 to design a set of test cases for the `ElevatorSimulation.java` program in Section 3.1.

28. What is a boundary test case for the algorithm in How To 3.1 on page 93? What is the expected output?

29. Using Figure 3 on page 97 as a guide, follow the process described in Section 3.6 to design a set of test cases for the `EarthquakeStrength.java` program in Section 3.3.

30. Suppose you are designing a part of a program for a medical robot that has a sensor returning an *x*- and *y*-location (measured in cm). You need to check whether the sensor location is inside the circle, outside the circle, or on the boundary (specifically, having a distance of less than 1 mm from the boundary). Assume the circle has center (0, 0) and a radius of 2 cm. Give a set of test cases.

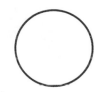

Practice It   Now you can try these exercises at the end of the chapter: R3.15, R3.16.

Make a Schedule and Make Time for Unexpected Problems

Commercial software is notorious for being delivered later than promised. For example, Microsoft originally promised that its Windows Vista operating system would be available late in 2003, then in 2005, then in March 2006; it finally was released in January 2007. Some of the early promises might not have been realistic. It was in Microsoft's interest to let prospective customers expect the imminent availability of the product. Had customers known the actual delivery date, they might have switched to a different product in the meantime. Undeniably, though, Microsoft had not anticipated the full complexity of the tasks it had set itself to solve.

Microsoft can delay the delivery of its product, but it is likely that you cannot. As a student or a programmer, you are expected to manage your time wisely and to finish your assignments on time. You can probably do simple programming exercises the night before the due date, but an assignment that looks twice as hard may well take four times as long, because more things can go wrong. You should therefore make a schedule whenever you start a programming project.

First, estimate realistically how much time it will take you to:

- Design the program logic.
- Develop test cases.
- Type the program in and fix syntax errors.
- Test and debug the program.

For example, for the income tax program I might estimate an hour for the design; 30 minutes for developing test cases; an hour for data entry and fixing syntax errors; and an hour for testing and debugging. That is a total of 3.5 hours. If I work two hours a day on this project, it will take me almost two days.

Make a schedule for your programming work and build in time for problems.

Then think of things that can go wrong. Your computer might break down. You might be stumped by a problem with the computer system. (That is a particularly important concern for beginners. It is *very* common to lose a day over a trivial problem just because it takes time to track down a person who knows the magic command to overcome it.) As a rule of thumb, *double* the time of your estimate. That is, you should start four days, not two days, before the due date. If nothing went wrong, great; you have the program done two days early. When the inevitable problem occurs, you have a cushion of time that protects you from embarrassment and failure.

Logging

Sometimes you run a program and you are not sure where it spends its time. To get a printout of the program flow, you can insert trace messages into the program, such as this one:

```
if (status == SINGLE)
{
   System.out.println("status is SINGLE");
   . . .
}
```

However, there is a problem with using System.out.println for trace messages. When you are done testing the program, you need to remove all print statements that produce trace messages. If you find another error, however, you need to stick the print statements back in.

To overcome this problem, you should use the Logger class, which allows you to turn off the trace messages without removing them from the program.

Instead of printing directly to System.out, use the global logger object that is returned by the call Logger.getGlobal(). (Prior to Java 7, you obtained the global logger as Logger.getLogger("global").) Then call the info method:

```
Logger.getGlobal().info("status is SINGLE");
```

By default, the message is printed. But if you call

```
Logger.getGlobal().setLevel(Level.OFF);
```

Logging messages can be deactivated when testing is complete.

at the beginning of the main method of your program, all log message printing is suppressed. Set the level to Level.INFO to turn logging of info messages on again. Thus, you can turn off the log messages when your program works fine, and you can turn them back on if you find another error. In other words, using Logger.getGlobal().info is just like System.out.println, except that you can easily activate and deactivate the logging.

The Logger class has many other options for industrial-strength logging. Check out the API documentation if you want to have more control over logging.

3.7 Boolean Variables and Operators

*A Boolean variable
is also called a flag
because it can be
either up (true) or
down (false).*

Java has two Boolean
operators that
combine conditions:
&& (*and*) and || (*or*).

Sometimes, you need to evaluate a logical condition in one part of a program and use it elsewhere. To store a condition that can be true or false, you use a *Boolean variable*. Boolean variables are named after the mathematician George Boole (1815–1864), a pioneer in the study of logic.

In Java, the boolean data type has exactly two values, denoted false and true. These values are not strings or integers; they are special values, just for Boolean variables. Here is a declaration of a Boolean variable:

```
boolean failed = true;
```

You can use the value later in your program to make a decision:

```
if (failed) // Only executed if failed has been set to true
{
    . . .
}
```

When you make complex decisions, you often need to combine Boolean values. An operator that combines Boolean conditions is called a **Boolean operator**. In Java, the && operator (called *and*) yields true only when both conditions are true. The || operator (called *or*) yields the result true if at least one of the conditions is true.

Suppose you write a program that processes temperature values, and you want to test whether a given temperature corresponds to liquid water. (At sea level, water freezes at 0 degrees Celsius and boils at 100 degrees.) Water is liquid if the temperature is greater than zero *and* less than 100:

```
if (temp > 0 && temp < 100) { System.out.println("Liquid"); }
```

The condition of the test has two parts, joined by the && operator. Each part is a Boolean value that can be true or false. The combined expression is true if both individual expressions are true. If either one of the expressions is false, then the result is also false (see Figure 8).

The Boolean operators && and || have a lower precedence than the relational operators. For that reason, you can write relational expressions on either side of the Boolean operators without using parentheses. For example, in the expression

```
temp > 0 && temp < 100
```

the expressions temp > 0 and temp < 100 are evaluated first. Then the && operator combines the results. Appendix B shows a table of the Java operators and their precedence.

A	B	A && B	A	B	A || B	A	!A
true	true	true	true	true	true	true	false
true	false	false	true	false	true	false	true
false	true	false	false	true	true		
false	false	false	false	false	false		

Figure 8 Boolean Truth Tables

At this geyser in Iceland, you can see ice, liquid water, and steam.

To invert a condition, use the ! (*not*) operator.

Conversely, let's test whether water is *not* liquid at a given temperature. That is the case when the temperature is at most 0 *or* at least 100. Use the || (*or*) operator to combine the expressions:

```
if (temp <= 0 || temp >= 100) { System.out.println("Not liquid"); }
```

Figure 9 shows flowcharts for these examples.

Sometimes you need to *invert* a condition with the *not* Boolean operator. The ! operator takes a single condition and evaluates to true if that condition is false and to false if the condition is true. In this example, output occurs if the value of the Boolean variable frozen is false:

```
if (!frozen) { System.out.println("Not frozen"); }
```

Table 5 illustrates additional examples of evaluating Boolean operators.

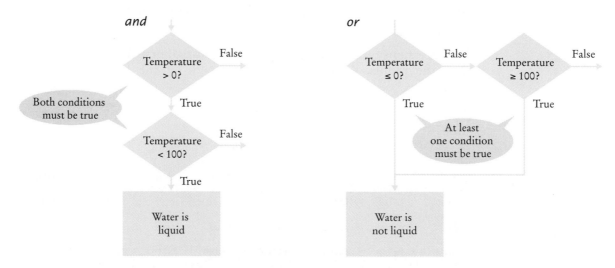

Figure 9 Flowcharts for *and* and *or* Combinations

Table 5 Boolean Operator Examples

Expression	Value	Comment
`0 < 200 && 200 < 100`	`false`	Only the first condition is true.
`0 < 200 || 200 < 100`	`true`	The first condition is true.
`0 < 200 || 100 < 200`	`true`	The `||` is not a test for "either-or". If both conditions are true, the result is true.
`0 < x && x < 100 || x == -1`	`(0 < x && x < 100)` `|| x == -1`	The `&&` operator has a higher precedence than the `||` operator (see Appendix B).
🚫 `0 < x < 100`	**Error**	**Error:** This expression does not test whether x is between 0 and 100. The expression `0 < x` is a Boolean value. You cannot compare a Boolean value with the integer 100.
🚫 `x && y > 0`	**Error**	**Error:** This expression does not test whether x and y are positive. The left-hand side of `&&` is an integer, x, and the right-hand side, `y > 0`, is a Boolean value. You cannot use `&&` with an integer argument.
`!(0 < 200)`	`false`	`0 < 200` is true, therefore its negation is `false`.
`frozen == true`	`frozen`	There is no need to compare a Boolean variable with true.
`frozen == false`	`!frozen`	It is clearer to use `!` than to compare with `false`.

31. Suppose x and y are two integers. How do you test whether both of them are zero?

32. How do you test whether at least one of them is zero?

33. How do you test whether *exactly one of them* is zero?

34. What is the value of `!!frozen`?

35. What is the advantage of using the type `boolean` rather than strings `"false"`/`"true"` or integers 0/1?

Practice It Now you can try these exercises at the end of the chapter: R3.29, P3.25, P3.27.

Common Error 3.5

Combining Multiple Relational Operators

Consider the expression

```
if (0 <= temp <= 100) // Error
```

This looks just like the mathematical test $0 \le temp \le 100$. But in Java, it is a compile-time error.

Let us dissect the condition. The first half, `0 <= temp`, is a test with an outcome true or false. The outcome of that test (true or false) is then compared against 100. This seems to make no sense. Is true larger than 100 or not? Can one compare truth values and numbers? In Java, you cannot. The Java compiler rejects this statement.

Instead, use && to combine two separate tests:

```
if (0 <= temp && temp <= 100) . . .
```

Another common error, along the same lines, is to write

```
if (input == 1 || 2) . . . // Error
```

to test whether input is 1 or 2. Again, the Java compiler flags this construct as an error. You cannot apply the || operator to numbers. You need to write two Boolean expressions and join them with the || operator:

```
if (input == 1 || input == 2) . . .
```

Common Error 3.6

Confusing && and || Conditions

It is a surprisingly common error to confuse *and* and *or* conditions. A value lies between 0 and 100 if it is at least 0 *and* at most 100. It lies outside that range if it is less than 0 *or* greater than 100. There is no golden rule; you just have to think carefully.

Often the *and* or *or* is clearly stated, and then it isn't too hard to implement it. But sometimes the wording isn't as explicit. It is quite common that the individual conditions are nicely set apart in a bulleted list, but with little indication of how they should be combined. Consider these instructions for filing a tax return. You can claim single filing status if any one of the following is true:

- You were never married.
- You were legally separated or divorced on the last day of the tax year.
- You were widowed, and did not remarry.

Since the test passes if *any one* of the conditions is true, you must combine the conditions with *or*. Elsewhere, the same instructions state that you may use the more advantageous status of married filing jointly if all five of the following conditions are true:

- Your spouse died less than two years ago and you did not remarry.
- You have a child whom you can claim as dependent.
- That child lived in your home for all of the tax year.
- You paid over half the cost of keeping up your home for this child.
- You filed a joint return with your spouse the year he or she died.

Because *all* of the conditions must be true for the test to pass, you must combine them with an *and*.

Special Topic 3.6

Short-Circuit Evaluation of Boolean Operators

The && and || operators are computed using short-circuit evaluation. In other words, logical expressions are evaluated from left to right, and evaluation stops as soon as the truth value is determined. When an && is evaluated and the first condition is false, the second condition is not evaluated, because it does not matter what the outcome of the second test is.

For example, consider the expression

```
quantity > 0 && price / quantity < 10
```

> The && and || operators are computed using *short-circuit evaluation:* As soon as the truth value is determined, no further conditions are evaluated.

Suppose the value of quantity is zero. Then the test quantity > 0 fails, and the second test is not attempted. That is just as well, because it is illegal to divide by zero.

Similarly, when the first condition of an || expression is true, then the remainder is not evaluated because the result must be true.

This process is called *short-circuit evaluation*.

In a short circuit, electricity travels along the path of least resistance. Similarly, short-circuit evaluation takes the fastest path for computing the result of a Boolean expression.

Special Topic 3.7

De Morgan's Law

Humans generally have a hard time comprehending logical conditions with *not* operators applied to *and/or* expressions. De Morgan's Law, named after the logician Augustus De Morgan (1806–1871), can be used to simplify these Boolean expressions.

Suppose we want to charge a higher shipping rate if we don't ship within the continental United States.

```
if (!(country.equals("USA") && !state.equals("AK") && !state.equals("HI")))
{
    shippingCharge = 20.00;
}
```

This test is a little bit complicated, and you have to think carefully through the logic. When it is *not* true that the country is USA *and* the state is not Alaska *and* the state is not Hawaii, then charge $20.00. Huh? It is not true that some people won't be confused by this code.

The computer doesn't care, but it takes human programmers to write and maintain the code. Therefore, it is useful to know how to simplify such a condition.

De Morgan's Law has two forms: one for the negation of an *and* expression and one for the negation of an *or* expression:

> De Morgan's law tells you how to negate && and || conditions.

!(A && B)	is the same as	!A || !B
!(A || B)	is the same as	!A && !B

Pay particular attention to the fact that the *and* and *or* operators are *reversed* by moving the *not* inward. For example, the negation of "the state is Alaska *or* it is Hawaii",

```
!(state.equals("AK") || state.equals("HI"))
```

is "the state is not Alaska *and* it is not Hawaii":

```
!state.equals("AK") && !state.equals("HI")
```

Now apply the law to our shipping charge computation:

```
!(country.equals("USA")
   && !state.equals("AK")
   && !state.equals("HI"))
```

is equivalent to

```
!country.equals("USA")
   || !!state.equals("AK")
   || !!state.equals("HI")
```

Because two ! cancel each other out, the result is the simpler test

```
!country.equals("USA")
   || state.equals("AK")
   || state.equals("HI")
```

In other words, higher shipping charges apply when the destination is outside the United States or to Alaska or Hawaii.

To simplify conditions with negations of *and* or *or* expressions, it is usually a good idea to apply De Morgan's Law to move the negations to the innermost level.

3.8 Application: Input Validation

Like a quality control worker, you want to make sure that user input is correct before processing it.

An important application for the if statement is *input validation*. Whenever your program accepts user input, you need to make sure that the user-supplied values are valid before you use them in your computations.

Consider our elevator simulation program. Assume that the elevator panel has buttons labeled 1 through 20 (but not 13). The following are illegal inputs:

- The number 13
- Zero or a negative number
- A number larger than 20
- An input that is not a sequence of digits, such as five

In each of these cases, we will want to give an error message and exit the program.

It is simple to guard against an input of 13:

```
if (floor == 13)
{
    System.out.println("Error: There is no thirteenth floor.");
}
```

Here is how you ensure that the user doesn't enter a number outside the valid range:

```
if (floor <= 0 || floor > 20)
{
    System.out.println("Error: The floor must be between 1 and 20.");
}
```

However, dealing with an input that is not a valid integer is a more serious problem. When the statement

```
floor = in.nextInt();
```

Call the hasNextInt or hasNextDouble method to ensure that the next input is a number.

is executed, and the user types in an input that is not an integer (such as five), then the integer variable floor is not set. Instead, a run-time exception occurs and the program is terminated. To avoid this problem, you should first call the hasNextInt method which checks whether the next input is an integer. If that method returns true, you can safely call nextInt. Otherwise, print an error message and exit the program.

```
if (in.hasNextInt())
{
    int floor = in.nextInt();
    Process the input value
}
```

```
else
{
    System.out.println("Error: Not an integer.");
}
```

Here is the complete elevator simulation program with input validation:

section_8/ElevatorSimulation2.java

```
 1  import java.util.Scanner;
 2
 3  /**
 4      This program simulates an elevator panel that skips the 13th floor, checking for
 5      input errors.
 6  */
 7  public class ElevatorSimulation2
 8  {
 9      public static void main(String[] args)
10      {
11          Scanner in = new Scanner(System.in);
12          System.out.print("Floor: ");
13          if (in.hasNextInt())
14          {
15              // Now we know that the user entered an integer
16
17              int floor = in.nextInt();
18
19              if (floor == 13)
20              {
21                  System.out.println("Error: There is no thirteenth floor.");
22              }
23              else if (floor <= 0 || floor > 20)
24              {
25                  System.out.println("Error: The floor must be between 1 and 20.");
26              }
27              else
28              {
29                  // Now we know that the input is valid
30
31                  int actualFloor = floor;
32                  if (floor > 13)
33                  {
34                      actualFloor = floor - 1;
35                  }
36
37                  System.out.println("The elevator will travel to the actual floor "
38                      + actualFloor);
39              }
40          }
41          else
42          {
43              System.out.println("Error: Not an integer.");
44          }
45      }
46  }
```

Program Run

```
Floor: 13
Error: There is no thirteenth floor.
```

36. In the `ElevatorSimulation2` program, what is the output when the input is

    a. 100?

    b. –1?

    c. 20?

    d. thirteen?

37. Your task is to rewrite lines 19–26 of the `ElevatorSimulation2` program so that there is a single `if` statement with a complex condition. What is the condition?

```
if (. . .)
{
    System.out.println("Error: Invalid floor number");
}
```

38. In the Sherlock Holmes story "The Adventure of the Sussex Vampire", the inimitable detective uttered these words: "Matilda Briggs was not the name of a young woman, Watson, … It was a ship which is associated with the giant rat of Sumatra, a story for which the world is not yet prepared." Over a hundred years later, researchers found giant rats in Western New Guinea, another part of Indonesia.

Suppose you are charged with writing a program that processes rat weights. It contains the statements

```
System.out.print("Enter weight in kg: ");
double weight = in.nextDouble();
```

What input checks should you supply?

When processing inputs, you want to reject values that are too large. But how large is too large? These giant rats, found in Western New Guinea, are about five times the size of a city rat.

39. Run the following test program and supply inputs 2 and three at the prompts. What happens? Why?

```
import java.util.Scanner

public class Test
{
    public static void main(String[] args)
    {
        Scanner in = new Scanner(System.in);
        System.out.print("Enter an integer: ");
        int m = in.nextInt();
        System.out.print("Enter another integer: ");
        int n = in.nextInt();
        System.out.println(m + " " + n);
    }
}
```

Practice It   Now you can try these exercises at the end of the chapter: R3.3, R3.32, P3.11.

VIDEO EXAMPLE 3.2   **The Genetic Code**

Watch this Video Example to see how to build a "decoder ring" for the genetic code.

Random Fact 3.2 Artificial Intelligence

When one uses a sophisticated computer program such as a tax preparation package, one is bound to attribute some intelligence to the computer. The computer asks sensible questions and makes computations that we find a mental challenge. After all, if doing one's taxes were easy, we wouldn't need a computer to do it for us.

As programmers, however, we know that all this apparent intelligence is an illusion. Human programmers have carefully "coached" the software in all possible scenarios, and it simply replays the actions and decisions that were programmed into it.

Would it be possible to write computer programs that are genuinely intelligent in some sense? From the earliest days of computing, there was a sense that the human brain might be nothing but an immense computer, and that it might well be feasible to program computers to imitate some processes of human thought. Serious research into *artificial intelligence* began in the mid-1950s, and the first twenty years brought some impressive successes. Programs that play chess—surely an activity that appears to require remarkable intellectual powers—have become so good that they now routinely beat all but the best human players. As far back as 1975, an *expert-system* program called Mycin gained fame for being better in diagnosing meningitis in patients than the average physician.

However, there were serious setbacks as well. From 1982 to 1992, the Japanese government embarked on a massive research project, funded at over 40 billion Japanese yen. It was known as the *Fifth-Generation Project*. Its goal was to develop new hardware and software to greatly improve the performance of expert system software. At its outset, the project created fear in other countries that the Japanese computer industry was about to become the undisputed leader in the field. However, the end results were disappointing and did little to bring

artificial intelligence applications to market.

From the very outset, one of the stated goals of the AI community was to produce software that could translate text from one language to another, for example from English to Russian. That undertaking proved to be enormously complicated. Human language appears to be much more subtle and interwoven with the human experience than had originally been thought. Even the grammar-checking tools that come with word-processing programs today are more of a gimmick than a useful tool, and analyzing grammar is just the first step in translating sentences.

The CYC (from en*cyc*lopedia) project, started by Douglas Lenat in 1984, tries to codify the implicit assumptions that underlie human speech and writing. The team members started out analyzing news articles and asked themselves what unmentioned facts are necessary to actually understand the sentences. For example, consider the sentence, "Last fall she enrolled in Michigan State". The reader automatically realizes that "fall" is not related to falling down in this context, but refers to the season. While there is a state of Michigan, here Michigan State denotes the university. A priori, a computer program has none of this

knowledge. The goal of the CYC project is to extract and store the requisite facts—that is, (1) people enroll in universities; (2) Michigan is a state; (3) many states have universities named X State University, often abbreviated as X State; (4) most people enroll in a university in the fall. By 1995, the project had codified about 100,000 common-sense concepts and about a million facts of knowledge relating them. Even this massive amount of data has not proven sufficient for useful applications.

In recent years, artificial intelligence technology has seen substantial advances. One of the most astounding examples is the outcome of a series of "grand challenges" for autonomous vehicles posed by the Defense Advanced Research Projects Agency (DARPA). Competitors were invited to submit a computer-controlled vehicle that had to complete an obstacle course without a human driver or remote control. The first event, in 2004, was a disappointment, with none of the entrants finishing the route. In 2005, five vehicles completed a grueling 212 km course in the Mojave desert. Stanford's Stanley came in first, with an average speed of 30 km/h. In 2007, DARPA moved the competition to an "urban" environment, an abandoned air force base. Vehicles had to be able to interact with each other, following California traffic laws. As Stanford's Sebastian Thrun explained: "In the last Grand Challenge, it didn't really matter whether an obstacle was a rock or a bush, because either way you'd just drive around it. The current challenge is to move from just sensing the environment to understanding it."

Winner of the 2007 DARPA Urban Challenge

Use the `if` statement to implement a decision.

- The `if` statement allows a program to carry out different actions depending on the nature of the data to be processed.

Implement comparisons of numbers and objects.

- Use relational operators (`<` `<=` `>` `>=` `==` `!=`) to compare numbers.
- Do not use the `==` operator to compare strings. Use the `equals` method instead.
- The `compareTo` method compares strings in lexicographic order.

Implement complex decisions that require multiple `if` statements.

- Multiple `if` statements can be combined to evaluate complex decisions.
- When using multiple `if` statements, test general conditions after more specific conditions.

Implement decisions whose branches require further decisions.

- When a decision statement is contained inside the branch of another decision statement, the statements are *nested*.
- Nested decisions are required for problems that have two levels of decision making.

Draw flowcharts for visualizing the control flow of a program.

- Flow charts are made up of elements for tasks, input/output, and decisions.
- Each branch of a decision can contain tasks and further decisions.
- Never point an arrow inside another branch.

Design test cases for your programs.

- Each branch of your program should be covered by a test case.
- It is a good idea to design test cases before implementing a program.
- Logging messages can be deactivated when testing is complete.

Use the Boolean data type to store and combine conditions that can be true or false.

- The Boolean type boolean has two values, false and true.
- Java has two Boolean operators that combinc conditions: && (*and*) and || (*or*).
- To invert a condition, use the ! (*not*) operator.
- The && and || operators are computed using *short-circuit evaluation:* As soon as the truth value is determined, no further conditions are evaluated.
- De Morgan's law tells you how to negate && and || conditions.

Apply if statements to detect whether user input is valid.

- Call the hasNextInt or hasNextDouble method to ensure that the next input is a number.

STANDARD LIBRARY ITEMS INTRODUCED IN THIS CHAPTER

```
java.lang.String                 java.util.logging.Level
   equals                           INFO
   compareTo                        OFF
java.util.Scanner               java.util.logging.Logger
   hasNextDouble                    getGlobal
   hasNextInt                       info
                                    setLevel
```

REVIEW EXERCISES

- **R3.1** What is the value of each variable after the if statement?

  a. int n = 1; int k = 2; int r = n;
     if (k < n) { r = k; }

  b. int n = 1; int k = 2; int r;
     if (n < k) { r = k; }
     else { r = k + n; }

  c. int n = 1; int k = 2; int r = k;
     if (r < k) { n = r; }
     else { k = n; }

  d. int n = 1; int k = 2; int r = 3;
     if (r < n + k) { r = 2 * n; }
     else { k = 2 * r; }

- **R3.2** Explain the difference between

  ```
  s = 0;
  if (x > 0) { s++; }
  if (y > 0) { s++; }
  ```

  and

  ```
  s = 0;
  if (x > 0) { s++; }
  else if (y > 0) { s++; }
  ```

•• R3.3 Find the errors in the following `if` statements.

a. `if x > 0 then System.out.print(x);`

b. `if (1 + x > Math.pow(x, Math.sqrt(2)) { y = y + x; }`

c. `if (x = 1) { y++; }`

d.
```
x = in.nextInt();
if (in.hasNextInt())
{
    sum = sum + x;
}
else
{
    System.out.println("Bad input for x");
}
```

e.
```
String letterGrade = "F";
if (grade >= 90) { letterGrade = "A"; }
if (grade >= 80) { letterGrade = "B"; }
if (grade >= 70) { letterGrade = "C"; }
if (grade >= 60) { letterGrade = "D"; }
```

• R3.4 What do these code fragments print?

a.
```
int n = 1;
int m = -1;
if (n < -m) { System.out.print(n); }
else { System.out.print(m); }
```

b.
```
int n = 1;
int m = -1;
if (-n >= m) { System.out.print(n); }
else { System.out.print(m); }
```

c.
```
double x = 0;
double y = 1;
if (Math.abs(x - y) < 1) { System.out.print(x); }
else { System.out.print(y); }
```

d.
```
double x = Math.sqrt(2);
double y = 2;
if (x * x == y) { System.out.print(x); }
else { System.out.print(y); }
```

•• R3.5 Suppose x and y are variables of type `double`. Write a code fragment that sets y to x if x is positive and to 0 otherwise.

•• R3.6 Suppose x and y are variables of type `double`. Write a code fragment that sets y to the absolute value of x without calling the `Math.abs` function. Use an `if` statement.

•• R3.7 Explain why it is more difficult to compare floating-point numbers than integers. Write Java code to test whether an integer n equals 10 and whether a floating-point number x is approximately equal to 10.

• R3.8 It is easy to confuse the = and == operators. Write a test program containing the statement

```
if (floor = 13)
```

What error message do you get? Write another test program containing the statement

```
count == 0;
```

What does your compiler do when you compile the program?

R3.9 Each square on a chess board can be described by a letter and number, such as g5 in this example:

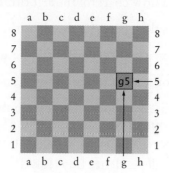

The following pseudocode describes an algorithm that determines whether a square with a given letter and number is dark (black) or light (white).

```
If the letter is an a, c, e, or g
    If the number is odd
        color = "black"
    Else
        color = "white"
Else
    If the number is even
        color = "black"
    Else
        color = "white"
```

Using the procedure in Programming Tip 3.5, trace this pseudocode with input g5.

R3.10 Give a set of four test cases for the algorithm of Exercise R3.9 that covers all branches.

R3.11 In a scheduling program, we want to check whether two appointments overlap. For simplicity, appointments start at a full hour, and we use military time (with hours 0–24). The following pseudocode describes an algorithm that determines whether the appointment with start time **start1** and end time **end1** overlaps with the appointment with start time **start2** and end time **end2**.

```
If start1 > start2
    s = start1
Else
    s = start2
If end1 < end2
    e = end1
Else
    e = end2
If s < e
    The appointments overlap.
Else
    The appointments don't overlap.
```

Trace this algorithm with an appointment from 10–12 and one from 11–13, then with an appointment from 10–11 and one from 12–13.

■ **R3.12** Draw a flow chart for the algorithm in Exercise R3.11.

■ **R3.13** Draw a flow chart for the algorithm in Exercise P3.17.

■ **R3.14** Draw a flow chart for the algorithm in Exercise P3.18.

■■ **R3.15** Develop a set of test cases for the algorithm in Exercise R3.11.

■■ **R3.16** Develop a set of test cases for the algorithm in Exercise P3.18.

■■ **R3.17** Write pseudocode for a program that prompts the user for a month and day and prints out whether it is one of the following four holidays:
   • New Year's Day (January 1)
   • Independence Day (July 4)
   • Veterans Day (November 11)
   • Christmas Day (December 25)

■■ **R3.18** Write pseudocode for a program that assigns letter grades for a quiz, according to the following table:

Score	Grade
90-100	A
80-89	B
70-79	C
60-69	D
< 60	F

■■ **R3.19** Explain how the lexicographic ordering of strings in Java differs from the ordering of words in a dictionary or telephone book. *Hint:* Consider strings such as IBM, wiley.com, Century 21, and While-U-Wait.

■■ **R3.20** Of the following pairs of strings, which comes first in lexicographic order?
   a. "Tom", "Jerry"
   b. "Tom", "Tomato"
   c. "church", "Churchill"
   d. "car manufacturer", "carburetor"
   e. "Harry", "hairy"
   f. "Java", " Car"
   g. "Tom", "Tom"
   h. "Car", "Carl"
   i. "car", "bar"

■ **R3.21** Explain the difference between an if/else if/else sequence and nested if statements. Give an example of each.

■■ **R3.22** Give an example of an if/else if/else sequence where the order of the tests does not matter. Give an example where the order of the tests matters.

■ **R3.23** Rewrite the condition in Section 3.3 to use < operators instead of >= operators. What is the impact on the order of the comparisons?

■■ **R3.24** Give a set of test cases for the tax program in Exercise P3.22. Manually compute the expected results.

- **R3.25** Make up a Java code example that shows the dangling else problem using the following statement: A student with a GPA of at least 1.5, but less than 2, is on probation. With less than 1.5, the student is failing.

- **R3.26** Complete the following truth table by finding the truth values of the Boolean expressions for all combinations of the Boolean inputs p, q, and r.

p	q	r	(p && q) || !r	!(p && (q || !r))
false	false	false		
false	false	true		
false	true	false		
. . .				
5 more combinations				
. . .				

- **R3.27** True or false? *A* && *B* is the same as *B* && *A* for any Boolean conditions *A* and *B*.

- **R3.28** The "advanced search" feature of many search engines allows you to use Boolean operators for complex queries, such as "(cats OR dogs) AND NOT pets". Contrast these search operators with the Boolean operators in Java.

- **R3.29** Suppose the value of b is false and the value of x is 0. What is the value of each of the following expressions?

  a. b && x == 0
  b. b || x == 0
  c. !b && x == 0
  d. !b || x == 0
  e. b && x != 0
  f. b || x != 0
  g. !b && x != 0
  h. !b || x != 0

- **R3.30** Simplify the following expressions. Here, b is a variable of type boolean.

  a. b == true
  b. b == false
  c. b != true
  d. b != false

- **R3.31** Simplify the following statements. Here, b is a variable of type boolean and n is a variable of type int.

  a. if (n == 0) { b = true; } else { b = false; }
  (Hint: What is the value of n == 0?)
  b. if (n == 0) { b = false; } else { b = true; }
  c. b = false; if (n > 1) { if (n < 2) { b = true; } }
  d. if (n < 1) { b = true; } else { b = n > 2; }

R3.32 What is wrong with the following program?

```
System.out.print("Enter the number of quarters: ");
int quarters = in.nextInt();
if (in.hasNextInt())
{
   total = total + quarters * 0.25;
   System.out.println("Total: " + total);
}
else
{
   System.out.println("Input error.");
}
```

PROGRAMMING EXERCISES

P3.1 Write a program that reads an integer and prints whether it is negative, zero, or positive.

P3.2 Write a program that reads a floating-point number and prints "zero" if the number is zero. Otherwise, print "positive" or "negative". Add "small" if the absolute value of the number is less than 1, or "large" if it exceeds 1,000,000.

P3.3 Write a program that reads an integer and prints how many digits the number has, by checking whether the number is ≥ 10, ≥ 100, and so on. (Assume that all integers are less than ten billion.) If the number is negative, first multiply it with –1.

P3.4 Write a program that reads three numbers and prints "all the same" if they are all the same, "all different" if they are all different, and "neither" otherwise.

P3.5 Write a program that reads three numbers and prints "increasing" if they are in increasing order, "decreasing" if they are in decreasing order, and "neither" otherwise. Here, "increasing" means "strictly increasing", with each value larger than its predecessor. The sequence 3 4 4 would not be considered increasing.

P3.6 Repeat Exercise P3.5, but before reading the numbers, ask the user whether increasing/decreasing should be "strict" or "lenient". In lenient mode, the sequence 3 4 4 is increasing and the sequence 4 4 4 is both increasing and decreasing.

P3.7 Write a program that reads in three integers and prints "in order" if they are sorted in ascending *or* descending order, or "not in order" otherwise. For example,

```
1 2 5    in order
1 5 2    not in order
5 2 1    in order
1 2 2    in order
```

P3.8 Write a program that reads four integers and prints "two pairs" if the input consists of two matching pairs (in some order) and "not two pairs" otherwise. For example,

```
1 2 2 1    two pairs
1 2 2 3    not two pairs
2 2 2 2    two pairs
```

• P3.9 Write a program that reads a temperature value and the letter C for Celsius or F for Fahrenheit. Print whether water is liquid, solid, or gaseous at the given temperature at sea level.

• P3.10 The boiling point of water drops by about one degree centigrade for every 300 meters (or 1,000 feet) of altitude. Improve the program of Exercise P3.9 to allow the user to supply the altitude in meters or feet.

• P3.11 Add error handling to Exercise P3.10. If the user does not enter a number when expected, or provides an invalid unit for the altitude, print an error message and end the program.

•• P3.12 Write a program that translates a letter grade into a number grade. Letter grades are A, B, C, D, and F, possibly followed by + or –. Their numeric values are 4, 3, 2, 1, and 0. There is no F+ or F–. A + increases the numeric value by 0.3, a – decreases it by 0.3. However, an A+ has value 4.0.

```
Enter a letter grade: B-
The numeric value is 2.7.
```

•• P3.13 Write a program that translates a number between 0 and 4 into the closest letter grade. For example, the number 2.8 (which might have been the average of several grades) would be converted to B–. Break ties in favor of the better grade; for example 2.85 should be a B.

•• P3.14 Write a program that takes user input describing a playing card in the following shorthand notation:

A	Ace
2 ... 10	Card values
J	Jack
Q	Queen
K	King
D	Diamonds
H	Hearts
S	Spades
C	Clubs

Your program should print the full description of the card. For example,

```
Enter the card notation: QS
Queen of Spades
```

•• P3.15 Write a program that reads in three floating-point numbers and prints the largest of the three inputs. For example:

```
Please enter three numbers: 4 9 2.5
The largest number is 9.
```

•• P3.16 Write a program that reads in three strings and sorts them lexicographically.

```
Enter three strings: Charlie Able Baker
Able
Baker
Charlie
```

•• **P3.17** When two points in time are compared, each given as hours (in military time, ranging from 0 and 23) and minutes, the following pseudocode determines which comes first.

```
If hour1 < hour2
    time1 comes first.
Else if hour1 and hour2 are the same
    If minute1 < minute2
        time1 comes first.
    Else if minute1 and minute2 are the same
        time1 and time2 are the same.
    Else
        time2 comes first.
Else
    time2 comes first.
```

Write a program that prompts the user for two points in time and prints the time that comes first, then the other time.

•• **P3.18** The following algorithm yields the season (Spring, Summer, Fall, or Winter) for a given month and day.

```
If month is 1, 2, or 3, season = "Winter"
Else if month is 4, 5, or 6, season = "Spring"
Else if month is 7, 8, or 9, season = "Summer"
Else if month is 10, 11, or 12, season = "Fall"
If month is divisible by 3 and day >= 21
    If season is "Winter", season = "Spring"
    Else if season is "Spring", season = "Summer"
    Else if season is "Summer", season = "Fall"
    Else season = "Winter"
```

Write a program that prompts the user for a month and day and then prints the season, as determined by this algorithm.

•• **P3.19** Write a program that reads in two floating-point numbers and tests whether they are the same up to two decimal places. Here are two sample runs.

```
Enter two floating-point numbers: 2.0 1.99998
They are the same up to two decimal places.
Enter two floating-point numbers: 2.0 1.98999
They are different.
```

••• **P3.20** Write a program that prompts for the day and month of the user's birthday and then prints a horoscope. Make up fortunes for programmers, like this:

```
Please enter your birthday (month and day): 6 16
Gemini are experts at figuring out the behavior of complicated programs.
You feel where bugs are coming from and then stay one step ahead. Tonight,
your style wins approval from a tough critic.
```

Each fortune should contain the name of the astrological sign. (You will find the names and date ranges of the signs at a distressingly large number of sites on the Internet.)

••P3.21 The original U.S. income tax of 1913 was quite simple. The tax was

- 1 percent on the first $50,000.
- 2 percent on the amount over $50,000 up to $75,000.
- 3 percent on the amount over $75,000 up to $100,000.
- 4 percent on the amount over $100,000 up to $250,000.
- 5 percent on the amount over $250,000 up to $500,000.
- 6 percent on the amount over $500,000.

There was no separate schedule for single or married taxpayers. Write a program that computes the income tax according to this schedule.

•••P3.22 Write a program that computes taxes for the following schedule.

If your status is Single and if the taxable income is over	but not over	the tax is	of the amount over
$0	$8,000	10%	$0
$8,000	$32,000	$800 + 15%	$8,000
$32,000		$4,400 + 25%	$32,000

If your status is Married and if the taxable income is over	but not over	the tax is	of the amount over
$0	$16,000	10%	$0
$16,000	$64,000	$1,600 + 15%	$16,000
$64,000		$8,800 + 25%	$64,000

•••P3.23 The TaxCalculator.java program uses a simplified version of the 2008 U.S. income tax schedule. Look up the tax brackets and rates for the current year, for both single and married filers, and implement a program that computes the actual income tax.

•••P3.24 *Unit conversion.* Write a unit conversion program that asks the users from which unit they want to convert (fl. oz, gal, oz, lb, in, ft, mi) and to which unit they want to convert (ml, l, g, kg, mm, cm, m, km). Reject incompatible conversions (such as gal → km). Ask for the value to be converted, then display the result:

```
Convert from? gal
Convert to? ml
Value? 2.5
2.5 gal = 9462.5 ml
```

•P3.25 Write a program that prompts the user to provide a single character from the alphabet. Print Vowel or Consonant, depending on the user input. If the user input is not a letter (between a and z or A and Z), or is a string of length > 1, print an error message.

■■■ **P3.26** *Roman numbers.* Write a program that converts a positive integer into the Roman number system. The Roman number system has digits

I	1
V	5
X	10
L	50
C	100
D	500
M	1,000

Numbers are formed according to the following rules:

a. Only numbers up to 3,999 are represented.

b. As in the decimal system, the thousands, hundreds, tens, and ones are expressed separately.

c. The numbers 1 to 9 are expressed as

I	1
II	2
III	3
IV	4
V	5
VI	6
VII	7
VIII	8
IX	9

As you can see, an I preceding a V or X is subtracted from the value, and you can never have more than three I's in a row.

d. Tens and hundreds are done the same way, except that the letters X, L, C and C, D, M are used instead of I, V, X, respectively.

Your program should take an input, such as 1978, and convert it to Roman numerals, MCMLXXVIII.

■■ **P3.27** Write a program that asks the user to enter a month (1 for January, 2 for February, and so on) and then prints the number of days in the month. For February, print "28 or 29 days".

```
Enter a month: 5
30 days
```

Do not use a separate if/else branch for each month. Use Boolean operators.

■■■ **P3.28** A year with 366 days is called a leap year. Leap years are necessary to keep the calendar synchronized with the sun because the earth revolves around the sun once every 365.25 days. Actually, that figure is not entirely precise, and for all dates after 1582 the *Gregorian correction* applies. Usually years that are divisible by 4 are leap years, for example 1996. However, years that are divisible by 100 (for example, 1900) are not leap years, but years that are divisible by 400 are leap years (for example,

2000). Write a program that asks the user for a year and computes whether that year is a leap year. Use a single `if` statement and Boolean operators.

■■■ **P3.29** French country names are feminine when they end with the letter e, masculine otherwise, except for the following which are masculine even though they end with e:

- le Belize
- le Cambodge
- le Mexique
- le Mozambique
- le Zaïre
- le Zimbabwe

Write a program that reads the French name of a country and adds the article: le for masculine or la for feminine, such as le Canada or la Belgique.

However, if the country name starts with a vowel, use l'; for example, l'Afghanistan.

For the following plural country names, use les:

- les Etats-Unis
- les Pays-Bas

■■■ **Business P3.30** Write a program to simulate a bank transaction. There are two bank accounts: checking and savings. First, ask for the initial balances of the bank accounts; reject negative balances. Then ask for the transactions; options are deposit, withdrawal, and transfer. Then ask for the account; options are checking and savings. Then ask for the amount; reject transactions that overdraw an account. At the end, print the balances of both accounts.

■■ **Business P3.31** Write a program that reads in the name and salary of an employee. Here the salary will denote an *hourly* wage, such as $9.25. Then ask how many hours the employee worked in the past week. Be sure to accept fractional hours. Compute the pay. Any overtime work (over 40 hours per week) is paid at 150 percent of the regular wage. Print a paycheck for the employee.

■■ **Business P3.32** When you use an automated teller machine (ATM) with your bank card, you need to use a personal identification number (PIN) to access your account. If a user fails more than three times when entering the PIN, the machine will block the card. Assume that the user's PIN is "1234" and write a program that asks the user for the PIN no more than three times, and does the following:

- If the user enters the right number, print a message saying, "Your PIN is correct", and end the program.
- If the user enters a wrong number, print a message saying, "Your PIN is incorrect" and, if you have asked for the PIN less than three times, ask for it again.
- If the user enters a wrong number three times, print a message saying "Your bank card is blocked" and end the program.

■ **Business P3.33** Calculating the tip when you go to a restaurant is not difficult, but your restaurant wants to suggest a tip according to the service diners receive. Write a program that calculates a tip according to the diner's satisfaction as follows:

- Ask for the diners' satisfaction level using these ratings: 1 = Totally satisfied, 2 = Satisfied, 3 = Dissatisfied.

- If the diner is totally satisfied, calculate a 20 percent tip.
- If the diner is satisfied, calculate a 15 percent tip.
- If the diner is dissatisfied, calculate a 10 percent tip.
- Report the satisfaction level and tip in dollars and cents.

■ Business P3.34   A supermarket awards coupons depending on how much a customer spends on groceries. For example, if you spend $50, you will get a coupon worth eight percent of that amount. The following table shows the percent used to calculate the coupon awarded for different amounts spent. Write a program that calculates and prints the value of the coupon a person can receive based on groceries purchased.

Here is a sample run:

```
Please enter the cost of your groceries: 14
You win a discount coupon of $ 1.12. (8% of your purchase)
```

Money Spent	Coupon Percentage
Less than $10	No coupon
From $10 to $60	8%
More than $60 to $150	10%
More than $150 to $210	12%
More than $210	14%

■ Science P3.35   Write a program that prompts the user for a wavelength value and prints a description of the corresponding part of the electromagnetic spectrum, as given in the following table.

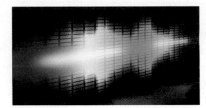

Electromagnetic Spectrum		
Type	Wavelength (m)	Frequency (Hz)
Radio Waves	$> 10^{-1}$	$< 3 \times 10^9$
Microwaves	10^{-3} to 10^{-1}	3×10^9 to 3×10^{11}
Infrared	7×10^{-7} to 10^{-3}	3×10^{11} to 4×10^{14}
Visible light	4×10^{-7} to 7×10^{-7}	4×10^{14} to 7.5×10^{14}
Ultraviolet	10^{-8} to 4×10^{-7}	7.5×10^{14} to 3×10^{16}
X-rays	10^{-11} to 10^{-8}	3×10^{16} to 3×10^{19}
Gamma rays	$< 10^{-11}$	$> 3 \times 10^{19}$

■ Science P3.36   Repeat Exercise P3.35, modifying the program so that it prompts for the frequency instead.

■■ Science P3.37 Repeat Exercise P3.35, modifying the program so that it first asks the user whether the input will be a wavelength or a frequency.

■■■ Science P3.38 A minivan has two sliding doors. Each door can be opened by either a dashboard switch, its inside handle, or its outside handle. However, the inside handles do not work if a child lock switch is activated. In order for the sliding doors to open, the gear shift must be in park, *and* the master unlock switch must be activated. (This book's author is the long-suffering owner of just such a vehicle.)

Your task is to simulate a portion of the control software for the vehicle. The input is a sequence of values for the switches and the gear shift, in the following order:

- Dashboard switches for left and right sliding door, child lock, and master unlock (0 for off or 1 for activated)
- Inside and outside handles on the left and right sliding doors (0 or 1)
- The gear shift setting (one of P N D 1 2 3 R).

A typical input would be 0 0 0 1 0 1 0 0 P.

Print "left door opens" and/or "right door opens" as appropriate. If neither door opens, print "both doors stay closed".

■ Science P3.39 Sound level L in units of decibel (dB) is determined by

$$L = 20 \log_{10}(p/p_0)$$

where p is the sound pressure of the sound (in Pascals, abbreviated Pa), and p_0 is a reference sound pressure equal to 20×10^{-6} Pa (where L is 0 dB). The following table gives descriptions for certain sound levels.

Threshold of pain	130 dB
Possible hearing damage	120 dB
Jack hammer at 1 m	100 dB
Traffic on a busy roadway at 10 m	90 dB
Normal conversation	60 dB
Calm library	30 dB
Light leaf rustling	0 dB

Write a program that reads a value and a unit, either dB or Pa, and then prints the closest description from the list above.

■■ Science P3.40 The electric circuit shown below is designed to measure the temperature of the gas in a chamber.

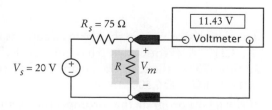

The resistor R represents a temperature sensor enclosed in the chamber. The resistance R, in Ω, is related to the temperature T, in °C, by the equation

$$R = R_0 + kT$$

In this device, assume $R_0 = 100\ \Omega$ and $k = 0.5$. The voltmeter displays the value of the voltage, V_m, across the sensor. This voltage V_m indicates the temperature, T, of the gas according to the equation

$$T = \frac{R}{k} - \frac{R_0}{k} = \frac{R_s}{k}\frac{V_m}{V_s - V_m} - \frac{R_0}{k}$$

Suppose the voltmeter voltage is constrained to the range $V_{min} = 12$ volts $\leq V_m \leq V_{max} = 18$ volts. Write a program that accepts a value of V_m and checks that it's between 12 and 18. The program should return the gas temperature in degrees Celsius when V_m is between 12 and 18 and an error message when it isn't.

■■■ Science P3.41

Crop damage due to frost is one of the many risks confronting farmers. The figure below shows a simple alarm circuit designed to warn of frost. The alarm circuit uses a device called a thermistor to sound a buzzer when the temperature drops below freezing. Thermistors are semiconductor devices that exhibit a temperature dependent resistance described by the equation

$$R = R_0 e^{\beta\left(\frac{1}{T} - \frac{1}{T_0}\right)}$$

where R is the resistance, in Ω, at the temperature T, in °K, and R_0 is the resistance, in Ω, at the temperature T_0, in °K. β is a constant that depends on the material used to make the thermistor.

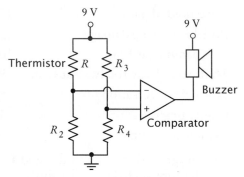

The circuit is designed so that the alarm will sound when

$$\frac{R_2}{R + R_2} < \frac{R_4}{R_3 + R_4}$$

The thermistor used in the alarm circuit has $R_0 = 33{,}192\ \Omega$ at $T_0 = 40$ °C, and $\beta = 3{,}310$ °K. (Notice that β has units of °K. The temperature in °K is obtained by adding 273° to the temperature in °C.) The resistors R_2, R_3, and R_4 have a resistance of 156.3 kΩ = 156,300 Ω.

Write a Java program that prompts the user for a temperature in °F and prints a message indicating whether or not the alarm will sound at that temperature.

- **Science P3.42** A mass $m = 2$ kilograms is attached to the end of a rope of length $r = 3$ meters. The mass is whirled around at high speed. The rope can withstand a maximum tension of $T = 60$ Newtons. Write a program that accepts a rotation speed v and determines whether such a speed will cause the rope to break. *Hint:* $T = mv^2/r$.

- **Science P3.43** A mass m is attached to the end of a rope of length $r = 3$ meters. The rope can only be whirled around at speeds of 1, 10, 20, or 40 meters per second. The rope can withstand a maximum tension of $T = 60$ Newtons. Write a program where the user enters the value of the mass m, and the program determines the greatest speed at which it can be whirled without breaking the rope. *Hint:* $T = mv^2/r$.

- ■ **Science P3.44** The average person can jump off the ground with a velocity of 7 mph without fear of leaving the planet. However, if an astronaut jumps with this velocity while standing on Halley's Comet, will the astronaut ever come back down? Create a program that allows the user to input a launch velocity (in mph) from the surface of Halley's Comet and determine whether a jumper will return to the surface. If not, the program should calculate how much more massive the comet must be in order to return the jumper to the surface.

Hint: Escape velocity is $v_{escape} = \sqrt{2\dfrac{GM}{R}}$, where $G = 6.67 \times 10^{-11} N\,m^2/kg^2$ is the gravitational constant, $M = 1.3 \times 10^{22}\,kg$ is the mass of Halley's comet, and $R = 1.153 \times 10^6\,m$ is its radius.

ANSWERS TO SELF-CHECK QUESTIONS

1. Change the if statement to
```
if (floor > 14)
{
    actualFloor = floor - 2;
}
```

2. 85. 90. 85.

3. The only difference is if originalPrice is 100. The statement in Self Check 2 sets discountedPrice to 90; this one sets it to 80.

4. 95. 100. 95.

5.
```
if (fuelAmount < 0.10 * fuelCapacity)
{
    System.out.println("red");
}
else
{
    System.out.println("green");
}
```

6. (a) and (b) are both true, (c) is false.

7. floor <= 13

8. The values should be compared with ==, not =.

9. input.equals("Y")

10. str.equals("") or str.length() == 0

11.
```
if (scoreA > scoreB)
{
    System.out.println("A won");
}
else if (scoreA < scoreB)
{
    System.out.println("B won");
}
else
{
    System.out.println("Game tied");
}
```

12.
```
if (x > 0) { s = 1; }
else if (x < 0) { s = -1; }
else { s = 0; }
```

13. You could first set s to one of the three values:
```
s = 0;
if (x > 0) { s = 1; }
else if (x < 0) { s = -1; }
```

14. The if (price <= 100) can be omitted (leaving just else), making it clear that the else branch is the sole alternative.

15. No destruction of buildings.

16. Add a branch before the final else:
```
else if (richter < 0)
{
    System.out.println("Error: Negative input");
}
```

17. 3200.

18. No. Then the computation is 0.10 × 32000 + 0.25 × (32000 − 32000).

19. No. Their individual tax is $5,200 each, and if they married, they would pay $10,400. Actually, taxpayers in higher tax brackets (which our program does not model) may pay higher taxes when they marry, a phenomenon known as the *marriage penalty*.

20. Change else in line 41 to
```
else if (maritalStatus.equals("m"))
```
and add another branch after line 52:
```
else
{
    System.out.println(
    "Error: marital status should be s or m.");
}
```

21. The higher tax rate is only applied on the income in the higher bracket. Suppose you are single and make $31,900. Should you try to get a $200 raise? Absolutely: you get to keep 90 percent of the first $100 and 75 percent of the next $100.

22.

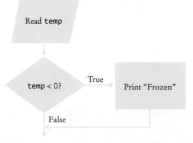

23. The "True" arrow from the first decision points into the "True" branch of the second decision, creating spaghetti code.

24. Here is one solution. In Section 3.7, you will see how you can combine the conditions for a more elegant solution.

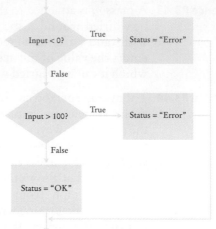

25.

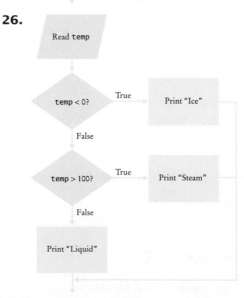

26.

27.

Test Case	Expected Output	Comment
12	12	Below 13th floor
14	13	Above 13th floor
13	?	The specification is not clear— See Section 3.8 for a version of this program with error handling

29. A boundary test case is a price of $128. A 16 percent discount should apply because the problem statement states that the larger discount applies if the price is *at least* $128. Thus, the expected output is $107.52.

30.

Test Case	Expected Output	Comment
9	Most structures fall	
7.5	Many buildings destroyed	
6.5	Many buildings ...	
5	Damage to poorly...	
3	No destruction...	
8.0	Most structures fall	Boundary case. In this program, boundary cases are not as significant because the behavior of an earthquake changes gradually.
-1		The specification is not clear—see Self Check 16 for a version of this program with error handling.

31.

Test Case	Expected Output	Comment
(0.5, 0.5)	inside	
(4, 2)	outside	
(0, 2)	on the boundary	Exactly on the boundary
(1.414, 1.414)	on the boundary	Close to the boundary
(0, 1.9)	inside	Not less than 1 mm from the boundary
(0, 2.1)	outside	Not less than 1 mm from the boundary

32. `x == 0 && y == 0`

33. `x == 0 || y == 0`

34. `(x == 0 && y != 0) || (y == 0 && x != 0)`

35. The same as the value of `frozen`.

36. You are guaranteed that there are no other values. With strings or integers, you would need to check that no values such as `"maybe"` or −1 enter your calculations.

37. (a) `Error: The floor must be between 1 and 20.`
(b) `Error: The floor must be between 1 and 20.`
(c) `19` (d) `Error: Not an integer.`

38. `floor == 13 || floor <= 0 || floor > 20`

39. Check for `in.hasNextDouble()`, to make sure a researcher didn't supply an input such as `oh my`. Check for `weight <= 0`, because any rat must surely have a positive weight. We don't know how giant a rat could be, but the New Guinea rats weighed no more than 2 kg. A regular house rat (*rattus rattus*) weighs up to 0.2 kg, so we'll say that any weight > 10 kg was surely an input error, perhaps confusing grams and kilograms. Thus, the checks are

```java
if (in.hasNextDouble())
{
   double weight = in.nextDouble();
   if (weight < 0)
   {
      System.out.println(
         "Error: Weight cannot be negative.");
   }
   else if (weight > 10)
   {
      System.out.println(
         "Error: Weight > 10 kg.");
   }
   else
   {
      Process valid weight.
   }
}
else
{
   System.out.print("Error: Not a number");
}
```

40. The second input fails, and the program terminates without printing anything.

CHAPTER 4

LOOPS

CHAPTER GOALS

To implement while, for, and do loops

To hand-trace the execution of a program

To become familiar with common
loop algorithms

To understand nested loops

To implement programs that read and process data sets

To use a computer for simulations

CHAPTER CONTENTS

4.1 THE WHILE LOOP 140

Syntax 4.1: while Statement 141

Common Error 4.1: Don't Think "Are We
There Yet?" 144

Common Error 4.2: Infinite Loops 145

Common Error 4.3: Off-by-One Errors 145

Random Fact 4.1: The First Bug 146

**4.2 PROBLEM SOLVING:
HAND-TRACING** 147

4.3 THE FOR LOOP 150

Syntax 4.2: for Statement 152

Programming Tip 4.1: Use for Loops for Their
Intended Purpose Only 155

Programming Tip 4.2: Choose Loop Bounds That
Match Your Task 155

Programming Tip 4.3: Count Iterations 156

4.4 THE DO LOOP 156

Programming Tip 4.4: Flowcharts for Loops 157

**4.5 APPLICATION: PROCESSING
SENTINEL VALUES** 158

Special Topic 4.1: The Loop-and-a-Half Problem
and the break Statement 160

Special Topic 4.2: Redirection of Input
and Output 161

Video Example 4.1: Evaluating a Cell
Phone Plan ✚

**4.6 PROBLEM SOLVING:
STORYBOARDS** 162

4.7 COMMON LOOP ALGORITHMS 165

How To 4.1: Writing a Loop 169

Worked Example 4.1: Credit Card Processing ✚

4.8 NESTED LOOPS 172

Worked Example 4.2: Manipulating the Pixels
in an Image ✚

**4.9 APPLICATION: RANDOM NUMBERS
AND SIMULATIONS** 176

Special Topic 4.3: Drawing Graphical Shapes 179

Video Example 4.2: Drawing a Spiral ✚

Random Fact 4.2: Software Piracy 182

In a loop, a part of a program is repeated over and over, until a specific goal is reached. Loops are important for calculations that require repeated steps and for processing input consisting of many data items. In this chapter, you will learn about loop statements in Java, as well as techniques for writing programs that process input and simulate activities in the real world.

4.1 The while Loop

In this section, you will learn about *loop statements* that repeatedly execute instructions until a goal has been reached.

Recall the investment problem from Chapter 1. You put $10,000 into a bank account that earns 5 percent interest per year. How many years does it take for the account balance to be double the original investment?

In Chapter 1 we developed the following algorithm for this problem:

Because the interest earned also earns interest, a bank balance grows exponentially.

Start with a year value of 0, a column for the interest, and a balance of $10,000.

year	interest	balance
0		$10,000

Repeat the following steps while the balance is less than $20,000.
  Add 1 to the year value.
  Compute the interest as balance x 0.05 (i.e., 5 percent interest).
  Add the interest to the balance.
Report the final year value as the answer.

You now know how to declare and update the variables in Java. What you don't yet know is how to carry out "Repeat steps while the balance is less than $20,000".

In a particle accelerator, subatomic particles traverse a loop-shaped tunnel multiple times, gaining the speed required for physical experiments. Similarly, in computer science, statements in a loop are executed while a condition is true.

Figure 1 Flowchart of a while Loop

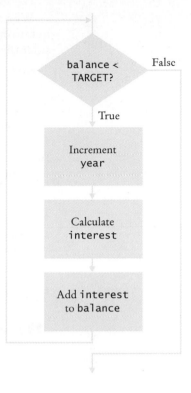

A loop executes instructions repeatedly while a condition is true.

In Java, the while statement implements such a repetition (see Syntax 4.1). It has the form

```
while (condition)
{
    statements
}
```

As long as the condition remains true, the statements inside the while statement are executed. These statements are called the **body** of the while statement.

In our case, we want to increment the year counter and add interest while the balance is less than the target balance of $20,000:

```
while (balance < TARGET)
{
    year++;
    double interest = balance * RATE / 100;
    balance = balance + interest;
}
```

A while statement is an example of a **loop**. If you draw a flowchart, the flow of execution loops again to the point where the condition is tested (see Figure 1).

Syntax 4.1 while Statement

```
Syntax     while (condition)
           {
               statements
           }
```

This variable is declared outside the loop and updated in the loop.

```
                             double balance = 0;
```

Beware of "off-by-one" errors in the loop condition. See page 145.

If the condition never becomes false, an infinite loop occurs. See page 145.

```
                             .
                             .
                             .
                             while (balance < TARGET)
                             {
```

Don't put a semicolon here! See page 86.

```
                                 double interest = balance * RATE / 100;
                                 balance = balance + interest;
```

These statements are executed while the condition is true.

This variable is created in each loop iteration.

```
                             }
```

Lining up braces is a good idea. See page 86.

Braces are not required if the body contains a single statement, but it's good to always use them. See page 86.

When you declare a variable *inside* the loop body, the variable is created for each iteration of the loop and removed after the end of each iteration. For example, consider the interest variable in this loop:

```
while (balance < TARGET)
{
    year++;
    double interest = balance * RATE / 100;
    balance = balance + interest;
} // interest no longer declared here
```

A new interest variable is created in each iteration.

In contrast, the balance and years variables were declared outside the loop body. That way, the same variable is used for all iterations of the loop.

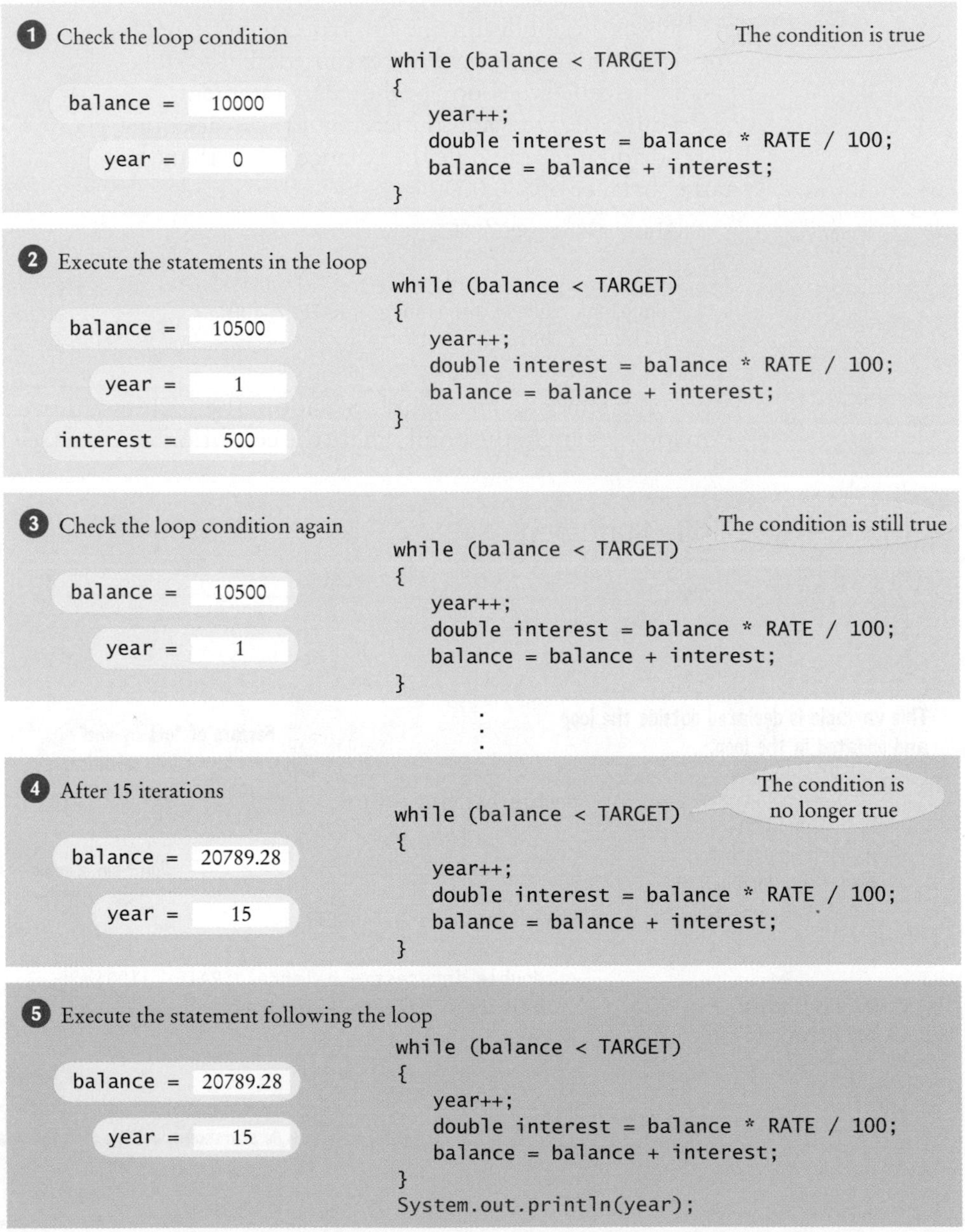

① Check the loop condition

balance = 10000

year = 0

```
while (balance < TARGET)
{
    year++;
    double interest = balance * RATE / 100;
    balance = balance + interest;
}
```

The condition is true

② Execute the statements in the loop

balance = 10500

year = 1

interest = 500

```
while (balance < TARGET)
{
    year++;
    double interest = balance * RATE / 100;
    balance = balance + interest;
}
```

③ Check the loop condition again

balance = 10500

year = 1

```
while (balance < TARGET)
{
    year++;
    double interest = balance * RATE / 100;
    balance = balance + interest;
}
```

The condition is still true

④ After 15 iterations

balance = 20789.28

year = 15

```
while (balance < TARGET)
{
    year++;
    double interest = balance * RATE / 100;
    balance = balance + interest;
}
```

The condition is no longer true

⑤ Execute the statement following the loop

balance = 20789.28

year = 15

```
while (balance < TARGET)
{
    year++;
    double interest = balance * RATE / 100;
    balance = balance + interest;
}
System.out.println(year);
```

Figure 2
Execution of the DoubleInvestment Loop

Here is the program that solves the investment problem. Figure 2 illustrates the program's execution.

section_1/DoubleInvestment.java

```java
 1   /**
 2       This program computes the time required to double an investment.
 3   */
 4   public class DoubleInvestment
 5   {
 6      public static void main(String[] args)
 7      {
 8         final double RATE = 5;
 9         final double INITIAL_BALANCE = 10000;
10         final double TARGET = 2 * INITIAL_BALANCE;
11
12         double balance = INITIAL_BALANCE;
13         int year = 0;
14
15         // Count the years required for the investment to double
16
17         while (balance < TARGET)
18         {
19            year++;
20            double interest = balance * RATE / 100;
21            balance = balance + interest;
22         }
23
24         System.out.println("The investment doubled after "
25            + year + " years.");
26      }
27   }
```

Program Run

```
The investment doubled after 15 years.
```

SELF CHECK

1. How many years does it take for the investment to triple? Modify the program and run it.

2. If the interest rate is 10 percent per year, how many years does it take for the investment to double? Modify the program and run it.

3. Modify the program so that the balance after each year is printed. How did you do that?

4. Suppose we change the program so that the condition of the while loop is
   ```java
   while (balance <= TARGET)
   ```
   What is the effect on the program? Why?

5. What does the following loop print?
   ```java
   int n = 1;
   while (n < 100)
   {
      n = 2 * n;
      System.out.print(n + " ");
   }
   ```

Practice It   Now you can try these exercises at the end of the chapter: R4.1, R4.5, P4.14.

Table 1 while Loop Examples

Loop	Output	Explanation

`i = 0; sum = 0;`
`while (sum < 10)`
`{`
   `i++; sum = sum + i;`
   Print `i` **and** `sum;`
`}`
	1 1
	2 3
	3 6
	4 10
		When sum is 10, the loop condition is false, and the loop ends.

`i = 0; sum = 0;`
`while (sum < 10)`
`{`
   `i++; sum = sum - i;`
   Print `i` **and** `sum;`
`}`
	1 -1
	2 -3
	3 -6
	4 -10
	. . .
		Because sum never reaches 10, this is an "infinite loop" (see Common Error 4.2 on page 145).

`i = 0; sum = 0;`
`while (sum < 0)`
`{`
   `i++; sum = sum - i;`
   Print `i` **and** `sum;`
`}`
	(No output)	The statement sum < 0 is false when the condition is first checked, and the loop is never executed.

`i = 0; sum = 0;`
`while (sum >= 10)`
`{`
   `i++; sum = sum + i;`
   Print `i` **and** `sum;`
`}`
	(No output)	The programmer probably thought, "Stop when the sum is at least 10." However, the loop condition controls when the loop is executed, not when it ends (see Common Error 4.1 on page 144).

`i = 0; sum = 0;`
`while (sum < 10) ;`
`{`
   `i++; sum = sum + i;`
   Print `i` **and** `sum;`
`}`
	(No output, program does not terminate)	Note the semicolon before the {. This loop has an empty body. It runs forever, checking whether sum < 0 and doing nothing in the body.

Common Error 4.1

Don't Think "Are We There Yet?"

When doing something repetitive, most of us want to know when we are done. For example, you may think, "I want to get at least $20,000," and set the loop condition to

`balance >= TARGET`

But the `while` loop thinks the opposite: How long am I allowed to keep going? The correct loop condition is

`while (balance < TARGET)`

In other words: "Keep at it while the balance is less than the target."

When writing a loop condition, don't ask, "Are we there yet?" The condition determines how long the loop will keep going.

Infinite Loops

A very annoying loop error is an *infinite loop:* a loop that runs forever and can be stopped only by killing the program or restarting the computer. If there are output statements in the program, then reams and reams of output flash by on the screen. Otherwise, the program just sits there and *hangs*, seeming to do nothing. On some systems, you can kill a hanging program by hitting Ctrl + C. On others, you can close the window in which the program runs.

A common reason for infinite loops is forgetting to update the variable that controls the loop:

```
int year = 1;
while (year <= 20)
{
    double interest = balance * RATE / 100;
    balance = balance + interest;
}
```

Like this hamster who can't stop running in the treadmill, an infinite loop never ends.

Here the programmer forgot to add a year++ command in the loop. As a result, the year always stays at 1, and the loop never comes to an end.

Another common reason for an infinite loop is accidentally incrementing a counter that should be decremented (or vice versa). Consider this example:

```
int year = 20;
while (year > 0)
{
    double interest = balance * RATE / 100;
    balance = balance + interest;
    year++;
}
```

The year variable really should have been decremented, not incremented. This is a common error because incrementing counters is so much more common than decrementing that your fingers may type the ++ on autopilot. As a consequence, year is always larger than 0, and the loop never ends. (Actually, year may eventually exceed the largest representable positive integer and *wrap around* to a negative number. Then the loop ends—of course, with a completely wrong result.)

Off-by-One Errors

Consider our computation of the number of years that are required to double an investment:

```
int year = 0;
while (balance < TARGET)
{
    year++;
    balance = balance * (1 + RATE / 100);
}
System.out.println("The investment doubled after "
    + year + " years.");
```

Should year start at 0 or at 1? Should you test for balance < TARGET or for balance <= TARGET? It is easy to be *off by one* in these expressions.

Some people try to solve **off-by-one errors** by randomly inserting +1 or -1 until the program seems to work—a terrible strategy. It can take a long time to compile and test all the various possibilities. Expending a small amount of mental effort is a real time saver.

Fortunately, off-by-one errors are easy to avoid, simply by thinking through a couple of test cases and using the information from the test cases to come up with a rationale for your decisions.

Should year start at 0 or at 1? Look at a scenario with simple values: an initial balance of $100 and an interest rate of 50 percent. After year 1, the balance is $150, and after year 2 it is $225, or over $200. So the investment doubled after 2 years. The loop executed two times, incrementing year each time. Hence year must start at 0, not at 1.

> An off-by-one error is a common error when programming loops. Think through simple test cases to avoid this type of error.

year	balance
0	$100
1	$150
2	$225

In other words, the `balance` variable denotes the balance after the end of the year. At the outset, the `balance` variable contains the balance after year 0 and not after year 1.

Next, should you use a < or <= comparison in the test? This is harder to figure out, because it is rare for the balance to be exactly twice the initial balance. There is one case when this happens, namely when the interest is 100 percent. The loop executes once. Now year is 1, and balance is exactly equal to 2 * `INITIAL_BALANCE`. Has the investment doubled after one year? It has. Therefore, the loop should not execute again. If the test condition is `balance < TARGET`, the loop stops, as it should. If the test condition had been `balance <= TARGET`, the loop would have executed once more.

In other words, you keep adding interest while the balance *has not yet doubled*.

Random Fact 4.1 The First Bug

According to legend, the first bug was found in the Mark II, a huge electromechanical computer at Harvard University. It really was caused by a bug—a moth was trapped in a relay switch.

Actually, from the note that the operator left in the log book next to the moth (see the photo), it appears as if the term "bug" had already been in active use at the time.

The pioneering computer scientist Maurice Wilkes wrote, "Somehow, at the Moore School and afterwards, one had always assumed there would be no particular difficulty in getting programs right. I can remember the exact instant in time at which it dawned on me that a great part of my future life would be spent finding mistakes in my own programs."

The First Bug

4.2 Problem Solving: Hand-Tracing

Hand-tracing is a simulation of code execution in which you step through instructions and track the values of the variables.

In Programming Tip 3.5, you learned about the method of hand-tracing. When you hand-trace code or pseudocode, you write the names of the variables on a sheet of paper, mentally execute each step of the code and update the variables.

It is best to have the code written or printed on a sheet of paper. Use a marker, such as a paper clip, to mark the current line. Whenever a variable changes, cross out the old value and write the new value below. When a program produces output, also write down the output in another column.

Consider this example. What value is displayed?

```java
int n = 1729;
int sum = 0;
while (n > 0)
{
   int digit = n % 10;
   sum = sum + digit;
   n = n / 10;
}
System.out.println(sum);
```

There are three variables: n, sum, and digit.

n	sum	digit

The first two variables are initialized with 1729 and 0 before the loop is entered.

```java
    int n = 1729;
⌐⌐  int sum = 0;
    while (n > 0)
    {
       int digit = n % 10;
       sum = sum + digit;
       n = n / 10;
    }
    System.out.println(sum);
```

n	sum	digit
1729	0	

Because n is greater than zero, enter the loop. The variable digit is set to 9 (the remainder of dividing 1729 by 10). The variable sum is set to 0 + 9 = 9.

```java
    int n = 1729;
    int sum = 0;
    while (n > 0)
    {
       int digit = n % 10;
⌐⌐     sum = sum + digit;
       n = n / 10;
    }
    System.out.println(sum);
```

n	sum	digit
1729	~~0~~	
	9	9

Finally, n becomes 172. (Recall that the remainder in the division 1729 / 10 is discarded because both arguments are integers.)

Cross out the old values and write the new ones under the old ones.

```
int n = 1729;
int sum = 0;
while (n > 0)
{
    int digit = n % 10;
    sum = sum + digit;
    n = n / 10;
}
System.out.println(sum);
```

n	sum	digit
~~1729~~	~~0~~	
172	9	9

Now check the loop condition again.

```
int n = 1729;
int sum = 0;
while (n > 0)
{
    int digit = n % 10;
    sum = sum + digit;
    n = n / 10;
}
System.out.println(sum);
```

Because n is still greater than zero, repeat the loop. Now digit becomes 2, sum is set to 9 + 2 = 11, and n is set to 17.

n	sum	digit
~~1729~~	~~0~~	
~~172~~	~~9~~	~~9~~
17	11	2

Repeat the loop once again, setting digit to 7, sum to 11 + 7 = 18, and n to 1.

n	sum	digit
~~1729~~	~~0~~	
~~172~~	~~9~~	~~9~~
~~17~~	~~11~~	~~2~~
1	18	7

Enter the loop for one last time. Now digit is set to 1, sum to 19, and n becomes zero.

n	sum	digit
~~1729~~	~~0~~	
~~172~~	~~9~~	~~9~~
~~17~~	~~11~~	~~2~~
~~1~~	~~18~~	~~7~~
0	19	1

```
    int n = 1729;
    int sum = 0;
    while (n > 0)
    {
        int digit = n % 10;
        sum = sum + digit;
        n = n / 10;
    }
    System.out.println(sum);
```

> Because n equals zero, this condition is not true.

The condition n > 0 is now false. Continue with the statement after the loop.

```
    int n = 1729;
    int sum = 0;
    while (n > 0)
    {
        int digit = n % 10;
        sum = sum + digit;
        n = n / 10;
    }
    System.out.println(sum);
```

n	sum	digit	output
1729	0		
172	9	9	
17	11	2	
1	18	7	
0	19	1	19

This statement is an output statement. The value that is output is the value of sum, which is 19.

Of course, you can get the same answer by just running the code. However, hand-tracing can give you an *insight* that you would not get if you simply ran the code. Consider again what happens in each iteration:

- We extract the last digit of n.
- We add that digit to sum.
- We strip the digit off n.

Hand-tracing can help you understand how an unfamiliar algorithm works.

In other words, the loop forms the sum of the digits in n. You now know what the loop does for any value of n, not just the one in the example. (Why would anyone want to form the sum of the digits? Operations of this kind are useful for checking the validity of credit card numbers and other forms of ID numbers—see Exercise P4.32.)

Hand-tracing can show errors in code or pseudocode.

Hand-tracing does not just help you understand code that works correctly. It is a powerful technique for finding errors in your code. When a program behaves in a way that you don't expect, get out a sheet of paper and track the values of the variables as you mentally step through the code.

You don't need a working program to do hand-tracing. You can hand-trace pseudocode. In fact, it is an excellent idea to hand-trace your pseudocode before you go to the trouble of translating it into actual code, to confirm that it works correctly.

SELF CHECK

6. Hand-trace the following code, showing the value of n and the output.
```
    int n = 5;
    while (n >= 0)
    {
        n--;
        System.out.print(n);
    }
```

7. Hand-trace the following code, showing the value of n and the output. What potential error do you notice?

```
int n = 1;
while (n <= 3)
{
    System.out.print(n + ", ");
    n++;
}
```

8. Hand-trace the following code, assuming that a is 2 and n is 4. Then explain what the code does for arbitrary values of a and n.

```
int r = 1;
int i = 1;
while (i <= n)
{
    r = r * a;
    i++;
}
```

9. Trace the following code. What error do you observe?

```
int n = 1;
while (n != 50)
{
    System.out.println(n);
    n = n + 10;
}
```

10. The following pseudocode is intended to count the number of digits in the number n:

count = 1
temp = n
while (temp > 10)
    Increment count.
    Divide temp by 10.0.

Trace the pseudocode for n = 123 and n = 100. What error do you find?

Practice It   Now you can try these exercises at the end of the chapter: R4.3, R4.6.

4.3 The for Loop

> The for loop is used when a value runs from a starting point to an ending point with a constant increment or decrement.

It often happens that you want to execute a sequence of statements a given number of times. You can use a while loop that is controlled by a counter, as in the following example:

```
int counter = 1; // Initialize the counter
while (counter <= 10) // Check the counter
{
    System.out.println(counter);
    counter++; // Update the counter
}
```

Because this loop type is so common, there is a special form for it, called the for loop (see Syntax 4.2).

```
for (int counter = 1; counter <= 10; counter++)
{
   System.out.println(counter);
}
```

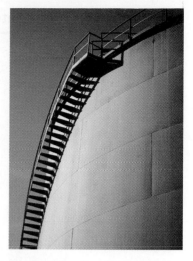

Some people call this loop *count-controlled*. In contrast, the while loop of the preceding section can be called an *event-controlled* loop because it executes until an event occurs; namely that the balance reaches the target. Another commonly used term for a count-controlled loop is *definite*. You know from the outset that the loop body will be executed a definite number of times; ten times in our example. In contrast, you do not know how many iterations it takes to accumulate a target balance. Such a loop is called *indefinite*.

The for loop neatly groups the initialization, condition, and update expressions together. However, it is important to realize that these expressions are not executed together (see Figure 3).

You can visualize the for loop as an orderly sequence of steps.

ANIMATION
The for *Loop*

- The initialization is executed once, before the loop is entered. **1**
- The condition is checked before each iteration. **2** **5**
- The update is executed after each iteration. **4**

1 Initialize counter

counter = 1

```
for (int counter = 1; counter <= 10; counter++)
{
   System.out.println(counter);
}
```

2 Check condition

counter = 1

```
for (int counter = 1; counter <= 10; counter++)
{
   System.out.println(counter);
}
```

3 Execute loop body

counter = 1

```
for (int counter = 1; counter <= 10; counter++)
{
   System.out.println(counter);
}
```

4 Update counter

counter = 2

```
for (int counter = 1; counter <= 10; counter++)
{
   System.out.println(counter);
}
```

5 Check condition again

counter = 2

```
for (int counter = 1; counter <= 10; counter++)
{
   System.out.println(counter);
}
```

Figure 3
Execution of a
for Loop

Syntax 4.2 for Statement

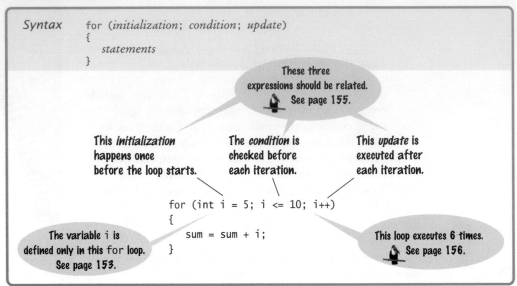

A for loop can count down instead of up:

```
for (int counter = 10; counter >= 0; counter--) . . .
```

The increment or decrement need not be in steps of 1:

```
for (int counter = 0; counter <= 10; counter = counter + 2) . . .
```

See Table 2 for additional variations.

So far, we have always declared the counter variable in the loop initialization:

```
for (int counter = 1; counter <= 10; counter++)
{
    . . .
}
// counter no longer declared here
```

Table 2 for Loop Examples

Loop	Values of i	Comment
for (i = 0; i <= 5; i++)	0 1 2 3 4 5	Note that the loop is executed 6 times. (See Programming Tip 4.3 on page 156.)
for (i = 5; i >= 0; i--)	5 4 3 2 1 0	Use i-- for decreasing values.
for (i = 0; i < 9; i = i + 2)	0 2 4 6 8	Use i = i + 2 for a step size of 2.
for (i = 0; i != 9; i = i + 2)	0 2 4 6 8 10 12 14 ... (infinite loop)	You can use < or <= instead of != to avoid this problem.
for (i = 1; i <= 20; i = i * 2)	1 2 4 8 16	You can specify any rule for modifying i, such as doubling it in every step.
for (i = 0; i < str.length(); i++)	0 1 2 ... until the last valid index of the string str	In the loop body, use the expression str.charAt(i) to get the ith character.

Such a variable is declared for all iterations of the loop, but you cannot use it after the loop. If you declare the counter variable before the loop, you can continue to use it after the loop:

```
int counter;
for (counter = 1; counter <= 10; counter++)
{
    . . .
}
// counter still declared here
```

Here is a typical use of the for loop. We want to print the balance of our savings account over a period of years, as shown in this table:

Year	Balance
1	10500.00
2	11025.00
3	11576.25
4	12155.06
5	12762.82

The for loop pattern applies because the variable year starts at 1 and then moves in constant increments until it reaches the target:

```
for (int year = 1; year <= nyears; year++)
{
    Update balance.
    Print year and balance.
}
```

Following is the complete program. Figure 4 shows the corresponding flowchart.

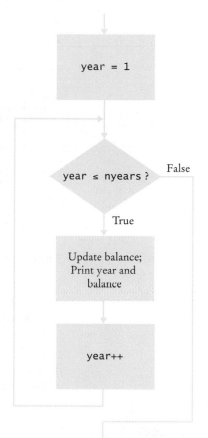

Figure 4 Flowchart of a for Loop

section_3/InvestmentTable.java

```
 1  import java.util.Scanner;
 2
 3  /**
 4     This program prints a table showing the growth of an investment.
 5  */
 6  public class InvestmentTable
 7  {
 8     public static void main(String[] args)
 9     {
10        final double RATE = 5;
11        final double INITIAL_BALANCE = 10000;
```

```
12        double balance = INITIAL_BALANCE;
13
14        System.out.print("Enter number of years: ");
15        Scanner in = new Scanner(System.in);
16        int nyears = in.nextInt();
17
18        // Print the table of balances for each year
19
20        for (int year = 1; year <= nyears; year++)
21        {
22           double interest = balance * RATE / 100;
23           balance = balance + interest;
24           System.out.printf("%4d %10.2f\n", year, balance);
25        }
26     }
27 }
```

Program Run

```
Enter number of years: 10
    1   10500.00
    2   11025.00
    3   11576.25
    4   12155.06
    5   12762.82
    6   13400.96
    7   14071.00
    8   14774.55
    9   15513.28
   10   16288.95
```

Another common use of the for loop is to traverse all characters of a string:

```
for (int i = 0; i < str.length(); i++)
{
   char ch = str.charAt(i);
   Process ch
}
```

Note that the counter variable i starts at 0, and the loop is terminated when i reaches the length of the string. For example, if str has length 5, i takes on the values 0, 1, 2, 3, and 4. These are the valid positions in the string.

SELF CHECK

11. Write the for loop of the InvestmentTable.java program as a while loop.

12. How many numbers does this loop print?
```
for (int n = 10; n >= 0; n--)
{
   System.out.println(n);
}
```

13. Write a for loop that prints all even numbers between 10 and 20 (inclusive).

14. Write a for loop that computes the sum of the integers from 1 to n.

15. How would you modify the for loop of the InvestmentTable.java program to print all balances until the investment has doubled?

Practice It   Now you can try these exercises at the end of the chapter: R4.4, R4.10, P4.8, P4.13.

Use **for** Loops for Their Intended Purpose Only

A for loop is an *idiom* for a loop of a particular form. A value runs from the start to the end, with a constant increment or decrement.

The compiler won't check whether the initialization, condition, and update expressions are related. For example, the following loop is legal:

```
// Confusing—unrelated expressions
for (System.out.print("Inputs: "); in.hasNextDouble(); sum = sum + x)
{
    x = in.nextDouble();
}
```

However, programmers reading such a for loop will be confused because it does not match their expectations. Use a while loop for iterations that do not follow the for idiom.

You should also be careful not to update the loop counter in the body of a for loop. Consider the following example:

```
for (int counter = 1; counter <= 100; counter++)
{
    if (counter % 10 == 0) // Skip values that are divisible by 10
    {
        counter++; // Bad style—you should not update the counter in a for loop
    }
    System.out.println(counter);
}
```

Updating the counter inside a for loop is confusing because the counter is updated *again* at the end of the loop iteration. In some loop iterations, counter is incremented once, in others twice. This goes against the intuition of a programmer who sees a for loop.

If you find yourself in this situation, you can either change from a for loop to a while loop, or implement the "skipping" behavior in another way. For example:

```
for (int counter = 1; counter <= 100; counter++)
{
    if (counter % 10 != 0) // Skip values that are divisible by 10
    {
        System.out.println(counter);
    }
}
```

Choose Loop Bounds That Match Your Task

Suppose you want to print line numbers that go from 1 to 10. Of course, you will use a loop:

```
for (int i = 1; i <= 10; i++)
```

The values for i are bounded by the relation $1 \le i \le 10$. Because there are $\le$ on both bounds, the bounds are called **symmetric**.

When traversing the characters in a string, it is more natural to use the bounds

```
for (int i = 0; i < str.length(); i++)
```

In this loop, i traverses all valid positions in the string. You can access the ith character as str.charAt(i). The values for i are bounded by $0 \le i < $ str.length(), with a $\le$ to the left and a $<$ to the right. That is appropriate, because str.length() is not a valid position. Such bounds are called **asymmetric**.

In this case, it is not a good idea to use symmetric bounds:

```
for (int i = 0; i <= str.length() - 1; i++) // Use < instead
```

The asymmetric form is easier to understand.

Count Iterations

Finding the correct lower and upper bounds for an iteration can be confusing. Should you start at 0 or at 1? Should you use <= b or < b as a termination condition?

Counting the number of iterations is a very useful device for better understanding a loop. Counting is easier for loops with asymmetric bounds. The loop

```
for (int i = a; i < b; i++)
```

is executed b - a times. For example, the loop traversing the characters in a string,

```
for (int i = 0; i < str.length(); i++)
```

runs str.length() times. That makes perfect sense, because there are str.length() characters in a string.

The loop with symmetric bounds,

```
for (int i = a; i <= b; i++)
```

is executed b - a + 1 times. That "+1" is the source of many programming errors.

For example,

```
for (int i = 0; i <= 10; i++)
```

runs 11 times. Maybe that is what you want; if not, start at 1 or use < 10.

One way to visualize this "+1" error is by looking at a fence. Each section has one fence post to the left, and there is a final post on the right of the last section. Forgetting to count the last value is often called a "fence post error".

How many posts do you need for a fence with four sections? It is easy to be "off by one" with problems such as this one.

4.4 The do Loop

Sometimes you want to execute the body of a loop at least once and perform the loop test after the body is executed. The do loop serves that purpose:

```
do
{
    statements
}
while (condition);
```

The body of the do loop is executed first, then the condition is tested.

Some people call such a loop a *post-test loop* because the condition is tested after completing the loop body. In contrast, while and for loops are *pre-test loops*. In those loop types, the condition is tested before entering the loop body.

A typical example for a do loop is input validation. Suppose you ask a user to enter a value < 100. If the user doesn't pay attention and enters a larger value, you ask again, until the value is correct. Of course, you cannot test the value until the user has entered it. This is a perfect fit for the do loop (see Figure 5):

Figure 5   Flowchart of a do Loop

```java
int value;
do
{
   System.out.print("Enter an integer < 100: ");
   value = in.nextInt();
}
while (value >= 100);
```

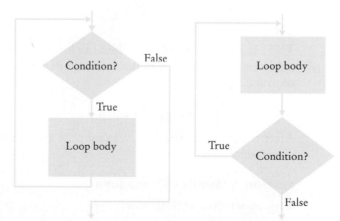

Prompt user
to enter
a value < 100

Copy the input
to value

value ≥ 100?

True

False

SELF CHECK

16. Suppose that we want to check for inputs that are at least 0 and at most 100. Modify the do loop for this check.

17. Rewrite the input check do loop using a while loop. What is the disadvantage of your solution?

18. Suppose Java didn't have a do loop. Could you rewrite any do loop as a while loop?

19. Write a do loop that reads integers and computes their sum. Stop when reading the value 0.

20. Write a do loop that reads integers and computes their sum. Stop when reading a zero or the same value twice in a row. For example, if the input is 1 2 3 4 4, then the sum is 14 and the loop stops.

Practice It   Now you can try these exercises at the end of the chapter: R4.9, R4.16, R4.17.

Programming Tip 4.4

Flowcharts for Loops

In Section 3.5, you learned how to use flowcharts to visualize the flow of control in a program. There are two types of loops that you can include in a flowchart; they correspond to a while loop and a do loop in Java. They differ in the placement of the condition—either before or after the loop body.

Condition? — False

True

Loop body

Loop body

Condition?

True

False

As described in Section 3.5, you want to avoid "spaghetti code" in your flowcharts. For loops, that means that you never want to have an arrow that points inside a loop body.

4.5 Application: Processing Sentinel Values

In this section, you will learn how to write loops that read and process a sequence of input values.

Whenever you read a sequence of inputs, you need to have some method of indicating the end of the sequence. Sometimes you are lucky and no input value can be zero. Then you can prompt the user to keep entering numbers, or 0 to finish the sequence. If zero is allowed but negative numbers are not, you can use –1 to indicate termination.

Such a value, which is not an actual input, but serves as a signal for termination, is called a **sentinel**.

Let's put this technique to work in a program that computes the average of a set of salary values. In our sample program, we will use –1 as a sentinel. An employee would surely not work for a negative salary, but there may be volunteers who work for free.

Inside the loop, we read an input. If the input is not –1, we process it. In order to compute the average, we need the total sum of all salaries, and the number of inputs.

In the military, a sentinel guards a border or passage. In computer science, a sentinel value denotes the end of an input sequence or the border between input sequences.

> A sentinel value denotes the end of a data set, but it is not part of the data.

```
salary = in.nextDouble();
if (salary != -1)
{
   sum = sum + salary;
   count++;
}
```

We stay in the loop while the sentinel value is not detected.

```
while (salary != -1)
{
   . . .
}
```

There is just one problem: When the loop is entered for the first time, no data value has been read. We must make sure to initialize salary with some value other than the sentinel:

```
double salary = 0;
// Any value other than –1 will do
```

After the loop has finished, we compute and print the average. Here is the complete program:

section_5/SentinelDemo.java

```
1   import java.util.Scanner;
2
3   /**
4      This program prints the average of salary values that are terminated with a sentinel.
5   */
```

```
 6   public class SentinelDemo
 7   {
 8      public static void main(String[] args)
 9      {
10         double sum = 0;
11         int count = 0;
12         double salary = 0;
13         System.out.print("Enter salaries, -1 to finish: ");
14         Scanner in = new Scanner(System.in);
15
16         // Process data until the sentinel is entered
17
18         while (salary != -1)
19         {
20            salary = in.nextDouble();
21            if (salary != -1)
22            {
23               sum = sum + salary;
24               count++;
25            }
26         }
27
28         // Compute and print the average
29
30         if (count > 0)
31         {
32            double average = sum / count;
33            System.out.println("Average salary: " + average);
34         }
35         else
36         {
37            System.out.println("No data");
38         }
39      }
40   }
```

Program Run

```
Enter salaries, -1 to finish: 10 10 40 -1
Average salary: 20
```

Some programmers don't like the "trick" of initializing the input variable with a value other than the sentinel. Another approach is to use a Boolean variable:

```
System.out.print("Enter salaries, -1 to finish: ");
boolean done = false;
while (!done)
{
   value = in.nextDouble();
   if (value == -1)
   {
      done = true;
   }
   else
   {
      Process value.
   }
}
```

You can use a Boolean variable to control a loop. Set the variable before entering the loop, then set it to the opposite to leave the loop.

Special Topic 4.1 on page 160 shows an alternative mechanism for leaving such a loop.

Now consider the case in which any number (positive, negative, or zero) can be an acceptable input. In such a situation, you must use a sentinel that is not a number (such as the letter Q). As you have seen in Section 3.8, the condition

```
in.hasNextDouble()
```

is `false` if the next input is not a floating-point number. Therefore, you can read and process a set of inputs with the following loop:

```
System.out.print("Enter values, Q to quit: ");
while (in.hasNextDouble())
{
   value = in.nextDouble();
   Process value.
}
```

SELF CHECK

21. What does the `SentinelDemo.java` program print when the user immediately types –1 when prompted for a value?

22. Why does the `SentinelDemo.java` program have *two* checks of the form

```
salary != -1
```

23. What would happen if the declaration of the `salary` variable in `SentinelDemo.java` was changed to

```
double salary = -1;
```

24. In the last example of this section, we prompt the user "Enter values, Q to quit." What happens when the user enters a different letter?

25. What is wrong with the following loop for reading a sequence of values?

```
System.out.print("Enter values, Q to quit: ");
do
{
   double value = in.nextDouble();
   sum = sum + value;
   count++;
}
while (in.hasNextDouble());
```

Practice It   Now you can try these exercises at the end of the chapter: R4.13, P4.27, P4.28.

Special Topic 4.1

The Loop-and-a-Half Problem and the break Statement

Consider again this loop for processing inputs until a sentinel value has been reached:

```
boolean done = false;
while (!done)
{
   double value = in.nextDouble();
   if (value == -1)
   {
      done = true;
   }
   else
   {
      Process value.
   }
}
```

The actual test for loop termination is in the middle of the loop, not at the top. This is called a **loop and a half** because one must go halfway into the loop before knowing whether one needs to terminate.

As an alternative, you can use the break reserved word.

```
while (true)
{
   double value = in.nextDouble();
   if (value == -1) { break; }
   Process value.
}
```

The break statement breaks out of the enclosing loop, independent of the loop condition. When the break statement is encountered, the loop is terminated, and the statement following the loop is executed.

In the loop-and-a-half case, break statements can be beneficial. But it is difficult to lay down clear rules as to when they are safe and when they should be avoided. We do not use the break statement in this book.

Special Topic 4.2

Redirection of Input and Output

Consider the SentinelDemo program that computes the average value of an input sequence. If you use such a program, then it is quite likely that you already have the values in a file, and it seems a shame that you have to type them all in again. The command line interface of your operating system provides a way to link a file to the input of a program, as if all the characters in the file had actually been typed by a user. If you type

> Use input redirection to read input from a file. Use output redirection to capture program output in a file.

```
java SentinelDemo < numbers.txt
```

the program is executed, but it no longer expects input from the keyboard. All input commands get their input from the file numbers.txt. This process is called *input redirection*.

Input redirection is an excellent tool for testing programs. When you develop a program and fix its bugs, it is boring to keep entering the same input every time you run the program. Spend a few minutes putting the inputs into a file, and use redirection.

You can also redirect output. In this program, that is not terribly useful. If you run

```
java SentinelDemo < numbers.txt > output.txt
```

the file output.txt contains the input prompts and the output, such as

```
Enter salaries, -1 to finish: Enter salaries, -1 to finish:
Enter salaries, -1 to finish: Enter salaries, -1 to finish:
Average salary: 15
```

However, redirecting output is obviously useful for programs that produce lots of output. You can format or print the file containing the output.

VIDEO EXAMPLE 4.1   ### Evaluating a Cell Phone Plan

In this Video Example, you will learn how to design a program that computes the cost of a cell phone plan from actual usage data.

✚ Available online in WileyPLUS and at www.wiley.com/college/horstmann.

4.6 Problem Solving: Storyboards

When you design a program that interacts with a user, you need to make a plan for that interaction. What information does the user provide, and in which order? What information will your program display, and in which format? What should happen when there is an error? When does the program quit?

This planning is similar to the development of a movie or a computer game, where *storyboards* are used to plan action sequences. A storyboard is made up of panels that show a sketch of each step. Annotations explain what is happening and note any special situations. Storyboards are also used to develop software—see Figure 6.

Making a storyboard is very helpful when you begin designing a program. You need to ask yourself which information you need in order to compute the answers that the program user wants. You need to decide how to present those answers. These are important considerations that you want to settle before you design an algorithm for computing the answers.

Let's look at a simple example. We want to write a program that helps users with questions such as "How many tablespoons are in a pint?" or "How many inches are 30 centimeters?"

What information does the user provide?

- The quantity and unit to convert from
- The unit to convert to

What if there is more than one quantity? A user may have a whole table of centimeter values that should be converted into inches.

What if the user enters units that our program doesn't know how to handle, such as ångström?

What if the user asks for impossible conversions, such as inches to gallons?

> A storyboard consists of annotated sketches for each step in an action sequence.

> Developing a storyboard helps you understand the inputs and outputs that are required for a program.

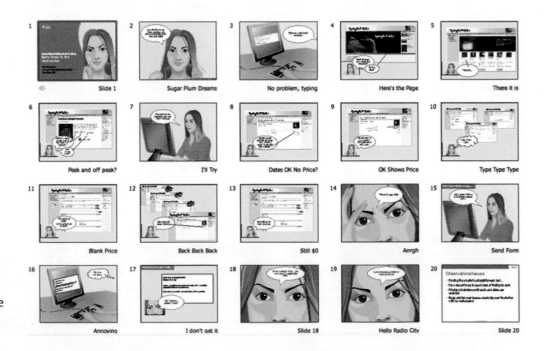

Figure 6
Storyboard for the Design of a Web Application

Let's get started with a storyboard panel. It is a good idea to write the user inputs in a different color. (Underline them if you don't have a color pen handy.)

Converting a Sequence of Values

What unit do you want to convert from? cm
What unit do you want to convert to? in
Enter values, terminated by zero ———————— Allows conversion of multiple values
30
30 cm = 11.81 in ————
100   ⌐ Format makes clear what got converted
100 cm = 39.37 in
0
What unit do you want to convert from?

The storyboard shows how we deal with a potential confusion. A user who wants to know how many inches are 30 centimeters may not read the first prompt carefully and specify inches. But then the output is "30 in = 76.2 cm", alerting the user to the problem.

The storyboard also raises an issue. How is the user supposed to know that "cm" and "in" are valid units? Would "centimeter" and "inches" also work? What happens when the user enters a wrong unit? Let's make another storyboard to demonstrate error handling.

Handling Unknown Units (needs improvement)

What unit do you want to convert from? om
What unit do you want to convert to? inches
Sorry, unknown unit.
What unit do you want to convert to? inch
Sorry, unknown unit.
What unit do you want to convert to? grrr

To eliminate frustration, it is better to list the units that the user can supply.

From unit (in, ft, mi, mm, cm, m, km, oz, lb, g, kg, tsp, tbsp, pint, gal): cm
To unit: in ——
           ⌐———— No need to list the units again

We switched to a shorter prompt to make room for all the unit names. Exercise R4.21 explores a different alternative.

There is another issue that we haven't addressed yet. How does the user quit the program? The first storyboard suggests that the program will go on forever.

We can ask the user after seeing the sentinel that terminates an input sequence.

> **Exiting the Program**
>
> From unit (in, ft, mi, mm, cm, m, km, oz, lb, g, kg, tsp, tbsp, pint, gal): cm
> To unit: in
> Enter values, terminated by zero
> 30
> 30 cm = 11.81 in
> 0
> More conversions (y, n)? n ⟵ Sentinel triggers the prompt to exit
> (Program exits)

As you can see from this case study, a storyboard is essential for developing a working program. You need to know the flow of the user interaction in order to structure your program.

SELF CHECK

26. Provide a storyboard panel for a program that reads a number of test scores and prints the average score. The program only needs to process one set of scores. Don't worry about error handling.

27. Google has a simple interface for converting units. You just type the question, and you get the answer.

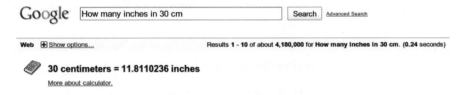

Make storyboards for an equivalent interface in a Java program. Show a scenario in which all goes well, and show the handling of two kinds of errors.

28. Consider a modification of the program in Self Check 26. Suppose we want to drop the lowest score before computing the average. Provide a storyboard for the situation in which a user only provides one score.

29. What is the problem with implementing the following storyboard in Java?

> **Computing Multiple Averages**
>
> Enter scores: 90 80 90 100 80
> The average is 88
> Enter scores: 100 70 70 100 80
> The average is 88
> Enter scores: -1 ⟵ -1 is used as a sentinel to exit the program
> (Program exits)

30. Produce a storyboard for a program that compares the growth of a $10,000 investment for a given number of years under two interest rates.

Practice It Now you can try these exercises at the end of the chapter: R4.21, R4.22, R4.23.

4.7 Common Loop Algorithms

In the following sections, we discuss some of the most common algorithms that are implemented as loops. You can use them as starting points for your loop designs.

4.7.1 Sum and Average Value

To compute an average, keep a total and a count of all values.

Computing the sum of a number of inputs is a very common task. Keep a *running total*, a variable to which you add each input value. Of course, the total should be initialized with 0.

```
double total = 0;
while (in.hasNextDouble())
{
    double input = in.nextDouble();
    total = total + input;
}
```

Note that the total variable is declared outside the loop. We want the loop to update a single variable. The input variable is declared inside the loop. A separate variable is created for each input and removed at the end of each loop iteration.

To compute an average, count how many values you have, and divide by the count. Be sure to check that the count is not zero.

```
double total = 0;
int count = 0;
while (in.hasNextDouble())
{
    double input = in.nextDouble();
    total = total + input;
    count++;
}
double average = 0;
if (count > 0)
{
    average = total / count;
}
```

4.7.2 Counting Matches

To count values that fulfill a condition, check all values and increment a counter for each match.

You often want to know how many values fulfill a particular condition. For example, you may want to count how many spaces are in a string. Keep a *counter*, a variable that is initialized with 0 and incremented whenever there is a match.

```
int spaces = 0;
for (int i = 0; i < str.length(); i++)
{
    char ch = str.charAt(i);
    if (ch == ' ')
    {
        spaces++;
    }
}
```

For example, if str is "My Fair Lady", spaces is incremented twice (when i is 2 and 7).

Note that the spaces variable is declared outside the loop. We want the loop to update a single variable. The ch variable is declared inside the loop. A separate variable is created for each iteration and removed at the end of each loop iteration.

This loop can also be used for scanning inputs. The following loop reads text, a word at a time, and counts the number of words with at most three letters:

```java
int shortWords = 0;
while (in.hasNext())
{
    String input = in.next();
    if (input.length() <= 3)
    {
        shortWords++;
    }
}
```

In a loop that counts matches, a counter is incremented whenever a match is found.

4.7.3 Finding the First Match

When you count the values that fulfill a condition, you need to look at all values. However, if your task is to find a match, then you can stop as soon as the condition is fulfilled.

Here is a loop that finds the first space in a string. Because we do not visit all elements in the string, a while loop is a better choice than a for loop:

```java
boolean found = false;
char ch = '?';
int position = 0;
while (!found && position < str.length())
{
    ch = str.charAt(position);
    if (ch == ' ') { found = true; }
    else { position++; }
}
```

If a match was found, then found is true, ch is the first matching character, and position is the index of the first match. If the loop did not find a match, then found remains false after the end of the loop.

Note that the variable ch is declared *outside* the while loop because you may want to use the input after the loop has finished. If it had been declared inside the loop body, you would not be able to use it outside the loop.

When searching, you look at items until a match is found.

4.7.4 Prompting Until a Match is Found

In the preceding example, we searched a string for a character that matches a condition. You can apply the same process to user input. Suppose you are asking a user to enter a positive value < 100. Keep asking until the user provides a correct input:

```
boolean valid = false;
double input = 0;
while (!valid)
{
   System.out.print("Please enter a positive value < 100: ");
   input = in.nextDouble();
   if (0 < input && input < 100) { valid = true; }
   else { System.out.println("Invalid input."); }
}
```

Note that the variable input is declared *outside* the while loop because you will want to use the input after the loop has finished.

4.7.5 Maximum and Minimum

To find the largest value, update the largest value seen so far whenever you see a larger one.

To compute the largest value in a sequence, keep a variable that stores the largest element that you have encountered, and update it when you find a larger one.

```
double largest = in.nextDouble();
while (in.hasNextDouble())
{
   double input = in.nextDouble();
   if (input > largest)
   {
      largest = input;
   }
}
```

This algorithm requires that there is at least one input.

To compute the smallest value, simply reverse the comparison:

```
double smallest = in.nextDouble();
while (in.hasNextDouble())
{
   double input = in.nextDouble();
   if (input < smallest)
   {
      smallest = input;
   }
}
```

To find the height of the tallest bus rider, remember the largest value so far, and update it whenever you see a taller one.

4.7.6 Comparing Adjacent Values

To compare adjacent inputs, store the preceding input in a variable.

When processing a sequence of values in a loop, you sometimes need to compare a value with the value that just preceded it. For example, suppose you want to check whether a sequence of inputs contains adjacent duplicates such as 1 7 2 9 9 4 9.

Now you face a challenge. Consider the typical loop for reading a value:

```java
double input;
while (in.hasNextDouble())
{
    input = in.nextDouble();
    . . .
}
```

How can you compare the current input with the preceding one? At any time, input contains the current input, overwriting the previous one.

The answer is to store the previous input, like this:

```java
double input = 0;
while (in.hasNextDouble())
{
    double previous = input;
    input = in.nextDouble();
    if (input == previous)
    {
        System.out.println("Duplicate input");
    }
}
```

When comparing adjacent values, store the previous value in a variable.

One problem remains. When the loop is entered for the first time, input has not yet been read. You can solve this problem with an initial input operation outside the loop:

```java
double input = in.nextDouble();
while (in.hasNextDouble())
{
    double previous = input;
    input = in.nextDouble();
    if (input == previous)
    {
        System.out.println("Duplicate input");
    }
}
```

ONLINE EXAMPLE

A program using common loop algorithms.

SELF CHECK

31. What total is computed when no user input is provided in the algorithm in Section 4.7.1?

32. How do you compute the total of all positive inputs?

33. What are the values of position and ch when no match is found in the algorithm in Section 4.7.3?

34. What is wrong with the following loop for finding the position of the first space in a string?

```java
boolean found = false;
for (int position = 0; !found && position < str.length(); position++)
{
```

```
        char ch = str.charAt(position);
        if (ch == ' ') { found = true; }
    }
```

35. How do you find the position of the *last* space in a string?

36. What happens with the algorithm in Section 4.7.5 when no input is provided at all? How can you overcome that problem?

Practice It   Now you can try these exercises at the end of the chapter: P4.5, P4.9, P4.10.

HOW TO 4.1   **Writing a Loop**

This How To walks you through the process of implementing a loop statement. We will illustrate the steps with the following example problem:

Read twelve temperature values (one for each month), and display the number of the month with the highest temperature. For example, according to http://worldclimate.com, the average maximum temperatures for Death Valley are (in order by month, in degrees Celsius):

  18.2 22.6 26.4 31.1 36.6 42.2 45.7 44.5 40.2 33.1 24.2 17.6

In this case, the month with the highest temperature (45.7 degrees Celsius) is July, and the program should display 7.

Step 1   Decide what work must be done *inside* the loop.

Every loop needs to do some kind of repetitive work, such as

- Reading another item.
- Updating a value (such as a bank balance or total).
- Incrementing a counter.

If you can't figure out what needs to go inside the loop, start by writing down the steps that you would take if you solved the problem by hand. For example, with the temperature reading problem, you might write

  Read first value.
  Read second value.
  If second value is higher than the first, set highest temperature to that value, highest month to 2.
  Read next value.
  If value is higher than the first and second, set highest temperature to that value, highest month to 3.
  Read next value.
  If value is higher than the highest temperature seen so far, set highest temperature to that value,
      highest month to 4.
  . . .

Now look at these steps and reduce them to a set of *uniform* actions that can be placed into the loop body. The first action is easy:

  Read next value.

The next action is trickier. In our description, we used tests "higher than the first", "higher than the first and second", "higher than the highest temperature seen so far". We need to settle on one test that works for all iterations. The last formulation is the most general.

Similarly, we must find a general way of setting the highest month. We need a variable that stores the current month, running from 1 to 12. Then we can formulate the second loop action:

If value is higher than the highest temperature, set highest temperature to that value,
highest month to current month.

Altogether our loop is

Repeat
    Read next value.
    If value is higher than the highest temperature,
        set highest temperature to that value,
        set highest month to current month.
    Increment current month.

Step 2   Specify the loop condition.

What goal do you want to reach in your loop? Typical examples are

- Has a counter reached its final value?
- Have you read the last input value?
- Has a value reached a given threshold?

In our example, we simply want the current month to reach 12.

Step 3   Determine the loop type.

We distinguish between two major loop types. A *count-controlled* loop is executed a definite number of times. In an *event-controlled* loop, the number of iterations is not known in advance—the loop is executed until some event happens.

Count-controlled loops can be implemented as `for` statements. For other loops, consider the loop condition. Do you need to complete one iteration of the loop body before you can tell when to terminate the loop? In that case, choose a `do` loop. Otherwise, use a `while` loop.

Sometimes, the condition for terminating a loop changes in the middle of the loop body. In that case, you can use a Boolean variable that specifies when you are ready to leave the loop. Follow this pattern:

```
boolean done = false;
while (!done)
{
   Do some work.
   If all work has been completed
   {
      done = true;
   }
   else
   {
    Do more work.
   }
}
```

Such a variable is called a **flag**.

In summary,

- If you know in advance how many times a loop is repeated, use a `for` loop.
- If the loop body must be executed at least once, use a `do` loop.
- Otherwise, use a `while` loop.

In our example, we read 12 temperature values. Therefore, we choose a `for` loop.

Step 4   Set up variables for entering the loop for the first time.

List all variables that are used and updated in the loop, and determine how to initialize them. Commonly, counters are initialized with 0 or 1, totals with 0.

In our example, the variables are

```
current month
highest value
highest month
```

We need to be careful how we set up the highest temperature value. We can't simply set it to 0. After all, our program needs to work with temperature values from Antarctica, all of which may be negative.

A good option is to set the highest temperature value to the first input value. Of course, then we need to remember to read in only 11 more values, with the current month starting at 2.

We also need to initialize the highest month with 1. After all, in an Australian city, we may never find a month that is warmer than January.

Step 5　Process the result after the loop has finished.

In many cases, the desired result is simply a variable that was updated in the loop body. For example, in our temperature program, the result is the highest month. Sometimes, the loop computes values that contribute to the final result. For example, suppose you are asked to average the temperatures. Then the loop should compute the sum, not the average. After the loop has completed, you are ready to compute the average: divide the sum by the number of inputs.

Here is our complete loop.

```
Read first value; store as highest value.
highest month = 1
For current month from 2 to 12
    Read next value.
    If value is higher than the highest value
        Set highest value to that value.
        Set highest month to current month.
```

Step 6　Trace the loop with typical examples.

Hand trace your loop code, as described in Section 4.2. Choose example values that are not too complex—executing the loop 3–5 times is enough to check for the most common errors. Pay special attention when entering the loop for the first and last time.

Sometimes, you want to make a slight modification to make tracing feasible. For example, when hand-tracing the investment doubling problem, use an interest rate of 20 percent rather than 5 percent. When hand-tracing the temperature loop, use 4 data values, not 12.

Let's say the data are 22.6 36.6 44.5 24.2. Here is the walkthrough:

current month	current value	highest month	highest value
		1	22.6
2	36.6	2	36.6
3	44.5	3	44.5
4	24.2		

The trace demonstrates that **highest month** and **highest value** are properly set.

Step 7　Implement the loop in Java.

Here's the loop for our example. Exercise P4.4 asks you to complete the program.

```java
double highestValue;
highestValue = in.nextDouble();
int highestMonth = 1;
```

```
for (int currentMonth = 2; currentMonth <= 12; currentMonth++)
{
   double nextValue = in.nextDouble();
   if (nextValue > highestValue)
   {
      highestValue = nextValue;
      highestMonth = currentMonth;
   }
}
System.out.println(highestMonth);
```

WORKED EXAMPLE 4.1   **Credit Card Processing**

This Worked Example uses a loop to remove spaces from a credit card number.

4.8 Nested Loops

When the body of a loop contains another loop, the loops are nested. A typical use of nested loops is printing a table with rows and columns.

In Section 3.4, you saw how to nest two if statements. Similarly, complex iterations sometimes require a **nested loop**: a loop inside another loop statement. When processing tables, nested loops occur naturally. An outer loop iterates over all rows of the table. An inner loop deals with the columns in the current row.

In this section you will see how to print a table. For simplicity, we will simply print the powers of x, x^n, as in the table at right.

Here is the pseudocode for printing the table:

Print table header.
For x from 1 to 10
　Print table row.
　Print new line.

How do you print a table row? You need to print a value for each exponent. This requires a second loop.

For n from 1 to 4
　Print x^n.

x^1	x^2	x^3	x^4
1	1	1	1
2	4	8	16
3	9	27	81
...	...	...	...
10	100	1000	10000

This loop must be placed inside the preceding loop. We say that the inner loop is *nested* inside the outer loop.

The hour and minute displays in a digital clock are an example of nested loops. The hours loop 12 times, and for each hour, the minutes loop 60 times.

➕ Available online in WileyPLUS and at www.wiley.com/college/horstmann.

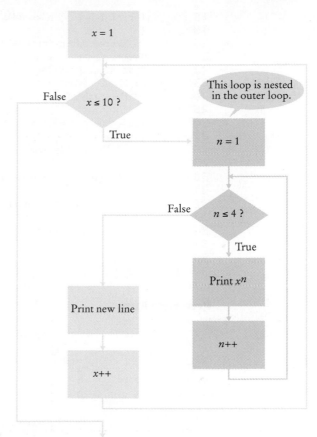

Figure 7
Flowchart of a Nested Loop

There are 10 rows in the outer loop. For each x, the program prints four columns in the inner loop (see Figure 7). Thus, a total of $10 \times 4 = 40$ values are printed.

Following is the complete program. Note that we also use loops to print the table header. However, those loops are not nested.

section_8/PowerTable.java

```
1   /**
2       This program prints a table of powers of x.
3   */
4   public class PowerTable
5   {
6      public static void main(String[] args)
7      {
8         final int NMAX = 4;
9         final double XMAX = 10;
10
11        // Print table header
12
13        for (int n = 1; n <= NMAX; n++)
14        {
15           System.out.printf("%10d", n);
16        }
17        System.out.println();
```

```
18      for (int n = 1; n <= NMAX; n++)
19      {
20         System.out.printf("%10s", "x ");
21      }
22      System.out.println();
23
24      // Print table body
25
26      for (double x = 1; x <= XMAX; x++)
27      {
28         // Print table row
29
30         for (int n = 1; n <= NMAX; n++)
31         {
32            System.out.printf("%10.0f", Math.pow(x, n));
33         }
34         System.out.println();
35      }
36   }
37 }
```

Program Run

1	2	3	4
x	x	x	x
1	1	1	1
2	4	8	16
3	9	27	81
4	16	64	256
5	25	125	625
6	36	216	1296
7	49	343	2401
8	64	512	4096
9	81	729	6561
10	100	1000	10000

SELF CHECK

37. Why is there a statement `System.out.println();` in the outer loop but not in the inner loop?

38. How would you change the program to display all powers from x^0 to x^5?

39. If you make the change in Self Check 38, how many values are displayed?

40. What do the following nested loops display?

```
for (int i = 0; i < 3; i++)
{
   for (int j = 0; j < 4; j++)
   {
      System.out.print(i + j);
   }
   System.out.println();
}
```

41. Write nested loops that make the following pattern of brackets:

```
[][][][]
[][][][]
[][][][]
```

Practice It Now you can try these exercises at the end of the chapter: R4.27, P4.19, P4.21.

Table 3 Nested Loop Examples		
Nested Loops	Output	Explanation

```for (i = 1; i <= 3; i++)```
 ```{```
    ```for (j = 1; j <= 4; j++) { Print "*" }```
    ```System.out.println();```
 ```}```
	```****```
	 ```****```
	 ```****```
		Prints 3 rows of 4 asterisks each.

```for (i = 1; i <= 4; i++)```
 ```{```
    ```for (j = 1; j <= 3; j++) { Print "*" }```
    ```System.out.println();```
 ```}```
	```***```
	 ```***```
	 ```***```
	 ```***```
		Prints 4 rows of 3 asterisks each.

```for (i = 1; i <= 4; i++)```
 ```{```
    ```for (j = 1; j <= i; j++) { Print "*" }```
    ```System.out.println();```
 ```}```
	```*```
	 ```**```
	 ```***```
	 ```****```
		Prints 4 rows of lengths 1, 2, 3, and 4.

```for (i = 1; i <= 3; i++)```
 ```{```
    ```for (j = 1; j <= 5; j++)```
    ```{```
       ```if (j % 2 == 0) { Print "*" }```
       ```else { Print "-" }```
    ```}```
    ```System.out.println();```
 ```}```
	```-*-*-```
	 ```-*-*-```
	 ```-*-*-```
		Prints asterisks in even columns, dashes in odd columns.

```for (i = 1; i <= 3; i++)```
 ```{```
    ```for (j = 1; j <= 5; j++)```
    ```{```
       ```if (i % 2 == j % 2) { Print "*" }```
       ```else { Print " " }```
    ```}```
    ```System.out.println();```
 ```}```
	```* * *```
	 ```* *```
	 ```* * *```
		Prints a checkerboard pattern.

WORKED EXAMPLE 4.2   Manipulating the Pixels in an Image

This Worked Example shows how to use nested loops for manipulating the pixels in an image. The outer loop traverses the rows of the image, and the inner loop accesses each pixel of a row.

⊕ Available online in WileyPLUS and at www.wiley.com/college/horstmann.

4.9 Application: Random Numbers and Simulations

In a simulation, you use the computer to simulate an activity.

A *simulation program* uses the computer to simulate an activity in the real world (or an imaginary one). Simulations are commonly used for predicting climate change, analyzing traffic, picking stocks, and many other applications in science and business. In many simulations, one or more loops are used to modify the state of a system and observe the changes. You will see examples in the following sections.

4.9.1 Generating Random Numbers

Many events in the real world are difficult to predict with absolute precision, yet we can sometimes know the average behavior quite well. For example, a store may know from experience that a customer arrives every five minutes. Of course, that is an average—customers don't arrive in five minute intervals. To accurately model customer traffic, you want to take that random fluctuation into account. Now, how can you run such a simulation in the computer?

You can introduce randomness by calling the random number generator.

The Java library has a *random number generator*, which produces numbers that appear to be completely random. Calling Math.random() yields a random floating-point number that is ≥ 0 and < 1. Call Math.random() again, and you get a different number.

The following program calls Math.random() ten times.

section_9_1/RandomDemo.java

```
1   /**
2       This program prints ten random numbers between 0 and 1.
3   */
4   public class RandomDemo
5   {
6      public static void main(String[] args)
7      {
8         for (int i = 1; i <= 10; i++)
9         {
10            double r = Math.random();
11            System.out.println(r);
12         }
13      }
14   }
```

Program Run

```
0.6513550469421886
0.920193662882893
0.6904776061289993
0.8862828776788884
0.7730177555323139
0.3020238718668635
0.0028504531690907164
0.9099983981705169
0.1151636530517488
0.1592258808929058
```

Actually, the numbers are not completely random. They are drawn from sequences of numbers that don't repeat for a long time. These sequences are actually computed from fairly simple formulas; they just behave like random numbers (see Exercise P4.25). For that reason, they are often called **pseudorandom** numbers.

4.9.2 Simulating Die Tosses

In actual applications, you need to transform the output from the random number generator into different ranges. For example, to simulate the throw of a die, you need random integers between 1 and 6.

Here is the general recipe for computing random integers between two bounds a and b. As you know from Programming Tip 4.3 on page 156, there are b - a + 1 values between a and b, including the bounds themselves. First compute

```
(int) (Math.random() * (b - a + 1))
```

to obtain a random integer between 0 and b - a, then add a, yielding a random value between a and b:

```
int r = (int) (Math.random() * (b - a + 1)) + a;
```

Here is a program that simulates the throw of a pair of dice:

section_9_2/Dice.java

```java
1   /**
2       This program simulates tosses of a pair of dice.
3   */
4   public class Dice
5   {
6      public static void main(String[] args)
7      {
8         for (int i = 1; i <= 10; i++)
9         {
10           // Generate two random numbers between 1 and 6
11
12           int d1 = (int) (Math.random() * 6) + 1;
13           int d2 = (int) (Math.random() * 6) + 1;
14           System.out.println(d1 + " " + d2);
15        }
16        System.out.println();
17     }
18  }
```

Program Run

```
5 1
2 1
1 2
5 1
1 2
6 4
4 4
6 1
6 3
5 2
```

4.9.3 The Monte Carlo Method

The Monte Carlo method is an ingenious method for finding approximate solutions to problems that cannot be precisely solved. (The method is named after the famous casino in Monte Carlo.) Here is a typical example. It is difficult to compute the number π, but you can approximate it quite well with the following simulation.

Simulate shooting a dart into a square surrounding a circle of radius 1. That is easy: generate random x and y coordinates between -1 and 1.

If the generated point lies inside the circle, we count it as a *hit*. That is the case when $x^2 + y^2 \leq 1$. Because our shots are entirely random, we expect that the ratio of *hits / tries* is approximately equal to the ratio of the areas of the circle and the square, that is, $\pi / 4$. Therefore, our estimate for π is $4 \times$ *hits / tries*. This method yields an estimate for π, using nothing but simple arithmetic.

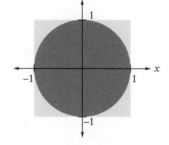

To generate a random floating-point value between -1 and 1, you compute:

```
double r = Math.random(); // 0 ≤ r < 1
double x = -1 + 2 * r; // −1 ≤ x < 1
```

As r ranges from 0 (inclusive) to 1 (exclusive), x ranges from $-1 + 2 \times 0 = -1$ (inclusive) to $-1 + 2 \times 1 = 1$ (exclusive). In our application, it does not matter that x never reaches 1. The points that fulfill the equation $x = 1$ lie on a line with area 0.

Here is the program that carries out the simulation:

section_9_3/MonteCarlo.java

```
1   /**
2       This program computes an estimate of pi by simulating dart throws onto a square.
3   */
4   public class MonteCarlo
5   {
6      public static void main(String[] args)
7      {
8         final int TRIES = 10000;
9
10        int hits = 0;
11        for (int i = 1; i <= TRIES; i++)
12        {
13           // Generate two random numbers between -1 and 1
14
15           double r = Math.random();
16           double x = -1 + 2 * r; // Between -1 and 1
17           r = Math.random();
18           double y = -1 + 2 * r;
19
```

```
20              // Check whether the point lies in the unit circle
21
22              if (x * x + y * y <= 1) { hits++; }
23          }
24
25          /*
26              The ratio hits / tries is approximately the same as the ratio
27              circle area / square area = pi / 4
28          */
29
30          double piEstimate = 4.0 * hits / TRIES;
31          System.out.println("Estimate for pi: " + piEstimate);
32      }
33  }
```

Program Run

```
Estimate for pi: 3.1504
```

SELF CHECK

42. How do you simulate a coin toss with the `Math.random()` method?

43. How do you simulate the picking of a random playing card?

44. Why does the loop body in `Dice.java` call `Math.random()` twice?

45. In many games, you throw a pair of dice to get a value between 2 and 12. What is wrong with this simulated throw of a pair of dice?

    ```
    int sum = (int) (Math.random() * 11) + 2;
    ```

46. How do you generate a random floating-point number ≥ 0 and < 100?

Practice It   Now you can try these exercises at the end of the chapter: R4.28, P4.7, P4.24.

Special Topic 4.3

Drawing Graphical Shapes

In Java, it is easy to produce simple drawings such as the one in Figure 8. By writing programs that draw such patterns, you can practice programming loops. For now, we give you a program outline into which you place your drawing code. The program outline also contains the necessary code for displaying a window containing your drawing. You need not look at that code now. It will be discussed in detail in Chapter 10.

Your drawing instructions go inside the draw method:

```
public class TwoRowsOfSquares
{
    public static void draw(Graphics g)
    {
        Drawing instructions
    }
    . . .
}
```

Figure 8   Two Rows of Squares

When the window is shown, the draw method is called, and your drawing instructions will be executed.

The draw method receives an object of type Graphics. The Graphics object has methods for drawing shapes. It also remembers the color that is used for drawing operations. You can think of the Graphics object as the equivalent of System.out for drawing shapes instead of printing values.

Table 4 shows useful methods of the Graphics class.

Table 4 Graphics Methods

Method	Result	Notes
g.drawRect(x, y, width, height)		(x, y) is the top left corner.
g.drawOval(x, y, width, height)		(x, y) is the top left corner of the box that bounds the ellipse. To draw a circle, use the same value for width and height.
g.fillRect(x, y, width, height)		The rectangle is filled in.
g.fillOval(x, y, width, height)		The oval is filled in.
g.drawLine(x1, y1, x2, y2)		(x1, y1) and (x2, y2) are the endpoints.
g.drawString("Message", x, y)	Message Basepoint Baseline	(x, y) is the basepoint.
g.setColor(color)	From now on, draw or fill methods will use this color.	Use Color.RED, Color.GREEN, Color.BLUE, and so on. (See Table 10.1 for a complete list of predefined colors.)

The program below draws the squares shown in Figure 8. When you want to produce your own drawings, make a copy of this program and modify it. Replace the drawing tasks in the draw method. Rename the class (for example, Spiral instead of TwoRowsOfSquares).

special_topic_3/TwoRowsOfSquares.java

```
1   import java.awt.Color;
2   import java.awt.Graphics;
3   import javax.swing.JFrame;
4   import javax.swing.JComponent;
5
6   /**
7      This program draws two rows of squares.
8   */
9   public class TwoRowsOfSquares
10  {
```

```
11  public static void draw(Graphics g)
12  {
13     final int width = 20;
14     g.setColor(Color.BLUE);
15
16     // Top row. Note that the top left corner of the drawing has coordinates (0, 0)
17     int x = 0;
18     int y = 0;
19     for (int i = 0; i < 10; i++)
20     {
21        g.fillRect(x, y, width, width);
22        x = x + 2 * width;
23     }
24     // Second row, offset from the first one
25     x = width;
26     y = width;
27     for (int i = 0; i < 10; i++)
28     {
29        g.fillRect(x, y, width, width);
30        x = x + 2 * width;
31     }
32  }
33
34  public static void main(String[] args)
35  {
36     // Do not look at the code in the main method
37     // Your code will go into the draw method above
38
39     JFrame frame = new JFrame();
40
41     final int FRAME_WIDTH = 400;
42     final int FRAME_HEIGHT = 400;
43
44     frame.setSize(FRAME_WIDTH, FRAME_HEIGHT);
45     frame.setDefaultCloseOperation(JFrame.EXIT_ON_CLOSE);
46
47     JComponent component = new JComponent()
48     {
49        public void paintComponent(Graphics graph)
50        {
51           draw(graph);
52        }
53     };
54
55     frame.add(component);
56     frame.setVisible(true);
57  }
58  }
```

VIDEO EXAMPLE 4.2   **Drawing a Spiral**

In this Video Example, you will see how to develop a program
that draws a spiral.

⊕ Available online in WileyPLUS and at www.wiley.com/college/horstmann.

Random Fact 4.2 Software Piracy

As you read this, you will have written a few computer programs and experienced firsthand how much effort it takes to write even the humblest of programs. Writing a real software product, such as a financial application or a computer game, takes a lot of time and money. Few people, and fewer companies, are going to spend that kind of time and money if they don't have a reasonable chance to make more money from their effort. (Actually, some companies give away their software in the hope that users will upgrade to more elaborate paid versions. Other companies give away the software that enables users to read and use files but sell the software needed to create those files. Finally, there are individuals who donate their time, out of enthusiasm, and produce programs that you can copy freely.)

When selling software, a company must rely on the honesty of its customers. It is an easy matter for an unscrupulous person to make copies of computer programs without paying for them. In most countries that is illegal. Most governments provide legal protection, such as copyright laws and patents, to encourage the development of new products. Countries that tolerate widespread piracy have found

that they have an ample cheap supply of foreign software, but no local manufacturers willing to design good software for their own citizens, such as word processors in the local script or financial programs adapted to the local tax laws.

When a mass market for software first appeared, vendors were enraged by the money they lost through piracy. They tried to fight back by various schemes to ensure that only the legitimate owner could use the software, such as *dongles*—devices that must be attached to a printer port before the software will run. Legitimate users hated these measures. They paid for the software, but they had to suffer through inconveniences, such as having multiple dongles stick out from their computer. In the United States, market pressures forced most vendors to give up on these copy protection schemes, but they are still commonplace in other parts of the world.

Because it is so easy and inexpensive to pirate software, and the chance of being found out is minimal, you have to make a moral choice for yourself. If a package that you would really like to have is too expensive for your budget, do you steal it, or do you stay

honest and get by with a more affordable product?

Of course, piracy is not limited to software. The same issues arise for other digital products as well. You may have had the opportunity to obtain copies of songs or movies without payment. Or you may have been frustrated by a copy protection device on your music player that made it difficult for you to listen to songs that you paid for. Admittedly, it can be difficult to have a lot of sympathy for a musical ensemble whose publisher charges a lot of money for what seems to have been very little effort on their part, at least when compared to the effort that goes into designing and implementing a software package. Nevertheless, it seems only fair that artists and authors receive some compensation for their efforts. How to pay artists, authors, and programmers fairly, without burdening honest customers, is an unsolved problem at the time of this writing, and many computer scientists are engaged in research in this area.

CHAPTER SUMMARY

Explain the flow of execution in a loop.

- A loop executes instructions repeatedly while a condition is true.
- An off-by-one error is a common error when programming loops. Think through simple test cases to avoid this type of error.

Use the technique of hand-tracing to analyze the behavior of a program.

- Hand-tracing is a simulation of code execution in which you step through instructions and track the values of the variables.
- Hand-tracing can help you understand how an unfamiliar algorithm works.
- Hand-tracing can show errors in code or pseudocode.

Use for loops for implementing count-controlled loops.

- The for loop is used when a value runs from a starting point to an ending point with a constant increment or decrement.

Choose between the while loop and the do loop.

- The do loop is appropriate when the loop body must be executed at least once.

Implement loops that read sequences of input data.

- A sentinel value denotes the end of a data set, but it is not part of the data.
- You can use a Boolean variable to control a loop. Set the variable to true before entering the loop, then set it to false to leave the loop.
- Use input redirection to read input from a file. Use output redirection to capture program output in a file.

Use the technique of storyboarding for planning user interactions.

- A storyboard consists of annotated sketches for each step in an action sequence.
- Developing a storyboard helps you understand the inputs and outputs that are required for a program.

Know the most common loop algorithms.

- To compute an average, keep a total and a count of all values.
- To count values that fulfill a condition, check all values and increment a counter for each match.
- If your goal is to find a match, exit the loop when the match is found.
- To find the largest value, update the largest value seen so far whenever you see a larger one.
- To compare adjacent inputs, store the preceding input in a variable.

Use nested loops to implement multiple levels of iteration.

- When the body of a loop contains another loop, the loops are nested. A typical use of nested loops is printing a table with rows and columns.

Apply loops to the implementation of simulations.

- In a simulation, you use the computer to simulate an activity.
- You can introduce randomness by calling the random number generator.

```
java.awt.Color              java.lang.Math
java.awt.Graphics              random
   drawLine
   drawOval
   drawRect
   drawString
   setColor
```

REVIEW EXERCISES

- **R4.1** Write a while loop that prints

    a. All squares less than n. For example, if n is 100, print 0 1 4 9 16 25 36 49 64 81.

    b. All positive numbers that are divisible by 10 and less than n. For example, if n is 100, print 10 20 30 40 50 60 70 80 90

    c. All powers of two less than n. For example, if n is 100, print 1 2 4 8 16 32 64.

- **R4.2** Write a loop that computes

    a. The sum of all even numbers between 2 and 100 (inclusive).

    b. The sum of all squares between 1 and 100 (inclusive).

    c. The sum of all odd numbers between a and b (inclusive).

    d. The sum of all odd digits of n. (For example, if n is 32677, the sum would be $3 + 7 + 7 = 17$.)

- **R4.3** Provide trace tables for these loops.

    a. ```
int i = 0; int j = 10; int n = 0;
while (i < j) { i++; j--; n++; }
```
    **b.** ```
int i = 0; int j = 0; int n = 0;
while (i < 10) { i++; n = n + i + j; j++; }
```
    c. ```
int i = 10; int j = 0; int n = 0;
while (i > 0) { i--; j++; n = n + i - j; }
```
    **d.** ```
int i = 0; int j = 10; int n = 0;
while (i != j) { i = i + 2; j = j - 2; n++; }
```

- **R4.4** What do these loops print?

    a. `for (int i = 1; i < 10; i++) { System.out.print(i + " "); }`
    b. `for (int i = 1; i < 10; i += 2) { System.out.print(i + " "); }`
    c. `for (int i = 10; i > 1; i--) { System.out.print(i + " "); }`
    d. `for (int i = 0; i < 10; i++) { System.out.print(i + " "); }`
    e. `for (int i = 1; i < 10; i = i * 2) { System.out.print(i + " "); }`
    f. `for (int i = 1; i < 10; i++) { if (i % 2 == 0) { System.out.print(i + " "); } }`

- **R4.5** What is an infinite loop? On your computer, how can you terminate a program that executes an infinite loop?

- **R4.6** Write a program trace for the pseudocode in Exercise P4.6, assuming the input values are 4 7 −2 −5 0.

•• R4.7 What is an "off-by-one" error? Give an example from your own programming experience.

• R4.8 What is a sentinel value? Give a simple rule when it is appropriate to use a numeric sentinel value.

• R4.9 Which loop statements does Java support? Give simple rules for when to use each loop type.

• R4.10 How many iterations do the following loops carry out? Assume that i is not changed in the loop body.

    a. `for (int i = 1; i <= 10; i++) . . .`
    b. `for (int i = 0; i < 10; i++) . . .`
    c. `for (int i = 10; i > 0; i--) . . .`
    d. `for (int i = -10; i <= 10; i++) . . .`
    e. `for (int i = 10; i >= 0; i++) . . .`
    f. `for (int i = -10; i <= 10; i = i + 2) . . .`
    g. `for (int i = -10; i <= 10; i = i + 3) . . .`

•• R4.11 Write pseudocode for a program that prints a calendar such as the following:

```
Su  M  T  W Th  F Sa
          1  2  3  4
 5  6  7  8  9 10 11
12 13 14 15 16 17 18
19 20 21 22 23 24 25
26 27 28 29 30 31
```

• R4.12 Write pseudocode for a program that prints a Celsius/Fahrenheit conversion table such as the following:

```
Celsius | Fahrenheit
--------+-----------
      0 |         32
     10 |         50
     20 |         68
    . . .         . . .
    100 |        212
```

• R4.13 Write pseudocode for a program that reads a student record, consisting of the student's first and last name, followed by a sequence of test scores and a sentinel of –1. The program should print the student's average score. Then provide a trace table for this sample input:

```
Harry Morgan 94 71 86 95 -1
```

•• R4.14 Write pseudocode for a program that reads a sequence of student records and prints the total score for each student. Each record has the student's first and last name, followed by a sequence of test scores and a sentinel of –1. The sequence is terminated by the word END. Here is a sample sequence:

```
Harry Morgan 94 71 86 95 -1
Sally Lin 99 98 100 95 90 -1
END
```

Provide a trace table for this sample input.

• R4.15 Rewrite the following for loop into a while loop.

```
int s = 0;
for (int i = 1; i <= 10; i++)
{
   s = s + i;
}
```

• R4.16 Rewrite the following do loop into a while loop.

```
int n = in.nextInt();
double x = 0;
double s;
do
{
   s = 1.0 / (1 + n * n);
   n++;
   x = x + s;
}
while (s > 0.01);
```

• R4.17 Provide trace tables of the following loops.

a.
```
int s = 1;
int n = 1;
while (s < 10) { s = s + n; }
n++;
```

b.
```
int s = 1;
for (int n = 1; n < 5; n++) { s = s + n; }
```

c.
```
int s = 1;
int n = 1;
do
{
   s = s + n;
   n++;
}
while (s < 10 * n);
```

• R4.18 What do the following loops print? Work out the answer by tracing the code, not by using the computer.

a.
```
int s = 1;
for (int n = 1; n <= 5; n++)
{
   s = s + n;
   System.out.print(s + " ");
}
```

b.
```
int s = 1;
for (int n = 1; s <= 10; System.out.print(s + " "))
{
   n = n + 2;
   s = s + n;
}
```

c.
```
int s = 1;
int n;
for (n = 1; n <= 5; n++)
{
   s = s + n;
   n++;
}
System.out.print(s + " " + n);
```

R4.19 What do the following program segments print? Find the answers by tracing the code, not by using the computer.

a.
```
int n = 1;
for (int i = 2; i < 5; i++) { n = n + i; }
System.out.print(n);
```

b.
```
int i;
double n = 1 / 2;
for (i = 2; i <= 5; i++) { n = n + 1.0 / i; }
System.out.print(i);
```

c.
```
double x = 1;
double y = 1;
int i = 0;
do
{
    y = y / 2;
    x = x + y;
    i++;
}
while (x < 1.8);
System.out.print(i);
```

d.
```
double x = 1;
double y = 1;
int i = 0;
while (y >= 1.5)
{
    x = x / 2;
    y = x + y;
    i++;
}
System.out.print(i);
```

R4.20 Give an example of a for loop where symmetric bounds are more natural. Give an example of a for loop where asymmetric bounds are more natural.

R4.21 Add a storyboard panel for the conversion program in Section 4.6 on page 162 that shows a scenario where a user enters incompatible units.

R4.22 In Section 4.6, we decided to show users a list of all valid units in the prompt. If the program supports many more units, this approach is unworkable. Give a storyboard panel that illustrates an alternate approach: If the user enters an unknown unit, a list of all known units is shown.

R4.23 Change the storyboards in Section 4.6 to support a menu that asks users whether they want to convert units, see program help, or quit the program. The menu should be displayed at the beginning of the program, when a sequence of values has been converted, and when an error is displayed.

R4.24 Draw a flow chart for a program that carries out unit conversions as described in Section 4.6.

R4.25 In Section 4.7.5, the code for finding the largest and smallest input initializes the largest and smallest variables with an input value. Why can't you initialize them with zero?

R4.26 What are nested loops? Give an example where a nested loop is typically used.

■■ **R4.27** The nested loops

```
for (int i = 1; i <= height; i++)
{
    for (int j = 1; j <= width; j++) { System.out.print("*"); }
    System.out.println();
}
```

display a rectangle of a given width and height, such as

```
****
****
****
```

Write a *single* for loop that displays the same rectangle.

■■ **R4.28** Suppose you design an educational game to teach children how to read a clock. How do you generate random values for the hours and minutes?

■■■ **R4.29** In a travel simulation, Harry will visit one of his friends that are located in three states. He has ten friends in California, three in Nevada, and two in Utah. How do you produce a random number between 1 and 3, denoting the destination state, with a probability that is proportional to the number of friends in each state?

PROGRAMMING EXERCISES

■ **P4.1** Write programs with loops that compute

a. The sum of all even numbers between 2 and 100 (inclusive).

b. The sum of all squares between 1 and 100 (inclusive).

c. All powers of 2 from 2^0 up to 2^{20}.

d. The sum of all odd numbers between a and b (inclusive), where a and b are inputs.

e. The sum of all odd digits of an input. (For example, if the input is 32677, the sum would be $3 + 7 + 7 = 17$.)

■■ **P4.2** Write programs that read a sequence of integer inputs and print

a. The smallest and largest of the inputs.

b. The number of even and odd inputs.

c. Cumulative totals. For example, if the input is 1 7 2 9, the program should print 1 8 10 19.

d. All adjacent duplicates. For example, if the input is 1 3 3 4 5 5 6 6 6 2, the program should print 3 5 6.

■■ **P4.3** Write programs that read a line of input as a string and print

a. Only the uppercase letters in the string.

b. Every second letter of the string.

c. The string, with all vowels replaced by an underscore.

d. The number of vowels in the string.

e. The positions of all vowels in the string.

■■ **P4.4** Complete the program in How To 4.1 on page 169. Your program should read twelve temperature values and print the month with the highest temperature.

•• P4.5 Write a program that reads a set of floating-point values. Ask the user to enter the values, then print

- the average of the values.
- the smallest of the values.
- the largest of the values.
- the range, that is the difference between the smallest and largest.

Of course, you may only prompt for the values once.

• P4.6 Translate the following pseudocode for finding the minimum value from a set of inputs into a Java program.

> Set a Boolean variable "first" to true.
> While another value has been read successfully
>   If first is true
>   Set the minimum to the value.
>   Set first to false.
>   Else if the value is less than the minimum
>   Set the minimum to the value.
> Print the minimum.

••• P4.7 Translate the following pseudocode for randomly permuting the characters in a string into a Java program.

> Read a word.
> Repeat word.length() times
>   Pick a random position i in the word, but not the last position.
>   Pick a random position j > i in the word.
>   Swap the letters at positions j and i.
> Print the word.

To swap the letters, construct substrings as follows:

first   i   middle   j   last

Then replace the string with

```
first + word.charAt(j) + middle + word.charAt(i) + last
```

•• P4.8 Write a program that reads a word and prints each character of the word on a separate line. For example, if the user provides the input "Harry", the program prints

```
H
a
r
r
y
```

•• P4.9 Write a program that reads a word and prints the word in reverse. For example, if the user provides the input "Harry", the program prints

```
yrraH
```

• P4.10 Write a program that reads a word and prints the number of vowels in the word. For this exercise, assume that a e i o u y are vowels. For example, if the user provides the input "Harry", the program prints 2 vowels.

■■■ P4.11 Write a program that reads a word and prints the number of syllables in the word. For this exercise, assume that syllables are determined as follows: Each sequence of adjacent vowels a e i o u y, except for the last e in a word, is a syllable. However, if that algorithm yields a count of 0, change it to 1. For example,

Word	Syllables
Harry	2
hairy	2
hare	1
the	1

■■■ P4.12 Write a program that reads a word and prints all substrings, sorted by length. For example, if the user provides the input "rum", the program prints

```
r
u
m
ru
um
rum
```

■ P4.13 Write a program that prints all powers of 2 from 2^0 up to 2^{20}.

■■ P4.14 Write a program that reads a number and prints all of its *binary digits:* Print the remainder number % 2, then replace the number with number / 2. Keep going until the number is 0. For example, if the user provides the input 13, the output should be

```
1
0
1
1
```

■■ P4.15 *Mean and standard deviation.* Write a program that reads a set of floating-point data values. Choose an appropriate mechanism for prompting for the end of the data set.

When all values have been read, print out the count of the values, the average, and the standard deviation. The average of a data set $\{x_1, \ldots, x_n\}$ is $\bar{x} = \sum x_i / n$, where $\sum x_i = x_1 + \ldots + x_n$ is the sum of the input values. The standard deviation is

$$s = \sqrt{\frac{\sum (x_i - \bar{x})^2}{n - 1}}$$

However, this formula is not suitable for the task. By the time the program has computed $\bar{x}$, the individual x_i are long gone. Until you know how to save these values, use the numerically less stable formula

$$s = \sqrt{\frac{\sum x_i^2 - \frac{1}{n}\left(\sum x_i\right)^2}{n - 1}}$$

You can compute this quantity by keeping track of the count, the sum, and the sum of squares as you process the input values.

•• **P4.16** The *Fibonacci numbers* are defined by the sequence

$$f_1 = 1$$
$$f_2 = 1$$
$$f_n = f_{n-1} + f_{n-2}$$

Fibonacci numbers describe the growth of a rabbit population.

Reformulate that as

```
fold1 = 1;
fold2 = 1;
fnew = fold1 + fold2;
```

After that, discard `fold2`, which is no longer needed, and set `fold2` to `fold1` and `fold1` to `fnew`. Repeat an appropriate number of times.

Implement a program that prompts the user for an integer n and prints the nth Fibonacci number, using the above algorithm.

••• **P4.17** *Factoring of integers.* Write a program that asks the user for an integer and then prints out all its factors. For example, when the user enters 150, the program should print

```
2
3
5
5
```

••• **P4.18** *Prime numbers.* Write a program that prompts the user for an integer and then prints out all prime numbers up to that integer. For example, when the user enters 20, the program should print

```
2
3
5
7
11
13
17
19
```

Recall that a number is a prime number if it is not divisible by any number except 1 and itself.

• **P4.19** Write a program that prints a multiplication table, like this:

```
 1   2   3   4   5   6   7   8   9  10
 2   4   6   8  10  12  14  16  18  20
 3   6   9  12  15  18  21  24  27  30
       . . .
10  20  30  40  50  60  70  80  90 100
```

•• **P4.20** Write a program that reads an integer and displays, using asterisks, a filled and hollow square, placed next to each other. For example if the side length is 5, the program should display

```
***** *****
***** *   *
***** *   *
***** *   *
***** *****
```

P4.21 Write a program that reads an integer and displays, using asterisks, a filled diamond of the given side length. For example, if the side length is 4, the program should display

```
   *
  ***
 *****
*******
 *****
  ***
   *
```

P4.22 *The game of Nim.* This is a well-known game with a number of variants. The following variant has an interesting winning strategy. Two players alternately take marbles from a pile. In each move, a player chooses how many marbles to take. The player must take at least one but at most half of the marbles. Then the other player takes a turn. The player who takes the last marble loses.

Write a program in which the computer plays against a human opponent. Generate a random integer between 10 and 100 to denote the initial size of the pile. Generate a random integer between 0 and 1 to decide whether the computer or the human takes the first turn. Generate a random integer between 0 and 1 to decide whether the computer plays *smart* or *stupid*. In stupid mode the computer simply takes a random legal value (between 1 and $n/2$) from the pile whenever it has a turn. In smart mode the computer takes off enough marbles to make the size of the pile a power of two minus 1—that is, 3, 7, 15, 31, or 63. That is always a legal move, except when the size of the pile is currently one less than a power of two. In that case, the computer makes a random legal move.

You will note that the computer cannot be beaten in smart mode when it has the first move, unless the pile size happens to be 15, 31, or 63. Of course, a human player who has the first turn and knows the winning strategy can win against the computer.

P4.23 *The Drunkard's Walk.* A drunkard in a grid of streets randomly picks one of four directions and stumbles to the next intersection, then again randomly picks one of four directions, and so on. You might think that on average the drunkard doesn't move very far because the choices cancel each other out, but that is actually not the case.

Represent locations as integer pairs (x, y). Implement the drunkard's walk over 100 intersections, starting at $(0, 0)$, and print the ending location.

P4.24 *The Monty Hall Paradox.* Marilyn vos Savant described the following problem (loosely based on a game show hosted by Monty Hall) in a popular magazine: "Suppose you're on a game show, and you're given the choice of three doors: Behind one door is a car; behind the others, goats. You pick a door, say No. 1, and the host, who knows what's behind the doors, opens another door, say No. 3, which has a goat. He then says to you, "Do you want to pick door No. 2?" Is it to your advantage to switch your choice?"

Ms. vos Savant proved that it is to your advantage, but many of her readers, including some mathematics professors, disagreed, arguing that the probability would not change because another door was opened.

Your task is to simulate this game show. In each iteration, randomly pick a door number between 1 and 3 for placing the car. Randomly have the player pick a door. Randomly have the game show host pick a door having a goat (but not the door that the player picked). Increment a counter for strategy 1 if the player wins by switching to the host's choice, and increment a counter for strategy 2 if the player wins by sticking with the original choice. Run 1,000 iterations and print both counters.

P4.25 A simple random generator is obtained by the formula

$$r_{new} = \left(a \cdot r_{old} + b\right)\%m$$

and then setting r_{old} to r_{new}. If m is chosen as 2^{32}, then you can compute

$$r_{new} = a \cdot r_{old} + b$$

because the truncation of an overflowing result to the int type is equivalent to computing the remainder.

Write a program that asks the user to enter a seed value for r_{old}. (Such a value is often called a *seed*). Then print the first 100 random integers generated by this formula, using $a = 32310901$ and $b = 1729$.

P4.26 *The Buffon Needle Experiment.* The following experiment was devised by Comte Georges-Louis Leclerc de Buffon (1707–1788), a French naturalist. A needle of length 1 inch is dropped onto paper that is ruled with lines 2 inches apart. If the needle drops onto a line, we count it as a *hit*. (See Figure 9.) Buffon discovered that the quotient *tries/hits* approximates π.

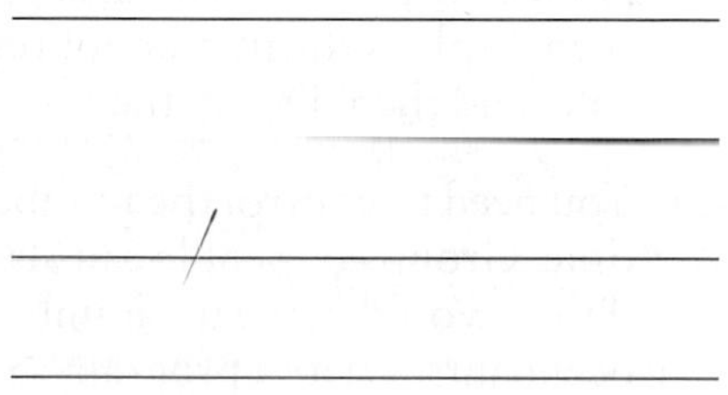

Figure 9
The Buffon Needle Experiment

For the Buffon needle experiment, you must generate two random numbers: one to describe the starting position and one to describe the angle of the needle with the x-axis. Then you need to test whether the needle touches a grid line.

Generate the *lower* point of the needle. Its x-coordinate is irrelevant, and you may assume its y-coordinate y_{low} to be any random number between 0 and 2. The angle α between the needle and the x-axis can be any value between 0 degrees and 180 degrees (π radians). The upper end of the needle has y-coordinate

$$y_{high} = y_{low} + \sin\alpha$$

The needle is a hit if y_{high} is at least 2, as shown in Figure 10. Stop after 10,000 tries and print the quotient *tries/hits*. (This program is not suitable for computing the value of π. You need π in the computation of the angle.)

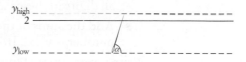

Figure 10
A Hit in the Buffon Needle Experiment

■■ Business P4.27 *Currency conversion.* Write a program that first asks the user to type today's price for one dollar in Japanese yen, then reads U.S. dollar values and converts each to yen. Use 0 as a sentinel.

■■ Business P4.28 Write a program that first asks the user to type in today's price of one dollar in Japanese yen, then reads U.S. dollar values and converts each to Japanese yen. Use 0 as the sentinel value to denote the end of dollar inputs. Then the program reads a sequence of yen amounts and converts them to dollars. The second sequence is terminated by another zero value.

■■ Business P4.29 Your company has shares of stock it would like to sell when their value exceeds a certain target price. Write a program that reads the target price and then reads the current stock price until it is at least the target price. Your program should use a Scanner to read a sequence of double values from standard input. Once the minimum is reached, the program should report that the stock price exceeds the target price.

■■ Business P4.30 Write an application to pre-sell a limited number of cinema tickets. Each buyer can buy as many as 4 tickets. No more than 100 tickets can be sold. Implement a program called TicketSeller that prompts the user for the desired number of tickets and then displays the number of remaining tickets. Repeat until all tickets have been sold, and then display the total number of buyers.

■■ Business P4.31 You need to control the number of people who can be in an oyster bar at the same time. Groups of people can always leave the bar, but a group cannot enter the bar if they would make the number of people in the bar exceed the maximum of 100 occupants. Write a program that reads the sizes of the groups that arrive or depart. Use negative numbers for departures. After each input, display the current number of occupants. As soon as the bar holds the maximum number of people, report that the bar is full and exit the program.

■■■ Business P4.32 *Credit Card Number Check.* The last digit of a credit card number is the *check digit*, which protects against transcription errors such as an error in a single digit or switching two digits. The following method is used to verify actual credit card numbers but, for simplicity, we will describe it for numbers with 8 digits instead of 16:

- Starting from the rightmost digit, form the sum of every other digit. For example, if the credit card number is 4358 9795, then you form the sum $5 + 7 + 8 + 3 = 23$.
- Double each of the digits that were not included in the preceding step. Add all digits of the resulting numbers. For example, with the number given above, doubling the digits, starting with the next-to-last one, yields 18 18 10 8. Adding all digits in these values yields $1 + 8 + 1 + 8 + 1 + 0 + 8 = 27$.
- Add the sums of the two preceding steps. If the last digit of the result is 0, the number is valid. In our case, $23 + 27 = 50$, so the number is valid.

Write a program that implements this algorithm. The user should supply an 8-digit number, and you should print out whether the number is valid or not. If it is not valid, you should print the value of the check digit that would make it valid.

·· Science P4.33 In a predator-prey simulation, you compute the populations of predators and prey, using the following equations:

$$prey_{n+1} = prey_n \times \left(1 + A - B \times pred_n\right)$$
$$pred_{n+1} = pred_n \times \left(1 - C + D \times prey_n\right)$$

Here, A is the rate at which prey birth exceeds natural death, B is the rate of predation, C is the rate at which predator deaths exceed births without food, and D represents predator increase in the presence of food.

Write a program that prompts users for these rates, the initial population sizes, and the number of periods. Then print the populations for the given number of periods. As inputs, try $A = 0.1$, $B = C = 0.01$, and $D = 0.00002$ with initial prey and predator populations of 1,000 and 20.

·· Science P4.34 *Projectile flight.* Suppose a cannonball is propelled straight into the air with a starting velocity v_0. Any calculus book will state that the position of the ball after t seconds is $s(t) = -\frac{1}{2}gt^2 + v_0 t$, where $g = 9.81 \text{ m/s}^2$ is the gravitational force of the earth. No calculus textbook ever mentions why someone would want to carry out such an obviously dangerous experiment, so we will do it in the safety of the computer.

In fact, we will confirm the theorem from calculus by a simulation. In our simulation, we will consider how the ball moves in very short time intervals Δt. In a short time interval the velocity v is nearly constant, and we can compute the distance the ball moves as $\Delta s = v \Delta t$. In our program, we will simply set

```
const double DELTA_T = 0.01;
```

and update the position by

```
s = s + v * DELTA_T;
```

The velocity changes constantly—in fact, it is reduced by the gravitational force of the earth. In a short time interval, $\Delta v = -g\Delta t$, we must keep the velocity updated as

```
v = v - g * DELTA_T;
```

In the next iteration the new velocity is used to update the distance.

Now run the simulation until the cannonball falls back to the earth. Get the initial velocity as an input (100 m/s is a good value). Update the position and velocity 100 times per second, but print out the position only every full second. Also printout the values from the exact formula $s(t) = -\frac{1}{2}gt^2 + v_0 t$ for comparison.

Note: You may wonder whether there is a benefit to this simulation when an exact formula is available. Well, the formula from the calculus book is *not* exact. Actually, the gravitational force diminishes the farther the cannonball is away from the surface of the earth. This complicates the algebra sufficiently that it is not possible to give an exact formula for the actual motion, but the computer simulation can simply be extended to apply a variable gravitational force. For cannonballs, the calculus-book formula is actually good enough, but computers are necessary to compute accurate trajectories for higher-flying objects such as ballistic missiles.

■■■ Science P4.35   A simple model for the hull of a ship is given by

$$|y| = \frac{B}{2}\left[1 - \left(\frac{2x}{L}\right)^2\right]\left[1 - \left(\frac{z}{T}\right)^2\right]$$

where B is the beam, L is the length, and T is the draft. (*Note:* There are two values of y for each x and z because the hull is symmetric from starboard to port.)

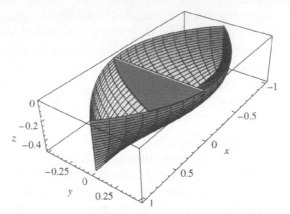

The cross-sectional area at a point x is called the "section" in nautical parlance. To compute it, let z go from 0 to $-T$ in n increments, each of size T/n. For each value of z, compute the value for y. Then sum the areas of trapezoidal strips. At right are the strips where $n = 4$.

Write a program that reads in values for B, L, T, x, and n and then prints out the cross-sectional area at x.

■ Science P4.36   Radioactive decay of radioactive materials can be modeled by the equation $A = A_0 e^{-t(\log 2/h)}$, where A is the amount of the material at time t, A_0 is the amount at time 0, and h is the half-life.

Technetium-99 is a radioisotope that is used in imaging of the brain. It has a half-life of 6 hours. Your program should display the relative amount A/A_0 in a patient body every hour for 24 hours after receiving a dose.

■■■ Science P4.37   The photo at left shows an electric device called a "transformer". Transformers are often constructed by wrapping coils of wire around a ferrite core. The figure below illustrates a situation that occurs in various audio devices such as cell phones and music players. In this circuit, a transformer is used to connect a speaker to the output of an audio amplifier.

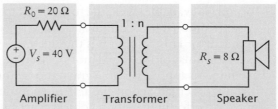

The symbol used to represent the transformer is intended to suggest two coils of wire. The parameter *n* of the transformer is called the "turns ratio" of the transformer. (The number of times that a wire is wrapped around the core to form a coil is called the number of turns in the coil. The turns ratio is literally the ratio of the number of turns in the two coils of wire.)

When designing the circuit, we are concerned primarily with the value of the power delivered to the speakers—that power causes the speakers to produce the sounds we want to hear. Suppose we were to connect the speakers directly to the amplifier without using the transformer. Some fraction of the power available from the amplifier would get to the speakers. The rest of the available power would be lost in the amplifier itself. The transformer is added to the circuit to increase the fraction of the amplifier power that is delivered to the speakers.

The power, P_s, delivered to the speakers is calculated using the formula

$$P_s = R_s \left(\frac{nV_s}{n^2 R_0 + R_s} \right)^2$$

Write a program that models the circuit shown and varies the turns ratio from 0.01 to 2 in 0.01 increments, then determines the value of the turns ratio that maximizes the power delivered to the speakers.

■ **Graphics P4.38** Write a program to plot the following face.

■ **Graphics P4.39** Write a graphical application that displays a checkerboard with 64 squares, alternating white and black.

■■■ **Graphics P4.40** Write a graphical application that draws a spiral, such as the following:

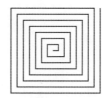

■■ **Graphics P4.41** It is easy and fun to draw graphs of curves with the Java graphics library. Simply draw 100 line segments joining the points $(x, f(x))$ and $(x + d, f(x + d))$, where x ranges from $x_{\min}$ to $x_{\max}$ and $d = (x_{\max} - x_{\min})/100$.
Draw the curve $f(x) = 0.00005x^3 - 0.03x^2 + 4x + 200$, where x ranges from 0 to 400 in this fashion.

■■■ **Graphics P4.42** Draw a picture of the "four-leaved rose" whose equation in polar coordinates is $r = \cos(2\theta)$. Let θ go from 0 to 2π in 100 steps. Each time, compute r and then compute the (x, y) coordinates from the polar coordinates by using the formula

$$x = r \cdot \cos(\theta), \ y = r \cdot \sin(\theta)$$

ANSWERS TO SELF-CHECK QUESTIONS

1. 23 years.

2. 7 years.

3. Add a statement

   ```
   System.out.println(balance);
   ```

   as the last statement in the while loop.

4. The program prints the same output. This is because the balance after 14 years is slightly below $20,000, and after 15 years, it is slightly above $20,000.

5. 2 4 8 16 32 64 128

   Note that the value 128 is printed even though it is larger than 100.

6. | n | output |
   |---|--------|
   | 5 | |
   | 4 | 4 |
   | 3 | 3 |
   | 2 | 2 |
   | 1 | 1 |
   | 0 | 0 |
   | -1 | -1 |

7. | n | output |
   |---|--------|
   | 1 | 1, |
   | 2 | 1, 2, |
   | 3 | 1, 2, 3, |
   | 4 | |

   There is a comma after the last value. Usually, commas are between values only.

8. | a | n | r | i |
   |---|---|---|---|
   | 2 | 4 | 1 | 1 |
   | | | 2 | 2 |
   | | | 4 | 3 |
   | | | 8 | 4 |
   | | | 16 | 5 |

   The code computes a^n.

9. | n | output |
   |---|--------|
   | 1 | 1 |
   | 11 | 11 |
   | 21 | 21 |
   | 31 | 31 |
   | 41 | 41 |
   | 51 | 51 |
   | 61 | 61 |
   | ... | |

   This is an infinite loop. n is never equal to 50.

10. | count | temp |
    |-------|------|
    | 1 | 123 |
    | 2 | 12.3 |
    | 3 | 1.23 |

This yields the correct answer. The number 123 has 3 digits.

count	temp
1	100
2	10.0

This yields the wrong answer. The number 100 also has 3 digits. The loop condition should have been

while (temp >= 10)

11. ```
    int year = 1;
    while (year <= nyears)
    {
       double interest = balance * RATE / 100;
       balance = balance + interest;
       System.out.printf("%4d %10.2f\n",
          year, balance);
       year++;
    }
    ```

12. 11 numbers: 10 9 8 7 6 5 4 3 2 1 0

13. ```
    for (int i = 10; i <= 20; i = i + 2)
    {
       System.out.println(i);
    }
    ```

14. ```
    int sum = 0;
    for (int i = 1; i <= n; i++)
    {
       sum = sum + i;
    }
    ```

15. ```
    for (int year = 1;
       balance <= 2 * INITIAL_BALANCE; year++)
    ```

    However, it is best not to use a for loop in this case because the loop condition does not relate to the year variable. A while loop would be a better choice.

16. ```
    do
    {
       System.out.print(
          "Enter a value between 0 and 100: ");
       value = in.nextInt();
    }
    while (value < 0 || value > 100);
    ```

17. ```
    int value = 100;
    while (value >= 100)
    {
       System.out.print("Enter a value < 100: ");
       value = in.nextInt();
    }
    ```

Here, the variable value had to be initialized with an artificial value to ensure that the loop is entered at least once.

18. Yes. The do loop

```
do { body } while (condition);
```

is equivalent to this while loop:

```
boolean first = true;
while (first || condition)
{
    body;
    first = false;
}
```

19.
```
int x;
int sum = 0;
do
{
    x = in.nextInt();
    sum = sum + x;
}
while (x != 0);
```

20.
```
int x = 0;
int previous;
do
{
    previous = x;
    x = in.nextInt();
    sum = sum + x;
}
while (x != 0 && previous != x);
```

21. `No data`

22. The first check ends the loop after the sentinel has been read. The second check ensures that the sentinel is not processed as an input value.

23. The while loop would never be entered. The user would never be prompted for input. Because count stays 0, the program would then print "No data".

24. The nextDouble method also returns false. A more accurate prompt would have been: "Enter values, a key other than a digit to quit." But that might be more confusing to the program user who would need now ponder which key to choose.

25. If the user doesn't provide any numeric input, the first call to in.nextDouble() will fail.

26. *Computing the average*

```
Enter scores, Q to quit: 90 80 90 100 80 Q
The average is 88
(Program exits)
```

27. *Simple conversion*

```
Your conversion question: How many in are 30 cm      Only one value can be converted
30 cm = 11.81 in
(Program exits)                                       Run program again for another question
```

Unknown unit

```
Your conversion question: How many inches are 30 cm?
Unknown unit: inches
Known units are in, ft, mi, mm, cm, m, km, oz, lb, g, kg, tsp, tbsp, pint, gal
(Program exits)
```

Program doesn't understand question syntax

```
Your conversion question: What is an ångström?
Please formulate your question as "How many (unit) are (value) (unit)?"
(Program exits)
```

28. *One score is not enough*

```
Enter scores, Q to quit: 90 Q
Error: At least two scores are required.
(Program exits)
```

29. It would not be possible to implement this interface using the Java features we have covered up to this point. There is no way for the program to know when the first set of inputs ends. (When you read numbers with value = in.nextDouble(), it is your choice whether to put them on a single line or multiple lines.)

30. *Comparing two interest rates*

```
First interest rate in percent: 5
Second interest rate in percent: 10
Years: 5
Year    5%         10%
0      10000.00   10000.00        This row clarifies that 1 means
1      10500.00   11000.00        the end of the first year
2      11025.00   12100.00
3      11576.25   13310.00
4      12155.06   14641.00
5      12762.82   16105.10
```

31. The total is zero.

32.
```
double total = 0;
while (in.hasNextDouble())
{
    double input = in.nextDouble();
    if (input > 0) { total = total + input; }
}
```

33. position is str.length() and ch is unchanged from its initial value, '?'. Note that ch must

be initialized with some value—otherwise the compiler will complain about a possibly uninitialized variable.

34. The loop will stop when a match is found, but you cannot access the match because neither position nor ch are defined outside the loop.

35. Start the loop at the end of string:

```
boolean found = false;
int i = str.length() - 1;
while (!found && i >= 0)
{
   char ch = str.charAt(i);
   if (ch == ' ') { found = true; }
   else { i--; }
}
```

36. The initial call to in.nextDouble() fails, terminating the program. One solution is to do all input in the loop and introduce a Boolean variable that checks whether the loop is entered for the first time.

```
double input = 0;
boolean first = true;
while (in.hasNextDouble())
{
   double previous = input;
   input = in.nextDouble();
   if (first) { first = false; }
   else if (input == previous)
   {
      System.out.println("Duplicate input");
   }
}
```

37. All values in the inner loop should be displayed on the same line.

38. Change lines 13, 18, and 30 to for (int n = 0; n <= NMAX; n++). Change NMAX to 5.

39. 60: The outer loop is executed 10 times, and the inner loop 6 times.

40.
```
0123
1234
2345
```

41.
```
for (int i = 1; i <= 3; i++)
{
   for (int j = 1; j <= 4; j++)
   {
      System.out.print("[]");
   }
   System.out.println();
}
```

42. Compute (int) (Math.random() * 2), and use 0 for heads, 1 for tails, or the other way around.

43. Compute (int) (Math.random() * 4) and associate the numbers 0 . . . 3 with the four suits. Then compute (int) (Math.random() * 13) and associate the numbers 0 . . . 12 with Jack, Ace, 2 . . . 10, Queen, and King.

44. We need to call it once for each die. If we printed the same value twice, the die tosses would not be independent.

45. The call will produce a value between 2 and 12, but all values have the same probability. When throwing a pair of dice, the number 7 is six times as likely as the number 2. The correct formula is

```
int sum = (int) (Math.random() * 6) + (int)
(Math.random() * 6) + 2;
```

46. Math.random() * 100.0

CHAPTER 5

METHODS

CHAPTER GOALS

To be able to implement methods

To become familiar with the concept of
parameter passing

To develop strategies for decomposing
complex tasks into simpler ones

To be able to determine the scope of a variable

To learn how to think recursively (optional)

CHAPTER CONTENTS

5.1 METHODS AS BLACK BOXES 202

5.2 IMPLEMENTING METHODS 204

Syntax 5.1: Static Method Declaration 205
Programming Tip 5.1: Method Comments 207

5.3 PARAMETER PASSING 207

Programming Tip 5.2: Do Not Modify Parameter
Variables 209
Common Error 5.1: Trying to Modify
Arguments 209

5.4 RETURN VALUES 210

Common Error 5.2: Missing Return Value 212
How To 5.1: Implementing a Method 212
Worked Example 5.1: Generating Random
Passwords ✚

**5.5 METHODS WITHOUT
RETURN VALUES** 214

**5.6 PROBLEM SOLVING: REUSABLE
METHODS** 215

**5.7 PROBLEM SOLVING: STEPWISE
REFINEMENT** 218

Programming Tip 5.3: Keep Methods Short 223
Programming Tip 5.4: Tracing Methods 223
Programming Tip 5.5: Stubs 224
Worked Example 5.2: Calculating a
Course Grade ✚

5.8 VARIABLE SCOPE 225

Video Example 5.1: Debugging ✚

**5.9 RECURSIVE METHODS
(OPTIONAL)** 228

How To 5.2: Thinking Recursively 231
Random Fact 5.1: The Explosive Growth of
Personal Computers 232
Video Example 5.2: Fully Justified Text ✚

A method packages a computation consisting of multiple steps into a form that can be easily understood and reused. (The person in the image to the left is in the middle of executing the method "make espresso".)

In this chapter, you will learn how to design and implement your own methods. Using the process of stepwise refinement, you will be able to break up complex tasks into sets of cooperating methods.

5.1 Methods as Black Boxes

A method is a named sequence of instructions.

A **method** is a sequence of instructions with a name. You have already encountered several methods. For example, the Math.pow method, which was introduced in Chapter 2, contains instructions to compute a power x^y. Moreover, every Java program has a method called main.

You *call* a method in order to execute its instructions. For example, consider the following program fragment:

```java
public static void main(String[] args)
{
    double result = Math.pow(2, 3);
    . . .
}
```

By using the expression Math.pow(2, 3), main *calls* the Math.pow method, asking it to compute 2^3. The instructions of the Math.pow method execute and compute the result. The Math.pow method *returns* its result back to main, and the main method resumes execution (see Figure 1).

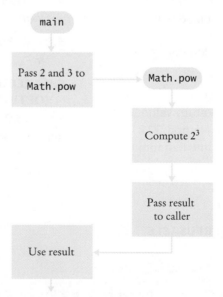

Figure 1 Execution Flow During a Method Call

Figure 2
The Math.pow Method
as a Black Box

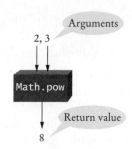

When another method calls the Math.pow method, it provides "inputs", such as the values 2 and 3 in the call Math.pow(2, 3). These values are called the **arguments** of the method call. Note that they are not necessarily inputs provided by a human user. They are simply the values for which we want the method to compute a result. The "output" that the Math.pow method computes is called the **return value**.

Arguments are supplied when a method is called.

Methods can receive multiple arguments, but they return only one value. It is also possible to have methods with no arguments. An example is the Math.random method that requires no argument to produce a random number.

The return value is the result that the method computes.

The return value of a method is returned to the calling method, where it is processed according to the statement containing the method call. For example, suppose your program contains a statement

```
double result = Math.pow(2, 3);
```

When the Math.pow method returns its result, the return value is stored in the variable result.

Do not confuse returning a value with producing program output. If you want the return value to be printed, you need to add a statement such as System.out.print(result).

At this point, you may wonder how the Math.pow method performs its job. For example, how does Math.pow compute that 2^3 is 8? By multiplying $2 \times 2 \times 2$? With logarithms? Fortunately, as a user of the method, you *don't need to know* how the method is implemented. You just need to know the *specification* of the method: If you provide arguments x and y, the method returns x^y. Engineers use the term *black box* for a device with a given specification but unknown implementation. You can think of Math.pow as a black box, as shown in Figure 2.

When you design your own methods, you will want to make them appear as black boxes to other programmers. Those programmers want to use your methods without knowing what goes on inside. Even if you are the only person working on a program, making each method into a black box pays off: there are fewer details that you need to keep in mind.

Although a thermostat is usually white, you can think of it as a "black box". The input is the desired temperature, and the output is a signal to the heater or air conditioner.

1. Consider the method call `Math.pow(3, 2)`. What are the arguments and return values?

2. What is the return value of the method call `Math.pow(Math.pow(2, 2), 2)`?

3. The `Math.ceil` method in the Java standard library is described as follows: The method receives a single argument a of type `double` and returns the smallest `double` value $\geq a$ that is an integer. What is the return value of `Math.ceil(2.3)`?

4. It is possible to determine the answer to Self Check 3 without knowing how the `Math.ceil` method is implemented. Use an engineering term to describe this aspect of the `Math.ceil` method.

Practice It Now you can try these exercises at the end of the chapter: R5.3, R5.6.

5.2 Implementing Methods

In this section, you will learn how to implement a method from a given specification. We will use a very simple example: a method to compute the volume of a cube with a given side length.

The `cubeVolume` method uses a given side length to compute the volume of a cube.

> When declaring a method, you provide a name for the method, a variable for each argument, and a type for the result.

When writing this method, you need to

- Pick a name for the method (`cubeVolume`).
- Declare a variable for each argument (`double sideLength`). These variables are called the **parameter variables**.
- Specify the type of the return value (`double`).
- Add the `public static` modifiers. We will discuss the meanings of these modifiers in Chapter 8. For now, you should simply add them to your methods.

Put all this information together to form the first line of the method's declaration:

```
public static double cubeVolume(double sideLength)
```

This line is called the **header** of the method. Next, specify the *body* of the method. The body contains the variable declarations and statements that are executed when the method is called.

The volume of a cube of side length s is $s \times s \times s$. However, for greater clarity, our parameter variable has been called `sideLength`, not s, so we need to compute `sideLength * sideLength * sideLength`.

We will store this value in a variable called `volume`:

```
double volume = sideLength * sideLength * sideLength;
```

In order to return the result of the method, use the `return` statement:

```
return volume;
```

The return *statement gives the method's result to the caller.*

The body of a method is enclosed in braces. Here is the complete method:

```
public static double cubeVolume(double sideLength)
{
    double volume = sideLength * sideLength * sideLength;
    return volume;
}
```

Let's put this method to use. We'll supply a main method that calls the cubeVolume method twice.

```
public static void main(String[] args)
{
    double result1 = cubeVolume(2);
    double result2 = cubeVolume(10);
    System.out.println("A cube with side length 2 has volume " + result1);
    System.out.println("A cube with side length 10 has volume " + result2);
}
```

When the method is called with different arguments, the method returns different results. Consider the call cubeVolume(2). The argument 2 corresponds to the sideLength parameter variable. Therefore, in this call, sideLength is 2. The method computes

Syntax 5.1   Static Method Declaration

Syntax   public static *returnType methodName*(*parameterType parameterName*, . . .)
           {
               method body
           }

Type of return value   Type of parameter variable

Name of method   Name of parameter variable

```
public static double cubeVolume(double sideLength)
```

Method body, executed when method is called.

```
{
    double volume = sideLength * sideLength * sideLength;
    return volume;
}
```

return **statement**
exits method and
returns result.

sideLength * sideLength * sideLength, or 2 * 2 * 2. When the method is called with a different argument, say 10, then the method computes 10 * 10 * 10.

Now we combine both methods into a test program. Note that both methods are contained in the same class. Also note the comment that describes the behavior of the cubeVolume method. (Programming Tip 5.1 describes the format of the comment.)

section_2/Cubes.java

```
1   /**
2       This program computes the volumes of two cubes.
3   */
4   public class Cubes
5   {
6      public static void main(String[] args)
7      {
8         double result1 = cubeVolume(2);
9         double result2 = cubeVolume(10);
10        System.out.println("A cube with side length 2 has volume " + result1);
11        System.out.println("A cube with side length 10 has volume " + result2);
12     }
13
14     /**
15         Computes the volume of a cube.
16         @param sideLength the side length of the cube
17         @return the volume
18     */
19     public static double cubeVolume(double sideLength)
20     {
21        double volume = sideLength * sideLength * sideLength;
22        return volume;
23     }
24  }
```

Program Run

```
A cube with side length 2 has volume 8
A cube with side length 10 has volume 1000
```

SELF CHECK

5. What is the value of cubeVolume(3)?

6. What is the value of cubeVolume(cubeVolume(2))?

7. Provide an alternate implementation of the body of the cubeVolume method by calling the Math.pow method.

8. Declare a method squareArea that computes the area of a square of a given side length.

9. Consider this method:

```
public static int mystery(int x, int y)
{
   double result = (x + y) / (y - x);
   return result;
}
```

What is the result of the call mystery(2, 3)?

Practice It   Now you can try these exercises at the end of the chapter: R5.1, R5.2, P5.5, P5.22.

Method Comments

Whenever you write a method, you should *comment* its behavior. Comments are for human readers, not compilers. The Java language provides a standard layout for method comments, called the **javadoc** convention, as shown here:

```
/**
    Computes the volume of a cube.
    @param sideLength the side length of the cube
    @return the volume
*/
public static double cubeVolume(double sideLength)
{
    double volume = sideLength * sideLength * sideLength;
    return volume;
}
```

> Method comments explain the purpose of the method, the meaning of the parameter variables and return value, as well as any special requirements.

Comments are enclosed in /** and */ delimiters. The first line of the comment describes the purpose of the method. Each @param clause describes a parameter variable and the @return clause describes the return value.

Note that the method comment does not document the implementation (*how* the method carries out its work) but rather the design (*what* the method does). The comment allows other programmers to use the method as a "black box".

5.3 Parameter Passing

> Parameter variables hold the arguments supplied in the method call.

In this section, we examine the mechanism of parameter passing more closely. When a method is called, variables are created for receiving the method's arguments. These variables are called **parameter variables**. (Another commonly used term is **formal parameters**.) The values that are supplied to the method when it is called are the **arguments** of the call. (These values are also commonly called the **actual parameters**.) Each parameter variable is initialized with the corresponding argument.

Consider the method call illustrated in Figure 3:

```
double result1 = cubeVolume(2);
```

A recipe for a fruit pie may say to use any kind of fruit. Here, "fruit" is an example of a parameter variable. Apples and cherries are examples of arguments.

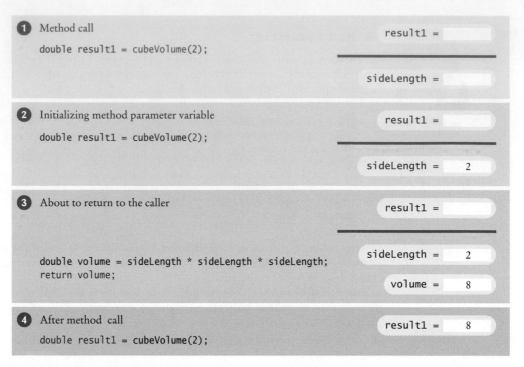

Figure 3   Parameter Passing

ANIMATION
Parameter Passing

- The parameter variable `sideLength` of the `cubeVolume` method is created when the method is called. **①**
- The parameter variable is initialized with the value of the argument that was passed in the call. In our case, `sideLength` is set to 2. **②**
- The method computes the expression `sideLength * sideLength * sideLength`, which has the value 8. That value is stored in the variable `volume`. **③**
- The method returns. All of its variables are removed. The return value is transferred to the *caller*, that is, the method calling the `cubeVolume` method. The caller puts the return value in the `result1` variable. **④**

Now consider what happens in a subsequent call, `cubeVolume(10)`. A new parameter variable is created. (Recall that the previous parameter variable was removed when the first call to `cubeVolume` returned.) It is initialized with 10, and the process repeats. After the second method call is complete, its variables are again removed.

SELF CHECK

10. What does this program print? Use a diagram like Figure 3 to find the answer.

```java
public static double mystery(int x, int y)
{
   double z = x + y;
   z = z / 2.0;
   return z;
}
public static void main(String[] args)
{
   int a = 5;
   int b = 7;
```

```
        System.out.println(mystery(a, b));
    }
```

11. What does this program print? Use a diagram like Figure 3 to find the answer.

```
public static int mystery(int x)
{
    int y = x * x;
    return y;
}
public static void main(String[] args)
{
    int a = 4;
    System.out.println(mystery(a + 1));
}
```

12. What does this program print? Use a diagram like Figure 3 to find the answer.

```
public static int mystery(int n)
{
    n++;
    n++;
    return n;
}
public static void main(String[] args)
{
    int a = 5;
    System.out.println(mystery(a));
}
```

Practice It   Now you can try these exercises at the end of the chapter: R5.5, R5.14, P5.8.

Programming Tip 5.2

Do Not Modify Parameter Variables

In Java, a parameter variable is just like any other variable. You can modify the values of the parameter variables in the body of a method. For example,

```
public static int totalCents(int dollars, int cents)
{
    cents = dollars * 100 + cents; // Modifies parameter variable
    return cents;
}
```

However, many programmers find this practice confusing (see Common Error 5.1). To avoid the confusion, simply introduce a separate variable:

```
public static int totalCents(int dollars, int cents)
{
    int result = dollars * 100 + cents;
    return result;
}
```

Common Error 5.1

Trying to Modify Arguments

The following method contains a common error: trying to modify an argument.

```
public static int addTax(double price, double rate)
{
    double tax = price * rate / 100;
    price = price + tax; // Has no effect outside the method
```

```
        return tax;
    }
```

Now consider this call:

```
    double total = 10;
    addTax(total, 7.5); // Does not modify total
```

When the addTax method is called, price is set to 10. Then price is changed to 10.75. When the method returns, all of its parameter variables are removed. Any values that have been assigned to them are simply forgotten. Note that total is *not* changed. In Java, a method can never change the contents of a variable that was passed as an argument.

5.4 Return Values

> The return statement terminates a method call and yields the method result.

You use the return statement to specify the result of a method. In the preceding examples, each return statement returned a variable. However, the return statement can return the value of any expression. Instead of saving the return value in a variable and returning the variable, it is often possible to eliminate the variable and return a more complex expression:

```
public static double cubeVolume(double sideLength)
{
    return sideLength * sideLength * sideLength;
}
```

When the return statement is processed, the method exits *immediately*. Some programmers find this behavior convenient for handling exceptional cases at the beginning of the method:

```
public static double cubeVolume(double sideLength)
{
    if (sideLength < 0) { return 0; }
    // Handle the regular case
    . . .
}
```

If the method is called with a negative value for sideLength, then the method returns 0 and the remainder of the method is not executed. (See Figure 4.)

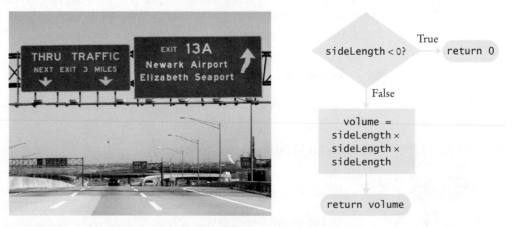

Figure 4   A return Statement Exits a Method Immediately

Every branch of a method needs to return a value. Consider the following incorrect method:

```java
public static double cubeVolume(double sideLength)
{
   if (sideLength >= 0)
   {
      return sideLength * sideLength * sideLength;
   } // Error—no return value if sideLength < 0
}
```

The compiler reports this as an error. A correct implementation is:

```java
public static double cubeVolume(double sideLength)
{
   if (sideLength >= 0)
   {
      return sideLength * sideLength * sideLength;
   }
   else
   {
      return 0;
   }
}
```

Many programmers dislike the use of multiple return statements in a method. You can avoid multiple returns by storing the method result in a variable that you return in the last statement of the method. For example:

```java
public static double cubeVolume(double sideLength)
{
   double volume;
   if (sideLength >= 0)
   {
      volume = sideLength * sideLength * sideLength;
   }
   else
   {
      volume = 0;
   }
   return volume;
}
```

ONLINE EXAMPLE

A program showing a method with multiple return statements.

SELF CHECK

13. Suppose we change the body of the cubeVolume method to

```java
if (sideLength <= 0) { return 0; }
return sideLength * sideLength * sideLength;
```

How does this method differ from the one described in this section?

14. What does this method do?

```java
public static boolean mystery (int n)
{
   if (n % 2 == 0) { return true };
   else { return false; }
}
```

15. Implement the mystery method of Self Check 14 with a single return statement.

Practice It   Now you can try these exercises at the end of the chapter: R5.13, P5.20.

Common Error 5.2

Missing Return Value

It is a compile-time error if some branches of a method return a value and others do not. Consider this example:

```
public static int sign(double number)
{
    if (number < 0) { return -1; }
    if (number > 0) { return 1; }
    // Error: missing return value if number equals 0
}
```

This method computes the sign of a number: –1 for negative numbers and +1 for positive numbers. If the argument is zero, however, no value is returned. The remedy is to add a statement return 0; to the end of the method.

HOW TO 5.1

Implementing a Method

A method is a computation that can be used multiple times with different arguments, either in the same program or in different programs. Whenever a computation is needed more than once, turn it into a method.

To illustrate this process, suppose that you are helping archaeologists who research Egyptian pyramids. You have taken on the task of writing a method that determines the volume of a pyramid, given its height and base length.

Step 1 Describe what the method should do.

Provide a simple English description, such as "Compute the volume of a pyramid whose base is a square."

Step 2 Determine the method's "inputs".

Make a list of *all* the parameters that can vary. It is common for beginners to implement methods that are overly specific. For example, you may know that the great pyramid of Giza, the largest of the Egyptian pyramids, has a height of 146 meters and a base length of 230 meters. You should *not* use these numbers in your calculation, even if the original problem only asked about the great pyramid. It is just as easy—and far more useful—to write a method that computes the volume of *any* pyramid.

> Turn computations that can be reused into methods.

In our case, the parameters are the pyramid's height and base length. At this point, we have enough information to document the method:

```
/**
    Computes the volume of a pyramid whose base is a square.
    @param height the height of the pyramid
    @param baseLength the length of one side of the pyramid's base
    @return the volume of the pyramid
*/
```

Step 3   Determine the types of the parameter variables and the return value.

The height and base length can both be floating-point numbers. Therefore, we will choose the type double for both parameter variables. The computed volume is also a floating-point number, yielding a return type of double. Therefore, the method will be declared as

```
public static double pyramidVolume(double height, double baseLength)
```

Step 4   Write pseudocode for obtaining the desired result.

In most cases, a method needs to carry out several steps to find the desired answer. You may need to use mathematical formulas, branches, or loops. Express your method in pseudocode.
An Internet search yields the fact that the volume of a pyramid is computed as

volume = 1/3 x height x base area

Because the base is a square, we have

base area = base length x base length

Using these two equations, we can compute the volume from the arguments.

Step 5   Implement the method body.

In our example, the method body is quite simple. Note the use of the return statement to return the result.

```
public static double pyramidVolume(double height, double baseLength)
{
   double baseArea = baseLength * baseLength;
   return height * baseArea / 3;
}
```

Step 6   Test your method.

After implementing a method, you should test it in isolation. Such a test is called a **unit test**. Work out test cases by hand, and make sure that the method produces the correct results. For example, for a pyramid with height 9 and base length 10, we expect the area to be 1/3 × 9 × 100 = 300. If the height is 0, we expect an area of 0.

```
public static void main(String[] args)
{
   System.out.println("Volume: " + pyramidVolume(9, 10));
   System.out.println("Expected: 300");
   System.out.println("Volume: " + pyramidVolume(0, 10));
   System.out.println("Expected: 0");
}
```

ONLINE EXAMPLE

➕ The program for calculating a pyramid's volume.

The output confirms that the method worked as expected:

```
Volume: 300
Expected: 300
Volume: 0
Expected: 0
```

WORKED EXAMPLE 5.1   Generating Random Passwords

This Worked Example creates a method that generates passwords of a given length with at least one digit and one special character.

Enter your current password: [   ]
Enter your new password: [   ]
Retype your new password: [   ]

➕   Available online in WileyPLUS and at www.wiley.com/college/horstmann.

5.5 Methods Without Return Values

Use a return type of void to indicate that a method does not return a value.

Sometimes, you need to carry out a sequence of instructions that does not yield a value. If that instruction sequence occurs multiple times, you will want to package it into a method. In Java, you use the return type void to indicate the absence of a return value.

Here is a typical example: Your task is to print a string in a box, like this:

A void *method returns no value, but it can produce output.*

```
-------
!Hello!
-------
```

However, different strings can be substituted for `Hello`. A method for this task can be declared as follows:

```java
public static void boxString(String contents)
```

Now you develop the body of the method in the usual way, by formulating a general method for solving the task.

Print a line that contains the - character n + 2 times, where n is the length of the string.
Print a line containing the contents, surrounded with a ! to the left and right.
Print another line containing the - character n + 2 times.

Here is the method implementation:

```java
/**
    Prints a string in a box.
    @param contents the string to enclose in a box
*/
public static void boxString(String contents)
{
    int n = contents.length();
    for (int i = 0; i < n + 2; i++) { System.out.print("-"); }
    System.out.println();
    System.out.println("!" + contents + "!");
    for (int i = 0; i < n + 2; i++) { System.out.print("-"); }
    System.out.println();
}
```

ONLINE EXAMPLE

A complete program demonstrating the boxString method.

Note that this method doesn't compute any value. It performs some actions and then returns to the caller.

Because there is no return value, you cannot use `boxString` in an expression. You can call

```java
boxString("Hello");
```

but not

```java
result = boxString("Hello"); // Error: boxString doesn't return a result.
```

If you want to return from a void method before reaching the end, you use a return statement without a value. For example,

```java
public static void boxString(String contents)
{
```

```
        int n = contents.length();
        if (n == 0)
        {
            return; // Return immediately
        }
        . . .
    }
```

16. How do you generate the following printout, using the `boxString` method?

```
-------
!Hello!
-------
-------
!World!
-------
```

17. What is wrong with the following statement?

```
System.out.print(boxString("Hello"));
```

18. Implement a method `shout` that prints a line consisting of a string followed by three exclamation marks. For example, `shout("Hello")` should print `Hello!!!`. The method should not return a value.

19. How would you modify the `boxString` method to leave a space around the string that is being boxed, like this:

```
---------
! Hello !
---------
```

20. The `boxString` method contains the code for printing a line of - characters twice. Place that code into a separate method `printLine`, and use that method to simplify `boxString`. What is the code of both methods?

Practice It   Now you can try these exercises at the end of the chapter: R5.4, P5.25.

5.6 Problem Solving: Reusable Methods

Eliminate replicated code or pseudocode by defining a method.

You have used many methods from the standard Java library. These methods have been provided as a part of the Java platform so that programmers need not recreate them. Of course, the Java library doesn't cover every conceivable need. You will often be able to save yourself time by designing your own methods that can be used for multiple problems.

When you write nearly identical code or pseudocode multiple times, either in the same program or in separate programs, consider introducing a method. Here is a typical example of code replication:

```
int hours;
do
{
    System.out.print("Enter a value between 0 and 23: ");
    hours = in.nextInt();
}
while (hours < 0 || hours > 23);
```

```
int minutes;
do
{
   System.out.print("Enter a value between 0 and 59: ");
   minutes = in.nextInt();
}
while (minutes < 0 || minutes > 59);
```

This program segment reads two variables, making sure that each of them is within a certain range. It is easy to extract the common behavior into a method:

```
/**
   Prompts a user to enter a value up to a given maximum until the user
   provides a valid input.
   @param high the largest allowable input
   @return the value provided by the user (between 0 and high, inclusive)
*/
public static int readIntUpTo(int high)
{
   int input;
   Scanner in = new Scanner(System.in);
   do
   {
      System.out.print("Enter a value between 0 and " + high + ": ");
      input = in.nextInt();
   }
   while (input < 0 || input > high);
   return input;
}
```

Then use this method twice:

```
int hours = readIntUpTo(23);
int minutes = readIntUpTo(59);
```

We have now removed the replication of the loop—it only occurs once, inside the method.

Note that the method can be reused in other programs that need to read integer values. However, we should consider the possibility that the smallest value need not always be zero.

Here is a better alternative:

Design your methods to be reusable. Supply parameter variables for the values that can vary when the method is reused.

```
/**
   Prompts a user to enter a value within a given range until the user
   provides a valid input.
   @param low the smallest allowable input
   @param high the largest allowable input
   @return the value provided by the user (between low and high, inclusive)
*/
public static int readIntBetween(int low, int high)
{
   int input;
   Scanner in = new Scanner(System.in);
   do
   {
      System.out.print("Enter a value between " + low + " and " + high + ": ");
      input = in.nextInt();
   }
   while (input < low || input > high);
   return input;
}
```

When carrying out the same task multiple times, use a method.

In our program, we call

```
int hours = readIntBetween(0, 23);
```

Another program can call

```
int month = readIntBetween(1, 12);
```

In general, you will want to provide parameter variables for the values that vary when a method is reused.

SELF CHECK

21. Consider the following statements:

```
int totalPennies = (int) Math.round(100 * total) % 100;
int taxPennies = (int) Math.round(100 * (total * taxRate)) % 100;
```

Introduce a method to reduce code duplication.

22. Consider this method that prints a page number on the left or right side of a page:

```
if (page % 2 == 0) { System.out.println(page); }
else { System.out.println("                              " + page); }
```

Introduce a method with return type boolean to make the condition in the if statement easier to understand.

23. Consider the following method that computes compound interest for an account with an initial balance of $10,000 and an interest rate of 5 percent:

```
public static double balance(int years) { return 10000 * Math.pow(1.05, years); }
```

How can you make this method more reusable?

24. The comment explains what the following loop does. Use a method instead.

```
// Counts the number of spaces
int spaces = 0;
for (int i = 0; i < input.length(); i++)
{
   if (input.charAt(i) == ' ') { spaces++; }
}
```

25. In Self Check 24, you were asked to implement a method that counts spaces. How can you generalize it so that it can count any character? Why would you want to do this?

Practice It Now you can try these exercises at the end of the chapter: R5.7, P5.21.

5.7 Problem Solving: Stepwise Refinement

Use the process of stepwise refinement to decompose complex tasks into simpler ones.

One of the most powerful strategies for problem solving is the process of **stepwise refinement**. To solve a difficult task, break it down into simpler tasks. Then keep breaking down the simpler tasks into even simpler ones, until you are left with tasks that you know how to solve.

Now apply this process to a problem of everyday life. You get up in the morning and simply must **get coffee**. How do you get coffee? You see whether you can get someone else, such as your mother or mate, to bring you some. If that fails, you must **make coffee**.

A production process is broken down into sequences of assembly steps.

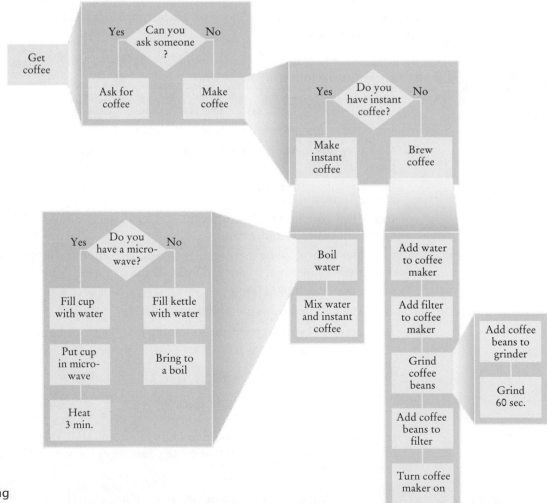

Figure 5
Flowchart of Coffee-Making Solution

How do you make coffee? If there is instant coffee available, you can **make instant coffee**. How do you make instant coffee? Simply **boil water** and mix the boiling water with the instant coffee. How do you boil water? If there is a microwave, then you fill a cup with water, place it in the microwave and heat it for three minutes. Otherwise, you fill a kettle with water and heat it on the stove until the water comes to a boil. On the other hand, if you don't have instant coffee, you must **brew coffee**. How do you brew coffee? You add water to the coffee maker, put in a filter, **grind coffee**, put the coffee in the filter, and turn the coffee maker on. How do you grind coffee? You add coffee beans to the coffee grinder and push the button for 60 seconds.

Figure 5 shows a flowchart view of the coffee-making solution. Refinements are shown as expanding boxes. In Java, you implement a refinement as a method. For example, a method `brewCoffee` would call `grindCoffee`, and `brewCoffee` would be called from a method `makeCoffee`.

Let us apply the process of stepwise refinement to a programming problem. When printing a check, it is customary to write the check amount both as a number ("$274.15") and as a text string ("two hundred seventy four dollars and 15 cents"). Doing so reduces the recipient's temptation to add a few digits in front of the amount.

For a human, this isn't particularly difficult, but how can a computer do this? There is no built-in method that turns 274 into "two hundred seventy four". We need to program this method. Here is the description of the method we want to write:

```
/**
    Turns a number into its English name.
    @param number a positive integer < 1,000
    @return the name of number (e.g., "two hundred seventy four")
*/
public static String intName(int number)
```

> When you discover that you need a method, write a description of the parameter variables and return values.

How can this method do its job? Consider a simple case first. If the number is between 1 and 9, we need to compute "one" ... "nine". In fact, we need the same computation *again* for the hundreds (two hundred). Any time you need something more than once, it is a good idea to turn that into a method. Rather than writing the entire method, write only the comment:

```
/**
    Turns a digit into its English name.
    @param digit an integer between 1 and 9
    @return the name of digit ("one" ... "nine")
*/
public static String digitName(int digit)
```

> A method may require simpler methods to carry out its work.

Numbers between 10 and 19 are special cases. Let's have a separate method `teenName` that converts them into strings "eleven", "twelve", "thirteen", and so on:

```
/**
    Turns a number between 10 and 19 into its English name.
    @param number an integer between 10 and 19
    @return the name of the number ("ten" ... "nineteen")
*/
public static String teenName(int number)
```

Next, suppose that the number is between 20 and 99. The name of such a number has two parts, such as "seventy four". We need a way of producing the first part, "twenty", "thirty", and so on. Again, we will put that computation into a separate method:

```
/**
    Gives the name of the tens part of a number between 20 and 99.
    @param number  an integer between 20 and 99
    @return  the name of the tens part of the number ("twenty" . . . "ninety")
*/
public static String tensName(int number)
```

Now let us write the pseudocode for the intName method. If the number is between 100 and 999, then we show a digit and the word "hundred" (such as "two hundred"). We then remove the hundreds, for example reducing 274 to 74. Next, suppose the remaining part is at least 20 and at most 99. If the number is evenly divisible by 10, we use tensName, and we are done. Otherwise, we print the tens with tensName (such as "seventy") and remove the tens, reducing 74 to 4. In a separate branch, we deal with numbers that are at between 10 and 19. Finally, we print any remaining single digit (such as "four").

> part = number (The part that still needs to be converted)
> name = "" (The name of the number)
>
> If part >= 100
>   name = name of hundreds in part + " hundred"
>   Remove hundreds from part.
>
> If part >= 20
>   Append tensName(part) to name.
>   Remove tens from part.
> Else if part >= 10
>   Append teenName(part) to name.
>   part = 0
>
> If (part > 0)
>   Append digitName(part) to name.

Translating the pseudocode into Java is straightforward. The result is shown in the source listing at the end of this section.

Note how we rely on helper methods to do much of the detail work. Using the process of stepwise refinement, we now need to consider these helper methods.

ANIMATION
Tracing a Method

Let's start with the digitName method. This method is so simple to implement that pseudocode is not really required. Simply use an if statement with nine branches:

```
public static String digitName(int digit)
{
    if (digit == 1) { return "one" };
    if (digit == 2) { return "two" };
    . . .
}
```

The teenName and tensName methods are similar.

This concludes the process of stepwise refinement. Here is the complete program:

section_7/IntegerName.java

```java
1   import java.util.Scanner;
2
3   /**
4      This program turns an integer into its English name.
5   */
6   public class IntegerName
7   {
8      public static void main(String[] args)
9      {
10        Scanner in = new Scanner(System.in);
11        System.out.print("Please enter a positive integer < 1000: ");
12        int input = in.nextInt();
13        System.out.println(intName(input));
14     }
15
16     /**
17        Turns a number into its English name.
18        @param number a positive integer < 1,000
19        @return the name of the number (e.g. "two hundred seventy four")
20     */
21     public static String intName(int number)
22     {
23        int part = number; // The part that still needs to be converted
24        String name = ""; // The name of the number
25
26        if (part >= 100)
27        {
28           name = digitName(part / 100) + " hundred";
29           part = part % 100;
30        }
31
32        if (part >= 20)
33        {
34           name = name + " " + tensName(part);
35           part = part % 10;
36        }
37        else if (part >= 10)
38        {
39           name = name + " " + teenName(part);
40           part = 0;
41        }
42
43        if (part > 0)
44        {
45           name = name + " " + digitName(part);
46        }
47
48        return name;
49     }
50
51     /**
52        Turns a digit into its English name.
53        @param digit an integer between 1 and 9
54        @return the name of digit ("one" ... "nine")
55     */
```

```
56      public static String digitName(int digit)
57      {
58         if (digit == 1) { return "one"; }
59         if (digit == 2) { return "two"; }
60         if (digit == 3) { return "three"; }
61         if (digit == 4) { return "four"; }
62         if (digit == 5) { return "five"; }
63         if (digit == 6) { return "six"; }
64         if (digit == 7) { return "seven"; }
65         if (digit == 8) { return "eight"; }
66         if (digit == 9) { return "nine"; }
67         return "";
68      }
69
70      /**
71         Turns a number between 10 and 19 into its English name.
72         @param number an integer between 10 and 19
73         @return the name of the given number ("ten" . . . "nineteen")
74      */
75      public static String teenName(int number)
76      {
77         if (number == 10) { return "ten"; }
78         if (number == 11) { return "eleven"; }
79         if (number == 12) { return "twelve"; }
80         if (number == 13) { return "thirteen"; }
81         if (number == 14) { return "fourteen"; }
82         if (number == 15) { return "fifteen"; }
83         if (number == 16) { return "sixteen"; }
84         if (number == 17) { return "seventeen"; }
85         if (number == 18) { return "eighteen"; }
86         if (number == 19) { return "nineteen"; }
87         return "";
88      }
89
90      /**
91         Gives the name of the tens part of a number between 20 and 99.
92         @param number an integer between 20 and 99
93         @return the name of the tens part of the number ("twenty" . . . "ninety")
94      */
95      public static String tensName(int number)
96      {
97         if (number >= 90) { return "ninety"; }
98         if (number >= 80) { return "eighty"; }
99         if (number >= 70) { return "seventy"; }
100        if (number >= 60) { return "sixty"; }
101        if (number >= 50) { return "fifty"; }
102        if (number >= 40) { return "forty"; }
103        if (number >= 30) { return "thirty"; }
104        if (number >= 20) { return "twenty"; }
105        return "";
106     }
107  }
```

Program Run

```
Please enter a positive integer < 1000: 729
seven hundred twenty nine
```

26. Explain how you can improve the `intName` method so that it can handle arguments up to 9999.

27. Why does line 40 set `part = 0`?

28. What happens when you call `intName(0)`? How can you change the `intName` method to handle this case correctly?

29. Trace the method call `intName(72)`, as described in Programming Tip 5.4.

30. Use the process of stepwise refinement to break down the task of printing the following table into simpler tasks.

```
+-----+-----------+
|  i  | i * i * i |
+-----+-----------+
|  1  |         1 |
|  2  |         8 |
   . . .       . . .
| 20  |      8000 |
+-----+-----------+
```

Practice It Now you can try these exercises at the end of the chapter: R5.12, P5.11, P5.24.

Programming Tip 5.3

Keep Methods Short

There is a certain cost for writing a method. You need to design, code, and test the method. The method needs to be documented. You need to spend some effort to make the method reusable rather than tied to a specific context. To avoid this cost, it is always tempting just to stuff more and more code in one place rather than going through the trouble of breaking up the code into separate methods. It is quite common to see inexperienced programmers produce methods that are several hundred lines long.

As a rule of thumb, a method that is so long that its code will not fit on a single screen in your development environment should probably be broken up.

Programming Tip 5.4

Tracing Methods

When you design a complex method, it is a good idea to carry out a manual walkthrough before entrusting your program to the computer.

Take an index card, or some other piece of paper, and write down the method call that you want to study. Write the name of the method and the names and values of the parameter variables, like this:

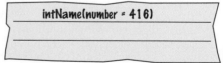

Then write the names and initial values of the method variables. Write them in a table, because you will update them as you walk through the code.

intName(number = 416)	
part	name
416	""

We enter the test part >= 100. part / 100 is 4 and part % 100 is 16. digitName(4) is easily seen to be "four". (Had digitName been complicated, you would have started another sheet of paper to figure out that method call. It is quite common to accumulate several sheets in this way.)

Now name has changed to name + " " + digitName(part / 100) + " hundred", that is "four hundred", and part has changed to part % 100, or 16.

intName(number = 416)	
part	name
~~416~~	~~""~~
16	"four hundred"

Now you enter the branch part >= 10. teenName(16) is sixteen, so the variables now have the values

intName(number = 416)	
part	name
~~416~~	~~""~~
~~16~~	~~"four hundred"~~
0	"four hundred sixteen"

Now it becomes clear why you need to set part to 0 in line 40. Otherwise, you would enter the next branch and the result would be "four hundred sixteen six". Tracing the code is an effective way to understand the subtle aspects of a method.

Programming Tip 5.5

Stubs

When writing a larger program, it is not always feasible to implement and test all methods at once. You often need to test a method that calls another, but the other method hasn't yet been implemented. Then you can temporarily replace the missing method with a **stub**. A stub is a method that returns a simple value that is sufficient for testing another method. Here are examples of stub methods:

Stubs are incomplete methods that can be used for testing.

```
/**
    Turns a digit into its English name.
    @param digit an integer between 1 and 9
    @return the name of digit ("one" . . . nine")
*/
public static String digitName(int digit)
{
    return "mumble";
}


/**
    Gives the name of the tens part of a number between 20 and 99.
    @param number an integer between 20 and 99
    @return the tens name of the number ("twenty" . . . "ninety")
```

```
*/
public static String tensName(int number)
{
    return "mumblety";
}
```

If you combine these stubs with the intName method and test it with an argument of 274, you will get a result of "mumble hundred mumblety mumble", which indicates that the basic logic of the intName method is working correctly.

WORKED EXAMPLE 5.2   **Calculating a Course Grade**

This Worked Example uses stepwise refinement to solve the problem of converting a set of letter grades into an average grade for a course.

5.8 Variable Scope

As your programs get larger and contain more variables, you may encounter problems where you cannot access a variable that is defined in a different part of your program, or where two variable definitions conflict with each other. In order to resolve these problems, you need to be familiar with the concept of *variable scope*.

> The scope of a variable is the part of the program in which it is visible.

The **scope** of a variable is the part of the program in which you can access it. For example, the scope of a method's parameter variable is the entire method. In the following code segment, the scope of the parameter variable sideLength is the entire cubeVolume method but not the main method.

```
public static void main(String[] args)
{
    System.out.println(cubeVolume(10));
}

public static double cubeVolume(double sideLength)
{
    return sideLength * sideLength * sideLength;
}
```

A variable that is defined within a method is called a **local variable**. When a local variable is declared in a block, its scope ranges from its declaration until the end of the block. For example, in the code segment below, the scope of the square variable is highlighted.

```
public static void main(String[] args)
{
    int sum = 0;
    for (int i = 1; i <= 10; i++)
    {
        int square = i * i;
        sum = sum + square;
    }
    System.out.println(sum);
}
```

➕ Available online in WileyPLUS and at www.wiley.com/college/horstmann.

The scope of a variable that is declared in a `for` statement extends to the end of the statement:

```java
public static void main(String[] args)
{
    int sum = 0;
    for (int i = 1; i <= 10; i++)
    {
        sum = sum + i * i;
    }
    System.out.println(sum);
}
```

Here is an example of a scope problem. The following code will not compile:

```java
public static void main(String[] args)
{
    double sideLength = 10;
    int result = cubeVolume();
    System.out.println(result);
}

public static double cubeVolume()
{
    return sideLength * sideLength * sideLength; // ERROR
}
```

Note the scope of the variable `sideLength`. The `cubeVolume` method attempts to read the variable, but it cannot—the scope of `sideLength` does not extend outside the `main` method. The remedy is to pass it as an argument, as we did in Section 5.2.

It is possible to use the same variable name more than once in a program. Consider the `result` variables in the following example:

```java
public static void main(String[] args)
{
    int result = square(3) + square(4);
    System.out.println(result);
}

public static int square(int n)
{
    int result = n * n;
    return result;
}
```

In the same way that there can be a street named "Main Street" in different cities, a Java program can have multiple variables with the same name.

Two local or parameter variables can have the same name, provided that their scopes do not overlap.

Each result variable is declared in a separate method, and their scopes do not overlap.

You can even have two variables with the same name in the same method, provided that their scopes do not overlap:

```java
public static void main(String[] args)
{
   int sum = 0;
   for (int i = 1; i <= 10; i++)
   {
      sum = sum + i;
   }

   for (int i = 1; i <= 10; i++)
   {
      sum = sum + i * i;
   }
   System.out.println(sum);
}
```

It is not legal to declare two variables with the same name in the same method in such a way that their scopes overlap. For example, the following is not legal:

```java
public static int sumOfSquares(int n)
{
   int sum = 0;
   for (int i = 1; i <= n; i++)
   {
      int n = i * i; // ERROR
      sum = sum + n;
   }
   return sum;
}
```

The scope of the local variable n is contained within the scope of the parameter variable n. In this case, you need to rename one of the variables.

SELF CHECK

Consider this sample program:

```java
1  public class Sample
2  {
3     public static void main(String[] args)
4     {
5        int x = 4;
6        x = mystery(x + 1);
7        System.out.println(s);
8     }
9
10    public static int mystery(int x)
11    {
12       int s = 0;
13       for (int i = 0; i < x; x++)
14       {
15          int x = i + 1;
16          s = s + x;
```

```
17          }
18          return s;
19      }
20  }
```

31. Which lines are in the scope of the variable i declared in line 13?

32. Which lines are in the scope of the parameter variable x declared in line 10?

33. The program declares two local variables with the same name whose scopes don't overlap. What are they?

34. There is a scope error in the mystery method. How do you fix it?

35. There is a scope error in the main method. What is it, and how do you fix it?

Practice It   Now you can try these exercises at the end of the chapter: R5.9, R5.10.

VIDEO EXAMPLE 5.1   **Debugging**

In this Video Example, you will learn how to use a debugger to find errors in a program.

5.9 Recursive Methods (Optional)

A recursive method is a method that calls itself. This is not as unusual as it sounds at first. Suppose you face the arduous task of cleaning up an entire house. You may well say to yourself, "I'll pick a room and clean it, and then I'll clean the other rooms." In other words, the cleanup task calls itself, but with a simpler input. Eventually, all the rooms will be cleaned.

Cleaning up a house can be solved recursively:
Clean one room, then clean up the rest.

➕ Available online in WileyPLUS and at www.wiley.com/college/horstmann.

In Java, a recursive method uses the same principle. Here is a typical example. We want to print triangle patterns like this:

```
[]
[][]
[][][]
[][][][]
```

Specifically, our task is to provide a method

```
public static void printTriangle(int sideLength)
```

The triangle given above is printed by calling `printTriangle(4)`. To see how recursion helps, consider how a triangle with side length 4 can be obtained from a triangle with side length 3.

```
[]
[][]
[][][]
[][][][]
```

Print the triangle with side length 3.
Print a line with four [].

More generally, here are the Java instructions for an arbitrary side length:

```java
public static void printTriangle(int sideLength)
{
    printTriangle(sideLength - 1);
    for (int i = 0; i < sideLength; i++)
    {
        System.out.print("[]");
    }
    System.out.println();
}
```

> A recursive computation solves a problem by using the solution of the same problem with simpler inputs.

There is just one problem with this idea. When the side length is 1, we don't want to call `printTriangle(0)`, `printTriangle(-1)`, and so on. The solution is simply to treat this as a special case, and not to print anything when `sideLength` is less than 1.

> For a recursion to terminate, there must be special cases for the simplest inputs.

```java
public static void printTriangle(int sideLength)
{
    if (sideLength < 1) { return; }
    printTriangle(sideLength - 1);
    for (int i = 0; i < sideLength; i++)
    {
        System.out.print("[]");
    }
    System.out.println();
}
```

Look at the `printTriangle` method one more time and notice how utterly reasonable it is. If the side length is 0, nothing needs to be printed. The next part is just as reasonable. Print the smaller triangle *and don't think about why that works*. Then print a row of `[]`. Clearly, the result is a triangle of the desired size.

There are two key requirements to make sure that the recursion is successful:

• Every recursive call must simplify the task in some way.

• There must be special cases to handle the simplest tasks directly.

The `printTriangle` method calls itself again with smaller and smaller side lengths. Eventually the side length must reach 0, and the method stops calling itself.

This set of Russian dolls looks similar to the call pattern of a recursive method.

Here is what happens when we print a triangle with side length 4:

- The call `printTriangle(4)` calls `printTriangle(3)`.
  - The call `printTriangle(3)` calls `printTriangle(2)`.
    - The call `printTriangle(2)` calls `printTriangle(1)`.
      - The call `printTriangle(1)` calls `printTriangle(0)`.
        - The call `printTriangle(0)` returns, doing nothing.
      - The call `printTriangle(1)` prints [].
    - The call `printTriangle(2)` prints [][].
  - The call `printTriangle(3)` prints [][][].
- The call `printTriangle(4)` prints [][][][].

ANIMATION
Tracing a Recursion

The call pattern of a recursive method looks complicated, and the key to the successful design of a recursive method is *not to think about it*.

Recursion is not really necessary to print triangle shapes. You can use nested loops, like this:

```java
public static void printTriangle(int sideLength)
{
   for (int i = 0; i < sideLength; i++)
   {
      for (int j = 0; j < i; j++)
      {
         System.out.print("[]");
      }
      System.out.println();
   }
}
```

ONLINE EXAMPLE

The complete TrianglePrinter program.

However, this pair of loops is a bit tricky. Many people find the recursive solution simpler to understand.

SELF CHECK

36. Consider this slight modification of the `printTriangle` method:
```java
public static void printTriangle(int sideLength)
{
   if (sideLength < 1) { return; }
   for (int i = 0; i < sideLength; i++)
   {
      System.out.print("[]");
```

```
    }
    System.out.println();
    printTriangle(sideLength - 1);
}
```

What is the result of `printTriangle(4)`?

37. Consider this recursive method:

```
public static int mystery(int n)
{
    if (n <= 0) { return 0; }
    return n + mystery(n - 1);
}
```

What is `mystery(4)`?

38. Consider this recursive method:

```
public static int mystery(int n)
{
    if (n <= 0) { return 0; }
    return mystery(n / 2) + 1;
}
```

What is `mystery(20)`?

39. Write a recursive method for printing n box shapes [] in a row.

40. The `intName` method in Section 5.7 accepted arguments < 1,000. Using a recursive call, extend its range to 999,999. For example an input of 12,345 should return `"twelve thousand three hundred forty five"`.

Practice It   Now you can try these exercises at the end of the chapter: R5.16, P5.16, P5.18.

HOW TO 5.2   Thinking Recursively

To solve a problem recursively requires a different mindset than to solve it by programming loops. In fact, it helps if you are, or pretend to be, a bit lazy and let others do most of the work for you. If you need to solve a complex problem, pretend that "someone else" will do most of the heavy lifting and solve the problem for all simpler inputs. Then you only need to figure out how you can turn the solutions with simpler inputs into a solution for the whole problem.

To illustrate the recursive thinking process, consider the problem of Section 4.2, computing the sum of the digits of a number. We want to design a method `digitSum` that computes the sum of the digits of an integer n.

For example, `digitSum(1729)` = 1 + 7 + 2 + 9 = 19

Step 1   Break the input into parts that can themselves be inputs to the problem.

In your mind, focus on a particular input or set of inputs for the task that you want to solve, and think how you can simplify the inputs. Look for simplifications that can be solved by the same task, and whose solutions are related to the original task.

In the digit sum problem, consider how we can simplify an input such as n = 1729. Would it help to subtract 1? After all, `digitSum(1729)` = `digitSum(1728)` + 1. But consider n = 1000. There seems to be no obvious relationship between `digitSum(1000)` and `digitSum(999)`.

A much more promising idea is to remove the last digit, that is, to compute n / 10 = 172. The digit sum of 172 is directly related to the digit sum of 1729.

> The key to finding a recursive solution is reducing the input to a simpler input for the same problem.

Step 2   Combine solutions with simpler inputs into a solution of the original problem.

In your mind, consider the solutions for the simpler inputs that you have discovered in Step 1. Don't worry *how* those solutions are obtained. Simply have faith that the solutions are readily available. Just say to yourself: These are simpler inputs, so someone else will solve the problem for me.

In the case of the digit sum task, ask yourself how you can obtain `digitSum(1729)` if you know `digitSum(172)`. You simply add the last digit (9) and you are done. How do you get the last digit? As the remainder `n % 10`. The value `digitSum(n)` can therefore be obtained as

> When designing a recursive solution, do not worry about multiple nested calls. Simply focus on reducing a problem to a slightly simpler one.

```
digitSum(n / 10) + n % 10
```

Don't worry how `digitSum(n / 10)` is computed. The input is smaller, and therefore it works.

Step 3   Find solutions to the simplest inputs.

A recursive computation keeps simplifying its inputs. To make sure that the recursion comes to a stop, you must deal with the simplest inputs separately. Come up with special solutions for them. That is usually very easy.

Look at the simplest inputs for the `digitSum` problem:

- A number with a single digit
- 0

Random Fact 5.1 The Explosive Growth of Personal Computers

In 1971, Marcian E. "Ted" Hoff, an engineer at Intel Corporation, was working on a chip for a manufacturer of electronic calculators. He realized that it would be a better idea to develop a *general-purpose* chip that could be *programmed* to interface with the keys and display of a calculator, rather than to do yet another custom design. Thus, the *microprocessor* was born. At the time, its primary application was as a controller for calculators, washing machines, and the like. It took years for the computer industry to notice that a genuine central processing unit was now available as a single chip.

Hobbyists were the first to catch on. In 1974 the first computer *kit,* the Altair 8800, was available from MITS Electronics for about $350. The kit consisted of the microprocessor, a circuit board, a very small amount of memory, toggle switches, and a row of display lights. Purchasers had to solder and assemble it, then program it in machine language through the toggle switches. It was not a big hit.

The first big hit was the Apple II. It was a real computer with a keyboard, a monitor, and a floppy disk drive. When it was first released, users had a $3,000 machine that could play Space Invaders, run a primitive bookkeeping program, or let users program it in BASIC. The original Apple II did not even support lowercase letters, making it worthless for word processing. The breakthrough came in 1979 with a new spreadsheet program, VisiCalc. In a spreadsheet, you enter financial data and their relationships into a grid of rows and columns (see the figure at right). Then you modify some of the data and watch in real time how the others change. For example, you can see how changing the mix of widgets in a manufacturing plant might affect estimated costs and profits. Middle managers in companies, who understood computers and were fed up with having to wait for hours or days to get their data runs back from the computing center, snapped up VisiCalc and the computer that was needed to run it. For them, the computer was a spreadsheet machine.

The next big hit was the IBM Personal Computer, ever after known as the PC. It was the first widely available personal computer that used Intel's 16-bit processor, the 8086, whose successors are still being used in personal computers today. The success of the PC was based not on any engineering breakthroughs but on the fact that it was easy to *clone*. IBM published the computer's specifications in order to encourage third parties to develop plug-in cards. Perhaps IBM did not foresee that functionally equivalent versions of their computer could be recreated by others, but a variety of PC clone vendors emerged, and ultimately IBM stopped selling personal computers.

IBM never produced an *operating system* for its PCs—that is, the software that organizes the interaction between the user and the computer, starts application programs, and manages disk storage and other resources. Instead, IBM offered customers the option of three separate operating systems. Most customers couldn't care less about the operating system.

A number with a single digit is its own digit sum, so you can stop the recursion when n < 10, and return n in that case. Or, you can be even lazier. If n has a single digit, then digitSum(n / 10) + n % 10 equals digitSum(0) + n. You can simply terminate the recursion when n is zero.

Step 4　Implement the solution by combining the simple cases and the reduction step.

Now you are ready to implement the solution. Make separate cases for the simple inputs that you considered in Step 3. If the input isn't one of the simplest cases, then implement the logic you discovered in Step 2.

Here is the complete digitSum method:

```
public static int digitSum(int n)
{
    if (n == 0) { return 0; } // Special case for terminating the recursion
    return digitSum(n / 10) + n % 10; // General case
}
```

VIDEO EXAMPLE 5.2　　**Fully Justified Text**

In printed books (such as this one), all but the last line of a paragraph have the same length. In this Video Example, you will see how to achieve this effect.

They chose the system that was able to launch most of the few applications that existed at the time. It happened to be DOS (Disk Operating System) by Microsoft. Microsoft licensed the same operating system to other hardware vendors and encouraged software companies to write DOS applications. A huge number of useful application programs for PC-compatible machines was the result.

PC applications were certainly useful, but they were not easy to learn. Every vendor developed a different *user interface:* the collection of keystrokes, menu options, and settings that a user needed to master to use a software package effectively. Data exchange between applications was difficult, because each program used a different data format. The Apple Macintosh changed all that in 1984. The designers of the Macintosh had the vision to supply an intuitive user interface with the computer and to force software developers to adhere to it. It took Microsoft and PC-compatible manufacturers years to catch up.

Most personal computers are used for accessing information from online sources, entertainment, word processing, and home finance. Some analysts predict that the personal computer will merge with the television set and cable network into an entertainment and information appliance.

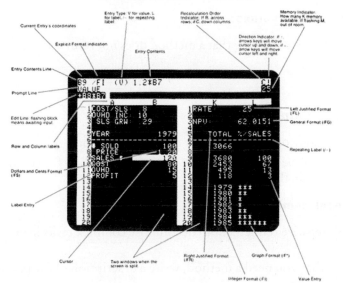

The Visicalc Spreadsheet Running on an Apple II

CHAPTER SUMMARY

Understand the concepts of methods, arguments, and return values.

- A method is a named sequence of instructions.
- Arguments are supplied when a method is called.
- The return value is the result that the method computes.

Be able to implement methods.

- When declaring a method, you provide a name for the method, a variable for each argument, and a type for the result.
- Method comments explain the purpose of the method, the meaning of the parameter variables and return value, as well as any special requirements.

Describe the process of parameter passing.

- Parameter variables hold the arguments supplied in the method call.

Describe the process of returning a value from a method.

- The return statement terminates a method call and yields the method result.
- Turn computations that can be reused into methods.

Design and implement methods without return values.

- Use a return type of void to indicate that a method does not return a value.

Develop methods that can be reused for multiple problems.

- Eliminate replicated code or pseudocode by defining a method.
- Design your methods to be reusable. Supply parameter variables for the values that can vary when the method is reused.

Apply the design principle of stepwise refinement.

- Use the process of stepwise refinement to decompose complex tasks into simpler ones.
- When you discover that you need a method, write a description of the parameter variables and return values.
- A method may require simpler methods to carry out its work.

Determine the scope of variables in a program.

- The scope of a variable is the part of the program in which it is visible.
- Two local or parameter variables can have the same name, provided that their scopes do not overlap.

Understand recursive method calls and implement simple recursive methods.

- A recursive computation solves a problem by using the solution of the same problem with simpler inputs.
- For a recursion to terminate, there must be special cases for the simplest inputs.
- The key to finding a recursive solution is reducing the input to a simpler input for the same problem.
- When designing a recursive solution, do not worry about multiple nested calls. Simply focus on reducing a problem to a slightly simpler one.

REVIEW EXERCISES

- **R5.1** In which sequence are the lines of the Cubes.java program in Section 5.2 executed, starting with the first line of main?

- **R5.2** Write method headers for methods with the following descriptions.
  - **a.** Computing the larger of two integers
  - **b.** Computing the smallest of three floating-point numbers
  - **c.** Checking whether an integer is a prime number, returning true if it is and false otherwise
  - **d.** Checking whether a string is contained inside another string
  - **e.** Computing the balance of an account with a given initial balance, an annual interest rate, and a number of years of earning interest
  - **f.** Printing the balance of an account with a given initial balance and an annual interest rate over a given number of years
  - **g.** Printing the calendar for a given month and year
  - **h.** Computing the weekday for a given day, month, and year (as a string such as "Monday")
  - **i.** Generating a random integer between 1 and n

- **R5.3** Give examples of the following methods from the Java library.
  - **a.** A method with a double argument and a double return value
  - **b.** A method with two double arguments and a double return value
  - **c.** A method with a String argument and a double return value
  - **d.** A method with no arguments and a double return value

- **R5.4** True or false?
  - **a.** A method has exactly one return statement.
  - **b.** A method has at least one return statement.

c. A method has at most one return value.

d. A method with return value void never has a return statement.

e. When executing a return statement, the method exits immediately.

f. A method with return value void must print a result.

g. A method without parameter variables always returns the same value.

•• R5.5 Consider these methods:

```
public static double f(double x) { return g(x) + Math.sqrt(h(x)); }
public static double g(double x) { return 4 * h(x); }
public static double h(double x) { return x * x + k(x) - 1; }
public static double k(double x) { return 2 * (x + 1); }
```

Without actually compiling and running a program, determine the results of the following method calls.

a. double x1 = f(2);

b. double x2 = g(h(2));

c. double x3 = k(g(2) + h(2));

d. double x4 = f(0) + f(1) + f(2);

e. double x5 = f(-1) + g(-1) + h(-1) + k(-1);

• R5.6 What is the difference between an argument and a return value? How many arguments can a method call have? How many return values?

•• R5.7 Design a method that prints a floating-point number as a currency value (with a $ sign and two decimal digits).

a. Indicate how the programs ch02/section_3/Volume2.java and ch04/section_3/InvestmentTable.java should change to use your method.

b. What change is required if the programs should show a different currency, such as euro?

•• Business R5.8 Write pseudocode for a method that translates a telephone number with letters in it (such as 1-800-FLOWERS) into the actual phone number. Use the standard letters on a phone pad.

•• R5.9 Describe the scope error in the following program and explain how to fix it.

```
public class Conversation
{
   public static void main(String[] args)
   {
      Scanner in = new Scanner(System.in);
```

```
        System.out.print("What is your first name? ");
        String input = in.next();
        System.out.println("Hello, " + input);
        System.out.print("How old are you? ");
        int input = in.nextInt();
        input++;
        System.out.println("Next year, you will be " + input);
    }
}
```

R5.10 For each of the variables in the following program, indicate the scope. Then determine what the program prints, without actually running the program.

```
1   public class Sample
2   {
3      public static void main(String[] args)
4      {
5         int i = 10;
6         int b = g(i);
7         System.out.println(b + i);
8      }
9
10     public static int f(int i)
11     {
12        int n = 0;
13        while (n * n <= i) { n++; }
14        return n - 1;
15     }
16
17     public static int g(int a)
18     {
19        int b = 0;
20        for (int n = 0; n < a; n++)
21        {
22           int i = f(n);
23           b = b + i;
24        }
25        return b;
26     }
27  }
```

R5.11 Use the process of stepwise refinement to describe the process of making scrambled eggs. Discuss what you do if you do not find eggs in the refrigerator.

R5.12 Perform a walkthrough of the intName method with the following arguments:

a. 5

b. 12

c. 21

d. 301

e. 324

f. 0

g. -2

R5.13 Consider the following method:

```
public static int f(int a)
{
    if (a < 0) { return -1; }
    int n = a;
```

```
          while (n > 0)
          {
             if (n % 2 == 0) // n is even
             {
                n = n / 2;
             }
             else if (n == 1) { return 1; }
             else { n = 3 * n + 1; }
          }
          return 0;
       }
```

Perform traces of the computations f(-1), f(0), f(1), f(2), f(10), and f(100).

■■■ **R5.14** Consider the following method that is intended to swap the values of two integers:

```
       public static void falseSwap(int a, int b)
       {
          int temp = a;
          a = b;
          b = temp;
       }

       public static void main(String[] args)
       {
          int x = 3;
          int y = 4;
          falseSwap(x, y);
          System.out.println(x + " " + y);
       }
```

Why doesn't the falseSwap method swap the contents of x and y?

■■■ **R5.15** Give pseudocode for a recursive method for printing all substrings of a given string. For example, the substrings of the string "rum" are "rum" itself, "ru", "um", "r", "u", "m", and the empty string. You may assume that all letters of the string are different.

■■■ **R5.16** Give pseudocode for a recursive method that sorts all letters in a string. For example, the string "goodbye" would be sorted into "bdegooy".

PROGRAMMING EXERCISES

■ **P5.1** Write the following methods and provide a program to test them.

   a. double smallest(double x, double y, double z), returning the smallest of the arguments

   b. double average(double x, double y, double z), returning the average of the arguments

■■ **P5.2** Write the following methods and provide a program to test them.

   a. boolean allTheSame(double x, double y, double z), returning true if the arguments are all the same

   b. boolean allDifferent(double x, double y, double z), returning true if the arguments are all different

   c. boolean sorted(double x, double y, double z), returning true if the arguments are sorted, with the smallest one coming first

■■ **P5.3** Write the following methods.

  a. int firstDigit(int n), returning the first digit of the argument

  b. int lastDigit(int n), returning the last digit of the argument

  c. int digits(int n), returning the number of digits of the argument

For example, firstDigit(1729) is 1, lastDigit(1729) is 9, and digits(1729) is 4. Provide a program that tests your methods.

■ **P5.4** Write a method

```
public static String middle(String str)
```

that returns a string containing the middle character in str if the length of str is odd, or the two middle characters if the length is even. For example, middle("middle") returns "dd".

■ **P5.5** Write a method

```
public static String repeat(String str, int n)
```

that returns the string str repeated n times. For example, repeat("ho", 3) returns "hohoho".

■■ **P5.6** Write a method

```
public static int countVowels(String str)
```

that returns a count of all vowels in the string str. Vowels are the letters a, e, i, o, and u, and their uppercase variants.

■■ **P5.7** Write a method

```
public static int countWords(String str)
```

that returns a count of all words in the string str. Words are separated by spaces. For example, countWords("Mary had a little lamb") should return 5.

■■ **P5.8** It is a well-known phenomenon that most people are easily able to read a text whose words have two characters flipped, provided the first and last letter of each word are not changed. For example,

> I dn'ot gvie a dman for a man taht can olny sepll a wrod one way. (Mrak Taiwn)

Write a method String scramble(String word) that constructs a scrambled version of a given word, randomly flipping two characters other than the first and last one. Then write a program that reads words and prints the scrambled words.

■ **P5.9** Write methods

```
public static double sphereVolume(double r)
public static double sphereSurface(double r)
public static double cylinderVolume(double r, double h)
public static double cylinderSurface(double r, double h)
public static double coneVolume(double r, double h)
public static double coneSurface(double r, double h)
```

that compute the volume and surface area of a sphere with radius r, a cylinder with a circular base with radius r and height h, and a cone with a circular base with radius r and height h. Then write a program that prompts the user for the values of r and h, calls the six methods, and prints the results.

•• P5.10 Write a method

```
public static double readDouble(String prompt)
```

that displays the prompt string, followed by a space, reads a floating-point number in, and returns it. Here is a typical usage:

```
salary = readDouble("Please enter your salary:");
percentageRaise = readDouble("What percentage raise would you like?");
```

•• P5.11 Enhance the `intName` method so that it works correctly for values < 1,000,000,000.

•• P5.12 Enhance the `intName` method so that it works correctly for negative values and zero. *Caution:* Make sure the improved method doesn't print 20 as `"twenty zero"`.

••• P5.13 For some values (for example, 20), the `intName` method returns a string with a leading space (`" twenty"`). Repair that blemish and ensure that spaces are inserted only when necessary. *Hint:* There are two ways of accomplishing this. Either ensure that leading spaces are never inserted, or remove leading spaces from the result before returning it.

••• P5.14 Write a method `String getTimeName(int hours, int minutes)` that returns the English name for a point in time, such as `"ten minutes past two"`, `"half past three"`, `"a quarter to four"`, or `"five o'clock"`. Assume that `hours` is between 1 and 12.

•• P5.15 Write a recursive method

```
public static String reverse(String str)
```

that computes the reverse of a string. For example, `reverse("flow")` should return `"wolf"`. *Hint:* Reverse the substring starting at the second character, then add the first character at the end. For example, to reverse `"flow"`, first reverse `"low"` to `"wol"`, then add the `"f"` at the end.

•• P5.16 Write a recursive method

```
public static boolean isPalindrome(String str)
```

that returns `true` if `str` is a palindrome, that is, a word that is the same when reversed. Examples of palindrome are "deed", "rotor", or "aibohphobia". *Hint:* A word is a palindrome if the first and last letters match and the remainder is also a palindrome.

•• P5.17 Use recursion to implement a method `public static boolean find(String str, String match)` that tests whether `match` is contained in `str`:

```
boolean b = find("Mississippi", "sip"); // Sets b to true
```

Hint: If `str` starts with `match`, then you are done. If not, consider the string that you obtain by removing the first character.

• P5.18 Use recursion to determine the number of digits in an integer `n`. *Hint:* If `n` is < 10, it has one digit. Otherwise, it has one more digit than `n / 10`.

• P5.19 Use recursion to compute a^n, where n is a positive integer. *Hint:* If n is 1, then $a^n = a$. If n is even, then $a^n = (a^{n/2})^2$. Otherwise, $a^n = a \times a^{n-1}$.

•• P5.20 *Leap years.* Write a method

```
public static boolean isLeapYear(int year)
```

that tests whether a year is a leap year: that is, a year with 366 days. Exercise P3.28 describes how to test whether a year is a leap year. In this exercise, use multiple `if` statements and `return` statements to return the result as soon as you know it.

•• **P5.21** In Exercise P3.26 you were asked to write a program to convert a number to its representation in Roman numerals. At the time, you did not know how to eliminate duplicate code, and as a consequence the resulting program was rather long. Rewrite that program by implementing and using the following method:

```
public static String romanDigit(int n, String one, String five, String ten)
```

That method translates one digit, using the strings specified for the one, five, and ten values. You would call the method as follows:

```
romanOnes = romanDigit(n % 10, "I", "V", "X");
n = n / 10;
romanTens = romanDigit(n % 10, "X", "L", "C");
. . .
```

•• **Business P5.22** Write a method that computes the balance of a bank account with a given initial balance and interest rate, after a given number of years. Assume interest is compounded yearly.

•• **Business P5.23** Write a program that prints instructions to get coffee, asking the user for input whenever a decision needs to be made. Decompose each task into a method, for example:

```
public static void brewCoffee()
{
    System.out.println("Add water to the coffee maker.");
    System.out.println("Put a filter in the coffee maker.");
    grindCoffee();
    System.out.println("Put the coffee in the filter.");
    . . .
}
```

•• **Business P5.24** Write a program that prints a paycheck. Ask the program user for the name of the employee, the hourly rate, and the number of hours worked. If the number of hours exceeds 40, the employee is paid "time and a half", that is, 150 percent of the hourly rate on the hours exceeding 40. Your check should look similar to that in the figure below. Use fictitious names for the payer and the bank. Be sure to use stepwise refinement and break your solution into several methods. Use the intName method to print the dollar amount of the check.

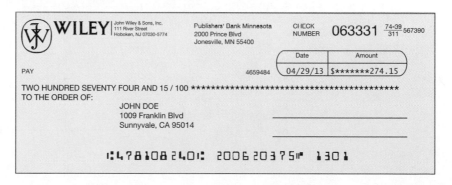

•• **Business P5.25** *Postal bar codes.* For faster sorting of letters, the United States Postal Service encourages companies that send large volumes of mail to use a bar code denoting the zip code (see Figure 6).

```
*************** ECRLOT ** CO57

CODE  C671RTS2
JOHN DOE                                    CO57
1009 FRANKLIN BLVD
SUNNYVALE      CA  95014 – 5143
```

||I.I.II.II.....II.I.I.I.I.I....II.I.I..II.I.I.I

Figure 6 A Postal Bar Code

The encoding scheme for a five-digit zip code is shown in Figure 7. There are full-height frame bars on each side. The five encoded digits are followed by a check digit, which is computed as follows: Add up all digits, and choose the check digit to make the sum a multiple of 10. For example, the zip code 95014 has a sum of 19, so the check digit is 1 to make the sum equal to 20.

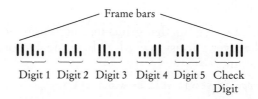

<table>
<tr><td></td><td></td><td></td><td>Frame bars</td><td></td><td></td></tr>
<tr><td>Digit 1</td><td>Digit 2</td><td>Digit 3</td><td>Digit 4</td><td>Digit 5</td><td>Check Digit</td></tr>
</table>

Figure 7 Encoding for Five-Digit Bar Codes

Each digit of the zip code, and the check digit, is encoded according to the table below, where 1 denotes a full bar and 0 a half bar:

Digit	Bar 1 (weight 7)	Bar 2 (weight 4)	Bar 3 (weight 2)	Bar 4 (weight 1)	Bar 5 (weight 0)
1	0	0	0	1	1
2	0	0	1	0	1
3	0	0	1	1	0
4	0	1	0	0	1
5	0	1	0	1	0
6	0	1	1	0	0
7	1	0	0	0	1
8	1	0	0	1	0
9	1	0	1	0	0
0	1	1	0	0	0

The digit can be easily computed from the bar code using the column weights 7, 4, 2, 1, 0. For example, 01100 is $0 \times 7 + 1 \times 4 + 1 \times 2 + 0 \times 1 + 0 \times 0 = 6$. The only exception is 0, which would yield 11 according to the weight formula.

Write a program that asks the user for a zip code and prints the bar code. Use : for half bars, | for full bars. For example, 95014 becomes

||:|:::|:|:|||::::::||:|::|:::|||

Provide these methods:

```
public static void printDigit(int d)
public static void printBarCode(int zipCode)
```

■■ **Business P5.26** Write a program that reads in a bar code (with : denoting half bars and | denoting full bars) and prints out the zip code it represents. Print an error message if the bar code is not correct.

■■ **Business P5.27** Write a program that converts a Roman number such as MCMLXXVIII to its decimal number representation. *Hint:* First write a method that yields the numeric value of each of the letters. Then use the following algorithm:

total = 0
While the roman number string is not empty
　If value(first character) is at least value(second character), or the string has length 1
　　Add value(first character) to total.
　　Remove the character.
　Else
　　Add the difference value(second character) - value(first character) to total.
　　Remove both characters.

■■ **Business P5.28** A non-governmental organization needs a program to calculate the amount of financial assistance for needy families. The formula is as follows:

- If the annual household income is between $30,000 and $40,000 and the household has at least three children, the amount is $1,000 per child.
- If the annual household income is between $20,000 and $30,000 and the household has at least two children, the amount is $1,500 per child.
- If the annual household income is less than $20,000, the amount is $2,000 per child.

Implement a method for this computation. Write a program that asks for the household income and number of children for each applicant, printing the amount returned by your method. Use –1 as a sentinel value for the input.

■■■ **Business P5.29** In a social networking service, a user has friends, the friends have other friends, and so on. We are interested in knowing how many people can be reached from a person by following a given number of friendship relations. This number is called the "degree of separation": one for friends, two for friends of friends, and so on. Because we do not have the data from an actual social network, we will simply use an average of the number of friends per user.

Write a recursive method

```
public static double reachablePeople(int degree, double averageFriendsPerUser)
```

Use that method in a program that prompts the user for the desired degree and average, and then prints the number of reachable people. This number should include the original user.

∎∎ Business P5.30 Having a secure password is a very important practice, when much of our information is stored online. Write a program that validates a new password, following these rules:

- The password must be at least 8 characters long.
- The password must have at least one uppercase and one lowercase letter
- The password must have at least one digit.

Write a program that asks for a password, then asks again to confirm it. If the passwords don't match or the rules are not fulfilled, prompt again. Your program should include a method that checks whether a password is valid.

∎∎∎ Science P5.31 You are designing an element for a control panel that displays a temperature value between 0 and 100. The element's color should vary continuously from blue (when the temperature is 0) to red (when the temperature is 100). Write a method `public static int colorForValue(double temperature)` that returns a color value for the given temperature. Colors are encoded as red/green/blue values, each between 0 and 255. The three colors are combined into a single integer, using the formula

```
color = 65536 × red + 256 × green + blue
```

Each of the intermediate colors should be fully saturated; that is, it should be on the outside of the color cube, along the path that goes from blue through cyan, green, and yellow to red.

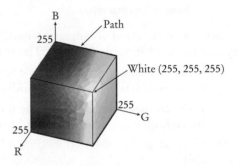

You need to know how to *interpolate* between values. In general, if an output y should vary from c to d as an input x varies from a to b, then y is computed as follows:

$$z = (x - a) / (b - a)$$

$$y = d\,z + c\,(1 - z)$$

If the temperature is between 0 and 25 degrees, interpolate between blue and cyan, whose (red, green, blue) components are (0, 0, 255) and (0, 255, 255). For temperature values between 25 and 50, interpolate between (0, 255, 255) and (0, 255, 0), which represents the color green. Do the same for the remaining two path segments.

You need to interpolate each color component separately and then combine the interpolated colors to a single integer.

Be sure to use appropriate helper methods to solve your task.

∎∎ Science P5.32 In a movie theater, the angle θ at which a viewer sees the picture on the screen depends on the distance x of the viewer from the screen. For a movie theater with the dimensions shown in the picture below, write a method that computes the angle for a given distance.

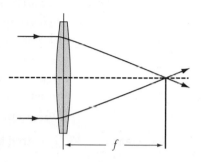

Next, provide a more general method that works for theaters with arbitrary dimensions.

■■ **Science P5.33** The effective focal length f of a lens of thickness d that has surfaces with radii of curvature R_1 and R_2 is given by

$$\frac{1}{f} = (n - 1)\left[\frac{1}{R_1} - \frac{1}{R_2} + \frac{(n - 1)d}{nR_1R_2}\right]$$

where n is the refractive index of the lens medium. Write a method that computes f in terms of the other parameters.

■■ **Science P5.34** A laboratory container is shaped like the frustum of a cone:

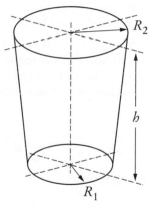

Write methods to compute the volume and surface area, using these equations:

$$V = \tfrac{1}{3}\pi h\left(R_1^2 + R_2^2 + R_1 R_2\right)$$

$$S = \pi\left(R_1 + R_2\right)\sqrt{\left(R_2 - R_1\right)^2 + h^2} + \pi R_1^2$$

■■ **Science P5.35** Electric wire, like that in the photo, is a cylindrical conductor covered by an insulating material. The resistance of a piece of wire is given by the formula

$$R = \frac{\rho L}{A} = \frac{4\rho L}{\pi d^2}$$

where ρ is the resistivity of the conductor, and L, A, and d are the length, cross-sectional area, and diameter of the wire. The resistivity of copper is $1.678 \times 10^{-8}\ \Omega$ m.

The wire diameter, *d*, is commonly specified by the American wire gauge (AWG), which is an integer, *n*. The diameter of an AWG *n* wire is given by the formula

$$d = 0.127 \times 92^{\frac{36-n}{39}} \text{ mm}$$

Write a method

```
public static double diameter(int wireGauge)
```

that accepts the wire gauge and returns the corresponding wire diameter. Write another method

```
public static double copperWireResistance(double length, int wireGauge)
```

that accepts the length and gauge of a piece of copper wire and returns the resistance of that wire. The resistivity of aluminum is 2.82×10^{-8} Ω m. Write a third method

```
public static double aluminumWireResistance(double length, int wireGauge)
```

that accepts the length and gauge of a piece of aluminum wire and returns the resistance of that wire.

Write a program to test these methods.

■■ Science P5.36 The drag force on a car is given by

$$F_D = \frac{1}{2}\rho v^2 A C_D$$

where ρ is the density of air (1.23 kg/m^3), *v* is the velocity in units of m/s, *A* is the projected area of the car (2.5 m^2), and C_D is the drag coefficient (0.2).

The amount of power in watts required to overcome such drag force is $P = F_D v$, and the equivalent horsepower required is Hp = $P / 746$. Write a program that accepts a car's velocity and computes the power in watts and in horsepower needed to overcome the resulting drag force. *Note:* 1 mph = 0.447 m/s.

ANSWERS TO SELF-CHECK QUESTIONS

1. The arguments are 3 and 2. The return value is 9.

2. The inner call to Math.pow returns $2^2 = 4$. Therefore, the outer call returns $4^2 = 16$.

3. 3.0

4. Users of the method can treat it as a *black box*.

5. 27

6. $8 \times 8 \times 8 = 512$

7. ```
double volume = Math.pow(sideLength, 3);
return volume;
```

8. ```
public static double squareArea(
      double sideLength)
{
    double area = sideLength * sideLength;
    return area;
}
```

9. (2 + 3) / (3 - 2) = 5

10. When the mystery method is called, x is set to 5, y is set to 7, and z becomes 12.0. Then z is changed to 6.0, and that value is returned and printed.

11. When the method is called, x is set to 5. Then y is set to 25, and that value is returned and printed.

12. When the method is called, n is set to 5. Then n is incremented twice, setting it to 7. That value is returned and printed.

13. It acts the same way: If sideLength is 0, it returns 0 directly instead of computing 0 × 0 × 0.

14. It returns true if n is even; false if n is odd.

15.
```java
public static boolean mystery(int n)
{
    return n % 2 == 0;
}
```

16.
```java
boxString("Hello");
boxString("World");
```

17. The `boxString` method does not return a value. Therefore, you cannot use it in a call to the print method.

18.
```java
public static void shout(String message)
{
    System.out.println(message ++ "!!!");
}
```

19.
```java
public static void boxString(String contents)
{
    int n = contents.length();
    for (int i = 0; i < n + 4; i++)
    {
        System.out.print("-");
    }
    System.out.println();
    System.out.println("! " + contents + " !");
    for (int i = 0; i < n + 4; i++)
    {
        System.out.print("-");
    }
    System.out.println()
}
```

20.
```java
public static void printLine(int count)
{
    for (int i = 0; i < count; i++)
    {
        System.out.print("-");
    }
    System.out.println();
}
public static void boxString(String contents)
{
    int n = contents.length();
    printLine(n + 2);
    System.out.println("!" + contents + "!");
    printLine(n + 2);
}
```

21.
```java
int totalPennies = getPennies(total);
int taxPennies = getPennies(total * taxRate);
```
where the method is defined as
```java
/**
    @param amount an amount in dollars and cents
    @return the number of pennies in the amount
*/
public static int getPennies(double amount)
{
    return (int) Math.round(100 * amount) % 100;
}
```

22.
```java
if (isEven(page)) . . .
```
where the method is defined as follows:
```java
public static boolean isEven(int n)
{
    return n % 2 == 0;
}
```

23. Add parameter variables so you can pass the initial balance and interest rate to the method:
```java
public static double balance(
    double initialBalance, double rate,
    int years)
{
    return initialBalance * pow(
        1 + rate / 100, years);
}
```

24.
```java
int spaces = countSpaces(input);
```
where the method is defined as follows:
```java
/**
    @param str any string
    @return the number of spaces in str
*/
public static int countSpaces(String str)
{
    int count = 0;
    for (int i = 0; i < str.length(); i++)
    {
        if (str.charAt(i) -- ' ')
        {
            count++;
        }
    }
    return count;
}
```

25. It is very easy to replace the space with any character.
```java
/**
    @param str any string
    @param ch a character whose occurrences
        should be counted
    @return the number of times that ch occurs
        in str
*/
public static int count(String str, char ch)
{
    int count = 0;
    for (int i = 0; i < str.length(); i++)
    {
        if (str.charAt(i) == ch) { count++; }
    }
    return count;
}
```
This is useful if you want to count other characters. For example, `count(input, ",")` counts the commas in the input.

26. Change line 28 to

```
name = name + digitName(part / 100)
    + " hundred";
```

In line 25, add the statement

```
if (part >= 1000)
{
    name = digitName(part / 1000) + "thousand ";
    part = part % 1000;
}
```

In line 18, change 1000 to 10000 in the comment.

27. In the case of "teens", we already have the last digit as part of the name.

28. Nothing is printed. One way of dealing with this case is to add the following statement before line 23.

```
if (number == 0) { return "zero"; }
```

29. Here is the approximate trace:

intName(number = 72)	
part	name
~~72~~	~~"seventy"~~
2	" seventy two"

Note that the string starts with a blank space. Exercise P5.13 asks you to eliminate it.

30. Here is one possible solution. Break up the task **print table** into **print header** and **print body**. The **print header** task calls **print separator**, prints the header cells, and calls **print separator** again. The **print body** task repeatedly calls **print row** and then calls **print separator**.

31. Lines 14–17.

32. Lines 11–19.

33. The variables x defined in lines 5 and 15.

34. Rename the local variable x that is declared in line 15, or rename the parameter variable x that is declared in line 10.

35. The main method accesses the local variable s of the mystery method. Assuming that the main method intended to print the last value of s before the method returned, it should simply print the return value that is stored in its local variable x.

36. [][][][]
[][][]
[][]
[]

37. $4 + 3 + 2 + 1 + 0 = 10$

38. mystery(10) + 1 = mystery(5) + 2 = mystery(2) + 3
= mystery(1) + 4 = mystery(0) + 5 = 5

39. The idea is to print one [], then print n - 1 of them.

```
public static void printBoxes(int n)
{
    if (n == 0) { return; }
    System.out.print("[]");
    printBoxes(n - 1);
}
```

40. Simply add the following to the beginning of the method:

```
if (part >= 1000)
{
    return intName(part / 1000) + " thousand "
        + intName(part % 1000);
}
```

CHAPTER 6

ARRAYS AND ARRAY LISTS

CHAPTER GOALS

To collect elements using arrays and array lists

To use the enhanced for loop for traversing arrays and array lists

To learn common algorithms for processing arrays and array lists

To work with two-dimensional arrays

CHAPTER CONTENTS

6.1 ARRAYS 250

Syntax 6.1: Arrays 251
Common Error 6.1: Bounds Errors 255
Common Error 6.2: Uninitialized Arrays 255
Programming Tip 6.1: Use Arrays for Sequences of Related Items 256
Random Fact 6.1: An Early Internet Worm 256

6.2 THE ENHANCED FOR LOOP 257

Syntax 6.2: The Enhanced for Loop 258

6.3 COMMON ARRAY ALGORITHMS 258

Common Error 6.3: Underestimating the Size of a Data Set 267
Special Topic 6.1: Sorting with the Java Library 267
Special Topic 6.2: Binary Search 267

6.4 USING ARRAYS WITH METHODS 268

Special Topic 6.3: Methods with a Variable Number of Parameters 272

6.5 PROBLEM SOLVING: ADAPTING ALGORITHMS 272

Programming Tip 6.2: Reading Exception Reports 274

How To 6.1: Working with Arrays 275
Worked Example 6.1: Rolling the Dice ✚

6.6 PROBLEM SOLVING: DISCOVERING ALGORITHMS BY MANIPULATING PHYSICAL OBJECTS 279

Video Example 6.1: Removing Duplicates from an Array ✚

6.7 TWO-DIMENSIONAL ARRAYS 282

Syntax 6.3: Two-Dimensional Array Declaration 283
Worked Example 6.2: A World Population Table ✚
Special Topic 6.4: Two-Dimensional Arrays with Variable Row Lengths 288
Special Topic 6.5: Multidimensional Arrays 289

6.8 ARRAY LISTS 289

Syntax 6.4: Array Lists 290
Common Error 6.4: Length and Size 299
Special Topic 6.6: The Diamond Syntax in Java 7 299
Video Example 6.2: Game of Life ✚

249

In many programs, you need to collect large numbers of values. In Java, you use the array and array list constructs for this purpose. Arrays have a more concise syntax, whereas array lists can automatically grow to any desired size. In this chapter, you will learn about arrays, array lists, and common algorithms for processing them.

6.1 Arrays

We start this chapter by introducing the array data type. Arrays are the fundamental mechanism in Java for collecting multiple values. In the following sections, you will learn how to declare arrays and how to access array elements.

6.1.1 Declaring and Using Arrays

Suppose you write a program that reads a sequence of values and prints out the sequence, marking the largest value, like this:

```
32
54
67.5
29
35
80
115 <= largest value
44.5
100
65
```

You do not know which value to mark as the largest one until you have seen them all. After all, the last value might be the largest one. Therefore, the program must first store all values before it can print them.

Could you simply store each value in a separate variable? If you know that there are ten values, then you could store the values in ten variables value1, value2, value3, ..., value10. However, such a sequence of variables is not very practical to use. You would have to write quite a bit of code ten times, once for each of the variables. In Java, an **array** is a much better choice for storing a sequence of values of the same type.

An array collects a sequence of values of the same type.

Here we create an array that can hold ten values of type double:

```
new double[10]
```

The number of elements (here, 10) is called the *length* of the array.

The new operator constructs the array. You will want to store the array in a variable so that you can access it later.

The type of an array variable is the type of the element to be stored, followed by []. In this example, the type is double[], because the element type is double.

Here is the declaration of an array variable of type double[] (see Figure 1):

```
double[] values;  ❶
```

When you declare an array variable, it is not yet initialized. You need to initialize the variable with the array:

```
double[] values = new double[10];  ❷
```

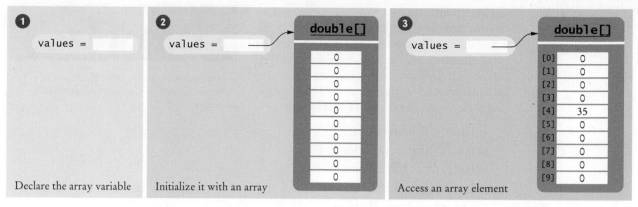

Figure 1 An Array of Size 10

Now `values` is initialized with an array of 10 numbers. By default, each number in the array is 0.

When you declare an array, you can specify the initial values. For example,

```
double[] moreValues = { 32, 54, 67.5, 29, 35, 80, 115, 44.5, 100, 65 };
```

When you supply initial values, you don't use the `new` operator. The compiler determines the length of the array by counting the initial values.

To access a value in an array, you specify which "slot" you want to use. That is done with the `[]` operator:

```
values[4] = 35; ❸
```

Now the number 4 slot of `values` is filled with 35 (see Figure 1). This "slot number" is called an *index*. Each slot in an array contains an *element*.

Because `values` is an array of `double` values, each element `values[i]` can be used like any variable of type `double`. For example, you can display the element with index 4 with the following command:

```
System.out.println(values[4]);
```

> Individual elements in an array are accessed by an integer index i, using the notation *array*[i].

> An array element can be used like any variable.

Syntax 6.1 Arrays

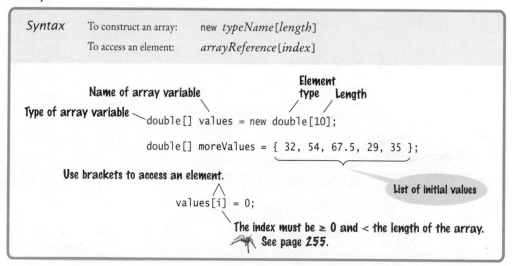

Syntax   To construct an array: new *typeName*[*length*]

         To access an element: *arrayReference*[*index*]

Type of array variable   Name of array variable   Element type   Length

```
double[] values = new double[10];
```

```
double[] moreValues = { 32, 54, 67.5, 29, 35 };
```

List of initial values

Use brackets to access an element.

```
values[i] = 0;
```

The index must be ≥ 0 and < the length of the array.
See page 255.

Before continuing, we must take care of an important detail of Java arrays. If you look carefully at Figure 1, you will find that the *fifth* element was filled when we changed values[4]. In Java, the elements of arrays are numbered *starting at 0*. That is, the legal elements for the values array are

Like a mailbox that is identified by a box number, an array element is identified by an index.

values[0], the first element

values[1], the second element

values[2], the third element

values[3], the fourth element

values[4], the fifth element

. . .

values[9], the tenth element

In other words, the declaration

```
double[] values = new double[10];
```

creates an array with ten elements. In this array, an index can be any integer ranging from 0 to 9.

An array index must be at least zero and less than the size of the array.

You have to be careful that the index stays within the valid range. Trying to access an element that does not exist in the array is a serious error. For example, if values has ten elements, you are not allowed to access values[20]. Attempting to access an element whose index is not within the valid index range is called a **bounds error**. The compiler does not catch this type of error. When a bounds error occurs at run time, it causes a run-time exception.

Here is a very common bounds error:

```
double[] values = new double[10];
values[10] = value;
```

A bounds error, which occurs if you supply an invalid array index, can cause your program to terminate.

There is no values[10] in an array with ten elements—the index can range from 0 to 9.

To avoid bounds errors, you will want to know how many elements are in an array. The expression values.length yields the length of the values array. Note that there are no parentheses following length.

Table 1 Declaring Arrays

`int[] numbers = new int[10];`	An array of ten integers. All elements are initialized with zero.
`final int LENGTH = 10;` `int[] numbers = new int[LENGTH];`	It is a good idea to use a named constant instead of a "magic number".
`int length = in.nextInt();` `double[] data = new double[length];`	The length need not be a constant.
`int[] squares = { 0, 1, 4, 9, 16 };`	An array of five integers, with initial values.
`String[] friends = { "Emily", "Bob", "Cindy" };`	An array of three strings.
🚫 `double[] data = new int[10];`	**Error:** You cannot initialize a double[] variable with an array of type int[].

Use the expression
array.length to find
the number of
elements in an array.

The following code ensures that you only access the array when the index variable
i is within the legal bounds:

```
if (0 <= i && i < values.length) { values[i] = value; }
```

Arrays suffer from a significant limitation: *their length is fixed.* If you start out with
an array of 10 elements and later decide that you need to add additional elements,
then you need to make a new array and copy all elements of the existing array into the
new array. We will discuss this process in detail in Section 6.3.9.

To visit all elements of an array, use a variable for the index. Suppose values has ten
elements and the integer variable i is set to 0, 1, 2, and so on, up to 9. Then the expression values[i] yields each element in turn. For example, this loop displays all elements
in the values array.

```
for (int i = 0; i < 10; i++)
{
    System.out.println(values[i]);
}
```

Note that in the loop condition the index is *less than* 10 because there is no element
corresponding to values[10].

6.1.2 Array References

If you look closely at Figure 1, you will note that the variable values does not store
any numbers. Instead, the array is stored elsewhere and the values variable holds a
reference to the array. (The reference denotes the location of the array in memory.)
When you access the elements in an array, you need not be concerned about the fact
that Java uses array references. This only becomes important when copying array
references.

When you copy an array variable into another, both variables refer to the same
array (see Figure 2).

An array reference
specifies the location
of an array. Copying
the reference yields a
second reference to
the same array.

```
int[] scores = { 10, 9, 7, 4, 5 };
int[] values = scores; // Copying array reference
```

You can modify the array through either of the variables:

```
scores[3] = 10;
System.out.println(values[3]); // Prints 10
```

Section 6.3.9 shows how you can make a copy of the *contents* of the array.

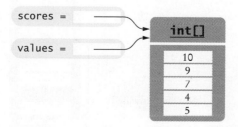

Figure 2
Two Array Variables Referencing the Same Array

6.1.3 Partially Filled Arrays

With a partially filled array, you need to remember how many elements are filled.

An array cannot change size at run time. This is a problem when you don't know in advance how many elements you need. In that situation, you must come up with a good guess on the maximum number of elements that you need to store. For example, we may decide that we sometimes want to store more than ten elements, but never more than 100:

```java
final int LENGTH = 100;
double[] values = new double[LENGTH];
```

In a typical program run, only a part of the array will be occupied by actual elements. We call such an array a **partially filled array**. You must keep a *companion variable* that counts how many elements are actually used. In Figure 3 we call the companion variable currentSize.

The following loop collects inputs and fills up the values array:

```java
int currentSize = 0;
Scanner in = new Scanner(System.in);
while (in.hasNextDouble())
{
   if (currentSize < values.length)
   {
      values[currentSize] = in.nextDouble();
      currentSize++;
   }
}
```

> With a partially filled array, keep a companion variable for the current size.

At the end of this loop, currentSize contains the actual number of elements in the array. Note that you have to stop accepting inputs if the currentSize companion variable reaches the array length.

To process the gathered array elements, you again use the companion variable, not the array length. This loop prints the partially filled array:

ONLINE EXAMPLE

A program demonstrating array operations.

```java
for (int i = 0; i < currentSize; i++)
{
   System.out.println(values[i]);
}
```

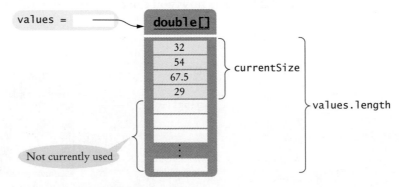

Figure 3 A Partially Filled Array

SELF CHECK

1. Declare an array of integers containing the first five prime numbers.

2. Assume the array primes has been initialized as described in Self Check 1. What does it contain after executing the following loop?

   ```
   for (int i = 0; i < 2; i++)
   {
      primes[4 - i] = primes[i];
   }
   ```

3. Assume the array primes has been initialized as described in Self Check 1. What does it contain after executing the following loop?

   ```
   for (int i = 0; i < 5; i++)
   {
      primes[i]++;
   }
   ```

4. Given the declaration

   ```
   int[] values = new int[10];
   ```

   write statements to put the integer 10 into the elements of the array values with the lowest and the highest valid index.

5. Declare an array called words that can hold ten elements of type String.

6. Declare an array containing two strings, "Yes", and "No".

7. Can you produce the output on page 250 without storing the inputs in an array, by using an algorithm similar to the algorithm for finding the maximum in Section 4.7.5?

Practice It Now you can try these exercises at the end of the chapter: R6.1, R6.2, R6.6, P6.1.

Common Error 6.1

Bounds Errors

Perhaps the most common error in using arrays is accessing a nonexistent element.

```
double[] values = new double[10];
values[10] = 5.4;
   // Error—values has 10 elements, and the index can range from 0 to 9
```

If your program accesses an array through an out-of-bounds index, there is no compiler error message. Instead, the program will generate an exception at run time.

Common Error 6.2

Uninitialized Arrays

A common error is to allocate an array variable, but not an actual array.

```
double[] values;
values[0] = 29.95; // Error—values not initialized
```

The Java compiler will catch this error. The remedy is to initialize the variable with an array:

```
double[] values = new double[10];
```

Use Arrays for Sequences of Related Items

Arrays are intended for storing sequences of values with the same meaning. For example, an array of test scores makes perfect sense:

```
int[] scores = new int[NUMBER_OF_SCORES];
```

But an array

```
int[] personalData = new int[3];
```

that holds a person's age, bank balance, and shoe size in positions 0, 1, and 2 is bad design. It would be tedious for the programmer to remember which of these data values is stored in which array location. In this situation, it is far better to use three separate variables.

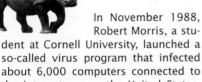

Random Fact 6.1 An Early Internet Worm

In November 1988, Robert Morris, a student at Cornell University, launched a so-called virus program that infected about 6,000 computers connected to the Internet across the United States. Tens of thousands of computer users were unable to read their e-mail or otherwise use their computers. All major universities and many high-tech companies were affected. (The Internet was much smaller then than it is now.)

The particular kind of virus used in this attack is called a *worm*. The worm program crawled from one computer on the Internet to the next. The worm would attempt to connect to finger, a program in the UNIX operating system for finding information on a user who has an account on a particular computer on the network. Like many programs in UNIX, finger was written in the C language. In order to store the user name, the finger program allocated an array of 512 characters, under the assumption that nobody would ever provide such a long input. Unfortunately, C does not check that an array index is less than the length of the array. If you write into an array using an index that is too large, you simply overwrite memory locations that belong to some other objects. In some versions of the finger program, the programmer had been lazy and had not checked whether the array holding the input characters was large enough

to hold the input. So the worm program purposefully filled the 512-character array with 536 bytes. The excess 24 bytes would overwrite a return address, which the attacker knew was stored just after the array. When that method was finished, it didn't return to its caller but to code supplied by the worm (see the figure, A "Buffer Overrun" Attack). That code ran under the same super-user privileges as finger, allowing the worm to gain entry into the remote system. Had the programmer who wrote finger been more conscientious, this particular attack would not be possible.

In Java, as in C, all programmers must be very careful not to overrun array boundaries. However, in Java, this error causes a run-time exception, and it never corrupts memory outside the array. This is one of the safety features of Java.

One may well speculate what would possess the virus author to spend many weeks to plan the antisocial act of breaking into thousands of computers and disabling them. It appears that the break-in was fully intended by the author, but the disabling of the computers was a bug, caused by continuous reinfection. Morris was sentenced to 3 years probation, 400 hours of community service, and a $10,000 fine.

In recent years, computer attacks have intensified and the motives have become more sinister. Instead

of disabling computers, viruses often steal financial data or use the attacked computers for sending spam e-mail. Sadly, many of these attacks continue to be possible because of poorly written programs that are susceptible to buffer overrun errors.

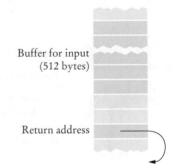

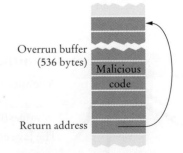

A "Buffer Overrun" Attack

6.2 The Enhanced for Loop

You can use the enhanced for loop to visit all elements of an array.

Often, you need to visit all elements of an array. The *enhanced for loop* makes this process particularly easy to program.

Here is how you use the enhanced for loop to total up all elements in an array named values:

```
double[] values = . . .;
double total = 0;
for (double element : values)
{
    total = total + element;
}
```

The loop body is executed for each element in the array values. At the beginning of each loop iteration, the next element is assigned to the variable element. Then the loop body is executed. You should read this loop as "for each element in values".

This loop is equivalent to the following for loop and an explicit index variable:

```
for (int i = 0; i < values.length; i++)
{
    double element = values[i];
    total = total + element;
}
```

Note an important difference between the enhanced for loop and the basic for loop. In the enhanced for loop, the *element variable* is assigned values[0], values[1], and so on. In the basic for loop, the *index variable* i is assigned 0, 1, and so on.

Use the enhanced for loop if you do not need the index values in the loop body.

Keep in mind that the enhanced for loop has a very specific purpose: getting the elements of a collection, from the beginning to the end. It is not suitable for all array algorithms. In particular, the enhanced for loop does not allow you to modify the contents of an array. The following loop does not fill an array with zeroes:

```
for (double element : values)
{
    element = 0; // ERROR: this assignment does not modify array elements
}
```

When the loop is executed, the variable element is set to values[0]. Then element is set to 0, then to values[1], then to 0, and so on. The values array is not modified. The remedy is simple: Use a basic for loop:

```
for (int i = 0; i < values.length; i++)
{
    values[i] = 0; // OK
}
```

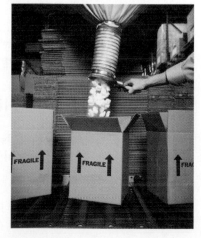

The enhanced for loop is a convenient mechanism for traversing all elements in a collection.

Syntax 6.2   The Enhanced for Loop

Syntax   for (*typeName variable* : *collection*)
{
   statements
}

This variable is set in each loop iteration.
It is only defined inside the loop.

An array

```
for (double element : values)
{
   sum = sum + element;
}
```

These statements
are executed for each
element.

The variable
contains an element,
not an index.

8. What does this enhanced for loop do?

```
int counter = 0;
for (double element : values)
{
   if (element == 0) { counter++; }
}
```

9. Write an enhanced for loop that prints all elements in the array values.

10. Write an enhanced for loop that multiplies all elements in a double[] array named factors, accumulating the result in a variable named product.

11. Why is the enhanced for loop not an appropriate shortcut for the following basic for loop?

```
for (int i = 0; i < values.length; i++) { values[i] = i * i; }
```

Practice It   Now you can try these exercises at the end of the chapter: R6.7, R6.8, R6.9.

6.3 Common Array Algorithms

In the following sections, we discuss some of the most common algorithms for working with arrays. If you use a partially filled array, remember to replace values.length with the companion variable that represents the current size of the array.

6.3.1 Filling

This loop fills an array with squares (0, 1, 4, 9, 16, ...). Note that the element with index 0 contains 0^2, the element with index 1 contains 1^2, and so on.

```
for (int i = 0; i < values.length; i++)
{
   values[i] = i * i;
}
```

6.3.2 Sum and Average Value

You have already encountered this algorithm in Section 4.7.1. When the values are located in an array, the code looks much simpler:

```
double total = 0;
for (double element : values)
{
   total = total + element;
}
double average = 0;
if (values.length > 0) { average = total / values.length; }
```

6.3.3 Maximum and Minimum

Use the algorithm from Section 4.7.5 that keeps a variable for the largest element already encountered. Here is the implementation of that algorithm for an array:

```
double largest = values[0];
for (int i = 1; i < values.length; i++)
{
   if (values[i] > largest)
   {
      largest = values[i];
   }
}
```

Note that the loop starts at 1 because we initialize largest with values[0].

To compute the smallest element, reverse the comparison.

These algorithms require that the array contain at least one element.

6.3.4 Element Separators

When separating elements, don't place a separator before the first element.

When you display the elements of an array, you usually want to separate them, often with commas or vertical lines, like this:

```
32 | 54 | 67.5 | 29 | 35
```

Note that there is one fewer separator than there are numbers. Print the separator before each element in the sequence *except the initial one* (with index 0) like this:

```
for (int i = 0; i < values.length; i++)
{
   if (i > 0)
   {
      System.out.print(" | ");
   }
   System.out.print(values[i]);
}
```

To print five elements, you need four separators.

If you want comma separators, you can use the Arrays.toString method. The expression

```
Arrays.toString(values)
```

returns a string describing the contents of the array values in the form

```
[32, 54, 67.5, 29, 35]
```

The elements are surrounded by a pair of brackets and separated by commas. This method can be convenient for debugging:

```
System.out.println("values=" + Arrays.toString(values));
```

6.3.5 Linear Search

To search for a specific element, visit the elements and stop when you encounter the match.

You often need to search for the position of a specific element in an array so that you can replace or remove it. Visit all elements until you have found a match or you have come to the end of the array. Here we search for the position of the first element in an array that is equal to 100:

```
int searchedValue = 100;
int pos = 0;
boolean found = false;
while (pos < values.length && !found)
{
   if (values[pos] == searchedValue)
   {
      found = true;
   }
   else
   {
      pos++;
   }
}
if (found) { System.out.println("Found at position: " + pos); }
else { System.out.println("Not found"); }
```

A linear search inspects elements in sequence until a match is found.

This algorithm is called **linear search** or *sequential search* because you inspect the elements in sequence. If the array is sorted, you can use the more efficient **binary search** algorithm—see Special Topic 6.2 on page 267.

6.3.6 Removing an Element

Suppose you want to remove the element with index pos from the array values. As explained in Section 6.1.3, you need a companion variable for tracking the number of elements in the array. In this example, we use a companion variable called currentSize.

If the elements in the array are not in any particular order, simply overwrite the element to be removed with the *last* element of the array, then decrement the current-Size variable. (See Figure 4.)

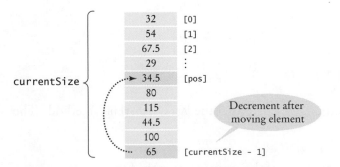

Figure 4
Removing an Element in an Unordered Array

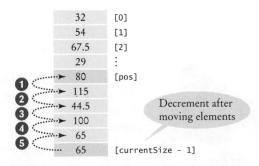

Figure 5
Removing an Element in an Ordered Array

```
values[pos] = values[currentSize - 1];
currentSize--;
```

The situation is more complex if the order of the elements matters. Then you must move all elements following the element to be removed to a lower index, and then decrement the variable holding the size of the array. (See Figure 5.)

```
for (int i = pos + 1; i < currentSize; i++)
{
    values[i - 1] = values[i];
}
currentSize--;
```

ANIMATION
Removing from an Array

6.3.7 Inserting an Element

In this section, you will see how to insert an element into an array. Note that you need a companion variable for tracking the array size, as explained in Section 6.1.3.

If the order of the elements does not matter, you can simply insert new elements at the end, incrementing the variable tracking the size.

```
if (currentSize < values.length)
{
    currentSize++;
    values[currentSize - 1] = newElement;
}
```

ANIMATION
Inserting into an Array

It is more work to insert an element at a particular position in the middle of an array. First, move all elements after the insertion location to a higher index. Then insert the new element (see Figure 7).

Note the order of the movement: When you remove an element, you first move the next element to a lower index, then the one after that, until you finally get to the end of the array. When you insert an element, you start at the end of the array, move that element to a higher index, then move the one before that, and so on until you finally get to the insertion location.

Before inserting an element, move elements to the end of the array *starting with the last one.*

```
if (currentSize < values.length)
{
    currentSize++;
    for (int i = currentSize - 1; i > pos; i--)
    {
        values[i] = values[i - 1];
    }
    values[pos] = newElement;
}
```

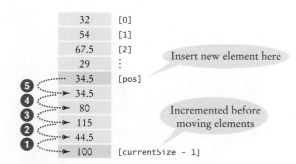

Figure 6
Inserting an Element in an Unordered Array

Figure 7
Inserting an Element in an Ordered Array

6.3.8 Swapping Elements

You often need to swap elements of an array. For example, you can sort an array by repeatedly swapping elements that are not in order.

Consider the task of swapping the elements at positions i and j of an array values. We'd like to set values[i] to values[j]. But that overwrites the value that is currently stored in values[i], so we want to save that first:

```
double temp = values[i];
values[i] = values[j];
```

Now we can set values[j] to the saved value.

```
values[j] = temp;
```

Figure 8 shows the process.

> Use a temporary variable when swapping two elements.

To swap two elements, you need a temporary variable.

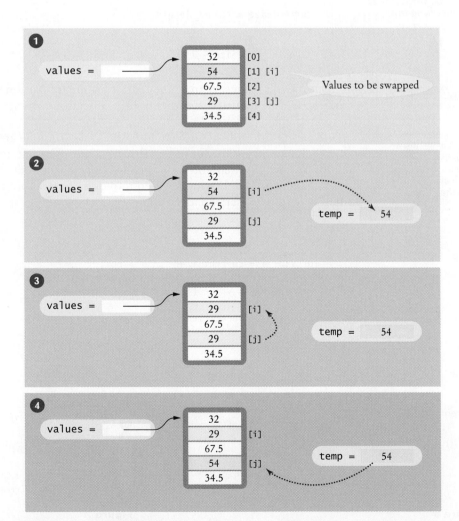

Figure 8 Swapping Array Elements

6.3.9 Copying Arrays

Array variables do not themselves hold array elements. They hold a reference to the actual array. If you copy the reference, you get another reference to the same array (see Figure 9):

```
double[] values = new double[6];
. . .  // Fill array
double[] prices = values; ❶
```

If you want to make a true copy of an array, call the Arrays.copyOf method (as shown in Figure 9).

```
double[] prices = Arrays.copyOf(values, values.length); ❷
```

The call Arrays.copyOf(values, n) allocates an array of length n, copies the first n elements of values (or the entire values array if n > values.length) into it, and returns the new array.

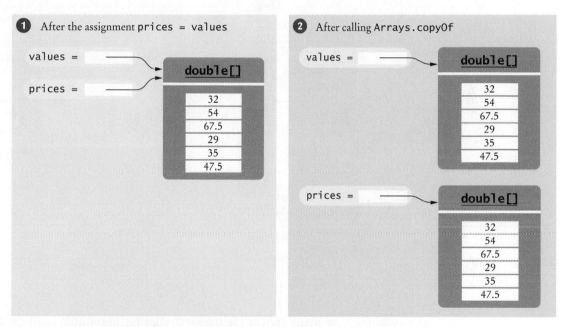

Figure 9 Copying an Array Reference versus Copying an Array

In order to use the Arrays class, you need to add the following statement to the top of your program:

```
import java.util.Arrays;
```

Another use for Arrays.copyOf is to grow an array that has run out of space. The following statements have the effect of doubling the length of an array (see Figure 10):

```
double[] newValues = Arrays.copyOf(values, 2 * values.length); ❶
values = newValues; ❷
```

The copyOf method was added in Java 6. If you use Java 5, replace

```
double[] newValues = Arrays.copyOf(values, n)
```

with

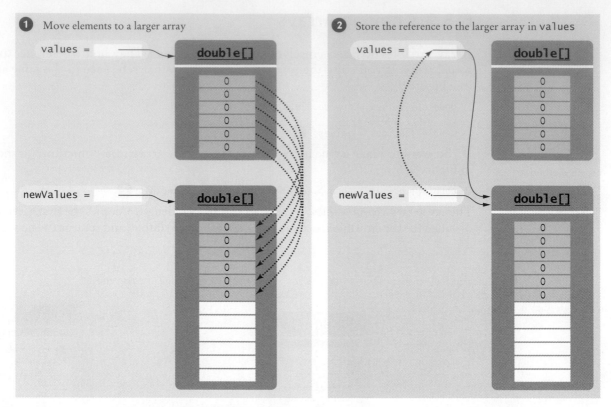

Figure 10 Growing an Array

```
double[] newValues = new double[n];
for (int i = 0; i < n && i < values.length; i++)
{
    newValues[i] = values[i];
}
```

6.3.10 Reading Input

If you know how many inputs the user will supply, it is simple to place them into an array:

```
double[] inputs = new double[NUMBER_OF_INPUTS];
for (i = 0; i < inputs.length; i++)
{
    inputs[i] = in.nextDouble();
}
```

However, this technique does not work if you need to read a sequence of arbitrary length. In that case, add the inputs to an array until the end of the input has been reached.

```
int currentSize = 0;
while (in.hasNextDouble() && currentSize < inputs.length)
{
    inputs[currentSize] = in.nextDouble();
    currentSize++;
}
```

Now `inputs` is a partially filled array, and the companion variable `currentSize` is set to the number of inputs.

However, this loop silently throws away inputs that don't fit into the array. A better approach is to grow the array to hold all inputs.

```java
double[] inputs = new double[INITIAL_SIZE];
int currentSize = 0;
while (in.hasNextDouble())
{
    // Grow the array if it has been completely filled
    if (currentSize >= inputs.length)
    {
        inputs = Arrays.copyOf(inputs, 2 * inputs.length); // Grow the inputs array
    }

    inputs[currentSize] = in.nextDouble();
    currentSize++;
}
```

When you are done, you can discard any excess (unfilled) elements:

```java
inputs = Arrays.copyOf(inputs, currentSize);
```

The following program puts these algorithms to work, solving the task that we set ourselves at the beginning of this chapter: to mark the largest value in an input sequence.

section_3/LargestInArray.java

```java
1   import java.util.Scanner;
2
3   /**
4       This program reads a sequence of values and prints them, marking the largest value.
5   */
6   public class LargestInArray
7   {
8       public static void main(String[] args)
9       {
10          final int LENGTH = 100;
11          double[] values = new double[LENGTH];
12          int currentSize = 0;
13
14          // Read inputs
15
16          System.out.println("Please enter values, Q to quit:");
17          Scanner in = new Scanner(System.in);
18          while (in.hasNextDouble() && currentSize < values.length)
19          {
20              values[currentSize] = in.nextDouble();
21              currentSize++;
22          }
23
24          // Find the largest value
25
26          double largest = values[0];
27          for (int i = 1; i < currentSize; i++)
28          {
29              if (values[i] > largest)
30              {
31                  largest = values[i];
32              }
33          }
```

```
34
35        // Print all values, marking the largest
36
37        for (int i = 0; i < currentSize; i++)
38        {
39           System.out.print(values[i]);
40           if (values[i] == largest)
41           {
42              System.out.print(" <== largest value");
43           }
44           System.out.println();
45        }
46     }
47  }
```

Program Run

```
Please enter values, Q to quit:
34.5 80 115 44.5 Q
34.5
80
115 <== largest value
44.5
```

SELF CHECK

12. Given these inputs, what is the output of the `LargestInArray` program?

```
20 10 20 Q
```

13. Write a loop that counts how many elements in an array are equal to zero.

14. Consider the algorithm to find the largest element in an array. Why don't we initialize `largest` and `i` with zero, like this?

```
double largest = 0;
for (int i = 0; i < values.length; i++)
{
   if (values[i] > largest)
   {
      largest = values[i];
   }
}
```

15. When printing separators, we skipped the separator before the initial element. Rewrite the loop so that the separator is printed *after* each element, except for the last element.

16. What is wrong with these statements for printing an array with separators?

```
System.out.print(values[0]);
for (int i = 1; i < values.length; i++)
{
   System.out.print(", " + values[i]);
}
```

17. When finding the position of a match, we used a `while` loop, not a `for` loop. What is wrong with using this loop instead?

```
for (pos = 0; pos < values.length && !found; pos++)
{
   if (values[pos] > 100)
   {
      found = true;
   }
```

```
    }
```

18. When inserting an element into an array, we moved the elements with larger index values, starting at the end of the array. Why is it wrong to start at the insertion location, like this?

```
for (int i = pos; i < currentSize - 1; i++)
{
    values[i + 1] = values[i];
}
```

Practice It   Now you can try these exercises at the end of the chapter: R6.17, R6.20, P6.15.

Common Error 6.3

Underestimating the Size of a Data Set

Programmers commonly underestimate the amount of input data that a user will pour into an unsuspecting program. Suppose you write a program to search for text in a file. You store each line in a string, and keep an array of strings. How big do you make the array? Surely nobody is going to challenge your program with an input that is more than 100 lines. Really? It is very easy to feed in the entire text of *Alice in Wonderland* or *War and Peace* (which are available on the Internet). All of a sudden, your program has to deal with tens or hundreds of thousands of lines. You either need to allow for large inputs or politely reject the excess input.

Special Topic 6.1

Sorting with the Java Library

Sorting an array efficiently is not an easy task. You will learn in Chapter 14 how to implement efficient sorting algorithms. Fortunately, the Java library provides an efficient sort method.

To sort an array values, call

```
Arrays.sort(values);
```

If the array is partially filled, call

```
Arrays.sort(values, 0, currentSize);
```

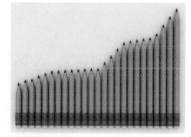

Special Topic 6.2

Binary Search

When an array is sorted, there is a much faster search algorithm than the linear search of Section 6.3.5.

Consider the following sorted array values.

[0]	[1]	[2]	[3]	[4]	[5]	[6]	[7]
1	5	8	9	12	17	20	32

We would like to see whether the number 15 is in the array. Let's narrow our search by finding whether the number is in the first or second half of the array. The last point in the first half of the values array, values[3], is 9, which is smaller than the number we are looking for. Hence, we should look in the second half of the array for a match, that is, in the sequence:

[0]	[1]	[2]	[3]	[4]	[5]	[6]	[7]
1	5	8	9	12	17	20	32

Now the last element of the first half of this sequence is 17; hence, the number must be located in the sequence:

```
[0] [1] [2] [3] [4] [5] [6] [7]
 1   5   8   9  12  17  20  32
```

The last element of the first half of this very short sequence is 12, which is smaller than the number that we are searching, so we must look in the second half:

```
[0] [1] [2] [3] [4] [5] [6] [7]
 1   5   8   9  12  17  20  32
```

We still don't have a match because $15 \neq 17$, and we cannot divide the subsequence further. If we wanted to insert 15 into the sequence, we would need to insert it just before values[5].

This search process is called a **binary search**, because we cut the size of the search in half in each step. That cutting in half works only because we know that the array is sorted. Here is an implementation in Java:

```java
boolean found = false;
int low = 0;
int high = values.length - 1;
int pos = 0;
while (low <= high && !found)
{
    pos = (low + high) / 2; // Midpoint of the subsequence
    if (values[pos] == searchedNumber) { found = true; }
    else if (values[pos] < searchedNumber) { low = pos + 1; } // Look in second half
    else { high = pos - 1; } // Look in first half
}
if (found) { System.out.println("Found at position " + pos); }
else { System.out.println("Not found. Insert before position " + pos); }
```

6.4 Using Arrays with Methods

In this section, we will explore how to write methods that process arrays.

Arrays can occur as method arguments and return values.

When you define a method with an array argument, you provide a parameter variable for the array. For example, the following method computes the sum of an array of floating-point numbers:

```java
public static double sum(double[] values)
{
    double total = 0;
    for (double element : values)
    {
        total = total + element;
    }
    return total;
}
```

This method visits the array elements, but it does not modify them. It is also possible to modify the elements of an array. The following method multiplies all elements of an array by a given factor:

```java
public static void multiply(double[] values, double factor)
{
    for (int i = 0; i < values.length; i++)
    {
```

```
            values[i] = values[i] * factor;
        }
    }
```

Figure 11 traces the method call

```
multiply(scores, 10);
```

Note these steps:

- The parameter variables `values` and `factor` are created. **1**
- The parameter variables are initialized with the arguments that are passed in the call. In our case, `values` is set to `scores` and `factor` is set to 10. Note that `values` and `scores` are references to the *same* array. **2**
- The method multiplies all array elements by 10. **3**
- The method returns. Its parameter variables are removed. However, `scores` still refers to the array with the modified elements. **4**

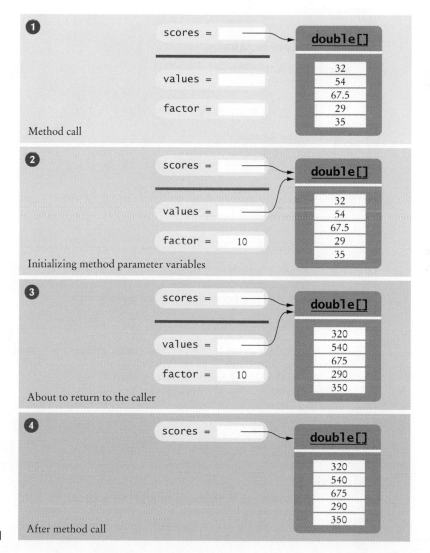

Figure 11
Trace of Call to
the `multiply` Method

A method can return an array. Simply build up the result in the method and return it. In this example, the squares method returns an array of squares from 0^2 up to $(n-1)^2$:

```java
public static int[] squares(int n)
{
   int[] result = new int[n];
   for (int i = 0; i < n; i++)
   {
      result[i] = i * i;
   }
   return result;
}
```

The following example program reads values from standard input, multiplies them by 10, and prints the result in reverse order. The program uses three methods:

- The readInputs method returns an array, using the algorithm of Section 6.3.10.
- The multiply method has an array argument. It modifies the array elements.
- The printReversed method also has an array argument, but it does not modify the array elements.

section_4/Reverse.java

```java
 1   import java.util.Scanner;
 2
 3   /**
 4      This program reads, scales, and reverses a sequence of numbers.
 5   */
 6   public class Reverse
 7   {
 8      public static void main(String[] args)
 9      {
10         double[] numbers = readInputs(5);
11         multiply(numbers, 10);
12         printReversed(numbers);
13      }
14
15      /**
16         Reads a sequence of floating-point numbers.
17         @param numberOfInputs the number of inputs to read
18         @return an array containing the input values
19      */
20      public static double[] readInputs(int numberOfInputs)
21      {
22         System.out.println("Enter " + numberOfInputs + " numbers: ");
23         Scanner in = new Scanner(System.in);
24         double[] inputs = new double[numberOfInputs];
25         for (int i = 0; i < inputs.length; i++)
26         {
27            inputs[i] = in.nextDouble();
28         }
29         return inputs;
30      }
31
32      /**
33         Multiplies all elements of an array by a factor.
34         @param values an array
35         @param factor the value with which element is multiplied
36      */
```

```
37    public static void multiply(double[] values, double factor)
38    {
39       for (int i = 0; i < values.length; i++)
40       {
41          values[i] = values[i] * factor;
42       }
43    }
44
45    /**
46       Prints an array in reverse order.
47       @param values an array of numbers
48       @return an array that contains the elements of values in reverse order
49    */
50    public static void printReversed(double[] values)
51    {
52       // Traverse the array in reverse order, starting with the last element
53       for (int i = values.length - 1; i >= 0; i--)
54       {
55          System.out.print(values[i] + " ");
56       }
57       System.out.println();
58    }
59 }
```

Program Run

```
Enter 5 numbers:
12 25 20 0 10
100.0 0.0 200.0 250.0 120.0
```

SELF CHECK

19. How do you call the squares method to compute the first five squares and store the result in an array numbers?

20. Write a method fill that fills all elements of an array of integers with a given value. For example, the call fill(scores, 10) should fill all elements of the array scores with the value 10.

21. Describe the purpose of the following method:

```
public static int[] mystery(int length, int n)
{
   int[] result = new int[length];
   for (int i = 0; i < result.length; i++)
   {
      result[i] = (int) (n * Math.random());
   }
   return result;
}
```

22. Consider the following method that reverses an array:

```
public static int[] reverse(int[] values)
{
   int[] result = new int[values.length];
   for (int i = 0; i < values.length; i++)
   {
      result[i] = values[values.length - 1 - i];
   }
   return result;
}
```

Suppose the reverse method is called with an array scores that contains the numbers 1, 4, and 9. What is the contents of scores after the method call?

23. Provide a trace diagram of the reverse method when called with an array that contains the values 1, 4, and 9.

Practice It   Now you can try these exercises at the end of the chapter: R6.25, P6.6, P6.7.

Special Topic 6.3

Methods with a Variable Number of Parameters

Starting with Java version 5.0, it is possible to declare methods that receive a variable number of parameters. For example, we can write a sum method that can compute the sum of any number of arguments:

```
int a = sum(1, 3); // Sets a to 4
int b = sum(1, 7, 2, 9); // Sets b to 19
```

The modified sum method must be declared as

```
public static void sum(int... values)
```

The ... symbol indicates that the method can receive any number of int arguments. The values parameter variable is actually an int[] array that contains all arguments that were passed to the method. The method implementation traverses the values array and processes the elements:

```
public void sum(int... values)
{
   int total = 0;
   for (int i = 0; i < values.length; i++) // values is an int[]
   {
      total = total + values[i];
   }
   return total;
}
```

6.5 Problem Solving: Adapting Algorithms

By combining fundamental algorithms, you can solve complex programming tasks.

In Section 6.3, you were introduced to a number of fundamental array algorithms. These algorithms form the building blocks for many programs that process arrays. In general, it is a good problem-solving strategy to have a repertoire of fundamental algorithms that you can combine and adapt.

Consider this example problem: You are given the quiz scores of a student. You are to compute the final quiz score, which is the sum of all scores after dropping the lowest one. For example, if the scores are

8   7   8.5   9.5   7   4   10

then the final score is 50.

We do not have a ready-made algorithm for this situation. Instead, consider which algorithms may be related. These include:

- Calculating the sum (Section 6.3.2)
- Finding the minimum value (Section 6.3.3)
- Removing an element (Section 6.3.6)

We can formulate a plan of attack that combines these algorithms:

> Find the minimum.
> Remove it from the array.
> Calculate the sum.

Let's try it out with our example. The minimum of

```
    [0] [1] [2] [3] [4] [5] [6]
    8   7  8.5 9.5  7   4   10
```

is 4. How do we remove it?

Now we have a problem. The removal algorithm in Section 6.3.6 locates the element to be removed by using the *position* of the element, not the value.

But we have another algorithm for that:

- Linear search (Section 6.3.5)

We need to fix our plan of attack:

> Find the minimum value.
> Find its position.
> Remove that position from the array.
> Calculate the sum.

Will it work? Let's continue with our example.

We found a minimum value of 4. Linear search tells us that the value 4 occurs at position 5.

```
    [0] [1] [2] [3] [4] [5] [6]
    8   7  8.5 9.5  7   4   10
```

We remove it:

```
    [0] [1] [2] [3] [4] [5]
    8   7  8.5 9.5  7   10
```

Finally, we compute the sum: $8 + 7 + 8.5 + 9.5 + 7 + 10 = 50$.

This walkthrough demonstrates that our strategy works.

Can we do better? It seems a bit inefficient to find the minimum and then make another pass through the array to obtain its position.

We can adapt the algorithm for finding the minimum to yield the position of the minimum. Here is the original algorithm:

```
double smallest = values[0];
for (int i = 1; i < values.length; i++)
{
   if (values[i] < smallest)
   {
      smallest = values[i];
   }
}
```

When we find the smallest value, we also want to update the position:

```
if (values[i] < smallest)
{
   smallest = values[i];
   smallestPosition = i;
}
```

In fact, then there is no reason to keep track of the smallest value any longer. It is simply `values[smallestPosition]`. With this insight, we can adapt the algorithm as follows:

```java
int smallestPosition = 0;
for (int i = 1; i < values.length; i++)
{
   if (values[i] < values[smallestPosition])
   {
      smallestPosition = i;
   }
}
```

ONLINE EXAMPLE

 A program that computes the final score using the adapted algorithm for finding the minimum.

With this adaptation, our problem is solved with the following strategy:

Find the position of the minimum.
Remove it from the array.
Calculate the sum.

The next section shows you a technique for discovering a new algorithm when none of the fundamental algorithms can be adapted to a task.

SELF CHECK

24. Section 6.3.6 has two algorithms for removing an element. Which of the two should be used to solve the task described in this section?

25. It isn't actually necessary to *remove* the minimum in order to compute the total score. Describe an alternative.

26. How can you print the number of positive and negative values in a given array, using one or more of the algorithms in Section 4.7?

27. How can you print all positive values in an array, separated by commas?

28. Consider the following algorithm for collecting all matches in an array:

```java
int matchesSize = 0;
for (int i = 0; i < values.length; i++)
{
   if (values[i] fulfills the condition)
   {
      matches[matchesSize] = values[i];
      matchesSize++;
   }
}
```

How can this algorithm help you with Self Check 27?

Practice It   Now you can try these exercises at the end of the chapter: R6.26, R6.27.

Programming Tip 6.2

Reading Exception Reports

You will sometimes have programs that terminate, reporting an "exception", such as

```
Exception in thread "main" java.lang.ArrayIndexOutOfBoundsException: 10
   at Homework1.processValues(Homework1.java:14)
   at Homework1.main(Homework1.java:36)
```

Quite a few students give up at that point, saying "it didn't work", or "my program died", without reading the error message. Admittedly, the format of the exception report is not very friendly. But, with some practice, it is easy to decipher it.

There are two pieces of useful information:

1. The name of the exception, such as `ArrayIndexOutOfBoundsException`
2. The `stack trace`, that is, the method calls that led to the exception, such as `Homework1.java:14` and `Homework1.java:36` in our example.

The name of the exception is always in the first line of the report, and it ends in `Exception`. If you get an `ArrayIndexOutOfBoundsException`, then there was a problem with an invalid array index. That is useful information.

To determine the line number of the offending code, look at the file names and line numbers. The first line of the stack trace is the method that actually generated the exception. The last line of the stack trace is a line in `main`. In our example, the exception was caused by line 14 of `Homework1.java`. Open up the file, go to that line, and look at it! Also look at the name of the exception. In most cases, these two pieces of information will make it completely obvious what went wrong, and you can easily fix your error.

Sometimes, the exception was thrown by a method that is in the standard library. Here is a typical example:

```
Exception in thread "main" java.lang.StringIndexOutOfBoundsException: String index
      out of range: -4
    at java.lang.String.substring(String.java:1444)
    at Homework2.main(Homework2.java:29)
```

The exception happened in the `substring` method of the `String` class, but the real culprit is the first method in a file that you wrote. In this example, that is `Homework2.main`, and you should look at line 29 of `Homework2.java`.

HOW TO 6.1   Working with Arrays

In many data processing situations, you need to process a sequence of values. This How To walks you through the steps for storing input values in an array and carrying out computations with the array elements.

Consider again the problem from Section 6.5: A final quiz score is computed by adding all the scores, except for the lowest one. For example, if the scores are

8   7   8.5   9.5   7   5   10

then the final score is 50.

Step 1   Decompose your task into steps.

You will usually want to break down your task into multiple steps, such as

- Reading the data into an array.
- Processing the data in one or more steps.
- Displaying the results.

When deciding how to process the data, you should be familiar with the array algorithms in Section 6.3. Most processing tasks can be solved by using one or more of these algorithms.

In our sample problem, we will want to read the data. Then we will remove the minimum and compute the total. For example, if the input is 8 7 8.5 9.5 7 5 10, we will remove the minimum of 5, yielding 8 7 8.5 9.5 7 10. The sum of those values is the final score of 50.

Thus, we have identified three steps:

Read inputs.
Remove the minimum.
Calculate the sum.

Step 2   Determine which algorithm(s) you need.

Sometimes, a step corresponds to exactly one of the basic array algorithms in Section 6.3. That is the case with calculating the sum (Section 6.3.2) and reading the inputs (Section 6.3.10). At other times, you need to combine several algorithms. To remove the minimum value, you can find the minimum value (Section 6.3.3), find its position (Section 6.3.5), and remove the element at that position (Section 6.3.6).

We have now refined our plan as follows:

Read inputs.
Find the minimum.
Find its position.
Remove the minimum.
Calculate the sum.

This plan will work—see Section 6.5. But here is an alternate approach. It is easy to compute the sum and subtract the minimum. Then we don't have to find its position. The revised plan is

Read inputs.
Find the minimum.
Calculate the sum.
Subtract the minimum.

Step 3   Use methods to structure the program.

Even though it may be possible to put all steps into the main method, this is rarely a good idea. It is better to make each processing step into a separate method. In our example, we will implement three methods:

- readInputs
- sum
- minimum

The main method simply calls these methods:

```
double[] scores = readInputs();
double total = sum(scores) - minimum(scores);
System.out.println("Final score: " + total);
```

Step 4   Assemble and test the program.

Place your methods into a class. Review your code and check that you handle both normal and exceptional situations. What happens with an empty array? One that contains a single element? When no match is found? When there are multiple matches? Consider these boundary conditions and make sure that your program works correctly.

In our example, it is impossible to compute the minimum if the array is empty. In that case, we should terminate the program with an error message *before* attempting to call the minimum method.

What if the minimum value occurs more than once? That means that a student had more than one test with the same low score. We subtract only one of the occurrences of that low score, and that is the desired behavior.

The following table shows test cases and their expected output:

Test Case	Expected Output	Comment
8 7 8.5 9.5 7 5 10	50	See Step 1.
8 7 7 9	24	Only one instance of the low score should be removed.
8	0	After removing the low score, no score remains.
(no inputs)	**Error**	That is not a legal input.

Here's the complete program (how_to_1/Scores.java):

```java
import java.util.Arrays;
import java.util.Scanner;

/**
    This program computes a final score for a series of quiz scores: the sum after dropping
    the lowest score. The program uses arrays.
*/
public class Scores
{
    public static void main(String[] args)
    {
        double[] scores = readInputs();
        if (scores.length == 0)
        {
            System.out.println("At least one score is required.");
        }
        else
        {
            double total = sum(scores) - minimum(scores);
            System.out.println("Final score: " + total);
        }
    }

    /**
        Reads a sequence of floating-point numbers.
        @return an array containing the numbers
    */
    public static double[] readInputs()
    {
        // Read the input values into an array

        final int INITIAL_SIZE = 10;
        double[] inputs = new double[INITIAL_SIZE];
        System.out.println("Please enter values, Q to quit:");
        Scanner in = new Scanner(System.in);
        int currentSize = 0;
        while (in.hasNextDouble())
        {
            // Grow the array if it has been completely filled
```

```java
            if (currentSize >= inputs.length)
            {
                inputs = Arrays.copyOf(inputs, 2 * inputs.length);
            }
            inputs[currentSize] = in.nextDouble();
            currentSize++;
        }

        return Arrays.copyOf(inputs, currentSize);
    }

    /**
        Computes the sum of the values in an array.
        @param values an array
        @return the sum of the values in values
    */
    public static double sum(double[] values)
    {
        double total = 0;
        for (double element : values)
        {
            total = total + element;
        }
        return total;
    }

    /**
        Gets the minimum value from an array.
        @param values an array of size >= 1
        @return the smallest element of values
    */
    public static double minimum(double[] values)
    {
        double smallest = values[0];
        for (int i = 1; i < values.length; i++)
        {
            if (values[i] < smallest)
            {
                smallest = values[i];
            }
        }
        return smallest;
    }
}
```

WORKED EXAMPLE 6.1   **Rolling the Dice**

This Worked Example shows how to analyze a set of die tosses to see whether the die is "fair".

➕ Available online in WileyPLUS and at www.wiley.com/college/horstmann.

6.6 Problem Solving: Discovering Algorithms by Manipulating Physical Objects

Manipulating physical objects can give you ideas for discovering algorithms.

In Section 6.5, you saw how to solve a problem by combining and adapting known algorithms. But what do you do when none of the standard algorithms is sufficient for your task? In this section, you will learn a technique for discovering algorithms by manipulating physical objects.

Consider the following task: You are given an array whose size is an even number, and you are to switch the first and the second half. For example, if the array contains the eight numbers

| 9 | 13 | 21 | 4 | 11 | 7 | 1 | 3 |

then you should change it to

| 11 | 7 | 1 | 3 | 9 | 13 | 21 | 4 |

Many students find it quite challenging to come up with an algorithm. They may know that a loop is required, and they may realize that elements should be inserted (Section 6.3.7) or swapped (Section 6.3.8), but they do not have sufficient intuition to draw diagrams, describe an algorithm, or write down pseudocode.

One useful technique for discovering an algorithm is to manipulate physical objects. Start by lining up some objects to denote an array. Coins, playing cards, or small toys are good choices.

Here we arrange eight coins:

> Use a sequence of coins, playing cards, or toys to visualize an array of values.

Now let's step back and see what we can do to change the order of the coins. We can remove a coin (Section 6.3.6):

Visualizing the removal of an array element

We can insert a coin (Section 6.3.7):

Visualizing the insertion of an array element

Or we can swap two coins (Section 6.3.8).

Visualizing the swapping of two coins

Go ahead—line up some coins and try out these three operations right now so that you get a feel for them.

Now how does that help us with our problem, switching the first and the second half of the array?

Let's put the first coin into place, by swapping it with the fifth coin. However, as Java programmers, we will say that we swap the coins in positions 0 and 4:

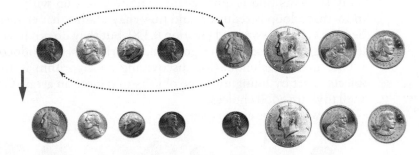

Next, we swap the coins in positions 1 and 5:

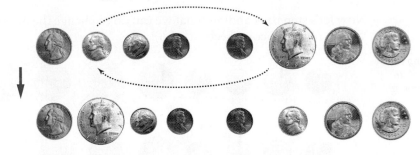

Two more swaps, and we are done:

Now an algorithm is becoming apparent:

```
i = 0
j = ... (we'll think about that in a minute)
While (don't know yet)
    Swap elements at positions i and j
    i++
    j++
```

Where does the variable j start? When we have eight coins, the coin at position zero is moved to position 4. In general, it is moved to the middle of the array, or to position **size / 2**.

And how many iterations do we make? We need to swap all coins in the first half. That is, we need to swap **size / 2** coins. The pseudocode is

```
i = 0
j = size / 2
While (i < size / 2)
    Swap elements at positions i and j
    i++
    j++
```

It is a good idea to make a walkthrough of the pseudocode (see Section 4.2). You can use paper clips to denote the positions of the variables i and j. If the walkthrough is successful, then we know that there was no "off-by-one" error in the pseudocode. Self Check 29 asks you to carry out the walkthrough, and Exercise P6.8 asks you to translate the pseudocode to Java. Exercise R6.28 suggests a different algorithm for switching the two halves of an array, by repeatedly removing and inserting coins.

You can use paper clips as position markers or counters.

Many people find that the manipulation of physical objects is less intimidating than drawing diagrams or mentally envisioning algorithms. Give it a try when you need to design a new algorithm!

SELF CHECK

29. Walk through the algorithm that we developed in this section, using two paper clips to indicate the positions for i and j. Explain why there are no bounds errors in the pseudocode.

30. Take out some coins and simulate the following pseudocode, using two paper clips to indicate the positions for i and j.

```
i = 0
j = size - 1
While (i < j)
    Swap elements at positions i and j
    i++
    j--
```

What does the algorithm do?

31. Consider the task of rearranging all elements in an array so that the even numbers come first. Otherwise, the order doesn't matter. For example, the array

1 4 14 2 1 3 5 6 23

could be rearranged to

4 2 14 6 1 5 3 23 1

Using coins and paperclips, discover an algorithm that solves this task by swapping elements, then describe it in pseudocode.

32. Discover an algorithm for the task of Self Check 31 that uses removal and insertion of elements instead of swapping.

33. Consider the algorithm in Section 4.7.4 that finds the largest element in a sequence of inputs—*not* the largest element in an array. Why is this algorithm better visualized by picking playing cards from a deck rather than arranging toy soldiers in a sequence?

Practice It   Now you can try these exercises at the end of the chapter: R6.28, R6.29, P6.8.

VIDEO EXAMPLE 6.1   **Removing Duplicates from an Array**

In this Video Example, we will discover an algorithm for removing duplicates from an array.

6.7 Two-Dimensional Arrays

It often happens that you want to store collections of values that have a two-dimensional layout. Such data sets commonly occur in financial and scientific applications. An arrangement consisting of rows and columns of values is called a *two-dimensional array*, or a *matrix*.

Let's explore how to store the example data shown in Figure 12: the medal counts of the figure skating competitions at the 2010 Winter Olympics.

	Gold	Silver	Bronze
Canada	1	0	1
China	1	1	0
Germany	0	0	1
Korea	1	0	0
Japan	0	1	1
Russia	0	1	1
United States	1	1	0

Figure 12 Figure Skating Medal Counts

➕ Available online in WileyPLUS and at www.wiley.com/college/horstmann.

6.7.1 Declaring Two-Dimensional Arrays

Use a two-dimensional array to store tabular data.

In Java, you obtain a two-dimensional array by supplying the number of rows and columns. For example, `new int[7][3]` is an array with seven rows and three columns. You store a reference to such an array in a variable of type `int[][]`. Here is a complete declaration of a two-dimensional array, suitable for holding our medal count data:

```java
final int COUNTRIES = 7;
final int MEDALS = 3;
int[][] counts = new int[COUNTRIES][MEDALS];
```

Alternatively, you can declare and initialize the array by grouping each row:

```java
int[][] counts =
   {
      { 1, 0, 1 },
      { 1, 1, 0 },
      { 0, 0, 1 },
      { 1, 0, 0 },
      { 0, 1, 1 },
      { 0, 1, 1 },
      { 1, 1, 0 }
   };
```

As with one-dimensional arrays, you cannot change the size of a two-dimensional array once it has been declared.

Syntax 6.3 **Two-Dimensional Array Declaration**

```
                                              Number of rows
          Name        Element type          Number of columns
                                           /  /
    double[][] tableEntries = new double[7][3];

                                          All values are initialized with 0.

       Name
          \
    int[][] data = {                       List of initial values
                     { 16, 3, 2, 13 },
                     { 5, 10, 11, 8 },
                     { 9, 6, 7, 12 },
                     { 4, 15, 14, 1 },
                   };
```

6.7.2 Accessing Elements

Individual elements in a two-dimensional array are accessed by using two index values, *array*[i][j].

To access a particular element in the two-dimensional array, you need to specify two index values in separate brackets to select the row and column, respectively (see Figure 13):

```java
int medalCount = counts[3][1];
```

To access all elements in a two-dimensional array, you use two nested loops. For example, the following loop prints all elements of counts:

```
for (int i = 0; i < COUNTRIES; i++)
{
    // Process the ith row
    for (int j = 0; j < MEDALS; j++)
    {
        // Process the jth column in the ith row
        System.out.printf("%8d", counts[i][j]);
    }
    System.out.println(); // Start a new line at the end of the row
}
```

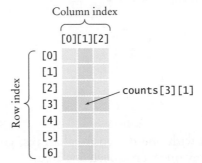

Figure 13
Accessing an Element in a
Two-Dimensional Array

6.7.3 Locating Neighboring Elements

Some programs that work with two-dimensional arrays need to locate the elements that are adjacent to an element. This task is particularly common in games. Figure 14 shows how to compute the index values of the neighbors of an element.

For example, the neighbors of counts[3][1] to the left and right are counts[3][0] and counts[3][2]. The neighbors to the top and bottom are counts[2][1] and counts[4][1].

You need to be careful about computing neighbors at the boundary of the array. For example, counts[0][1] has no neighbor to the top. Consider the task of computing the sum of the neighbors to the top and bottom of the element count[i][j]. You need to check whether the element is located at the top or bottom of the array:

```
int total = 0;
if (i > 0) { total = total + counts[i - 1][j]; }
if (i < ROWS - 1) { total = total + counts[i + 1][j]; }
```

[i - 1][j - 1]	[i - 1][j]	[i - 1][j + 1]
[i][j - 1]	[i][j]	[i][j + 1]
[i + 1][j - 1]	[i + 1][j]	[i + 1][j + 1]

Figure 14
Neighboring Locations in a
Two-Dimensional Array

6.7.4 Computing Row and Column Totals

A common task is to compute row or column totals. In our example, the row totals give us the total number of medals won by a particular country.

Finding the right index values is a bit tricky, and it is a good idea to make a quick sketch. To compute the total of row i, we need to visit the following elements:

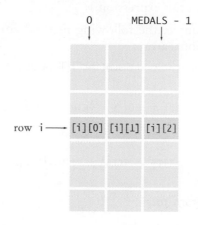

As you can see, we need to compute the sum of counts[i][j], where j ranges from 0 to MEDALS - 1. The following loop computes the total:

```
int total = 0;
for (int j = 0; j < MEDALS; j++)
{
   total = total + counts[i][j];
}
```

Computing column totals is similar. Form the sum of counts[i][j], where i ranges from 0 to COUNTRIES - 1.

```
int total = 0;
for (int i = 0; i < COUNTRIES; i++)
{
   total = total + counts[i][j];
}
```

ANIMATION
Tracing a Nested Loop in a 2D Array

6.7.5 Two-Dimensional Array Parameters

When you pass a two-dimensional array to a method, you will want to recover the dimensions of the array. If values is a two-dimensional array, then

- values.length is the number of rows.
- values[0].length is the number of columns. (See Special Topic 6.4 for an explanation of this expression.)

For example, the following method computes the sum of all elements in a two-dimensional array:

```java
public static int sum(int[][] values)
{
   int total = 0;
   for (int i = 0; i < values.length; i++)
   {
      for (int j = 0; j < values[0].length; j++)
      {
         total = total + values[i][j];
      }
   }
   return total;
}
```

Working with two-dimensional arrays is illustrated in the following program. The program prints out the medal counts and the row totals.

section_7/Medals.java

```java
1   /**
2      This program prints a table of medal winner counts with row totals.
3   */
4   public class Medals
5   {
6      public static void main(String[] args)
7      {
8         final int COUNTRIES = 7;
9         final int MEDALS = 3;
10
11         String[] countries =
12            {
13               "Canada",
14               "China",
15               "Germany",
16               "Korea",
17               "Japan",
18               "Russia",
19               "United States"
20            };
21
22         int[][] counts =
23            {
24               { 1, 0, 1 },
25               { 1, 1, 0 },
26               { 0, 0, 1 },
27               { 1, 0, 0 },
28               { 0, 1, 1 },
29               { 0, 1, 1 },
30               { 1, 1, 0 }
```

```
31              };
32
33          System.out.println("        Country    Gold Silver Bronze    Total");
34
35          // Print countries, counts, and row totals
36          for (int i = 0; i < COUNTRIES; i++)
37          {
38              // Process the ith row
39              System.out.printf("%15s", countries[i]);
40
41              int total = 0;
42
43              // Print each row element and update the row total
44              for (int j = 0; j < MEDALS; j++)
45              {
46                  System.out.printf("%8d", counts[i][j]);
47                  total = total + counts[i][j];
48              }
49
50              // Display the row total and print a new line
51              System.out.printf("%8d\n", total);
52          }
53      }
54 }
```

Program Run

Country	Gold	Silver	Bronze	Total
Canada	1	0	1	2
China	1	1	0	2
Germany	0	0	1	1
Korea	1	0	0	1
Japan	0	1	1	2
Russia	0	1	1	2
United States	1	1	0	2

SELF CHECK

34. What results do you get if you total the columns in our sample data?

35. Consider an 8 × 8 array for a board game:

```
int[][] board = new int[8][8];
```

Using two nested loops, initialize the board so that zeroes and ones alternate, as on a checkerboard:

```
0 1 0 1 0 1 0 1
1 0 1 0 1 0 1 0
0 1 0 1 0 1 0 1
. . .
1 0 1 0 1 0 1 0
```

Hint: Check whether i + j is even.

36. Declare a two-dimensional array for representing a tic-tac-toe board. The board has three rows and columns and contains strings "x", "o", and " ".

37. Write an assignment statement to place an "x" in the upper-right corner of the tic-tac-toe board in Self Check 36.

38. Which elements are on the diagonal joining the upper-left and the lower-right corners of the tic-tac-toe board in Self Check 36?

Practice It   Now you can try these exercises at the end of the chapter: R6.30, P6.18, P6.19.

WORKED EXAMPLE 6.2   A World Population Table

This Worked Example shows how to print world population data in a table with row and column headers, and with totals for each of the data columns.

Special Topic 6.4

Two-Dimensional Arrays with Variable Row Lengths

When you declare a two-dimensional array with the command

```
int[][] a = new int[3][3];
```

then you get a 3 × 3 matrix that can store 9 elements:

```
a[0][0] a[0][1] a[0][2]
a[1][0] a[1][1] a[1][2]
a[2][0] a[2][1] a[2][2]
```

In this matrix, all rows have the same length.

In Java it is possible to declare arrays in which the row length varies. For example, you can store an array that has a triangular shape, such as:

```
b[0][0]
b[1][0] b[1][1]
b[2][0] b[2][1] b[2][2]
```

To allocate such an array, you must work harder. First, you allocate space to hold three rows. Indicate that you will manually set each row by leaving the second array index empty:

```
double[][] b = new double[3][];
```

Then allocate each row separately (see Figure 15):

```
for (int i = 0; i < b.length; i++)
{
   b[i] = new double[i + 1];
}
```

You can access each array element as b[i][j]. The expression b[i] selects the ith row, and the [j] operator selects the jth element in that row.

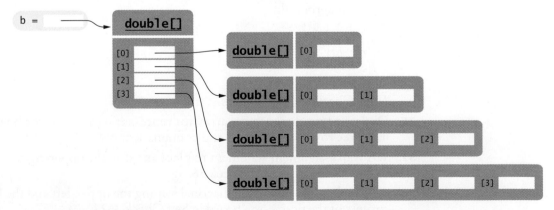

Figure 15   A Triangular Array

➕ Available online in WileyPLUS and at *www.wiley.com/college/horstmann*.

Note that the number of rows is b.length, and the length of the ith row is b[i].length. For example, the following pair of loops prints a ragged array:

```java
for (int i = 0; i < b.length; i++)
{
   for (int j = 0; j < b[i].length; j++)
   {
      System.out.print(b[i][j]);
   }
   System.out.println();
}
```

Alternatively, you can use two enhanced for loops:

```java
for (double[] row : b)
{
   for (double element : row)
   {
      System.out.print(element);
   }
   System.out.println();
}
```

Naturally, such "ragged" arrays are not very common.

Java implements plain two-dimensional arrays in exactly the same way as ragged arrays: as arrays of one-dimensional arrays. The expression new int[3][3] automatically allocates an array of three rows, and three arrays for the rows' contents.

Special Topic 6.5

Multidimensional Arrays

You can declare arrays with more than two dimensions. For example, here is a three-dimensional array:

```java
int[][][] rubiksCube = new int[3][3][3];
```

Each array element is specified by three index values:

```java
rubiksCube[i][j][k]
```

6.8 Array Lists

An array list stores a sequence of values whose size can change.

When you write a program that collects inputs, you don't always know how many inputs you will have. In such a situation, an **array list** offers two significant advantages:

- Array lists can grow and shrink as needed.
- The ArrayList class supplies methods for common tasks, such as inserting and removing elements.

In the following sections, you will learn how to work with array lists.

An array list expands to hold as many elements as needed.

Syntax 6.4   Array Lists

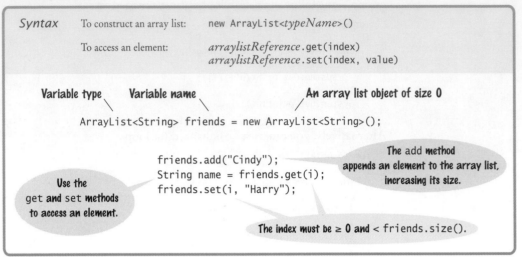

Syntax   To construct an array list: `new ArrayList<typeName>()`

To access an element: `arraylistReference.get(index)`
`arraylistReference.set(index, value)`

Variable type   **Variable name**   **An array list object of size 0**

`ArrayList<String> friends = new ArrayList<String>();`

`friends.add("Cindy");`
`String name = friends.get(i);`
`friends.set(i, "Harry");`

Use the get and set methods to access an element.

The add method appends an element to the array list, increasing its size.

The index must be ≥ 0 and < `friends.size()`.

6.8.1 Declaring and Using Array Lists

The following statement declares an array list of strings:

```
ArrayList<String> names = new ArrayList<String>();
```

The `ArrayList` class is contained in the java.util package. In order to use array lists in your program, you need to use the statement `import java.util.ArrayList`.

> The `ArrayList` class is a generic class: `ArrayList<Type>` collects elements of the specified type.

The type `ArrayList<String>` denotes an array list of `String` elements. The angle brackets around the `String` type tell you that `String` is a **type parameter**. You can replace `String` with any other class and get a different array list type. For that reason, `ArrayList` is called a **generic class**. However, you cannot use primitive types as type parameters—there is no `ArrayList<int>` or `ArrayList<double>`. Section 6.8.5 shows how you can collect numbers in an array list.

It is a common error to forget the initialization:

```
ArrayList<String> names;
names.add("Harry"); // Error—names not initialized
```

Here is the proper initialization:

```
ArrayList<String> names = new ArrayList<String>();
```

Note the `()` after `new ArrayList<String>` on the right-hand side of the initialization. It indicates that the **constructor** of the `ArrayList<String>` class is being called. We will discuss constructors in Chapter 8.

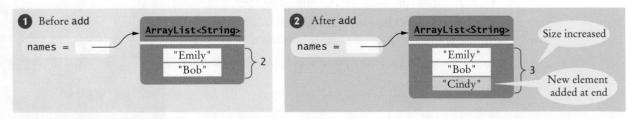

1 Before add

`names =`

ArrayList<String>

"Emily"
"Bob"   } 2

2 After add

`names =`

ArrayList<String>

"Emily"
"Bob"
"Cindy"   } 3

Size increased

New element added at end

Figure 16 Adding an Element with add

When the `ArrayList<String>` is first constructed, it has size 0. You use the `add` method to add an element to the end of the array list.

```
names.add("Emily"); // Now names has size 1 and element "Emily"
names.add("Bob"); // Now names has size 2 and elements "Emily", "Bob"
names.add("Cindy"); // names has size 3 and elements "Emily", "Bob", and "Cindy"
```

> Use the `size` method to obtain the current size of an array list.

The size increases after each call to `add` (see Figure 16). The `size` method yields the current size of the array list.

To obtain an array list element, use the `get` method, not the `[]` operator. As with arrays, index values start at 0. For example, `names.get(2)` retrieves the name with index 2, the third element in the array list:

```
String name = names.get(2);
```

> Use the `get` and `set` methods to access an array list element at a given index.

As with arrays, it is an error to access a nonexistent element. A very common bounds error is to use the following:

```
int i = names.size();
name = names.get(i);  // Error
```

The last valid index is `names.size() - 1`.

To set an array list element to a new value, use the set method.

```
names.set(2, "Carolyn");
```

An array list has methods for adding and removing elements in the middle.

This call sets position 2 of the names array list to "Carolyn", overwriting whatever value was there before.

The set method overwrites existing values. It is different from the `add` method, which adds a new element to the array list.

You can insert an element in the middle of an array list. For example, the call `names.add(1, "Ann")` adds a new element at position 1 and moves all elements with index 1 or larger by one position. After each call to the `add` method, the size of the array list increases by 1 (see Figure 17).

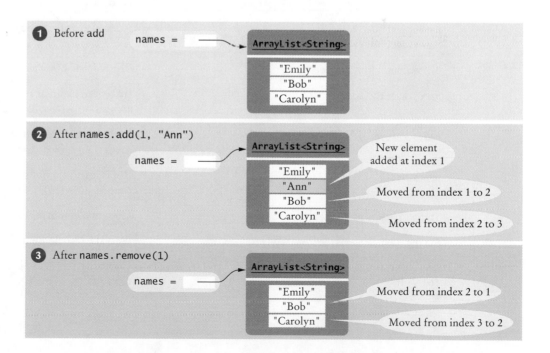

Figure 17 Adding and Removing Elements in the Middle of an Array List

Use the add and remove methods to add and remove array list elements.

Conversely, the remove method removes the element at a given position, moves all elements after the removed element down by one position, and reduces the size of the array list by 1. Part 3 of Figure 17 illustrates the result of names.remove(1).

With an array list, it is very easy to get a quick printout. Simply pass the array list to the println method:

```
System.out.println(names); // Prints [Emily, Bob, Carolyn]
```

6.8.2 Using the Enhanced for Loop with Array Lists

You can use the enhanced for loop to visit all elements of an array list. For example, the following loop prints all names:

```
ArrayList<String> names = . . . ;
for (String name : names)
{
    System.out.println(name);
}
```

This loop is equivalent to the following basic for loop:

```
for (int i = 0; i < names.size(); i++)
{
    String name = names.get(i);
    System.out.println(name);
}
```

Table 2 Working with Array Lists

`ArrayList<String> names = new ArrayList<String>();`	Constructs an empty array list that can hold strings.
`names.add("Ann");` `names.add("Cindy");`	Adds elements to the end.
`System.out.println(names);`	Prints [Ann, Cindy].
`names.add(1, "Bob");`	Inserts an element at index 1. names is now [Ann, Bob, Cindy].
`names.remove(0);`	Removes the element at index 0. names is now [Bob, Cindy].
`names.set(0, "Bill");`	Replaces an element with a different value. names is now [Bill, Cindy].
`String name = names.get(i);`	Gets an element.
`String last = names.get(names.size() - 1);`	Gets the last element.

`ArrayList<Integer> squares = new ArrayList<Integer>();`
`for (int i = 0; i < 10; i++)`
`{`
`    squares.add(i * i);`
`}`
	Constructs an array list holding the first ten squares.

6.8.3 Copying Array Lists

As with arrays, you need to remember that array list variables hold references. Copying the reference yields two references to the same array list (see Figure 18).

```
ArrayList<String> friends = names;
friends.add("Harry");
```

Now both `names` and `friends` reference the same array list to which the string `"Harry"` was added.

If you want to make a copy of an array list, construct the copy and pass the original list into the constructor:

```
ArrayList<String> newNames = new ArrayList<String>(names);
```

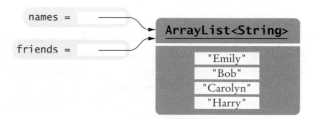

Figure 18   Copying an Array List Reference

6.8.4 Array Lists and Methods

Like arrays, array lists can be method arguments and return values. Here is an example: a method that receives a list of strings and returns the reversed list.

```
public static ArrayList<String> reverse(ArrayList<String> names)
{
   // Allocate a list to hold the method result
   ArrayList<String> result = new ArrayList<String>();

   // Traverse the names list in reverse order, starting with the last element
   for (int i = names.size() - 1; i >= 0; i--)
   {
      // Add each name to the result
      result.add(names.get(i));
   }
   return result;
}
```

If this method is called with an array list containing the names Emily, Bob, Cindy, it returns a new array list with the names Cindy, Bob, Emily.

6.8.5 Wrappers and Auto-boxing

To collect numbers in array lists, you must use wrapper classes.

In Java, you cannot directly insert primitive type values—numbers, characters, or boolean values   into array lists. For example, you cannot form an `ArrayList<double>`. Instead, you must use one of the **wrapper classes** shown in the following table.

Primitive Type	Wrapper Class
byte	Byte
boolean	Boolean
char	Character
double	Double
float	Float
int	Integer
long	Long
short	Short

For example, to collect `double` values in an array list, you use an `ArrayList<Double>`. Note that the wrapper class names start with uppercase letters, and that two of them differ from the names of the corresponding primitive type: `Integer` and `Character`.

Conversion between primitive types and the corresponding wrapper classes is automatic. This process is called **auto-boxing** (even though *auto-wrapping* would have been more consistent).

For example, if you assign a `double` value to a `Double` variable, the number is automatically "put into a box" (see Figure 19).

```
Double wrapper = 29.95;
```

Conversely, wrapper values are automatically "unboxed" to primitive types.

```
double x = wrapper;
```

Because boxing and unboxing is automatic, you don't need to think about it. Simply remember to use the wrapper type when you declare array lists of numbers. From then on, use the primitive type and rely on auto-boxing.

```
ArrayList<Double> values = new ArrayList<Double>();
values.add(29.95);
double x = values.get(0);
```

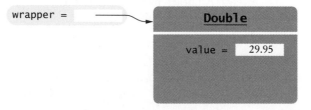

Figure 19   A Wrapper Class Variable

Like truffles that must be in a wrapper to be sold,
a number must be placed in a wrapper to be stored in an array list.

6.8.6 Using Array Algorithms with Array Lists

The array algorithms in Section 6.3 can be converted to array lists simply by using the array list methods instead of the array syntax (see Table 3 on page 297). For example, this code snippet finds the largest element in an array:

```
double largest = values[0];
for (int i = 1; i < values.length; i++)
{
   if (values[i] > largest)
   {
      largest = values[i];
   }
}
```

Here is the same algorithm, now using an array list:

```
double largest = values.get(0);
for (int i = 1; i < values.size(); i++)
{
   if (values.get(i) > largest)
   {
      largest = values.get(i);
   }
}
```

6.8.7 Storing Input Values in an Array List

When you collect an unknown number of inputs, array lists are *much* easier to use than arrays. Simply read inputs and add them to an array list:

```
ArrayList<Double> inputs = new ArrayList<Double>();
while (in.hasNextDouble())
{
   inputs.add(in.nextDouble());
}
```

6.8.8 Removing Matches

It is easy to remove elements from an array list, by calling the remove method. A common processing task is to remove all elements that match a particular condition. Suppose, for example, that we want to remove all strings of length < 4 from an array list.

Of course, you traverse the array list and look for matching elements:

```
ArrayList<String> words = ...;
for (int i = 0; i < words.size(); i++)
{
   String word = words.get(i);
   if (word.length() < 4)
   {
      Remove the element at index i.
   }
}
```

But there is a subtle problem. After you remove the element, the for loop increments i, skipping past the *next* element.

Consider this concrete example, where words contains the strings "Welcome", "to", "the", "island!". When i is 1, we remove the word "to" at index 1. Then i is incremented to 2, and the word "the", which is now at position 1, is never examined.

i	words
~~0~~	~~"Welcome", "to", "the", "island"~~
~~1~~	"Welcome", "the", "island"
2	

We should not increment the index when removing a word. The appropriate pseudo-code is

If the element at index i matches the condition
    Remove the element.
Else
    Increment i.

Because we don't always increment the index, a for loop is not appropriate for this algorithm. Instead, use a while loop:

```
int i = 0;
while (i < words.size())
{
    String word = words.get(i);
    if (word.length() < 4)
    {
        words.remove(i);
    }
    else
    {
        i++;
    }
}
```

6.8.9 Choosing Between Array Lists and Arrays

For most programming tasks, array lists are easier to use than arrays. Array lists can grow and shrink. On the other hand, arrays have a nicer syntax for element access and initialization.

Which of the two should you choose? Here are some recommendations.

- If the size of a collection never changes, use an array.
- If you collect a long sequence of primitive type values and you are concerned about efficiency, use an array.
- Otherwise, use an array list.

ONLINE EXAMPLE

A version of the Scores program using an array list.

The following program shows how to mark the largest value in a sequence of values. This program uses an array list. Note how the program is an improvement over the array version on page 265. This program can process input sequences of arbitrary length.

Table 3 Comparing Array and Array List Operations

Operation	Arrays	Array Lists
Get an element.	`x = values[4];`	`x = values.get(4)`
Replace an element.	`values[4] = 35;`	`values.set(4, 35);`
Number of elements.	`values.length`	`values.size()`
Number of filled elements.	`currentSize` (companion variable, see Section 6.1.3)	`values.size()`
Remove an element.	See Section 6.3.6	`values.remove(4);`
Add an element, growing the collection.	See Section 6.3.7	`values.add(35);`
Initializing a collection.	`int[] values = { 1, 4, 9 };`	No initializer list syntax; call add three times.

section_8/LargestInArrayList.java

```java
1   import java.util.ArrayList;
2   import java.util.Scanner;
3
4   /**
5      This program reads a sequence of values and prints them, marking the largest value.
6   */
7   public class LargestInArrayList
8   {
9      public static void main(String[] args)
10     {
11        ArrayList<Double> values = new ArrayList<Double>();
12
13        // Read inputs
14
15        System.out.println("Please enter values, Q to quit:");
16        Scanner in = new Scanner(System.in);
17        while (in.hasNextDouble())
18        {
19           values.add(in.nextDouble());
20        }
21
22        // Find the largest value
23
24        double largest = values.get(0);
25        for (int i = 1; i < values.size(); i++)
26        {
27           if (values.get(i) > largest)
28           {
29              largest = values.get(i);
30           }
31        }
32
33        // Print all values, marking the largest
34
```

```
35        for (double element : values)
36        {
37           System.out.print(element);
38           if (element == largest)
39           {
40              System.out.print(" <== largest value");
41           }
42           System.out.println();
43        }
44     }
45  }
```

Program Run

```
Please enter values, Q to quit:
35 80 115 44.5 Q
35
80
115 <== largest value
44.5
```

SELF CHECK

39. Declare an array list primes of integers that contains the first five prime numbers (2, 3, 5, 7, and 11).

40. Given the array list primes declared in Self Check 39, write a loop to print its elements in reverse order, starting with the last element.

41. What does the array list names contain after the following statements?

```
ArrayList<String> names = new ArrayList<String>;
names.add("Bob");
names.add(0, "Ann");
names.remove(1);
names.add("Cal");
```

42. What is wrong with this code snippet?

```
ArrayList<String> names;
names.add(Bob);
```

43. Consider this method that appends the elements of one array list to another.

```
public static void append(ArrayList<String> target, ArrayList<String> source)
{
   for (int i = 0; i < source.size(); i++)
   {
      target.add(source.get(i));
   }
}
```

What are the contents of names1 and names2 after these statements?

```
ArrayList<String> names1 = new ArrayList<String>();
names1.add("Emily");
names1.add("Bob");
names1.add("Cindy");
ArrayList<String> names2 = new ArrayList<String>();
names2.add("Dave");
append(names1, names2);
```

44. Suppose you want to store the names of the weekdays. Should you use an array list or an array of seven strings?

45. The section_8 directory of your source code contains an alternate implementation of the problem solution in How To 6.1 on page 275. Compare the array and array list implementations. What is the primary advantage of the latter?

Practice It   Now you can try these exercises at the end of the chapter: R6.10, R6.34, P6.21, P6.23.

Common Error 6.4

Length and Size

Unfortunately, the Java syntax for determining the number of elements in an array, an array list, and a string is not at all consistent.

Data Type	Number of Elements
Array	`a.length`
Array list	`a.size()`
String	`a.length()`

It is a common error to confuse these. You just have to remember the correct syntax for every data type.

Special Topic 6.6

The Diamond Syntax in Java 7

Java 7 introduces a convenient syntax enhancement for declaring array lists and other generic classes. In a statement that declares and constructs an array list, you need not repeat the type parameter in the constructor. That is, you can write

```
ArrayList<String> names = new ArrayList<>();
```

instead of

```
ArrayList<String> names = new ArrayList<String>();
```

This shortcut is called the "diamond syntax" because the empty brackets <> look like a diamond shape.

VIDEO EXAMPLE 6.2   **Game of Life**

Conway's *Game of Life* simulates the growth of a population, using only two simple rules. This Video Example shows you how to implement this famous "game".

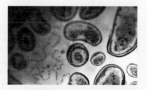

✚ Available online in WileyPLUS and at www.wiley.com/college/horstmann.

CHAPTER SUMMARY

Use arrays for collecting values.

- An array collects a sequence of values of the same type.
- Individual elements in an array are accessed by an integer index i, using the notation *array*[i].
- An array element can be used like any variable.
- An array index must be at least zero and less than the size of the array.
- A bounds error, which occurs if you supply an invalid array index, can cause your program to terminate.
- Use the expression *array*.length to find the number of elements in an array.
- An array reference specifies the location of an array. Copying the reference yields a second reference to the same array.
- With a partially filled array, keep a companion variable for the current size.

Know when to use the enhanced for loop.

- You can use the enhanced for loop to visit all elements of an array.
- Use the enhanced for loop if you do not need the index values in the loop body.

Know and use common array algorithms.

- When separating elements, don't place a separator before the first element.
- A linear search inspects elements in sequence until a match is found.
- Before inserting an element, move elements to the end of the array *starting with the last one*.
- Use a temporary variable when swapping two elements.
- Use the Arrays.copyOf method to copy the elements of an array into a new array.

Implement methods that process arrays.

- Arrays can occur as method arguments and return values.

Combine and adapt algorithms for solving a programming problem.

- By combining fundamental algorithms, you can solve complex programming tasks.
- You should be familiar with the implementation of fundamental algorithms so that you can adapt them.

Discover algorithms by manipulating physical objects.

- Use a sequence of coins, playing cards, or toys to visualize an array of values.
- You can use paper clips as position markers or counters.

Use two-dimensional arrays for data that is arranged in rows and columns.

- Use a two-dimensional array to store tabular data.
- Individual elements in a two-dimensional array are accessed by using two index values, *array*[i][j].

Use array lists for managing collections whose size can change.

- An array list stores a sequence of values whose size can change.
- The ArrayList class is a generic class: ArrayList<*Type*> collects elements of the specified type.
- Use the size method to obtain the current size of an array list.
- Use the get and set methods to access an array list element at a given index.
- Use the add and remove methods to add and remove array list elements.
- To collect numbers in array lists, you must use wrapper classes.

STANDARD LIBRARY ITEMS INTRODUCED IN THIS CHAPTER

```
java.lang.Boolean          java.util.ArrayList<E>
java.lang.Double               add
java.lang.Integer              get
java.util.Arrays               remove
    copyOf                     set
    toString                   size
```

REVIEW EXERCISES

■■ **R6.1** Write code that fills an array values with each set of numbers below.

a.	1	2	3	4	5	6	7	8	9	10	
b.	0	2	4	6	8	10	12	14	16	18	20
c.	1	4	9	16	25	36	49	64	81	100	
d.	0	0	0	0	0	0	0	0	0	0	
e.	1	4	9	16	9	7	4	9	11		
f.	0	1	0	1	0	1	0	1	0	1	
g.	0	1	2	3	4	0	1	2	3	4	

■■ R6.2 Consider the following array:

```
int[] a = { 1, 2, 3, 4, 5, 4, 3, 2, 1, 0 };
```

What is the value of total after the following loops complete?

a. int total = 0;
   for (int i = 0; i < 10; i++) { total = total + a[i]; }

b. int total = 0;
   for (int i = 0; i < 10; i = i + 2) { total = total + a[i]; }

c. int total = 0;
   for (int i = 1; i < 10; i = i + 2) { total = total + a[i]; }

d. int total = 0;
   for (int i = 2; i <= 10; i++) { total = total + a[i]; }

e. int total = 0;
   for (int i = 1; i < 10; i = 2 * i) { total = total + a[i]; }

f. int total = 0;
   for (int i = 9; i >= 0; i--) { total = total + a[i]; }

g. int total = 0;
   for (int i = 9; i >= 0; i = i - 2) { total = total + a[i]; }

h. int total = 0;
   for (int i = 0; i < 10; i++) { total = a[i] - total; }

■■ R6.3 Consider the following array:

```
int[] a = { 1, 2, 3, 4, 5, 4, 3, 2, 1, 0 };
```

What are the contents of the array a after the following loops complete?

a. for (int i = 1; i < 10; i++) { a[i] = a[i - 1]; }

b. for (int i = 9; i > 0; i--) { a[i] = a[i - 1]; }

c. for (int i = 0; i < 9; i++) { a[i] = a[i + 1]; }

d. for (int i = 8; i >= 0; i--) { a[i] = a[i + 1]; }

e. for (int i = 1; i < 10; i++) { a[i] = a[i] + a[i - 1]; }

f. for (int i = 1; i < 10; i = i + 2) { a[i] = 0; }

g. for (int i = 0; i < 5; i++) { a[i + 5] = a[i]; }

h. for (int i = 1; i < 5; i++) { a[i] = a[9 - i]; }

■■■ R6.4 Write a loop that fills an array values with ten random numbers between 1 and 100. Write code for two nested loops that fill values with ten *different* random numbers between 1 and 100.

■■ R6.5 Write Java code for a loop that simultaneously computes both the maximum and minimum of an array.

■ R6.6 What is wrong with each of the following code segments?

a. int[] values = new int[10];
   for (int i = 1; i <= 10; i++)
   {
      values[i] = i * i;
   }

b. int[] values;
   for (int i = 0; i < values.length; i++)
   {
      values[i] = i * i;
   }

•• R6.7 Write enhanced for loops for the following tasks.

  a. Printing all elements of an array in a single row, separated by spaces.

  b. Computing the product of all elements in an array.

  c. Counting how many elements in an array are negative.

•• R6.8 Rewrite the following loops without using the enhanced for loop construct. Here, values is an array of floating-point numbers.

  a. `for (double x : values) { total = total + x; }`

  b. `for (double x : values) { if (x == target) { return true; } }`

  c. `int i = 0;`
  `for (double x : values) { values[i] = 2 * x; i++; }`

•• R6.9 Rewrite the following loops, using the enhanced for loop construct. Here, values is an array of floating-point numbers.

  a. `for (int i = 0; i < values.length; i++) { total = total + values[i]; }`

  b. `for (int i = 1; i < values.length; i++) { total = total + values[i]; }`

  c. `for (int i = 0; i < values.length; i++)`
  `{`
  `    if (values[i] == target) { return i; }`
  `}`

• R6.10 What is wrong with each of the following code segments?

  a. `ArrayList<int> values = new ArrayList<int>();`

  b. `ArrayList<Integer> values = new ArrayList();`

  c. `ArrayList<Integer> values = new ArrayList<Integer>;`

  d. `ArrayList<Integer> values = new ArrayList<Integer>();`
  `for (int i = 1; i <= 10; i++)`
  `{`
  `    values.set(i - 1, i * i);`
  `}`

  e. `ArrayList<Integer> values;`
  `for (int i = 1; i <= 10; i++)`
  `{`
  `    values.add(i * i);`
  `}`

• R6.11 What is an index of an array? What are the legal index values? What is a bounds error?

• R6.12 Write a program that contains a bounds error. Run the program. What happens on your computer?

• R6.13 Write a loop that reads ten numbers and a second loop that displays them in the opposite order from which they were entered.

• R6.14 Trace the flow of the linear search loop in Section 6.3.5, where values contains the elements 80 90 100 120 110. Show two columns, for pos and found. Repeat the trace when values contains 80 90 100 70.

• R6.15 Trace both mechanisms for removing an element described in Section 6.3.6. Use an array values with elements 110 90 100 120 80, and remove the element at index 2.

■■ **R6.16** For the operations on partially filled arrays below, provide the header of a method. Do not implement the methods.

    a. Sort the elements in decreasing order.

    b. Print all elements, separated by a given string.

    c. Count how many elements are less than a given value.

    d. Remove all elements that are less than a given value.

    e. Place all elements that are less than a given value in another array.

■ **R6.17** Trace the flow of the loop in Section 6.3.4 with the given example. Show two columns, one with the value of i and one with the output.

■ **R6.18** Consider the following loop for collecting all elements that match a condition; in this case, that the element is larger than 100.

```
ArrayList<Double> matches = new ArrayList<Double>();
for (double element : values)
{
   if (element > 100)
   {
      matches.add(element);
   }
}
```

Trace the flow of the loop, where values contains the elements 110 90 100 120 80. Show two columns, for element and matches.

■ **R6.19** Trace the flow of the loop in Section 6.3.5, where values contains the elements 80 90 100 120 110. Show two columns, for pos and found. Repeat the trace when values contains the elements 80 90 120 70.

■■ **R6.20** Trace the algorithm for removing an element described in Section 6.3.6. Use an array values with elements 110 90 100 120 80, and remove the element at index 2.

■■ **R6.21** Give pseudocode for an algorithm that rotates the elements of an array by one position, moving the initial element to the end of the array, like this:

■■ **R6.22** Give pseudocode for an algorithm that removes all negative values from an array, preserving the order of the remaining elements.

■■ **R6.23** Suppose values is a *sorted* array of integers. Give pseudocode that describes how a new value can be inserted in its proper position so that the resulting array stays sorted.

■■■ **R6.24** A *run* is a sequence of adjacent repeated values. Give pseudocode for computing the length of the longest run in an array. For example, the longest run in the array with elements

    1 2 5 5 3 1 2 4 3 2 2 2 2 3 6 5 5 6 3 1

has length 4.

■■■ R6.25 What is wrong with the following method that aims to fill an array with random numbers?

```
public static void fillWithRandomNumbers(double[] values)
{
    double[] numbers = new double[values.length];
    for (int i = 0; i < numbers.length; i++)
    {
        numbers[i] = Math.random();
    }
    values = numbers;
}
```

■■ R6.26 You are given two arrays denoting x- and y-coordinates of a set of points in the plane. For plotting the point set, we need to know the x- and y-coordinates of the smallest rectangle containing the points.

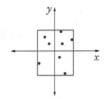

How can you obtain these values from the fundamental algorithms in Section 6.3?

■ R6.27 Solve the problem described in Section 6.5 by sorting the array first. How do you need to modify the algorithm for computing the total?

■■ R6.28 Solve the task described in Section 6.6 using an algorithm that removes and inserts elements instead of switching them. Write the pseudocode for the algorithm, assuming that methods for removal and insertion exist. Act out the algorithm with a sequence of coins and explain why it is less efficient than the swapping algorithm developed in Section 6.6.

■■ R6.29 Develop an algorithm for finding the most frequently occurring value in an array of numbers. Use a sequence of coins. Place paper clips below each coin that count how many other coins of the same value are in the sequence. Give the pseudocode for an algorithm that yields the correct answer, and describe how using the coins and paper clips helped you find the algorithm.

■■ R6.30 Write Java statements for performing the following tasks with an array declared as

```
int[][] values = new int[ROWS][COLUMNS];
```

- Fill all entries with 0.
- Fill elements alternately with 0s and 1s in a checkerboard pattern.
- Fill only the elements at the top and bottom row with zeroes.
- Compute the sum of all elements.
- Print the array in tabular form.

■■ R6.31 Write pseudocode for an algorithm that fills the first and last column as well as the first and last row of a two-dimensional array of integers with −1.

■ R6.32 Section 6.8.8 shows that you must be careful about updating the index value when you remove elements from an array list. Show how you can avoid this problem by traversing the array list backwards.

■■ **R6.33** True or false?

    a. All elements of an array are of the same type.

    b. Arrays cannot contain strings as elements.

    c. Two-dimensional arrays always have the same number of rows and columns.

    d. Elements of different columns in a two-dimensional array can have different types.

    e. A method cannot return a two-dimensional array.

    f. A method cannot change the length of an array argument.

    g. A method cannot change the number of columns of an argument that is a two-dimensional array.

■■ **R6.34** How do you perform the following tasks with array lists in Java?

    a. Test that two array lists contain the same elements in the same order.

    b. Copy one array list to another.

    c. Fill an array list with zeroes, overwriting all elements in it.

    d. Remove all elements from an array list.

■ **R6.35** True or false?

    a. All elements of an array list are of the same type.

    b. Array list index values must be integers.

    c. Array lists cannot contain strings as elements.

    d. Array lists can change their size, getting larger or smaller.

    e. A method cannot return an array list.

    f. A method cannot change the size of an array list argument.

PROGRAMMING EXERCISES

■■ **P6.1** Write a program that initializes an array with ten random integers and then prints four lines of output, containing

- Every element at an even index.
- Every even element.
- All elements in reverse order.
- Only the first and last element.

■■ **P6.2** Write array methods that carry out the following tasks for an array of integers. For each method, provide a test program.

    a. Swap the first and last elements in the array.

    b. Shift all elements by one to the right and move the last element into the first position. For example, 1 4 9 16 25 would be transformed into 25 1 4 9 16.

    c. Replace all even elements with 0.

    d. Replace each element except the first and last by the larger of its two neighbors.

  e. Remove the middle element if the array length is odd, or the middle two elements if the length is even.

  f. Move all even elements to the front, otherwise preserving the order of the elements.

  g. Return the second-largest element in the array.

  h. Return true if the array is currently sorted in increasing order.

  i. Return true if the array contains two adjacent duplicate elements.

  j. Return true if the array contains duplicate elements (which need not be adjacent).

■ **P6.3** Modify the `LargestInArray.java` program in Section 6.3 to mark both the smallest and the largest elements.

■■ **P6.4** Write a method `sumWithoutSmallest` that computes the sum of an array of values, except for the smallest one, in a single loop. In the loop, update the sum and the smallest value. After the loop, return the difference.

■ **P6.5** Write a method `public static void removeMin` that removes the minimum value from a partially filled array without calling other methods.

■■ **P6.6** Compute the *alternating sum* of all elements in an array. For example, if your program reads the input

$$1 \quad 4 \quad 9 \quad 16 \quad 9 \quad 7 \quad 4 \quad 9 \quad 11$$

then it computes

$$1 - 4 + 9 - 16 + 9 - 7 + 4 - 9 + 11 = -2$$

■ **P6.7** Write a method that reverses the sequence of elements in an array. For example, if you call the method with the array

$$1 \quad 4 \quad 9 \quad 16 \quad 9 \quad 7 \quad 4 \quad 9 \quad 11$$

then the array is changed to

$$11 \quad 9 \quad 4 \quad 7 \quad 9 \quad 16 \quad 9 \quad 4 \quad 1$$

■ **P6.8** Write a method that implements the algorithm developed in Section 6.6.

■■ **P6.9** Write a method

```
public static boolean equals(int[] a, int[] b)
```

that checks whether two arrays have the same elements in the same order.

■■ **P6.10** Write a method

```
public static boolean sameSet(int[] a, int[] b)
```

that checks whether two arrays have the same elements in some order, ignoring duplicates. For example, the two arrays

$$1 \quad 4 \quad 9 \quad 16 \quad 9 \quad 7 \quad 4 \quad 9 \quad 11$$

and

$$11 \quad 11 \quad 7 \quad 9 \quad 16 \quad 4 \quad 1$$

would be considered identical. You will probably need one or more helper methods.

■■■ **P6.11** Write a method

```
public static boolean sameElements(int[] a, int[] b)
```

that checks whether two arrays have the same elements in some order, with the same multiplicities. For example,

1 4 9 16 9 7 4 9 11

and

11 1 4 9 16 9 7 4 9

would be considered identical, but

1 4 9 16 9 7 4 9 11

and

11 11 7 9 16 4 1 4 9

would not. You will probably need one or more helper methods.

■■ **P6.12** A *run* is a sequence of adjacent repeated values. Write a program that generates a sequence of 20 random die tosses in an array and that prints the die values, marking the runs by including them in parentheses, like this:

```
1 2 (5 5) 3 1 2 4 3 (2 2 2 2) 3 6 (5 5) 6 3 1
```

Use the following pseudocode:

```
Set a boolean variable inRun to false.
For each valid index i in the array
    If inRun
        If values[i] is different from the preceding value
            Print ).
            inRun = false.
    If not inRun
        If values[i] is the same as the following value
            Print (.
            inRun = true.
    Print values[i].
If inRun, print ).
```

■■ **P6.13** Write a program that generates a sequence of 20 random die tosses in an array and that prints the die values, marking only the longest run, like this:

```
1 2 5 5 3 1 2 4 3 (2 2 2 2) 3 6 5 5 6 3 1
```

If there is more than one run of maximum length, mark the first one.

■■ **P6.14** Write a program that generates a sequence of 20 random values between 0 and 99 in an array, prints the sequence, sorts it, and prints the sorted sequence. Use the sort method from the standard Java library.

■■■ **P6.15** Write a program that produces ten random permutations of the numbers 1 to 10. To generate a random permutation, you need to fill an array with the numbers 1 to 10 so that no two entries of the array have the same contents. You could do it by brute force, by generating random values until you have a value that is not yet in the array. But that is inefficient. Instead, follow this algorithm.

> Make a second array and fill it with the numbers 1 to 10.
> Repeat 10 times
>   Pick a random element from the second array.
>   Remove it and append it to the permutation array.

■■ P6.16 It is a well-researched fact that men in a restroom generally prefer to maximize their distance from already occupied stalls, by occupying the middle of the longest sequence of unoccupied places.

For example, consider the situation where ten stalls are empty.

_ _ _ _ _ _ _ _ _ _

The first visitor will occupy a middle position:

_ _ _ _ _ X _ _ _ _

The next visitor will be in the middle of the empty area at the left.

_ _ X _ _ X _ _ _ _

Write a program that reads the number of stalls and then prints out diagrams in the format given above when the stalls become filled, one at a time. *Hint:* Use an array of boolean values to indicate whether a stall is occupied.

■■■ P6.17 In this assignment, you will model the game of *Bulgarian Solitaire*. The game starts with 45 cards. (They need not be playing cards. Unmarked index cards work just as well.) Randomly divide them into some number of piles of random size. For example, you might start with piles of size 20, 5, 1, 9, and 10. In each round, you take one card from each pile, forming a new pile with these cards. For example, the sample starting configuration would be transformed into piles of size 19, 4, 8, 9, and 5. The solitaire is over when the piles have size 1, 2, 3, 4, 5, 6, 7, 8, and 9, in some order. (It can be shown that you always end up with such a configuration.)

In your program, produce a random starting configuration and print it. Then keep applying the solitaire step and print the result. Stop when the solitaire final configuration is reached.

■■■ P6.18 *Magic squares.* An $n \times n$ matrix that is filled with the numbers 1, 2, 3, . . ., n^2 is a magic square if the sum of the elements in each row, in each column, and in the two diagonals is the same value.

16	3	2	13
5	10	11	8
9	6	7	12
4	15	14	1

Write a program that reads in 16 values from the keyboard and tests whether they form a magic square when put into a 4 × 4 array. You need to test two features:

1. Does each of the numbers 1, 2, ..., 16 occur in the user input?

2. When the numbers are put into a square, are the sums of the rows, columns, and diagonals equal to each other?

▪▪▪ P6.19 Implement the following algorithm to construct magic $n \times n$ squares; it works only if n is odd.

> Set row = n – 1, column = n / 2.
> For k = 1 ... n * n
>   Place k at [row][column].
>   Increment row and column.
>   If the row or column is n, replace it with 0.
>   If the element at [row][column] has already been filled
>   Set row and column to their previous values.
>   Decrement row.

Here is the 5×5 square that you get if you follow this method:

11	18	25	2	9
10	12	19	21	3
4	6	13	20	22
23	5	7	14	16
17	24	1	8	15

Write a program whose input is the number n and whose output is the magic square of order n if n is odd.

▪▪ P6.20 Write a method that computes the average of the neighbors of a two-dimensional array element in the eight directions shown in Figure 14.

```
public static double neighborAverage(int[][] values, int row, int column)
```

However, if the element is located at the boundary of the array, only include the neighbors that are in the array. For example, if row and column are both 0, there are only three neighbors.

▪▪ P6.21 Write a program that reads a sequence of input values and displays a bar chart of the values, using asterisks, like this:

```
**********************
*******************************************
**************************
*************************
**************
```

You may assume that all values are positive. First figure out the maximum value. That value's bar should be drawn with 40 asterisks. Shorter bars should use proportionally fewer asterisks.

▪▪▪ P6.22 Improve the program of Exercise P6.21 to work correctly when the data set contains negative values.

▪▪ P6.23 Improve the program of Exercise P6.21 by adding captions for each bar. Prompt the user for the captions and data values. The output should look like this:

```
      Egypt **********************
     France *******************************************
      Japan **************************
    Uruguay *************************
Switzerland **************
```

■■ P6.24 A theater seating chart is implemented as a two-dimensional array of ticket prices, like this:

```
10 10 10 10 10 10 10 10 10 10
10 10 10 10 10 10 10 10 10 10
10 10 10 10 10 10 10 10 10 10
10 10 20 20 20 20 20 20 10 10
10 10 20 20 20 20 20 20 10 10
10 10 20 20 20 20 20 20 10 10
20 20 30 30 40 40 30 30 20 20
20 30 30 40 50 50 40 30 30 20
30 40 50 50 50 50 50 50 40 30
```

Write a program that prompts users to pick either a seat or a price. Mark sold seats by changing the price to 0. When a user specifies a seat, make sure it is available. When a user specifies a price, find any seat with that price.

■■■ P6.25 Write a program that plays tic-tac-toe. The tic-tac-toe game is played on a 3 × 3 grid as in the photo at right. The game is played by two players, who take turns. The first player marks moves with a circle, the second with a cross. The player who has formed a horizontal, vertical, or diagonal sequence of three marks wins. Your program should draw the game board, ask the user for the coordinates of the next mark, change the players after every successful move, and pronounce the winner.

■ P6.26 Write a method

```
public static ArrayList<Integer> append(ArrayList<Integer> a, ArrayList<Integer> b)
```

that appends one array list after another. For example, if a is

1   4   9   16

and b is

9   7   4   9   11

then append returns the array list

1   4   9   16   9   7   4   9   11

■■ P6.27 Write a method

```
public static ArrayList<Integer> merge(ArrayList<Integer> a, ArrayList<Integer> b)
```

that merges two array lists, alternating elements from both array lists. If one array list is shorter than the other, then alternate as long as you can and then append the remaining elements from the longer array list. For example, if a is

1   4   9   16

and b is

9   7   4   9   11

then merge returns the array list

1   9   4   7   9   4   16   9   11

•• P6.28 Write a method

```
public static ArrayList<Integer> mergeSorted(ArrayList<Integer> a,
    ArrayList<Integer> b)
```

that merges two *sorted* array lists, producing a new sorted array list. Keep an index into each array list, indicating how much of it has been processed already. Each time, append the smallest unprocessed element from either array list, then advance the index. For example, if a is

$$1 \quad 4 \quad 9 \quad 16$$

and b is

$$4 \quad 7 \quad 9 \quad 9 \quad 11$$

then mergeSorted returns the array list

$$1 \quad 4 \quad 4 \quad 7 \quad 9 \quad 9 \quad 9 \quad 11 \quad 16$$

•• Business P6.29 A pet shop wants to give a discount to its clients if they buy one or more pets and at least five other items. The discount is equal to 20 percent of the cost of the other items, but not the pets.

Implement a method

```
public static void discount(double[] prices, boolean[] isPet, int nItems)
```

The method receives information about a particular sale. For the ith item, prices[i] is the price before any discount, and isPet[i] is true if the item is a pet.

Write a program that prompts a cashier to enter each price and then a Y for a pet or N for another item. Use a price of –1 as a sentinel. Save the inputs in an array. Call the method that you implemented, and display the discount.

•• Business P6.30 A supermarket wants to reward its best customer of each day, showing the customer's name on a screen in the supermarket. For that purpose, the customer's purchase amount is stored in an ArrayList<Double> and the customer's name is stored in a corresponding ArrayList<String>.

Implement a method

```
public static String nameOfBestCustomer(ArrayList<Double> sales,
    ArrayList<String> customers)
```

that returns the name of the customer with the largest sale.

Write a program that prompts the cashier to enter all prices and names, adds them to two array lists, calls the method that you implemented, and displays the result. Use a price of 0 as a sentinel.

••• Business P6.31 Improve the program of Exercise P6.30 so that it displays the top customers, that is, the topN customers with the largest sales, where topN is a value that the user of the program supplies.

Implement a method

```
public static ArrayList<String> nameOfBestCustomers(ArrayList<Double> sales,
    ArrayList<String> customers, int topN)
```

If there were fewer than topN customers, include all of them.

■■ **Science P6.32** Sounds can be represented by an array of "sample values" that describe the intensity of the sound at a point in time. The program `ch06/sound/SoundEffect.java` reads a sound file (in WAV format), calls a method process for processing the sample values, and saves the sound file. Your task is to implement the process method by introducing an echo. For each sound value, add the value from 0.2 seconds ago. Scale the result so that no value is larger than 32767.

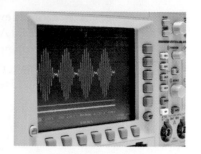

■■■ **Science P6.33** You are given a two-dimensional array of values that give the height of a terrain at different points in a square. Write a method

```
public static void floodMap(double[][] heights, double waterLevel)
```

that prints out a flood map, showing which of the points in the terrain would be flooded if the water level was the given value. In the flood map, print a * for each flooded point and a space for each point that is not flooded.

Here is a sample map:

Then write a program that reads one hundred terrain height values and shows how the terrain gets flooded when the water level increases in ten steps from the lowest point in the terrain to the highest.

■■ **Science P6.34** Sample values from an experiment often need to be smoothed out. One simple approach is to replace each value in an array with the average of the value and its two neighboring values (or one neighboring value if it is at either end of the array). Implement a method

```
public static void smooth(double[] values, int size)
```

that carries out this operation. You should not create another array in your solution.

■■ **Science P6.35** Modify the `ch06/animation/BlockAnimation.java` program to show an animated sine wave. In the ith frame, shift the sine wave by i degrees.

■■■ **Science P6.36** Write a program that models the movement of an object with mass m that is attached to an oscillating spring. When a spring is displaced from its equilibrium position by an amount x, Hooke's law states that the restoring force is

$$F = -kx$$

where k is a constant that depends on the spring. (Use 10 N/m for this simulation.)

Start with a given displacement x (say, 0.5 meter). Set the initial velocity v to 0. Compute the acceleration a

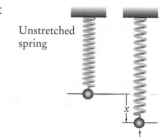

Unstretched spring

from Newton's law ($F = ma$) and Hooke's law, using a mass of 1 kg. Use a small time interval $\Delta t = 0.01$ second. Update the velocity—it changes by $a\Delta t$. Update the displacement—it changes by $v\Delta t$.

Every ten iterations, plot the spring displacement as a bar, where 1 pixel represents 1 cm. Use the technique in Special Topic 4.3 for creating an image.

•• Graphics P6.37 Using the technique of Special Topic 4.3, generate the image of a checkerboard.

• Graphics P6.38 Using the technique of Special Topic 4.3, generate the image of a sine wave. Draw a line of pixels for every five degrees.

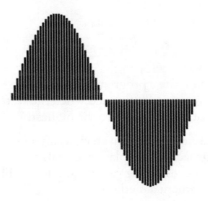

ANSWERS TO SELF-CHECK QUESTIONS

1. `int[] primes = { 2, 3, 5, 7, 11 };`

2. `2, 3, 5, 3, 2`

3. `3, 4, 6, 8, 12`

4. `values[0] = 10;`
`values[9] = 10;`

or better: `values[values.length - 1] = 10;`

5. `String[] words = new String[10];`

6. `String[] words = { "Yes", "No" };`

7. No. Because you don't store the values, you need to print them when you read them. But you don't know where to add the <= until you have seen all values.

8. It counts how many elements of `values` are zero.

9. ```
for (double x : values)
{
    System.out.println(x);
}
```

**10.** ```
double product = 1;
for (double f : factors)
{
    product = product * f;
```

}

11. The loop writes a value into `values[i]`. The enhanced for loop does not have the index variable `i`.

12. ```
20 <== largest value
10
20 <== largest value
```

13. ```
int count = 0;
for (double x : values)
{
    if (x == 0) { count++; }
}
```

14. If all elements of values are negative, then the result is incorrectly computed as 0.

15. ```
for (int i = 0; i < values.length; i++)
{
    System.out.print(values[i]);
    if (i < values.lenqth - 1)
    {
        System.out.print(" | ");
    }
}
```

Now you know why we set up the loop the other way.

16. If the array has no elements, then the program terminates with an exception.

17. If there is a match, then pos is incremented before the loop exits.

18. This loop sets all elements to `values[pos]`.

19. `int[] numbers = squares(5);`

20. ```
public static void fill(int[] values, int value)
{
    for (int i = 0; i < values.length; i++)
    {
        values[i] = value; }
}
```

21. The method returns an array whose length is given in the first argument. The array is filled with random integers between 0 and n - 1.

22. The contents of scores is unchanged. The reverse method returns a new array with the reversed numbers.

23.

values	result	i
[1, 4, 9]	[0, 0, 0]	0
	[9, 0, 0]	1
	[9, 4, 0]	2
	[9, 4, 1]	

24. Use the first algorithm. The order of elements does not matter when computing the sum.

25. **Find the minimum value.**
Calculate the sum.
Subtract the minimum value.

26. Use the algorithm for counting matches (Section 4.7.2) twice, once for counting the positive values and once for counting the negative values.

27. You need to modify the algorithm in Section 6.3.4.
```
boolean first = true;
for (int i = 0; i < values.length; i++)
{
    if (values[i] > 0))
    {
        if (first) { first = false; }
        else { System.out.print(", "); }
    }
    System.out.print(values[i]);
}
```

Note that you can no longer use i > 0 as the criterion for printing a separator.

28. Use the algorithm to collect all positive elements in an array, then use the algorithm in Section 6.3.4 to print the array of matches.

29. The paperclip for i assumes positions 0, 1, 2, 3. When i is incremented to 4, the condition i < size / 2 becomes false, and the loop ends. Similarly, the paperclip for j assumes positions 4, 5, 6, 7, which are the valid positions for the second half of the array.

30. It reverses the elements in the array.

31. Here is one solution. The basic idea is to move all odd elements to the end. Put one paper clip at the beginning of the array and one at the end. If the element at the first paper clip is odd, swap it with the one at the other paper clip and move that paper clip to the left. Otherwise, move the first paper clip to the right. Stop when the two paper clips meet. Here is the pseudocode:

i = 0

j = size - 1

```
While (i < j)
   If (a[i] is odd)
      Swap elements at positions i and j.
      j--
   Else
      i++
```

32. Here is one solution. The idea is to remove all odd elements and move them to the end. The trick is to know when to stop. Nothing is gained by moving odd elements into the area that already contains moved elements, so we want to mark that area with another paper clip.

```
i = 0
moved = size
While (i < moved)
   If (a[i] is odd)
      Remove the element at position i and add it
         at the end.
      moved--
```

33. When you read inputs, you get to see values one at a time, and you can't peek ahead. Picking cards one at a time from a deck of cards simulates this process better than looking at a sequence of items, all of which are revealed.

34. You get the total number of gold, silver, and bronze medals in the competition. In our example, there are four of each.

35.
```
for (int i = 0; i < 8; i++)
{
   for (int j = 0; j < 8; j++)
   {
      board[i][j] = (i + j) % 2;
   }
}
```

36. `String[][] board = new String[3][3];`

37. `board[0][2] = "x";`

38. `board[0][0], board[1][1], board[2][2]`

39.
```
ArrayList<Integer> primes =
   new ArrayList<Integer>();
primes.add(2);
primes.add(3);
primes.add(5);
primes.add(7);
primes.add(11);
```

40.
```
for (int i = primes.size() - 1; i >= 0; i--)
{
   System.out.println(primes.get(i));
}
```

41. `"Ann", "Cal"`

42. The `names` variable has not been initialized.

43. `names1` contains "Emily", "Bob", "Cindy", "Dave"; `names2` contains "Dave"

44. Because the number of weekdays doesn't change, there is no disadvantage to using an array, and it is easier to initialize:

```
String[] weekdayNames = { "Monday", "Tuesday",
   "Wednesday", "Thursday", "Friday",
   "Saturday", "Sunday" };
```

45. Reading inputs into an array list is much easier.

CHAPTER **7**

INPUT/OUTPUT AND EXCEPTION HANDLING

CHAPTER GOALS

To read and write text files

To process command line arguments

To throw and catch exceptions

To implement programs that propagate checked exceptions

CHAPTER CONTENTS

7.1 READING AND WRITING TEXT FILES 318

Common Error 7.1: Backslashes in File Names 321

Common Error 7.2: Constructing a Scanner with a String 321

Special Topic 7.1: Reading Web Pages 321

Special Topic 7.2: File Dialog Boxes 321

Special Topic 7.3: Reading and Writing Binary Data 322

7.2 TEXT INPUT AND OUTPUT 323

Special Topic 7.4: Regular Expressions 330

Video Example 7.1: Computing a Document's Readability ⊕

7.3 COMMAND LINE ARGUMENTS 330

How To 7.1: Processing Text Files 333

Random Fact 7.1: Encryption Algorithms 336

Worked Example 7.1: Analyzing Baby Names ⊕

7.4 EXCEPTION HANDLING 337

Syntax 7.1: Throwing an Exception 338

Syntax 7.2: Catching Exceptions 341

Syntax 7.3: The throws Clause 343

Syntax 7.4: The finally Clause 344

Programming Tip 7.1: Throw Early, Catch Late 345

Programming Tip 7.2: Do Not Squelch Exceptions 345

Programming Tip 7.3: Do Not Use catch and finally in the Same try Statement 346

Special Topic 7.5: Automatic Resource Management in Java 7 346

Random Fact 7.2: The Ariane Rocket Incident 347

7.5 APPLICATION: HANDLING INPUT ERRORS 347

Video Example 7.2: Detecting Accounting Fraud ⊕

In this chapter, you will learn how to read and write files—a very useful skill for processing real world data. As an application, you will learn how to encrypt data. (The Enigma machine shown at left is an encryption device used by Germany in World War II. Pioneering British computer scientists broke the code and were able to intercept encoded messages, which was a significant help in winning the war.) The remainder of this chapter tells you how your programs can report and recover from problems, such as missing files or malformed content, using the exception-handling mechanism of the Java language.

7.1 Reading and Writing Text Files

We begin this chapter by discussing the common task of reading and writing files that contain text. Examples of text files include not only files that are created with a simple text editor, such as Windows Notepad, but also Java source code and HTML files.

In Java, the most convenient mechanism for reading text is to use the Scanner class. You already know how to use a Scanner for reading console input. To read input from a disk file, the Scanner class relies on another class, File, which describes disk files and directories. (The File class has many methods that we do not discuss in this book; for example, methods that delete or rename a file.)

To begin, construct a File object with the name of the input file:

> Use the Scanner class for reading text files.

```
File inputFile = new File("input.txt");
```

Then use the File object to construct a Scanner object:

```
Scanner in = new Scanner(inputFile);
```

This Scanner object reads text from the file input.txt. You can use the Scanner methods (such as nextInt, nextDouble, and next) to read data from the input file.

For example, you can use the following loop to process numbers in the input file:

```
while (in.hasNextDouble())
{
    double value = in.nextDouble();
    Process value.
}
```

To write output to a file, you construct a PrintWriter object with the desired file name, for example

> When writing text files, use the PrintWriter class and the print/ println/printf methods.

```
PrintWriter out = new PrintWriter("output.txt");
```

If the output file already exists, it is emptied before the new data are written into it. If the file doesn't exist, an empty file is created.

The PrintWriter class is an enhancement of the PrintStream class that you already know—System.out is a PrintStream object. You can use the familiar print, println, and printf methods with any PrintWriter object:

```
out.println("Hello, World!");
out.printf("Total: %8.2f\n", total);
```

Close all files when you are done processing them.

When you are done processing a file, be sure to *close* the Scanner or PrintWriter:

```
in.close();
out.close();
```

If your program exits without closing the PrintWriter, some of the output may not be written to the disk file.

The following program puts these concepts to work. It reads a file containing numbers, and writes the numbers to another file, lined up in a column and followed by their total.

For example, if the input file has the contents

```
32 54 67.5 29 35 80
115 44.5 100 65
```

then the output file is

```
        32.00
        54.00
        67.50
        29.00
        35.00
        80.00
       115.00
        44.50
       100.00
        65.00
Total:  622.00
```

There is one additional issue that we need to tackle. If the input or output file for a Scanner doesn't exist, a FileNotFoundException occurs when the Scanner object is constructed. The compiler insists that we specify what the program should do when that happens. Similarly, the PrintWriter constructor generates this exception if it cannot open the file for writing. (This can happen if the name is illegal or the user does not have the authority to create a file in the given location.) In our sample program, we want to terminate the main method if the exception occurs. To achieve this, we label the main method with a throws declaration:

```
public static void main(String[] args) throws FileNotFoundException
```

You will see in Section 7.4 how to deal with exceptions in a more professional way.

The File, PrintWriter, and FileNotFoundException classes are contained in the java.io package.

section_1/Total.java

```
 1   import java.io.File;
 2   import java.io.FileNotFoundException;
 3   import java.io.PrintWriter;
 4   import java.util.Scanner;
 5
 6   /**
 7      This program reads a file with numbers, and writes the numbers to another
 8      file, lined up in a column and followed by their total.
 9   */
10   public class Total
11   {
12      public static void main(String[] args) throws FileNotFoundException
13      {
```

```
14        // Prompt for the input and output file names
15
16        Scanner console = new Scanner(System.in);
17        System.out.print("Input file: ");
18        String inputFileName = console.next();
19        System.out.print("Output file: ");
20        String outputFileName = console.next();
21
22        // Construct the Scanner and PrintWriter objects for reading and writing
23
24        File inputFile = new File(inputFileName);
25        Scanner in = new Scanner(inputFile);
26        PrintWriter out = new PrintWriter(outputFileName);
27
28        // Read the input and write the output
29
30        double total = 0;
31
32        while (in.hasNextDouble())
33        {
34            double value = in.nextDouble();
35            out.printf("%15.2f\n", value);
36            total = total + value;
37        }
38
39        out.printf("Total: %8.2f\n", total);
40
41        in.close();
42        out.close();
43    }
44 }
```

SELF CHECK

1. What happens when you supply the same name for the input and output files to the Total program? Try it out if you are not sure.

2. What happens when you supply the name of a nonexistent input file to the Total program? Try it out if you are not sure.

3. Suppose you wanted to add the total to an existing file instead of writing a new file. Self Check 1 indicates that you cannot simply do this by specifying the same file for input and output. How can you achieve this task? Provide the pseudo-code for the solution.

4. How do you modify the program so that it shows the average, not the total, of the inputs?

5. How can you modify the Total program so that it writes the values in two columns, like this:

```
    32.00    54.00
    67.50    29.00
    35.00    80.00
   115.00    44.50
   100.00    65.00
Total:      622.00
```

Practice It   Now you can try these exercises at the end of the chapter: R7.1, R7.2, P7.1.

Backslashes in File Names

When you specify a file name as a string literal, and the name contains backslash characters (as in a Windows file name), you must supply each backslash twice:

```
File inputFile = new File("c:\\homework\\input.dat");
```

A single backslash inside a quoted string is an **escape character** that is combined with the following character to form a special meaning, such as \n for a newline character. The \\ combination denotes a single backslash.

When a user supplies a file name to a program, however, the user should not type the backslash twice.

Constructing a Scanner with a String

When you construct a PrintWriter with a string, it writes to a file:

```
PrintWriter out = new PrintWriter("output.txt");
```

However, this does *not* work for a Scanner. The statement

```
Scanner in = new Scanner("input.txt"); // Error?
```

does *not* open a file. Instead, it simply reads through the string: in.next() returns the string "input.txt". (This is occasionally useful—see Section 7.2.4.)

You must simply remember to use File objects in the Scanner constructor:

```
Scanner in = new Scanner(new File("input.txt")); // OK
```

Reading Web Pages

You can read the contents of a web page with this sequence of commands:

```
String address = "http://horstmann.com/index.html";
URL pageLocation = new URL(address);
Scanner in = new Scanner(pageLocation.openStream());
```

Now simply read the contents of the web page with the Scanner in the usual way. The URL constructor and the openStream method can throw an IOException, so you need to tag the main method with throws IOException. (See Section 7.4.3 for more information on the throws clause.)

The URL class is contained in the java.net package.

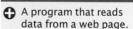

ONLINE EXAMPLE

A program that reads data from a web page.

File Dialog Boxes

In a program with a graphical user interface, you will want to use a file dialog box (such as the one shown in the figure below) whenever the users of your program need to pick a file. The JFileChooser class implements a file dialog box for the Swing user-interface toolkit.

The JFileChooser class has many options to fine-tune the display of the dialog box, but in its most basic form it is quite simple: Construct a file chooser object; then call the showOpenDialog or showSaveDialog method. Both methods show the same dialog box, but the button for selecting a file is labeled "Open" or "Save", depending on which method you call.

For better placement of the dialog box on the screen, you can specify the user-interface component over which to pop up the dialog box. If you don't care where the dialog box pops up, you can simply pass null. The showOpenDialog and showSaveDialog methods return either JFileChooser.APPROVE_OPTION, if the user has chosen a file, or JFileChooser.CANCEL_OPTION, if the user canceled the selection. If a file was chosen, then you call the getSelectedFile method to obtain a File object that describes the file. Here is a complete example:

ONLINE EXAMPLE

A program that demonstrates how to use a file chooser.

```java
JFileChooser chooser = new JFileChooser();
Scanner in = null;
if (chooser.showOpenDialog(null) == JFileChooser.APPROVE_OPTION)
{
    File selectedFile = chooser.getSelectedFile();
    in = new Scanner(selectedFile);
    . . .
}
```

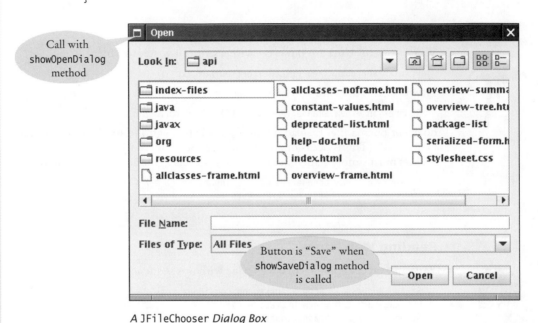

A JFileChooser *Dialog Box*

Special Topic 7.3

Reading and Writing Binary Data

You use the Scanner and PrintWriter classes to read and write text files. Text files contain sequences of characters. Other files, such as images, are not made up of characters but of bytes. A **byte** is a fundamental storage unit in a computer—a number consisting of eight binary digits. (A byte can represent unsigned integers between 0 and 255 or signed integers between −128 and 127.) The Java library has a different set of classes, called streams, for working with binary files. While modifying binary files is quite challenging and beyond the scope of this book, we give you a simple example of copying binary data from a web site to a file.

You use an InputStream to read binary data. For example,

```java
URL imageLocation = new URL("http://horstmann.com/java4everyone/duke.gif");
InputStream in = imageLocation.openStream();
```

To write binary data to a file, use a FileOutputStream:

```java
FileOutputStream out = new FileOutputStream("duke.gif");
```

The read method of an input stream reads a single byte and returns −1 when no further input is available. The `write` method of an output stream writes a single byte.

The following loop copies all bytes from an input stream to an output stream:

```
boolean done = false;
while (!done)
{
   int input = in.read(); // -1 or a byte between 0 and 255
   if (input == -1) { done = true; }
   else { out.write(input); }
}
```

7.2 Text Input and Output

In the following sections, you will learn how to process text with complex contents, and you will learn how to cope with challenges that often occur with real data.

7.2.1 Reading Words

The next method of the Scanner class reads the next string. Consider the loop

The next method reads a string that is delimited by white space.

```
while (in.hasNext())
{
   String input = in.next();
   System.out.println(input);
}
```

If the user provides the input:

```
Mary had a little lamb
```

this loop prints each word on a separate line:

```
Mary
had
a
little
lamb
```

However, the words can contain punctuation marks and other symbols. The next method returns any sequence of characters that is not white space. *White space* includes spaces, tab characters, and the newline characters that separate lines. For example, the following strings are considered "words" by the next method:

```
snow.
1729
C++
```

(Note the period after snow—it is considered a part of the word because it is not white space.)

Here is precisely what happens when the next method is executed. Input characters that are white space are *consumed*—that is, removed from the input. However, they do not become part of the word. The first character that is not white space becomes the first character of the word. More characters are added until either another white space character occurs, or the end of the input file has been reached. However, if the end of the input file is reached before any character was added to the word, a "no such element exception" occurs.

Sometimes, you want to read just the words and discard anything that isn't a letter. You achieve this task by calling the useDelimiter method on your Scanner object:

```
Scanner in = new Scanner(. . .);
in.useDelimiter("[^A-Za-z]+");
```

Here, we set the character pattern that separates words to "any sequence of characters other than letters". (See Special Topic 7.4.) With this setting, punctuation and numbers are not included in the words returned by the next method.

7.2.2 Reading Characters

Sometimes, you want to read a file one character at a time. You will see an example in Section 7.3 where we encrypt the characters of a file. You achieve this task by calling the useDelimiter method on your Scanner object with an empty string:

```
Scanner in = new Scanner(. . .);
in.useDelimiter("");
```

Now each call to next returns a string consisting of a single character. Here is how you can process the characters:

```
while (in.hasNext())
{
    char ch = in.next().charAt(0);
    Process ch.
}
```

7.2.3 Classifying Characters

The Character class has methods for classifying characters.

When you read a character, or when you analyze the characters in a word or line, you often want to know what kind of character it is. The Character class declares several useful methods for this purpose. Each of them has an argument of type char and returns a boolean value (see Table 1).

For example, the call

```
Character.isDigit(ch)
```

returns true if ch is a digit ('0' ... '9' or a digit in another writing system—see Random Fact 2.2), false otherwise.

Table 1 Character Testing Methods

Method	Examples of Accepted Characters
isDigit	0, 1, 2
isLetter	A, B, C, a, b, c
isUpperCase	A, B, C
isLowerCase	a, b, c
isWhiteSpace	space, newline, tab

7.2.4 Reading Lines

The nextLine method reads an entire line.

When each line of a file is a data record, it is often best to read entire lines with the nextLine method:

```
String line = in.nextLine();
```

The next input line (without the newline character) is placed into the string line. You can then take the line apart for further processing.

The hasNextLine method returns true if there is at least one more line in the input, false when all lines have been read. To ensure that there is another line to process, call the hasNextLine method before calling nextLine.

Here is a typical example of processing lines in a file. A file with population data from the CIA Fact Book site (https://www.cia.gov/library/publications/the-world-factbook/index.html) contains lines such as the following:

```
China    1330044605
India    1147995898
United States 303824646
. . .
```

Because some country names have more than one word, it would be tedious to read this file using the next method. For example, after reading United, how would your program know that it needs to read another word before reading the population count?

Instead, read each input line into a string:

```
while (in.hasNextLine())
{
    String line = nextLine();
    Process line.
}
```

Use the isDigit and isWhiteSpace methods introduced to find out where the name ends and the number starts.

Locate the first digit:

```
int i = 0;
while (!Character.isDigit(line.charAt(i))) { i++; }
```

Then extract the country name and population:

```
String countryName = line.substring(0, i);
String population = line.substring(i);
```

However, the country name contains one or more spaces at the end. Use the trim method to remove them:

```
countryName = countryName.trim();
```

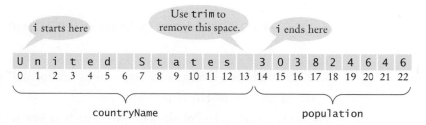

The trim method returns the string with all white space at the beginning and end removed.

There is one additional problem. The population is stored in a string, not a number. In Section 7.2.6, you will see how to convert the string to a number.

7.2.5 Scanning a String

In the preceding section, you saw how to break a string into parts by looking at individual characters. Another approach is occasionally easier. You can use a Scanner object to read the characters from a string:

```
Scanner lineScanner = new Scanner(line);
```

Then you can use lineScanner like any other Scanner object, reading words and numbers:

```
String countryName = lineScanner.next(); // Read first word
// Add more words to countryName until number encountered
while (!lineScanner.hasNextInt())
{
   countryName = countryName + " " + lineScanner.next();
}
int populationValue = lineScanner.nextInt();
```

7.2.6 Converting Strings to Numbers

Sometimes you have a string that contains a number, such as the population string in Section 7.2.4. For example, suppose that the string is the character sequence "303824646". To get the integer value 303824646, you use the Integer.parseInt method:

```
int populationValue = Integer.parseInt(population);
   // populationValue is the integer 303824646
```

To convert a string containing floating-point digits to its floating-point value, use the Double.parseDouble method. For example, suppose input is the string "3.95".

```
double price = Double.parseDouble(input);
   // price is the floating-point number 3.95
```

If a string contains the digits of a number, you use the Integer.parseInt or Double.parseDouble method to obtain the number value.

You need to be careful when calling the Integer.parseInt and Double.parseDouble methods. The argument must be a string containing the digits of an integer, without any additional characters. Not even spaces are allowed! In our situation, we happen to know that there won't be any spaces at the beginning of the string, but there might be some at the end. Therefore, we use the trim method:

```
int populationValue = Integer.parseInt(population.trim());
```

How To 7.1 on page 333 continues this example.

7.2.7 Avoiding Errors When Reading Numbers

You have used the nextInt and nextDouble methods of the Scanner class many times, but here we will have a look at what happens in "abnormal" situations. Suppose you call

```
int value = in.nextInt();
```

The nextInt method recognizes numbers such as 3 or -21. However, if the input is not a properly formatted number, an "input mismatch exception" occurs. For example, consider an input containing the characters

```
21st  century
```

White space is consumed and the word 21st is read. However, this word is not a properly formatted number, causing an input mismatch exception in the nextInt method.

If there is no input at all when you call nextInt or nextDouble, a "no such element exception" occurs. To avoid exceptions, use the hasNextInt method to screen the input when reading an integer. For example,

```
if (in.hasNextInt())
{
   int value = in.nextInt();
   . . .
}
```

Similarly, you should call the hasNextDouble method before calling nextDouble.

7.2.8 Mixing Number, Word, and Line Input

The nextInt, nextDouble, and next methods *do not* consume the white space that follows the number or word. This can be a problem if you alternate between calling nextInt/nextDouble/next and nextLine. Suppose a file contains country names and population values in this format:

```
China
1330044605
India
1147995898
United States
303824646
```

Now suppose you read the file with these instructions:

```
while (in.hasNextLine())
{
   String countryName = in.nextLine();
   int population = in.nextInt();
   Process the country name and population.
}
```

Initially, the input contains

```
China\n1330044605\nIndia\n
```

After the first call to the nextLine method, the input contains

```
1330044605\nIndia\n
```

After the call to nextInt, the input contains

```
\nIndia\n
```

Note that the nextInt call did *not* consume the newline character. Therefore, the second call to nextLine reads an empty string!

The remedy is to add a call to nextLine after reading the population value:

```
String countryName = in.nextLine();
int population = in.nextInt();
in.nextLine(); // Consume the newline
```

The call to nextLine consumes any remaining white space *and* the newline character.

7.2.9 Formatting Output

When you write numbers or strings, you often want to control how they appear. For example, dollar amounts are usually formatted with two significant digits, such as

```
Cookies:       3.20
```

You know from Section 2.3.2 how to achieve this output with the `printf` method. In this section, we discuss additional options of the `printf` method.

Suppose you need to print a table of items and prices, each stored in an array, such as this one:

```
Cookies:       3.20
Linguine:      2.95
Clams:        17.29
```

Note that the item strings line up to the left, whereas the numbers line up to the right. By default, the `printf` method lines up values to the right. To specify left alignment, you add a hyphen (-) before the field width:

```
System.out.printf("%-10s%10.2f", items[i] + ":", prices[i]);
```

Here, we have two format specifiers.

- `%-10s` formats a left-justified string. The string `items[i] + ":"` is padded with spaces so it becomes ten characters wide. The - indicates that the string is placed on the left, followed by sufficient spaces to reach a width of 10.

- `%10.2f` formats a floating-point number, also in a field that is ten characters wide. However, the spaces appear to the left and the value to the right.

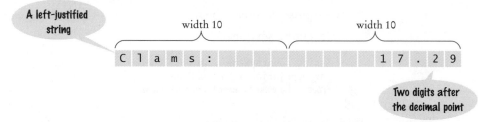

A construct such as `%-10s` or `%10.2f` is called a *format specifier:* it describes how a value should be formatted.

Table 2 Format Flags

Flag	Meaning	Example
-	Left alignment	1.23 followed by spaces
0	Show leading zeroes	001.23
+	Show a plus sign for positive numbers	+1.23
(	Enclose negative numbers in parentheses	(1.23)
,	Show decimal separators	12,300
^	Convert letters to uppercase	1.23E+1

Table 3 Format Types		
Code	Type	Example
d	Decimal integer	123
f	Fixed floating-point	12.30
e	Exponential floating-point	1.23e+1
g	General floating-point (exponential notation is used for very large or very small values)	12.3
s	String	Tax:

A format specifier has the following structure:

- The first character is a %
- Next, there are optional "flags" that modify the format, such as - to indicate left alignment. See Table 2 for the most common format flags.
- Next is the field width, the total number of characters in the field (including the spaces used for padding), followed by an optional precision for floating-point numbers.
- The format specifier ends with the format type, such as f for floating-point values or s for strings. There are quite a few format types—Table 3 shows the most important ones.

SELF CHECK

6. Suppose the input contains the characters Hello, World!. What are the values of word and input after this code fragment?

   ```
   String word = in.next();
   String input = in.nextLine();
   ```

7. Suppose the input contains the characters 995.0 Fred. What are the values of number and input after this code fragment?

   ```
   int number = 0;
   if (in.hasNextInt()) { number = in.nextInt(); }
   String input = in.next();
   ```

8. Suppose the input contains the characters 6E6 6,995.00. What are the values of x1 and x2 after this code fragment?

   ```
   double x1 = in.nextDouble();
   double x2 = in.nextDouble();
   ```

9. Your input file contains a sequence of numbers, but sometimes a value is not available and is marked as N/A. How can you read the numbers and skip over the markers?

10. How can you remove spaces from the country name in Section 7.2.4 without using the trim method?

Practice It Now you can try these exercises at the end of the chapter: P7.2, P7.4, P7.5.

Regular Expressions

Regular expressions describe character patterns. For example, numbers have a simple form. They contain one or more digits. The regular expression describing numbers is [0-9]+. The set [0-9] denotes any digit between 0 and 9, and the + means "one or more".

The search commands of professional programming editors understand regular expressions. Moreover, several utility programs use regular expressions to locate matching text. A commonly used program that uses regular expressions is *grep* (which stands for "global regular expression print"). You can run grep from a command line or from inside some compilation environments. Grep is part of the UNIX operating system, and versions are available for Windows. It needs a regular expression and one or more files to search. When grep runs, it displays a set of lines that match the regular expression.

Suppose you want to find all magic numbers (see Programming Tip 2.2) in a file.

```
grep [0-9]+ Homework.java
```

lists all lines in the file Homework.java that contain sequences of digits. That isn't terribly useful; lines with variable names x1 will be listed. OK, you want sequences of digits that do *not* immediately follow letters:

```
grep [^A-Za-z][0-9]+ Homework.java
```

The set [^A-Za-z] denotes any characters that are *not* in the ranges A to Z and a to z. This works much better, and it shows only lines that contain actual numbers.

The useDelimiter method of the Scanner class accepts a regular expression to describe delimiters—the blocks of text that separate words. As already mentioned, if you set the delimiter pattern to [^A-Za-z]+, a delimiter is a sequence of one or more characters that are not letters.

For more information on regular expressions, consult one of the many tutorials on the Internet by pointing your search engine to "regular expression tutorial".

VIDEO EXAMPLE 7.1

Computing a Document's Readability

In this Video Example, we develop a program that computes the Flesch Readability Index for a document.

7.3 Command Line Arguments

Depending on the operating system and Java development environment used, there are different methods of starting a program—for example, by selecting "Run" in the compilation environment, by clicking on an icon, or by typing the name of the program at the prompt in a command shell window. The latter method is called "invoking the program from the command line". When you use this method, you must of course type the name of the program, but you can also type in additional information that the program can use. These additional strings are called **command line arguments**. For example, if you start a program with the command line

```
java ProgramClass -v input.dat
```

then the program receives two command line arguments: the strings "-v" and "input. dat". It is entirely up to the program what to do with these strings. It is customary to interpret strings starting with a hyphen (-) as program options.

➕ Available online in WileyPLUS and at www.wiley.com/college/horstmann.

Should you support command line arguments for your programs, or should you prompt users, perhaps with a graphical user interface? For a casual and infrequent user, an interactive user interface is much better. The user interface guides the user along and makes it possible to navigate the application without much knowledge. But for a frequent user, a command line interface has a major advantage: it is easy to automate. If you need to process hundreds of files every day, you could spend all your time typing file names into file chooser dialog boxes. However, by using batch files or shell scripts (a feature of your computer's operating system), you can automatically call a program many times with different command line arguments.

Your program receives its command line arguments in the args parameter of the main method:

```java
public static void main(String[] args)
```

In our example, args is an array of length 2, containing the strings

```java
args[0]:    "-v"
args[1]:    "input.dat"
```

> Programs that start from the command line receive the command line arguments in the main method.

Let us write a program that *encrypts* a file—that is, scrambles it so that it is unreadable except to those who know the decryption method. Ignoring 2,000 years of progress in the field of encryption, we will use a method familiar to Julius Caesar, replacing A with a D, B with an E, and so on (see Figure 1).

The program takes the following command line arguments:

- An optional -d flag to indicate decryption instead of encryption
- The input file name
- The output file name

For example,

```java
java CaesarCipher input.txt encrypt.txt
```

encrypts the file input.txt and places the result into encrypt.txt.

```java
java CaesarCipher -d encrypt.txt output.txt
```

decrypts the file encrypt.txt and places the result into output.txt.

The emperor Julius Caesar used a simple scheme to encrypt messages.

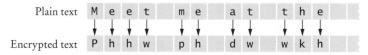

Plain text M e e t   m e   a t   t h e

Encrypted text P h h w   p h   d w   w k h

Figure 1 Caesar Cipher

section_3/CaesarCipher.java

```java
1    import java.io.File;
2    import java.io.FileNotFoundException;
3    import java.io.PrintWriter;
4    import java.util.Scanner;
```

```
 5
 6   /**
 7       This program encrypts a file using the Caesar cipher.
 8   */
 9   public class CaesarCipher
10   {
11      public static void main(String[] args) throws FileNotFoundException
12      {
13         final int DEFAULT_KEY = 3;
14         int key = DEFAULT_KEY;
15         String inFile = "";
16         String outFile = "";
17         int files = 0; // Number of command line arguments that are files
18
19         for (int i = 0; i < args.length; i++)
20         {
21            String arg = args[i];
22            if (arg.charAt(0) == '-')
23            {
24               // It is a command line option
25
26               char option = arg.charAt(1);
27               if (option == 'd') { key = -key; }
28               else { usage(); return; }
29            }
30            else
31            {
32               // It is a file name
33
34               files++;
35               if (files == 1) { inFile = arg; }
36               else if (files == 2) { outFile = arg; }
37            }
38         }
39         if (files != 2) { usage(); return; }
40
41         Scanner in = new Scanner(new File(inFile));
42         in.useDelimiter(""); // Process individual characters
43         PrintWriter out = new PrintWriter(outFile);
44
45         while (in.hasNext())
46         {
47            char from = in.next().charAt(0);
48            char to = encrypt(from, key);
49            out.print(to);
50         }
51         in.close();
52         out.close();
53      }
54
55      /**
56          Encrypts upper- and lowercase characters by shifting them
57          according to a key.
58          @param ch the letter to be encrypted
59          @param key the encryption key
60          @return the encrypted letter
61      */
62      public static char encrypt(char ch, int key)
63      {
64         int base = 0;
```

```
65        if ('A' <= ch && ch <= 'Z') { base = 'A'; }
66        else if ('a' <= ch && ch <= 'z') { base = 'a'; }
67        else { return ch; } // Not a letter
68        int offset = ch - base + key;
69        final int LETTERS = 26; // Number of letters in the Roman alphabet
70        if (offset > LETTERS) { offset = offset - LETTERS; }
71        else if (offset < 0) { offset = offset + LETTERS; }
72        return (char) (base + offset);
73     }
74
75     /**
76        Prints a message describing proper usage.
77     */
78     public static void usage()
79     {
80        System.out.println("Usage: java CaesarCipher [-d] infile outfile");
81     }
82  }
```

SELF CHECK

11. If the program is invoked with java CaesarCipher -d file1.txt, what are the elements of args?

12. Trace the program when it is invoked as in Self Check 11.

13. Will the program run correctly if the program is invoked with java CaesarCipher file1.txt file2.txt -d? If so, why? If not, why not?

14. Encrypt CAESAR using the Caesar cipher.

15. How can you modify the program so that the user can specify an encryption key other than 3 with a -k option, for example

    java CaesarCipher -k15 input.txt output.txt

Practice It   Now you can try these exercises at the end of the chapter: R7.4, P7.8, P7.9.

HOW TO 7.1   **Processing Text Files**

Processing text files that contain real data can be surprisingly challenging. This How To gives you step-by-step guidance.

As an example, we will consider this task: Read two country data files, worldpop.txt and worldarea.txt (supplied with the book's companion code). Both files contain the same countries in the same order. Write a file world_pop_density.txt that contains country names and population densities (people per square km), with the country names aligned left and the numbers aligned right:

```
Afghanistan                   50.56
Akrotiri                     127.64
Albania                      125.91
Algeria                       14.18
American Samoa               288.92
. . .
```

Singapore is one of the most densely populated countries in the world.

Step 1   Understand the processing task.

As always, you need to have a clear understanding of the task before designing a solution. Can you carry out the task by hand (perhaps with smaller input files)? If not, get more information about the problem.

One important aspect that you need to consider is whether you can process the data as it becomes available, or whether you need to store it first. For example, if you are asked to write out sorted data, you first need to collect all input, perhaps by placing it in an array list. However, it is often possible to process the data "on the go", without storing it.

In our example, we can read each file a line at a time and compute the density for each line because our input files store the population and area data in the same order.

The following pseudocode describes our processing task.

```
While there are more lines to be read
    Read a line from each file.
    Extract the country name.
    population = number following the country name in the line from the first file
    area = number following the country name in the line from the second file
    If area != 0
        density = population / area
    Print country name and density.
```

Step 2   Determine which files you need to read and write.

This should be clear from the problem. In our example, there are two input files, the population data and the area data, and one output file.

Step 3   Choose a mechanism for obtaining the file names.

There are three options:

- Hard-coding the file names (such as `"worldpop.txt"`).
- Asking the user:
  ```
  Scanner in = new Scanner(System.in);
  System.out.print("Enter filename: ");
  String inFile = in.nextLine();
  ```
- Using command-line arguments for the file names.

In our example, we use hard-coded file names for simplicity.

Step 4   Choose between line, word, and character-based input.

As a rule of thumb, read lines if the input data is grouped by lines. That is the case with tabular data, such as in our example, or when you need to report line numbers.

When gathering data that can be distributed over several lines, then it makes more sense to read words. Keep in mind that you lose all white space when you read words.

Reading characters is mostly useful for tasks that require access to individual characters. Examples include analyzing character frequencies, changing tabs to spaces, or encryption.

Step 5   With line-oriented input, extract the required data.

It is simple to read a line of input with the `nextLine` method. Then you need to get the data out of that line. You can extract substrings, as described in Section 7.2.4.

Typically, you will use methods such as `Character.isWhitespace` and `Character.isDigit` to find the boundaries of substrings.

If you need any of the substrings as numbers, you must convert them, using `Integer.parseInt` or `Double.parseDouble`.

Step 6   Use methods to factor out common tasks.

Processing input files usually has repetitive tasks, such as skipping over white space or extracting numbers from strings. It really pays off to develop a set of methods to handle these tedious operations.

In our example, we have two common tasks that call for helper methods: extracting the country name and the value that follows. We will implement methods

```
public static String extractCountry(String line)
public static double extractValue(String line)
```

These methods are implemented as described in Section 7.2.4.

Here is the complete source code (how_to_1/PopulationDensity.java).

```java
import java.io.File;
import java.io.FileNotFoundException;
import java.io.PrintWriter;
import java.util.Scanner;

/**
    This program reads data files of country populations and areas and prints the
    population density for each country.
*/
public class PopulationDensity
{
    public static void main(String[] args) throws FileNotFoundException
    {
        // Construct Scanner objects for input files

        Scanner in1 = new Scanner(new File("worldpop.txt"));
        Scanner in2 = new Scanner(new File("worldarea.txt"));

        // Construct PrintWriter for the output file

        PrintWriter out = new PrintWriter("world_pop_density.txt");

        // Read lines from each file

        while (in1.hasNextLine() && in2.hasNextLine())
        {
            String line1 = in1.nextLine();
            String line2 = in2.nextLine();

            // Extract country and associated value
            String country = extractCountry(line1);
            double population = extractValue(line1);
            double area = extractValue(line2);

            // Compute and print the population density
            double density = 0;
            if (area != 0) // Protect against division by zero
            {
                density = population / area;
            }
            out.printf("%-40s%15.2f\n", country, density);
        }

        in1.close();
        in2.close();
        out.close();
    }
```

```
/**
    Extracts the country from an input line.
    @param line  a line containing a country name, followed by a number
    @return  the country name
*/
public static String extractCountry(String line)
{
    int i = 0; // Locate the start of the first digit
    while (!Character.isDigit(line.charAt(i))) { i++; }
    return line.substring(0, i).trim(); // Extract the country name
}


/**
    Extracts the value from an input line.
    @param line  a line containing a country name, followed by a value
    @return  the value associated with the country
*/
public static double extractValue(String line)
{
    int i = 0; // Locate the start of the first digit
    while (!Character.isDigit(line.charAt(i))) { i++; }
    // Extract and convert the value
    return Double.parseDouble(line.substring(i).trim());
}
}
```

Random Fact 7.1 Encryption Algorithms

The exercises at the end of this chapter give a few algorithms for encrypting text. Don't actually use any of those methods to send secret messages to your lover. Any skilled cryptographer can *break* these schemes in a very short time—that is, reconstruct the original text without knowing the secret keyword.

In 1978, Ron Rivest, Adi Shamir, and Leonard Adleman introduced an encryption method that is much more powerful. The method is called *RSA encryption*, after the last names of its inventors. The exact scheme is too complicated to present here, but it is not actually difficult to follow. You can find the details in http://theory.lcs.mit.edu/~rivest/rsapaper.pdf.

RSA is a remarkable encryption method. There are two keys: a public key and a private key. (See the figure.) You can print the public key on your business card (or in your e-mail signature block) and give it to any-

one. Then anyone can send you messages that only you can decrypt. Even though everyone else knows the public key, and even if they intercept all the messages coming to you, they cannot break the scheme and actually read the messages. In 1994, hundreds of researchers, collaborating over the Internet, cracked an RSA message encrypted with a 129-digit key. Messages encrypted with a key of 230 digits or more are expected to be secure.

The inventors of the algorithm obtained a *patent* for it. A patent is a deal that society makes with an inventor. For a period of 20 years, the inventor has an exclusive right for its commercialization, may collect royalties from others wishing to manufacture the invention, and may even stop competitors from using it altogether. In return, the inventor must publish the invention, so that others may learn from it, and must relinquish all claim to it after the monopoly period ends. The presumption is that in the absence

of patent law, inventors would be reluctant to go through the trouble of inventing, or they would try to cloak their techniques to prevent others from copying their devices.

There has been some controversy about the RSA patent. Had there not been patent protection, would the inventors have published the method anyway, thereby giving the benefit to society without the cost of the 20-year monopoly? In this case, the answer is probably yes. The inventors were academic researchers, who live on salaries rather than sales receipts and are usually rewarded for their discoveries by a boost in their reputation and careers. Would their followers have been as active in discovering (and patenting) improvements? There is no way of knowing, of course. Is an algorithm even patentable, or is it a mathematical fact that belongs to nobody? The patent office did take the latter attitude for a long time. The RSA inventors and many others described their

Analyzing Baby Names

In this Worked Example, you will use data from the Social Security Administration to analyze the most popular baby names.

7.4 Exception Handling

There are two aspects to dealing with program errors: *detection* and *handling*. For example, the Scanner constructor can detect an attempt to read from a non-existent file. However, it cannot handle that error. A satisfactory way of handling the error might be to terminate the program, or to ask the user for another file name. The Scanner class cannot choose between these alternatives. It needs to report the error to another part of the program.

In Java, *exception handling* provides a flexible mechanism for passing control from the point of error detection to a handler that can deal with the error. In the following sections, we will look into the details of this mechanism.

inventions in terms of imaginary electronic devices, rather than algorithms, to circumvent that restriction. Nowadays, the patent office will award software patents.

There is another interesting aspect to the RSA story. A programmer, Phil Zimmermann, developed a program called PGP (for *Pretty Good Privacy*) that is based on RSA. Anyone can use the program to encrypt messages, and decryption is not feasible even with the most powerful computers. You can get a copy of a free PGP implementation from the GNU project (http://www.gnupg.org). The existence of strong encryption methods bothers the United States government to no end. Criminals and foreign agents can send communications that the police and intelligence agencies cannot decipher. The government considered charging Zimmermann with breaching a law that forbids the unauthorized export of munitions, arguing that he should have known that his program would appear on the Internet. There have been serious proposals to make it illegal for private citizens to use these encryption methods, or to keep the keys secret from law enforcement.

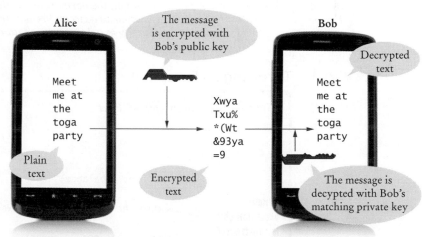

Public-Key Encryption

7.4.1 Throwing Exceptions

To signal an exceptional condition, use the throw statement to throw an exception object.

When you detect an error condition, your job is really easy. You just *throw* an appropriate exception object, and you are done. For example, suppose someone tries to withdraw too much money from a bank account.

```java
if (amount > balance)
{
    // Now what?
}
```

First look for an appropriate exception class. The Java library provides many classes to signal all sorts of exceptional conditions. Figure 2 shows the most useful ones. (The classes are arranged as a tree-shaped hierarchy, with more specialized classes at the bottom of the tree. We will discuss such hierarchies in more detail in Chapter 9.)

Look around for an exception type that might describe your situation. How about the ArithmeticException? Is it an arithmetic error to have a negative balance? No—Java can deal with negative numbers. Is the amount to be withdrawn illegal? Indeed it is. It is just too large. Therefore, let's throw an IllegalArgumentException.

```java
if (amount > balance)
{
    throw new IllegalArgumentException("Amount exceeds balance");
}
```

When you throw an exception, processing continues in an exception handler.

When you throw an exception, execution does not continue with the next statement but with an **exception handler**. That is the topic of the next section.

When you throw an exception, the normal control flow is terminated. This is similar to a circuit breaker that cuts off the flow of electricity in a dangerous situation.

Syntax 7.1   Throwing an Exception

Syntax   throw *exceptionObject*;

Most exception objects can be constructed with an error message.

A new exception object is constructed, then thrown.

```java
if (amount > balance)
{
    throw new IllegalArgumentException("Amount exceeds balance");
}
balance = balance - amount;
```

This line is not executed when the exception is thrown.

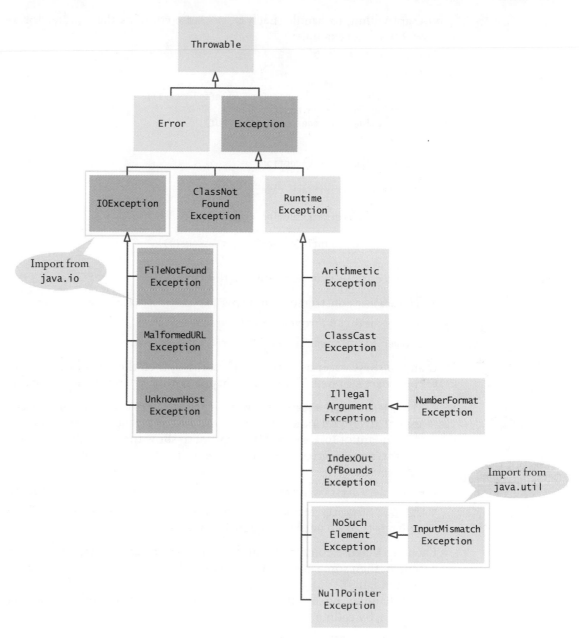

Figure 2   A Part of the Hierarchy of Exception Classes

7.4.2 Catching Exceptions

Place the statements
that can cause an
exception inside a
try block, and the
handler inside a
catch clause.

Every exception should be handled somewhere in your program. If an exception has
no handler, an error message is printed, and your program terminates. Of course,
such an unhandled exception is confusing to program users.

You handle exceptions with the try/catch statement. Place the statement into a
location of your program that knows how to handle a particular exception. The try
block contains one or more statements that may cause an exception of the kind that

you are willing to handle. Each catch clause contains the handler for an exception type. Here is an example:

```
try
{
    String filename = . . .;
    Scanner in = new Scanner(new File(filename));
    String input = in.next();
    int value = Integer.parseInt(input);
    . . .
}
catch (IOException exception)
{
    exception.printStackTrace();
}
catch (NumberFormatException exception)
{
    System.out.println(exception.getMessage());
}
```

Three exceptions may be thrown in this try block:

- The Scanner constructor can throw a FileNotFoundException.
- Scanner.next can throw a NoSuchElementException.
- Integer.parseInt can throw a NumberFormatException.

If any of these exceptions is actually thrown, then the rest of the instructions in the try block are skipped. Here is what happens for the various exception types:

ANIMATION
Exception Handling

- If a FileNotFoundException is thrown, then the catch clause for the IOException is executed. (If you look at Figure 2, you will note that FileNotFoundException is a descendant of IOException.) If you want to show the user a different message for a FileNotFoundException, you must place the catch clause *before* the clause for an IOException.
- If a NumberFormatException occurs, then the second catch clause is executed.
- A NoSuchElementException is *not caught* by any of the catch clauses. The exception remains thrown until it is caught by another try block.

Each catch clause contains a handler. When the catch (IOException exception) block is executed, then some method in the try block has failed with an IOException (or one of its descendants).
In this handler, we produce a printout of the chain of method calls that led to the exception, by calling

```
exception.printStackTrace()
```

You should only catch those exceptions that you can handle.

Syntax 7.2   Catching Exceptions

Syntax
```
try
{
    statement
    statement
    . . .
}
catch (ExceptionClass exceptionObject)
{
    statement
    statement
    . . .
}
```

```
try
{
    Scanner in = new Scanner(new File("input.txt"));
    String input = in.next();
    process(input);
}
catch (IOException exception)
{
    System.out.println("Could not open input file");
}
catch (Exception except)
{
    System.out.println(except.getMessage);
}
```

This constructor can throw a FileNotFoundException.

This is the exception that was thrown.

When an IOException is thrown, execution resumes here.

Additional catch clauses can appear here. Place more specific exceptions before more general ones.

A FileNotFoundException is a special case of an IOException.

In the second exception handler, we call exception.getMessage() to retrieve the message associated with the exception. When the parseInt method throws a NumberFormatException, the message contains the string that it was unable to format. When you throw an exception, you can provide your own message string. For example, when you call

```
throw new IllegalArgumentException("Amount exceeds balance");
```

the message of the exception is the string provided in the constructor.

In these sample catch clauses, we merely inform the user of the source of the problem. Often, it is better to give the user another chance to provide a correct input—see Section 7.5 for a solution.

7.4.3 Checked Exceptions

In Java, the exceptions that you can throw and catch fall into three categories.

- Internal errors are reported by descendants of the type Error. One example is the OutOfMemoryError, which is thrown when all available computer memory has been used up. These are fatal errors that happen rarely, and we will not consider them in this book.

- Descendants of RuntimeException, such as as IndexOutOfBoundsException or Illegal-ArgumentException indicate errors in your code. They are called **unchecked exceptions**.

- All other exceptions are **checked exceptions**. These exceptions indicate that something has gone wrong for some external reason beyond your control. In Figure 2, the checked exceptions are shaded in a darker color.

Why have two kinds of exceptions? A checked exception describes a problem that can occur, no matter how careful you are. For example, an IOException can be caused by forces beyond your control, such as a disk error or a broken network connection. The compiler takes checked exceptions very seriously and ensures that they are handled. Your program will not compile if you don't indicate how to deal with a checked exception.

The unchecked exceptions, on the other hand, are your fault. The compiler does not check whether you handle an unchecked exception, such as an IndexOutOfBounds-Exception. After all, you should check your index values rather than install a handler for that exception.

If you have a handler for a checked exception in the same method that may throw it, then the compiler is satisfied. For example,

```
try
{
    File inFile = new File(filename);
    Scanner in = new Scanner(inFile); // Throws FileNotFoundException
    . . .
}
catch (FileNotFoundException exception) // Exception caught here
{
    . . .
}
```

However, it commonly happens that the current method *cannot handle* the exception. In that case, you need to tell the compiler that you are aware of this exception and that you want your method to be terminated when it occurs. You supply a method with a throws clause.

```
public static String readData(String filename) throws FileNotFoundException
{
    File inFile = new File(filename);
    Scanner in = new Scanner(inFile);
    . . .
}
```

The throws clause signals the caller of your method that it may encounter a FileNotFoundException. Then the caller needs to make the same decision—handle the exception, or declare that the exception may be thrown.

It sounds somehow irresponsible not to handle an exception when you know that it happened. Actually, the opposite is true. Java provides an exception handling facility so that an exception can be sent to the *appropriate* handler. Some methods detect errors, some methods handle them, and some methods just pass them along. The throws clause simply ensures that no exceptions get lost along the way.

Just as trucks with large or hazardous loads carry warning signs, the throws *clause warns the caller that an exception may occur.*

Syntax 7.3   The throws Clause

Syntax   *modifiers returnType methodName(parameterType parameterName, . . .)*
                 throws *ExceptionClass, ExceptionClass, . . .*

```
public static String readData(String filename)
        throws FileNotFoundException, NumberFormatException
```

You must specify all checked exceptions that this method may throw.

You may also list unchecked exceptions.

7.4.4 The finally Clause

Once a try block is entered, the statements in a finally clause are guaranteed to be executed, whether or not an exception is thrown.

Occasionally, you need to take some action whether or not an exception is thrown. The finally construct is used to handle this situation. Here is a typical situation.

It is important to close a PrintWriter to ensure that all output is written to the file. In the following code segment, we open a stream, call one or more methods, and then close the stream:

```
PrintWriter out = new PrintWriter(filename);
writeData(out);
out.close(); // May never get here
```

Now suppose that one of the methods before the last line throws an exception. Then the call to close is never executed! You solve this problem by placing the call to close inside a finally clause:

```
PrintWriter out = new PrintWriter(filename);
try
{
    writeData(out);
}
finally
{
    out.close();
}
```

In a normal case, there will be no problem. When the try block is completed, the finally clause is executed, and the writer is closed. However, if an exception occurs, the finally clause is also executed before the exception is passed to its handler.

Use the finally clause whenever you need to do some clean up, such as closing a file, to ensure that the clean up happens no matter how the method exits.

ONLINE EXAMPLE

A program that demonstrates throwing and catching exceptions.

All visitors to a foreign country have to go through passport control, no matter what happened on their trip. Similarly, the code in a finally clause is always executed, even when an exception has occurred.

Syntax 7.4 The finally Clause

```
Syntax     try
           {
               statement
               statement
               . . .
           }
           finally
           {
               statement
               statement
               . . .
           }
```

This variable must be declared outside the `try` block so that the `finally` clause can access it.

```
PrintWriter out = new PrintWriter(filename);
try
```

This code may throw exceptions.

```
{
    writeData(out);
}
finally
```

This code is always executed, even if an exception occurs.

```
{
    out.close();
}
```

SELF CHECK

16. Suppose balance is 100 and amount is 200. What is the value of balance after these statements?

```
if (amount > balance)
{
    throw new IllegalArgumentException("Amount exceeds balance");
}
balance = balance - amount;
```

17. When depositing an amount into a bank account, we don't have to worry about overdrafts—except when the amount is negative. Write a statement that throws an appropriate exception in that case.

18. Consider the method

```
public static void main(String[] args)
{
    try
    {
        Scanner in = new Scanner(new File("input.txt"));
        int value = in.nextInt();
        System.out.println(value);
    }
    catch (IOException exception)
    {
        System.out.println("Error opening file.");
    }
}
```

Suppose the file with the given file name exists and has no contents. Trace the flow of execution.

19. Why is an `ArrayIndexOutOfBoundsException` not a checked exception?

20. Is there a difference between catching checked and unchecked exceptions?

21. What is wrong with the following code, and how can you fix it?

```java
public static void writeAll(String[] lines, String filename)
{
    PrintWriter out = new PrintWriter(filename);
    for (String line : lines)
    {
        out.println(line.toUpperCase());
    }
    out.close();
}
```

Practice It   Now you can try these exercises at the end of the chapter: R7.7, R7.8, R7.9.

Programming Tip 7.1

Throw Early, Catch Late

When a method detects a problem that it cannot solve, it is better to throw an exception rather than try to come up with an imperfect fix. For example, suppose a method expects to read a number from a file, and the file doesn't contain a number. Simply using a zero value would be a poor choice because it hides the actual problem and perhaps causes a different problem elsewhere.

> Throw an exception as soon as a problem is detected. Catch it only when the problem can be handled.

Conversely, a method should only catch an exception if it can really remedy the situation. Otherwise, the best remedy is simply to have the exception propagate to its caller, allowing it to be caught by a competent handler.

These principles can be summarized with the slogan "throw early, catch late".

Programming Tip 7.2

Do Not Squelch Exceptions

When you call a method that throws a checked exception and you haven't specified a handler, the compiler complains. In your eagerness to continue your work, it is an understandable impulse to shut the compiler up by squelching the exception:

```java
try
{
    Scanner in = new Scanner(new File(filename));
    // Compiler complained about FileNotFoundException
    . . .
}
catch (FileNotFoundException e) {} // So there!
```

The do-nothing exception handler fools the compiler into thinking that the exception has been handled. In the long run, this is clearly a bad idea. Exceptions were designed to transmit problem reports to a competent handler. Installing an incompetent handler simply hides an error condition that could be serious.

Programming Tip 7.3

Do Not Use catch and finally in the Same try Statement

It is possible to have a finally clause following one or more catch clauses. Then the code in the finally clause is executed whenever the try block is exited in any of three ways:

1. After completing the last statement of the try block
2. After completing the last statement of a catch clause, if this try block caught an exception
3. When an exception was thrown in the try block and not caught

It is tempting to combine catch and finally clauses, but the resulting code can be hard to understand, and it is often incorrect. Instead, use two statements:

- a try/finally statement to close resources
- a separate try/catch statement to handle errors

For example,

```
try
{
    PrintWriter out = new PrintWriter(filename);
    try
    {
        Write output.
    }
    finally
    {
        out.close();
    }
}
catch (IOException exception)
{
    Handle exception.
}
```

Note that the nested statements work correctly if the PrintWriter constructor throws an exception, too.

Special Topic 7.5

Automatic Resource Management in Java 7

In Java 7, you can use a new form of the try block that automatically closes a PrintWriter or Scanner object. Here is the syntax:

```
try (PrintWriter out = new PrintWriter(filename))
{
    Write output to out.
}
```

The close method is automatically invoked on the out object when the try block ends, whether or not an exception has occurred. A finally statement is not required.

Random Fact 7.2 The Ariane Rocket Incident

The European Space Agency (ESA), Europe's counterpart to NASA, had developed a rocket model called Ariane that it had successfully used several times to launch satellites and scientific experiments into space. However, when a new version, the Ariane 5, was launched on June 4, 1996, from ESA's launch site in Kourou, French Guiana, the rocket veered off course about 40 seconds after liftoff. Flying at an angle of more than 20 degrees, rather than straight up, exerted such an aerodynamic force that the boosters separated, which triggered the automatic self-destruction mechanism. The rocket blew itself up.

The ultimate cause of this accident was an unhandled exception! The rocket contained two identical devices (called inertial reference systems) that processed flight data from measuring devices and turned the data into information about the rocket position.

The onboard computer used the position information for controlling the boosters. The same inertial reference systems and computer software had worked fine on the Ariane 4.

However, due to design changes to the rocket, one of the sensors measured a larger acceleration force than had been encountered in the Ariane 4. That value, expressed as a floating-point value, was stored in a 16-bit integer (like a short variable in Java). Unlike Java, the Ada language, used for the device software, generates an exception if a floating-point number is too large to be converted to an integer. Unfortunately, the programmers of the device had decided that this situation would never happen and didn't provide an exception handler.

When the overflow did happen, the exception was triggered and, because there was no handler, the device shut itself off. The onboard computer sensed the failure and switched over to the backup device. However, that device had shut itself off for exactly the same reason, something that the designers of the rocket had not expected. They figured that the devices might fail for mechanical reasons, and the chance of two devices having the same mechanical failure was considered remote. At that point, the rocket was without reliable position information and went off course.

Perhaps it would have been better if the software hadn't been so thorough? If it had ignored the overflow, the device wouldn't have been shut off. It would have computed bad data. But then the device would have reported wrong position data, which could have been just as fatal. Instead, a correct implementation should have caught overflow exceptions and come up with some strategy to recompute the flight data. Clearly, giving up was not a reasonable option in this context.

The advantage of the exception-handling mechanism is that it makes these issues explicit to programmers—something to think about when you curse the Java compiler for complaining about uncaught exceptions.

The Explosion of the Ariane Rocket

7.5 Application: Handling Input Errors

This section walks through an example program that includes exception handling. The program, DataAnalyzer.java, asks the user for the name of a file. The file is expected to contain data values. The first line of the file should contain the total number of values, and the remaining lines contain the data. A typical input file looks like this:

```
3
1.45
-2.1
0.05
```

When designing a program, ask yourself what kinds of exceptions can occur.

What can go wrong? There are two principal risks.

- The file might not exist.
- The file might have data in the wrong format.

Who can detect these faults? The `Scanner` constructor will throw an exception when the file does not exist. The methods that process the input values need to throw an exception when they find an error in the data format.

What exceptions can be thrown? The `Scanner` constructor throws a `FileNotFoundException` when the file does not exist, which is appropriate in our situation. When there are fewer data items than expected, or when the file doesn't start with the count of values, the program will throw an `NoSuchElementException`. Finally, when there are more inputs than expected, an `IOException` should be thrown.

For each exception, you need to decide which part of your program can competently handle it.

Who can remedy the faults that the exceptions report? Only the `main` method of the `DataAnalyzer` program interacts with the user, so it catches the exceptions, prints appropriate error messages, and gives the user another chance to enter a correct file:

```
// Keep trying until there are no more exceptions
boolean done = false;
while (!done)
{
   try
   {
      Prompt user for file name.

      double[] data = readFile(filename);

      Process data.

      done = true;
   }
   catch (FileNotFoundException exception)
   {
      System.out.println("File not found.");
   }
   catch (NoSuchElementException exception)
   {
      System.out.println("File contents invalid.");
   }
   catch (IOException exception)
   {
      exception.printStackTrace();
   }
}
```

The first two `catch` clauses in the `main` method give a human-readable error report if bad data was encountered or the file was not found. However, if another `IOException` occurs, then it prints a stack trace so that a programmer can diagnose the problem.

The following `readFile` method constructs the `Scanner` object and calls the `readData` method. It does not handle any exceptions. If there is a problem with the input file, it simply passes the exception to its caller.

```
public static double[] readFile(String filename) throws IOException
{
   File inFile = new File(filename);
   Scanner in = new Scanner(inFile);
   try
   {
```

```
            return readData(in);
        }
        finally
        {
            in.close();
        }
    }
```

Note how the `finally` clause ensures that the file is closed even when an exception occurs.

Also note that the `throws` clause of the `readFile` method need not include the `File-NotFoundException` class because it is a special case of an `IOException`.

The `readData` method reads the number of values, constructs an array, and fills it with the data values.

```
public static double[] readData(Scanner in) throws IOException
{
    int numberOfValues = in.nextInt(); // May throw NoSuchElementException
    double[] data = new double[numberOfValues];

    for (int i = 0; i < numberOfValues; i++)
    {
        data[i] = in.nextDouble(); // May throw NoSuchElementException
    }

    if (in.hasNext())
    {
        throw new IOException("End of file expected");
    }
    return data;
}
```

As discussed in Section 7.2.7, the calls to the `nextInt` and `nextDouble` methods can throw a `NoSuchElementException` when there is no input at all or an `InputMismatchException` if the input is not a number. As you can see from Figure 2 on page 340, an `InputMismatchException` is a special case of a `NoSuchElementException`.

You need not declare the `NoSuchElementException` in the `throws` clause because it is not a checked exception, but you can include it for greater clarity.

There are three potential errors:

- The file might not start with an integer.
- There might not be a sufficient number of data values.
- There might be additional input after reading all data values.

In the first two cases, the `Scanner` throws a `NoSuchElementException`. Note again that this is *not* a checked exception—we could have avoided it by calling `hasNextInt`/`hasNextDouble` first. However, this method does not know what to do in this case, so it allows the exception to be sent to a handler elsewhere.

When we find that there is additional unexpected input, we throw an `IOException`. To see the exception handling at work, look at a specific error scenario.

1. `main` calls `readFile`.
2. `readFile` calls `readData`.
3. `readData` calls `Scanner.nextInt`.
4. There is no integer in the input, and `Scanner.nextInt` throws a `NoSuchElement-Exception`.

5. `readData` has no catch clause. It terminates immediately.

6. `readFile` has no catch clause. It terminates immediately after executing the `finally` clause and closing the file.

7. The first catch clause in `main` is for a `FileNotFoundException`. The exception that is currently being thrown is a `NoSuchElementException`, and this handler doesn't apply.

8. The next catch clause is for a `NoSuchElementException`, and execution resumes here. That handler prints a message to the user. Afterward, the user is given another chance to enter a file name. Note that the statements for processing the data have been skipped.

This example shows the separation between error detection (in the `readData` method) and error handling (in the `main` method). In between the two is the `readFile` method, which simply passes the exceptions along.

section_5/DataAnalyzer.java

```java
1   import java.io.File;
2   import java.io.FileNotFoundException;
3   import java.io.IOException;
4   import java.util.Scanner;
5   import java.util.NoSuchElementException;
6
7   /**
8      This program processes a file containing a count followed by data values.
9      If the file doesn't exist or the format is incorrect, you can specify another file.
10  */
11  public class DataAnalyzer
12  {
13     public static void main(String[] args)
14     {
15        Scanner in = new Scanner(System.in);
16
17        // Keep trying until there are no more exceptions
18
19        boolean done = false;
20        while (!done)
21        {
22           try
23           {
24              System.out.print("Please enter the file name: ");
25              String filename = in.next();
26
27              double[] data = readFile(filename);
28
29              // As an example for processing the data, we compute the sum
30
31              double sum = 0;
32              for (double d : data) { sum = sum + d; }
33              System.out.println("The sum is " + sum);
34
35              done = true;
36           }
37           catch (FileNotFoundException exception)
38           {
39              System.out.println("File not found.");
```

```
40          }
41          catch (NoSuchElementException exception)
42          {
43             System.out.println("File contents invalid.");
44          }
45          catch (IOException exception)
46          {
47             exception.printStackTrace();
48          }
49       }
50    }
51
52    /**
53       Opens a file and reads a data set.
54       @param filename the name of the file holding the data
55       @return the data in the file
56    */
57    public static double[] readFile(String filename) throws IOException
58    {
59       File inFile = new File(filename);
60       Scanner in = new Scanner(inFile);
61       try
62       {
63          return readData(in);
64       }
65       finally
66       {
67          in.close();
68       }
69    }
70
71    /**
72       Reads a data set.
73       @param in the scanner that scans the data
74       @return the data set
75    */
76    public static double[] readData(Scanner in) throws IOException
77    {
78       int numberOfValues = in.nextInt(); // May throw NoSuchElementException
79       double[] data = new double[numberOfValues];
80
81       for (int i = 0; i < numberOfValues; i++)
82       {
83          data[i] = in.nextDouble(); // May throw NoSuchElementException
84       }
85
86       if (in.hasNext())
87       {
88          throw new IOException("End of file expected");
89       }
90       return data;
91    }
92 }
```

22. Why doesn't the readFile method catch any exceptions?

23. Consider the try/finally statement in the readFile method. Why was the in variable declared outside the try block?

24. Suppose the user specifies a file that exists and is empty. Trace the flow of execution in the DataAnalyzer program.

25. Why didn't the readData method call hasNextInt/hasNextDouble to ensure that the NoSuchElementException is not thrown?

Practice It   Now you can try these exercises at the end of the chapter: R7.15, R7.16, P7.13.

VIDEO EXAMPLE 7.2   **Detecting Accounting Fraud**

In this Video Example, you will see how to detect accounting fraud by analyzing digit distributions. You will learn how to read data from the Internet and handle exceptional situations.

CHAPTER SUMMARY

Develop programs that read and write files.

- Use the Scanner class for reading text files.
- When writing text files, use the PrintWriter class and the print/println/printf methods.
- Close all files when you are done processing them.

Be able to process text in files.

- The next method reads a string that is delimited by white space.
- The Character class has methods for classifying characters.
- The nextLine method reads an entire line.
- If a string contains the digits of a number, you use the Integer.parseInt or Double.parseDouble method to obtain the number value.

Process the command line arguments of a program.

- Programs that start from the command line receive the command line arguments in the main method.

Use exception handling to transfer control from an error location to an error handler.

- To signal an exceptional condition, use the throw statement to throw an exception object.
- When you throw an exception, processing continues in an exception handler.
- Place the statements that can cause an exception inside a try block, and the handler inside a catch clause.

⊕ Available online in WileyPLUS and at www.wiley.com/college/horstmann.

- Checked exceptions are due to external circumstances that the programmer cannot prevent. The compiler checks that your program handles these exceptions.
- Add a throws clause to a method that can throw a checked exception.
- Once a try block is entered, the statements in a finally clause are guaranteed to be executed, whether or not an exception is thrown.

- Throw an exception as soon as a problem is detected. Catch it only when the problem can be handled.

Use exception handling in a program that processes input.

- When designing a program, ask yourself what kinds of exceptions can occur.
- For each exception, you need to decide which part of your program can competently handle it.

STANDARD LIBRARY ITEMS INTRODUCED IN THIS CHAPTER

java.io.File
java.io.FileNotFoundException
java.io.IOException
java.io.PrintWriter
  close
java.lang.Character
  isDigit
  isLetter
  isLowerCase
  isUpperCase
  isWhiteSpace
java.lang.Double
  parseDouble
java.lang.Error
java.lang.Integer
  parseInt
java.lang.IllegalArgumentException
java.lang.NullPointerException

java.lang.NumberFormatException
java.lang.RuntimeException
java.lang.Throwable
  getMessage
  printStackTrace
java.net.URL
  openStream
java.util.InputMismatchException
java.util.NoSuchElementException
java.util.Scanner
  close
  hasNextLine
  nextLine
  useDelimiter
javax.swing.JFileChooser
  getSelectedFile
  showOpenDialog
  showSaveDialog

REVIEW EXERCISES

• • R7.1 What happens if you try to open a file for reading that doesn't exist? What happens if you try to open a file for writing that doesn't exist?

• • R7.2 What happens if you try to open a file for writing, but the file or device is write-protected (sometimes called read-only)? Try it out with a short test program.

• R7.3 How do you open a file whose name contains a backslash, like c:temp\output.dat?

• R7.4 If a program Woozle is started with the command

```
java Woozle -Dname=piglet -I\eeyore -v heff.txt a.txt lump.txt
```

what are the values of args[0], args[1], and so on?

• R7.5 What is the difference between throwing an exception and catching an exception?

■ R7.6   What is a checked exception? What is an unchecked exception? Give an example for each. Which exceptions do you need to declare with the `throws` reserved word?

■■ R7.7   Why don't you need to declare that your method might throw an `IndexOutOfBounds-Exception`?

■■ R7.8   When your program executes a `throw` statement, which statement is executed next?

■■ R7.9   What happens if an exception does not have a matching `catch` clause?

■■ R7.10   What can your program do with the exception object that a `catch` clause receives?

■■ R7.11   Is the type of the exception object always the same as the type declared in the `catch` clause that catches it? If not, why not?

■ R7.12   What is the purpose of the `finally` clause? Give an example of how it can be used.

■■ R7.13   What happens when an exception is thrown, the code of a `finally` clause executes, and that code throws an exception of a different kind than the original one? Which one is caught by a surrounding `catch` clause? Write a sample program to try it out.

■■ R7.14   Which exceptions can the `next` and `nextInt` methods of the `Scanner` class throw? Are they checked exceptions or unchecked exceptions?

■■ R7.15   Suppose the program in Section 7.5 reads a file containing the following values:

```
1
2
3
4
```

What is the outcome? How could the program be improved to give a more accurate error report?

■■ R7.16   Can the `readFile` method in Section 7.5 throw a `NullPointerException`? If so, how?

PROGRAMMING EXERCISES

■ P7.1   Write a program that carries out the following tasks:

> Open a file with the name hello.txt.
> Store the message "Hello, World!" in the file.
> Close the file.
> Open the same file again.
> Read the message into a string variable and print it.

■ P7.2   Write a program that reads a file containing text. Read each line and send it to the output file, preceded by *line numbers*. If the input file is

```
Mary had a little lamb
Whose fleece was white as snow.
And everywhere that Mary went,
The lamb was sure to go!
```

then the program produces the output file

```
/* 1 */ Mary had a little lamb
/* 2 */ Whose fleece was white as snow.
/* 3 */ And everywhere that Mary went,
/* 4 */ The lamb was sure to go!
```

The line numbers are enclosed in /* */ delimiters so that the program can be used for numbering Java source files.

Prompt the user for the input and output file names.

■ **P7.3** Repeat Exercise P7.2, but allow the user to specify the file name on the command-line. If the user doesn't specify any file name, then prompt the user for the name.

■ **P7.4** Write a program that reads a file containing two columns of floating-point numbers. Prompt the user for the file name. Print the average of each column.

■■ **P7.5** Write a program that asks the user for a file name and prints the number of characters, words, and lines in that file.

■■ **P7.6** Write a program Find that searches all files specified on the command line and prints out all lines containing a specified word. For example, if you call

```
java Find ring report.txt address.txt Homework.java
```

then the program might print

```
report.txt: has broken up an international ring of DVD bootleggers that
address.txt: Kris Kringle, North Pole
address.txt: Homer Simpson, Springfield
Homework.java: String filename;
```

The specified word is always the first command line argument.

■■ **P7.7** Write a program that checks the spelling of all words in a file. It should read each word of a file and check whether it is contained in a word list. A word list is available on most Linux systems in the file /usr/share/dict/words. (If you don't have access to a Linux system, your instructor should be able to get you a copy.) The program should print out all words that it cannot find in the word list.

■■ **P7.8** Write a program that replaces each line of a file with its reverse. For example, if you run

```
java Reverse HelloPrinter.java
```

then the contents of HelloPrinter.java are changed to

```
retnirPolleH ssalc cilbup
{
)sgra ][gnirtS(niam diov citats cilbup
{
wodniw elosnoc eht ni gniteerg a yalpsiD //

;)"!dlroW ,olleH"(nltnirp.tuo.metsyS
}
}
```

Of course, if you run Reverse twice on the same file, you get back the original file.

■■ **P7.9** Write a program that reads each line in a file, reverses its lines, and writes them to another file. For example, if the file input.txt contains the lines

```
Mary had a little lamb
Its fleece was white as snow
And everywhere that Mary went
The lamb was sure to go.
```

and you run

```
reverse input.txt output.txt
```

then output.txt contains

```
The lamb was sure to go.
And everywhere that Mary went
Its fleece was white as snow
Mary had a little lamb
```

■■ **P7.10** Get the data for names in prior decades from the Social Security Administration. Paste the table data in files named babynames80s.txt, etc. Modify the worked_example_1/BabyNames.java program so that it prompts the user for a file name. The numbers in the files have comma separators, so modify the program to handle them. Can you spot a trend in the frequencies?

■■ **P7.11** Write a program that reads in worked_example_1/babynames.txt and produces two files, boynames.txt and girlnames.txt, separating the data for the boys and girls.

■■■ **P7.12** Write a program that reads a file in the same format as worked_example_1/babynames.txt and prints all names that are both boy and girl names (such as Alexis or Morgan).

■■ **P7.13** Write a program that asks the user to input a set of floating-point values. When the user enters a value that is not a number, give the user a second chance to enter the value. After two chances, quit reading input. Add all correctly specified values and print the sum when the user is done entering data. Use exception handling to detect improper inputs.

■■ **P7.14** Using the mechanism described in Special Topic 7.1, write a program that reads all data from a web page and writes them to a file. Prompt the user for the web page URL and the file.

■■ **P7.15** Using the mechanism described in Special Topic 7.1, write a program that reads all data from a web page and prints all hyperlinks of the form

   `<a href="`*link*`">`*link text*`</a>`

Extra credit if your program can follow the links that it finds and find links in those web pages as well. (This is the method that search engines such as Google use to find web sites.)

■■ **Business P7.16** A hotel salesperson enters sales in a text file. Each line contains the following, separated by semicolons: The name of the client, the service sold (such as Dinner, Conference, Lodging, and so on), the amount of the sale, and the date of that event. Write a program that reads such a file and displays the total amount for each service category. Display an error if the file does not exist or the format is incorrect.

■■ **Business P7.17** Write a program that reads a text file as described in Exercise P7.16, and that writes a separate file for each service category, containing the entries for that category. Name the output files Dinner.txt, Conference.txt, and so on.

■■ **Business P7.18** A store owner keeps a record of daily cash transactions in a text file. Each line contains three items: The invoice number, the cash amount, and the letter P if the amount was paid or R if it was received. Items are separated by spaces. Write a program that prompts the store owner for the amount of cash at the beginning and end of the day, and the name of the file. Your program should check whether the actual amount of cash at the end of the day equals the expected value.

■■■ **Science P7.19** After the switch in the figure below closes, the voltage (in volts) across the capacitor is represented by the equation

$$v(t) = B\left(1 - e^{-t/(RC)}\right)$$

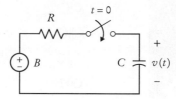

Suppose the parameters of the electric circuit are $B = 12$ volts, $R = 500\ \Omega$, and $C = 0.25\ \mu F$. Consequently

$$v(t) = 12\left(1 - e^{-0.008t}\right)$$

where t has units of μs. Read a file params.txt containing the values for B, R, C, and the starting and ending values for t. Write a file rc.txt of values for the time t and the corresponding capacitor voltage $v(t)$, where t goes from the given starting value to the given ending value in 100 steps. In our example, if t goes from 0 to 1,000 μs, the twelfth entry in the output file would be:

    110   7.02261

■■■ **Science P7.20** The figure below shows a plot of the capacitor voltage from the circuit shown in Exercise P7.19. The capacitor voltage increases from 0 volts to B volts. The "rise time" is defined as the time required for the capacitor voltage to change from $v_1 = 0.05 \times B$ to $v_2 = 0.95 \times B$.

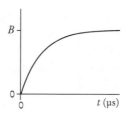

The file rc.txt contains a list of values of time t and the corresponding capacitor voltage $v(t)$. A time in μs and the corresponding voltage in volts are printed on the same line. For example, the line

    110   7.02261

indicates that the capacitor voltage is 7.02261 volts when the time is 110 μs. The time is increasing in the data file.

Write a program that reads the file rc.txt and uses the data to calculate the rise time. Approximate B by the voltage in the last line of the file, and find the data points that are closest to $0.05 \times B$ and $0.95 \times B$.

■■ **Science P7.21** Suppose a file contains bond energies and bond lengths for covalent bonds in the following format:

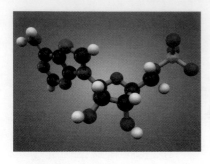

Single, double, or triple bond	Bond energy (kJ/mol)	Bond length (nm)
C|C	370	0.154
C||C	680	0.13
C|||C	890	0.12
C|H	435	0.11
C|N	305	0.15
C|O	360	0.14
C|F	450	0.14
C|Cl	340	0.18
O|H	500	0.10
O|O	220	0.15
O|Si	375	0.16
N|H	430	0.10
N|O	250	0.12
F|F	160	0.14
H|H	435	0.074

Write a program that accepts data from one column and returns the corresponding data from the other columns in the stored file. If input data matches different rows, then return all matching row data. For example, a bond length input of 0.12 should return triple bond C\|\|\|C and bond energy 890 kJ/mol *and* single bond N\|O and bond energy 250 kJ/mol.

ANSWERS TO SELF-CHECK QUESTIONS

1. When the `PrintWriter` object is created, the output file is emptied. Sadly, that is the same file as the input file. The input file is now empty and the `while` loop exits immediately.

2. The program throws a `FileNotFoundException` and terminates.

3. Open a scanner for the file.
   For each number in the scanner
     Add the number to an array.
   Close the scanner.
   Set total to 0.
   Open a print writer for the file.
   For each number in the array
     Write the number to the print writer.
     Add the number to total.
   Write total to the print writer.
   Close the print writer.

4. Add a variable count that is incremented whenever a number is read. In the end, print the average, not the total, as

   ```
   out.printf("Average: %8.2f\n", total / count);
   ```

   Because the string `"Average"` is three characters longer than `"Total"`, change the other output to `out.printf("%18.2f\n", value)`.

5. Add a variable count that is incremented whenever a number is read. Only write a new line when it is even.

   ```
   count++;
   out.printf("%8.2f", value);
   if (count % 2 == 0) { out.println(); }
   ```

   At the end of the loop, write a new line if count is odd, then write the total:

   ```
   if (count % 2 == 1) { out.println(); }
   out.printf("Total: %10.2f\n", total);
   ```

6. word is `"Hello,"` and input is `"World!"`

7. Because 995.0 is not an integer, the call `in.hasNextInt()` returns false, and the call `in.nextInt()` is skipped. The value of `number` stays 0, and input is set to the string `"995.0"`.

8. x1 is set to 6000000. Because a comma is not considered a part of a floating-point number in Java, the second call to `nextDouble` causes an input mismatch exception and x2 is not set.

9. Read them as strings, and convert those strings to numbers that are not equal to N/A:

   ```
   String input = in.next();
   if (!input.equals("N/A"))
   {
       double value = Double.parseDouble(input);
       Process value.
   }
   ```

10. Locate the last character of the country name:

    ```
    int j = i - 1;
    while (!Character.isWhiteSpace(line.charAt(j)))
    {
        j--;
    }
    ```

    Then extract the country name:

    ```
    String countryName = line.substring(0, j + 1);
    ```

11. args[0] is `"-d"` and args[1] is `"file1.txt"`

12.

key	inFile	outFile	i	arg
~~3~~	~~null~~	null	~~0~~	~~-d~~
-3	file1.txt		~~1~~	file1.txt
			2	

    Then the program prints a message

    ```
    Usage: java CaesarCipher [-d] infile outfile
    ```

13. The program will run correctly. The loop that parses the options does not depend on the positions in which the options appear.

14. FDHVDU

15. Add the lines

    ```
    else if (option == 'k')
    {
        key = Integer.parseInt(
            args[i].substring(2));
    }
    ```

    after line 27 and update the usage information.

16. It is still 100. The last statement was not executed because the exception was thrown.

17. ```
    if (amount < 0)
    {
        throw new IllegalArgumentException(
            "Negative amount");
    }
    ```
    ```

18. The Scanner constructor succeeds because the file exists. The nextInt method throws a NoSuchElementException. This is *not* an IOException. Therefore, the error is not caught. Because there is no other handler, an error message is printed and the program terminates.

19. Because programmers should simply check that their array index values are valid instead of trying to handle an ArrayIndexOutOfBounds-Exception.

20. No. You can catch both exception types in the same way, as you can see in the code example on page 339.

21. There are two mistakes. The PrintWriter constructor can throw a FileNotFoundException. You should supply a throws clause. And if one of the array elements is null, a NullPointerException is thrown. In that case, the out.close() statement is never executed. You should use a try/finally statement.

22. The exceptions are better handled in the main method.

23. If it had been declared inside the try block, its scope would only have extended until the end of the try block, and it would not have been accessible in the finally clause.

24. main calls readFile, which calls readData. The call in.nextInt() throws a NoSuchElementException. The readFile method doesn't catch it, so it propagates back to main, where it is caught. An error message is printed, and the user can specify another file.

25. We *want* to throw that exception, so that someone else can handle the problem of a bad data file.

OBJECTS AND CLASSES

To understand the concepts of classes, objects, and encapsulation

To implement instance variables, methods, and constructors

To be able to design, implement, and test your own classes

To understand the behavior of object references, static variables, and static methods

8.1 OBJECT-ORIENTED PROGRAMMING 362

8.2 IMPLEMENTING A SIMPLE CLASS 364
Syntax 8.1: Instance Variable Declaration 365

8.3 SPECIFYING THE PUBLIC INTERFACE OF A CLASS 367
Special Topic 8.1: The javadoc Utility 370

8.4 DESIGNING THE DATA REPRESENTATION 371

8.5 IMPLEMENTING INSTANCE METHODS 372
Syntax 8.2: Instance Methods 373
Programming Tip 8.1: All Instance Variables Should Be Private; Most Methods Should Be Public 374

8.6 CONSTRUCTORS 375
Syntax 8.3: Constructors 376
Common Error 8.1: Forgetting to Initialize Object References in a Constructor 378
Common Error 8.2: Trying to Call a Constructor 379
Common Error 8.3: Declaring a Constructor as void 379

Special Topic 8.2: Overloading 380

8.7 TESTING A CLASS 380
How To 8.1: Implementing a Class 382
Worked Example 8.1: Implementing a Bank Account Class ✛
Video Example 8.1: Paying Off a Loan ✛

8.8 PROBLEM SOLVING: TRACING OBJECTS 386

8.9 PROBLEM SOLVING: PATTERNS FOR OBJECT DATA 388
Video Example 8.2: Modeling a Robot Escaping from a Maze ✛
Random Fact 8.1: Electronic Voting Machines 394

8.10 OBJECT REFERENCES 395
Special Topic 8.3: Calling One Constructor from Another 399

8.11 STATIC VARIABLES AND METHODS 400
Random Fact 8.2: Open Source and Free Software 402

This chapter introduces you to object-oriented programming, an important technique for writing complex programs. In an object-oriented program, you don't simply manipulate numbers and strings, but you work with objects that are meaningful for your application. Objects with the same behavior (such as the windmills to the left) are grouped into classes. A programmer provides the desired behavior by specifying and implementing methods for these classes. In this chapter, you will learn how to discover, specify, and implement your own classes, and how to use them in your programs.

8.1 Object-Oriented Programming

You have learned how to structure your programs by decomposing tasks into methods. This is an excellent practice, but experience shows that it does not go far enough. It is difficult to understand and update a program that consists of a large collection of methods.

To overcome this problem, computer scientists invented **object-oriented programming**, a programming style in which tasks are solved by collaborating objects. Each object has its own set of data, together with a set of methods that act upon the data.

You have already experienced this programming style when you used strings, the System.out object, or a Scanner object. Each of these objects has a set of methods. For example, you can use the length and substring methods to work with String objects.

When you develop an object-oriented program, you create your own objects that describe what is important in your application. For example, in a student database you might work with Student and Course objects. Of course, then you must supply methods for these objects.

> A class describes a set of objects with the same behavior.

In Java, a programmer doesn't implement a single object. Instead, the programmer provides a **class**. A class describes a set of objects with the same behavior. For example, the String class describes the behavior of all strings. The class specifies how

A Car class describes passenger vehicles that can carry 4–5 people and a small amount of luggage.

a string stores its characters, which methods can be used with strings, and how the methods are implemented.

In contrast, the `PrintStream` class describes the behavior of objects that can be used to produce output. One such object is `System.out`, and you have seen in Chapter 7 how to create `PrintStream` objects that send output to a file.

Each class defines a specific set of methods that you can use with its objects. For example, when you have a `String` object, you can invoke the `length` method:

```
"Hello, World".length()
```

We say that the `length` method is a method of the `String` class. The `PrintStream` class has a different set of methods. For example, the call

```
System.out.length()
```

would be illegal—the `PrintStream` class has no `length` method. However, `PrintStream` has a `println` method, and the call

```
out.println("Hello, World!")
```

is legal.

The set of all methods provided by a class, together with a description of their behavior, is called the **public interface** of the class.

When you work with an object of a class, you do not know how the object stores its data, or how the methods are implemented. You need not know how a `String` organizes a character sequence, or how a `PrintWriter` object sends data to a file. All you need to know is the public interface—which methods you can apply, and what these methods do. The process of providing a public interface, while hiding the implementation details, is called **encapsulation**.

When you design your own classes, you will use encapsulation. That is, you will specify a set of public methods and hide the implementation details. Other programmers on your team can then use your classes without having to know their implementations, just as you are able to make use of the `String` and `PrintStream` classes.

If you work on a program that is being developed over a long period of time, it is common for implementation details to change, usually to make objects more efficient or more capable. When the implementation is hidden, the improvements do not affect the programmers that use the objects.

> Every class has a public interface: a collection of methods through which the objects of the class can be manipulated.

> Encapsulation is the act of providing a public interface and hiding the implementation details.

> Encapsulation enables changes in the implementation without affecting users of a class.

You can drive a car by operating the steering wheel and pedals, without knowing how the engine works. Similarly, you use an object through its methods. The implementation is hidden.

A driver of an electric car doesn't have to learn new controls even though the car engine is very different. Neither does the programmer who uses an object with an improved implementation—as long as the same methods are used.

SELF CHECK

1. Is the method call `"Hello, World".println()` legal? Why or why not?
2. When using a `String` object, you do not know how it stores its characters. How can you access them?
3. Describe a way in which a `String` object might store its characters.
4. Suppose the providers of your Java compiler decide to change the way that a `String` object stores its characters, and they update the `String` method implementations accordingly. Which parts of your code do you need to change when you get the new compiler?

Practice It   Now you can try these exercises at the end of the chapter: R8.1, R8.4.

8.2 Implementing a Simple Class

In this section, we look at the implementation of a very simple class. You will see how objects store their data, and how methods access the data of an object. Knowing how a very simple class operates will help you design and implement more complex classes later in this chapter.

Our first example is a class that models a *tally counter*, a mechanical device that is used to count people—for example, to find out how many people attend a concert or board a bus (see Figure 1).

Whenever the operator pushes a button, the counter value advances by one. We model this operation with a `count` method. A physical counter has a display to show the current value. In our simulation, we use a `getValue` method instead.

Figure 1   A Tally Counter

Here is an example of using the Counter class. First, we construct an object of the class:

```
Counter tally = new Counter();
```

In Java, you use the new operator to construct objects. We will discuss object construction in more detail in Section 8.6.

Next, we invoke methods on our object. First, we invoke the count method twice, simulating two button pushes. Then we invoke the getValue method to check how many times the button was pushed.

```
tally.count();
tally.count();
int result = tally.getValue(); // Sets result to 2
```

We can invoke the methods again, and the result will be different.

```
tally.count();
tally.count();
result = tally.getValue(); // Sets result to 4
```

As you can see, the tally object remembers the effect of prior method calls.

When implementing the Counter class, we need to specify how each counter object stores its data. In this simple example, that is very straightforward. Each counter needs a variable that keeps track of how many times the counter has been advanced.

An object stores its data in **instance variables**. An *instance* of a class is an object of the class. Thus, an instance variable is a storage location that is present in each object of the class.

You specify instance variables in the class declaration:

> An object's instance variables store the data required for executing its methods.

```
public class Counter
{
   private int value;
   . . .
}
```

An instance variable declaration consists of the following parts:

- An **modifier** (private)
- The **type** of the instance variable (such as int)
- The name of the instance variable (such as value)

Syntax 8.1 Instance Variable Declaration

Syntax
```
public class ClassName
{
    private typeName variableName;
    . . .
}
```

```
public class Counter
{
    private int value;
    . . .
}
```

Instance variables should always be private.

Each object of this class has a separate copy of this instance variable.

Type of the variable

Each object of a class has its own set of instance variables. For example, if concertCounter and boardingCounter are two objects of the Counter class, then each object has its own value variable (see Figure 2).

As you will see in Section 8.6, the instance variable value is set to 0 when a Counter object is constructed.

Next, let us have a quick look at the implementation of the methods of the Counter class. The count method advances the counter value by 1.

```
public void count()
{
    value = value + 1;
}
```

We will cover the syntax of the method header in Section 8.3. For now, focus on the body of the method inside the braces.

Note how the count method increments the instance variable value. *Which* instance variable? The one belonging to the object on which the method is invoked. For example, consider the call

```
concertCounter.count();
```

This call advances the value variable of the concertCounter object.

The methods that you invoke on an object are called **instance methods** to distinguish them from the static methods of Chapter 5.

Finally, look at the other instance method of the Counter class. The getValue method returns the current value:

```
public int getValue()
{
    return value;
}
```

This method is required so that users of the Counter class can find out how often a particular counter has been clicked. A user cannot simply access the value instance variable. That variable has been declared with the access specifier private.

The private specifier restricts access to the methods of the *same class*. For example, the value variable can be accessed by the count and getValue methods of the Counter class but not a method of another class. Those other methods need to use the getValue method if they want to find out the counter's value, or the count method if they want to change it.

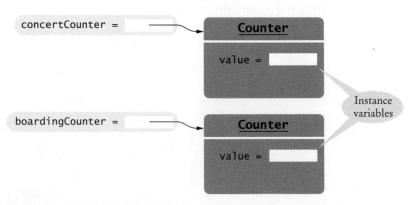

Figure 2 Instance Variables

These clocks have common behavior, but each of them has a different state. Similarly, objects of a class can have their instance variables set to different values.

Private instance variables are an essential part of encapsulation. They allow a programmer to hide the implementation of a class from a class user.

5. Supply the body of a method `public void reset()` that resets the counter back to zero.

6. Consider a change to the implementation of the counter. Instead of using an integer counter, we use a string of | characters to keep track of the clicks, just like a human might do.

```java
public class Counter
{
   private String strokes = "";
   public void count()
   {
      strokes = strokes + "|";
   }
   . . .
}
```

   How do you implement the `getValue` method with this data representation?

7. Suppose another programmer has used the original `Counter` class. What changes does that programmer have to make in order to use the modified class?

8. Suppose you use a class `Clock` with private instance variables `hours` and `minutes`. How can you access these variables in your program?

Practice It   Now you can try these exercises at the end of the chapter: P8.1, P8.2.

8.3 Specifying the Public Interface of a Class

When designing a class, you start by specifying its **public interface**. The public interface of a class consists of all methods that a user of the class may want to apply to its objects.

Let's consider a simple example. We want to use objects that simulate cash registers. A cashier who rings up a sale presses a key to start the sale, then rings up each item. A display shows the amount owed as well as the total number of items purchased.

In our simulation, we want to call the following methods on a cash register object:

- Add the price of an item.
- Get the total amount owed, and the count of items purchased.
- Clear the cash register to start a new sale.

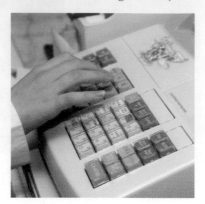

Here is an outline of the CashRegister class. We supply comments for all of the methods to document their purpose.

```
/**
    A simulated cash register that tracks the item
    count and the total amount due.
*/
public class CashRegister
{
    private data—see Section 8.4

    /**
        Adds an item to this cash register.
        @param price the price of this item
    */
    public void addItem(double price)
    {
        implementation—see Section 8.5
    }

    /**
        Gets the price of all items in the current sale.
        @return the total price
    */
    public double getTotal()
    {
        implementation—see Section 8.5
    }

    /**
        Gets the number of items in the current sale.
        @return the item count
    */
    public int getCount()
    {
        implementation—see Section 8.5
    }

    /**
        Clears the item count and the total.
    */
    public void clear()
    {
        implementation—see Section 8.5
    }
}
```

The method declarations and comments make up the *public interface* of the class. The data and the method bodies make up the *private implementation* of the class.

Note that the methods of the CashRegister class are instance methods. They are *not* declared as static. You invoke them on objects (or instances) of the CashRegister class.

Figure 3
An Object Reference
and an Object

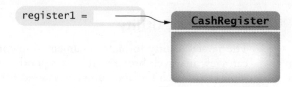

To see an instance method in action, we first need to construct an object:

```
CashRegister register1 = new CashRegister();
    // Constructs a CashRegister object
```

This statement initializes the register1 variable with a reference to a new CashRegister object—see Figure 3. (We discuss the process of object construction in Section 8.6 and object references in Section 8.10.)

Once the object has been constructed, we are ready to invoke a method:

```
register1.addItem(1.95); // Invokes a method
```

> A mutator method changes the object on which it operates.

When you look at the public interface of a class, it is useful to classify its methods as *mutators* and *accessors*. A **mutator** method modifies the object on which it operates. The CashRegister class has two mutators: addItem and clear. After you call either of these methods, the object has changed. You can observe that change by calling the getTotal or getCount method.

> An accessor method does not change the object on which it operates.

An **accessor** method queries the object for some information without changing it. The CashRegister class has two accessors: getTotal and getCount. Applying either of these methods to a CashRegister object simply returns a value and does not modify the object. For example, the following statement prints the current total and count:

```
System.out.println(register1.getTotal()) + " " + register1.getCount());
```

Now we know *what* a CashRegister object can do, but not *how* it does it. Of course, to use CashRegister objects in our programs, we don't need to know.

In the next sections, you will see how the CashRegister class is implemented.

SELF CHECK

9. What does the following code segment print?

```
CashRegister reg = new CashRegister();
reg.clear();
reg.addItem(0.95);
reg.addItem(0.95);
System.out.println(reg.getCount() + " " + reg.getTotal());
```

10. What is wrong with the following code segment?

```
CashRegister reg = new CashRegister();
reg.clear();
reg.addItem(0.95);
System.out.println(reg.getAmountDue());
```

11. Declare a method getDollars of the CashRegister class that yields the amount of the total sale as a dollar value without the cents.

12. Name two accessor methods of the String class.

13. Is the nextInt method of the Scanner class an accessor or a mutator?

14. Provide documentation comments for the Counter class of Section 8.2.

Practice It   Now you can try these exercises at the end of the chapter: R8.2, R8.8.

Special Topic 8.1

The `javadoc` Utility

The javadoc utility formats documentation comments into a neat set of documents that you can view in a web browser. It makes good use of the seemingly repetitive phrases. The first sentence of each method comment is used for a *summary table* of all methods of your class (see Figure 4). The @param and @return comments are neatly formatted in the detail description of each method (see Figure 5). If you omit any of the comments, then javadoc generates documents that look strangely empty.

This documentation format may look familiar. It is the same format that is used in the official Java documentation. The programmers who implement the Java library use javadoc themselves. They too document every class, every method, every parameter, and every return value, and then use javadoc to extract the documentation.

Many integrated programming environments can execute javadoc for you. Alternatively, you can invoke the javadoc utility from a shell window, by issuing the command

```
javadoc MyClass.java
```

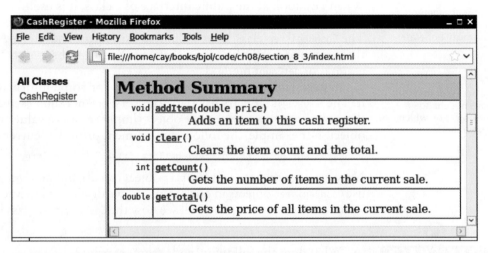

Figure 4   A Method Summary Generated by `javadoc`

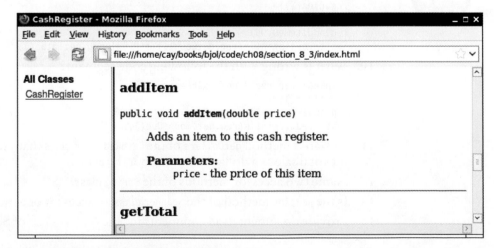

Figure 5   Method Detail Generated by `javadoc`

The javadoc utility produces files such as MyClass.html in HTML format, which you can inspect in a browser. You can use hyperlinks to navigate to other classes and methods.

You can run javadoc before implementing any methods. Just leave all the method bodies empty. Don't run the compiler—it would complain about missing return values. Simply run javadoc on your file to generate the documentation for the public interface that you are about to implement.

The javadoc tool is wonderful because it does one thing right: It allows you to put the documentation *together with your code*. That way, when you update your programs, you can see right away which documentation needs to be updated. Hopefully, you will update it right then and there. Afterward, run javadoc again and get updated information that is timely and nicely formatted.

8.4 Designing the Data Representation

An object stores its data in **instance variables**. These are variables that are declared inside the class (see Syntax 8.1).

When implementing a class, you have to determine which data each object needs to store. The object needs to have all the information necessary to carry out any method call.

Go through all methods and consider their data requirements. It is a good idea to start with the accessor methods. For example, a CashRegister object must be able to return the correct value for the getTotal method. That means, it must either store all entered prices and compute the total in the method call, or it must store the total.

For each accessor method, an object must either store or compute the result.

Now apply the same reasoning to the getCount method. If the cash register stores all entered prices, it can count them in the getCount method. Otherwise, you need to have a variable for the count.

The addItem method receives a price as an argument, and it must record the price. If the CashRegister object stores an array of entered prices, then the addItem method appends the price. On the other hand, if we decide to store just the item total and count, then the addItem method updates these two variables.

Finally, the clear method must prepare the cash register for the next sale, either by emptying the array of prices or by setting the total and count to zero.

Commonly, there is more than one way of representing the data of an object, and you must make a choice.

We have now discovered two different ways of representing the data that the object needs. Either of them will work, and we have to make a choice. We will choose the simpler one: variables for the total price and the item count. (Other options are explored in Exercises P8.16 and P8.17.)

```
int itemCount;
double totalPrice;
```

Like a wilderness explorer who needs to carry all items that may be needed, an object needs to store the data required for any method calls.

The instance variables are declared in the class, but outside any methods, with the private modifier:

```java
public class CashRegister
{
    private int itemCount;
    private double totalPrice;
    . . .
}
```

Be sure that your data representation supports method calls in any order.

Note that method calls can come in *any order*. For example, consider the CashRegister class. After calling

```java
register1.getTotal()
```

a program can make another call to

```java
register1.addItem(1.95)
```

You should not assume that you can clear the sum in a call to getTotal. Your data representation should allow for method calls that come in arbitrary order, in the same way that occupants of a car can push the various buttons and levers in any order they choose.

ONLINE EXAMPLE

The CashRegister class with instance variables.

SELF CHECK

15. What is wrong with this code segment?

```java
CashRegister register2 = new CashRegister();
register2.clear();
register2.addItem(0.95);
System.out.println(register2.totalPrice);
```

16. Consider a class Time that represents a point in time, such as 9 A.M. or 3:30 P.M. Give two sets of instance variables that can be used for implementing the Time class. (*Hint for the second set:* Military time.)

17. Suppose the implementor of the Time class changes from one implementation strategy to another, keeping the public interface unchanged. What do the programmers who use the Time class need to do?

18. Consider a class Grade that represents a letter grade, such as A+ or B. Give two different sets of instance variables that can be used for implementing the Grade class.

Practice It Now you can try these exercises at the end of the chapter: R8.6, R8.16.

8.5 Implementing Instance Methods

When implementing a class, you need to provide the bodies for all methods. Implementing an instance method is very similar to implementing a static method, with one essential difference: You can access the instance variables of the class in the method body.

For example, here is the implementation of the addItem method of the CashRegister class. (You can find the remaining methods at the end of the next section.)

```java
public void addItem(double price)
{
    itemCount++;
    totalPrice = totalPrice + price;
}
```

Syntax 8.2 Instance Methods

```
Syntax    modifiers returnType methodName(parameterType parameterName, . . . )
          {
              method body
          }
```

```
public class CashRegister
{
    . . .
    public void addItem(double price)
    {
        itemCount++;
        totalPrice = totalPrice + price;
    }
    . . .
}
```

Explicit parameter

Instance variables of the implicit parameter

The object on which a method is applied is the implicit parameter.

Whenever you use an instance variable, such as itemCount or totalPrice, in a method, it denotes that instance variable *of the object on which the method was invoked.* For example, consider the call

```
register1.addItem(1.95);
```

The first statement in the addItem method is

```
itemCount++;
```

Which itemCount is incremented? In this call, it is the itemCount of the register1 object. (See Figure 6.)

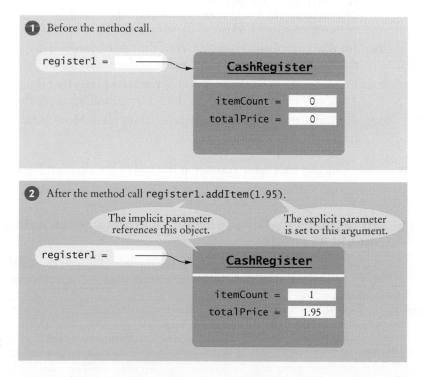

① Before the method call.

```
register1 =
```

CashRegister

| itemCount = | 0 |
| totalPrice = | 0 |

② After the method call register1.addItem(1.95).

The implicit parameter references this object.

The explicit parameter is set to this argument.

```
register1 =
```

CashRegister

| itemCount = | 1 |
| totalPrice = | 1.95 |

Figure 6
Implicit and Explicit Parameters

When an item is added, it affects the instance variables of the cash register object on which the method is invoked.

ONLINE EXAMPLE

The CashRegister class with method implementations.

Explicit parameters of a method are listed in the method declaration.

The object on which a method is invoked is called the **implicit parameter** of the method. In Java, you do not actually write the implicit parameter in the method declaration. For that reason, the parameter is called "implicit".

In contrast, parameters that are explicitly mentioned in the method declaration, such as the totalPrice parameter variable, are called **explicit parameters**. Every method has exactly one implicit parameter and zero or more explicit parameters.

SELF CHECK

19. What are the values of register1.itemCount, register1.totalPrice, register2.itemCount, and register2.totalPrice after these statements?

```
CashRegister register1 = new CashRegister();
register1.addItem(0.90);
register1.addItem(0.95);
CashRegister register2 = new CashRegister();
register2.addItem(1.90);
```

20. Implement a method getDollars of the CashRegister class that yields the amount of the total sale as a dollar value without the cents.

21. Consider the substring method of the String class that is described in Section 2.5.6. How many parameters does it have, and what are their types?

22. Consider the length method of the String class. How many parameters does it have, and what are their types?

Practice It Now you can try these exercises at the end of the chapter: R8.10, P8.16, P8.17, P8.18.

Programming Tip 8.1

All Instance Variables Should Be Private; Most Methods Should Be Public

It is possible to declare instance variables as public, but you should not do that in your own code. Always use encapsulation, with private instance variables that are manipulated with methods.

Typically, methods are public. However, sometimes you have a method that is used only as a helper method by other methods. In that case, you can make the helper method private. Simply use the private reserved word when declaring the method.

8.6 Constructors

A constructor initializes the instance variables of an object.

A constructor is invoked when an object is created with the new operator.

The name of a constructor is the same as the class name.

A **constructor** initializes the instance variables of an object. The constructor is automatically called whenever an object is created with the new operator.

You have seen the new operator in Chapter 2. It is used whenever a new object is required. For example, the expression new Scanner(System.in) in the statement

```
Scanner in = new Scanner(System.in);
```

constructs a new object of the Scanner class. Specifically, a constructor of the Scanner class is called with the argument System.in. That constructor initializes the Scanner object.

The name of a constructor is identical to the name of its class. For example:

```
public class CashRegister
{
    . . .

    /**
        Constructs a cash register with cleared item count and total.
    */
    public CashRegister() // A constructor
    {
        itemCount = 0;
        totalPrice = 0;
    }
}
```

Constructors never return values, but you do not use the void reserved word when declaring them.

A class can have multiple constructors.

Many classes have more than one constructor. This allows you to declare objects in different ways. Consider for example a BankAccount class that has two constructors:

```
public class BankAccount
{
    . . .

    /**
        Constructs a bank account with a zero balance.
    */
    public BankAccount() { . . . }

    /**
        Constructs a bank account with a given balance.
        @param initialBalance the initial balance
    */
    public BankAccount(double initialBalance) { . . . }
}
```

Both constructors have the same name as the class, BankAccount. The first constructor has no parameter variables, whereas the second constructor has a parameter variable of type double.

The compiler picks the constructor that matches the construction arguments.

When you construct an object, the compiler chooses the constructor that matches the arguments that you supply. For example,

```
BankAccount joesAccount = new BankAccount();
    // Uses BankAccount() constructor
BankAccount lisasAccount = new BankAccount(499.95);
    // Uses BankAccount(double) constructor
```

Syntax 8.3 Constructors

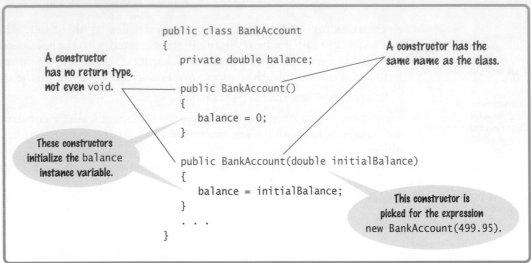

A constructor
has no return type,
not even void.

A constructor has the
same name as the class.

These constructors
initialize the balance
instance variable.

```
public class BankAccount
{
    private double balance;

    public BankAccount()
    {
        balance = 0;
    }

    public BankAccount(double initialBalance)
    {
        balance = initialBalance;
    }
    . . .
}
```

This constructor is
picked for the expression
new BankAccount(499.95).

By default, numbers
are initialized as 0,
Booleans as false,
and object references
as null.

If you do not initialize an instance variable in a constructor, it is automatically set to a default value:

- Numbers are set to zero.
- Boolean variables are initialized as false.
- Object and array references are set to the special value null that indicates that no object is associated with the variable (see Section 8.10). This is usually not desirable, and you should initialize object references in your constructors (see Common Error 8.1 on page 378).

In this regard, instance variables differ from local variables declared inside methods. The computer reports an error if you use a local variable that has not been explicitly initialized.

If you do not provide
a constructor, a
constructor with
no arguments
is generated.

If you do not supply any constructor for a class, the compiler automatically generates a constructor. That constructor has no arguments, and it initializes all instance variables with their default values. Therefore, every class has at least one constructor.

You have now encountered all concepts that are necessary to implement the CashRegister class.

*A constructor is like a set of
assembly instructions for an object.*

The complete code for the class is given here. In the next section, you will see how to test the class.

section_6/CashRegister.java

```java
1   /**
2       A simulated cash register that tracks the item count and
3       the total amount due.
4   */
5   public class CashRegister
6   {
7       private int itemCount;
8       private double totalPrice;
9
10      /**
11          Constructs a cash register with cleared item count and total.
12      */
13      public CashRegister()
14      {
15          itemCount = 0;
16          totalPrice = 0;
17      }
18
19      /**
20          Adds an item to this cash register.
21          @param price the price of this item
22      */
23      public void addItem(double price)
24      {
25          itemCount++;
26          totalPrice = totalPrice + price;
27      }
28
29      /**
30          Gets the price of all items in the current sale.
31          @return the total amount
32      */
33      public double getTotal()
34      {
35          return totalPrice;
36      }
37
38      /**
39          Gets the number of items in the current sale.
40          @return the item count
41      */
42      public int getCount()
43      {
44          return itemCount;
45      }
46
47      /**
48          Clears the item count and the total.
49      */
50      public void clear()
51      {
52          itemCount = 0;
53          totalPrice = 0;
54      }
55  }
```

23. Consider this class:

```java
public class Person
{
    private String name;

    public Person(String firstName, String lastName)
    {
        name = lastName + ", " + firstName;
    }
    . . .
}
```

If an object is constructed as

```java
Person harry = new Person("Harry", "Morgan");
```

what is its `name` instance variable?

24. Provide an implementation for a `Person` constructor so that after the call

```java
Person p = new Person();
```

the `name` instance variable of `p` is "unknown".

25. What happens if you supply no constructor for the `CashRegister` class?

26. Consider the following class:

```java
public class Item
{
    private String description;
    private double price;

    public Item() { . . . }
    // Additional methods omitted
}
```

Provide an implementation for the constructor. Be sure that no instance variable is set to `null`.

27. Which constructors should be supplied in the `Item` class so that each of the following declarations compiles?

a. `Item item2 = new Item("Corn flakes");`

b. `Item item3 = new Item(3.95);`

c. `Item item4 = new Item("Corn flakes", 3.95);`

d. `Item item1 = new Item();`

e. `Item item5;`

Practice It Now you can try these exercises at the end of the chapter: R8.12, P8.4, P8.5.

Common Error 8.1

Forgetting to Initialize Object References in a Constructor

Just as it is a common error to forget to initialize a local variable, it is easy to forget about instance variables. Every constructor needs to ensure that all instance variables are set to appropriate values.

If you do not initialize an instance variable, the Java compiler will initialize it for you. Numbers are initialized with 0, but object references—such as string variables—are set to the `null` reference.

Of course, 0 is often a convenient default for numbers. However, null is hardly ever a convenient default for objects. Consider this "lazy" constructor for a modified version of the BankAccount class:

```java
public class BankAccount
{
   private double balance;
   private String owner;
   . . .
   public BankAccount(double initialBalance)
   {
      balance = initialBalance;
   }
}
```

In this case, balance is initialized, but the owner variable is set to a null reference. This can be a problem—it is illegal to call methods on the null reference.

To avoid this problem, it is a good idea to initialize every instance variable:

```java
public BankAccount(double initialBalance)
{
   balance = initialBalance;
   owner = "None";
}
```

Common Error 8.2

Trying to Call a Constructor

A constructor is not a method. You must use it in combination with the new reserved word:

```java
CashRegister register1 = new CashRegister();
```

After an object has been constructed, you cannot invoke the constructor on that object again. For example, you cannot call the constructor to clear an object:

```java
. . .
register1.CashRegister(); // Error
```

It is true that the constructor can set a *new* CashRegister object to the cleared state, but you cannot invoke a constructor on an *existing* object. However, you can replace the object with a new one:

```java
register1 = new CashRegister(); // OK
```

Common Error 8.3

Declaring a Constructor as void

Do not use the void reserved word when you declare a constructor:

```java
public void BankAccount()  // Error—don't use void!
```

This would declare a method with return type void and *not* a constructor. Unfortunately, the Java compiler does not consider this a syntax error.

Overloading

When the same method name is used for more than one method, then the name is **overloaded**. In Java you can overload method names provided that the parameter types are different. For example, you can declare two methods, both called print:

```
public void print(CashRegister register)
public void print(BankAccount account)
```

When the print method is called,

```
print(x);
```

the compiler looks at the type of x. If x is a CashRegister object, the first method is called. If x is an BankAccount object, the second method is called. If x is neither, the compiler generates an error.

We have not used the overloading feature in this book. Instead, we gave each method a unique name, such as printRegister or printAccount. However, we have no choice with constructors. Java demands that the name of a constructor equal the name of the class. If a class has more than one constructor, then that name must be overloaded.

8.7 Testing a Class

In the preceding section, we completed the implementation of the CashRegister class. What can you do with it? Of course, you can compile the file CashRegister.java. However, you can't *execute* the CashRegister class. It doesn't contain a main method. That is normal—most classes don't contain a main method. They are meant to be combined with a class that has a main method.

> A unit test verifies that a class works correctly in isolation, outside a complete program.

In the long run, your class may become a part of a larger program that interacts with users, stores data in files, and so on. However, before integrating a class into a program, it is always a good idea to test it in isolation. Testing in isolation, outside a complete program, is called **unit testing**.

To test your class, you have two choices. Some interactive development environments, such as BlueJ (http://bluej.org) and Dr. Java (http://drjava.org), have commands for constructing objects and invoking methods. Then you can test a class simply by constructing an object, calling methods, and verifying that you get the expected return values. Figure 7 shows the result of calling the getTotal method on a CashRegister object in BlueJ.

An engineer tests a part in isolation. This is an example of unit testing.

> To test a class, use an environment for interactive testing, or write a tester class to execute test instructions.

Alternatively, you can write a *tester class*. A tester class is a class with a main method that contains statements to run methods of another class. A tester class typically carries out the following steps:

1. Construct one or more objects of the class that is being tested.
2. Invoke one or more methods.
3. Print out one or more results.
4. Print the expected results.

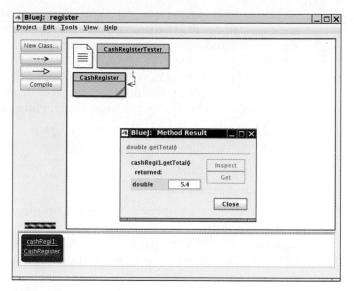

Figure 7   The Return Value of the `getTotal` Method in BlueJ

Here is a class to run methods of the CashRegister class. The main method constructs an object of type CashRegister, invokes the addItem method three times, and then displays the result of the getCount and getTotal methods.

section_7/CashRegisterTester.Java

```
1   /**
2         This program tests the CashRegister class.
3   */
4   public class CashRegisterTester
5   {
6      public static void main(String[] args)
7      {
8         CashRegister register1 = new CashRegister();
9         register1.addItem(1.95);
10        register1.addItem(0.95);
11        register1.addItem(2.50);
12        System.out.println(register1.getCount());
13        System.out.println("Expected: 3");
14        System.out.printf("%.2f\n", register1.getTotal());
15        System.out.println("Expected: 5.40");
16     }
17  }
```

Program Run

```
3
Expected: 3
5.40
Expected: 5.40
```

In our sample program, we add three items totaling $5.40. When displaying the method results, we also display messages that describe the values we expect to see.

Determining the expected result in advance is an important part of testing.

This is a very important step. You want to spend some time thinking about what the expected result is before you run a test program. This thought process will help you understand how your program should behave, and it can help you track down errors at an early stage.

To produce a program, you need to combine the CashRegister and CashRegisterTester classes. The details for building the program depend on your compiler and development environment. In most environments, you need to carry out these steps:

1. Make a new subfolder for your program.
2. Make two files, one for each class.
3. Compile both files.
4. Run the test program.

Many students are surprised that such a simple program contains two classes. However, this is normal. The two classes have entirely different purposes. The CashRegister class describes objects that model cash registers. The CashRegisterTester class runs a test that puts a CashRegister object through its paces.

SELF CHECK

28. How would you enhance the tester class to test the clear method?
29. When you run the CashRegisterTester program, how many objects of class CashRegister are constructed? How many objects of type CashRegisterTester?
30. Why is the CashRegisterTester class unnecessary in development environments that allow interactive testing, such as BlueJ?

Practice It   Now you can try these exercises at the end of the chapter: P8.10, P8.11, P8.21.

HOW TO 8.1   **Implementing a Class**

A very common task is to implement a class whose objects can carry out a set of specified actions. This How To walks you through the necessary steps.

As an example, consider a class Menu. An object of this class can display a menu such as

```
1) Open new account
2) Log into existing account
3) Help
4) Quit
```

Then the menu waits for the user to supply a value. If the user does not supply a valid value, the menu is redisplayed, and the user can try again.

Step 1   Get an informal list of the responsibilities of your objects.

Be careful that you restrict yourself to features that are actually required in the problem. With real-world items, such as cash registers or bank accounts, there are potentially dozens of features that might be worth implementing. But your job is not to faithfully model the real world. You need to determine only those responsibilities that you need for solving your specific problem.

In the case of the menu, you need to

Display the menu.
Get user input.

Now look for hidden responsibilities that aren't part of the problem description. How do objects get created? Which mundane activities need to happen, such as clearing the cash register at the beginning of each sale?

In the menu example, consider how a menu is produced. The programmer creates an empty menu object and then adds options "Open new account", "Help", and so on. That is another responsibility:

Add an option.

Step 2   Specify the public interface.

Turn the list in Step 1 into a set of methods, with specific types for the parameter variables and the return values. Many programmers find this step simpler if they write out method calls that are applied to a sample object, like this:

```
Menu mainMenu = new Menu();
mainMenu.addOption("Open new account");
// Add more options
int input = mainMenu.getInput();
```

Now we have a specific list of methods.

- `void addOption(String option)`

- `int getInput()`

What about displaying the menu? There is no sense in displaying the menu without also asking the user for input. However, `getInput` may need to display the menu more than once if the user provides a bad input. Thus, `display` is a good candidate for a private method.

To complete the public interface, you need to specify the constructors. Ask yourself what information you need in order to construct an object of your class. Sometimes you will want two constructors: one that sets all instance variables to a default and one that sets them to user-supplied values.

In the case of the menu example, we can get by with a single constructor that creates an empty menu.

Here is the public interface:

```
public class Menu
{
    public Menu() { . . . }
    public void addOption(String option) { . . . }
    public int getInput() { . . . }
}
```

Step 3   Document the public interface.

Supply a documentation comment for the class, then comment each method.

```
/**
    A menu that is displayed on a console.
*/
public class Menu
{
    /**
        Constructs a menu with no options.
    */
    public Menu() { . . . }

    /**
        Adds an option to the end of this menu.
        @param option the option to add
    */
    public void addOption(String option) { . . . }
```

```
/**
   Displays the menu, with options numbered starting with 1,
   and prompts the user for input. Repeats until a valid input
   is supplied.
   @return the number that the user supplied
*/
public int getInput() { . . . }
}
```

Step 4 Determine instance variables.

Ask yourself what information an object needs to store to do its job. The object needs to be able to process every method using just its instance variables and the method arguments.

Go through each method, perhaps starting with a simple one or an interesting one, and ask yourself what the object needs to carry out the method's task. Which data items are required in addition to the method arguments? Make instance variables for those data items.

In our example, let's start with the addOption method. We clearly need to store the added menu option so that the menu can be displayed later. How should we store the options? As an array list of strings? As one long string? Both approaches can be made to work. We will use an array list here. Exercise P8.3 asks you to implement the other approach.

```
public class Menu
{
   private ArrayList<String> options;
   . . .
}
```

Now consider the getInput method. It shows the stored options and reads an integer. When checking that the input is valid, we need to know the number of menu items. Because we store them in an array list, the number of menu items is simply obtained as the size of the array list. If you stored the menu items in one long string, you might want to keep another instance variable that stores the item count.

We will also need a scanner to read the user input, which we will add as another instance variable:

```
private Scanner in;
```

Step 5 Implement constructors and methods.

Implement the constructors and methods in your class, one at a time, starting with the easiest ones. For example, here is the implementation of the addOption method:

```
public void addOption(String option)
{
   options.add(option);
}
```

Here is the getInput method. This method is a bit more sophisticated. It loops until a valid input has been obtained, displaying the menu options before reading the input.

```
public int getInput()
{
   int input;
   do
   {
      for (int i = 0; i < options.size(); i++)
      {
         int choice = i + 1;
         System.out.println(choice + ") " + options.get(i));
      }
      input = in.nextInt();
   }
   while (input < 1 || input > options.size());
```

```
        return input;
    }
```

Finally, we need to supply a constructor to initialize the instance variables:

```
public Menu()
{
    options = new ArrayList<String>();
    in = new Scanner(System.in);
}
```

If you find that you have trouble with the implementation of some of your methods, you may need to rethink your choice of instance variables. It is common for a beginner to start out with a set of instance variables that cannot accurately describe the state of an object. Don't hesitate to go back and rethink your implementation strategy.

Once you have completed the implementation, compile your class and fix any compiler errors.

Step 6   Test your class.

Write a short tester program and execute it. The tester program should carry out the method calls that you found in Step 2.

```
public class MenuTester
{
    public static void main(String[] args)
    {
        Menu mainMenu = new Menu();
        mainMenu.addOption("Open new account");
        mainMenu.addOption("Log into existing account");
        mainMenu.addOption("Help");
        mainMenu.addOption("Quit");
        int input = mainMenu.getInput();
        System.out.println("Input: " + input);
    }
}
```

Program Run

```
1) Open new account
2) Log into existing account
3) Help
4) Quit
5
1) Open new account
2) Log into existing account
3) Help
4) Quit
3
Input: 3
```

ONLINE EXAMPLE

The complete Menu and MenuTester classes.

WORKED EXAMPLE 8.1   **Implementing a Bank Account Class**

This Worked Example shows how to develop a class that simulates a bank account.

Available online in WileyPLUS and at www.wiley.com/college/horstmann.

Paying Off a Loan

When you take out a loan, the bank tells you how much you need to pay and for how long. Where do these numbers come from? This Video Example uses a Loan object to demonstrate how a loan is paid off.

8.8 Problem Solving: Tracing Objects

You have seen how the technique of hand-tracing is useful for understanding how a program works. When your program contains objects, it is useful to adapt the technique so that you gain a better understanding about object data and encapsulation.

> Write the methods on the front of a card, and the instance variables on the back.

Use an index card or a sticky note for each object. On the front, write the methods that the object can execute. On the back, make a table for the values of the instance variables.

Here is a card for a CashRegister object:

CashRegister reg1		itemCount	totalPrice
clear			
addItem(price)			
getTotal			
getCount			

front   *back*

In a small way, this gives you a feel for encapsulation. An object is manipulated through its public interface (on the front of the card), and the instance variables are hidden in the back.

When an object is constructed, fill in the initial values of the instance variables:

itemCount	totalPrice
0	0

> Update the values of the instance variables when a mutator method is called.

Whenever a mutator method is executed, cross out the old values and write the new ones below. Here is what happens after a call to the addItem method:

itemCount	totalPrice
~~0~~	~~0~~
1	19.95

✚ Available online in WileyPLUS and at www.wiley.com/college/horstmann.

If you have more than one object in your program, you will have multiple cards, one for each object:

itemCount	totalPrice
~~0~~	~~0~~
1	19.95

itemCount	totalPrice
~~0~~	~~0~~
1	19.95
2	34.95

These diagrams are also useful when you design a class. Suppose you are asked to enhance the `CashRegister` class to compute the sales tax. Add a method `getSalesTax` to the front of the card. Now turn the card over, look over the instance variables, and ask yourself whether the object has sufficient information to compute the answer. Remember that each object is an autonomous unit. Any data value that can be used in a computation must be

- An instance variable.
- A method argument.
- A static variable (uncommon; see Section 8.11).

To compute the sales tax, we need to know the tax rate and the total of the taxable items. (Food items are usually not subject to sales tax.) We don't have that information available. Let us introduce additional instance variables for the tax rate and the taxable total. The tax rate can be set in the constructor (assuming it stays fixed for the lifetime of the object). When adding an item, we need to be told whether the item is taxable. If so, we add its price to the taxable total.

For example, consider the following statements.

```
CashRegister reg2(7.5); // 7.5 percent sales tax
reg2.addItem(3.95, false); // Not taxable
reg2.addItem(19.95, true); // Taxable
```

When you record the effect on a card, it looks like this:

itemCount	totalPrice	taxableTotal	taxRate
~~0~~	~~0~~	~~0~~	7.5
~~1~~	~~3.95~~		
2	23.90	19.95	

With this information, it becomes easy to compute the tax. It is **taxableTotal x taxRate / 100**. Tracing the object helped us understand the need for additional instance variables.

SELF CHECK

31.   Consider a `Car` class that simulates fuel consumption in a car. We will assume a fixed efficiency (in miles per gallon) that is supplied in the constructor. There are methods for adding gas, driving a given distance, and checking the amount of gas

left in the tank. Make a card for a Car object, choosing suitable instance variables and showing their values after the object was constructed.

32. Trace the following method calls:

```
Car myCar(25);
myCar.addGas(20);
myCar.drive(100);
myCar.drive(200);
myCar.addGas(5);
```

33. Suppose you are asked to simulate the odometer of the car, by adding a method `getMilesDriven`. Add an instance variable to the object's card that is suitable for computing this method.

34. Trace the methods of Self Check 32, updating the instance variable that you added in Self Check 33.

Practice It   Now you can try these exercises at the end of the chapter: R8.13, R8.14, R8.15.

8.9 Problem Solving: Patterns for Object Data

When you design a class, you first consider the needs of the programmers who use the class. You provide the methods that the users of your class will call when they manipulate objects. When you implement the class, you need to come up with the instance variables for the class. It is not always obvious how to do this. Fortunately, there is a small set of recurring patterns that you can adapt when you design your own classes. We introduce these patterns in the following sections.

8.9.1 Keeping a Total

An instance variable for the total is updated in methods that increase or decrease the total amount.

Many classes need to keep track of a quantity that can go up or down as certain methods are called. Examples:

- A bank account has a balance that is increased by a deposit, decreased by a withdrawal.
- A cash register has a total that is increased when an item is added to the sale, cleared after the end of the sale.
- A car has gas in the tank, which is increased when fuel is added and decreased when the car drives.

In all of these cases, the implementation strategy is similar. Keep an instance variable that represents the current total. For example, for the cash register:

```
private double totalPrice;
```

Locate the methods that affect the total. There is usually a method to increase it by a given amount.

```
public void addItem(double price)
{
    totalPrice = totalPrice + price;
}
```

Depending on the nature of the class, there may be a method that reduces or clears the total. In the case of the cash register, there is a clear method:

```
public void clear()
{
    total = 0;
}
```

There is usually a method that yields the current total. It is easy to implement:

```
public double getTotal()
{
    return totalPrice;
}
```

All classes that manage a total follow the same basic pattern. Find the methods that affect the total and provide the appropriate code for increasing or decreasing it. Find the methods that report or use the total, and have those methods read the current total.

8.9.2 Counting Events

A counter that counts events is incremented in methods that correspond to the events.

You often need to count how often certain events occur in the life of an object. For example:

- In a cash register, you want to know how many items have been added in a sale.
- A bank account charges a fee for each transaction; you need to count them.

Keep a counter, such as

```
private int itemCount;
```

Increment the counter in those methods that correspond to the events that you want to count.

```
public void addItem(double price)
{
    totalPrice = totalPrice + price;
    itemCount++;
}
```

You may need to clear the counter, for example at the end of a sale or a statement period.

```
public void clear()
{
    total = 0;
    itemCount = 0;
}
```

There may or may not be a method that reports the count to the class user. The count may only be used to compute a fee or an average. Find out which methods in your class make use of the count, and read the current value in those methods.

8.9.3 Collecting Values

Some objects collect numbers, strings, or other objects. For example, each multiple-choice question has a number of choices. A cash register may need to store all prices of the current sale.

An object can collect other objects in an array or array list.

Use an array list or an array to store the values. (An array list is usually simpler because you won't need to track the number of values.) For example,

```
public class Question
{
    private ArrayList<String> choices;
    . . .
}
```

In the constructor, initialize the instance variable to an empty collection:

```
public Question()
{
    choices = new ArrayList<String>();
}
```

A shopping cart object needs to manage a collection of items.

You need to supply some mechanism for adding values. It is common to provide a method for appending a value to the collection:

```
public void add(String question)
{
    choices.add(question);
}
```

The user of a Question object can call this method multiple times to add the various choices.

8.9.4 Managing Properties of an Object

An object property can be accessed with a getter method and changed with a setter method.

A property is a value of an object that an object user can set and retrieve. For example, a Student object may have a name and an ID.

Provide an instance variable to store the property's value and methods to get and set it.

```
public class Student
{
    private String name;
    . . .
    public String getName() { return name; }
    public void setName(String newName) { name = newName; }
    . . .
}
```

It is common to add error checking to the setter method. For example, we may want to reject a blank name:

```
public void setName(String newName)
{
    if (newName.length() > 0) { name = newName; }
}
```

Some properties should not change after they have been set in the constructor. For example, a student's ID may be fixed (unlike the student's name, which may change). In that case, don't supply a setter method.

```
public class Student
{
```

```
      private int id;
      . . .
      public Student(int anId) { id = anId; }
      public String getId() { return id; }
      // No setId method
      . . .
   }
```

8.9.5 Modeling Objects with Distinct States

> If your object can have one of several states that affect the behavior, supply an instance variable for the current state.

Some objects have behavior that varies depending on what has happened in the past. For example, a Fish object may look for food when it is hungry and ignore food after it has eaten. Such an object would need to remember whether it has recently eaten.

Supply an instance variable that models the state, together with some constants for the state values:

```
public class Fish
{
   private int hungry;

   public static final int NOT_HUNGRY = 0;
   public static final int SOMEWHAT_HUNGRY = 1;
   public static final int VERY_HUNGRY = 2;
   . . .
}
```

(Alternatively, you can use an enumeration—see Special Topic 3.4.)

Determine which methods change the state. In this example, a fish that has just eaten food, won't be hungry. But as the fish moves, it will get hungrier.

```
public void eat()
{
   hungry = NOT_HUNGRY;
   . . .
}

public void move()
{
   . . .
   if (hungry < VERY_HUNGRY) { hungry++; }
}
```

If a fish is in a hungry state,
its behavior changes.

Finally, determine where the state affects behavior. A fish that is very hungry will want to look for food first.

```
public void move()
{
   if (hungry == VERY_HUNGRY)
   {
      Look for food.
   }
   . . .
}
```

8.9.6 Describing the Position of an Object

To model a moving object, you need to store and update its position.

Some objects move around during their lifetime, and they remember their current position. For example,

- A train drives along a track and keeps track of the distance from the terminus.
- A simulated bug living on a grid crawls from one grid location to the next, or makes 90 degree turns to the left or right.
- A cannonball is shot into the air, then descends as it is pulled by the gravitational force.

Such objects need to store their position. Depending on the nature of their movement, they may also need to store their orientation or velocity.

If the object moves along a line, you can represent the position as a distance from a fixed point.

```
private double distanceFromTerminus;
```

If the object moves in a grid, remember its current location and direction in the grid:

```
private int row;
private int column;
private int direction; // 0 = North, 1 = East, 2 = South, 3 = West
```

When you model a physical object such as a cannonball, you need to track both the position and the velocity, possibly in two or three dimensions. Here we model a cannonball that is shot upward into the air:

```
private double zPosition;
private double zVelocity;
```

There will be methods that update the position. In the simplest case, you may be told by how much the object moves:

```
public void move(double distanceMoved)
{
   distanceFromTerminus = distanceFromTerminus + distanceMoved;
}
```

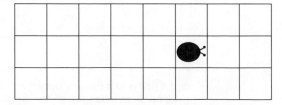

A bug in a grid needs to store its row, column, and direction.

If the movement happens in a grid, you need to update the row or column, depending on the current orientation.

```
public void moveOneUnit()
{
   if (direction == NORTH) { row--; }
   else if (direction == EAST) { column++; }
   . . .
}
```

Exercise P8.25 shows you how to update the position of a physical object with known velocity.

Whenever you have a moving object, keep in mind that your program will *simulate* the actual movement in some way. Find out the rules of that simulation, such as movement along a line or in a grid with integer coordinates. Those rules determine how to represent the current position. Then locate the methods that move the object, and update the positions according to the rules of the simulation.

SELF CHECK

35. Suppose we want to count the number of transactions in a bank account in a statement period, and we add a counter to the BankAccount class:

```
public class BankAccount
{
   private int transactionCount;
   . . .
}
```

In which methods does this counter need to be updated?

36. In the example in Section 8.9.3, why is the add method required? That is, why can't the user of a Question object just call the add method of the ArrayList<String> class?

37. Suppose we want to enhance the CashRegister class in Section 8.6 to track the prices of all purchased items for printing a receipt. Which instance variable should you provide? Which methods should you modify?

38. Consider an Employee class with properties for tax ID number and salary. Which of these properties should have only a getter method, and which should have getter and setter methods?

39. Look at the direction instance variable in the bug example in Section 8.9.6. This is an example of which pattern?

Practice It Now you can try these exercises at the end of the chapter: P8.6, P8.7, P8.12.

VIDEO EXAMPLE 8.2 **Modeling a Robot Escaping from a Maze**

In this Video Example, we will program classes that model a robot escaping from a maze.

✚ Available online in WileyPLUS and at www.wiley.com/college/horstmann.

Random Fact 8.1 Electronic Voting Machines

In the 2000 presidential elections in the United States, votes were tallied by a variety of machines. Some machines processed cardboard ballots into which voters punched holes to indicate their choices (see below). When voters were not careful, remains of paper—the now infamous "chads"—were partially stuck in the punch cards, causing votes to be miscounted. A manual recount was necessary, but it was not carried out everywhere due to time constraints and procedural wrangling. The election was very close, and there remain doubts in the minds of many people whether the election outcome would have been different if the voting machines had accurately counted the intent of the voters.

Punch Card Ballot

Subsequently, voting machine manufacturers have argued that electronic voting machines would avoid the problems caused by punch cards or optically scanned forms. In an electronic voting machine, voters indicate their preferences by pressing buttons or touching icons on a computer screen. Typically, each voter is presented with a summary screen for review before casting the ballot. The process is very similar to using a bank's automated teller machine.

It seems plausible that these machines make it more likely that a vote is counted in the same way that the voter intends. However, there has been significant controversy surrounding some types of electronic voting machines. If a machine simply records the votes and prints out the totals after the election has been completed, then how do you know that the machine worked correctly? Inside the machine is a computer that executes a program, and, as you may know from your own experience, programs can have bugs.

In fact, some electronic voting machines do have bugs. There have been isolated cases where machines reported tallies that were impossible. When a machine reports far more or far fewer votes than voters, then it is clear that it malfunctioned. Unfortunately, it is then impossible to find out the actual votes. Over time, one would expect these bugs to be fixed in the software. More insidiously, if the results are plausible, nobody may ever investigate.

Many computer scientists have spoken out on this issue and confirmed that it is impossible, with today's technology, to tell that software is error free and has not been tampered with. Many of them recommend that electronic voting machines should employ a *voter verifiable audit trail*. (A good source of information is http://verifiedvoting.org.) Typically, a voter-verifiable machine prints out a ballot. Each voter has a chance to review the printout, and then deposits it in an old-fashioned ballot box. If there is a problem with the electronic equipment, the printouts can be scanned or counted by hand.

As this book is written, this concept is strongly resisted both by manufacturers of electronic voting machines and by their customers, the cities and counties that run elections. Manufacturers are reluctant to increase the cost of the machines because they may not be able to pass the cost increase on to their customers, who tend to have tight budgets. Election officials fear problems with malfunctioning printers, and some of them have publicly stated that they actually prefer equipment that eliminates bothersome recounts.

What do you think? You probably use an automated bank teller machine to get cash from your bank account. Do you review the paper record that the machine issues? Do you check your bank statement? Even if you don't, do you put your faith in other people who double-check their balances, so that the bank won't get away with widespread cheating?

Is the integrity of banking equipment more important or less important than that of voting machines? Won't every voting process have some room for error and fraud anyway? Is the added cost for equipment, paper, and staff time reasonable to combat a potentially slight risk of malfunction and fraud? Computer scientists cannot answer these questions—an informed society must make these tradeoffs. But, like all professionals, they have an obligation to speak out and give accurate testimony about the capabilities and limitations of computing equipment.

Touch Screen Voting Machine

8.10 Object References

In Java, a variable whose type is a class does not actually hold an object. It merely holds the *memory location* of an object. The object itself is stored elsewhere—see Figure 8.

An object reference specifies the location of an object.

We use the technical term **object reference** to denote the memory location of an object. When a variable contains the memory location of an object, we say that it *refers* to an object. For example, after the statement

```
CashRegister reg1 = new CashRegister();
```

the variable reg1 refers to the CashRegister object that the new operator constructed. Technically speaking, the new operator returned a reference to the new object, and that reference is stored in the reg1 variable.

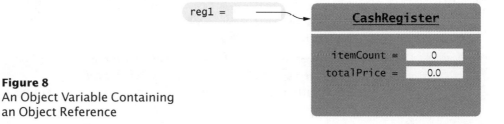

Figure 8
An Object Variable Containing
an Object Reference

8.10.1 Shared References

Multiple object variables can contain references to the same object.

You can have two (or more) object variables that store references to the same object, for example by assigning one to the other.

```
CashRegister reg2 = reg1;
```

Now you can access the same CashRegister object both as reg1 and as reg2, as shown in Figure 9.

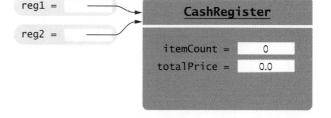

Figure 9
Two Object Variables
Referring to the Same Object

Primitive type variables store values. Object variables store references.

In this regard, object variables differ from variables for primitive types (numbers, characters, and boolean values). When you declare

```
int num1 = 0;
```

then the num1 variable holds the number 0, not a reference to the number (see Figure 10).

num1 = 0

Figure 10 A Variable of Type int Stores a Number

ANIMATION
Object References

You can see the difference between primitive type variables and object variables when you make a copy of a variable. When you copy a number, the original and the copy of the number are independent values. But when you copy an object reference, both the original and the copy are references to the same object.

Consider the following code, which copies a number and then changes the copy (see Figure 11):

```java
int num1 = 0; ①
int num2 = num1; ②
num2++; ③
```

Now the variable num1 contains the value 0, and num2 contains 1.

Now consider the seemingly analogous code with CashRegister objects (see Figure 12):

```java
CashRegister reg1 = new CashRegister(); ①
CashRegister reg2 = reg1; ②
reg2.addItem(2.95); ③
```

Because reg1 and reg2 refer to the same cash register after step ②, both variables now refer to a cash register with item count 1 and total price 2.95.

> When copying an object reference, you have two references to the same object.

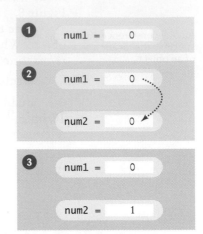

Figure 11 Copying Numbers

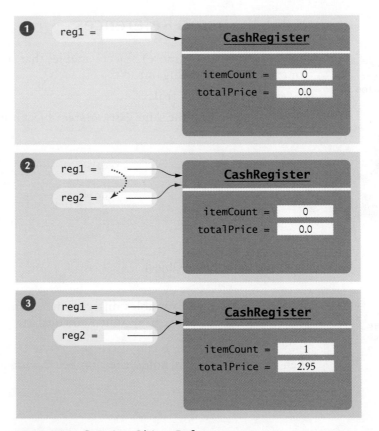

Figure 12 Copying Object References

There is a reason for the difference between numbers and objects. In the computer, each number requires a small amount of memory. But objects can be very large. It is far more efficient to manipulate only the memory location.

8.10.2 The null Reference

The null reference refers to no object.

An object reference can have the special value null if it refers to no object at all. It is common to use the null value to indicate that a value has never been set. For example,

```
String middleInitial = null; // No middle initial
```

You use the == operator (and not equals) to test whether an object reference is a null reference:

```
if (middleInitial == null)
{
    System.out.println(firstName + " " + lastName);
}
else
{
    System.out.println(firstName + " " + middleInitial + ". " + lastName);
}
```

Note that the null reference is not the same as the empty string "". The empty string is a valid string of length 0, whereas a null indicates that a String variable refers to no string at all.

It is an error to invoke a method on a null reference. For example,

```
CashRegister reg = null;
System.out.println(reg.getTotal()); // Error—cannot invoke a method on null
```

This code causes a "null pointer exception" at run time.

The null reference is the default value for an object reference that is contained inside another object or an array of objects. In order to avoid run-time errors, you need to replace these null references with references to actual objects.

For example, suppose you construct an array of bank accounts:

```
BankAccount[] accounts = new BankAccount[NACCOUNTS];
```

You now have an array filled with null references. If you want an array of actual bank accounts, you need to construct them:

```
for (int i = 0; i < accounts.length; i++)
{
    accounts[i] = new BankAccount();
}
```

8.10.3 The this Reference

In a method, the this reference refers to the implicit parameter.

Every instance method receives the implicit parameter in a variable called this.
For example, consider the method call

```
reg1.addItem(2.95);
```

When the method is called, the parameter variable this refers to the same object as reg1 (see Figure 13).

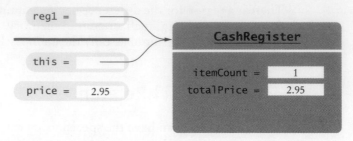

Figure 13 The Implicit Parameter of a Method Call

You don't usually need to use the this reference, but you can. For example, you can write the addItem method like this:

```
void addItem(double price)
{
   this.itemCount++;
   this.totalPrice = this.totalPrice + price;
}
```

Some programmers like to use the this reference to make it clear that itemCount and totalPrice are instance variables and not local variables. You may want to try it out and see if you like that style.

There is another situation where the this reference can make your programs easier to read. Consider a constructor or instance method that calls another instance method *on the same object*. For example, the CashRegister constructor can call the clear method instead of duplicating its code:

```
public CashRegister()
{
   clear();
}
```

This call is easier to understand when you use the this reference:

```
public CashRegister()
{
   this.clear();
}
```

It is now more obvious that the method is invoked on the object that is being constructed.

Finally, some people like to use the this reference in constructors. Here is a typical example:

```
public class Student
{
   private int id;
   private String name;

   public Student(int id, String name)
   {
      this.id = id;
      this.name = name;
   }
}
```

The expression id refers to the parameter variable, and this.id to the instance variable. In general, if both a local variable and an instance variable have the same name, you can access the local variable by its name, and the instance variable with the this reference.

You can implement the constructor without using the this reference. Simply choose other names for the parameter variables:

```java
public Student(int anId, String aName)
{
    id = anId;
    name = aName;
}
```

SELF CHECK

40. Suppose we have a variable
    ```java
    String greeting = "Hello";
    ```
    What is the effect of this statement?
    ```java
    String greeting2 = greeting;
    ```

41. After calling `String greeting3 = greeting2.toUpperCase()`, what are the contents of greeting and greeting2?

42. What is the value of s.length() if s is

    a. the empty string ""?

    b. null?

43. What is the type of this in the call greeting.substring(1, 4)?

44. Supply a method addItems(int quantity, double price) in the CashRegister class to add multiple instances of the same item. Your implementation should repeatedly call the addItem method. Use the this reference.

Practice It   Now you can try these exercises at the end of the chapter: R8.19, R8.20.

Special Topic 8.3

Calling One Constructor from Another

Consider the BankAccount class outlined in Section 8.6. It has two constructors: a constructor without arguments to initialize the balance with zero, and another constructor to supply an initial balance. Rather than explicitly setting the balance to zero, one constructor can call another constructor of the same class instead. There is a shorthand notation to achieve this result:

```java
public class BankAccount
{
    public BankAccount (double initialBalance)
    {
        balance = initialBalance;
    }

    public BankAccount()
    {
        this(0);
    }
    . . .
}
```

The command this(0); means "Call another constructor of this class and supply the value 0". Such a call to another constructor can occur only as the *first line in a constructor*.

> This syntax is a minor convenience. We will not use it in this book. Actually, the use of the reserved word this is a little confusing. Normally, this denotes a reference to the implicit parameter, but if this is followed by parentheses, it denotes a call to another constructor of this class.

8.11 Static Variables and Methods

A static variable belongs to the class, not to any object of the class.

Sometimes, a value properly belongs to a class, not to any object of the class. You use a **static variable** for this purpose. Here is a typical example: We want to assign bank account numbers sequentially. That is, we want the bank account constructor to construct the first account with number 1001, the next with number 1002, and so on. To solve this problem, we need to have a single value of lastAssignedNumber that is a property of the *class*, not any object of the class. Such a variable is called a static variable, because you declare it using the static reserved word.

The reserved word static *is a holdover from the C++ language. Its use in Java has no relationship to the normal use of the term.*

```
public class BankAccount
{
    private double balance;
    private int accountNumber;
    private static int lastAssignedNumber = 1000;

    public BankAccount()
    {
        lastAssignedNumber++;
        accountNumber = lastAssignedNumber;
    }
    . . .
}
```

Every BankAccount object has its own balance and accountNumber instance variables, but there is only a single copy of the lastAssignedNumber variable (see Figure 14). That variable is stored in a separate location, outside any BankAccount objects.

Like instance variables, static variables should always be declared as private to ensure that methods of other classes do not change their values. However, static *constants* may be either private or public. For example, the BankAccount class can define a public constant value, such as

```
public class BankAccount
{
    public static final double OVERDRAFT_FEE = 29.95;
    . . .
}
```

Methods from any class can refer to such a constant as BankAccount.OVERDRAFT_FEE.

A static method is not invoked on an object.

Sometimes a class defines methods that are not invoked on an object. Such a method is called a **static method**. A typical example of a static method is the sqrt method in the Math class. Because numbers aren't objects, you can't invoke methods on them. For example, if x is a number, then the call x.sqrt() is not legal in Java.

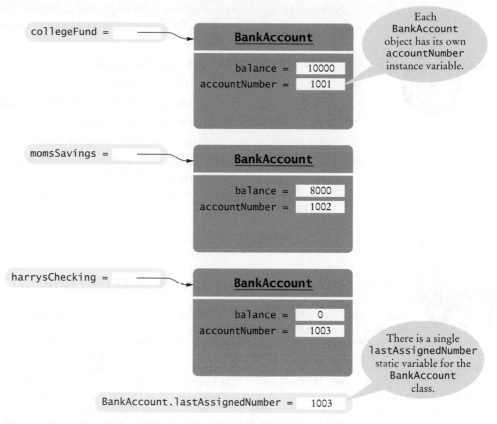

Figure 14   A Static Variable and Instance Variables

Therefore, the Math class provides a static method that is invoked as Math.sqrt(x). No object of the Math class is constructed. The Math qualifier simply tells the compiler where to find the sqrt method.

You can define your own static methods for use in other classes. Here is an example:

```
public class Financial
{
    /**
        Computes a percentage of an amount.
        @param percentage the percentage to apply
        @param amount the amount to which the percentage is applied
        @return the requested percentage of the amount
    */
    public static double percentOf(double percentage, double amount)
    {
        return (percentage / 100) * amount;
    }
}
```

When calling this method, supply the name of the class containing it:

```
double tax = Financial.percentOf(taxRate, total);
```

ONLINE EXAMPLE

A program with static methods and variables.

You had to use static methods in Chapter 5 before you knew how to implement your own objects. However, in object-oriented programming, static methods are not very common.

Nevertheless, the main method is always static. When the program starts, there aren't any objects. Therefore, the first method of a program must be a static method.

SELF CHECK

45. Name two static variables of the System class.

46. Name a static constant of the Math class.

47. The following method computes the average of an array of numbers:

```
public static double average(double[] values)
```

Why should it not be defined as an instance method?

48. Harry tells you that he has found a great way to avoid those pesky objects: Put all code into a single class and declare all methods and variables static. Then main can call the other static methods, and all of them can access the static variables. Will Harry's plan work? Is it a good idea?

Practice It   Now you can try these exercises at the end of the chapter: P8.14, P8.15.

Random Fact 8.2 Open Source and Free Software

Most companies that produce software regard the source code as a trade secret. After all, if customers or competitors had access to the source code, they could study it and create similar programs without paying the original vendor. For the same reason, customers dislike secret source code. If a company goes out of business or decides to discontinue support for a computer program, its users are left stranded. They are unable to fix bugs or adapt the program to a new operating system. Nowadays, some software packages are distributed with "open source" or "free software" licenses. Here, the term "free" doesn't refer to price, but to the freedom to inspect and modify the source code. Richard Stallman, a famous computer scientist and winner of a MacArthur "genius" grant, pioneered the concept of free software. He is the inventor of the Emacs text editor and the originator of the GNU project that aims to create an entirely free version of a UNIX compatible operating system. All programs of the GNU project are licensed under the General Public License or GPL. The GPL allows you to make as many copies as you wish, make any modifications to the source, and redistribute the original and modified programs, charging nothing at all or whatever the market will bear. In return, you must agree that your modifications also fall under the GPL. You must give out the source code to any changes that you distribute, and anyone else can distribute them under the same conditions. The GPL, and similar open source licenses, form a social contract. Users of the software enjoy the freedom to use and modify the software, and in return they are obligated to share any improvements that they make. Many programs, such as the Linux operating system and the GNU C++ compiler, are distributed under the GPL.

Some commercial software vendors have attacked the GPL as "viral" and "undermining the commercial software sector". Other companies have a more nuanced strategy, producing proprietary software while also contributing to open source projects.

Frankly, open source is not a panacea and there is plenty of room for the commercial software sector. Open source software often lacks the polish of commercial software because many of the programmers are volunteers who are interested in solving their own problems, not in making a product that is easy to use by others. Some product categories are not available at all as open source software because the development work is unattractive when there is little promise of commercial gain. Open source software has been most successful in areas that are of interest to programmers, such as the Linux operating system, Web servers, and programming tools.

On the positive side, the open software community can be very competitive and creative. It is quite common to see several competing projects that take ideas from each other, all rapidly becoming more capable. Having many programmers involved, all reading the source code, often means that bugs tend to get squashed quickly. Eric Raymond describes open source development in his famous article "The Cathedral and the Bazaar" (http://catb.org/~esr/writings/cathedral-bazaar/cathedral-bazaar/index.html). He writes "Given enough eyeballs, all bugs are shallow".

Richard Stallman, a pioneer of the free source movement.

CHAPTER SUMMARY

Understand the concepts of classes, objects, and encapsulation.

- A class describes a set of objects with the same behavior.
- Every class has a public interface: a collection of methods through which the objects of the class can be manipulated.
- Encapsulation is the act of providing a public interface and hiding the implementation details.
- Encapsulation enables changes in the implementation without affecting users of a class.

Understand instance variables and method implementations of a simple class.

- An object's instance variables store the data required for executing its methods.
- Each object of a class has its own set of instance variables.
- An instance method can access the instance variables of the object on which it acts.
- A private instance variable can only be accessed by the methods of its own class.

Write method headers that describe the public interface of a class.

- You can use method headers and method comments to specify the public interface of a class.
- A mutator method changes the object on which it operates.
- An accessor method does not change the object on which it operates.

Choose an appropriate data representation for a class.

- For each accessor method, an object must either store or compute the result.
- Commonly, there is more than one way of representing the data of an object, and you must make a choice.
- Be sure that your data representation supports method calls in any order.

Provide the implementation of instance methods for a class.

- The object on which a method is applied is the implicit parameter.
- Explicit parameters of a method are listed in the method declaration.

Design and implement constructors.

- A constructor initializes the instance variables of an object.
- A constructor is invoked when an object is created with the new operator.
- The name of a constructor is the same as the class name.
- A class can have multiple constructors.
- The compiler picks the constructor that matches the construction arguments.

- By default, numbers are initialized as 0, Booleans as `false`, and object references as `null`.
- If you do not provide a constructor, a constructor with no arguments is generated.

Write tests that verify that a class works correctly.

- A unit test verifies that a class works correctly in isolation, outside a complete program.
- To test a class, use an environment for interactive testing, or write a tester class to execute test instructions.
- Determining the expected result in advance is an important part of testing.

Use the technique of object tracing for visualizing object behavior.

- Write the methods on the front of a card, and the instance variables on the back.
- Update the values of the instance variables when a mutator method is called.

Use patterns to design the data representation of a class.

- An instance variable for the total is updated in methods that increase or decrease the total amount.
- A counter that counts events is incremented in methods that correspond to the events.
- An object can collect other objects in an array or array list.
- An object property can be accessed with a getter method and changed with a setter method.
- If your object can have one of several states that affect the behavior, supply an instance variable for the current state.
- To model a moving object, you need to store and update its position.

Describe the behavior of object references.

- An object reference specifies the location of an object.
- Multiple object variables can contain references to the same object.
- Primitive type variables store values. Object variables store references.
- When copying an object reference, you have two references to the same object.
- The `null` reference refers to no object.
- In a method, the `this` reference refers to the implicit parameter.

Understand the behavior of static variables and methods.

- A static variable belongs to the class, not to any object of the class.
- A static method is not invoked on an object.

REVIEW EXERCISES

- **R8.1** What is encapsulation? Why is it useful?

- **R8.2** What values are returned by the calls `reg1.getCount()`, `reg1.getTotal()`, `reg2.getCount()`, and `reg2.getTotal()` after these statements?

  ```
  CashRegister reg1 = new CashRegister();
  reg1.addItem(3.25);
  reg1.addItem(1.95);
  CashRegister reg2 = new CashRegister();
  reg2.addItem(3.25);
  reg2.clear();
  ```

- **R8.3** Consider the `Menu` class in How To 8.1 on page 382. What is displayed when the following calls are executed?

  ```
  Menu simpleMenu = new Menu();
  simpleMenu.addOption("Ok");
  simpleMenu.addOption("Cancel");
  int response = simpleMenu.getInput();
  ```

- **R8.4** What is the *public interface* of a class? How does it differ from the *implementation* of a class?

- **R8.5** Consider the data representation of a cash register that keeps track of sales tax in Section 8.8. Instead of tracking the taxable total, track the total sales tax. Redo the walkthrough with this change.

- **R8.6** Suppose the `CashRegister` needs to support a method `void undo()` that undoes the addition of the preceding item. This enables a cashier to quickly undo a mistake. What instance variables should you add to the `CashRegister` class to support this modification?

- **R8.7** What is an instance method, and how does it differ from a static method?

- **R8.8** What is a mutator method? What is an accessor method?

- **R8.9** What is an implicit parameter? How does it differ from an explicit parameter?

- **R8.10** How many implicit parameters can an instance method have? How many implicit parameters can a static method have? How many explicit parameters can an instance method have?

- **R8.11** What is a constructor?

- **R8.12** How many constructors can a class have? Can you have a class with no constructors? If a class has more than one constructor, which of them gets called?

- **R8.13** Using the object tracing technique described in Section 8.8, trace the program at the end of Section 8.7.

- **R8.14** Using the object tracing technique described in Section 8.8, trace the program in Worked Example 8.1.

- **R8.15** Design a modification of the `BankAccount` class in Worked Example 8.1 in which the first five transactions per month are free and a $1 fee is charged for every additional transaction. Provide a method that deducts the fee at the end of a month. What additional instance variables do you need? Using the object tracing technique described in Section 8.8, trace a scenario that shows how the fees are computed over two months.

■■■ R8.16 Instance variables are "hidden" by declaring them as private, but they aren't hidden very well at all. Anyone can read the class declaration. Explain to what extent the private reserved word hides the private implementation of a class.

■■■ R8.17 You can read the itemCount instance variable of the CashRegister class with the getCount accessor method. Should there be a setCount mutator method to change it? Explain why or why not.

■■■ R8.18 In a static method, it is easy to differentiate between calls to instance methods and calls to static methods. How do you tell them apart? Why is it not as easy for methods that are called from an instance method?

■■ R8.19 What is the this reference? Why would you use it?

■■ R8.20 What is the difference between the number zero, the null reference, the value false, and the empty string?

PROGRAMMING EXERCISES

■ P8.1 We want to add a button to the tally counter in Section 8.2 that allows an operator to undo an accidental button click. Provide a method

```
public void undo()
```

that simulates such a button. As an added precaution, make sure that the operator cannot click the undo button more often than the count button.

■ P8.2 Simulate a tally counter that can be used to admit a limited number of people. First, the limit is set with a call

```
public void setLimit(int maximum)
```

If the count button was clicked more often than the limit, simulate an alarm by printing out a message "Limit exceeded".

■■■ P8.3 Reimplement the Menu class so that it stores all menu items in one long string. *Hint:* Keep a separate counter for the number of options. When a new option is added, append the option count, the option, and a newline character.

■■ P8.4 Implement a class Address. An address has a house number, a street, an optional apartment number, a city, a state, and a postal code. Supply two constructors: one with an apartment number and one without. Supply a print method that prints the address with the street on one line and the city, state, and zip code on the next line. Supply a method public boolean comesBefore(Address other) that tests whether this address comes before another when the addresses are compared by postal code.

■ P8.5 Implement a class SodaCan with methods getSurfaceArea() and get-Volume(). In the constructor, supply the height and radius of the can.

■■ P8.6 Implement a class Car with the following properties. A car has a certain fuel efficiency (measured in miles/gallon) and a certain amount of fuel in the gas tank. The efficiency is specified in the constructor, and the initial fuel level is 0. Supply a method drive that simulates driving the car for a certain distance, reducing the fuel level in the gas tank, and methods getGas-Level, to return the current fuel level, and addGas, to tank up. Sample usage:

```
Car myHybrid = new Car(50); // 50 miles per gallon
myHybrid.addGas(20); // Tank 20 gallons
myHybrid.drive(100); // Drive 100 miles
System.out.println(myHybrid.getGasLevel()); // Print fuel remaining
```

■■ **P8.7** Implement a class Student. For the purpose of this exercise, a student has a name and a total quiz score. Supply an appropriate constructor and methods getName(), addQuiz(int score), getTotalScore(), and getAverageScore(). To compute the latter, you also need to store the *number of quizzes* that the student took.

■■ **P8.8** Modify the Student class of Exercise P8.7 to compute grade point averages. Methods are needed to add a grade and get the current GPA. Specify grades as elements of a class Grade. Supply a constructor that constructs a grade from a string, such as "B+". You will also need a method that translates grades into their numeric values (for example, "B+" becomes 3.3).

■■■ **P8.9** Declare a class ComboLock that works like the combination lock in a gym locker, as shown here. The lock is constructed with a combination—three numbers between 0 and 39. The reset method resets the dial so that it points to 0. The turnLeft and turnRight methods turn the dial by a given number of ticks to the left or right. The open method attempts to open the lock. The lock opens if the user first turned it right to the first number in the combination, then left to the second, and then right to the third.

```
public class ComboLock
{
    . . .
    public ComboLock(int secret1, int secret2, int secret3) { . . . }
    public void reset() { . . . }
    public void turnLeft(int ticks) { . . . }
    public void turnRight(int ticks) { . . . }
    public boolean open() { . . . }
}
```

■■ **P8.10** Implement a VotingMachine class that can be used for a simple election. Have methods to clear the machine state, to vote for a Democrat, to vote for a Republican, and to get the tallies for both parties.

■■ **P8.11** Provide a class for authoring a simple letter. In the constructor, supply the names of the sender and the recipient:

```
public Letter(String from, String to)
```

Supply a method

```
public void addLine(String line)
```

to add a line of text to the body of the letter. Supply a method

```
public String getText()
```

that returns the entire text of the letter. The text has the form:

Dear *recipient name*:
blank line
first line of the body
second line of the body
. . .

> *last line of the body*
> *blank line*
> Sincerely,
> *blank line*
> *sender name*

Also supply a main method that prints this letter.

```
Dear John:

I am sorry we must part.
I wish you all the best.

Sincerely,

Mary
```

Construct an object of the Letter class and call addLine twice.

■■ P8.12 Write a class Bug that models a bug moving along a horizontal line. The bug moves either to the right or left. Initially, the bug moves to the right, but it can turn to change its direction. In each move, its position changes by one unit in the current direction. Provide a constructor

```
public Bug(int initialPosition)
```

and methods

- public void turn()
- public void move()
- public int getPosition()

Sample usage:

```
Bug bugsy = new Bug(10);
bugsy.move(); // Now the position is 11
bugsy.turn();
bugsy.move(); // Now the position is 10
```

Your main method should construct a bug, make it move and turn a few times, and print the actual and expected positions.

■■ P8.13 Implement a class Moth that models a moth flying in a straight line. The moth has a position, the distance from a fixed origin. When the moth moves toward a point of light, its new position is halfway between its old position and the position of the light source. Supply a constructor

```
public Moth(double initialPosition)
```

and methods

- public void moveToLight(double lightPosition)
- public void getPosition()

Your main method should construct a moth, move it toward a couple of light sources, and check that the moth's position is as expected.

■■■ P8.14 Write static methods

- public static double sphereVolume(double r)
- public static double sphereSurface(double r)
- public static double cylinderVolume(double r, double h)
- public static double cylinderSurface(double r, double h)

- `public static double coneVolume(double r, double h)`
- `public static double coneSurface(double r, double h)`

that compute the volume and surface area of a sphere with a radius r, a cylinder with a circular base with radius r and height h, and a cone with a circular base with radius r and height h. Place them into a class `Geometry`. Then write a program that prompts the user for the values of r and h, calls the six methods, and prints the results.

■■ P8.15 Solve Exercise P8.14 by implementing classes `Sphere`, `Cylinder`, and `Cone`. Which approach is more object-oriented?

■■ Business P8.16 Reimplement the `CashRegister` class so that it keeps track of the price of each added item in an `ArrayList<Double>`. Remove the `itemCount` and `totalPrice` instance variables. Reimplement the `clear`, `addItem`, `getTotal`, and `getCount` methods. Add a method `displayAll` that displays the prices of all items in the current sale.

■■ Business P8.17 Reimplement the `CashRegister` class so that it keeps track of the total price as an integer: the total cents of the price. For example, instead of storing 17.29, store the integer 1729. Such an implementation is commonly used because it avoids the accumulation of roundoff errors. Do not change the public interface of the class.

■■ Business P8.18 After closing time, the store manager would like to know how much business was transacted during the day. Modify the `CashRegister` class to enable this functionality. Supply methods `getSalesTotal` and `getSalesCount` to get the total amount of all sales and the number of sales. Supply a method `resetSales` that resets any counters and totals so that the next day's sales start from zero.

■■ Business P8.19 Implement a class `Portfolio`. This class has two objects, `checking` and `savings`, of the type `BankAccount` that was developed in Worked Example 8.1 (ch08/worked_example_1/BankAccount.java in your code files). Implement four methods:

- `public void deposit(double amount, String account)`
- `public void withdraw(double amount, String account)`
- `public void transfer(double amount, String account)`
- `public double getBalance(String account)`

Here the account string is "S" or "C". For the deposit or withdrawal, it indicates which account is affected. For a transfer, it indicates the account from which the money is taken; the money is automatically transferred to the other account.

■■ Business P8.20 Design and implement a class `Country` that stores the name of the country, its population, and its area. Then write a program that reads in a set of countries and prints

- The country with the largest area.
- The country with the largest population.
- The country with the largest population density (people per square kilometer (or mile)).

■■ Business P8.21 Design a class `Message` that models an e-mail message. A message has a recipient, a sender, and a message text. Support the following methods:

- A constructor that takes the sender and recipient
- A method `append` that appends a line of text to the message body
- A method `toString` that makes the message into one long string like this: `"From: Harry Morgan\nTo: Rudolf Reindeer\n . . ."`

Write a program that uses this class to make a message and print it.

■■ **Business P8.22** Design a class `Mailbox` that stores e-mail messages, using the `Message` class of Exercise P8.21. Implement the following methods:

- `public void addMessage(Message m)`
- `public Message getMessage(int i)`
- `public void removeMessage(int i)`

■■ **Business P8.23** Design a `Customer` class to handle a customer loyalty marketing campaign. After accumulating $100 in purchases, the customer receives a $10 discount on the next purchase. Provide methods

- `void makePurchase(double amount)`
- `boolean discountReached()`

Provide a test program and test a scenario in which a customer has earned a discount and then made over $90, but less than $100 in purchases. This should not result in a second discount. Then add another purchase that results in the second discount.

■■■ **Business P8.24** The Downtown Marketing Association wants to promote downtown shopping with a loyalty program similar to the one in Exercise P8.23. Shops are identified by a number between 1 and 20. Add a new parameter variable to the `makePurchase` method that indicates the shop. The discount is awarded if a customer makes purchases in at least three different shops, spending a total of $100 or more.

■■■ **Science P8.25** Design a class `Cannonball` to model a cannonball that is fired into the air. A ball has

- An x- and a y-position.
- An x- and a y-velocity.

Supply the following methods:

- A constructor with an x-position (the y-position is initially 0)
- A method `move(double sec)` that moves the ball to the next position (First compute the distance traveled in sec seconds, using the current velocities, then update the x- and y-positions; then update the y-velocity by taking into account the gravitational acceleration of -9.81 m/s^2; the x-velocity is unchanged.)
- Methods `getX` and `getY` that get the current location of the cannonball
- A method `shoot` whose arguments are the angle α and initial velocity v (Compute the x-velocity as $v \cos \alpha$ and the y-velocity as $v \sin \alpha$; then keep calling `move` with a time interval of 0.1 seconds until the y-position is 0; call `getX` and `getY` after every move and display the position.)

Use this class in a program that prompts the user for the starting angle and the initial velocity. Then call `shoot`.

■■ **Science P8.26** The colored bands on the top-most resistor shown in the photo below indicate a resistance of 6.2 kΩ ±5 percent. The resistor tolerance of ±5 percent indicates the acceptable variation in the resistance. A 6.2 kΩ ±5 percent resistor could have a resistance as small as 5.89 kΩ or as large as 6.51 kΩ. We say that 6.2 kΩ is the *nominal value* of the resistance and that the actual value of the resistance can be any value between 5.89 kΩ and 6.51 kΩ.

Write a program that represents a resistor as a class. Provide a single constructor that accepts values for the nominal resistance and tolerance and then determines the actual value randomly. The class should provide public methods to get the nominal resistance, tolerance, and the actual resistance.

Write a `main` method for the program that demonstrates that the class works properly by displaying actual resistances for ten 330 Ω ±10 percent resistors.

■■ **Science P8.27** In the `Resistor` class from Exercise P8.26, supply a method that returns a description of the "color bands" for the resistance and tolerance. A resistor has four color bands:

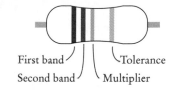

First band / Second band / Multiplier / Tolerance

- The first band is the first significant digit of the resistance value.
- The second band is the second significant digit of the resistance value.
- The third band is the decimal multiplier.
- The fourth band indicates the tolerance.

Color	Digit	Multiplier	Tolerance
Black	0	$\times 10^0$	—
Brown	1	$\times 10^1$	±1%
Red	2	$\times 10^2$	±2%
Orange	3	$\times 10^3$	—
Yellow	4	$\times 10^4$	—
Green	5	$\times 10^5$	±0.5%
Blue	6	$\times 10^6$	±0.25%
Violet	7	$\times 10^7$	±0.1%
Gray	8	$\times 10^8$	±0.05%
White	9	$\times 10^9$	—
Gold	—	$\times 10^{-1}$	±5%
Silver	—	$\times 10^{-2}$	±10%
None	—	—	±20%

For example (using the values from the table as a key), a resistor with red, violet, green, and gold bands (left to right) will have 2 as the first digit, 7 as the second digit, a multiplier of 10^5, and a tolerance of ±5 percent, for a resistance of 2,700 kΩ, plus or minus 5 percent.

■ ■ ■ **Science P8.28** The figure below shows a frequently used electric circuit called a "voltage divider". The input to the circuit is the voltage v_i. The output is the voltage v_o. The output of a voltage divider is proportional to the input, and the constant of proportionality is called the "gain" of the circuit. The voltage divider is represented by the equation

$$G = \frac{v_o}{v_i} = \frac{R_2}{R_1 + R_2}$$

where G is the gain and R_1 and R_2 are the resistances of the two resistors that comprise the voltage divider.

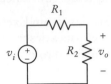

Manufacturing variations cause the actual resistance values to deviate from the nominal values, as described in Exercise P8.26. In turn, variations in the resistance values cause variations in the values of the gain of the voltage divider. We calculate the *nominal value of the gain* using the nominal resistance values and the *actual value of the gain* using actual resistance values.

Write a program that contains two classes, `VoltageDivider` and `Resistor`. The `Resistor` class is described in Exercise P8.26. The `VoltageDivider` class should have two instance variables that are objects of the `Resistor` class. Provide a single constructor that accepts two `Resistor` objects, nominal values for their resistances, and the resistor tolerance. The class should provide public methods to get the nominal and actual values of the voltage divider's gain.

Write a `main` method for the program that demonstrates that the class works properly by displaying nominal and actual gain for ten voltage dividers each consisting of 5% resistors having nominal values $R_1 = 250\ \Omega$ and $R_2 = 750\ \Omega$.

ANSWERS TO SELF-CHECK QUESTIONS

1. No—the object `"Hello, World"` belongs to the `String` class, and the `String` class has no `println` method.

2. Through the `substring` and `charAt` methods.

3. As an `ArrayList<Character>`. As a char array.

4. None. The methods will have the same effect, and your code could not have manipulated `String` objects in any other way.

5. ```
   public void reset()
   {
       value = 0;
   }
   ```

6. ```
   public int getValue()
   {
   ```

```
           return strokes.length();
   }
```

7. None—the public interface has not changed.

8. You cannot access the instance variables directly. You must use the methods provided by the `Clock` class.

9. `2 1.90`

10. There is no method named `getAmountDue`.

11. `public int getDollars();`

12. `length`, `substring`. In fact, all methods of the `String` class are accessors.

13. A mutator. Getting the next number removes it from the input, thereby modifying it. Not

convinced? Consider what happens if you call the `nextInt` method twice. You will usually get two different numbers. But if you call an accessor twice on an object (without a mutation between the two calls), you are sure to get the same result.

14.
```
/**
    This class models a tally counter.
*/
public class Counter
{
    private int value;

    /**
        Gets the current value of this counter.
        @return the current value
    */
    public int getValue()
    {
        return value;
    }

    /**
        Advances the value of this counter by 1.
    */
    public void count()
    {
        value = value + 1;
    }
}
```

15. The code tries to access a private instance variable.

16. (1) `int hours;` // Between 1 and 12
`int minutes;` // Between 0 and 59
`boolean pm;` // True for P.M., false for A.M.

(2) `int hours;` // Military time, between 0 and 23
`int minutes;` // Between 0 and 59

(3) `int totalMinutes` // Between 0 and 60 * 24 - 1

17. They need not change their programs at all because the public interface has not changed. They need to recompile with the new version of the `Time` class.

18. (1) `String letterGrade;` // "A+", "B"

(2) `double numberGrade;` // 4.3, 3.0

19. 2 1.85 1 1.90

20.
```
public int getDollars()
{
    int dollars = (int) totalPrice;
        // Truncates cents
    return dollars;
}
```

21. Three parameters: two explicit parameters of type `int`, and one implicit parameter of type `String`.

22. One parameter: the implicit parameter of type `String`. The method has no explicit parameters.

23. `"Morgan, Harry"`

24. `public Person() { name = "unknown"; }`

25. A constructor is generated that has the same effect as the constructor provided in this section. It sets both instance variables to zero.

26.
```
public Item()
{
    price = 0;
    description = "";
}
```

The `price` instance variable need not be initialized because it is set to zero by default, but it is clearer to initialize it explicitly.

27. (a) `Item(String)` (b) `Item(double)`
(c) `Item(String, double)` (d) `Item()`
(e) No constructor has been called.

28. Add these lines:
```
register1.clear();
System.out.println(register1.getCount());
System.out.println("Expected: 0");
System.out.printf("%.2f\n",
    register1.getTotal());
System.out.println("Expected: 0.00");
```

29. 1, 0

30. These environments allow you to call methods on an object without creating a `main` method.

31.

front

back

32.

gasLeft	milesPerGallon
~~0~~	25
~~20~~	
~~16~~	
~~8~~	
13	

33.

gasLeft	milesPerGallon	totalMiles
0	25	0

34.

gasLeft	milesPerGallon	totalMiles
~~0~~	25	0
~~20~~		
~~16~~		100
~~8~~		300
13		

35. It needs to be incremented in the deposit and withdraw methods. There also needs to be some method to reset it after the end of a statement period.

36. The ArrayList<String> instance variable is private, and the class users cannot acccess it.

37. Add an ArrayList<Double> prices. In the addItem method, add the current price. In the reset method, replace the array list with an empty one. Also supply a method printReceipt that prints the prices.

38. The tax ID of an employee does not change, and no setter method should be supplied. The salary of an employee can change, and both getter and setter methods should be supplied.

39. It is an example of the "state pattern" described in Section 8.9.5. The direction is a state that changes when the bug turns, and it affects how the bug moves.

40. Both greeting and greeting2 refer to the same string "Hello".

41. They both still refer to the string "Hello". The toUpperCase method computes the string "HELLO", but it is not a mutator—the original string is unchanged.

42. (a) 0

(b) A null pointer exception is thrown.

43. It is a reference of type String.

44.
```
public void addItems(int quantity, double price)
{
    for (int i = 1; i <= quantity; i++)
    {
        this.addItem(price);
    }
}
```

45. System.in and System.out

46. Math.PI

47. The method needs no data of any object. The only required input is the values argument.

48. Yes, it works. Static methods can call each other and access static variables—any method can. But it is a terrible idea. A program that consists of a single class with many methods is hard to understand.

INHERITANCE AND INTERFACES

CHAPTER GOALS

CHAPTER GOALS

To learn about inheritance

To implement subclasses that inherit and override superclass methods

To understand the concept of polymorphism

To be familiar with the common superclass Object and its methods

To work with interface types

CHAPTER CONTENTS

9.1 INHERITANCE HIERARCHIES 416

Programming Tip 9.1: Use a Single Class for Variation in Values, Inheritance for Variation in Behavior 420

9.2 IMPLEMENTING SUBCLASSES 420

Syntax 9.1: Subclass Declaration 422

Common Error 9.1: Replicating Instance Variables from the Superclass 423

Common Error 9.2: Confusing Super- and Subclasses 424

9.3 OVERRIDING METHODS 424

Common Error 9.3: Accidental Overloading 428

Common Error 9.4: Forgetting to Use super When Invoking a Superclass Method 429

Special Topic 9.1: Calling the Superclass Constructor 429

Syntax 9.2: Constructor with Superclass Initializer 430

9.4 POLYMORPHISM 430

Special Topic 9.2: Dynamic Method Lookup and the Implicit Parameter 433

Special Topic 9.3: Abstract Classes 434

Special Topic 9.4: Final Methods and Classes 435

Special Topic 9.5: Protected Access 436

How To 9.1: Developing an Inheritance Hierarchy 436

Worked Example 9.1: Implementing an Employee Hierarchy for Payroll Processing ✚

Video Example 9.1: Building a Discussion Board ✚

9.5 OBJECT: THE COSMIC SUPERCLASS 441

Syntax 9.3: The instanceof Operator 445

Common Error 9.5: Don't Use Type Tests 446

Special Topic 9.6: Inheritance and the toString Method 446

Special Topic 9.7: Inheritance and the equals Method 447

9.6 INTERFACE TYPES 448

Syntax 9.4: Interface Types 449

Common Error 9.6: Forgetting to Declare Implementing Methods as Public 453

Special Topic 9.8: Constants in Interfaces 453

Special Topic 9.9: Function Objects 454

Video Example 9.2: Drawing Geometric Shapes ✚

Objects from related classes usually share common behavior. For example, shovels, rakes, and clippers all perform gardening tasks. In this chapter, you will learn how the notion of inheritance expresses the relationship between specialized and general classes. By using inheritance, you will be able to share code between classes and provide services that can be used by multiple classes.

9.1 Inheritance Hierarchies

A subclass inherits data and behavior from a superclass.

In object-oriented design, **inheritance** is a relationship between a more general class (called the **superclass**) and a more specialized class (called the **subclass**). The subclass inherits data and behavior from the superclass. For example, consider the relationships between different kinds of vehicles depicted in Figure 1.

Every car *is a* vehicle. Cars share the common traits of all vehicles, such as the ability to transport people from one place to another. We say that the class Car inherits from the class Vehicle. In this relationship, the Vehicle class is the superclass and the Car class is the subclass. In Figure 2, the superclass and subclass are joined with an arrow that points to the superclass.

You can always use a subclass object in place of a superclass object.

Suppose we have an algorithm that manipulates a Vehicle object. Because a car is a special kind of vehicle, we can use a Car object in such an algorithm, and it will work correctly. The **substitution principle** states that you can always use a subclass object when a superclass object is expected. For example, consider a method that takes an argument of type Vehicle:

```
void processVehicle(Vehicle v)
```

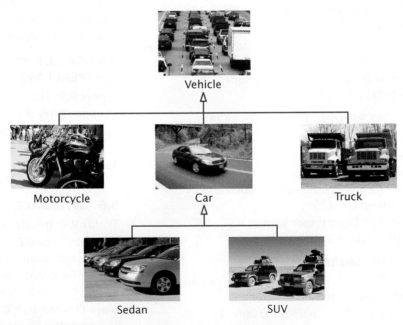

Figure 1 An Inheritance Hierarchy of Vehicle Classes

Figure 2
An Inheritance Diagram

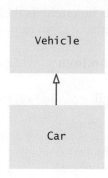

Because Car is a subclass of Vehicle, you can call that method with a Car object:

```
Car myCar = new Car(. . .);
processVehicle(myCar);
```

Why provide a method that processes Vehicle objects instead of Car objects? That method is more useful because it can handle *any* kind of vehicle (including Truck and Motorcycle objects). In general, when we group classes into an inheritance hierarchy, we can share common code among the classes.

In this chapter, we will consider a simple hierarchy of classes. Most likely, you have taken computer-graded quizzes. A quiz consists of questions, and there are different kinds of questions:

- Fill-in-the-blank
- Choice (single or multiple)
- Numeric (where an approximate answer is ok; e.g., 1.33 when the actual answer is 4/3)
- Free response

We will develop a simple but flexible quiz-taking program to illustrate inheritance.

Figure 3 shows an inheritance hierarchy for these question types.

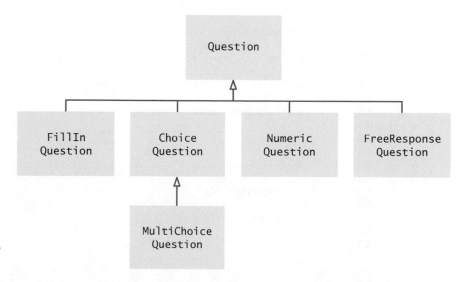

Figure 3
Inheritance Hierarchy
of Question Types

At the root of this hierarchy is the Question type. A question can display its text, and it can check whether a given response is a correct answer.

section_1/Question.java

```java
1  /**
2      A question with a text and an answer.
3  */
4  public class Question
5  {
6     private String text;
7     private String answer;
8
9     /**
10        Constructs a question with empty question and answer.
11     */
12     public Question()
13     {
14        text = "";
15        answer = "";
16     }
17
18     /**
19        Sets the question text.
20        @param questionText the text of this question
21     */
22     public void setText(String questionText)
23     {
24        text = questionText;
25     }
26
27     /**
28        Sets the answer for this question.
29        @param correctResponse the answer
30     */
31     public void setAnswer(String correctResponse)
32     {
33        answer = correctResponse;
34     }
35
36     /**
37        Checks a given response for correctness.
38        @param response the response to check
39        @return true if the response was correct, false otherwise
40     */
41     public boolean checkAnswer(String response)
42     {
43        return response.equals(answer);
44     }
45
46     /**
47        Displays this question.
48     */
49     public void display()
50     {
51        System.out.println(text);
52     }
53  }
```

This question class is very basic. It does not handle multiple-choice questions, numeric questions, and so on. In the following sections, you will see how to form subclasses of the Question class.

Here is a simple test program for the Question class:

section_1/QuestionDemo1.java

```java
1   import java.util.ArrayList;
2   import java.util.Scanner;
3
4   /**
5       This program shows a simple quiz with one question.
6   */
7   public class QuestionDemo1
8   {
9       public static void main(String[] args)
10      {
11          Scanner in = new Scanner(System.in);
12
13          Question q = new Question();
14          q.setText("Who was the inventor of Java?");
15          q.setAnswer("James Gosling");
16
17          q.display();
18          System.out.print("Your answer: ");
19          String response = in.nextLine();
20          System.out.println(q.checkAnswer(response));
21      }
22  }
```

Program Run

```
Who was the inventor of Java?
Your answer: James Gosling
true
```

SELF CHECK

1. Consider classes Manager and Employee. Which should be the superclass and which should be the subclass?

2. What are the inheritance relationships between classes BankAccount, Checking-Account, and SavingsAccount?

3. Figure 7.2 shows an inheritance diagram of exception classes in Java. List all superclasses of the class RuntimeException.

4. Consider the method doSomething(Car c). List all vehicle classes from Figure 1 whose objects *cannot* be passed to this method.

5. Should a class Quiz inherit from the class Question? Why or why not?

Practice It   Now you can try these exercises at the end of the chapter: R9.1, R9.7, R9.9.

Use a Single Class for Variation in Values, Inheritance for Variation in Behavior

The purpose of inheritance is to model objects with different *behavior*. When students first learn about inheritance, they have a tendency to overuse it, by creating multiple classes even though the variation could be expressed with a simple instance variable.

Consider a program that tracks the fuel efficiency of a fleet of cars by logging the distance traveled and the refueling amounts. Some cars in the fleet are hybrids. Should you create a subclass HybridCar? Not in this application. Hybrids don't behave any differently than other cars when it comes to driving and refueling. They just have a better fuel efficiency. A single Car class with an instance variable

```
double milesPerGallon;
```

is entirely sufficient.

However, if you write a program that shows how to repair different kinds of vehicles, then it makes sense to have a separate class HybridCar. When it comes to repairs, hybrid cars behave differently from other cars.

9.2 Implementing Subclasses

In this section, you will see how to form a subclass and how a subclass automatically inherits functionality from its superclass.

Suppose you want to write a program that handles questions such as the following:

```
In which country was the inventor of Java born?
1. Australia
2. Canada
3. Denmark
4. United States
```

You could write a ChoiceQuestion class from scratch, with methods to set up the question, display it, and check the answer. But you don't have to. Instead, use inheritance and implement ChoiceQuestion as a subclass of the Question class (see Figure 4).

In Java, you form a subclass by specifying what makes the subclass different from its superclass.

> A subclass inherits all methods that it does not override.

Subclass objects automatically have the instance variables that are declared in the superclass. You only declare instance variables that are not part of the superclass objects.

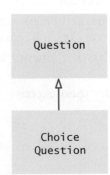

Figure 4
The ChoiceQuestion Class is a Subclass of the Question Class

Like the manufacturer of a stretch limo, who starts with a regular car and modifies it, a programmer makes a subclass by modifying another class.

> A subclass can override a superclass method by providing a new implementation.

The subclass inherits all public methods from the superclass. You declare any methods that are *new* to the subclass, and *change* the implementation of inherited methods if the inherited behavior is not appropriate. When you supply a new implementation for an inherited method, you **override** the method.

A `ChoiceQuestion` object differs from a `Question` object in three ways:

- Its objects store the various choices for the answer.
- There is a method for adding answer choices.
- The `display` method of the `ChoiceQuestion` class shows these choices so that the respondent can choose one of them.

When the `ChoiceQuestion` class inherits from the `Question` class, it needs to spell out these three differences:

```java
public class ChoiceQuestion extends Question
{
    // This instance variable is added to the subclass
    private ArrayList<String> choices;

    // This method is added to the subclass
    public void addChoice(String choice, boolean correct) { . . . }

    // This method overrides a method from the superclass
    public void display() { . . . }
}
```

> The extends reserved word indicates that a class inherits from a superclass.

The reserved word `extends` denotes inheritance.

Figure 5 shows the layout of a `ChoiceQuestion` object. It has the `text` and `answer` instance variables that are declared in the `Question` superclass, and it adds an additional instance variable, `choices`.

The `addChoice` method is specific to the `ChoiceQuestion` class. You can only apply it to `ChoiceQuestion` objects, not general `Question` objects.

In contrast, the `display` method is a method that already exists in the superclass. The subclass overrides this method, so that the choices can be properly displayed.

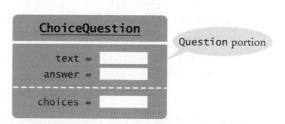

Figure 5 Data Layout of Subclass Object

Syntax 9.1 Subclass Declaration

Syntax   public class *SubclassName* extends *SuperclassName*
{
    instance variables
    methods
}

The reserved word extends
denotes inheritance.

Declare instance variables
that are added to
the subclass.

Subclass   Superclass

public class ChoiceQuestion extends Question
{
    private ArrayList<String> choices

Declare methods that are
added to the subclass.

    public void addChoice(String choice, boolean correct) { . . . }

Declare methods that
the subclass overrides.

    public void display() { . . . }
}

All other methods of the Question class are automatically inherited by the Choice-
Question class.

You can call the inherited methods on a subclass object:

```
choiceQuestion.setAnswer("2");
```

However, the private instance variables of the superclass are inaccessible. Because
these variables are private data of the superclass, only the superclass has access to
them. The subclass has no more access rights than any other class.

In particular, the ChoiceQuestion methods cannot directly access the instance variable answer. These methods must use the public interface of the Question class to access
its private data, just like every other method.

To illustrate this point, let's implement the addChoice method. The method has two
arguments: the choice to be added (which is appended to the list of choices), and a
Boolean value to indicate whether this choice is correct. For example,

```
question.addChoice("Canada", true);
```

The first argument is added to the choices variable. If the second argument is true, then
the answer instance variable becomes the number of the current choice. For example, if
choices.size() is 2, then answer is set to the string "2".

```
public void addChoice(String choice, boolean correct)
{
    choices.add(choice);
    if (correct)
    {
        // Convert choices.size() to string
        String choiceString = "" + choices.size();
        setAnswer(choiceString);
    }
}
```

You can't just access the answer variable in the superclass. Fortunately, the Question class has a setAnswer method. You can call that method. On which object? The

question that you are currently modifying—that is, the implicit parameter of the ChoiceQuestion.addChoice method. As you saw in Chapter 8, if you invoke a method on the implicit parameter, you don't have to specify the implicit parameter and can write just the method name:

```
setAnswer(choiceString);
```

If you prefer, you can make it clear that the method is executed on the implicit parameter:

```
this.setAnswer(choiceString);
```

SELF CHECK

6. Suppose q is an object of the class Question and cq an object of the class Choice-Question. Which of the following calls are legal?

   a. q.setAnswer(response)

   b. cq.setAnswer(response)

   c. q.addChoice(choice, true)

   d. cq.addChoice(choice, true)

7. Suppose the class Employee is declared as follows:

```
public class Employee
{
    private String name;
    private double baseSalary;

    public void setName(String newName) { . . . }
    public void setBaseSalary(double newSalary) { . . . }
    public String getName() { . . . }
    public double getSalary() { . . . }
}
```

   Declare a class Manager that inherits from the class Employee and adds an instance variable bonus for storing a salary bonus. Omit constructors and methods.

8. Which instance variables does the Manager class from Self Check 7 have?

9. In the Manager class, provide the method header (but not the implementation) for a method that overrides the getSalary method from the class Employee.

10. Which methods does the Manager class from Self Check 9 inherit?

Practice It   Now you can try these exercises at the end of the chapter: R9.3, P9.6, P9.10.

Common Error 9.1

Replicating Instance Variables from the Superclass

A subclass has no access to the private instance variables of the superclass.

```
public ChoiceQuestion(String questionText)
{
    text = questionText; // Error—tries to access private superclass variable
}
```

When faced with a compiler error, beginners commonly "solve" this issue by adding *another* instance variable with the same name to the subclass:

```
public class ChoiceQuestion extends Question
{
```

```
        private ArrayList<String> choices;
        private String text; // Don't!
        . . .
    }
```

Sure, now the constructor compiles, but it doesn't set the correct text! Such a ChoiceQuestion object has two instance variables, both named text. The constructor sets one of them, and the display method displays the other.

ChoiceQuestion

text =
answer =

choices =
text =

Question portion

Common Error 9.2

Confusing Super- and Subclasses

If you compare an object of type ChoiceQuestion with an object of type Question, you find that

- The reserved word extends suggests that the ChoiceQuestion object is an extended version of a Question.
- The ChoiceQuestion object is larger; it has an added instance variable, choices.
- The ChoiceQuestion object is more capable; it has an addChoice method.

It seems a superior object in every way. So why is ChoiceQuestion called the *subclass* and Question the *superclass*?

The *super/sub* terminology comes from set theory. Look at the set of all questions. Not all of them are ChoiceQuestion objects; some of them are other kinds of questions. Therefore, the set of ChoiceQuestion objects is a *subset* of the set of all Question objects, and the set of Question objects is a *superset* of the set of ChoiceQuestion objects. The more specialized objects in the subset have a richer state and more capabilities.

9.3 Overriding Methods

An overriding method can extend or replace the functionality of the superclass method.

The subclass inherits the methods from the superclass. If you are not satisfied with the behavior of an inherited method, you *override* it by specifying a new implementation in the subclass.

Consider the display method of the ChoiceQuestion class. It overrides the superclass display method in order to show the choices for the answer. This method *extends* the functionality of the superclass version. This means that the subclass method carries out the action of the superclass method (in our case, displaying the question text), and it also does some additional work (in our case, displaying the choices). In other cases, a subclass method *replaces* the functionality of a superclass method, implementing an entirely different behavior.

Let us turn to the implementation of the display method of the ChoiceQuestion class. The method needs to

- Display the question text.
- Display the answer choices.

The second part is easy because the answer choices are an instance variable of the subclass.

```java
public class ChoiceQuestion
{
   . . .
   public void display()
   {
      // Display the question text
      . . .
      // Display the answer choices
      for (int i = 0; i < choices.size(); i++)
      {
         int choiceNumber = i + 1;
         System.out.println(choiceNumber + ": " + choices.get(i));
      }
   }
}
```

But how do you get the question text? You can't access the text variable of the superclass directly because it is private.

Instead, you can call the display method of the superclass, by using the reserved word super:

Use the reserved word super to call a superclass method.

```java
public void display()
{
   // Display the question text
   super.display(); // OK
   // Display the answer choices
   . . .
}
```

If you omit the reserved word super, then the method will not work as intended.

```java
public void display()
{
   // Display the question text
   display(); // Error—invokes this.display()
   . . .
}
```

ANIMATION
Inheritance

Because the implicit parameter this is of type ChoiceQuestion, and there is a method named display in the ChoiceQuestion class, that method will be called—but that is just the method you are currently writing! The method would call itself over and over.

Here is the complete program that lets you take a quiz consisting of two Choice-Question objects. We construct both objects and pass them to a method presentQuestion. That method displays the question to the user and checks whether the user response is correct.

section_3/QuestionDemo2.java

```java
1   import java.util.Scanner;
2
3   /**
4      This program shows a simple quiz with two choice questions.
5   */
6   public class QuestionDemo2
7   {
8      public static void main(String[] args)
9      {
```

```
10        ChoiceQuestion first = new ChoiceQuestion();
11        first.setText("What was the original name of the Java language?");
12        first.addChoice("*7", false);
13        first.addChoice("Duke", false);
14        first.addChoice("Oak", true);
15        first.addChoice("Gosling", false);
16
17        ChoiceQuestion second = new ChoiceQuestion();
18        second.setText("In which country was the inventor of Java born?");
19        second.addChoice("Australia", false);
20        second.addChoice("Canada", true);
21        second.addChoice("Denmark", false);
22        second.addChoice("United States", false);
23
24        presentQuestion(first);
25        presentQuestion(second);
26     }
27
28     /**
29        Presents a question to the user and checks the response.
30        @param q the question
31     */
32     public static void presentQuestion(ChoiceQuestion q)
33     {
34        q.display();
35        System.out.print("Your answer: ");
36        Scanner in = new Scanner(System.in);
37        String response = in.nextLine();
38        System.out.println(q.checkAnswer(response));
39     }
40  }
```

section_3/ChoiceQuestion.java

```
1   import java.util.ArrayList;
2
3   /**
4      A question with multiple choices.
5   */
6   public class ChoiceQuestion extends Question
7   {
8      private ArrayList<String> choices;
9
10     /**
11        Constructs a choice question with no choices.
12     */
13     public ChoiceQuestion()
14     {
15        choices = new ArrayList<String>();
16     }
17
18     /**
19        Adds an answer choice to this question.
20        @param choice the choice to add
21        @param correct true if this is the correct choice, false otherwise
22     */
23     public void addChoice(String choice, boolean correct)
24     {
```

```
25        choices.add(choice);
26        if (correct)
27        {
28           // Convert choices.size() to string
29           String choiceString = "" + choices.size();
30           setAnswer(choiceString);
31        }
32     }
33
34     public void display()
35     {
36        // Display the question text
37        super.display();
38        // Display the answer choices
39        for (int i = 0; i < choices.size(); i++)
40        {
41           int choiceNumber = i + 1;
42           System.out.println(choiceNumber + ": " + choices.get(i));
43        }
44     }
45  }
```

Program Run

```
What was the original name of the Java language?
1: *7
2: Duke
3: Oak
4: Gosling
Your answer: *7
false
In which country was the inventor of Java born?
1: Australia
2: Canada
3: Denmark
4: United States
Your answer: 2
true
```

SELF CHECK

11. What is wrong with the following implementation of the display method?

```
public class ChoiceQuestion
{
   . . .
   public void display()
   {
      System.out.println(text);
      for (int i = 0; i < choices.size(); i++)
      {
         int choiceNumber = i + 1;
         System.out.println(choiceNumber + ": " + choices.get(i));
      }
   }
}
```

12. What is wrong with the following implementation of the display method?

```
public class ChoiceQuestion
{
```

```
   . . .
   public void display()
   {
      this.display();
      for (int i = 0; i < choices.size(); i++)
      {
         int choiceNumber = i + 1;
         System.out.println(choiceNumber + ": " + choices.get(i));
      }
   }
}
```

13. Look again at the implementation of the addChoice method that calls the setAnswer method of the superclass. Why don't you need to call super.setAnswer?

14. In the Manager class of Self Check 7, override the getName method so that managers have a * before their name (such as *Lin, Sally).

15. In the Manager class of Self Check 9, override the getSalary method so that it returns the sum of the salary and the bonus.

Practice It   Now you can try these exercises at the end of the chapter: P9.1, P9.2, P9.11.

Common Error 9.3

Accidental Overloading

In Java, two methods can have the same name, provided they differ in their parameter types. For example, the PrintStream class has methods called println with headers

```
void println(int x)
```

and

```
void println(String x)
```

These are different methods, each with its own implementation. The Java compiler considers them to be completely unrelated. We say that the println name is **overloaded**. This is different from overriding, where a subclass method provides an implementation of a method whose parameter variables have the *same* types.

If you mean to override a method but use a parameter variable with a different type, then you accidentally introduce an overloaded method. For example,

```
public class ChoiceQuestion extends Question
{
   . . .
   public void display(PrintStream out)
   // Does not override void display()
   {
      . . .
   }
}
```

The compiler will not complain. It thinks that you want to provide a method just for PrintStream arguments, while inheriting another method void display().

When overriding a method, be sure to check that the types of the parameter variables match exactly.

Common Error 9.4

Forgetting to Use super When Invoking a Superclass Method

A common error in extending the functionality of a superclass method is to forget the reserved word super. For example, to compute the salary of a manager, get the salary of the underlying Employee object and add a bonus:

```java
public class Manager
{
    . . .
    public double getSalary()
    {
        double baseSalary = getSalary();
            // Error: should be super.getSalary()
        return baseSalary + bonus;
    }
}
```

Here getSalary() refers to the getSalary method applied to the implicit parameter of the method. The implicit parameter is of type Manager, and there is a getSalary method in the Manager class. Calling that method is a recursive call, which will never stop. Instead, you must tell the compiler to invoke the superclass method.

Whenever you call a superclass method from a subclass method with the same name, be sure to use the reserved word super.

Special Topic 9.1

Calling the Superclass Constructor

Consider the process of constructing a subclass object. A subclass constructor can only initialize the instance variables of the subclass. But the superclass instance variables also need to be initialized. Unless you specify otherwise, the superclass instance variables are initialized with the constructor of the superclass that has no arguments.

> Unless specified otherwise, the subclass constructor calls the superclass constructor with no arguments.

In order to specify another constructor, you use the super reserved word, together with the arguments of the superclass constructor, as the *first statement* of the subclass constructor.

For example, suppose the Question superclass had a constructor for setting the question text. Here is how a subclass constructor could call that superclass constructor:

> To call a superclass constructor, use the super reserved word in the first statement of the subclass constructor.

```java
public ChoiceQuestion(String questionText)
{
    super(questionText);
    choices = new ArrayList<String>();
}
```

In our example program, we used the superclass constructor with no arguments. However, if all superclass constructors have arguments, you must use the super syntax and provide the arguments for a superclass constructor.

> The constructor of a subclass can pass arguments to a superclass constructor, using the reserved word super.

When the reserved word super is followed by a parenthesis, it indicates a call to the superclass constructor. When used in this way, the constructor call must be *the first statement of the subclass constructor*. If super is followed by a period and a method name, on the other hand, it indicates a call to a superclass method, as you saw in the preceding section. Such a call can be made anywhere in any subclass method.

Syntax 9.2 Constructor with Superclass Initializer

Syntax   public *ClassName*(*parameterType parameterName*, . . .)
             {
                 super(*arguments*);
                 . . .
             }

The superclass
constructor
is called first.

public ChoiceQuestion(String questionText)
{
    super(questionText);
    choices = new ArrayList<String>;
}

If you omit the superclass constructor call, the superclass constructor with no arguments is invoked.

The constructor
body can contain
additional statements.

9.4 Polymorphism

In this section, you will learn how to use inheritance for processing objects of different types in the same program.

Consider our first sample program. It presented two Question objects to the user. The second sample program presented two ChoiceQuestion objects. Can we write a program that shows a mixture of both question types?

With inheritance, this goal is very easy to realize. In order to present a question to the user, we need not know the exact type of the question. We just display the question and check whether the user supplied the correct answer. The Question superclass has methods for this purpose. Therefore, we can simply declare the parameter variable of the presentQuestion method to have the type Question:

```
public static void presentQuestion(Question q)
{
    q.display();
    System.out.print("Your answer: ");
    Scanner in = new Scanner(System.in);
    String response = in.nextLine();
    System.out.println(q.checkAnswer(response));
}
```

As discussed in Section 9.1, we can substitute a subclass object whenever a superclass object is expected:

```
ChoiceQuestion second = new ChoiceQuestion();
. . .
presentQuestion(second); // OK to pass a ChoiceQuestion
```

A subclass reference
can be used when a
superclass reference
is expected.

When the presentQuestion method executes, the object references stored in second and q refer to the same object of type ChoiceQuestion (see Figure 6).

However, the *variable* q knows less than the full story about the object to which it refers (see Figure 7).

Because q is a variable of type Question, you can call the display and checkAnswer methods. You cannot call the addChoice method, though—it is not a method of the Question superclass.

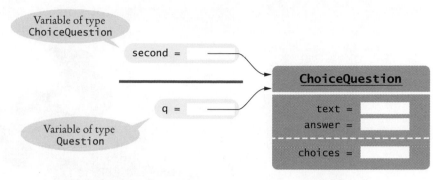

Figure 6 Variables of Different Types Referring to the Same Object

ANIMATION
Polymorphism

This is as it should be. After all, it happens that in this method call, q refers to a ChoiceQuestion. In another method call, q might refer to a plain Question or an entirely different subclass of Question.

Now let's have a closer look inside the presentQuestion method. It starts with the call

```
q.display(); // Does it call Question.display or ChoiceQuestion.display?
```

Which display method is called? If you look at the program output on page 433, you will see that the method called depends on the contents of the parameter variable q. In the first case, q refers to a Question object, so the Question.display method is called. But in the second case, q refers to a ChoiceQuestion, so the ChoiceQuestion.display method is called, showing the list of choices.

In Java, method calls *are always determined by the type of the actual object*, not the type of the variable containing the object reference. This is called **dynamic method lookup**.

Dynamic method lookup allows us to treat objects of different classes in a uniform way. This feature is called **polymorphism**. We ask multiple objects to carry out a task, and each object does so in its own way.

Polymorphism ("having multiple shapes") allows us to manipulate objects that share a set of tasks, even though the tasks are executed in different ways.

Polymorphism makes programs *easily extensible*. Suppose we want to have a new kind of question for calculations, where we are willing to accept an approximate answer. All we need to do is to declare a new class NumericQuestion that extends Question, with its own checkAnswer method. Then we can call the presentQuestion method with a mixture of plain questions, choice questions, and numeric questions. The presentQuestion method need not be changed at all! Thanks to dynamic method lookup, method calls to the display and checkAnswer methods automatically select the correct method of the newly declared classes.

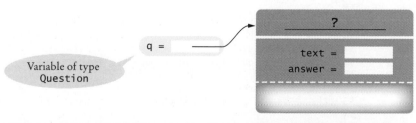

Figure 7 A Question Reference Can Refer to an Object of Any Subclass of Question

In the same way that vehicles can differ in their method of locomotion,
polymorphic objects carry out tasks in different ways.

section_4/QuestionDemo3.java

```java
1   import java.util.Scanner;
2
3   /**
4      This program shows a simple quiz with two question types.
5   */
6   public class QuestionDemo3
7   {
8      public static void main(String[] args)
9      {
10        Question first = new Question();
11        first.setText("Who was the inventor of Java?");
12        first.setAnswer("James Gosling");
13
14        ChoiceQuestion second = new ChoiceQuestion();
15        second.setText("In which country was the inventor of Java born?");
16        second.addChoice("Australia", false);
17        second.addChoice("Canada", true);
18        second.addChoice("Denmark", false);
19        second.addChoice("United States", false);
20
21        presentQuestion(first);
22        presentQuestion(second);
23     }
24
25     /**
26        Presents a question to the user and checks the response.
27        @param q the question
28     */
29     public static void presentQuestion(Question q)
30     {
31        q.display();
32        System.out.print("Your answer: ");
33        Scanner in = new Scanner(System.in);
34        String response = in.nextLine();
35        System.out.println(q.checkAnswer(response));
36     }
37  }
```

Program Run

```
Who was the inventor of Java?
Your answer: Bjarne Stroustrup
false
In which country was the inventor of Java born?
1: Australia
2: Canada
3: Denmark
4: United States
Your answer: 2
true
```

SELF CHECK

16. Assuming `SavingsAccount` is a subclass of `BankAccount`, which of the following code fragments are valid in Java?

    a. `BankAccount account = new SavingsAccount();`

    b. `SavingsAccount account2 = new BankAccount();`

    c. `BankAccount account = null;`

    d. `SavingsAccount account2 = account;`

17. If `account` is a variable of type `BankAccount` that holds a non-null reference, what do you know about the object to which `account` refers?

18. Declare an array `quiz` that can hold a mixture of `Question` and `ChoiceQuestion` objects.

19. Consider the code fragment

    ```
    ChoiceQuestion cq = . . .; // A non-null value
    cq.display();
    ```

    Which actual method is being called?

20. Is the method call `Math.sqrt(2)` resolved through dynamic method lookup?

Practice It Now you can try these exercises at the end of the chapter: R9.6, P9.4, P9.20.

Special Topic 9.2

Dynamic Method Lookup and the Implicit Parameter

Suppose we add the `presentQuestion` method to the `Question` class itself:

```
void presentQuestion()
{
    display();
    System.out.print("Your answer: ");
    Scanner in = new Scanner(System.in);
    String response = in.nextLine();
    System.out.println(checkAnswer(response));
}
```

Now consider the call

```
ChoiceQuestion cq = new ChoiceQuestion();
cq.setText("In which country was the inventor of Java born?");
. . .
cq.presentQuestion();
```

Which `display` and `checkAnswer` method will the `presentQuestion` method call? If you look inside the code of the `presentQuestion` method, you can see that these methods are executed on the implicit parameter.

```java
public class Question
{
    public void presentQuestion()
    {
        this.display();
        System.out.print("Your answer: ");
        Scanner in = new Scanner(System.in);
        String response = in.nextLine();
        System.out.println(this.checkAnswer(response));
    }
}
```

The implicit parameter `this` in our call is a reference to an object of type `ChoiceQuestion`. Because of dynamic method lookup, the `ChoiceQuestion` versions of the `display` and `checkAnswer` methods are called automatically. This happens even though the `presentQuestion` method is declared in the `Question` class, which has *no knowledge* of the `ChoiceQuestion` class.

As you can see, polymorphism is a very powerful mechanism. The `Question` class supplies a `presentQuestion` method that specifies the common nature of presenting a question, namely to display it and check the response. How the displaying and checking are carried out is left to the subclasses.

Special Topic 9.3

Abstract Classes

When you extend an existing class, you have the choice whether or not to override the methods of the superclass. Sometimes, it is desirable to *force* programmers to override a method. That happens when there is no good default for the superclass, and only the subclass programmer can know how to implement the method properly.

Here is an example: Suppose the First National Bank of Java decides that every account type must have some monthly fees. Therefore, a `deductFees` method should be added to the `Account` class:

```java
public class Account
{
    public void deductFees() { . . . }
    . . .
}
```

But what should this method do? Of course, we could have the method do nothing. But then a programmer implementing a new subclass might simply forget to implement the `deductFees` method, and the new account would inherit the do-nothing method of the superclass. There is a better way—declare the `deductFees` method as an **abstract method**:

```java
public abstract void deductFees();
```

An abstract method has no implementation. This forces the implementors of subclasses to specify concrete implementations of this method. (Of course, some subclasses might decide to implement a do-nothing method, but then that is their choice—not a silently inherited default.)

You cannot construct objects of classes with abstract methods. For example, once the `Account` class has an abstract method, the compiler will flag an attempt to create a `new Account()` as an error.

> An abstract method is a method whose implementation is not specified.

> An abstract class is a class that cannot be instantiated.

A class for which you cannot create objects is called an **abstract class**. A class for which you can create objects is sometimes called a **concrete class**. In Java, you must declare all abstract classes with the reserved word abstract:

```
public abstract class Account
{
    public abstract void deductFees();
    . . .
}

public class SavingsAccount extends Account // Not abstract
{
    . . .
    public void deductFees() // Provides an implementation
    {
        . . .
    }
}
```

Note that you cannot construct an *object* of an abstract class, but you can still have an *object reference* whose type is an abstract class. Of course, the actual object to which it refers must be an instance of a concrete subclass:

```
Account anAccount; // OK
anAccount = new Account(); // Error—Account is abstract
anAccount = new SavingsAccount(); // OK
anAccount = null; // OK
```

The reason for using abstract classes is to force programmers to create subclasses. By specifying certain methods as abstract, you avoid the trouble of coming up with useless default methods that others might inherit by accident.

Special Topic 9.4

Final Methods and Classes

In Special Topic 9.3 you saw how you can force other programmers to create subclasses of abstract classes and override abstract methods. Occasionally, you may want to do the opposite and *prevent* other programmers from creating subclasses or from overriding certain methods. In these situations, you use the final reserved word. For example, the String class in the standard Java library has been declared as

```
public final class String { . . . }
```

That means that nobody can extend the String class. When you have a reference of type String, it must contain a String object, never an object of a subclass.

You can also declare individual methods as final:

```
public class SecureAccount extends BankAccount
{
    . . .
    public final boolean checkPassword(String password)
    {
        . . .
    }
}
```

This way, nobody can override the checkPassword method with another method that simply returns true.

Protected Access

We ran into a hurdle when trying to implement the display method of the ChoiceQuestion class. That method wanted to access the instance variable text of the superclass. Our remedy was to use the appropriate method of the superclass to display the text.

Java offers another solution to this problem. The superclass can declare an instance variable as *protected*:

```
public class Question
{
    protected String text;
    . . .
}
```

Protected data in an object can be accessed by the methods of the object's class and all its subclasses. For example, ChoiceQuestion inherits from Question, so its methods can access the protected instance variables of the Question superclass.

Some programmers like the protected access feature because it seems to strike a balance between absolute protection (making instance variables private) and no protection at all (making instance variables public). However, experience has shown that protected instance variables are subject to the same kinds of problems as public instance variables. The designer of the superclass has no control over the authors of subclasses. Any of the subclass methods can corrupt the superclass data. Furthermore, classes with protected variables are hard to modify. Even if the author of the superclass would like to change the data implementation, the protected variables cannot be changed, because someone somewhere out there might have written a subclass whose code depends on them.

In Java, protected variables have another drawback—they are accessible not just by subclasses, but also by other classes in the same package (see Section 12.4 for information about packages).

It is best to leave all data private. If you want to grant access to the data to subclass methods only, consider making the *accessor* method protected.

Developing an Inheritance Hierarchy

When you work with a set of classes, some of which are more general and others more specialized, you want to organize them into an inheritance hierarchy. This enables you to process objects of different classes in a uniform way.

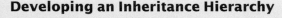

As an example, we will consider a bank that offers customers the following account types:

- A savings account that earns interest. The interest compounds monthly and is computed on the minimum monthly balance.

- A checking account that has no interest, gives you three free withdrawals per month, and charges a $1 transaction fee for each additional withdrawal.

The program will manage a set of accounts of both types, and it should be structured so that other account types can be added without affecting the main processing loop. Supply a menu

```
D)eposit  W)ithdraw  M)onth end  Q)uit
```

For deposits and withdrawals, query the account number and amount. Print the balance of the account after each transaction.

In the "Month end" command, accumulate interest or clear the transaction counter, depending on the type of the bank account. Then print the balance of all accounts.

Step 1   List the classes that are part of the hierarchy.

In our case, the problem description yields two classes: SavingsAccount and CheckingAccount. Of course, you could implement each of them separately. But that would not be a good idea because the classes would have to repeat common functionality, such as updating an account balance. We need another class that can be responsible for that common functionality. The problem statement does not explicitly mention such a class. Therefore, we need to discover it. Of course, in this case, the solution is simple. Savings accounts and checking accounts are special cases of a bank account. Therefore, we will introduce a common superclass BankAccount.

Step 2   Organize the classes into an inheritance hierarchy.

Draw an inheritance diagram that shows super- and subclasses. Here is one for our example:

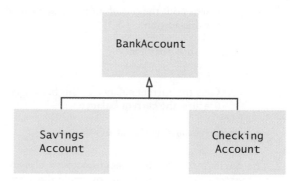

Step 3   Determine the common responsibilities.

In Step 2, you will have identified a class at the base of the hierarchy. That class needs to have sufficient responsibilities to carry out the tasks at hand. To find out what those tasks are, write pseudocode for processing the objects.

```
For each user command
    If it is a deposit or withdrawal
        Deposit or withdraw the amount from the specified account.
        Print the balance.
    If it is month end processing
        For each account
            Call month end processing.
            Print the balance.
```

From the pseudocode, we obtain the following list of common responsibilities that every bank account must carry out:

```
Deposit money.
Withdraw money.
Get the balance.
Carry out month end processing.
```

Step 4   Decide which methods are overridden in subclasses.

For each subclass and each of the common responsibilities, decide whether the behavior can be inherited or whether it needs to be overridden. Be sure to declare any methods that are inherited or overridden in the root of the hierarchy.

```java
public class BankAccount
{
    . . .
```

```
      /**
          Makes a deposit into this account.
          @param amount the amount of the deposit
      */
      public void deposit(double amount) { . . . }

      /**
          Makes a withdrawal from this account, or charges a penalty if
          sufficient funds are not available.
          @param amount the amount of the withdrawal
      */
      public void withdraw(double amount) { . . . }

      /**
          Carries out the end of month processing that is appropriate
          for this account.
      */
      public void monthEnd() { . . . }

      /**
          Gets the current balance of this bank account.
          @return the current balance
      */
      public double getBalance() { . . . }
   }
```

The SavingsAccount and CheckingAccount classes both override the monthEnd method. The SavingsAccount class must also override the withdraw method to track the minimum balance. The CheckingAccount class must update a transaction count in the withdraw method.

Step 5 Declare the public interface of each subclass.

Typically, subclasses have responsibilities other than those of the superclass. List those, as well as the methods that need to be overridden. You also need to specify how the objects of the subclasses should be constructed.

In this example, we need a way of setting the interest rate for the savings account. In addition, we need to specify constructors and overridden methods.

```
   public class SavingsAccount extends BankAccount
   {
      . . .
      /**
          Constructs a savings account with a zero balance.
      */
      public SavingsAccount() { . . . }

      /**
          Sets the interest rate for this account.
          @param rate the monthly interest rate in percent
      */
      public void setInterestRate(double rate) { . . . }

      // These methods override superclass methods
      public void withdraw(double amount) { . . . }
      public void monthEnd() { . . . }
   }

   public class CheckingAccount extends BankAccount
   {
      . . .
      /**
```

Constructs a checking account with a zero balance.
```
*/
public CheckingAccount() { . . . }

// These methods override superclass methods
public void withdraw(double amount) { . . . }
public void monthEnd() { . . . }
}
```

Step 6   Identify instance variables.

List the instance variables for each class. If you find an instance variable that is common to all classes, be sure to place it in the base of the hierarchy.

All accounts have a balance. We store that value in the BankAccount superclass:

```
public class BankAccount
{
    private double balance;
    . . .
}
```

The SavingsAccount class needs to store the interest rate. It also needs to store the minimum monthly balance, which must be updated by all withdrawals.

```
public class SavingsAccount extends BankAccount
{
    private double interestRate;
    private double minBalance;
    . . .
}
```

The CheckingAccount class needs to count the withdrawals, so that the charge can be applied after the free withdrawal limit is reached.

```
public class CheckingAccount extends BankAccount
{
    private int withdrawals;
    . . .
}
```

Step 7   Implement constructors and methods.

The methods of the BankAccount class update or return the balance.

```
public void deposit(double amount)
{
    balance = balance + amount;
}

public void withdraw(double amount)
{
    balance = balance - amount;
}

public double getBalance()
{
    return balance;
}
```

At the level of the BankAccount superclass, we can say nothing about end of month processing. We choose to make that method do nothing:

```
public void monthEnd()
{
}
```

In the `withdraw` method of the `SavingsAccount` class, the minimum balance is updated. Note the call to the superclass method:

```java
public void withdraw(double amount)
{
   super.withdraw(amount);
   double balance = getBalance();
   if (balance < minBalance)
   {
      minBalance = balance;
   }
}
```

In the `monthEnd` method of the `SavingsAccount` class, the interest is deposited into the account. We must call the `deposit` method because we have no direct access to the `balance` instance variable. The minimum balance is reset for the next month.

```java
public void monthEnd()
{
   double interest = minBalance * interestRate / 100;
   deposit(interest);
   minBalance = getBalance();
}
```

The `withdraw` method of the `CheckingAccount` class needs to check the withdrawal count. If there have been too many withdrawals, a charge is applied. Again, note how the method invokes the superclass method:

```java
public void withdraw(double amount)
{
   final int FREE_WITHDRAWALS = 3;
   final int WITHDRAWAL_FEE = 1;

   super.withdraw(amount);
   withdrawals++;
   if (withdrawals > FREE_WITHDRAWALS)
   {
      super.withdraw(WITHDRAWAL_FEE);
   }
}
```

End of month processing for a checking account simply resets the withdrawal count.

```java
public void monthEnd()
{
   withdrawals = 0;
}
```

Step 8   Construct objects of different subclasses and process them.

In our sample program, we allocate 5 checking accounts and 5 savings accounts and store their addresses in an array of bank accounts. Then we accept user commands and execute deposits, withdrawals, and monthly processing.

```java
BankAccount[] accounts = . . .;
. . .
Scanner in = new Scanner(System.in);
boolean done = false;
while (!done)
{
   System.out.print("D)eposit  W)ithdraw  M)onth end  Q)uit: ");
   String input = in.next();
   if (input.equals("D") || input.equals("W")) // Deposit or withdrawal
   {
```

```
        System.out.print("Enter account number and amount: ");
        int num = in.nextInt();
        double amount = in.nextDouble();

        if (input.equals("D")) { accounts[num].deposit(amount); }
        else { accounts[num].withdraw(amount); }

        System.out.println("Balance: " + accounts[num].getBalance());
     }
     else if (input.equals("M")) // Month end processing
     {
        for (int n = 0; n < accounts.length; n++)
        {
           accounts[n].monthEnd();
           System.out.println(n + " " + accounts[n].getBalance());
        }
     }
     else if (input == "Q")
     {
        done = true;
     }
  }
```

ONLINE EXAMPLE

➕ The complete program with BankAccount, SavingsAccount, and CheckingAccount classes.

WORKED EXAMPLE 9.1

Implementing an Employee Hierarchy for Payroll Processing

This Worked Example shows how to implement payroll processing that works for different kinds of employees.

VIDEO EXAMPLE 9.1

Building a Discussion Board

In this Video Example, we will build a discussion board for students and instructors.

9.5 Object: The Cosmic Superclass

In Java, every class that is declared without an explicit extends clause automatically extends the class Object. That is, the class Object is the direct or indirect superclass of *every* class in Java (see Figure 8). The Object class defines several very general methods, including

- toString, which yields a string describing the object (Section 9.5.1).
- equals, which compares objects with each other (Section 9.5.2).
- hashCode, which yields a numerical code for storing the object in a set (see Special Topic 15.1).

➕ Available online in WileyPLUS and at www.wiley.com/college/horstmann.

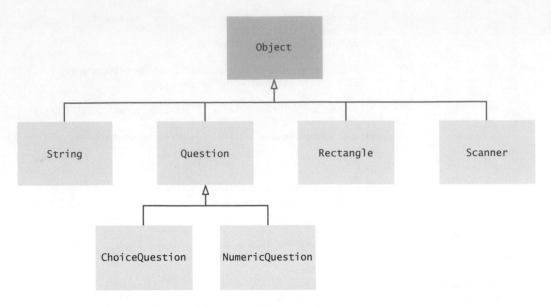

Figure 8 The Object Class Is the Superclass of Every Java Class

9.5.1 Overriding the toString Method

The toString method returns a string representation for each object. It is often used for debugging. For example, consider the Rectangle class in the standard Java library. Its toString method shows the state of a rectangle:

```
Rectangle box = new Rectangle(5, 10, 20, 30);
String s = box.toString();
   // Sets s to "java.awt.Rectangle[x=5,y=10,width=20,height=30]"
```

The toString method is called automatically whenever you concatenate a string with an object. Here is an example:

```
"box=" + box;
```

On one side of the + concatenation operator is a string, but on the other side is an object reference. The Java compiler automatically invokes the toString method to turn the object into a string. Then both strings are concatenated. In this case, the result is the string

```
"box=java.awt.Rectangle[x=5,y=10,width=20,height=30]"
```

The compiler can invoke the toString method, because it knows that *every* object has a toString method: Every class extends the Object class, and that class declares toString.

As you know, numbers are also converted to strings when they are concatenated with other strings. For example,

```
int age = 18;
String s = "Harry's age is " + age;
   // Sets s to "Harry's age is 18"
```

In this case, the toString method is *not* involved. Numbers are not objects, and there is no toString method for them. Fortunately, there is only a small set of primitive types, and the compiler knows how to convert them to strings.

Let's try the `toString` method for the `BankAccount` class:

```
BankAccount momsSavings = new BankAccount(5000);
String s = momsSavings.toString(); // Sets s to something like "BankAccount@d24606bf"
```

That's disappointing—all that's printed is the name of the class, followed by the **hash code**, a seemingly random code. The hash code can be used to tell objects apart—different objects are likely to have different hash codes. (See Special Topic 15.1 for the details.)

> Override the toString method to yield a string that describes the object's state.

We don't care about the hash code. We want to know what is *inside* the object. But, of course, the `toString` method of the `Object` class does not know what is inside the `BankAccount` class. Therefore, we have to override the method and supply our own version in the `BankAccount` class. We'll follow the same format that the `toString` method of the `Rectangle` class uses: first print the name of the class, and then the values of the instance variables inside brackets.

```java
public class BankAccount
{
   . . .
   public String toString()
   {
      return "BankAccount[balance=" + balance + "]";
   }
}
```

This works better:

```
BankAccount momsSavings = new BankAccount(5000);
String s = momsSavings.toString(); // Sets s to "BankAccount[balance=5000]"
```

9.5.2 The equals Method

> The equals method checks whether two objects have the same contents.

In addition to the `toString` method, the `Object` class also provides an `equals` method, whose purpose is to check whether two objects have the same contents:

```
if (stamp1.equals(stamp2)) . . .      // Contents are the same—see Figure 9
```

This is different from the test with the `==` operator, which tests whether two references are identical, referring to the *same object:*

```
if (stamp1 == stamp2) . . .      // Objects are the same—see Figure 10
```

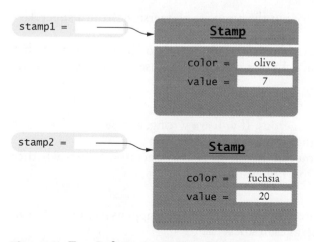

Figure 9 Two References to Equal Objects

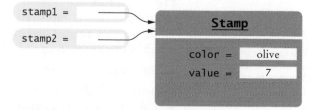

Figure 10 Two References to the Same Object

Let's implement the `equals` method for a `Stamp` class. You need to override the `equals` method of the `Object` class:

```
public class Stamp
{
    private String color;
    private int value;
    . . .
    public boolean equals(Object otherObject)
    {
        . . .
    }
    . . .
}
```

The equals *method checks whether two objects have the same contents.*

Now you have a slight problem. The `Object` class knows nothing about stamps, so it declares the `otherObject` parameter variable of the `equals` method to have the type `Object`. When overriding the method, you are not allowed to change the type of the parameter variable. Cast the parameter variable to the class `Stamp`:

```
Stamp other = (Stamp) otherObject;
```

Then you can compare the two stamps:

```
public boolean equals(Object otherObject)
{
    Stamp other = (Stamp) otherObject;
    return color.equals(other.color)
        && value == other.value;
}
```

Note that this `equals` method can access the instance variables of *any* `Stamp` object: the access `other.color` is perfectly legal.

9.5.3 The `instanceof` Operator

As you have seen, it is legal to store a subclass reference in a superclass variable:

```
ChoiceQuestion cq = new ChoiceQuestion();
Question q = cq; // OK
Object obj = cq; // OK
```

Very occasionally, you need to carry out the opposite conversion, from a superclass reference to a subclass reference.

For example, you may have a variable of type `Object`, and you happen to know that it actually holds a `Question` reference. In that case, you can use a cast to convert the type:

> If you know that an object belongs to a given class, use a cast to convert the type.

```
Question q = (Question) obj;
```

However, this cast is somewhat dangerous. If you are wrong, and `obj` actually refers to an object of an unrelated type, then a "class cast" exception is thrown.

To protect against bad casts, you can use the `instanceof` operator. It tests whether an object belongs to a particular type. For example,

> The `instanceof` operator tests whether an object belongs to a particular type.

```
obj instanceof Question
```

returns `true` if the type of `obj` is convertible to `Question`. This happens if `obj` refers to an actual `Question` or to a subclass such as `ChoiceQuestion`.

Syntax 9.3   The `instanceof` Operator

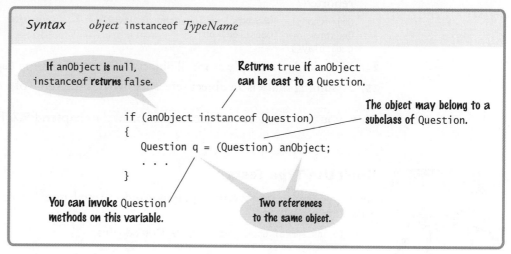

Syntax   *object* `instanceof` *TypeName*

If `anObject` is `null`, `instanceof` **returns** `false`.

Returns `true` **if** `anObject` **can be cast to a** `Question`.

The object may belong to a subclass of `Question`.

```
if (anObject instanceof Question)
{
    Question q = (Question) anObject;
    . . .
}
```

You can invoke `Question` methods on this variable.

Two references to the same object.

Using the `instanceof` operator, a safe cast can be programmed as follows:

```
if (obj instanceof Question)
{
    Question q = (Question) obj;
}
```

Note that `instanceof` is *not* a method. It is an operator, just like + or <. However, it does not operate on numbers. To the left is an object, and to the right a type name.

Do *not* use the `instanceof` operator to bypass polymorphism:

```
if (q instanceof ChoiceQuestion) // Don't do this—see Common Error 9.5 on page 446
{
    // Do the task the ChoiceQuestion way
}
else if (q instanceof Question)
{
    // Do the task the Question way
}
```

ONLINE EXAMPLE

A program that demonstrates the `toString` method and the `instanceof` operator.

In this case, you should implement a method `doTheTask` in the `Question` class, override it in `ChoiceQuestion`, and call

```
q.doTheTask();
```

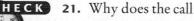

SELF CHECK

21. Why does the call

```
System.out.println(System.out);
```

produce a result such as `java.io.PrintStream@7a84e4`?

22. Will the following code fragment compile? Will it run? If not, what error is reported?

```
Object obj = "Hello";
System.out.println(obj.length());
```

23. Will the following code fragment compile? Will it run? If not, what error is reported?

```java
Object obj = "Who was the inventor of Java?";
Question q = (Question) obj;
q.display();
```

24. Why don't we simply store all objects in variables of type Object?

25. Assuming that x is an object reference, what is the value of x instanceof Object?

Practice It   Now you can try these exercises at the end of the chapter: P9.7, P9.8, P9.12.

Common Error 9.5

Don't Use Type Tests

Some programmers use specific type tests in order to implement behavior that varies with each class:

```java
if (q instanceof ChoiceQuestion) // Don't do this
{
    // Do the task the ChoiceQuestion way
}
else if (q instanceof Question)
{
    // Do the task the Question way
}
```

This is a poor strategy. If a new class such as NumericQuestion is added, then you need to revise all parts of your program that make a type test, adding another case:

```java
else if (q instanceof NumericQuestion)
{
    // Do the task the NumericQuestion way
}
```

In contrast, consider the addition of a class NumericQuestion to our quiz program. *Nothing* needs to change in that program because it uses polymorphism, not type tests.

    Whenever you find yourself trying to use type tests in a hierarchy of classes, reconsider and use polymorphism instead. Declare a method doTheTask in the superclass, override it in the subclasses, and call

```java
q.doTheTask();
```

Special Topic 9.6

Inheritance and the toString Method

You just saw how to write a toString method: Form a string consisting of the class name and the names and values of the instance variables. However, if you want your toString method to be usable by subclasses of your class, you need to work a bit harder. Instead of hardcoding the class name, call the getClass method (which every class inherits from the Object class) to obtain an object that describes a class and its properties. Then invoke the getName method to get the name of the class:

```java
public String toString()
{
    return getClass().getName() + "[balance=" + balance + "]";
}
```

Then the toString method prints the correct class name when you apply it to a subclass, say a SavingsAccount.

```
SavingsAccount momsSavings = . . . ;
System.out.println(momsSavings);
// Prints "SavingsAccount[balance=10000]"
```

Of course, in the subclass, you should override `toString` and add the values of the subclass instance variables. Note that you must call `super.toString` to get the instance variables of the superclass—the subclass can't access them directly.

```
public class SavingsAccount extends BankAccount
{
   . . .
   public String toString()
   {
      return super.toString() + "[interestRate=" + interestRate + "]";
   }
}
```

Now a savings account is converted to a string such as `SavingsAccount[balance= 10000][interestRate=5]`. The brackets show which variables belong to the superclass.

Special Topic 9.7

Inheritance and the `equals` Method

You just saw how to write an `equals` method: Cast the `otherObject` parameter variable to the type of your class, and then compare the instance variables of the implicit parameter and the explicit parameter.

But what if someone called `stamp1.equals(x)` where `x` wasn't a `Stamp` object? Then the bad cast would generate an exception. It is a good idea to test whether `otherObject` really is an instance of the `Stamp` class. The easiest test would be with the `instanceof` operator. However, that test is not specific enough. It would be possible for `otherObject` to belong to some subclass of `Stamp`. To rule out that possibility, you should test whether the two objects belong to the same class. If not, return false.

```
if (getClass() != otherObject.getClass()) { return false; }
```

Moreover, the Java language specification demands that the `equals` method return false when `otherObject` is `null`.

Here is an improved version of the `equals` method that takes these two points into account:

```
public boolean equals(Object otherObject)
{
   if (otherObject == null) { return false; }
   if (getClass() != otherObject.getClass()) { return false; }
   Stamp other = (Stamp) otherObject;
   return color.equals(other.color) && value == other.value;
}
```

When you implement `equals` in a subclass, you should first call `equals` in the superclass to check whether the superclass instance variables match. Here is an example:

```
public CollectibleStamp extends Stamp
{
   private int year;
   . . .
   public boolean equals(Object otherObject)
   {
      if (!super.equals(otherObject)) { return false; }
      CollectibleStamp other = (CollectibleStamp) otherObject;
      return year == other.year;
   }
}
```

9.6 Interface Types

It is often possible to design a general and reusable mechanism for processing objects by focusing on the essential operations that an algorithm needs. You use *interface types* to express these operations.

9.6.1 Defining an Interface

Consider the following method that computes the average balance in an array of BankAccount objects:

```
public static double average(BankAccount[] objects)
{
   if (objects.length == 0) { return 0; }
   double sum = 0;
   for (BankAccount obj : objects)
   {
      sum = sum + obj.getBalance();
   }
   return sum / objects.length;
}
```

Now suppose you have an array of Country objects and want to determine the average of the areas:

```
public static double average(Country[] objects)
{
   if (objects.length == 0) { return 0; }
   double sum = 0;
   for (Country obj : objects)
   {
      sum = sum + obj.getArea();
   }
   return sum / objects.length;
}
```

Clearly, the algorithm for computing the result is the same in both cases, but the details of measurement differ. How can we write a *single* method that computes the averages of both bank accounts and countries?

This standmixer provides the "rotation" service to any attachment that conforms to a common interface. Similarly, the average *method at the end of this section works with any class that implements a common interface.*

Syntax 9.4   Interface Types

| Syntax | Declaring: | ```
public interface InterfaceName
{
    method declarations
}
``` |
|--------|------------|---|
|        | Implementing: | ```
public class ClassName implements InterfaceName, InterfaceName, . . .
{
    instance variables
    methods
}
``` |

Interface methods are always public.

```
public interface Measurable
{
    double getMeasure();
}
```

Interface methods have no implementation.

```
public class BankAccount implements Measurable
{
    . . .
```

A class can implement one or more interface types.

Other BankAccount methods.

```
    public double getMeasure()
    {
        return balance;
    }
}
```

Implementation for the method that was declared in the interface type.

Suppose that the classes agree on a single method getMeasure that obtains the measure to be used in the data analysis. For bank accounts, getMeasure returns the balance. For countries, getMeasure returns the area. Other classes can participate too, provided that their getMeasure method returns an appropriate value.

Then we can implement a single method that computes

```
sum = sum + obj.getMeasure();
```

What is the type of the variable obj? Any class that has a getMeasure method.

In Java, an **interface type** is used to specify required operations. We will declare an interface type that we call Measurable:

```
public interface Measurable
{
    double getMeasure();
}
```

> A Java interface type contains the return types, names, and parameter variables of a set of methods.

The interface declaration lists all methods that the interface type requires. The Measurable interface type requires a single method, but in general, an interface type can require multiple methods. (Note that the Measurable type is not a type in the standard library—it is a type that was created specifically for this book.)

An interface type is similar to a class, but there are several important differences:

> Unlike a class, an interface type provides no implementation.

- All methods in an interface type are *abstract*; that is, they have a name, parameter variables, and a return type, but they don't have an implementation.
- All methods in an interface type are automatically public.
- An interface type cannot have instance variables.
- An interface type cannot have static methods.

We can use the interface type `Measurable` to implement a "universal" method for computing averages:

```java
public static double average(Measurable[] objects)
{
    if (objects.length == 0) { return 0; }
    double sum = 0;
    for (Measurable obj : objects)
    {
        sum = sum + obj.getMeasure();
    }
    return sum / objects.length;
}
```

9.6.2 Implementing an Interface

The average method is usable for objects of any class that **implements** the `Measurable` interface. A class implements an interface type if it declares the interface in an `implements` clause, and if it implements the method or methods that the interface requires. Let's modify the `BankAccount` class to implement the `Measurable` interface.

```java
public class BankAccount implements Measurable
{
    public double getMeasure()
    {
        return balance;
    }
    . . .
}
```

Note that the class must declare the method as `public`, whereas the interface type need not—all methods in an interface type are public.

Similarly, it is an easy matter to implement a `Country` class that implements the `Measurable` interface.

```java
public class Country implements Measurable
{
    public double getMeasure()
    {
        return area;
    }
    . . .
}
```

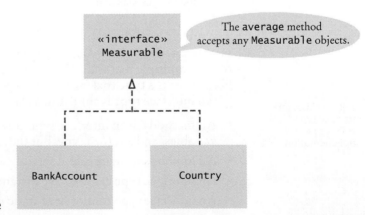

Figure 11
Classes that Implement
the Measurable Interface

A reference to a BankAccount or Country can be converted to a Measurable reference. The sample program at the end of this section shows how the same average method can compute the average of a collection of bank accounts or countries.

In summary, the Measurable interface expresses what all measurable objects have in common. This commonality makes it possible to write methods such as average that are usable for many classes.

Figure 11 shows a diagram of the classes and interfaces in this program. A dotted arrow with a triangular tip denotes the "implements" relationship.

section_6/MeasurableDemo.java

```java
 1  /**
 2      This program demonstrates the measurable BankAccount and Country classes.
 3  */
 4  public class MeasurableDemo
 5  {
 6     public static void main(String[] args)
 7     {
 8        Measurable[] accounts = new Measurable[3];
 9        accounts[0] = new BankAccount(0);
10        accounts[1] = new BankAccount(10000);
11        accounts[2] = new BankAccount(2000);
12
13        System.out.println("Average balance: "
14           + average(accounts));
15
16        Measurable[] countries = new Measurable[3];
17        countries[0] = new Country("Uruguay", 176220);
18        countries[1] = new Country("Thailand", 514000);
19        countries[2] = new Country("Belgium", 30510);
20
21        System.out.println("Average area: "
22           + average(countries));
23     }
24
25     /**
26         Computes the average of the measures of the given objects.
27         @param objects an array of Measurable objects
28         @return the average of the measures
29     */
30     public static double average(Measurable[] objects)
31     {
32        if (objects.length == 0) { return 0; }
33        double sum = 0;
34        for (Measurable obj : objects)
35        {
36           sum = sum + obj.getMeasure();
37        }
38        return sum / objects.length;
39     }
40  }
```

Program Run

```
Average balance: 4000.0
Average area: 240243.33333333334
```

9.6.3 The Comparable Interface

Implement the Comparable interface so that objects of your class can be compared, for example, in a sort method.

In the preceding sections, we defined the Measurable interface and provided an average method that works with any classes implementing that interface. In this section, you will learn about the Comparable interface of the standard Java library.

The Measurable interface is used for measuring a single object. The Comparable interface is more complex because comparisons involve two objects. The interface declares a compareTo method. The call

```
a.compareTo(b)
```

must return a negative number if a should come before b, zero if a and b are the same, and a positive number otherwise.

The Comparable interface has a single method:

```java
public interface Comparable
{
    int compareTo(Object otherObject);
}
```

For example, the BankAccount class can implement Comparable like this:

```java
public class BankAccount implements Comparable
{
    . . .
    public int compareTo(Object otherObject)
    {
        BankAccount other = (BankAccount) otherObject;
        if (balance < other.balance) { return -1; }
        if (balance > other.balance) { return 1; }
        return 0;
    }
    . . .
}
```

This compareTo method compares bank accounts by their balance. Note that the compareTo method has a parameter variable of type Object. To turn it into a BankAccount reference, we use a cast:

```java
BankAccount other = (BankAccount) otherObject;
```

Once the BankAccount class implements the Comparable interface, you can sort an array of bank accounts with the Arrays.sort method:

```java
BankAccount[] accounts = new BankAccount[3];
accounts[0] = new BankAccount(10000);
accounts[1] = new BankAccount(0);
accounts[2] = new BankAccount(2000);
Arrays.sort(accounts);
```

The compareTo *method checks whether another object is larger or smaller.*

The accounts array is now sorted by increasing balance.

26. Suppose you want to use the average method to find the average salary of Employee objects. What condition must the Employee class fulfill?

27. Why can't the average method have a parameter variable of type Object[]?

28. Why can't you use the average method to find the average length of String objects?

29. What is wrong with this code?

```
Measurable meas = new Measurable();
System.out.println(meas.getMeasure());
```

30. How can you sort an array of Country objects by increasing area?

31. Can you use the Arrays.sort method to sort an array of String objects? Check the API documentation for the String class.

Practice It Now you can try these exercises at the end of the chapter: R9.14, P9.15, P9.16.

Common Error 9.6

Forgetting to Declare Implementing Methods as Public

The methods in an interface are not declared as public, because they are public by default. However, the methods in a class are *not* public by default. It is a common error to forget the public reserved word when declaring a method from an interface:

```
public class BankAccount implements Measurable
{
    double getMeasure() // Oops—should be public
    {
        return balance;
    }
    . . .
}
```

Then the compiler complains that the method has a weaker access level, namely package access instead of public access (see Section 12.4). The remedy is to declare the method as public.

Special Topic 9.8

Constants in Interfaces

Interfaces cannot have instance variables, but it is legal to specify **constants**.

When declaring a constant in an interface, you can (and should) omit the reserved words public static final, because all variables in an interface are automatically public static final. For example,

```
public interface Measurable
{
    double OUNCES_PER_LITER = 33.814;
    . . .
}
```

To use this constant in your programs, add the interface name:

```
Measurable.OUNCES_PER_LITER
```

Special Topic 9.9

Function Objects

In the preceding section, you saw how the `Measurable` interface type makes it possible to provide services that work for many classes—provided they are willing to implement the interface type. But what can you do if a class does not do so? For example, we might want to compute the average length of a collection of strings, but `String` does not implement `Measurable`.

Let's rethink our approach. The `average` method needs to measure each object. When the objects are required to be of type `Measurable`, the responsibility for measuring lies with the objects themselves, which is the cause of the limitation that we noted. It would be better if another object could carry out the measurement. Let's move the measurement method into a different interface:

```
public interface Measurer
{
    double measure(Object anObject);
}
```

The `measure` method measures an object and returns its measurement. We use a parameter variable of type `Object`, the "lowest common denominator" of all classes in Java, because we do not want to restrict which classes can be measured.

We add a parameter variable of type `Measurer` to the `average` method:

```
public static double average(Object[] objects, Measurer meas)
{
    if (objects.length == 0) { return 0; }
    double sum = 0;
    for (Object obj : objects)
    {
        sum = sum + meas.measure(obj);
    }
    return sum / objects.length;
}
```

When calling the method, you need to supply a `Measurer` object. That is, you need to implement a class with a `measure` method, and then create an object of that class. Let's do that for measuring strings:

```
public class StringMeasurer implements Measurer
{
    public double measure(Object obj)
    {
        String str = (String) obj; // Cast obj to String type
        return str.length();
    }
}
```

Note that the `measure` method must accept an argument of type `Object`, even though this particular measurer just wants to measure strings. The parameter variable must have the same type as in the `Measurer` interface. Therefore, the `Object` parameter variable is cast to the `String` type.

Finally, we are ready to compute the average length of an array of strings:

```
String[] words = { "Mary", "had", "a", "little", "lamb" };
Measurer lengthMeasurer = new StringMeasurer();
double result = average(words, lengthMeasurer); // result is set to 3.6
```

An object such as `lengthMeasurer` is called a *function object*. The sole purpose of the object is to execute a single method, in our case `measure`. (In mathematics, as well as many other programming languages, the term "function" is used where Java uses "method".)

The `Comparator` interface, discussed in Special Topic 14.5, is another example of an interface for function objects.

VIDEO EXAMPLE 9.2 **Drawing Geometric Shapes**

In this Video Example, you will see how to use inheritance to describe and draw different geometric shapes.

CHAPTER SUMMARY

Explain the notions of inheritance, superclass, and subclass.

- A subclass inherits data and behavior from a superclass.
- You can always use a subclass object in place of a superclass object.

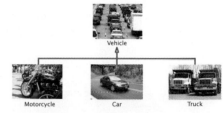

Implement subclasses in Java.

- A subclass inherits all methods that it does not override.
- A subclass can override a superclass method by providing a new implementation.
- The extends reserved word indicates that a class inherits from a superclass.

Implement methods that override methods from a superclass.

- An overriding method can extend or replace the functionality of the superclass method.
- Use the reserved word super to call a superclass method.
- Unless specified otherwise, the subclass constructor calls the superclass constructor with no arguments.
- To call a superclass constructor, use the super reserved word in the first statement of the subclass constructor.
- The constructor of a subclass can pass arguments to a superclass constructor, using the reserved word super.

Use polymorphism for processing objects of related types.

- A subclass reference can be used when a superclass reference is expected.
- Polymorphism ("having multiple shapes") allows us to manipulate objects that share a set of tasks, even though the tasks are executed in different ways.
- An abstract method is a method whose implementation is not specified.
- An abstract class is a class that cannot be instantiated.

Use the toString method and instanceof operator with objects.

- Override the toString method to yield a string that describes the object's state.
- The equals method checks whether two objects have the same contents.

➕ Available online in WileyPLUS and at www.wiley.com/college/horstmann.

- If you know that an object belongs to a given class, use a cast to convert the type.
- The instanceof operator tests whether an object belongs to a particular type.

Use interface types for algorithms that process objects of different classes.

- A Java interface type contains the return types, names, and parameter variables of a set of methods.
- Unlike a class, an interface type provides no implementation.
- By using an interface type for a parameter variable, a method can accept objects from many classes.
- The implements reserved word indicates which interfaces a class implements.
- Implement the Comparable interface so that objects of your class can be compared, for example, in a sort method.

REVIEW EXERCISES

· R9.1 Identify the superclass and subclass in each of the following pairs of classes.

    a. Employee, Manager
    b. GraduateStudent, Student
    c. Person, Student
    d. Employee, Professor
    e. BankAccount, CheckingAccount
    f. Vehicle, Car
    g. Vehicle, Minivan
    h. Car, Minivan
    i. Truck, Vehicle

· R9.2 Consider a program for managing inventory in a small appliance store. Why isn't it useful to have a superclass SmallAppliance and subclasses Toaster, CarVacuum, TravelIron, and so on?

· R9.3 Which methods does the ChoiceQuestion class inherit from its superclass? Which methods does it override? Which methods does it add?

· R9.4 Which methods does the SavingsAccount class in How To 9.1 inherit from its superclass? Which methods does it override? Which methods does it add?

· R9.5 List the instance variables of a CheckingAccount object from How To 9.1.

·· R9.6 Suppose the class Sub extends the class Sandwich. Which of the following assignments are legal?

```
Sandwich x = new Sandwich();
Sub y = new Sub();
```

    a. x = y;
    b. y = x;
    c. y = new Sandwich();
    d. x = new Sub();

R9.7 Draw an inheritance diagram that shows the inheritance relationships between these classes.

- Person
- Employee
- Student
- Instructor
- Classroom
- Object

R9.8 In an object-oriented traffic simulation system, we have the classes listed below. Draw an inheritance diagram that shows the relationships between these classes.

- Vehicle
- Car
- Truck
- Sedan
- Coupe
- PickupTruck
- SportUtilityVehicle
- Minivan
- Bicycle
- Motorcycle

R9.9 What inheritance relationships would you establish among the following classes?

- Student
- Professor
- TeachingAssistant
- Employee
- Secretary
- DepartmentChair
- Janitor
- SeminarSpeaker
- Person
- Course
- Seminar
- Lecture
- ComputerLab

R9.10 How does a cast such as (BankAccount) x differ from a cast of number values such as (int) x?

R9.11 Which of these conditions returns true? Check the Java documentation for the inheritance patterns. Recall that System.out is an object of the PrintStream class.

    a. System.out instanceof PrintStream
    b. System.out instanceof OutputStream
    c. System.out instanceof LogStream
    d. System.out instanceof Object
    e. System.out instanceof Closeable
    f. System.out instanceof Writer

R9.12 Suppose C is a class that implements the interfaces I and J. Which of the following assignments require a cast?

```
C c = . . .;
I i = . . .;
J j = . . .;
```

    a. c = i;
    b. j = c;
    c. i = j;

R9.13 Suppose C is a class that implements the interfaces I and J, and i is declared as

```
I i = new C();
```

Which of the following statements will throw an exception?

    a. `C c = (C) i;`
    b. `J j = (J) i;`
    c. `i = (I) null;`

■■ R9.14 Suppose the class `Sandwich` implements the `Edible` interface, and you are given the variable declarations

```
Sandwich sub = new Sandwich();
Rectangle cerealBox = new Rectangle(5, 10, 20, 30);
Edible e = null;
```

Which of the following assignment statements are legal?

    a. `e = sub;`
    b. `sub = e;`
    c. `sub = (Sandwich) e;`
    d. `sub = (Sandwich) cerealBox;`
    e. `e = cerealBox;`
    f. `e = (Edible) cerealBox;`
    g. `e = (Rectangle) cerealBox;`
    h. `e = (Rectangle) null;`

PROGRAMMING EXERCISES

■■ P9.1 Add a class `NumericQuestion` to the question hierarchy of Section 9.1. If the response and the expected answer differ by no more than 0.01, then accept the response as correct.

■■ P9.2 Add a class `FillInQuestion` to the question hierarchy of Section 9.1. Such a question is constructed with a string that contains the answer, surrounded by _ _, for example, `"The inventor of Java was _James Gosling_"`. The question should be displayed as

    `The inventor of Java was _____`

■ P9.3 Modify the `checkAnswer` method of the `Question` class so that it does not take into account different spaces or upper/lowercase characters. For example, the response `"JAMES gosling"` should match an answer of `"James Gosling"`.

■■ P9.4 Add a class `AnyCorrectChoiceQuestion` to the question hierarchy of Section 9.1 that allows multiple correct choices. The respondent should provide any one of the correct choices. The answer string should contain all of the correct choices, separated by spaces. Provide instructions in the question text.

■■ P9.5 Add a class `MultiChoiceQuestion` to the question hierarchy of Section 9.1 that allows multiple correct choices. The respondent should provide all correct choices, separated by spaces. Provide instructions in the question text.

■■ P9.6 Add a method `addText` to the `Question` superclass and provide a different implementation of `ChoiceQuestion` that calls `addText` rather than storing an array list of choices.

■ P9.7 Provide `toString` methods for the `Question` and `ChoiceQuestion` classes.

- ▪▪ **P9.8** Implement a superclass `Person`. Make two classes, `Student` and `Instructor`, that inherit from `Person`. A person has a name and a year of birth. A student has a major, and an instructor has a salary. Write the class declarations, the constructors, and the methods `toString` for all classes. Supply a test program that tests these classes and methods.

- ▪▪ **P9.9** Make a class `Employee` with a name and salary. Make a class `Manager` inherit from `Employee`. Add an instance variable, named `department`, of type `String`. Supply a method `toString` that prints the manager's name, department, and salary. Make a class `Executive` inherit from `Manager`. Supply appropriate `toString` methods for all classes. Supply a test program that tests these classes and methods.

- ▪▪ **P9.10** The `Rectangle` class of the standard Java library does not supply a method to compute the area or the perimeter of a rectangle. Provide a subclass `BetterRectangle` of the `Rectangle` class that has `getPerimeter` and `getArea` methods. *Do not add any instance variables.* In the constructor, call the `setLocation` and `setSize` methods of the `Rectangle` class. Provide a program that tests the methods that you supplied.

- ▪▪▪ **P9.11** Repeat Exercise P9.10, but in the `BetterRectangle` constructor, invoke the superclass constructor.

- ▪▪ **P9.12** A labeled point has *x*- and *y*-coordinates and a string label. Provide a class `LabeledPoint` with a constructor `LabeledPoint(int x, int y, String label)` and a `toString` method that displays x, y, and the label.

- ▪▪ **P9.13** Reimplement the `LabeledPoint` class of Exercise P9.12 by storing the location in a `java.awt.Point` object. Your `toString` method should invoke the `toString` method of the `Point` class.

- ▪▪ **P9.14** Modify the `SodaCan` class of Exercise P8.5 to implement the `Measurable` interface. The measure of a soda can should be its surface area. Write a program that computes the average surface area of an array of soda cans.

- ▪▪ **P9.15** A person has a name and a height in centimeters. Use the `average` method in Section 9.6 to process a collection of `Person` objects.

- ▪▪▪ **P9.16** Write a method

  ```
  public static Measurable maximum(Measurable[] objects)
  ```

  that returns the object with the largest measure. Use that method to determine the country with the largest area from an array of countries.

- ▪▪▪ **P9.17** Declare an interface `Filter` as follows:

  ```
  public interface Filter
  {
      boolean accept(Object x);
  }
  ```

  Write a method

  ```
  public static ArrayList<Object> collectAll(ArrayList<Object> objects, Filter f)
  ```

  that returns all objects in the `objects` array that are accepted by the given filter.
  Provide a class `ShortWordFilter` whose `filter` method accepts all strings of length < 5.
  Then write a program that reads all words from `System.in`, puts them into an `ArrayList<Object>`, calls `collectAll`, and prints a list of the short words.

■■■ **P9.18** The System.out.printf method has predefined formats for printing integers, floating-point numbers, and other data types. But it is also extensible. If you use the S format, you can print any class that implements the Formattable interface. That interface has a single method:

```
void formatTo(Formatter formatter, int flags, int width, int precision)
```

In this exercise, you should make the BankAccount class implement the Formattable interface. Ignore the flags and precision and simply format the bank balance, using the given width. In order to achieve this task, you need to get an Appendable reference like this:

```
Appendable a = formatter.out();
```

Appendable is another interface with a method

```
void append(CharSequence sequence)
```

CharSequence is yet another interface that is implemented by (among others) the String class. Construct a string by first converting the bank balance into a string and then padding it with spaces so that it has the desired width. Pass that string to the append method.

■■■ **P9.19** Enhance the formatTo method of Exercise P9.18 by taking into account the precision.

■■ **Business P9.20** Change the CheckingAccount class in How To 9.1 so that a $1 fee is levied for deposits or withdrawals in excess of three free monthly transactions. Place the code for computing the fee into a separate method that you call from the deposit and withdraw methods.

■■ **Business P9.21** Implement a superclass Appointment and subclasses Onetime, Daily, and Monthly. An appointment has a description (for example, "see the dentist") and a date. Write a method occursOn(int year, int month, int day) that checks whether the appointment occurs on that date. For example, for a monthly appointment, you must check whether the day of the month matches. Then fill an array of Appointment objects with a mixture of appointments. Have the user enter a date and print out all appointments that occur on that date.

■■ **Business P9.22** Improve the appointment book program of Exercise P9.21. Give the user the option to add new appointments. The user must specify the type of the appointment, the description, and the date.

■■■ **Business P9.23** Improve the appointment book program of Exercises P9.21 and P9.22 by letting the user save the appointment data to a file and reload the data from a file. The saving part is straightforward: Make a method save. Save the type, description, and date to a file. The loading part is not so easy. First determine the type of the appointment to be loaded, create an object of that type, and then call a load method to load the data.

■■■ **Science P9.24** In this problem, you will model a circuit consisting of an arbitrary configuration of resistors. Provide a superclass Circuit with a instance method getResistance. Provide a subclass Resistor representing a single resistor. Provide subclasses Serial and Parallel, each of which contains an ArrayList<Circuit>. A Serial circuit models a series of circuits, each of which can be a single resistor or another circuit. Similarly, a

`Parallel` circuit models a set of circuits in parallel. For example, the following circuit is a `Parallel` circuit containing a single resistor and one `Serial` circuit:

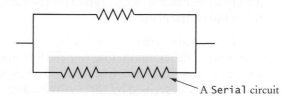

A `Serial` circuit

Use Ohm's law to compute the combined resistance.

■■ Science P9.25 Part (a) of the figure below shows a symbolic representation of an electric circuit called an *amplifier*. The input to the amplifier is the voltage v_i and the output is the voltage v_o. The output of an amplifier is proportional to the input. The constant of proportionality is called the "gain" of the amplifier.

Parts (b), (c), and (d) show schematics of three specific types of amplifier: the *inverting amplifier*, *noninverting amplifier*, and *voltage divider amplifier*. Each of these three amplifiers consists of two resistors and an op amp. The value of the gain of each amplifier depends on the values of its resistances. In particular, the gain, g, of the inverting amplifier is given by $g = -\dfrac{R_2}{R_1}$. Similarly the gains of the noninverting amplifier and voltage divider amplifier are given by $g = 1 + \dfrac{R_2}{R_1}$ and $g = \dfrac{R_2}{R_1 + R_2}$, respectively.

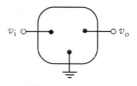

(a) Amplifier

(b) Inverting amplifier

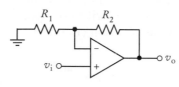

(c) Noninverting amplifier

(d) Voltage divider amplifier

Write a Java program that represents the amplifier as a superclass and represents the inverting, noninverting, and voltage divider amplifiers as subclasses. Give the subclass two methods, `getGain` and a `getDescription` method that returns a string identifying the amplifier. Each subclass should have a constructor with two arguments, the resistances of the amplifier.

The subclasses need to override the `getGain` and `getDescription` methods of the superclass.

Supply a class that demonstrates that the subclasses all work properly for sample values of the resistances.

■■ Science P9.26 Resonant circuits are used to select a signal (e.g., a radio station or TV channel) from among other competing signals. Resonant circuits are characterized by the frequency response shown in the figure below. The resonant frequency response is completely described by three parameters: the resonant frequency, ω_0, the bandwidth, B, and the gain at the resonant frequency, k.

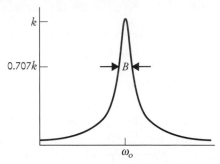

Frequency (rad/s, log scale)

Two simple resonant circuits are shown in the figure below. The circuit in (a) is called a *parallel resonant circuit*. The circuit in (b) is called a *series resonant circuit*. Both resonant circuits consist of a resistor having resistance R, a capacitor having capacitance C, and an inductor having inductance L.

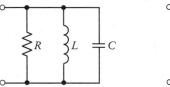

(a) Parallel resonant circuit   (b) Series resonant circuit

These circuits are designed by determining values of R, C, and L that cause the resonant frequency response to be described by specified values of ω_0, B, and k. The design equations for the parallel resonant circuit are:

$$R = k, \quad C = \frac{1}{BR}, \text{ and } \quad L = \frac{1}{\omega_0^2 C}$$

Similarly, the design equations for the series resonant circuit are:

$$R = \frac{1}{k}, \quad L = \frac{R}{B}, \text{ and } \quad C = \frac{1}{\omega_0^2 L}$$

Write a Java program that represents `ResonantCircuit` as a superclass and represents the `SeriesResonantCircuit` and `ParallelResonantCircuit` as subclasses. Give the superclass three private instance variables representing the parameters ω_0, B, and k of the resonant frequency response. The superclass should provide public instance methods to get and set each of these variables. The superclass should also provide a `display` method that prints a description of the resonant frequency response.

Each subclass should provide a method that designs the corresponding resonant circuit. The subclasses should also override the `display` method of the superclass to print descriptions of both the frequency response (the values of ω_o, B, and k) and the circuit (the values of R, C, and L).

All classes should provide appropriate constructors.

Supply a class that demonstrates that the subclasses all work properly.

ANSWERS TO SELF-CHECK QUESTIONS

1. Because every manager is an employee but not the other way around, the `Manager` class is more specialized. It is the subclass, and `Employee` is the superclass.

2. `CheckingAccount` and `SavingsAccount` both inherit from the more general class `BankAccount`.

3. `Exception`, `Throwable`

4. Vehicle, truck, motorcycle

5. It shouldn't. A quiz isn't a question; it *has* questions.

6. a, b, d

7.
```
public class Manager extends Employee
{
    private double bonus;
    // Constructors and methods omitted
}
```

8. `name`, `baseSalary`, and `bonus`

9.
```
public class Manager extends Employee
{
    . . .
    public double getSalary() { . . . }
}
```

10. `getName`, `setName`, `setBaseSalary`

11. The method is not allowed to access the instance variable text from the superclass.

12. The type of the `this` reference is `ChoiceQuestion`. Therefore, the `display` method of `ChoiceQuestion` is selected, and the method calls itself.

13. Because there is no ambiguity. The subclass doesn't have a `setAnswer` method.

14.
```
public String getName()
{
    return "*" + super.getName();
}
```

15.
```
public double getSalary()
{
    return super.getSalary() + bonus;
}
```

16. a only.

17. It belongs to the class `BankAccount` or one of its subclasses.

18. `Question[] quiz = new Question[SIZE];`

19. You cannot tell from the fragment—cq may be initialized with an object of a subclass of `ChoiceQuestion`. The `display` method of whatever object cq references is invoked.

20. No. This is a static method of the `Math` class. There is no implicit parameter object that could be used to dynamically look up a method.

21. Because the implementor of the `PrintStream` class did not supply a `toString` method.

22. The second line will not compile. The class `Object` does not have a method `length`.

23. The code will compile, but the second line will throw a class cast exception because `Question` is not a subclass of `String`.

24. There are only a few methods that can be invoked on variables of type `Object`.

25. The value is `false` if x is `null` and `true` otherwise.

26. It must implement the `Measurable` interface and provide a `getMeasure` method returning the salary.

27. The `Object` class doesn't have a `getMeasure` method.

28. You cannot modify the `String` class to implement `Measurable`—it is a library class. See Special Topic 9.9 for a solution.

29. Measurable is not a class. You cannot construct objects of type Measurable.

30. Have the Country class implement the Comparable interface, as shown below, and call Arrays.sort.

```
public class Country implements Comparable
{
   . . .
   public int compareTo(Object otherObject)
   {
      Country other = (Country) otherObject;
      if (area < other.area) return -1;
      if (area > other.area) return 1;
      return 0;
   }
}
```

31. Yes, you can, because String implements the Comparable interface type.

GRAPHICAL USER INTERFACES

To implement simple graphical user interfaces

To add buttons, text fields, and other components to a frame window

To handle events that are generated by buttons

To write programs that display simple drawings

10.1 FRAME WINDOWS 466

Special Topic 10.1: Adding the main Method to the Frame Class 470

10.2 EVENTS AND EVENT HANDLING 470

Common Error 10.1: Modifying Parameter Types in the Implementing Method 478

Common Error 10.2: Forgetting to Attach a Listener 478

Programming Tip 10.1: Don't Use a Frame as a Listener 478

Special Topic 10.2: Local Inner Classes 479

Special Topic 10.3: Anonymous Inner Classes 480

10.3 PROCESSING TEXT INPUT 481

10.4 CREATING DRAWINGS 487

Common Error 10.3: Forgetting to Repaint 496

Common Error 10.4: By Default, Components Have Zero Width and Height 497

How To 10.1: Drawing Graphical Shapes 497

Worked Example 10.1: Coding a Bar Chart Creator ⊕

Video Example 10.1: Solving Crossword Puzzles ⊕

In this chapter, you will learn how to write graphical user-interface applications that contain buttons, text components, and graphical components such as charts. You will be able to process the events that are generated by button clicks, process the user input, and update the textual and graphical output.

10.1 Frame Windows

A graphical application shows information inside a **frame**: a window with a title bar, as shown in Figure 1. In the following sections, you will learn how to display a frame and how to place user-interface components inside it.

A graphical user interface is displayed inside a frame.

10.1.1 Displaying a Frame

> To show a frame, construct a JFrame object, set its size, and make it visible.

To show a frame, carry out the following steps:

1. Construct an object of the JFrame class:

   ```
   JFrame frame = new JFrame();
   ```

2. Set the size of the frame:

   ```
   final int FRAME_WIDTH = 300;
   final int FRAME_HEIGHT = 400;
   frame.setSize(FRAME_WIDTH, FRAME_HEIGHT);
   ```

   This frame will be 300 pixels wide and 400 pixels tall. If you omit this step the frame will be 0 by 0 pixels, and you won't be able to see it. (Pixels are the tiny dots from which digital images are composed.)

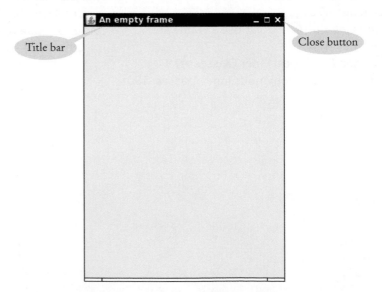

Figure 1 A Frame Window

3. If you'd like, set the title of the frame:

```
frame.setTitle("An empty frame");
```

If you omit this step, the title bar is simply left blank.

4. Set the "default close operation":

```
frame.setDefaultCloseOperation(JFrame.EXIT_ON_CLOSE);
```

When the user closes the frame, the program automatically exits. Don't omit this step. If you do, the program keeps running even after the frame is closed.

5. Make the frame visible:

```
frame.setVisible(true);
```

The simple program below shows all of these steps. It produces the empty frame shown in Figure 1.

The JFrame class is a part of the javax.swing package. Swing is the nickname for the graphical user-interface library in Java. The "x" in javax denotes the fact that Swing started out as a Java *extension* before it was added to the standard library.

section_1_1/EmptyFrameViewer.java

```
1   import javax.swing.JFrame;
2
3   /**
4      This program displays an empty frame.
5   */
6   public class EmptyFrameViewer
7   {
8      public static void main(String[] args)
9      {
10        JFrame frame = new JFrame();
11
12        final int FRAME_WIDTH = 300;
13        final int FRAME_HEIGHT = 400;
14        frame.setSize(FRAME_WIDTH, FRAME_HEIGHT);
15        frame.setTitle("An empty frame");
16        frame.setDefaultCloseOperation(JFrame.EXIT_ON_CLOSE);
17
18        frame.setVisible(true);
19      }
20   }
```

10.1.2 Adding User-Interface Components to a Frame

An empty frame is not very interesting. You will want to add some user-interface components, such as buttons and text labels. However, if you add components directly to the frame, they get placed on top of each other.

When building a graphical user interface, you add components to a frame.

Use a JPanel to group multiple user-interface components together.

If you have more than one component, put them into a **panel** (a container for other user-interface components), and then add the panel to the frame:

```
JPanel panel = new JPanel();
panel.add(button);
panel.add(label);
frame.add(panel);
```

You first construct the components, providing the text that should appear on them:

```
JButton button = new JButton("Click me!");
JLabel label = new JLabel("Hello, World!");
```

Then you add the components to the frame, as shown above. Figure 2 shows the result. When you run the program, you can click the button, but nothing will happen. You will see in Section 10.2 how to attach an action to a button.

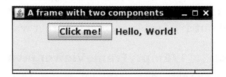

Figure 2   A Frame with a Button and a Label

section_1_2/FIlledFrameViewer.java

```java
1    import javax.swing.JButton;
2    import javax.swing.JFrame;
3    import javax.swing.JLabel;
4    import javax.swing.JPanel;
5
6    /**
7        This program shows a frame that is filled with two components.
8    */
9    public class FilledFrameViewer
10   {
11      public static void main(String[] args)
12      {
13         JFrame frame = new JFrame();
14
15         JButton button = new JButton("Click me!");
16         JLabel label = new JLabel("Hello, World!");
17
18         JPanel panel = new JPanel();
19         panel.add(button);
20         panel.add(label);
21         frame.add(panel);
22
23         final int FRAME_WIDTH = 300;
24         final int FRAME_HEIGHT = 100;
25         frame.setSize(FRAME_WIDTH, FRAME_HEIGHT);
26         frame.setTitle("A frame with two components");
27         frame.setDefaultCloseOperation(JFrame.EXIT_ON_CLOSE);
28
29         frame.setVisible(true);
30      }
31   }
```

10.1.3 Using Inheritance to Customize Frames

Declare a JFrame subclass for a complex frame.

As you add more user-interface components to a frame, the frame can get quite complex. Your programs will become easier to understand when you use inheritance for complex frames.

To do so, design a subclass of JFrame. Store the components as instance variables. Initialize them in the constructor of your subclass. This approach makes it easy to add helper methods for organizing your code.

It is also a good idea to set the frame size in the frame constructor. The frame usually has a better idea of the preferred size than the program displaying it.

For example,

In Java, you can use inheritance to customize a frame.

```java
public class FilledFrame extends JFrame
{
   // Use instance variables for components
   private JButton button;
   private JLabel label;

   private static final int FRAME_WIDTH = 300;
   private static final int FRAME_HEIGHT = 100;

   public FilledFrame()
   {
      // Now we can use a helper method
      createComponents();

      // It is a good idea to set the size in the frame constructor
      setSize(FRAME_WIDTH, FRAME_HEIGHT);
   }

   private void createComponents()
   {
      button = new JButton("Click me!");
      label = new JLabel("Hello, World!");
      JPanel panel = new JPanel();
      panel.add(button);
      panel.add(label);
      add(panel);
   }
}
```

Of course, we still need a class with a main method:

```java
public class FilledFrameViewer2
{
   public static void main(String[] args)
   {
      JFrame frame = new FilledFrame();
      frame.setTitle("A frame with two components");
      frame.setDefaultCloseOperation(JFrame.EXIT_ON_CLOSE);
      frame.setVisible(true);
   }
}
```

ONLINE EXAMPLE

The complete FilledFrame program.

1. How do you display a square frame with a title bar that reads "Hello, World!"?
2. How can a program display two frames at once?
3. How can a program show a frame with two buttons labeled Yes and No?
4. Why does the `FilledFrameViewer2` class declare the frame variable to have class `JFrame`, not `FilledFrame`?
5. How many Java source files are required by the application in Section 10.1.3 when we use inheritance to declare the frame class?
6. Why does the `createComponents` method of `FilledFrame` call `add(panel)`, whereas the main method of `FilledFrameViewer` calls `frame.add(panel)`?

Practice It   Now you can try these exercises at the end of the chapter: R10.1, R10.4, P10.1.

Special Topic 10.1

Adding the `main` Method to the Frame Class

Have another look at the `FilledFrame` and `FilledFrameViewer2` classes. Some programmers prefer to combine these two classes, by adding the `main` method to the frame class:

```java
public class FilledFrame extends JFrame
{
    . . .
    public static void main(String[] args)
    {
        JFrame frame = new FilledFrame();
        frame.setTitle("A frame with two components");
        frame.setDefaultCloseOperation(JFrame.EXIT_ON_CLOSE);
        frame.setVisible(true);
    }

    public FilledFrame()
    {
        createComponents();
        setSize(FRAME_WIDTH, FRAME_HEIGHT);
    }
    . . .
}
```

This is a convenient shortcut that you will find in many programs, but it does not separate the responsibilities between the frame class and the program.

10.2 Events and Event Handling

In an application that interacts with the user through a console window, user input is under control of the program. The program asks the user for input in a specific order. For example, a program might ask the user to supply first a name, then a dollar amount. But the programs that you use every day on your computer don't work like that. In a program with a modern **graphical user interface**, the *user* is in control. The user can use both the mouse and the keyboard and can manipulate many parts of the user interface in any desired order. For example, the user can enter information into text fields, pull down menus, click buttons, and drag scroll bars in any order. The program must react to the user commands in whatever order they arrive. Having to deal with many possible inputs in random order is quite a bit harder than simply forcing the user to supply input in a fixed order.

In the following sections, you will learn how to write Java programs that can react to user-interface events.

10.2.1 Listening to Events

Whenever the user of a graphical program types characters or uses the mouse anywhere inside one of the windows of the program, the program receives a notification that an **event** has occurred. For example, whenever the mouse moves a tiny interval over a window, a "mouse move" event is generated. Clicking a button or selecting a menu item generates an "action" event.

Most programs don't want to be flooded by irrelevant events. For example, when a button is clicked with the mouse, the mouse moves over the button, then the mouse button is pressed, and finally the button is released. Rather than receiving all these mouse events, a program can indicate that it only cares about button clicks, not about the underlying mouse events. On the other hand, if the mouse input is used

In an event-driven user interface, the program receives an event whenever the user manipulates an input component.

for drawing shapes on a virtual canvas, a program needs to closely track mouse events.

Every program must indicate which events it needs to receive. It does that by installing **event listener** objects. These objects are instances of classes that you must provide. The methods of your event listener classes contain the instructions that you want to have executed when the events occur.

To install a listener, you need to know the **event source**. The event source is the user-interface component, such as a button, that generates a particular event. You add an event listener object to the appropriate event sources. Whenever the event occurs, the event source calls the appropriate methods of all attached event listeners.

This sounds somewhat abstract, so let's run through an extremely simple program that prints a message whenever a button is clicked. Button listeners must belong to a class that implements the ActionListener interface:

```java
public interface ActionListener
{
    void actionPerformed(ActionEvent event);
}
```

This particular interface has a single method, actionPerformed. It is your job to supply a class whose actionPerformed method contains the instructions that you want executed whenever the button is clicked. Here is a very simple example of such a listener class:

section_2_1/ClickListener.java

```java
1   import java.awt.event.ActionEvent;
2   import java.awt.event.ActionListener;
3
```

```
4    /**
5        An action listener that prints a message.
6    */
7    public class ClickListener implements ActionListener
8    {
9        public void actionPerformed(ActionEvent event)
10       {
11           System.out.println("I was clicked.");
12       }
13   }
```

We ignore the event parameter variable of the actionPerformed method—it contains additional details about the event, such as the time at which it occurred. Note that the event handling classes are defined in the java.awt.event package. (AWT is the Abstract Window Toolkit, the Java library for dealing with windows and events.)

Once the listener class has been declared, we need to construct an object of the class and add it to the button:

Attach an ActionListener to each button so that your program can react to button clicks.

```
ActionListener listener = new ClickListener();
button.addActionListener(listener);
```

Whenever the button is clicked, the Java event handling library calls

```
listener.actionPerformed(event);
```

As a result, the message is printed.

You can test this program out by opening a console window, starting the Button-Viewer1 program from that console window, clicking the button, and watching the messages in the console window (see Figure 3).

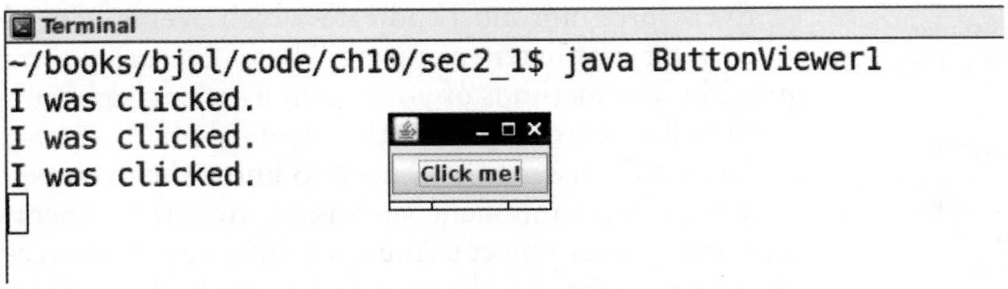

Figure 3 Implementing an Action Listener

section_2_1/ButtonFrame1.java

```
1    import java.awt.event.ActionListener;
2    import javax.swing.JButton;
3    import javax.swing.JFrame;
4    import javax.swing.JPanel;
5
6    /**
7        This frame demonstrates how to install an action listener.
8    */
9    public class ButtonFrame1 extends JFrame
10   {
11       private static final int FRAME_WIDTH = 100;
12       private static final int FRAME_HEIGHT = 60;
13
```

```
14        public ButtonFrame1()
15        {
16            createComponents();
17            setSize(FRAME WIDTH, FRAME_HEIGHT);
18        }
19
20        private void createComponents()
21        {
22            JButton button = new JButton("Click me!");
23            JPanel panel = new JPanel();
24            panel.add(button);
25            add(panel);
26
27            ActionListener listener = new ClickListener();
28            button.addActionListener(listener);
29        }
30    }
```

section_2_1/ButtonViewer1.java

```
1    import javax.swing.JFrame;
2
3    /**
4       This program demonstrates how to install an action listener.
5    */
6    public class ButtonViewer1
7    {
8        public static void main(String[] args)
9        {
10            JFrame frame = new ButtonFrame1();
11            frame.setDefaultCloseOperation(JFrame.EXIT_ON_CLOSE);
12            frame.setVisible(true);
13        }
14    }
```

10.2.2 Using Inner Classes for Listeners

An inner class is a class that is declared inside another class.

In the preceding section, you saw how to specify button actions. The code for the button action is placed into a listener class. It is common to implement listener classes as **inner classes** like this:

```
public class ButtonFrame2 extends JFrame
{
    . . .
    // This inner class is declared inside the frame class
    class ClickListener implements ActionListener
    {
        . . .
    }

    private void createComponents()
    {
        button = new JButton("Click me!");
        ActionListener listener = new ClickListener();
        button.addActionListener(listener);
        . . .
    }
}
```

An inner class is simply a class that is declared inside another class.

There are two advantages to making a listener class into an inner class. First, listener classes tend to be very short. You can put the inner class close to where it is needed, without cluttering up the remainder of the project. Moreover, inner classes have a very attractive feature: Their methods can access instance variables and methods of the surrounding class.

This feature is particularly useful when implementing event handlers. It allows the inner class to access variables without having to receive them as constructor or method arguments.

Let's look at an example. Instead of printing the message "I was clicked", we want to show it in a label. If we make the action listener into an inner class of the frame class, its actionPerformed method can access the label instance variable and call the setText method, which changes the label text.

```java
public class ButtonFrame2 extends JFrame
{
    private JButton button;
    private JLabel label;
    . . .
    class ClickListener implements ActionListener
    {
        public void actionPerformed(ActionEvent event)
        {
            // Accesses label variable from surrounding class
            label.setText("I was clicked");
        }
    }
    . . .
}
```

Having the listener as a regular class is unattractive—the listener would need to be constructed with a reference to the label field (see Exercise P10.5).

section_2_2/ButtonFrame2.java

```java
1   import java.awt.event.ActionEvent;
2   import java.awt.event.ActionListener;
3   import javax.swing.JButton;
4   import javax.swing.JFrame;
5   import javax.swing.JLabel;
6   import javax.swing.JPanel;
7
8   public class ButtonFrame2 extends JFrame
9   {
10      private JButton button;
11      private JLabel label;
12
13      private static final int FRAME_WIDTH = 300;
14      private static final int FRAME_HEIGHT = 100;
15
16      public ButtonFrame2()
17      {
18          createComponents();
19          setSize(FRAME_WIDTH, FRAME_HEIGHT);
20      }
21
```

```
22      /**
23          An action listener that changes the label text.
24      */
25      class ClickListener implements ActionListener
26      {
27          public void actionPerformed(ActionEvent event)
28          {
29              label.setText("I was clicked.");
30          }
31      }
32
33      private void createComponents()
34      {
35          button = new JButton("Click me!");
36          ActionListener listener = new ClickListener();
37          button.addActionListener(listener);
38
39          label = new JLabel("Hello, World!");
40
41          JPanel panel = new JPanel();
42          panel.add(button);
43          panel.add(label);
44          add(panel);
45      }
46  }
```

10.2.3 Application: Showing Growth of an Investment

In this section, we will build a practical application with a graphical user interface. A frame displays the amount of money in a bank account. Whenever the user clicks a button, 5 percent interest is added, and the new balance is displayed (see Figure 4).

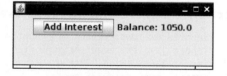

Figure 4
Clicking the Button
Grows the Investment

We need a button and a label for the user interface. We also need to store the current balance:

```
public class InvestmentFrame extends JFrame
{
    private JButton button;
    private JLabel resultLabel;
    private double balance;

    private static final double INTEREST_RATE = 5;
    private static final double INITIAL_BALANCE = 1000;
    . . .
}
```

We initialize the balance when the frame is constructed. Then we add the button and label to a panel, and the panel to the frame:

```
public InvestmentFrame()
{
```

```
      balance = INITIAL_BALANCE;

      createComponents();
      setSize(FRAME_WIDTH, FRAME_HEIGHT);
   }
```

Now we are ready for the hard part—the event listener that handles button clicks. As in the preceding section, it is necessary to declare a class that implements the Action-Listener interface, and to place the button action into the actionPerformed method. Our listener class adds interest and displays the new balance:

```
class AddInterestListener implements ActionListener
{
   public void actionPerformed(ActionEvent event)
   {
      double interest = balance * INTEREST_RATE / 100;
      balance = balance + interest;
      resultLabel.setText("Balance: " + balance);
   }
}
```

We make this class an inner class so that it can access the balance and resultLabel instance variables.

Finally, we need to add an instance of the listener class to the button:

```
private void createComponents()
{
   button = new JButton("Add Interest");
   ActionListener listener = new AddInterestListener();
   button.addActionListener(listener);
   . . .
}
```

Here is the complete program. It demonstrates how to add multiple components to a frame, by using a panel, and how to implement listeners as inner classes.

section_2_3/InvestmentFrame.java

```
1   import java.awt.event.ActionEvent;
2   import java.awt.event.ActionListener;
3   import javax.swing.JButton;
4   import javax.swing.JFrame;
5   import javax.swing.JLabel;
6   import javax.swing.JPanel;
7
8   public class InvestmentFrame extends JFrame
9   {
10     private JButton button;
11     private JLabel resultLabel;
12     private double balance;
13
14     private static final int FRAME_WIDTH = 300;
15     private static final int FRAME_HEIGHT = 100;
16
17     private static final double INTEREST_RATE = 5;
18     private static final double INITIAL_BALANCE = 1000;
19
20     public InvestmentFrame()
21     {
22        balance = INITIAL_BALANCE;
```

```
23
24        createComponents();
25        setSize(FRAME_WIDTH, FRAME_HEIGHT);
26     }
27
28     /**
29        Adds interest to the balance and updates the display.
30     */
31     class AddInterestListener implements ActionListener
32     {
33        public void actionPerformed(ActionEvent event)
34        {
35           double interest = balance * INTEREST_RATE / 100;
36           balance = balance + interest;
37           resultLabel.setText("Balance: " + balance);
38        }
39     }
40
41     private void createComponents()
42     {
43        button = new JButton("Add Interest");
44        ActionListener listener = new AddInterestListener();
45        button.addActionListener(listener);
46
47        resultLabel = new JLabel("Balance: " + balance);
48
49        JPanel panel = new JPanel();
50        panel.add(button);
51        panel.add(resultLabel);
52        add(panel);
53     }
54 }
```

section_2_3/InvestmentViewer.java

```
1  import javax.swing.JFrame;
2
3  /**
4     This program shows the growth of an investment.
5  */
6  public class InvestmentViewer
7  {
8     public static void main(String[] args)
9     {
10        JFrame frame = new InvestmentFrame();
11        frame.setDefaultCloseOperation(JFrame.EXIT_ON_CLOSE);
12        frame.setVisible(true);
13     }
14 }
```

SELF CHECK

7. Which objects are the event source and the event listener in the ButtonViewer program?

8. Why is it legal to assign a ClickListener object to a variable of type ActionListener?

9. When do you call the actionPerformed method?

10. Why would an inner class method want to access a variable from a surrounding scope?

11. How do you place the "Balance: . . ." message to the left of the "Add Interest" button?

Practice It   Now you can try these exercises at the end of the chapter: R10.7, P10.2, P10.5.

Common Error 10.1

Modifying Parameter Types in the Implementing Method

When you implement an interface, you must declare each method *exactly* as it is specified in the interface. Accidentally making small changes to the parameter variable types is a common error. Here is the classic example,

```
class MyListener implements ActionListener
{
    public void actionPerformed()
    // Oops . . . forgot ActionEvent parameter variable
    {
        . . .
    }
}
```

As far as the compiler is concerned, this class fails to provide the method

```
public void actionPerformed(ActionEvent event)
```

You have to read the error message carefully and pay attention to the parameter variable and return types to find your error.

Common Error 10.2

Forgetting to Attach a Listener

If you run your program and find that your buttons seem to be dead, double-check that you attached the button listener. The same holds for other user-interface components. It is a surprisingly common error to program the listener class and the event handler action without actually attaching the listener to the event source.

Programming Tip 10.1

Don't Use a Frame as a Listener

In this book, we use inner classes for event listeners. That approach works for many different event types. Once you master the technique, you don't have to think about it anymore. Many development environments automatically generate code with inner classes, so it is a good idea to be familiar with them.

However, some programmers bypass the event listener classes and turn a frame into a listener, like this:

```
public class InvestmentFrame extends JFrame
    implements ActionListener  // This approach is not recommended
{
    . . .
    public InvestmentFrame()
    {
        button = new JButton("Add Interest");
        button.addActionListener(this);
        . . .
```

```
        }

        public void actionPerformed(ActionEvent event)
        {
        }
        . . .
    }
```

Now the `actionPerformed` method is a part of the `InvestmentFrame` class rather than part of a separate listener class. The listener is installed as this.

We don't recommend this technique. If the viewer class contains two buttons that each generate action events, then the `actionPerformed` method must investigate the event source, which leads to code that is tedious and error-prone.

Special Topic 10.2

Local Inner Classes

An inner class can be declared completely inside a method. For example,

```
public static void main(String[] args)
{
    . . .
    class ClickListener implements ActionListener
    {
        public void actionPerformed(ActionEvent event)
        {
            . . .
        }
    }

    JButton button = new JButton("Click me");
    button.addActionListener(new ClickListener());
    . . .
}
```

This places the inner class exactly where you need it, next to the button.

The methods of a class that is defined inside a method can access the variables of the enclosing method, provided they are declared as `final`. For example,

```
public static void main(String[] args)
{
    final JLabel label = new JLabel("Hello, World!");
    . . .
    class ClickListener implements ActionListener
    {
        public void actionPerformed(ActionEvent event)
        {
            label.setText("I was clicked");
            // Accesses label variable from enclosing method
        }
    }
    . . .
    button.addActionListener(new ClickListener());
}
```

That sounds quite restrictive, but it is usually not an issue if the variable is an object reference. Keep in mind that an object variable is `final` when the variable always refers to the same object. The state of the object can change, but the variable can't refer to a different object. For example, in our program, we never intended to have the `label` variable refer to multiple labels, so there was no harm in declaring it as `final`.

However, you can't change a numeric or Boolean local variable from an inner class. For example, the following would not work:

```java
public static void main(String[] args)
{
   final double balance = INITIAL_BALANCE;
   . . .
   class AddInterestListener implements ActionListener
   {
      public void actionPerformed(ActionEvent event)
      {
         double interest = balance * (1 + INTEREST_RATE);
         balance = balance + interest;
            // Error: Can't modify a final numeric variable
      }
   }
   . . .
}
```

The remedy is to use an object instead:

```java
public static void main(String[] args)
{
   final BankAccount account = new BankAccount();
   account.deposit(INITIAL_BALANCE);
   . . .
   class AddInterestListener implements ActionListener
   {
      public void actionPerformed(ActionEvent event)
      {
         double interest = balance * (1 + INTEREST_RATE);
         account.deposit(interest);
            // Ok—we don't change the reference, just the object's state
      }
   }
   . . .
}
```

Special Topic 10.3

Anonymous Inner Classes

An entity is anonymous if it does not have a name. In a program, something that is only used once doesn't usually need a name. For example, you can replace

```java
String buttonLabel = "Add Interest";
JButton button = new JButton(buttonLabel);
```

with

```java
JButton button = new JButton("Add Interest");
```

The string "Add Interest" is an anonymous object. Programmers like anonymous objects, because they don't have to go through the trouble of coming up with a name. If you have struggled with the decision whether to call a label l, label, or buttonLabel, you'll understand this sentiment.

Event listeners often give rise to a similar situation. You construct a single object of an event listener class. Afterward, the class is never used again. In Java, it is possible to declare an anonymous class if all you ever need is a single object of the class.

Here is an example:

```
button = new JButton("Add Interest");
button.addActionListener(new ActionListener()
    {
        public void actionPerformed(ActionEvent event)
        {
            double interest = balance * (1 + INTEREST_RATE);
            account.deposit(interest);
        }
    });
```

This means: Define a class that implements the ActionListener interface with the given action-Performed method. Construct an object of that class and pass it to the addActionListener method.

Many programmers like this style because it is so compact. Moreover, GUI builders in integrated development environments often generate code of this form.

10.3 Processing Text Input

We continue our discussion with graphical user interfaces that accept text input. Of course, a graphical application can receive text input by calling the showInputDialog method of the JOptionPane class, but popping up a separate dialog box for each input is not a natural user interface. Most graphical programs collect text input through **text components** (see Figures 5 and 7). In the following two sections, you will learn how to add text components to a graphical application, and how to read what the user types into them.

10.3.1 Text Fields

Use a JTextField component for reading a single line of input. Place a JLabel next to each text field.

The JTextField class provides a text field for reading a single line of text. When you construct a text field, you need to supply the width—the approximate number of characters that you expect the user to type.

```
final int FIELD_WIDTH = 10;
rateField = new JTextField(FIELD_WIDTH);
```

Users can type additional characters, but then a part of the contents of the field becomes invisible.

You will want to label each text field so that the user knows what to type into it. Construct a JLabel object for each label:

```
JLabel rateLabel = new JLabel("Interest Rate: ");
```

You want to give the user an opportunity to enter all information into the text fields before processing it. Therefore, you should supply a button that the user can press to indicate that the input is ready for processing.

Figure 5
An Application
with a Text Field

When that button is clicked, its `actionPerformed` method should read the user input from each text field, using the `getText` method of the `JTextField` class. The `getText` method returns a `String` object. In our sample program, we turn the string into a number, using the `Double.parseDouble` method. After updating the account, we show the balance in another label.

```
class AddInterestListener implements ActionListener
{
   public void actionPerformed(ActionEvent event)
   {
      double rate = Double.parseDouble(rateField.getText());
      double interest = balance * rate / 100;
      balance = balance + interest;
      resultLabel.setText("Balance: " + balance);
   }
}
```

The following application is a useful prototype for a graphical user-interface front end for arbitrary calculations. You can easily modify it for your own needs. Place input components into the frame. In the `actionPerformed` method, carry out the needed calculations. Display the result in a label.

section_3_1/InvestmentFrame2.java

```
1   import java.awt.event.ActionEvent;
2   import java.awt.event.ActionListener;
3   import javax.swing.JButton;
4   import javax.swing.JFrame;
5   import javax.swing.JLabel;
6   import javax.swing.JPanel;
7   import javax.swing.JTextField;
8
9   /**
10     A frame that shows the growth of an investment with variable interest.
11  */
12  public class InvestmentFrame2 extends JFrame
13  {
14     private static final int FRAME_WIDTH = 450;
15     private static final int FRAME_HEIGHT = 100;
16
17     private static final double DEFAULT_RATE = 5;
18     private static final double INITIAL_BALANCE = 1000;
19
20     private JLabel rateLabel;
21     private JTextField rateField;
22     private JButton button;
23     private JLabel resultLabel;
24     private double balance;
25
26     public InvestmentFrame2()
27     {
28        balance = INITIAL_BALANCE;
29
30        resultLabel = new JLabel("Balance: " + balance);
31
32        createTextField();
33        createButton();
34        createPanel();
35
```

```
36            setSize(FRAME_WIDTH, FRAME_HEIGHT);
37        }
38
39        private void createTextField()
40        {
41            rateLabel = new JLabel("Interest Rate: ");
42
43            final int FIELD_WIDTH = 10;
44            rateField = new JTextField(FIELD_WIDTH);
45            rateField.setText("" + DEFAULT_RATE);
46        }
47
48        /**
49            Adds interest to the balance and updates the display.
50        */
51        class AddInterestListener implements ActionListener
52        {
53            public void actionPerformed(ActionEvent event)
54            {
55                double rate = Double.parseDouble(rateField.getText());
56                double interest = balance * rate / 100;
57                balance = balance + interest;
58                resultLabel.setText("Balance: " + balance);
59            }
60        }
61
62        private void createButton()
63        {
64            button = new JButton("Add Interest");
65
66            ActionListener listener = new AddInterestListener();
67            button.addActionListener(listener);
68        }
69
70        private void createPanel()
71        {
72            panel = new JPanel();
73            panel.add(rateLabel);
74            panel.add(rateField);
75            panel.add(button);
76            panel.add(resultLabel);
77            add(panel);
78        }
79    }
```

10.3.2 Text Areas

Use a JTextArea to show multiple lines of text.

In the preceding section, you saw how to construct text fields. A text field holds a single line of text. To display multiple lines of text, use the JTextArea class.

You can use a text area for reading or displaying multi-line text.

When constructing a text area, you can specify the number of rows and columns:

```
final int ROWS = 10; // Lines of text
final int COLUMNS = 30; // Characters in each row
JTextArea textArea = new JTextArea(ROWS, COLUMNS);
```

Use the setText method to set the text of a text field or text area. The append method adds text to the end of a text area. Use newline characters to separate lines, like this:

```
textArea.append(balance + "\n");
```

If you want to use a text field or text area for display purposes only, call the set-Editable method like this

```
textArea.setEditable(false);
```

Now the user can no longer edit the contents of the field, but your program can still call setText and append to change it.

As shown in Figure 6, the JTextField and JTextArea classes are subclasses of the class JTextComponent. The methods setText and setEditable are declared in the JText-Component class and inherited by JTextField and JTextArea. However, the append method is declared in the JTextArea class.

To add scroll bars to a text area, use a JScrollPane, like this:

```
JTextArea textArea = new JTextArea(ROWS, COLUMNS);
JScrollPane scrollPane = new JScrollPane(textArea);
```

You can add scroll bars to any component with a JScrollPane.

Then add the scroll pane to the panel. Figure 7 shows the result.

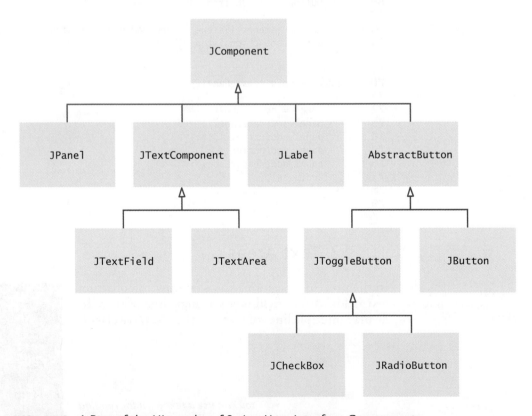

Figure 6 A Part of the Hierarchy of Swing User-Interface Components

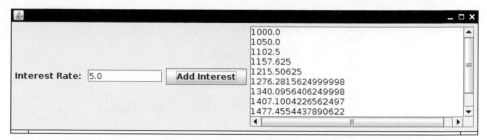

Figure 7 The Investment Application with a Text Area Inside Scroll Bars

The following sample program puts these concepts together. A user can enter numbers into the interest rate text field and then click on the "Add Interest" button. The interest rate is applied, and the updated balance is appended to the text area. The text area has scroll bars and is not editable.

This program is similar to the previous investment viewer program, but it keeps track of all the bank balances, not just the last one.

section_3_2/InvestmentFrame3.java

```java
1   import java.awt.event.ActionEvent;
2   import java.awt.event.ActionListener;
3   import javax.swing.JButton;
4   import javax.swing.JFrame;
5   import javax.swing.JLabel;
6   import javax.swing.JPanel;
7   import javax.swing.JScrollPane;
8   import javax.swing.JTextArea;
9   import javax.swing.JTextField;
10
11  /**
12     A frame that shows the growth of an investment with variable interest,
13     using a text area.
14  */
15  public class InvestmentFrame3 extends JFrame
16  {
17     private static final int FRAME_WIDTH = 400;
18     private static final int FRAME_HEIGHT = 250;
19
20     private static final int AREA_ROWS = 10;
21     private static final int AREA_COLUMNS = 30;
22
23     private static final double DEFAULT_RATE = 5;
24     private static final double INITIAL_BALANCE = 1000;
25
26     private JLabel rateLabel;
27     private JTextField rateField;
28     private JButton button;
29     private JTextArea resultArea;
30     private double balance;
31
32     public InvestmentFrame3()
33     {
34        balance = INITIAL_BALANCE;
35        resultArea = new JTextArea(AREA_ROWS, AREA_COLUMNS);
```

```
36       resultArea.setText(balance + "\n");
37       resultArea.setEditable(false);
38
39       createTextField();
40       createButton();
41       createPanel();
42
43       setSize(FRAME_WIDTH, FRAME_HEIGHT);
44    }
45
46    private void createTextField()
47    {
48       rateLabel = new JLabel("Interest Rate: ");
49
50       final int FIELD_WIDTH = 10;
51       rateField = new JTextField(FIELD_WIDTH);
52       rateField.setText("" + DEFAULT_RATE);
53    }
54
55    class AddInterestListener implements ActionListener
56    {
57       public void actionPerformed(ActionEvent event)
58       {
59          double rate = Double.parseDouble(rateField.getText());
60          double interest = balance * rate / 100;
61          balance = balance + interest;
62          resultArea.append(balance + "\n");
63       }
64    }
65
66    private void createButton()
67    {
68       button = new JButton("Add Interest");
69
70       ActionListener listener = new AddInterestListener();
71       button.addActionListener(listener);
72    }
73
74    private void createPanel()
75    {
76       JPanel = new JPanel();
77       panel.add(rateLabel);
78       panel.add(rateField);
79       panel.add(button);
80       JScrollPane scrollPane = new JScrollPane(resultArea);
81       panel.add(scrollPane);
82       add(panel);
83    }
84 }
```

SELF CHECK

12. What happens if you omit the first JLabel object in the program of Section 10.3.1?

13. If a text field holds an integer, what expression do you use to read its contents?

14. What is the difference between a text field and a text area?

15. Why did the InvestmentFrame3 program call resultArea.setEditable(false)?

16. How would you modify the `InvestmentFrame3` program if you didn't want to use scroll bars?

Practice It Now you can try these exercises at the end of the chapter: R10.13, P10.9, P10.10.

10.4 Creating Drawings

You often want to include simple drawings such as graphs or charts in your programs. The Java library does not have any standard components for this purpose, but it is fairly easy to make your own drawings. The following sections show how.

10.4.1 Drawing on a Component

We start out with a simple bar chart (see Figure 8) that is composed of three rectangles.

You can make simple drawings out of lines, rectangles, and circles.

> In order to display a drawing, provide a class that extends the `JComponent` class.

You cannot draw directly onto a frame. Instead, you add a component to the frame and draw on the component. To do so, extend the `JComponent` class and override its `paintComponent` method.

```
public class ChartComponent extends JComponent
{
    public void paintComponent(Graphics g)
    {
        Drawing instructions
    }
}
```

> Place drawing instructions inside the `paintComponent` method. That method is called whenever the component needs to be repainted.

When the component is shown for the first time, its `paintComponent` method is called automatically. The method is also called when the window is resized, or when it is shown again after it was hidden.

The `paintComponent` method receives an object of type `Graphics`. The `Graphics` object stores the graphics state—the current color, font, and so on, that are used for drawing operations. The `Graphics` class has methods for drawing geometric shapes. The call

```
g.fillRect(x, y, width, height)
```

draws a solid rectangle with upper-left corner (x, y) and the given width and height.

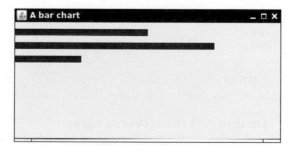

Figure 8 Drawing a Bar Chart

The Graphics class has methods to draw rectangles and other shapes.

Here we draw three rectangles. They line up on the left because they all have $x = 0$. They also all have the same height.

```java
public class ChartComponent extends JComponent
{
    public void paintComponent(Graphics g)
    {
        g.fillRect(0, 10, 200, 10);
        g.fillRect(0, 30, 300, 10);
        g.fillRect(0, 50, 100, 10);
    }
}
```

Note that the coordinate system is different from the one used in mathematics. The origin $(0, 0)$ is at the upper-left corner of the component, and the y-coordinate grows downward.

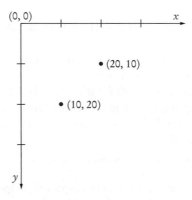

Here is the source code for the ChartComponent class. As you can see from the import statements, the Graphics class is part of the java.awt package.

section_4_1/ChartComponent.java

```java
1   import java.awt.Graphics;
2   import javax.swing.JComponent;
3
4   /**
5      A component that draws a bar chart.
6   */
7   public class ChartComponent extends JComponent
8   {
9      public void paintComponent(Graphics g)
10     {
11        g.fillRect(0, 10, 200, 10);
12        g.fillRect(0, 30, 300, 10);
13        g.fillRect(0, 50, 100, 10);
14     }
15  }
```

Now we need to add the component to a frame, and show the frame. Because the frame is so simple, we don't make a frame subclass. Here is the viewer class:

section_4_1/ChartViewer.java

```java
1   import javax.swing.JComponent;
2   import javax.swing.JFrame;
```

```
 3
 4   public class ChartViewer
 5   {
 6      public static void main(String[] args)
 7      {
 8         JFrame frame = new JFrame();
 9
10         frame.setSize(400, 200);
11         frame.setTitle("A bar chart");
12         frame.setDefaultCloseOperation(JFrame.EXIT_ON_CLOSE);
13
14         JComponent component = new ChartComponent();
15         frame.add(component);
16
17         frame.setVisible(true);
18      }
19   }
```

10.4.2 Ovals, Lines, Text, and Color

In the preceding section, you learned how to write a program that draws rectangles. Now we turn to additional graphical elements that allow you to draw quite a few interesting pictures.

To draw an oval, you specify its *bounding box* (see Figure 9) in the same way that you would specify a rectangle, namely by the x- and y-coordinates of the top-left corner and the width and height of the box. Then the call

```
g.drawOval(x, y, width, height);
```

draws the outline of an oval. To draw a circle, simply set the width and height to the same values:

```
g.drawOval(x, y, diameter, diameter);
```

Notice that (x, y) is the top-left corner of the bounding box, not the center of the circle.

If you want to fill the inside of an oval, use the fillOval method instead. Conversely, if you want only the outline of a rectangle, with no filling, use the drawRect method.

Use drawRect, drawOval, and drawLine to draw geometric shapes.

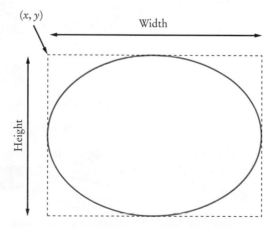

Figure 9   An Oval and Its Bounding Box

Figure 10
Basepoint and Baseline

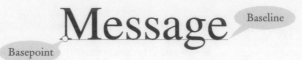

To draw a line, call the drawLine method with the *x*- and *y*-coordinates of both end points:

```
g.drawLine(x1, y1, x2, y2);
```

You often want to put text inside a drawing, for example, to label some of the parts. Use the drawString method of the Graphics class to draw a string anywhere in a window. You must specify the string and the *x*- and *y*-coordinates of the basepoint of the first character in the string (see Figure 10). For example,

```
g.drawString("Message", 50, 100);
```

> The drawString method draws a string, starting at its basepoint.

When you first start drawing, all shapes and strings are drawn with a black pen. To change the color, you need to supply an object of type Color. Java uses the RGB color model. That is, you specify a color by the amounts of the primary colors—red, green, and blue—that make up the color. The amounts are given as integers between 0 (primary color not present) and 255 (maximum amount present). For example,

```
Color magenta = new Color(255, 0, 255);
```

constructs a Color object with maximum red, no green, and maximum blue, yielding a bright purple color called magenta.

Table 1 Predefined Colors		
Color		RGB Values
Color.BLACK		0, 0, 0
Color.BLUE		0, 0, 255
Color.CYAN		0, 255, 255
Color.GRAY		128, 128, 128
Color.DARKGRAY		64, 64, 64
Color.LIGHTGRAY		192, 192, 192
Color.GREEN		0, 255, 0
Color.MAGENTA		255, 0, 255
Color.ORANGE		255, 200, 0
Color.PINK		255, 175, 175
Color.RED		255, 0, 0
Color.WHITE		255, 255, 255
Color.YELLOW		255, 255, 0

For your convenience, a variety of colors have been predefined in the Color class. Table 1 shows those predefined colors and their RGB values. For example, Color.PINK has been predefined to be the same color as new Color(255, 175, 175).

To draw a shape in a different color, first set the color of the Graphics object, then call the drawing method:

> When you set a new color in the graphics context, it is used for subsequent drawing operations.

```
g.setColor(Color.YELLOW);
g.fillOval(350, 25, 35, 20); // Fills the oval in yellow
```

The following program puts all these shapes to work, creating a simple chart (see Figure 11).

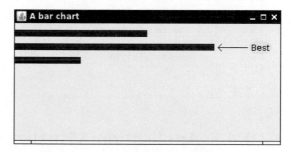

Figure 11 A Bar Chart with a Label

section_4_2/ChartComponent2.java

```java
1   import java.awt.Color;
2   import java.awt.Graphics;
3   import javax.swing.JComponent;
4
5   /**
6      A component that draws a demo chart.
7   */
8   public class ChartComponent2 extends JComponent
9   {
10     public void paintComponent(Graphics g)
11     {
12        // Draw the bars
13        g.fillRect(0, 10, 200, 10);
14        g.fillRect(0, 30, 300, 10);
15        g.fillRect(0, 50, 100, 10);
16
17        // Draw the arrow
18        g.drawLine(350, 35, 305, 35);
19        g.drawLine(305, 35, 310, 30);
20        g.drawLine(305, 35, 310, 40);
21
22        // Draw the highlight and the text
23        g.setColor(Color.YELLOW);
24        g.fillOval(350, 25, 35, 20);
25        g.setColor(Color.BLACK);
26        g.drawString("Best", 355, 40);
27     }
28   }
```

section_4_2/ChartViewer2.java

```java
1   import javax.swing.JComponent;
2   import javax.swing.JFrame;
3
4   public class ChartViewer2
5   {
6      public static void main(String[] args)
7      {
8         JFrame frame = new JFrame();
9
10        frame.setSize(400, 200);
11        frame.setTitle("A bar chart");
12        frame.setDefaultCloseOperation(JFrame.EXIT_ON_CLOSE);
13
14        JComponent component = new ChartComponent2();
15        frame.add(component);
16
17        frame.setVisible(true);
18     }
19  }
```

10.4.3 Application: Visualizing the Growth of an Investment

In this section, we will add a bar chart to the investment program of Section 10.3. Whenever the user clicks on the "Add Interest" button, another bar is added to the bar chart (see Figure 12).

The chart class of the preceding section produced a fixed bar chart. We will develop an improved version that can draw a chart with any values. The chart keeps an array list of the values:

```java
public class ChartComponent extends JComponent
{
    private ArrayList<Double> values;
    private double maxValue;
    . . .
}
```

When drawing the bars, we need to scale the values to fit into the chart. For example, if the investment program adds a value such as 10050 to the chart, we don't want to draw a bar that is 10,050 pixels long. In order to scale the values, we need to know the largest value that should still fit inside the chart. We will ask the user of the chart component to provide that maximum in the constructor:

```java
public ChartComponent(double max)
{
    values = new ArrayList<Double>();
    maxValue = max;
}
```

We compute the width of a bar as

```java
int barWidth = (int) (getWidth() * value / maxValue);
```

The getWidth method returns the width of the component in pixels. If the value to be drawn equals maxValue, the bar stretches across the entire component width.

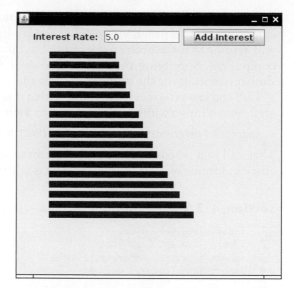

Figure 12 Clicking on the "Add Interest" Button Adds a Bar to the Chart

Here is the complete `paintComponent` method. We stack the bars horizontally and leave small gaps between them:

```java
public void paintComponent(Graphics g)
{
   final int GAP = 5;
   final int BAR_HEIGHT = 10;

   int y = GAP;
   for (double value : values)
   {
      int barWidth = (int) (getWidth() * value / maxValue);
      g.fillRect(0, y, barWidth, BAR_HEIGHT);
      y = y + BAR_HEIGHT + GAP;
   }
}
```

Whenever the user clicks the "Add Interest" button, a value is added to the array list. Afterward, it is essential to call the `repaint` method:

```java
public void append(double value)
{
   values.add(value);
   repaint();
}
```

The call to `repaint` forces a call to the `paintComponent` method. The `paintComponent` method redraws the component. Then the graph is drawn again, now showing the appended value.

Why not call `paintComponent` directly? The simple answer is that you can't—you don't have a `Graphics` object that you can pass as an argument. Instead, you need to ask the Swing library to make the call to `paintComponent` at its earliest convenience. That is what the `repaint` method does.

Call the repaint method whenever the state of a painted component changes.

When placing a painted component into a panel, you need to specify its preferred size.

We need to address another issue with painted components. If you place a painted component into a panel, you need to specify its preferred size. Otherwise, the panel will assume that the preferred size is 0 by 0 pixels, and you won't be able to see the component. Specifying the preferred size of a painted component is conceptually similar to specifying the number of rows and columns in a text area.

Call the setPreferredSize method with a Dimension object as argument. A Dimension argument wraps a width and a height into a single object. The call has the form

```
chart.setPreferredSize(new Dimension(CHART_WIDTH, CHART_HEIGHT));
```

That's all that is required to add a diagram to an application. Here is the code for the chart and frame classes; the viewer class is with the book's companion code.

section_4_3/ChartComponent.java

```
1   import java.awt.Color;
2   import java.awt.Graphics;
3   import java.util.ArrayList;
4   import javax.swing.JComponent;
5
6   /**
7      A component that draws a chart.
8   */
9   public class ChartComponent extends JComponent
10  {
11     private ArrayList<Double> values;
12     private double maxValue;
13
14     public ChartComponent(double max)
15     {
16        values = new ArrayList<Double>();
17        maxValue = max;
18     }
19
20     public void append(double value)
21     {
22        values.add(value);
23        repaint();
24     }
25
26     public void paintComponent(Graphics g)
27     {
28        final int GAP = 5;
29        final int BAR_HEIGHT = 10;
30
31        int y = GAP;
32        for (double value : values)
33        {
34           int barWidth = (int) (getWidth() * value / maxValue);
35           g.fillRect(0, y, barWidth, BAR_HEIGHT);
36           y = y + BAR_HEIGHT + GAP;
37        }
38     }
39  }
```

section_4_3/InvestmentFrame4.java

```
1   import java.awt.Dimension;
2   import java.awt.event.ActionEvent;
```

```
 3   import java.awt.event.ActionListener;
 4   import javax.swing.JButton;
 5   import javax.swing.JFrame;
 6   import javax.swing.JLabel;
 7   import javax.swing.JPanel;
 8   import javax.swing.JTextField;
 9
10   /**
11      A frame that shows the growth of an investment with variable interest,
12      using a bar chart.
13   */
14   public class InvestmentFrame4 extends JFrame
15   {
16      private static final int FRAME_WIDTH = 400;
17      private static final int FRAME_HEIGHT = 400;
18
19      private static final int CHART_WIDTH = 300;
20      private static final int CHART_HEIGHT = 300;
21
22      private static final double DEFAULT_RATE = 5;
23      private static final double INITIAL_BALANCE = 1000;
24
25      private JLabel rateLabel;
26      private JTextField rateField;
27      private JButton button;
28      private ChartComponent chart;
29      private double balance;
30
31      public InvestmentFrame4()
32      {
33         balance = INITIAL_BALANCE;
34         chart = new ChartComponent(3 * INITIAL_BALANCE);
35         chart.setPreferredSize(new Dimension(CHART_WIDTH, CHART_HEIGHT));
36         chart.append(INITIAL_BALANCE);
37
38         createTextField();
39         createButton();
40         createPanel();
41
42         setSize(FRAME_WIDTH, FRAME_HEIGHT);
43      }
44
45      private void createTextField()
46      {
47         rateLabel = new JLabel("Interest Rate: ");
48
49         final int FIELD_WIDTH = 10;
50         rateField = new JTextField(FIELD_WIDTH);
51         rateField.setText("" + DEFAULT_RATE);
52      }
53
54      class AddInterestListener implements ActionListener
55      {
56         public void actionPerformed(ActionEvent event)
57         {
58            double rate = Double.parseDouble(rateField.getText());
59            double interest = balance * rate / 100;
60            balance = balance + interest;
61            chart.append(balance);
62         }
```

```
63        }
64
65        private void createButton()
66        {
67           button = new JButton("Add Interest");
68
69           ActionListener listener = new AddInterestListener();
70           button.addActionListener(listener);
71        }
72
73        private void createPanel()
74        {
75           JPanel panel = new JPanel();
76           panel.add(rateLabel);
77           panel.add(rateField);
78           panel.add(button);
79           panel.add(chart);
80           add(panel);
81        }
82     }
```

SELF CHECK

17. How do you modify the program in Section 10.4.1 to draw two squares?

18. What happens if you call `fillOval` instead `fillRect` in the program of Section 10.4.1?

19. Give instructions to draw a circle with center (100, 100) and radius 25.

20. Give instructions to draw a letter "V" by drawing two line segments.

21. Give instructions to draw a string consisting of the letter "V".

22. What are the RGB color values of `Color.BLUE`?

23. How do you draw a yellow square on a red background?

24. What would happen in the investment viewer program if we simply painted each bar as

   `g.fillRect(0, y, value, BAR_HEIGHT);`

   in the `paintComponent` method of the `ChartComponent` class?

25. What would happen if you omitted the call to `repaint` in the `append` method of the `ChartComponent` class?

26. What would happen if you omitted the call to `chart.setPreferredSize` in the `InvestmentFrame4` constructor?

Practice It   Now you can do: R10.18, P10.17, P10.18.

Common Error 10.3

Forgetting to Repaint

When you change the data in a painted component, the component is not automatically painted with the new data. You must call the `repaint` method of the component. Your component's `paintComponent` method will then be invoked. Note that you should not call the `paintComponent` method directly.

The best place to call `repaint` is in the method of your component that modifies the data values:

```
void changeData(. . .)
{
    Update data values
    repaint();
}
```

This is a concern only for your own painted components. When you make a change to a standard Swing component such as a `JLabel`, the component is automatically repainted.

Common Error 10.4

By Default, Components Have Zero Width and Height

You must be careful when you add a painted component, such as a component displaying a chart, to a panel. The default size for a `JComponent` is 0 by 0 pixels, and the component will not be visible. The remedy is to call the `setPreferredSize` method:

```
chart.setPreferredSize(new Dimension(CHART_WIDTH, CHART_HEIGHT));
```

This is an issue only for painted components. Buttons, labels, and so on, know how to compute their preferred size.

HOW TO 10.1

Drawing Graphical Shapes

Suppose you want to write a program that displays graphical shapes such as cars, aliens, charts, or any other images that can be obtained from rectangles, lines, and ellipses. These instructions give you a step-by-step procedure for decomposing a drawing into parts and implementing a program that produces the drawing.

In this How To we will create a program to draw a national flag.

Step 1 Determine the shapes that you need for the drawing.

You can use the following shapes:

- Squares and rectangles
- Circles and ellipses
- Lines

The outlines of these shapes can be drawn in any color, and you can fill the insides of these shapes with any color. You can also use text to label parts of your drawing.

Some national flag designs consist of three equally wide sections of different colors, side by side, as in the Italian flag shown below.

You could draw such a flag using three rectangles. But if the middle rectangle is white, as it is, for example, in the flag of Italy (green, white, red), it is easier and looks better to draw a line on the top and bottom of the middle portion:

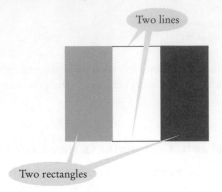

Step 2 Find the coordinates for the shapes.

You now need to find the exact positions for the geometric shapes.

- For rectangles, you need the x- and y-position of the top-left corner, the width, and the height.
- For ellipses, you need the top-left corner, width, and height of the bounding rectangle.
- For lines, you need the x- and y-positions of the starting point and the end point.
- For text, you need the x- and y-position of the basepoint.

A commonly-used size for a window is 300 by 300 pixels. You may not want the flag crammed all the way to the top, so perhaps the upper-left corner of the flag should be at point (100, 100).

Many flags, such as the flag of Italy, have a width : height ratio of 3 : 2. (You can often find exact proportions for a particular flag by doing a bit of Internet research on one of several Flags of the World sites.) For example, if you make the flag 90 pixels wide, then it should be 60 pixels tall. (Why not make it 100 pixels wide? Then the height would be $100 \cdot 2 / 3 \approx 67$, which seems more awkward.)

Now you can compute the coordinates of all the important points of the shape:

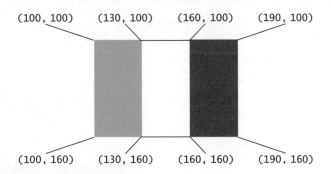

Step 3 Write Java statements to draw the shapes.

In our example, there are two rectangles and two lines:

```
g.setColor(Color.GREEN);
g.fillRect(100, 100, 30, 60);

g.setColor(Color.RED);
g.fillRect(160, 100, 30, 60);
```

```
g.setColor(Color.BLACK);
g.drawLine(130, 100, 160, 100);
g.drawLine(130, 160, 160, 160);
```

If you are more ambitious, then you can express the coordinates in terms of a few variables. In the case of the flag, we have arbitrarily chosen the top-left corner and the width. All other coordinates follow from those choices. If you decide to follow the ambitious approach, then the rectangles and lines are determined as follows:

```
g.fillRect(xLeft, yTop, width / 3, width * 2 / 3);
. . .
g.fillRect(xLeft + 2 * width / 3, yTop, width / 3, width * 2 / 3);
. . .
g.drawLine(xLeft + width / 3, yTop, xLeft + width * 2 / 3, yTop);
g.drawLine(xLeft + width / 3, yTop + width * 2 / 3,
    xLeft + width * 2 / 3, yTop + width * 2 / 3);
```

Step 4   Consider using methods or classes for repetitive steps.

Do you need to draw more than one flag? Perhaps with different sizes? Then it is a good idea to design a method or class, so you won't have to repeat the same drawing instructions.
For example, you can write a method

```
void drawItalianFlag(Graphics g, int xLeft, int yTop, int width)
{
    Draw a flag at the given location and size
}
```

Place the instructions from the preceding step into this method. Then you can call

```
drawItalianFlag(g, 10, 10, 100);
drawItalianFlag(g, 10, 125, 150);
```

in the paintComponent method to draw two flags.

Step 5   Place the drawing instructions in the paintComponent method.

```
public class ItalianFlagComponent extends JComponent
{
    public void paintComponent(Graphics g)
    {
        Drawing instructions
    }
}
```

If your drawing is simple, simply place all drawing statements here. Otherwise, call the methods you created in Step 4.

Step 6   Write the viewer class.

Provide a viewer class, with a main method in which you construct a frame, add your component, and make your frame visible. The viewer class is completely routine; you only need to change a single line to show a different component.

```
public class ItalianFlagViewer
{
    public static void main(String[] args)
    {
        JFrame frame = new JFrame();

        frame.setSize(300, 400);
        frame.setDefaultCloseOperation(JFrame.EXIT_ON_CLOSE);

        JComponent component = new ItalianFlagComponent();
        frame.add(component);
```

ONLINE EXAMPLE

The complete flag
drawing program.

```
            frame.setVisible(true);
        }
    }
```

WORKED EXAMPLE 10.1   Coding a Bar Chart Creator

In this Worked Example, we will develop a simple program for creating bar charts. The user
enters labels and values for the bars, and the program displays the chart.

VIDEO EXAMPLE 10.1   Solving Crossword Puzzles

In this Video Example, we develop a program that finds words for
solving a crossword puzzle.

CHAPTER SUMMARY

Display frames and add components inside frames.

- To show a frame, construct a JFrame object, set its size, and make
  it visible.
- Use a JPanel to group multiple user-interface components together.
- Declare a JFrame subclass for a complex frame.

Explain the event concept and handle button events.

- User-interface events include key presses, mouse moves, button clicks, menu
  selections, and so on.
- An event listener belongs to a class created by the application programmer. Its
  methods describe the actions to be taken when an event occurs.
- Event sources report on events. When an event occurs, the event source notifies
  all event listeners.
- Attach an ActionListener to each button so that your program
  can react to button clicks.
- Methods of an inner class can access variables from the
  surrounding class.

Use text components for reading text input.

- Use a JTextField component for reading a single line of input. Place a JLabel next to
  each text field.
- Use a JTextArea to show multiple lines of text.
- You can add scroll bars to any component with a JScrollPane.

Available online in WileyPLUS and at www.wiley.com/college/horstmann.

Create simple drawings with rectangles, ovals, lines, and text.

- In order to display a drawing, provide a class that extends the JComponent class.
- Place drawing instructions inside the paintComponent method. That method is called whenever the component needs to be repainted.
- The Graphics class has methods to draw rectangles and other shapes.
- Use drawRect, drawOval, and drawLine to draw geometric shapes.
- The drawString method draws a string, starting at its basepoint.
- When you set a new color in the graphics context, it is used for subsequent drawing operations.
- Call the repaint method whenever the state of a painted component changes.
- When placing a painted component into a panel, you need to specify its preferred size.

STANDARD LIBRARY ITEMS INTRODUCED IN THIS CHAPTER

java.awt.Color
java.awt.Component
  addMouseListener
  getHeight
  getWidth
  repaint
  setPreferredSize
  setSize
  setVisible
java.awt.Container
  add
java.awt.Dimension
java.awt.Frame
  setTitle

java.awt.Graphics
  setColor
  drawLine
  drawOval
  drawRect
  drawString
  fillOval
  fillRect
java.awt.event.ActionEvent
java.awt.event.ActionListener
  actionPerformed
javax.swing.AbstractButton
  addActionListener
javax.swing.JComponent
  paintComponent

javax.swing.JFrame
  setDefaultCloseOperation
javax.swing.JButton
javax.swing.JLabel
javax.swing.JPanel
javax.swing.JScrollPane
javax.swing.JTextArea
  append
javax.swing.JTextField
javax.swing.text.JTextComponent
  getText
  isEditable
  setEditable
  setText

REVIEW EXERCISES

- **R10.1** What is the difference between a frame and a panel?

- **R10.2** From a programmer's perspective, what is the most important difference between the user interface of a console application and a graphical application?

- **R10.3** Why are separate viewer and frame classes used for graphical programs?

- **R10.4** What happens if you add a button and a label directly to a JFrame without using a JPanel? What happens if you add the label first? Try it out, by modifying the program in Section 10.1.2, and report your observations.

- **R10.5** What is an event object? An event source? An event listener?

- **R10.6** Who calls the actionPerformed method of an event listener? When does the call to the actionPerformed method occur?

■■ **R10.7** You can exit a graphical program by calling System.exit(0). Describe how to provide an Exit button that functions in the same way as closing the window. Should you still call setDefaultCloseOperation on the frame?

■ **R10.8** How would you add a counter to the program in Section 10.2.1 that prints how often the button has been clicked? Where is the counter updated?

■■ **R10.9** How would you add a counter to the program in Section 10.2.2 that shows how often the button has been clicked? Where is the counter updated? Where is it displayed?

■■■ **R10.10** How would you reorganize the InvestmentViewer program in Section 10.2.3 if you needed to make AddInterestListener into a top-level class (that is, not an inner class)?

■■■ **R10.11** Why are we using inner classes for event listeners? If Java did not have inner classes, could we still implement event listeners? How?

■■■ **R10.12** Is it a requirement to use inheritance for frames, as described in Section 10.1.3? (*Hint:* Consider Special Topic 10.1.)

■ **R10.13** What is the difference between a label, a text field, and a text area?

■■ **R10.14** Name a method that is declared in JTextArea, a method that JTextArea inherits from JTextComponent, and a method that JTextArea inherits from JComponent.

■■ **R10.15** Why did the program in Section 10.3.2 use a text area and not a label to show how the interest accumulates? How could you have achieved a similar effect with an array of labels?

■■ **R10.16** Who calls the paintComponent method of a component? When does the call to the paintComponent method occur?

■ **R10.17** In the program of Section 10.4.2, why was the oval drawn before the string?

■■ **R10.18** How would you modify the chart component in Section 10.4.3 to draw a vertical bar chart? (*Careful:* The y-values grow downward.)

■■ **R10.19** How do you specify a text color?

■■ **R10.20** What is the difference between the paintComponent and repaint methods?

■■ **R10.21** Explain why the call to the getWidth method in the ChartComponent class has no explicit parameter.

■ **R10.22** How would you modify the drawItalianFlag method in How To 10.1 to draw any flag with a white vertical stripe in the middle and two arbitrary colors to the left and right?

PROGRAMMING EXERCISES

■ **P10.1** Write a program that shows a square frame filled with 100 buttons labeled 1 to 100. Nothing needs to happen when you press any of the buttons.

■ **P10.2** Enhance the ButtonViewer1 program in Section 10.2.1 so that it prints a message "I was clicked n times!" whenever the button is clicked. The value n should be incremented with each click.

•• P10.3 Enhance the ButtonViewer1 program in Section 10.2.1 so that it has two buttons, each of which prints a message "I was clicked *n* times!" whenever the button is clicked. Each button should have a separate click count.

•• P10.4 Enhance the ButtonViewer1 program in Section 10.2.1 so that it has two buttons labeled A and B, each of which prints a message "Button *x* was clicked!", where *x* is A or B.

•• P10.5 Implement a ButtonViewer1 program as in Exercise P10.3 using only a single listener class. *Hint:* Pass the button label to the constructor of the listener.

• P10.6 Enhance the ButtonViewer1 program so that it prints the date and time at which the button was clicked. *Hint:* System.out.println(new java.util.Date()) prints the current date and time.

••• P10.7 Implement the ClickListener in the ButtonViewer2 program of Section 10.2.2 as a regular class (that is, not an inner class). *Hint:* Store a reference to the label. Add a constructor to the listener class that sets the reference.

•• P10.8 Add error handling to the program in Section 10.3.2. If the interest rate is not a floating-point number, or if it less than 0, display an error message, using a JOption-Pane (see Special Topic 2.5).

• P10.9 Write a graphical application simulating a bank account. Supply text fields and buttons for depositing and withdrawing money, and for displaying the current balance in a label.

• P10.10 Write a graphical application describing an earthquake, as in Section 3.3. Supply a text field and button for entering the strength of the earthquake. Display the earthquake description in a label.

• P10.11 Write a graphical application for computing statistics of a data set. Supply a text field and button for adding floating-point values, and display the current minimum, maximum, and average in a label.

• P10.12 Write an application with three labeled text fields, one each for the initial amount of a savings account, the annual interest rate, and the number of years. Add a button "Calculate" and a read-only text area to display the balance of the savings account after the end of each year.

•• P10.13 In the application from Exercise P10.12, replace the text area with a bar chart that shows the balance after the end of each year.

• P10.14 Write a graphics program that draws your name in red, contained inside a blue rectangle. Provide a class NameViewer and a class NameComponent.

•• P10.15 Write a graphics program that draws 12 strings, one each for the 12 standard colors, besides Color.WHITE, each in its own color. Provide a class ColorNameViewer and a class ColorNameComponent.

•• P10.16 Write a program that draws two solid squares: one in pink and one in purple. Use a standard color for one of them and a custom color for the other. Provide a class TwoSquareViewer and a class TwoSquareComponent.

•• P10.17 Write a program to plot the following face. Provide a class FaceViewer and a class Face-Component.

•• P10.18 Draw a "bull's eye"—a set of concentric rings in alternating black and white colors. *Hint:* Fill a black circle, then fill a smaller white circle on top, and so on. Your program should be composed of classes BullsEyeComponent and BullsEyeViewer.

•• P10.19 Write a program that draws a picture of a house. It could be as simple as the accompanying figure, or if you like, make it more elaborate (3-D, skyscraper, marble columns in the entryway, whatever).

•• P10.20 Extend Exercise P10.19 by supplying a drawHouse method in which you can specify the position and size. Then populate your frame with a few houses of different sizes.

•• P10.21 Extend Exercise P10.20 so that you can make the houses appear in different colors. The color should be passed as an argument to the drawHouse method. Populate your frame with houses of different colors.

•• P10.22 Improve the output quality of the investment application in Section 10.3.2. Format the numbers with two decimal digits, using the String.format method. Set the font of the text area to a fixed width font, using the call

```
textArea.setFont(new Font(Font.MONOSPACED, Font.PLAIN, 12));
```

•• P10.23 Write a program that draws a 3D view of a cylinder.

•• P10.24 Write a program to plot the string "HELLO", using only lines and circles. Do not call drawString, and do not use System.out. Make classes LetterH, LetterE, LetterL, and LetterO.

•• P10.25 Modify the drawItalianFlag method in How To 10.1 to draw any flag with three horizontal colored stripes. Write a program that displays the German and Hungarian flags.

P10.26 Write a program that displays the Olympic rings. Color the rings in the Olympic colors. Provide a method drawRing that draws a ring of a given position and color.

P10.27 Write a program that prompts the user to enter an integer in a text field. When a Draw button is clicked, draw as many rectangles at random positions in a component as the user requested.

P10.28 Write a program that asks the user to enter an integer n into a text field. When a Draw button is clicked, draw an n-by-n grid in a component.

P10.29 Write a program that has a Draw button and a component in which a random mixture of rectangles, ellipses, and lines, with random positions, is displayed each time the Draw button is clicked.

P10.30 Make a bar chart to plot the following data set. Label each bar. Provide a class BarChartViewer and a class BarChartComponent.

Bridge Name	Longest Span (ft)
Golden Gate	4,200
Brooklyn	1,595
Delaware Memorial	2,150
Mackinac	3,800

P10.31 Write a program that draws a clock face with a time that the user enters in two text fields (one for the hours, one for the minutes).

Hint: You need to determine the angles of the hour hand and the minute hand. The angle of the minute hand is easy; the minute hand travels 360 degrees in 60 minutes. The angle of the hour hand is harder; it travels 360 degrees in 12 × 60 minutes.

P10.32 Write a program that fills the window with a large ellipse, with a black outline and filled with your favorite color. The ellipse should touch the window boundaries, even if the window is resized.

Business P10.33 Implement a graphical application that simulates a cash register. Provide a text field for the item price and two buttons for adding the item to the sale, one for taxable items and one for nontaxable items. In a text area, display the register tape that lists all items (labeling the taxable items with a *), followed by the amount due. Provide another button for starting a new sale.

Business P10.34 Write a graphical application to implement a currency converter between euros and U.S. dollars, and vice versa. Provide two text fields for the euro and dollar amounts. Between them, place two buttons labeled > and < for updating the field on the right or left. For this exercise, use a conversion rate of 1 euro = 1.42 U.S. dollars.

■■ **Business P10.35** Write a graphical application that produces a restaurant bill. Provide buttons for ten popular dishes or drink items. (You decide on the items and their prices.) Provide text fields for entering less popular items and prices. In a text area, show the bill, including tax and a suggested tip.

ANSWERS TO SELF-CHECK QUESTIONS

1. Modify the `EmptyFrameViewer` program as follows:

```
final int FRAME_WIDTH = 300;
final int FRAME_HEIGHT = 300;
. . .
frame.setTitle("Hello, World!");
```

2. Construct two `JFrame` objects, set each of their sizes, and call `setVisible(true)` on each of them.

3. Add the following panel to the frame:

```
JButton button1 = new JButton("Yes");
JButton button2 = new JButton("No");
JPanel panel = new JPanel();
panel.add(button1);
panel.add(button2);
```

4. There was no need to invoke any methods that are specific to `FilledFrame`. It is always a good idea to use the most general type when declaring a variable.

5. Two: `FilledFrameViewer2`, `FilledFrame`.

6. It's an instance method of `FilledFrame`, so the frame is the implicit parameter.

7. The `button` object is the event source. The `listener` object is the event listener.

8. The `ClickListener` class implements the `Action-Listener` interface.

9. You don't. The Swing library calls the method when the button is clicked.

10. Direct access is simpler than the alternative— passing the variable as an argument to a constructor or method.

11. First add `label` to the `panel`, then add `button`.

12. Then the text field is not labeled, and the user will not know its purpose.

13. `Integer.parseInt(textField.getText())`

14. A text field holds a single line of text; a text area holds multiple lines.

15. The text area is intended to display the program output. It does not collect user input.

16. Don't construct a `JScrollPane` but add the `resultArea` object directly to the panel.

17. Here is one possible solution:

```
g.fillRect(0, 0, 50, 50);
g.fillRect(0, 100, 50, 50);
```

18. The program shows three very elongated ellipses instead of the rectangles.

19. `g.drawOval(75, 75, 50, 50);`

20. `g.drawLine(0, 0, 10, 30);`
     `g.drawLine(10, 30, 20, 0);`

21. `g.drawString("V", 0, 30);`

22. 0, 0, 255

23. First fill a big red square, then fill a small yellow square inside:

```
g.setColor(Color.RED);
g.fillRect(0, 0, 200, 200);
g.setColor(Color.YELLOW);
g.fillRect(50, 50, 100, 100);
```

24. All the bars would stretch all the way to the right of the component since they would be much longer than the component's width.

25. The chart would not be repainted when the user hits the "Add Interest" button.

26. The chart would be shown at size 0 by 0; that is, it would be invisible.

THE BASIC LATIN AND LATIN-1 SUBSETS OF UNICODE

This appendix lists the Unicode characters that are most commonly used for processing Western European languages. A complete listing of Unicode characters can be found at http://unicode.org.

Table 1 Selected Control Characters			
Character	Code	Decimal	Escape Sequence
Tab	'\u0009'	9	'\t'
Newline	'\u000A'	10	'\n'
Return	'\u000D'	13	'\r'
Space	'\u0020'	32	

Table 2 The Basic Latin (ASCII) Subset of Unicode

Char.	Code	Dec.	Char.	Code	Dec.	Char.	Code	Dec.
			@	'\u0040'	64	`	'\u0060'	96
!	'\u0021'	33	A	'\u0041'	65	a	'\u0061'	97
"	'\u0022'	34	B	'\u0042'	66	b	'\u0062'	98
#	'\u0023'	35	C	'\u0043'	67	c	'\u0063'	99
$	'\u0024'	36	D	'\u0044'	68	d	'\u0064'	100
%	'\u0025'	37	E	'\u0045'	69	e	'\u0065'	101
&	'\u0026'	38	F	'\u0046'	70	f	'\u0066'	102
'	'\u0027'	39	G	'\u0047'	71	g	'\u0067'	103
(	'\u0028'	40	H	'\u0048'	72	h	'\u0068'	104
)	'\u0029'	41	I	'\u0049'	73	i	'\u0069'	105
*	'\u002A'	42	J	'\u004A'	74	j	'\u006A'	106
+	'\u002B'	43	K	'\u004B'	75	k	'\u006B'	107
,	'\u002C'	44	L	'\u004C'	76	l	'\u006C'	108
-	'\u002D'	45	M	'\u004D'	77	m	'\u006D'	109
.	'\u002E'	46	N	'\u004E'	78	n	'\u006E'	110
/	'\u002F'	47	O	'\u004F'	79	o	'\u006F'	111
0	'\u0030'	48	P	'\u0050'	80	p	'\u0070'	112
1	'\u0031'	49	Q	'\u0051'	81	q	'\u0071'	113
2	'\u0032'	50	R	'\u0052'	82	r	'\u0072'	114
3	'\u0033'	51	S	'\u0053'	83	s	'\u0073'	115
4	'\u0034'	52	T	'\u0054'	84	t	'\u0074'	116
5	'\u0035'	53	U	'\u0055'	85	u	'\u0075'	117
6	'\u0036'	54	V	'\u0056'	86	v	'\u0076'	118
7	'\u0037'	55	W	'\u0057'	87	w	'\u0077'	119
8	'\u0038'	56	X	'\u0058'	88	x	'\u0078'	120
9	'\u0039'	57	Y	'\u0059'	89	y	'\u0079'	121
:	'\u003A'	58	Z	'\u005A'	90	z	'\u007A'	122
;	'\u003B'	59	[	'\u005B'	91	{	'\u007B'	123
<	'\u003C'	60	\'	'\u005C'	92	|	'\u007C'	124
=	'\u003D'	61	]	'\u005D'	93	}	'\u007D'	125
>	'\u003E'	62	^	'\u005E'	94	~	'\u007E'	126
?	'\u003F'	63	_	'\u005F'	95			

Table 3 The Latin-1 Subset of Unicode

Char.	Code	Dec.	Char.	Code	Dec.	Char.	Code	Dec.
			À	`'\u00C0'`	192	à	`'\u00E0'`	224
¡	`'\u00A1'`	161	Á	`'\u00C1'`	193	á	`'\u00E1'`	225
¢	`'\u00A2'`	162	Â	`'\u00C2'`	194	â	`'\u00E2'`	226
£	`'\u00A3'`	163	Ã	`'\u00C3'`	195	ã	`'\u00E3'`	227
¤	`'\u00A4'`	164	Ä	`'\u00C4'`	196	ä	`'\u00E4'`	228
¥	`'\u00A5'`	165	Å	`'\u00C5'`	197	å	`'\u00E5'`	229
¦	`'\u00A6'`	166	Æ	`'\u00C6'`	198	æ	`'\u00E6'`	230
§	`'\u00A7'`	167	Ç	`'\u00C7'`	199	ç	`'\u00E7'`	231
¨	`'\u00A8'`	168	È	`'\u00C8'`	200	è	`'\u00E8'`	232
©	`'\u00A9'`	169	É	`'\u00C9'`	201	é	`'\u00E9'`	233
ª	`'\u00AA'`	170	Ê	`'\u00CA'`	202	ê	`'\u00EA'`	234
«	`'\u00AB'`	171	Ë	`'\u00CB'`	203	ë	`'\u00EB'`	235
¬	`'\u00AC'`	172	Ì	`'\u00CC'`	204	ì	`'\u00EC'`	236
	`'\u00AD'`	173	Í	`'\u00CD'`	205	í	`'\u00ED'`	237
®	`'\u00AE'`	174	Î	`'\u00CE'`	206	î	`'\u00EE'`	238
¯	`'\u00AF'`	175	Ï	`'\u00CF'`	207	ï	`'\u00EF'`	239
°	`'\u00B0'`	176	Ð	`'\u00D0'`	208	ð	`'\u00F0'`	240
±	`'\u00B1'`	177	Ñ	`'\u00D1'`	209	ñ	`'\u00F1'`	241
²	`'\u00B2'`	178	Ò	`'\u00D2'`	210	ò	`'\u00F2'`	242
³	`'\u00B3'`	179	Ó	`'\u00D3'`	211	ó	`'\u00F3'`	243
´	`'\u00B4'`	180	Ô	`'\u00D4'`	212	ô	`'\u00F4'`	244
µ	`'\u00B5'`	181	Õ	`'\u00D5'`	213	õ	`'\u00F5'`	245
¶	`'\u00B6'`	182	Ö	`'\u00D6'`	214	ö	`'\u00F6'`	246
·	`'\u00B7'`	183	×	`'\u00D7'`	215	÷	`'\u00F7'`	247
¸	`'\u00B8'`	184	Ø	`'\u00D8'`	216	ø	`'\u00F8'`	248
¹	`'\u00B9'`	185	Ù	`'\u00D9'`	217	ù	`'\u00F9'`	249
º	`'\u00BA'`	186	Ú	`'\u00DA'`	218	ú	`'\u00FA'`	250
»	`'\u00BB'`	187	Û	`'\u00DB'`	219	û	`'\u00FB'`	251
¼	`'\u00BC'`	188	Ü	`'\u00DC'`	220	ü	`'\u00FC'`	252
½	`'\u00BD'`	189	Ý	`'\u00DD'`	221	ý	`'\u00FD'`	253
¾	`'\u00BE'`	190	Þ	`'\u00DE'`	222	þ	`'\u00FE'`	254
¿	`'\u00BF'`	191	ß	`'\u00DF'`	223	ÿ	`'\u00FF'`	255

JAVA OPERATOR SUMMARY

The Java operators are listed in groups of decreasing *precedence* in the table below. The horizontal lines in the table indicate a change in operator precedence. Operators with higher precedence bind more strongly than those with lower precedence. For example, x + y * z means x + (y * z) because the * operator has higher precedence than the + operator. Looking at the table below, you can tell that x && y || z means (x && y) || z because the || operator has lower precedence.

The *associativity* of an operator indicates whether it groups left to right, or right to left. For example, the - operator binds left to right. Therefore, x - y - z means (x - y) - z. But the = operator binds right to left, and x = y = z means x = (y = z).

Operator	Description	Associativity
.	Access class feature	
[]	Array subscript	Left to right
()	Function call	
++	Increment	
--	Decrement	
!	Boolean *not*	
~	Bitwise *not*	
+ *(unary)*	(Has no effect)	Right to left
- *(unary)*	Negative	
(*TypeName*)	Cast	
new	Object allocation	
*	Multiplication	
/	Division or integer division	Left to right
%	Integer remainder	
+	Addition, string concatenation	Left to right
-	Subtraction	
<<	Shift left	
>>	Right shift with sign extension	Left to right
>>>	Right shift with zero extension	

Operator	Description	Associativity
<	Less than	
<=	Less than or equal	
>	Greater than	Left to right
>=	Greater than or equal	
instanceof	Tests whether an object's type is a given type or a subtype thereof	
==	Equal	Left to right
!=	Not equal	
&	Bitwise *and*	Left to right
^	Bitwise exclusive *or*	Left to right
|	Bitwise *or*	Left to right
&&	Boolean "short circuit" *and*	Left to right
||	Boolean "short circuit" *or*	Left to right
? :	Conditional	Right to left
=	Assignment	Right to left
op=	Assignment with binary operator (*op* is one of +, -, *, /, &, |, ^, <<, >>, >>>)	

JAVA RESERVED WORD SUMMARY

Reserved Word	Description
abstract	An abstract class or method
assert	An assertion that a condition is fulfilled
boolean	The Boolean type
break	Breaks out of the current loop or labeled statement
byte	The 8-bit signed integer type
case	A label in a switch statement
catch	The handler for an exception in a try block
char	The 16-bit Unicode character type
class	Defines a class
const	Not used
continue	Skip the remainder of a loop body
default	The default label in a switch statement
do	A loop whose body is executed at least once
double	The 64-bit double-precision floating-point type
else	The alternative clause in an if statement
enum	An enumeration type
extends	Indicates that a class is a subclass of another class
final	A value that cannot be changed after it has been initialized, a method that cannot be overridden, or a class that cannot be extended
finally	A clause of a try block that is always executed
float	The 32-bit single-precision floating-point type
for	A loop with initialization, condition, and update expressions
goto	Not used
if	A conditional branch statement
implements	Indicates that a class realizes an interface

Reserved Word	Description
import	Allows the use of class names without the package name
instanceof	Tests whether an object's type is a given type or a subtype thereof
int	The 32-bit integer type
interface	An abstract type with only abstract methods and constants
long	The 64-bit integer type
native	A method implemented in non-Java code
new	Allocates an object
package	A collection of related classes
private	A feature that is accessible only by methods of the same class
protected	A feature that is accessible only by methods of the same class, a subclass, or another class in the same package
public	A feature that is accessible by all methods
return	Returns from a method
short	The 16-bit integer type
static	A feature that is defined for a class, not for individual instances
strictfp	Use strict rules for floating-point computations
super	Invoke the superclass constructor or a superclass method
switch	A selection statement
synchronized	A block of code that is accessible to only one thread at a time
this	The implicit parameter of a method; or invocation of another constructor of the same class
throw	Throws an exception
throws	The exceptions that a method may throw
transient	Instance variables that should not be serialized
try	A block of code with exception handlers or a finally handler
void	Tags a method that doesn't return a value
volatile	A variable that may be accessed by multiple threads without synchronization
while	A loop statement

THE JAVA LIBRARY

This appendix lists all classes and methods from the standard Java library that are used in this book.

In the following inheritance hierarchy, superclasses that are not used in this book are shown in gray type. Some classes implement interfaces not covered in this book; they are omitted. Classes are sorted first by package, then alphabetically within a package.

```
java.lang.Object
    java.awt.BorderLayout
    java.awt.Color
    java.awt.Component
        java.awt.Container
            javax.swing.JComponent
                javax.swing.AbstractButton
                    javax.swing.JButton
                    javax.swing.JMenuItem
                        javax.swing.JMenu
                    javax.swing.JToggleButton
                        javax.swing.JCheckBox
                        javax.swing.JRadioButton
                javax.swing.JComboBox
                javax.swing.JFileChooser
                javax.swing.JLabel
                javax.swing.JMenuBar
                javax.swing.JPanel
                javax.swing.JOptionPane
                javax.swing.JScrollPane
                javax.swing.JSlider
                javax.swing.text.JTextComponent
                    javax.swing.JTextArea
                    javax.swing.JTextField
            java.awt.Window
                java.awt.Frame
                    javax.swing.JFrame
    java.awt.Dimension2D
        java.awt.Dimension
    java.awt.FlowLayout
    java.awt.Font
    java.awt.Graphics
    java.awt.GridLayout
    java.awt.event.MouseAdapter implements MouseListener
    java.io.File implements Comparable<File>
    java.io.InputStream
        java.io.FileInputStream
    java.io.OutputStream
        java.io.FileOutputStream
        java.io.FilterOutputStream
            java.io.PrintStream
    java.io.Writer
        java.io.PrintWriter
```

```
java.lang.Boolean implements Comparable<Boolean>
java.lang.Character implements Comparable<Character>
java.lang.Class
java.lang.Math
java.lang.Number
   java.math.BigDecimal implements Comparable<BigDecimal>
   java.math.BigInteger implements Comparable<BigInteger>
   java.lang.Double implements Comparable<Double>
   java.lang.Integer implements Comparable<Integer>
java.lang.String implements Comparable<String>
java.lang.System
java.lang.Throwable
   java.lang.Error
   java.lang.Exception
      java.lang.InterruptedException
      java.io.IOException
         java.io.EOFException
         java.io.FileNotFoundException
      java.lang.RuntimeException
         java.lang.IllegalArgumentException
            java.lang.NumberFormatException
         java.lang.IllegalStateException
         java.util.NoSuchElementException
            java.util.InputMismatchException
         java.lang.NullPointerException
java.text.Format
   java.text.DateFormat
java.util.AbstractCollection<E>
   java.util.AbstractList<E>
      java.util.AbstractSequentialList<E>
         java.util.LinkedList<E> implements List<E>, Queue<E>
      java.util.ArrayList<E> implements List<E>
   java.util.AbstractQueue<E>
      java.util.PriorityQueue<E>
   java.util.AbstractSet<E>
      java.util.HashSet<E> implements Set<E>
      java.util.TreeSet<E>implements SortedSet<E>
java.util.AbstractMap<K, V>
   java.util.HashMap<K, V> implements Map<K, V>
   java.util.TreeMap<K, V>, Map<K, V>
java.util.Arrays
java.util.Collections
java.util.Calendar
   java.util.GregorianCalendar
java.util.Dictionary<K, V>
   java.util.Hashtable<K, V>
      java.util.Properties
java.util.EventObject
   java.awt.AWTEvent
      java.awt.event.ActionEvent
      java.awt.event.ComponentEvent
         java.awt.event.InputEvent
            java.awt.event.KeyEvent
            java.awt.event.MouseEvent
   javax.swing.event.ChangeEvent
java.util.Random
java.util.Scanner
java.util.logging.Level
```

```
            java.util.logging.Logger
            javax.swing.ButtonGroup
            javax.swing.ImageIcon
            javax.swing.Keystroke
            javax.swing.Timer
            javax.swing.border.AbstractBorder
                javax.swing.border.EtchedBorder
                javax.swing.border.TitledBorder
        java.lang.Comparable<T>
        java.util.Collection<E>
            java.util.List<E>
            java.util.Set<E>
                java.util.SortedSet<E>
        java.util.Comparator<T>
        java.util.EventListener
            java.awt.event.ActionListener
            java.awt.event.KeyListener
            java.awt.event.MouseListener
            javax.swing.event.ChangeListener
        java.util.Iterator<E>
            java.util.ListIterator<E>
        java.util.Map<K, V>
        java.util.Queue<E> extends Collection<E>
```

In the following descriptions, the phrase "this object" ("this component", "this container", and so forth) means the object (component, container, and so forth) on which the method is invoked (the implicit parameter, `this`).

Package `java.awt`

Class `java.awt.BorderLayout`

- `BorderLayout()`
  This constructs a border layout. A border layout has five regions for adding components, called `"NORTH"`, `"EAST"`, `"SOUTH"`, `"WEST"`, and `"CENTER"`.

- `static final int CENTER`
  This value identifies the center position of a border layout.

- `static final int EAST`
  This value identifies the east position of a border layout.

- `static final int NORTH`
  This value identifies the north position of a border layout.

- `static final int SOUTH`
  This value identifies the south position of a border layout.

- `static final int WEST`
  This value identifies the west position of a border layout.

Class `java.awt.Color`

- `Color(int red, int green, int blue)`
  This creates a color with the specified red, green, and blue values between 0 and 255.
  Parameters: red The red component
                     green The green component
                     blue The blue component

Class `java.awt.Component`

- `void addKeyListener(KeyListener listener)`
  This method adds a key listener to the component.
  Parameters: listener The key listener to be added

- `void addMouseListener(MouseListener listener)`
  This method adds a mouse listener to the component.
  Parameters: listener The mouse listener to be added

- `int getHeight()`
  This method gets the height of this component.
  Returns: The height in pixels

- `int getWidth()`
  This method gets the width of this component.
  Returns: The width in pixels

- `void repaint()`
  This method repaints this component by scheduling a call to the paint method.

- `void setFocusable(boolean focusable)`
  This method controls whether or not the component can receive input focus.
  Parameters: focusable true to have focus, or false to lose focus

- `void setPreferredSize(Dimension preferredSize)`
  This method sets the preferred size of this component.

- `void setSize(int width, int height)`
  This method sets the size of this component.
  Parameters: width the component width
                     height the component height

- `void setVisible(boolean visible)`
  This method shows or hides the component.
  Parameters: visible true to show the component, or false to hide it

Class `java.awt.Container`

- `void add(Component c)`
- `void add(Component c, Object position)`
  These methods add a component to the end of this container. If a position is given, the layout manager is called to position the component.
  Parameters: c The component to be added
                     position An object expressing position information for the layout manager

- void **setLayout**(LayoutManager manager)
  This method sets the layout manager for this container.
  Parameters: manager A layout manager

Class java.awt.Dimension

- **Dimension**(int width, int height)
  This constructs a Dimension object with the given width and height.
  Parameters: width The width
  height The height

Class java.awt.FlowLayout

- **FlowLayout**()
  This constructs a new flow layout. A flow layout places as many components as possible in a row, without changing their size, and starts new rows when necessary.

Class java.awt.Font

- **Font**(String name, int style, int size)
  This constructs a font object from the specified name, style, and point size.
  Parameters: name The font name, either a font face name or a logical font name, which must be one of "Dialog", "DialogInput", "Monospaced", "Serif", or "SansSerif"
  style One of Font.PLAIN, Font.ITALIC, Font.BOLD, or Font.ITALIC+Font.BOLD
  size The point size of the font

Class java.awt.Frame

- void **setTitle**(String title)
  This method sets the frame title.
  Parameters: title The title to be displayed in the border of the frame

Class java.awt.Graphics

- void **drawLine**(int x1, int y1, int x2, int y2)
  Draws a line between two points
  Parameters: x1, y1 The starting point
  x2, y2 The endpoint
- void **drawOval**(int x, int y, int width, int height)
- void **fillOval**(int x, int y, int width, int height)
  Parameters: x1, y1 The top-left corner of the bounding rectangle
  width, height The width and height of the bounding rectangle
- void **drawRect**(int x, int y, int width, int height)
- void **fillRect**(int x, int y, int width, int height)
  Parameters: x1, y1 The top-left corner of the rectangle
  width, height The width and height of the rectangle

- void **drawString**(String s, int x, int y)
  This method draws a string in the current font and color.
  Parameters: s   The string to draw
                              x, y   The basepoint of the first character in the string

- void **setColor**(Color c)
  This method sets the current color. After the method call, all graphics operations use this color.
  Parameters: c   The new drawing color

Class java.awt.GridLayout

- **GridLayout**(int rows, int cols)
  This constructor creates a grid layout with the specified number of rows and columns. The components in a grid layout are arranged in a grid with equal widths and heights. One, but not both, of rows and cols can be zero, in which case any number of objects can be placed in a row or in a column, respectively.
  Parameters: rows   The number of rows in the grid
                              cols   The number of columns in the grid

Class java.awt.Rectangle

- **Rectangle**()
  This constructs a rectangle with a top-left corner at (0, 0) and width and height set to 0.

- **Rectangle**(int x, int y, int width, int height)
  This constructs a rectangle with given top-left corner and size.
  Parameters: x, y   The top-left corner
                              width   The width
                              height   The height

- double **getHeight**()
- double **getWidth**()
  These methods get the height and width of the rectangle.

- double **getX**()
- double **getY**()
  These methods get the x- and y-coordinates of the top-left corner of the rectangle.

- void **grow**(int dw, int dh)
  This method adjusts the width and height of this rectangle.
  Parameters: dw   The amount to add to the width (can be negative)
                              dh   The amount to add to the height (can be negative)

- Rectangle **intersection**(Rectangle other)
  This method computes the intersection of this rectangle with the specified rectangle.
  Parameters: other   A rectangle
  Returns: The largest rectangle contained in both this and other

- void **setLocation**(int x, int y)
  This method moves this rectangle to a new location.
  Parameters: x, y   The new top-left corner

- void **setSize**(int width, int height)
  This method sets the width and height of this rectangle to new values.
  Parameters: width The new width
                      height The new height

- void **translate**(int dx, int dy)
  This method moves this rectangle.
  Parameters: dx The distance to move along the x-axis
                      dy The distance to move along the y-axis

- Rectangle **union**(Rectangle other)
  This method computes the union of this rectangle with the specified rectangle. This is not the set-theoretic union but the smallest rectangle that contains both this and other.
  Parameters: other A rectangle
  Returns: The smallest rectangle containing both this and other

Package java.awt.event

Interface java.awt.event.ActionListener

- void **actionPerformed**(ActionEvent e)
  The event source calls this method when an action occurs.

Class java.awt.event.KeyEvent

This event is passed to the KeyListener methods. Use the KeyStroke class to obtain the key information from the key event.

Interface java.awt.event.KeyListener

- void **keyPressed**(KeyEvent e)
- void **keyReleased**(KeyEvent e)
  These methods are called when a key has been pressed or released.

- void **keyTyped**(KeyEvent e)
  This method is called when a keystroke has been composed by pressing and releasing one or more keys.

Class java.awt.event.MouseEvent

- int **getX**()
  This method returns the horizontal position of the mouse as of the time the event occurred.
  Returns: The x-position of the mouse

- int **getY**()
  This method returns the vertical position of the mouse as of the time the event occurred.
  Returns: The y-position of the mouse

Interface java.awt.event.MouseListener

- void **mouseClicked**(MouseEvent e)
  This method is called when the mouse has been clicked (that is, pressed and released in quick succession).

- void **mouseEntered**(MouseEvent e)
  This method is called when the mouse has entered the component to which this listener was added.

- void **mouseExited**(MouseEvent e)
  This method is called when the mouse has exited the component to which this listener was added.

- void **mousePressed**(MouseEvent e)
  This method is called when a mouse button has been pressed.

- void **mouseReleased**(MouseEvent e)
  This method is called when a mouse button has been released.

Package java.io

Class java.io.EOFException

- **EOFException**(String message)
  This constructs an "end of file" exception object.
  Parameters: message   The detail message

Class java.io.File

- **File**(String name)
  This constructs a File object that describes a file (which may or may not exist) with the given name.
  Parameters: name   The name of the file

- static final String pathSeparator
  The sytem-dependent separator between path names. A colon (:) in Linux or Mac OS X; a semicolon (;) in Windows.

Class java.io.FileInputStream

- **FileInputStream**(File f)
  This constructs a file input stream and opens the chosen file. If the file cannot be opened for reading, a FileNotFoundException is thrown.
  Parameters: f   The file to be opened for reading

- **FileInputStream**(String name)
  This constructs a file input stream and opens the named file. If the file cannot be opened for reading, a FileNotFoundException is thrown.
  Parameters: name   The name of the file to be opened for reading

Class java.io.FileNotFoundException

This exception is thrown when a file could not be opened.

Class java.io.FileOutputStream

- **FileOutputStream**(File f)
  This constructs a file output stream and opens the chosen file. If the file cannot be opened for writing, a FileNotFoundException is thrown.
  Parameters: f The file to be opened for writing

- **FileOutputStream**(String name)
  This constructs a file output stream and opens the named file. If the file cannot be opened for writing, a FileNotFoundException is thrown.
  Parameters: name The name of the file to be opened for writing

Class java.io.InputStream

- void **close**()
  This method closes this input stream (such as a FileInputStream) and releases any system resources associated with the stream.

- int **read**()
  This method reads the next byte of data from this input stream.
  Returns: The next byte of data, or –1 if the end of the stream is reached

Class java.io.InputStreamReader

- **InputStreamReader**(InputStream in)
  This constructs a reader from a specified input stream.
  Parameters: in The stream to read from

Class java.io.IOException

This type of exception is thrown when an input/output error is encountered.

Class java.io.OutputStream

- void **close**()
  This method closes this output stream (such as a FileOutputStream) and releases any system resources associated with this stream. A closed stream cannot perform output operations and cannot be reopened.

- void **write**(int b)
  This method writes the lowest byte of b to this output stream.
  Parameters: b The integer whose lowest byte is written

Class java.io.PrintStream / Class java.io.PrintWriter

- **PrintStream**(String name)
- **PrintWriter**(String name)
  This constructs a PrintStream or PrintWriter and opens the named file. If the file cannot be opened for writing, a FileNotFoundException is thrown.
  Parameters: name The name of the file to be opened for writing

- void **close**()
  This method closes this stream or writer and releases any associated system resources.
- void **print**(int x)
- void **print**(double x)
- void **print**(Object x)
- void **print**(String x)
- void **println**()
- void **println**(int x)
- void **println**(double x)
- void **println**(Object x)
- void **println**(String x)

  These methods print a value to this PrintStream or PrintWriter. The println methods print a newline after the value. Objects are printed by converting them to strings with their toString methods.

  Parameters: x   The value to be printed

- PrintStream **printf**(String format, Object... values)
- Printwriter **printf**(String format, Object... values)

  These methods print the format string to this PrintStream or PrintWriter, substituting the given values for placeholders that start with %.

  Parameters: format   The format string
                  values   The values to be printed. You can supply any number of values

  Returns: The implicit parameter

Package java.lang

Class java.lang.Boolean

- **Boolean**(boolean value)
  This constructs a wrapper object for a boolean value.
  Parameters: value   The value to store in this object

- boolean **booleanValue**()
  This method returns the value stored in this Boolean object.
  Returns: The Boolean value of this object

Class java.lang.Character

- static boolean **isDigit**(ch)
  This method tests whether a given character is a Unicode digit.
  Parameters: ch   The character to test
  Returns: true if the character is a digit

- static boolean **isLetter**(ch)
  This method tests whether a given character is a Unicode letter.
  Parameters: ch   The character to test
  Returns: true if the character is a letter

- static boolean **isLowerCase**(ch)
  This method tests whether a given character is a lowercase Unicode letter.
  Parameters: ch The character to test
  Returns: true if the character is a lowercase letter

- static boolean **isUpperCase**(ch)
  This method tests whether a given character is an uppercase Unicode letter.
  Parameters: ch The character to test
  Returns: true if the character is an uppercase letter

Class java.lang.Class

- static Class **forName**(String className)
  This method loads a class with a given name. Loading a class initializes its static fields.
  Parameters: className The name of the class to load
  Returns: The type descriptor of the class

Interface java.lang.Comparable<T>

- int **compareTo**(T other)
  This method compares this object with the other object.
  Parameters: other The object to be compared
  Returns: A negative integer if this object is less than the other, zero if they are equal, or a positive integer otherwise

Class java.lang.Double

- **Double**(double value)
  This constructs a wrapper object for a double-precision floating-point number.
  Parameters: value The value to store in this object

- double **doubleValue**()
  This method returns the floating-point value stored in this Double wrapper object.
  Returns: The value stored in the object

- static double **parseDouble**(String s)
  This method returns the floating-point number that the string represents. If the string cannot be interpreted as a number, a NumberFormatException is thrown.
  Parameters: s The string to be parsed
  Returns: The value represented by the string argument

Class java.lang.Error

This is the superclass for all unchecked system errors.

Class java.lang.IllegalArgumentException

- **IllegalArgumentException**()
  This constructs an IllegalArgumentException with no detail message.

Class java.lang.IllegalStateException

This exception is thrown if the state of an object indicates that a method cannot currently be applied.

Class java.lang.Integer

- **Integer**(int value)
  This constructs a wrapper object for an integer.
  Parameters: value The value to store in this object

- int **intValue**()
  This method returns the integer value stored in this wrapper object.
  Returns: The value stored in the object

- static int **parseInt**(String s)
  This method returns the integer that the string represents. If the string cannot be interpreted as an integer, a NumberFormatException is thrown.
  Parameters: s The string to be parsed
  Returns: The value represented by the string argument

- static Integer **parseInt**(String s, int base)
  This method returns the integer value that the string represents in a given number system. If the string cannot be interpreted as an integer, a NumberFormatException is thrown.
  Parameters: s The string to be parsed
  base The base of the number system (such as 2 or 16)
  Returns: The value represented by the string argument

- static String **toString**(int i)
- static String **toString**(int i, int base)
  This method creates a string representation of an integer in a given number system. If no base is given, a decimal representation is created.
  Parameters: i An integer number
  base The base of the number system (such as 2 or 16)
  Returns: A string representation of the argument in the specified number system

- static final int MAX_VALUE
  This constant is the largest value of type int.

- static final int MIN_VALUE
  This constant is the smallest (negative) value of type int.

Class java.lang.InterruptedException

This exception is thrown to interrupt a thread, usually with the intention of terminating it.

Class java.lang.Math

- static double **abs**(double x)
  This method returns the absolute value $|x|$.
  Parameters: x A floating-point value
  Returns: The absolute value of the argument

- `static double` **`acos`**`(double x)`
  This method returns the angle with the given cosine, $\cos^{-1} x \in [0, \pi]$.
  Parameters: x A floating-point value between −1 and 1
  Returns: The arc cosine of the argument, in radians
- `static double` **`asin`**`(double x)`
  This method returns the angle with the given sine, $\sin^{-1} x \in [-\pi/2, \pi/2]$.
  Parameters: x A floating-point value between −1 and 1
  Returns: The arc sine of the argument, in radians
- `static double` **`atan`**`(double x)`
  This method returns the angle with the given tangent, $\tan^{-1} x$ $(-\pi/2, \pi/2)$.
  Parameters: x A floating-point value
  Returns: The arc tangent of the argument, in radians
- `static double` **`atan2`**`(double y, double x)`
  This method returns the arc tangent, $\tan^{-1}(y/x) \in (-\pi, \pi)$. If x can equal zero, or if it is necessary to distinguish "northwest" from "southeast" and "northeast" from "southwest", use this method instead of `atan(y/x)`.
  Parameters: y, x Two floating-point values
  Returns: The angle, in radians, between the points (0,0) and (x,y)
- `static double` **`ceil`**`(double x)`
  This method returns the smallest integer $\geq x$ (as a `double`).
  Parameters: x A floating-point value
  Returns: The smallest integer greater than or equal to the argument
- `static double` **`cos`**`(double radians)`
  This method returns the cosine of an angle given in radians.
  Parameters: radians An angle, in radians
  Returns: The cosine of the argument
- `static double` **`exp`**`(double x)`
  This method returns the value e^x, where e is the base of the natural logarithms.
  Parameters: x A floating-point value
  Returns: e^x
- `static double` **`floor`**`(double x)`
  This method returns the largest integer $\leq x$ (as a `double`).
  Parameters: x A floating-point value
  Returns: The largest integer less than or equal to the argument
- `static double` **`log`**`(double x)`
- `static double` **`log10`**`(double x)`
  This method returns the natural (base e) or decimal (base 10) logarithm of x, $\ln x$.
  Parameters: x A number greater than 0.0
  Returns: The natural logarithm of the argument
- `static int` **`max`**`(int x, int y)`
- `static double` **`max`**`(double x, double y)`
  These methods return the larger of the given arguments.
  Parameters: x, y Two integers or floating-point values
  Returns: The maximum of the arguments

- `static int min(int x, int y)`
- `static double min(double x, double y)`

  These methods return the smaller of the given arguments.

  Parameters: x, y   Two integers or floating-point values

  Returns: The minimum of the arguments

- `static double pow(double x, double y)`

  This method returns the value x^y ($x > 0$, or $x = 0$ and $y > 0$, or $x < 0$ and y is an integer).

  Parameters: x, y   Two floating-point values

  Returns: The value of the first argument raised to the power of the second argument

- `static long round(double x)`

  This method returns the closest `long` integer to the argument.

  Parameters: x   A floating-point value

  Returns: The argument rounded to the nearest `long` value

- `static double sin(double radians)`

  This method returns the sine of an angle given in radians.

  Parameters: radians   An angle, in radians

  Returns: The sine of the argument

- `static double sqrt(double x)`

  This method returns the square root of x, $\sqrt{x}$.

  Parameters: x   A nonnegative floating-point value

  Returns: The square root of the argument

- `static double tan(double radians)`

  This method returns the tangent of an angle given in radians.

  Parameters: radians   An angle, in radians

  Returns: The tangent of the argument

- `static double toDegrees(double radians)`

  This method converts radians to degrees.

  Parameters: radians   An angle, in radians

  Returns: The angle in degrees

- `static double toRadians(double degrees)`

  This methods converts degrees to radians.

  Parameters: degrees   An angle, in degrees

  Returns: The angle in radians

- `static final double E`

  This constant is the value of e, the base of the natural logarithms.

- `static final double PI`

  This constant is the value of π.

Class java.lang.NullPointerException

This exception is thrown when a program tries to use an object through a `null` reference.

Class java.lang.NumberFormatException

This exception is thrown when a program tries to parse the numerical value of a string that is not a number.

Class java.lang.Object

- boolean **equals**(Object other)

  This method tests whether this and the other object are equal. This method tests only whether the object references are to the same object. Subclasses should redefine this method to compare the instance variables.

  Parameters: other   The object with which to compare

  Returns: True if the objects are equal, false otherwise

- String **toString**()

  This method returns a string representation of this object. This method produces only the class name and locations of the objects. Subclasses should redefine this method to print the instance variables.

  Returns: A string describing this object

Class java.lang.RuntimeException

This is the superclass for all unchecked exceptions.

Class java.lang.String

- int **compareTo**(String other)

  This method compares this string and the other string lexicographically.

  Parameters: other   The other string to be compared

  Returns: A value less than 0 if this string is lexicographically less than the other, 0 if the strings are equal, and a value greater than 0 otherwise

- boolean **equals**(String other)

- boolean **equalsIgnoreCase**(String other)

  These methods test whether two strings are equal, or whether they are equal when letter case is ignored.

  Parameters: other   The other string to be compared

  Returns: true if the strings are equal

- static String **format**(String format, Object... values)

  This method formats the given string by substituting placeholders beginning with % with the given values.

  Parameters: format   The string with the placeholders

                        values   The values to be substituted for the placeholders

  Returns: The formatted string, with the placeholders replaced by the given values

- int **length**()

  This method returns the length of this string.

  Returns: The count of characters in this string

- String **replace**(String match, String replacement)
  This method replaces matching substrings with a given replacement.
  Parameters: match The string whose matches are to be replaced
                      replacement The string with which matching substrings are
                      replaced
  Returns: A string that is identical to this string, with all matching sub-
                      strings replaced by the given replacement

- String **substring**(int begin)
- String **substring**(int begin, int pastEnd)
  These methods return a new string that is a substring of this string, made up of
  all characters starting at position begin and up to either position pastEnd - 1, if it is
  given, or the end of the string.
  Parameters: begin The beginning index, inclusive
                      pastEnd The ending index, exclusive
  Returns: The specified substring

- String **toLowerCase**()
  This method returns a new string that consists of all characters in this string con-
  verted to lowercase.
  Returns: A string with all characters in this string converted to lowercase

- String **toUpperCase**()
  This method returns a new string that consists of all characters in this string con-
  verted to uppercase.
  Returns: A string with all characters in this string converted to uppercase

Class java.lang.System

- static long **currentTimeMillis**()
  This method returns the difference, measured in milliseconds, between the cur-
  rent time and midnight, Universal Time, January 1, 1970.
  Returns: The current time in milliseconds since January 1, 1970.

- static void **exit**(int status)
  This method terminates the program.
  Parameters: status Exit status. A nonzero status code indicates abnormal
                      termination

- static final InputStream in
  This object is the "standard input" stream. Reading from this stream typically
  reads keyboard input.

- static final PrintStream out
  This object is the "standard output" stream. Printing to this stream typically
  sends output to the console window.

Class java.lang.Throwable

This is the superclass of exceptions and errors.

- Throwable()
  This constructs a Throwable with no detail message.

- String **getMessage**()
  This method gets the message that describes the exception or error.
  Returns: The message

- void **printStackTrace**()
  This method prints a stack trace to the "standard error" stream. The stack trace contains a printout of this object and of all calls that were pending at the time it was created.

Package java.math

Class java.math.BigDecimal

- **BigDecimal**(String value)
  This constructs an arbitrary-precision floating-point number from the digits in the given string.
  Parameters: value   A string representing the floating-point number

- BigDecimal **add**(BigDecimal other)
- BigDecimal **multiply**(BigDecimal other)
- BigDecimal **subtract**(BigDecimal other)
  These methods return a BigDecimal whose value is the sum, difference, product, or quotient of this number and the other.
  Parameters: other   The other number
  Returns: The result of the arithmetic operation

Class java.math.BigInteger

- **BigInteger**(String value)
  This constructs an arbitrary-precision integer from the digits in the given string.
  Parameters: value   A string representing an arbitrary-precision integer

- BigInteger **add**(BigInteger other)
- BigInteger **divide**(BigInteger other)
- BigInteger **mod**(BigInteger other)
- BigInteger **multiply**(BigInteger other)
- BigInteger **subtract**(BigInteger other)
  These methods return a BigInteger whose value is the sum, quotient, remainder, product, or difference of this number and the other.
  Parameters: other   The other number
  Returns: The result of the arithmetic operation

Package java.text

Class java.text.DateFormat

- String **format**(Date aDate)
  This method formats a date.
  Parameters: aDate   The date to format
  Returns: A string containing the formatted date

- static DateFormat **getTimeInstance**()
  This method returns a formatter that formats only the time portion of a date.
  Returns: The formatter object

- void **setTimeZone**(TimeZone zone)
  This method sets the time zone to be used when formatting dates.
  Parameters: zone   The time zone to use

Package java.util

Class java.util.ArrayList<E>

- **ArrayList**()
  This constructs an empty array list.

- boolean **add**(E element)
  This method appends an element to the end of this array list.
  Parameters: element   The element to add
  Returns: true (This method returns a value because it overrides a method
                      in the List interface.)

- void **add**(int index, E element)
  This method inserts an element into this array list at the given position.
  Parameters: index   Insert position
                      element   The element to insert

- E **get**(int index)
  This method gets the element at the specified position in this array list.
  Parameters: index   Position of the element to return
  Returns: The requested element

- E **remove**(int index)
  This method removes the element at the specified position in this array list and
  returns it.
  Parameters: index   Position of the element to remove
  Returns: The removed element

- E **set**(int index, E element)
  This method replaces the element at a specified position in this array list.
  Parameters: index   Position of element to replace
                      element   Element to be stored at the specified position
  Returns: The element previously at the specified position

- `int size()`
  This method returns the number of elements in this array list.
  Returns: The number of elements in this array list

Class java.util.Arrays

- `static int binarySearch(Object[] a, Object key)`
  This method searches the specified array for the specified object using the binary search algorithm. The array elements must implement the `Comparable` interface. The array must be sorted in ascending order.
  Parameters: a The array to be searched
                    key The value to be searched for
  Returns: The position of the search key, if it is contained in the array; otherwise, $-index - 1$, where *index* is the position where the element may be inserted

- `static T[] copyOf(T[] a, int newLength)`
  This method copies the elements of the array a, or the first `newLength` elements if `a.length > newLength`, into an array of length `newLength` and returns that array. `T` can be a primitive type, class, or interface type.
  Parameters: a The array to be copied
                    key The value to be searched for
  Returns: The position of the search key, if it is contained in the array; otherwise, $-index - 1$, where *index* is the position where the element may be inserted

- `static void sort(Object[] a)`
  This method sorts the specified array of objects into ascending order. Its elements must implement the `Comparable` interface.
  Parameters: a The array to be sorted

- `static String toString(T[] a)`
  This method creates and returns a string containing the array elements. `T` can be a primitive type, class, or interface type.
  Parameters: a An array
  Returns: A string containing a comma-separated list of string representations of the array elements, surrounded by brackets.

Class java.util.Calendar

- `int get(int field)`
  This method returns the value of the given field.
  Parameters: field   One of `Calendar.YEAR`, `Calendar.MONTH`, `Calendar.DAY_OF_MONTH`, `Calendar.HOUR`, `Calendar.MINUTE`, `Calendar.SECOND`, or `Calendar.MILLISECOND`

Interface java.util.Collection<E>

- `boolean add(E element)`
  This method adds an element to this collection.
  Parameters: element The element to add
  Returns: `true` if adding the element changes the collection

- `boolean` **contains**`(E element)`
  This method tests whether an element is present in this collection.
  Parameters: `element`   The element to find
  Returns: `true` if the element is contained in the collection
- `Iterator` **iterator**`()`
  This method returns an iterator that can be used to traverse the elements of this collection.
  Returns: An object of a class implementing the `Iterator` interface
- `boolean` **remove**`(E element)`
  This method removes an element from this collection.
  Parameters: `element`   The element to remove
  Returns: `true` if removing the element changes the collection
- `int` **size**`()`
  This method returns the number of elements in this collection.
  Returns: The number of elements in this collection

Class java.util.Collections

- `static <T> int` **binarySearch**`(List<T> a, T key)`
  This method searches the specified list for the specified object using the binary search algorithm. The list elements must implement the `Comparable` interface. The list must be sorted in ascending order.
  Parameters: `a`   The list to be searched
                   `key`   The value to be searched for
  Returns: The position of the search key, if it is contained in the list; otherwise, $-index - 1$, where $index$ is the position where the element may be inserted
- `static <T> void` **sort**`(List<T> a)`
  This method sorts the specified list of objects into ascending order. Its elements must implement the `Comparable` interface.
  Parameters: `a`   The list to be sorted

Interface java.util.Comparator<T>

- `int` **compare**`(T first, T second)`
  This method compares the given objects.
  Parameters: `first, second`   The objects to be compared
  Returns: A negative integer if the first object is less than the second, zero if they are equal, or a positive integer otherwise

Class java.util.EventObject

- `Object` **getSource**`()`
  This method returns a reference to the object on which this event initially occurred.
  Returns: The source of this event

Class java.util.GregorianCalendar

- GregorianCalendar()
  This constructs a calendar object that represents the current date and time.
- GregorianCalendar(int year, int month, int day)
  This constructs a calendar object that represents the start of the given date.
  Parameters: year, month, day   The given date

Class java.util.HashMap<K, V>

- HashMap<K, V>()
  This constructs an empty hash map.

Class java.util.HashSet<E>

- HashSet<E>()
  This constructs an empty hash set.

Class java.util.InputMismatchException

This exception is thrown if the next available input item does not match the type of the requested item.

Class java.util.Iterator<E>

- boolean hasNext()
  This method checks whether the iterator is past the end of the list.
  Returns: true if the iterator is not yet past the end of the list
- E next()
  This method moves the iterator over the next element in the linked list. This method throws an exception if the iterator is past the end of the list.
  Returns: The object that was just skipped over
- void remove()
  This method removes the element that was returned by the last call to next or previous. This method throws an exception if there was an add or remove operation after the last call to next or previous.

Interface java.util.LinkedList<E>

- void addFirst(E element)
- void addLast(E element)
  These methods add an element before the first or after the last element in this list.
  Parameters: element   The element to be added
- E getFirst()
- E getLast()
  These methods return a reference to the specified element from this list.
  Returns: The first or last element

- E `removeFirst()`
- E `removeLast()`

These methods remove the specified element from this list.

Returns: A reference to the removed element

Interface java.util.List<E>

- ListIterator<E> `listIterator()`

This method gets an iterator to visit the elements in this list.

Returns: An iterator that points before the first element in this list

Interface java.util.ListIterator<E>

Objects implementing this interface are created by the `listIterator` methods of list classes.

- void **add**(E element)

This method adds an element after the iterator position and moves the iterator after the new element.

Parameters: element The element to be added

- boolean **hasPrevious**()

This method checks whether the iterator is before the first element of the list.

Returns: true if the iterator is not before the first element of the list

- E **previous**()

This method moves the iterator over the previous element in the linked list. This method throws an exception if the iterator is before the first element of the list.

Returns: The object that was just skipped over

- void **set**(E element)

This method replaces the element that was returned by the last call to next or previous. This method throws an exception if there was an add or remove operation after the last call to next or previous.

Parameters: element The element that replaces the old list element

Interface java.util.Map<K, V>

- V **get**(K key)

Gets the value associated with a key in this map.

Parameters: key The key for which to find the associated value

Returns: The value associated with the key, or null if the key is not present in the map

- Set<K> **keySet**()

This method returns all keys this map.

Returns: A set of all keys in this map

- V **put**(K key, V value)

This method associates a value with a key in this map.

Parameters: key The lookup key

value The value to associate with the key

Returns: The value previously associated with the key, or null if the key was not present in the map

- V **remove**(K key)

  This method removes a key and its associated value from this map.

  Parameters:　　key　The lookup key

  Returns:　　　　The value previously associated with the key, or null if the key was not present in the map

Class java.util.NoSuchElementException

This exception is thrown if an attempt is made to retrieve a value that does not exist.

Class java.util.PriorityQueue<E>

- **PriorityQueue**<E>()

  This constructs an empty priority queue. The element type E must implement the Comparable interface.

- E **remove**()

  This method removes the smallest element in the priority queue.

  Returns:　　　　The removed value

Class java.util.Properties

- String **getProperty**(String key)

  This method gets the value associated with a key in this properties map.

  Parameters:　　key　The key for which to find the associated value

  Returns:　　　　The value, or null if the key is not present in the map

- void **load**(InputStream in)

  This method loads a set of key/value pairs into this properties map from a stream.

  Parameters:　　in　The stream from which to read the key/value pairs (it must be a sequence of lines of the form key=value)

Interface java.util.Queue<E>

- E **peek**()

  Gets the element at the head of the queue without removing it.

  Returns:　　　　The head element or null if the queue is empty

Class java.util.Random

- **Random**()

  This constructs a new random number generator.

- double **nextDouble**()

  This method returns the next pseudorandom, uniformly distributed floating-point number between 0.0 (inclusive) and 1.0 (exclusive) from this random number generator's sequence.

  Returns:　　　　The next pseudorandom floating-point number

- int **nextInt**(int n)

  This method returns the next pseudorandom, uniformly distributed integer between 0 (inclusive) and the specified value (exclusive) drawn from this random number generator's sequence.

  Parameters: n   Number of values to draw from

  Returns: The next pseudorandom integer

Class java.util.Scanner

- **Scanner**(File in)
- **Scanner**(InputStream in)
- **Scanner**(Reader in)

  These construct a scanner that reads from the given file, input stream, or reader.

  Parameters: in   The file, input stream, or reader from which to read

- void **close**()

  This method closes this scanner and releases any associated system resources.

- boolean **hasNext**()
- boolean **hasNextDouble**()
- boolean **hasNextInt**()
- boolean **hasNextLine**()

  These methods test whether it is possible to read any non-empty string, a floating-point value, an integer, or a line, as the next item.

  Returns: true if it is possible to read an item of the requested type, false otherwise (either because the end of the file has been reached, or because a number type was tested and the next item is not a number)

- String **next**()
- double **nextDouble**()
- int **nextInt**()
- String **nextLine**()

  These methods read the next whitespace-delimited string, floating-point value, integer, or line.

  Returns: The value that was read

- Scanner **useDelimiter**(String pattern)

  Sets the pattern for the delimiters between input tokens.

  Parameters: pattern   A regular expression for the delimiter pattern

  Returns: This scanner

Interface java.util.Set<E>

This interface describes a collection that contains no duplicate elements.

Class java.util.TreeMap<K, V>

- TreeMap<K, V>()

  This constructs an empty tree map. The iterator of a TreeMap visits the entries in sorted order.

Class java.util.TreeSet<E>

* `TreeSet<E>()`
  This constructs an empty tree set.

Package java.util.logging

Class java.util.logging.Level

* `static final int INFO`
  This value indicates informational logging.
* `static final int OFF`
  This value indicates logging of no messages.

Class java.util.logging.Logger

* `static Logger getGlobal()`
  This method gets the global logger. For Java 5 and 6, use `getLogger("global")` instead.
  Returns: The global logger that, by default, displays messages with level `INFO` or a higher severity on the console.
* `void info(String message)`
  This method logs an informational message.
  Parameters: `message` The message to log
* `void setLevel(Level aLevel)`
  This method sets the logging level. Logging messages with a lesser severity than the current level are ignored.
  Parameters: `aLevel` The minimum level for logging messages

Package javax.swing

Class javax.swing.AbstractButton

* `void addActionListener(ActionListener listener)`
  This method adds an action listener to the button.
  Parameters: `listener` The action listener to be added
* `boolean isSelected()`
  This method returns the selection state of the button.
  Returns: `true` if the button is selected
* `void setSelected(boolean state)`
  This method sets the selection state of the button. This method updates the button but does not trigger an action event.
  Parameters: `state` `true` to select, `false` to deselect

Class javax.swing.ButtonGroup

- void **add**(AbstractButton button)
  This method adds the button to the group.
  Parameters: button The button to add

Class javax.swing.ImageIcon

- **ImageIcon**(String filename)
  This constructs an image icon from the specified graphics file.
  Parameters: filename A string specifying a file name

Class javax.swing.JButton

- **JButton**(String label)
  This constructs a button with the given label.
  Parameters: label The button label

Class javax.swing.JCheckBox

- **JCheckBox**(String text)
  This constructs a check box with the given text, which is initially deselected.
  (Use the setSelected method to make the box selected; see the javax.swing.
  AbstractButton class.)
  Parameters: text The text displayed next to the check box

Class javax.swing.JComboBox

- **JComboBox**()
  This constructs a combo box with no items.

- void **addItem**(Object item)
  This method adds an item to the item list of this combo box.
  Parameters: item The item to add

- Object **getSelectedItem**()
  This method gets the currently selected item of this combo box.
  Returns: The currently selected item

- boolean **isEditable**()
  This method checks whether the combo box is editable. An editable combo box
  allows the user to type into the text field of the combo box.
  Returns: true if the combo box is editable

- void **setEditable**(boolean state)
  This method is used to make the combo box editable or not.
  Parameters: state true to make editable, false to disable editing

- void **setSelectedItem**(Object item)
  This method sets the item that is shown in the display area of the combo box as
  selected.
  Parameters: item The item to be displayed as selected

Package javax.swing

Class `javax.swing.JComponent`

- protected void **paintComponent**(Graphics g)
  Override this method to paint the surface of a component. Your method needs to call super.paintComponent(g).
  Parameters: g   The graphics context used for drawing
- void **setBorder**(Border b)
  This method sets the border of this component.
  Parameters: b   The border to surround this component
- void **setFont**(Font f)
  Sets the font used for the text in this component.
  Parameters: f   A font

Class `javax.swing.JFileChooser`

- **JFileChooser**()
  This constructs a file chooser.
- File **getSelectedFile**()
  This method gets the selected file from this file chooser.
  Returns: The selected file
- int **showOpenDialog**(Component parent)
  This method displays an "Open File" file chooser dialog box.
  Parameters: parent   The parent component or null
  Returns: The return state of this file chooser after it has been closed by the user: either APPROVE_OPTION or CANCEL_OPTION. If APPROVE_OPTION is returned, call getSelectedFile() on this file chooser to get the file
- int **showSaveDialog**(Component parent)
  This method displays a "Save File" file chooser dialog box.
  Parameters: parent   The parent component or null
  Returns: The return state of the file chooser after it has been closed by the user: either APPROVE_OPTION or CANCEL_OPTION

Class `javax.swing.JFrame`

- void **setDefaultCloseOperation**(int operation)
  This method sets the default action for closing the frame.
  Parameters: operation   The desired close operation. Choose among DO_NOTHING_ON_CLOSE, HIDE_ON_CLOSE (the default), DISPOSE_ON_CLOSE, or EXIT_ON_CLOSE
- void **setJMenuBar**(JMenuBar mb)
  This method sets the menu bar for this frame.
  Parameters: mb   The menu bar. If mb is null, then the current menu bar is removed
- static final int EXIT_ON_CLOSE
  This value indicates that when the user closes this frame, the application is to exit.

Class javax.swing.JLabel

- `JLabel(String text)`
- `JLabel(String text, int alignment)`

  These containers create a JLabel instance with the specified text and horizontal alignment.

  Parameters: text The label text to be displayed by the label

                        alignment One of SwingConstants.LEFT, SwingConstants.CENTER, or

                                  SwingConstants.RIGHT

Class javax.swing.JMenu

- `JMenu()`

  This constructs a menu with no items.

- `JMenuItem add(JMenuItem menuItem)`

  This method appends a menu item to the end of this menu.

  Parameters: menuItem The menu item to be added

  Returns: The menu item that was added

Class javax.swing.JMenuBar

- `JMenuBar()`

  This constructs a menu bar with no menus.

- `JMenu add(JMenu menu)`

  This method appends a menu to the end of this menu bar.

  Parameters: menu The menu to be added

  Returns: The menu that was added

Class javax.swing.JMenuItem

- `JMenuItem(String text)`

  This constructs a menu item.

  Parameters: text The text to appear in the menu item

Class javax.swing.JOptionPane

- `static String showInputDialog(Object prompt)`

  This method brings up a modal input dialog box, which displays a prompt and waits for the user to enter an input in a text field, preventing the user from doing anything else in this program.

  Parameters: prompt The prompt to display

  Returns: The string that the user typed

- `static void showMessageDialog(Component parent, Object message)`

  This method brings up a confirmation dialog box that displays a message and waits for the user to confirm it.

  Parameters: parent The parent component or null

                        message The message to display

Class javax.swing.JPanel

This class is a component without decorations. It can be used as an invisible container for other components.

Class javax.swing.JRadioButton

- **JRadioButton**(String text)

  This constructs a radio button having the given text that is initially deselected. (Use the setSelected method to select it; see the javax.swing.AbstractButton class.)

  Parameters: text The string displayed next to the radio button

Class javax.swing.JScrollPane

- **JScrollPane**(Component c)

  This constructs a scroll pane around the given component.

  Parameters: c The component that is decorated with scroll bars

Class javax.swing.JSlider

- **JSlider**(int min, int max, int value)

  This constructor creates a horizontal slider using the specified minimum, maximum, and value.

  Parameters: min The smallest possible slider value
  max The largest possible slider value
  value The initial value of the slider

- void **addChangeListener**(ChangeListener listener)

  This method adds a change listener to the slider.

  Parameters: listener The change listener to add

- int **getValue**()

  This method returns the slider's value.

  Returns: The current value of the slider

Class javax.swing.JTextArea

- **JTextArea**()

  This constructs an empty text area.

- **JTextArea**(int rows, int columns)

  This constructs an empty text area with the specified number of rows and columns.

  Parameters: rows The number of rows
  columns The number of columns

- void **append**(String text)

  This method appends text to this text area.

  Parameters: text The text to append

Class javax.swing.JTextField

- **JTextField**()
  This constructs an empty text field.
- **JTextField**(int columns)
  This constructs an empty text field with the specified number of columns.
  Parameters: columns   The number of columns

Class javax.swing.KeyStroke

- static KeyStroke **getKeyStrokeForEvent**(KeyEvent event)
  Gets a KeyStroke object describing the key stroke that caused the event.
  Parameters: event   The key event to be analyzed
  Returns: A KeyStroke object. Call toString on this object to get a string
                     representation such as "pressed LEFT"

Class javax.swing.Timer

- **Timer**(int millis, ActionListener listener)
  This constructs a timer that notifies an action listener whenever a time interval has
  elapsed.
  Parameters: millis   The number of milliseconds between timer notifications
                     listener   The object to be notified when the time interval has
                              elapsed
- void **start**()
  This method starts the timer. Once the timer has started, it begins notifying its
  listener.
- void **stop**()
  This method stops the timer. Once the timer has stopped, it no longer notifies its
  listener.

Package javax.swing.border

Class javax.swing.border.EtchedBorder

- **EtchedBorder**()
  This constructor creates a lowered etched border.

Class javax.swing.border.TitledBorder

- **TitledBorder**(Border b, String title)
  This constructor creates a titled border that adds a title to a given border.
  Parameters: b   The border to which the title is added
                     title   The title the border should display

Package `javax.swing.event`

Class `javax.swing.event.ChangeEvent`

Components such as sliders emit change events when they are manipulated by the user.

Interface `javax.swing.event.ChangeListener`

- void **stateChanged**(ChangeEvent e)

  This event is called when the event source has changed its state.

  Parameters: e   A change event

Package `javax.swing.text`

Class `javax.swing.text.JTextComponent`

- String **getText**()

  This method returns the text contained in this text component.

  Returns: The text

- boolean **isEditable**()

  This method checks whether this text component is editable.

  Returns: true if the component is editable

- void **setEditable**(boolean state)

  This method is used to make this text component editable or not.

  Parameters: state   true to make editable, false to disable editing

- void **setText**(String text)

  This method sets the text of this text component to the specified text. If the argument is the empty string, the old text is deleted.

  Parameters: text   The new text to be set

GLOSSARY

Abstract class   A class that cannot be instantiated.

Abstract method   A method with a name, parameter variable types, and return type but without an implementation.

Accessor method   A method that accesses an object but does not change it.

Aggregation   The *has-a* relationship between classes.

Algorithm   An unambiguous, executable, and terminating specification of a way to solve a problem.

Anonymous class   A class that does not have a name.

Anonymous object   An object that is not stored in a named variable.

API (Application Programming Interface)   A code library for building programs.

API Documentation   Information about each class in the Java library.

Applet   A graphical Java program that executes inside a web browser or applet viewer.

Argument   A value supplied in a method call, or one of the values combined by an operator.

Array   A collection of values of the same type stored in contiguous memory locations, each of which can be accessed by an integer index.

Array list   A Java class that implements a dynamically-growable array of objects.

Assignment   Placing a new value into a variable.

Association   A relationship between classes in which one can navigate from objects of one class to objects of the other class, usually by following object references.

Asymmetric bounds   Bounds that include the starting index but not the ending index.

Attribute   A named property that an object is responsible for maintaining.

Auto-boxing   Automatically converting a primitive type value into a wrapper type object.

Balanced tree   A tree in which each subtree has the property that the number of descendants to the left is approximately the same as the number of descendants to the right.

Big-Oh notation   The notation $g(n) = O(f(n))$, which denotes that the function g grows at a rate that is bounded by the growth rate of the function f with respect to n. For example, $10n^2 + 100n - 1000 = O(n^2)$.

Binary file   A file in which values are stored in their binary representation and cannot be read as text.

Binary operator   An operator that takes two arguments, for example + in $x + y$.

Binary search   A fast algorithm for finding a value in a sorted array. It narrows the search down to half of the array in every step.

Binary search tree   A binary tree in which *each* subtree has the property that all left descendants are smaller than the value stored in the root, and all right descendants are larger.

Bit   Binary digit; the smallest unit of information, having two possible values: 0 and 1. A data element consisting of n bits has 2^n possible values.

Black-box testing   Testing a method without knowing its implementation.

Block   A group of statements bracketed by {}.

Boolean operator   An operator that can be applied to Boolean values. Java has three Boolean operators: &&, ||, and !.

Boolean type   A type with two possible values: true and false.

Border layout   A layout management scheme in which components are placed into the center or one of the four borders of their container.

Boundary test case   A test case involving values that are at the outer boundary of the set of legal values. For example, if a method is expected to work for all nonnegative integers, then 0 is a boundary test case.

Bounds error   Trying to access an array element that is outside the legal range.

break statement   A statement that terminates a loop or switch statement.

Bug   A programming error.

Byte   A number made up of eight bits. Essentially all currently manufactured computers use a byte as the smallest unit of storage in memory.

Bytecode   Instructions for the Java virtual machine.

Call stack   The ordered set of all methods that currently have been called but not yet terminated, starting with the current method and ending with main.

Case sensitive   Distinguishing upper- and lowercase characters.

Cast   Explicitly converting a value from one type to a different type. For example, the cast from a floating-point number x to an integer is expressed in Java by the cast notation (int) x.

catch clause   A part of a try block that is executed when a matching exception is thrown by any statement in the try block.

Central processing unit (CPU)   The part of a computer that executes the machine instructions.

Character   A single letter, digit, or symbol.

Check box   A user-interface component that can be used for a binary selection.

Checked exception   An exception that the compiler checks. All checked exceptions must be declared or caught.

Class   A programmer-defined data type.

Collection   A data structure that provides a mechanism for adding, removing, and locating elements.

Collaborator   A class on which another class depends.

Combo box   A user-interface component that combines a text field with a drop-down list of selections.

Command line   The line the user types to start a program in DOS or UNIX or a command window in Windows. It consists of the program name followed by any necessary arguments.

Comment   An explanation to help the human reader understand a section of a program; ignored by the compiler.

Compiler   A program that translates code in a high-level language (such as Java) to machine instructions (such as bytecode for the Java virtual machine).

Compile-time error   An error that is detected when a program is compiled.

Component   See **User-interface component**

Composition   An aggregation relationship where the aggregated objects do not have an existence independent of the containing object.

Computer program   A sequence of instructions that is executed by a computer.

Concatenation   Placing one string after another to form a new string.

Concrete class   A class that can be instantiated.

Console program   A Java program that does not have a graphical window. A console program reads input from the keyboard and writes output to the terminal screen.

Constant   A value that cannot be changed by a program. In Java, constants are defined with the reserved word final.

Constructor   A sequence of statements for initializing a newly instantiated object.

Container   A user-interface component that can hold other components and present them together to the user. Also, a data structure, such as a list, that can hold a collection of objects and present them individually to a program.

Content pane   The part of a Swing frame that holds the user-interface components of the frame.

Coupling   The degree to which classes are related to each other by dependency.

CRC card   An index card representing a class that lists its responsibilities and collaborating classes.

De Morgan's Law   A law about logical operations that describes how to negate expressions formed with *and* and *or* operations.

Debugger   A program that lets a user run another program one or a few steps at a time, stop execution, and inspect the variables in order to analyze it for bugs.

Dependency   The *uses* relationship between classes, in which one class needs services provided by another class.

Directory   A structure on a disk that can hold files or other directories; also called a folder.

Dot notation   The notation *object.method(arguments)* or *object.variable* used to invoke a method or access a variable.

Doubly-linked list   A linked list in which each link has a reference to both its predecessor and successor links.

Dynamic method lookup   Selecting a method to be invoked at run time. In Java, dynamic method lookup considers the class of the implicit parameter object to select the appropriate method.

Editor   A program for writing and modifying text files.

Encapsulation   The hiding of implementation details.

Enumeration type   A type with a finite number of values, each of which has its own symbolic name.

Escape character   A character in text that is not taken literally but has a special meaning when combined with the character or characters that follow it. The \ character is an escape character in Java strings.

Escape sequence   A sequence of characters that starts with an escape character, such as \n or \".

Event See **User-interface event**

Event class A class that contains information about an event, such as its source.

Event adapter A class that implements an event listener interface by defining all methods to do nothing.

Event handler A method that is executed when an event occurs.

Event listener An object that is notified by an event source when an event occurs.

Event source An object that can notify other classes of events.

Exception A class that signals a condition that prevents the program from continuing normally. When such a condition occurs, an object of the exception class is thrown.

Exception handler A sequence of statements that is given control when an exception of a particular type has been thrown and caught.

Explicit parameter A parameter of a method other than the object on which the method is invoked.

Expression A syntactical construct that is made up of constants, variables, method calls, and the operators combining them.

Extension The last part of a file name, which specifies the file type. For example, the extension .java denotes a Java file.

Fibonacci numbers The sequence of numbers 1, 1, 2, 3, 5, 8, 13, ..., in which every term is the sum of its two predecessors.

File A sequence of bytes that is stored on disk.

`finally` **clause** A part of a try block that is executed no matter how the try block is exited.

Flag See **Boolean type**

Floating-point number A number that can have a fractional part.

Flow layout A layout management scheme in which components are laid out left to right.

Folder See **Directory**

Font A set of character shapes in a particular style and size.

Frame A window with a border and a title bar.

Garbage collection Automatic reclamation of memory occupied by objects that are no longer referenced.

Generic class A class with one or more type parameters.

Generic programming Providing program components that can be reused in a wide variety of situations.

Graphics context A class through which a programmer can cause shapes to appear on a window or off-screen bitmap.

grep The "global regular expression print" search program, useful for finding all strings matching a pattern in a set of files.

Grid layout A layout management scheme in which components are placed into a two-dimensional grid.

GUI (Graphical User Interface) A user interface in which the user supplies inputs through graphical components such as buttons, menus, and text fields.

Hard disk A device that stores information on rotating platters with magnetic coating.

Hardware   The physical equipment for a computer or another device.

Hash code   A value that is computed by a hash function.

Hash collision   Two different objects for which a hash function computes identical values.

Hash function   A function that computes an integer value from an object in such a way that different objects are likely to yield different values.

Hash table   A data structure in which elements are mapped to array positions according to their hash function values.

Hashing   Applying a hash function to a set of objects.

Heapsort algorithm   A sorting algorithm that inserts the values to be sorted into a heap.

High-level programming language   A programming language that provides an abstract view of a computer and allows programmers to focus on their problem domain.

HTML (Hypertext Markup Language)   The language in which web pages are described.

HTTP (Hypertext Transfer Protocol)   The protocol that defines communication between web browsers and web servers.

IDE (Integrated Development Environment)   A programming environment that includes an editor, compiler, and debugger.

Implementing an interface   Implementing a class that defines all methods specified in the interface.

Implicit parameter   The object on which a method is invoked. For example, in the call x.f(y), the object x is the implicit parameter of the method f.

Importing a class or package   Indicating the intention of referring to a class, or all classes in a package, by the simple name rather than the qualified name.

Inheritance   The *is-a* relationship between a more general superclass and a more specialized subclass.

Initialization   Setting a variable to a well-defined value when it is created.

Inner class   A class that is defined inside another class.

Instance method   A method with an implicit parameter; that is, a method that is invoked on an instance of a class.

Instance of a class   An object whose type is that class.

Instance variable   A variable defined in a class for which every object of the class has its own value.

Instantiation of a class   Construction of an object of that class.

Integer   A number that cannot have a fractional part.

Integer division   Taking the quotient of two integers and discarding the remainder. In Java the / symbol denotes integer division if both arguments are integers. For example, 11/4 is 2, not 2.75.

Interface   A type with no instance variables, only abstract methods and constants.

Internet   A worldwide collection of networks, routing equipment, and computers using a common set of protocols that define how participants interact with each other.

Iterator   An object that can inspect all elements in a container such as a linked list.

javadoc   The documentation generator in the Java SDK. It extracts documentation comments from Java source files and produces a set of linked HTML files.

JDK   The Java software development kit that contains the Java compiler and related development tools.

JVM   The Java Virtual Machine.

Layout manager   A class that arranges user-interface components inside a container.

Lazy evaluation   Deferring the computation of a value until it is needed, thereby avoiding the computation if the value is never needed.

Lexicographic ordering   Ordering strings in the same order as in a dictionary, by skipping all matching characters and comparing the first non-matching characters of both strings. For example, "orbit" comes before "orchid" in lexicographic ordering. Note that in Java, unlike a dictionary, the ordering is case sensitive: Z comes before a.

Library   A set of precompiled classes that can be included in programs.

Linear search   Searching a container (such as an array or list) for an object by inspecting each element in turn.

Linked list   A data structure that can hold an arbitrary number of objects, each of which is stored in a link object, which contains a pointer to the next link.

Literal   A constant value in a program that is explicitly written as a number, such as –2 or 6.02214115E23 or as a character sequence, such as "Harry".

Local variable   A variable whose scope is a block.

Logging   Sending messages that trace the progress of a program to a file or window.

Logical operator   See **Boolean operator**.

Logic error   An error in a syntactically correct program that causes it to act differently from its specification. (A form of run-time error.)

Loop   A sequence of instructions that is executed repeatedly.

Loop and a half   A loop whose termination decision is neither at the beginning nor at the end.

Machine code   Instructions that can be executed directly by the CPU.

Magic number   A number that appears in a program without explanation.

main method   The method that is first called when a Java application executes.

Map   A data structure that keeps associations between key and value objects.

Memory location   A value that specifies the location of data in computer memory.

Merge sort   A sorting algorithm that first sorts two halves of a data structure and then merges the sorted subarrays together.

Method   A sequence of statements that has a name, may have parameter variables, and may return a value. A method can be invoked any number of times, with different values for its parameter variables.

Modifier   A reserved word that indicates the accessibility of a feature, such as private or public.

Modulus   The % operator that computes the remainder of an integer division.

Mutator method   A method that changes the state of an object.

Mutual recursion   Cooperating methods that call each other.

Name clash   Accidentally using the same name to denote two program features in a way that cannot be resolved by the compiler.

Nested loop   A loop that is contained in another loop.

Networks   An interconnected system of computers and other devices.

new operator   An operator that allocates new objects.

Newline   The '\n' character, which indicates the end of a line.

Null reference   A reference that does not refer to any object.

Number literal   A constant value in a program this is explicitly written as a number, such as −2 or 6.02214115E23.

Object   A value of a class type.

Object-oriented programming   Designing a program by discovering objects, their properties, and their relationships.

Object reference   A value that denotes the location of an object in memory. In Java, a variable whose type is a class contains a reference to an object of that class.

Off-by-one error   A common programming error in which a value is one larger or smaller than it should be.

Operating system   The software that launches application programs and provides services (such as a file system) for those programs.

Operator   A symbol denoting a mathematical or logical operation, such as + or &&.

Operator associativity   The rule that governs in which order operators of the same precedence are executed. For example, in Java the - operator is left-associative because a - b - c is interpreted as (a - b) - c, and - is right-associative because a = b = c is interpreted as a = (b = c).

Operator precedence   The rule that governs which operator is evaluated first. For example, in Java the && operator has a higher precedence than the || operator. Hence a || b && c is interpreted as a || (b && c). (See Appendix B.)

Overloading   Giving more than one meaning to a method name.

Overriding   Redefining a method in a subclass.

Package   A collection of related classes. The import statement is used to access one or more classes in a package.

Panel   A user-interface component with no visual appearance. It can be used to group other components.

Parallel arrays   Arrays of the same length, in which corresponding elements are logically related.

Parameter   An item of information that is specified to a method when the method is called. For example, in the call System.out.println("Hello, World!"), the parameters are the implicit parameter System.out and the explicit parameter "Hello, World!".

Parameter passing   Specifying expressions to be arguments for a method when it is called.

Parameter variable   A variable of a method that is initialized with a value when the method is called.

Partially filled array   An array that is not filled to capacity, together with a companion variable that indicates the number of elements actually stored.

Permutation   A rearrangement of a set of values.

Polymorphism   Selecting a method among several methods that have the same name on the basis of the actual types of the implicit parameters.

Postfix operator   A unary operator that is written after its argument.

Prefix operator   A unary operator that is written before its argument.

Primitive type   In Java, a number type or `boolean`.

Priority queue   An abstract data type that enables efficient insertion of elements and efficient removal of the smallest element.

Programming   The act of designing and implementing computer programs.

Project   A collection of source files and their dependencies.

Prompt   A string that tells the user to provide input.

Pseudocode   A high-level description of the actions of a program or algorithm, using a mixture of English and informal programming language syntax.

Pseudorandom number   A number that appears to be random but is generated by a mathematical formula.

Public interface   The features (methods, variables, and nested types) of a class that are accessible to all clients.

Queue   A collection of items with "first-in, first-out" retrieval.

Quicksort   A generally fast sorting algorithm that picks an element, called the pivot, partitions the sequence into the elements smaller than the pivot and those larger than the pivot, and then recursively sorts the subsequences.

Radio button   A user-interface component that can be used for selecting one of several options.

RAM (random-access memory)   Electronic circuits in a computer that can store code and data of running programs.

Random access   The ability to access any value directly without having to read the values preceding it.

Recursion   A method for computing a result by decomposing the inputs into simpler values and applying the same method to them.

Recursive method   A method that can call itself with simpler values. It must handle the simplest values without calling itself.

Redirection   Linking the input or output of a program to a file instead of the keyboard or display.

Reference   See **Object reference**

Regular expression   A string that defines a set of matching strings according to their content. Each part of a regular expression can be a specific required character; one of a set of permitted characters such as `[abc]`, which can be a range such as `[a-z]`; any character not in a set of forbidden characters, such as `[^0-9]`; a repetition of one or more matches, such as `[0-9]+`, or zero or more, such as `[ACGT]`; one of a set of alternatives, such as `and|et|und`; or various other possibilities. For example, `"[A-Za-z][0-9]+"` matches `"Cloud9"` or `"007"` but not `"Jack"`.

Relational operator   An operator that compares two values, yielding a Boolean result.

Reserved word   A word that has a special meaning in a programming language and therefore cannot be used as a name by the programmer.

Return value   The value returned by a method through a return statement.

Reverse Polish notation   A style of writing expressions in which the operators are written following the operands, such as 2 3 4 * + for 2 + 3 * 4.

Roundoff error   An error introduced by the fact that the computer can store only a finite number of digits of a floating-point number.

Run-time error   An error in a syntactically correct program that causes it to act differently from its specification.

Run-time stack   The data structure that stores the local variables of all called methods as a program runs.

Scope   The part of a program in which a variable is defined.

Secondary storage   Storage that persists without electricity, e.g., a hard disk.

Selection sort   A sorting algorithm in which the smallest element is repeatedly found and removed until no elements remain.

Sentinel   A value in input that is not to be used as an actual input value but to signal the end of input.

Sequential access   Accessing values one after another without skipping over any of them.

Sequential search   See **Linear search**

Set   An unordered collection that allows efficient addition, location, and removal of elements.

Shadowing   Hiding a variable by defining another one with the same name.

Shell script   A file that contains commands for running programs and manipulating files. Typing the name of the shell script file on the command line causes those commands to be executed.

Shell window   A window for interacting with an operating system through textual commands.

Short-circuit evaluation   Evaluating only a part of an expression if the remainder cannot change the result.

Sign bit   The bit of a binary number that indicates whether the number is positive or negative.

Software   The intangible instructions and data that are necessary for operating a computer or another device.

Source code   Instructions in a programming language that need to be translated before execution on a computer.

Source file   A file containing instructions in a programming language such as Java.

Stack   A data structure with "last-in, first-out" retrieval. Elements can be added and removed only at one position, called the top of the stack.

Stack trace   A printout of the call stack, listing all currently pending method calls.

State   The current value of an object, which is determined by the cumulative action of all methods that were invoked on it.

State diagram   A diagram that depicts state transitions and their causes.

Statement   A syntactical unit in a program. In Java a statement is either a simple statement, a compound statement, or a block.

Static method   A method with no implicit parameter.

Static variable   A variable defined in a class that has only one value for the whole class, and which can be accessed and changed by any method of that class.

Stepwise refinement   The process of solving a problem that starts out with a subdivision into steps, then continues by further subdividing those steps.

String   A sequence of characters.

Stub   A method with no or minimal functionality.

Subclass   A class that inherits variables and methods from a superclass but adds instance variables, adds methods, or redefines methods.

Substitution principle   The principle that a subclass object can be used in place of any superclass object.

Superclass   A general class from which a more specialized class (a subclass) inherits.

Swing   A Java toolkit for implementing graphical user interfaces.

Symmetric bounds   Bounds that include the starting index and the ending index.

Syntax   Rules that define how to form instructions in a particular programming language.

Syntax diagram   A graphical representation of grammar rules.

Syntax error   An instruction that does not follow the programming language rules and is rejected by the compiler. (A form of compile-time error.)

Tab character   The '\t' character, which advances the next character on the line to the next one of a set of fixed positions known as tab stops.

Ternary operator   An operator with three arguments. Java has one ternary operator, `a ? b : c`.

Text field   A user-interface component that allows a user to provide text input.

Text file   A file in which values are stored in their text representation.

Throwing an exception   Indicating an abnormal condition by terminating the normal control flow of a program and transferring control to a matching catch clause.

throws specifier   Indicates the types of the checked exceptions that a method may throw.

Token   A sequence of consecutive characters from an input source that belongs together for the purpose of analyzing the input. For example, a token can be a sequence of characters other than white space.

Trace message   A message that is printed during a program run for debugging purposes.

Tree   A data structure consisting of nodes, each of which has a list of child nodes, and one of which is distinguished as the root node.

try block   A block of statements that contains exception processing clauses. A try block contains at least one catch or finally clause.

Turing machine   A very simple model of computation that is used in theoretical computer science to explore computability of problems.

Two-dimensional array   A tabular arrangement of elements in which an element is specified by a row and a column index.

Type   A named set of values and the operations that can be carried out with them.

Type parameter A parameter in a generic class or method that can be replaced with an actual type.

Unary operator An operator with one argument.

Unchecked exception An exception that the compiler doesn't check.

Unicode A standard code that assigns code values consisting of two bytes to characters used in scripts around the world. Java stores all characters as their Unicode values.

Unified Modeling Language (UML) A notation for specifying, visualizing, constructing, and documenting the artifacts of software systems.

Uninitialized variable A variable that has not been set to a particular value. In Java, using an uninitialized local variable is a syntax error.

Unit test A test of a method by itself, isolated from the remainder of the program.

URL (uniform resource locator) A pointer to an information resource (such as a web page or an image) on the World Wide Web.

User-interface component A building block for a graphical user interface, such as a button or a text field. User-interface components are used to present information to the user and allow the user to enter information to the program.

User-interface event A notification to a program that a user action such as a key press, mouse move, or menu selection has occurred.

Variable A symbol in a program that identifies a storage location that can hold different values.

Virtual machine A program that simulates a CPU that can be implemented efficiently on a variety of actual machines. A given program in Java bytecode can be executed by any Java virtual machine, regardless of which CPU is used to run the virtual machine itself.

void A reserved word indicating no type or an unknown type.

Walkthrough A step-by-step manual simulation of a computer program.

White space Any sequence of only space, tab, and newline characters.

Wrapper class A class that contains a primitive type value, such as `Integer`.

INDEX

Symbols

( ) (parentheses)
    enclosing arguments, 13
    in expressions, unbalanced, 46–47
\ (backslash)
    escape character, 60, 321
    in string literals, 321
= (equal sign)
    assignment statement, 34
    vs. equal signs (==), 89
== (equal signs)
    comparing strings, 90, 92
    equal operator, 88–89
    vs. equal sign (=), 89
% (percent sign)
    in format specifiers, 329
    modulus operator, description, 42
    modulus operator, online example, 45
, (comma)
    separating arguments, 13
    show decimal separators, 328
: (colon), path separator, 522
{ } (braces)
    layout, 86
    matching, 86
    readability, 86
&& (ampersands), *and* operator
    definition, 111
    flowchart, 112
    negating, 115–116
    vs. *or* operator, 114
    short-circuit evaluation, 114–115
* (asterisk), multiplication operator, 41
^ (caret), convert letters to uppercase, 328*t*
$ (dollar sign), in variable names, 33
" (double quote), String character
    delimiter, 61
! (exclamation point), *not* operator, 112
!= (exclamation point, equal), *not equal*
    operator, 88–89
> (greater than), comparison operator, 88–89
>= (greater than, equal), comparison
    operator, 88–89
((left paren), enclose negative numbers in
    parentheses, 328
< (less than), comparison operator, 88–89
<= (less than, equal), comparison
    operator, 88–89

? (question mark), conditional operator, 87.
    See also if statements
' (single quote), character literal
    delimiter, 61
_ (underscore), in variable names, 33
|| (vertical lines), *or* operator
    definition, 111
    flowchart, 112
    negating, 115–116
    vs. *and* operator, 114
    short-circuit evaluation, 114–115
/ (slash), division operator, 41, 42
/**...*/ (slash asterisks...)
    explanatory comment delimiter, 36
    method comment delimiter, 207
/*...*/ (slash asterisk...), long comment
    delimiter, 36
// (slashes), short comment delimiter, 35–36
+ (plus sign)
    addition operator, 41
    concatenation operator, 59–60
    for positive numbers, 328
++ (plus signs), increment operator, 41
- (hyphen), indicating program options, 330
- (minus sign)
    left alignment, 328
    subtraction operator, 41
-- (minus signs), decrement operator, 41
; (semicolon)
    after an if condition, 86–87
    ending Java statements, 12–13
    omitting, 14
    path separator, 522
2D arrays. See arrays, two-dimensional

A

abs method, Math class, 44*t*, 526
absolute values, computing, 44*t*, 526
abstract classes, 434–435
AbstractButton class, 539
accessor methods
    data representation, 371–372
    definition, 369
accounting fraud detection,
    video example, 352
acos method, Math class, 527
ActionListener class, 521

actionPerformed method, ActionListener
    class, 471–475, 521
actual parameters. *See* arguments
add method
    ArrayList<E> class, 291, 532
    with big number objects, 40
    BigDecimal class, 531
    BigInteger class, 531
    ButtonGroup class, 540
    Collection<E> class, 533
    Container class, 518
    JMenu class, 542
    JMenuBar class, 542
    ListIterator<E> class, 536
addActionListener method, AbstractButton
    class, 481, 539
addChangeListener method, JSlider class, 543
addFirst method, LinkedList<E> class, 535
addItem method, JComboBox class, 540
addKeyListener method, Component class, 518
addLast method, LinkedList<E> class, 535
addMouseListener method, Component
    class, 518
Adleman, Leonard, 336
algorithms
    for array lists, 295. *See also* arrays,
        common algorithms
    for arrays. *See* arrays, common
        algorithms
    definition, 19
    encryption, 336
    for loops. *See* loops, common algorithms
algorithms, designing
    executable steps, 19
    overview, 16–18
    pseudocode, 18, 20–21
    terminating steps, 19
    unambiguous steps, 19
algorithms, examples
    comparison shopping for cars, 20–21
    dividing household expenses (video
        example), 21
    investment problem, 17–18
aligning text with
    format specifiers, 328
    tabs, 87
alphabets, international, 66
Altair 8800 computer kit, 232
ampersands (&&), *and* operator
    definition, 111
    flowchart, 112
    negating, 115–116
    vs. or operator, 114
    short-circuit evaluation, 114–115

anonymous inner classes, 480–481
API (application programming interface),
    definition, 53
API documentation, 53
append method, JTextArea class, 484, 543
appending
    array list elements, 532
    text to text areas, 484, 543
Apple II computer, 232
Apple Macintosh computer, 233
applets. *See* programs
application programmers, 53
application programming interface (API),
    definition, 53
applications. *See* programs
Arabic characters, 66
arc cosine, computing, 527
arc sine, computing, 527
arc tangent, computing, 527
args parameter, 331
arguments, methods
    definition, 203
    modifying, 209–210
arguments, passing to methods
    from the command line, 330–333
    overview, 207–209
    syntax, 13
Ariane rocket incident, 347
arithmetic. *See also* numbers
    combining with assignment
        statements, 47
    expressions. *See* expressions
arithmetic operations
    * (asterisk), multiplication operator, 41
    -- (minus signs), decrement operator, 4
        (percent sign), modulus, 42
    ++ (plus signs), increment operator, 41
    / (slash), division operator, 41, 42
    abs method, Math class, 44*t*
    cos method, Math class, 43*t*
    exp method, Math class, 43*t*
    log method, Math class, 43*t*
    log10 method, Math class, 44*t*
    max method, Math class, 44*t*
    min method, Math class, 44*t*
    PI constant, Math class, 45*t*
    pow method, Math class, 43*t*
    round method, Math class, 44*t*
    sin method, Math class, 43*t*
    sqrt method, Math class, 43*t*
    tan method, Math class, 43*t*
    toDegrees method, Math class, 43*t*
    toRadians method, Math class, 43*t*

array lists. *See also* arrays; collections
  algorithms, 295. *See also* arrays, common
      algorithms
  vs. arrays, 296–297
  auto-boxing, 294
  constructors, 290–291
  copying, 293
  creating, 290–292, 532
  definition, 289
  diamond syntax, 299
  inserting primitive type values, 293–294
  maximum value, finding, 295
  as method arguments and return
      values, 293
  overview, 290–292
  storing input values, 295
  syntax, 290
  type parameter, repeating, 299
  wrapper classes, 293–294
array lists, elements
  appending, 532
  counting, 299, 533
  getting, 532
  inserting, 532
  removing, 295–296, 532
  replacing, 532
array references
  copying, 253, 263–264
  definition, 253
ArrayIndexOutOfBoundsException class, 275
ArrayList<E> class, 290–292, 532–533
arrays. *See also* array lists; collections
  vs. array lists, 296–297
  averaging values, 259
  common algorithms, 258–266
  companion variables, 254–255
  converting to strings, 533
  copying, 263–264, 533
  declaring, 250–253
  elements of, 251
  filling, 257–258
  maximum/minimum value, finding, 259
  multidimensional, 289. *See also* arrays,
      two-dimensional
  online example, 254
  overview, 250–253
  partially filled, 254–255
  reading input, 264–267
  slot numbers. *See* indexes
  summing values, 259
  syntax, 251
  traversing, 257–258
  uses for, 256

arrays, common algorithms. *See also* array
    lists, algorithms
  adapting to new purposes, 272–274
  animation, 261
  averaging values, 259
  copying array references, 263–264
  copying arrays, 263–264
  element separators, 259–260
  increasing size of, 263–264
  inserting elements, 261, 279
  linear search, 260
  maximum/minimum value, finding, 259
  online example, 281
  reading input, 264–267
  removing elements, 260–261, 279
  simulating with physical objects,
      279–282
  sorting by swapping elements, 262
  summing values, 259
  swapping elements, 262, 279–281
arrays, elements
  accessing, 251, 253
  animation, 261
  counting, 299
  definition, 251
  inserting, 261, 279
  multiplying by a given factor, 268–271
  removing, 260–261, 279
  removing duplicates (video example), 282
  reversing, 270–271
  separators, 259–260
  swapping, 262, 279–281
arrays, examples
  counting medal winners, 286–287
  quiz scores, 275–278
  rolling dice, 278
arrays, indexes
  bounds errors, 252–253, 255, 275
  definition, 251
  starting number, 252
arrays, initializing
  default values, 250–251
  uninitialized arrays, 255
  with zeros, 257–258
arrays, length
  definition, 250
  increasing, 263–264
  size requirements, estimating, 267
arrays, searching
  binary search, 267–268, 533
  linear search, 260
arrays, sorting
  with the Arrays.sort method, 267, 533
  by swapping elements, 262

arrays, two-dimensional. *See also
    multidimensional arrays*
    accessing elements, 283–284
    animation, 285
    declaring, 283
    definition, 282
    locating neighboring elements, 284
    passing as argument to a
        method, 286–287
    syntax, 283
    totaling rows and columns, 285
    tracing a nested loop (animation), 285
arrays, with methods
    passing as arguments to methods,
        268–269, 286–287
    returning values from methods, 270
    sample program, 270–271
Arrays class, 533
artificial intelligence, 119
asin method, Math class, 527
assignment statements
    assigning values to variables, 34
    combining with arithmetic, 47
    sample program, 36
asterisk (*), multiplication operator, 41
asymmetric bounds, 155
atan method, Math class, 527
atan2 method, Math class, 527
average method, 450–451
averages, calculating, 259, 449–454

B

baby names analysis
    worked example, 337
backing up files, 11
bank account worked example, 385
bar charts, drawing on user-interface
        components, 487–489, 492–496, 500
BigDecimal class, 40, 531
BigInteger class, 40, 531
binary data, reading, 322–323
binary search, 267–268
binarySearch method
    Arrays class, 533
    Collections class, 534
black boxes, methods as, 202–203
Boole, George, 111
Boolean class, 294, 524
Boolean variables and operators
    controlling loops, 159–160
    De Morgan's Law, 115–116
    inverting conditions, 112, 115–116
    online example, 112

overview, 111–116. *See also specific
    variables and operators*
    truth tables, 111
booleanValue method, Boolean class, 524
BorderLayout class, 517
borders, user-interface components, 517,
        541, 544
boundary conditions, testing, 108
bounding boxes, drawing on user-interface
        components, 489
bounds errors, 252–253, 255, 275
bounds for loops, choosing, 155
boxString method
    online example, 214
    printing a string in a box, 214–215
braces ({ })
    layout, 86
    matching, 86
    readability, 86
branching, if statements
    animation, 96, 100
    code duplication, 88
    multiple alternatives, 96–99
    nesting branches, 100–102, 104
branching, switch statements, 99
break statements
    in loops, 160–161
    in switch statements, 99
buffer overrun attack, 256
bugs, first actual case, 146. *See also
        debugging*
button groups, 468, 540
button labels, 468, 540
ButtonFrame1.java class, 472–473
ButtonFrame2.java class, 474–475
ButtonGroup class, 540
buttons, 468, 539
buttons, detecting. *See* events
ButtonViewer1.java class, 473
by-hand computations. *See* tracing code
Byte class, 294
byte type, 40*t*
bytes, definition, 322

C

CaesarCipher.java class, 331–333
Caesar's cipher, 331–333
Calendar class, 533. *See also* GregorianCalendar
    class
calendars, 533, 535
calling methods. *See* methods, calling
camel case, 33
capital letters. *See* case sensitivity
car shopping, example, 20–21

caret (^), convert letters to uppercase, 328*t*
cars, self-driving, 119
case sensitivity
    definition, 9
    Java programming language, 9
    misspelling words, 16
    variables, 33
cash register simulation, 367–369
CashRegister.java class
    online examples, 372, 387
    sample program, 368–369, 377–378
CashRegisterTester.java class, 381–382
cast operator
    converting double to int, 44–45
    syntax, 44
casting data types, 444–446
catch clause, 339–341, 346
catching exceptions, 339–344, 345
"The Cathedral and the Bazaar," 402
ceil method, Math class, 527
ceiling value, computing, 527
cell phone plans, evaluating (video
        example), 161
central processing unit (CPU), 3
ChangeEvent class, 545
ChangeListener class, 545
char type
    characters, 59
    description, 40*t*
Character class, 294, 324, 524–525
character literals, delimiting, 61
characters. *See also* strings
    Arabic, 66
    char type, 59
    Chinese, 66
    classifying, 324
    definition, 59
    Egyptian hieroglyphics, 66
    German, 66
    Greek, 66
    Hebrew, 66
    international alphabets, 66
    Korean, 66
    reading from a string, 326
    reading text files, 324
    returning from strings, 61. *See also*
        substrings
    Russian, 66
    sorting, 93
    Thai, 66
    Unicode, 66
charAt method, 61
ChartComponent2.java class, 491–492
ChartComponent.java class, 488, 494

ChartViewer2.java class, 492
ChartViewer.java class, 488–489
check boxes, 540
checked exceptions, 341–343
Chinese characters, 66
ChoiceQuestion.java class, 426–427
Class class, 525
class files, definition, 9
classes. *See also specific classes*
    abstract, 434–435
    API documentation, 53
    bank account worked example, 385
    concrete, 435
    declaring, 12
    definition, 12, 362
    final, 435
    generic, 290
    implementing, How To, 382–385
    importing from packages, 49
    vs. interface types, 449
    listener, 473–475
    loading, 525
    main methods, 380
    naming conventions, 33
    private implementation, 367–369
    public. *See* public classes
    tester, 380–382
    testing, 380–382
    unit testing, 380–382
classes, inner
    anonymous, 480–481
    declaring inside a method, 479–480
    definition, 474
    as event listeners, 473–475
    local, 479–480
classes, public interface
    definition, 363
    hiding implementation details. *See*
        encapsulation
    implementing, 364–367
    specifying, 367–369
ClickListener.java class, 471–472
close method
    automatic invocation, 346
    closing a file, 319, 523
    InputStream class, 523
    OutputStream class, 523
    PrintStream class, 524
    PrintWriter class, 524
    Scanner class, 538
code duplication
    branching if statements, 88
    eliminating, 215–217
collecting values, instance variables for,
        389–390

Collection<E> class, 533–534
collections. *See also* array lists; arrays
    duplicate elements, 538
    searching, 534
    sorting, 534
collections, elements
    adding, 533
    counting, 534
    no duplicates, 538
    removing, 534
    testing for, 534
    traversing, 534
Collections class, 534
colon (:), path separator, 522
color
    predefined palette, 490
    user-interface components, 489–492,
        518, 520
Color class, 491–492, 518
combo boxes, 540
comma (,)
    separating arguments, 13
    show decimal separators, 328
command line arguments, 330–333
comments
    /*...*/ (slash asterisk...), long comment
        delimiter, 36
    /**...*/ (slash asterisks...), explanatory
        comment delimiter, 36
    // (slashes), short comment delimiter,
        35–36
    definition, 35
    generating documentation from. *See*
        javadoc utility
    methods, 207
    purpose of, 35–37
companion variables, 254–255
Comparable<T> class, 452, 525
Comparator<T> class, 534
compare method, Comparator<T> class, 534
compareTo method
    Comparable<T> class, 525
    lexicographic ordering of strings, 92–93
    String class, 529
comparison shopping for cars,
        example, 20–21
comparisons
    floating-point numbers, 91–92
    lexicographic (dictionary) order of
        strings, 92–93, 529
    numbers, 88–92
    objects, 452, 525, 529, 534
    online example, 90
    precedence, 90

strings, 88–92, 529
    syntax, 89
    testing if results are close enough, 91–92
comparisons, relational operators
    combining, 113–114
    overview, 88
    summary of, 89t. *See also specific*
        operators
compile-time errors, 15
compiling programs
    animation, 10
    compilation process (animation), 10
    identifying text strings, 13
    in an integrated development
        environment, 9
    source code, 9
    video example, 11
Component class, 518
computations, by hand. *See* tracing code
computer programs. *See* programs
computers
    Altair 8800 kit, 232
    Apple II, 232
    Apple Macintosh, 233
    ENIAC (electronic numerical integrator
        and computer), 5
    human beings as, 5
    IBM Personal Computer, 232–233
    Macintosh, 233
    personal computers, history of, 232–233
computers, components of
    CPU (central processing unit), 3
    hard disks, 3
    input, 4
    networks, 4
    output, 4
    primary storage, 3
    secondary storage, 3
    storage, 3
    storage devices. *See specific devices*
    transistors, 3
concatenating strings, 59–60
concrete classes, 435
conditional operator, (?), 87
confirmation dialog boxes, 542
console window
    in an integrated development
        environment, 8
    writing to, 530
constants. *See also* variables
    declaring, 35
    definition, 35
    distinguishing from variables, 35
    interface types, 453

magic numbers, 39
named, 35
sample program, 36
constructors
array lists, 290–291
clearing objects, 379
default values, 376
definition, 375
multiple per class, 375
naming, 375
new reserved word, 379
returning values, 375
with superclass initializer, 430
syntax, 376
uninitialized, 376
void reserved word, 379
constructors, calling
to clear objects, 379
with new reserved word, 375
one from another, 399–400
for superclasses, 429–430
consuming white space, 323–324, 327
Container class, 518–519
containers
adding user-interface components, 518
layout manager, setting, 519
contains method, Collection<E> class, 534
converting number types. See cast operator
copy protection schemes, 182
copying
array lists, 293
array references, 263–264
arrays, 263–264
object references, 396
copyOf method, Arrays class, 263–264, 533
cos method, Math class, 43t, 527
cosine, computing, 43t, 527
cost of stamps, example, 56
count-controlled loops. See for loops
Counter.java class
example, 365–367
online example, 366
syntax, 365
counters
hardware, example, 364–367
software, in loops. See loops, counters
CounterTester program, online example, 366
counting
array list elements, 299, 533
collection elements, 534
events, instance variables for, 389
medal winners, example, 286–287
course grade calculation example, 225
coverage, testing, 108

CPU (central processing unit), 3
credit card processing, example, 172
crossword puzzles (video example), 500
Cubes.java class, 206
current time, in milliseconds, 530
currentTimeMillis method, System class, 530
CYC project, 119

D
dangling else problem, 104
DARPA urban challenge, 119
data sets, estimating size, 267–268
data types
numbers, summary of, 40t. See also
specific types
primitive, 64
testing, 444–446
DataAnalyzer.java class, 347–351
date and time
calendars, 533, 535
current time, in milliseconds, 530
formatting, 532
Gregorian calendar, 535
time zone, setting, 532
DateFormat class, 532
De Morgan's Law, 115–116
debugging
bugs, first actual case, 146
overriding toString method, 442–443
separating array elements, 260
string representation of objects, 442–443
video example, 228
decisions. See Boolean variables and
operators; comparisons; conditional
operator; if statements
declaring
array lists, 290–292
arrays, 250–253
classes, 12
constants, 35
loop counters, 152–153
main method, 12
two-dimensional arrays, 283
variables, 30–32
decrementing/incrementing loop
counters, 152
definite loops. See for loops
degrees, converting to radians, 528
Denver airport luggage handling system, 95
dialog boxes
choosing file names from a list, 321–322
confirmation, 542
input, 542
for input/output, 65

dialog boxes (continued)
online example, 65, 322
Open File, 541
Save File, 541
diamond syntax, 299
Dice.java class, 177
dictionary (lexicographic) order of strings, 92–93, 529
die tosses, simulating, 177
digits, testing for, 324t
digitSum method
online example, 233
summing the digits of an integer, 231–233
Dimension class, 494, 519
directories, definition, 10. *See also* folders
discount price calculation
online example, 95
sample program, 93–95
discussion board, video example, 441
distance computations, video example, 65
divide method, BigInteger class, 531
dividing household expenses, video example, 21
division, floating-point numbers, 46
division, intege (percent sign), modulus, 42
/ (slash), division operator, 41, 42
accidental, 46
remainders, 42
video example, 47
do loops. *See also* loops
input validation, 156–157
online example, 156
overview, 156–157
documentation
generating from code comments. *See* javadoc utility
online example, 368
dollar sign ($), in variable names, 33
dongles, 182
DOS (disk operating system), 233
dot notation, 64
Double class, 294, 525
double quote ("), String character delimiter, 61
double type. *See also* floating-point numbers
assigning to an integer, 44
converting to int, 44–45
description, 40t
DoubleInvestment.java class, 143
doubleValue method, Double class, 525
draw method, 179
drawing
bar charts, 487–489, 492–496, 500

bounding boxes, 489
color, 489–492
default width and height, 497
geometric shapes (video example), 455
graphical shapes, How To, 497–500
lines, 489–492, 519
online example, 500
ovals, 489–492, 519
overview, 179–180
rectangles, 519, 520
repainting changes, 493–496
sample program, 180–181
spirals (video example), 181
squares, 180–181
strings, 520
text, 489–492
drawLine method, Graphics class, 180, 489–492, 519
drawOval method, Graphics class, 180, 489–492, 519
drawRect method, Graphics class, 180, 489–492, 519
drawString method, Graphics class, 180, 490–492, 520
duplicate variable names, 226–227
dynamic method lookup, 431, 433–434

E

E constant, 528
earthquakes
Loma Prieta, 96
online example, 98
printing descriptions of, sample program, 96–98
Eckert, J. Presper, 5
editors, in an integrated development environment, 8
Egyptian hieroglyphics, 66
electronic voting machines, 394
elevator simulator, 84–85, 116–118
ElevatorSimulation2.java class, 117–118
ElevatorSimulation.java class, 84–85
else statements, dangling else problem, 104
empty strings, 59
EmptyFrameViewer.java class, 467
encapsulation, definition, 363
encryption
algorithms, 336
Caesar's cipher, 331–333
Enigma machine, 318
PGP (Pretty Good Privacy), 337
private keys, 336
public keys, 336
RSA encryption, 336

sample program, 331–333
end-of-file exception, 522
enhanced for loops, 257–258
ENIAC (electronic numerical integrator and computer), 5
Enigma encryption machine, 318
enumeration types, 105
EOFException class, 522
equal sign (=)
    assignment statement, 34
    vs. equal signs (==), 89
equal signs (==)
    comparing strings, 90, 92
    equal operator, 88–89
    vs. equal sign (=), 89
equals method
    Object class, 443–444, 447, 529. *See also* instanceof operator
    String class, 529
    testing strings for equality, 90
equalsIgnoreCase method, String class, 529
Error class, 341, 525
errors. *See also* exceptions
    compile-time, 15
    detecting, 337
    handling. *See* exception handling
    misspelled words, 16
    run-time, 15
    stack trace printout, 531
escape sequences, 60–61
EtchedBorder class, 544
event handling, 472. *See also* events
event listeners
    action listeners, 471–472, 521, 539
    frames as, 478–479
    for horizontal sliders, 543, 545
    inner classes as, 473–475
    keystrokes, 518, 521
    mouse actions, 518, 521–522
    mouse position, 521
    omitting, 478
    overview, 471–473
event sources, 471–473
event-controlled loops. *See* while loops
EventObject class, 534
events. *See also* event handling; java.awt. event package
    listening to, 471–473
    source object, getting, 534
    user-interface, 470–471
exception handlers, 338–341
exception handling. *See also specific exceptions*
    animation, 340

catch clause, 339–341, 346
catching exceptions, 339–344, 345
checked exceptions, 341–343
definition, 337
end of file, 522
finally clause, 343–344, 346
flowchart, 339
input errors, sample program, 347–351
online example, 343
squelching exceptions, 345
superclass. *See* Error class
syntax, 338, 341
throwing exceptions, 338–339, 345
throws clause, 342–343
unchecked exceptions, 341–343
exception reports
    error messages, 275
    reading and interpreting, 274–275
exceptions. *See also* errors
    array index out of bounds, 275
    definition, 15
    end of file, 522
    file not found, 319–320, 340, 523
    illegal argument, 338, 525
    illegal state, 526
    input mismatch, 349, 535
    input/output, 321
    interrupting a thread, 526
    no such element, 340, 537
    null pointer, 528
    number format, 340, 529
    runtime, 341, 529
    throwing, 338–339, 345, 530–531
exclamation point, equal (!=), *not equal operator*, 88–89
exclamation point (!), *not* operator, 112
executable steps, 19
exit method, System class, 530
exp method, Math class, 43*t*, 527
expert systems, 119
explicit parameters, 374
exponential floating-point, formatting, 329
exponentiation, 43*t*, 527–528
expressions
    definition, 41
    order of operations, 41
    spaces in, 47
    unbalanced parentheses, 46–47

F

federal tax rate schedule, 100*t*
Fifth-Generation Project, 119
file chooser, 321–322, 541
File class, 318, 522

file names
    backslashes, as string literals, 321
    choosing from a list, 321
`FileInputStream` class, 522
`FileNotFoundException` class, 319–320,
        340, 523
`FileOutputStream` class, 322–323
files. *See also* folders
    definition, 10
    making backup copies, 11
`FilledFrame` program, online example, 469
`FilledFrameViewer.java` class, 468
filling arrays, 254–255, 257–258
filling graphic images
    ovals, 180, 489–492, 519
    rectangles, 180, 519
`fillOval` method, `Graphics` class, 180,
        489–492, 519
`fillRect` method, `Graphics` class, 180, 519
final classes, 435
final reserved word, omitting, 453
final variables, 35
finally clause, 343–344, 346
fixed floating-point, formatting, 329
flags. *See* Boolean variables and operators
`Float` class, 294
float type
    description, 40*t*
    vs. `double`, 39
floating-point bug, Pentium computers, 48
floating-point numbers. *See also* `double` type
    assigning to an integer, 44
    comparing, roundoff errors, 91
    comparisons, 91–92
    converting to integer, 44–45. *See also* cast
        operator
    definition, 32
    division, 46
    float type, 39
    formatting, 329
    mixing with integers, 41
    reading, 50
    rounding, 45
`floor` method, `Math` class, 527
floor value, computing, 527
flowcharts. *See also* storyboards
    elements of, 105–106
    overview, 106–108
    spaghetti code, 106
`FlowLayout` class, 519
folders. *See also* files
    definition, 10
    hierarchical organization, 10
`Font` class, 519

font objects, constructing, 519
fonts, user-interface components, 541
for each loops, 257–258
for loops. *See also* loops
    animation, 151
    overview, 150–151
    sample program, 153–154
    syntax, 152
for loops, enhanced
    traversing array lists, 292
    traversing arrays, 257–258
formal parameters. *See* parameter variables
format flags, 328–329
format method
    `DateFormat` class, 532
    `String` class, 529
format specifiers, 328–329
formatting date and time, 532
formatting output
    , (comma), show decimal separators, 328
    ^ (caret), convert letters to uppercase, 328
    ((left paren), enclose negative numbers
        in parentheses, 328
    - (minus sign), left alignment, 328
    + (plus sign), for positive numbers, 328
    decimal integers, 329
    exponential floating-point, 329
    fixed floating-point, 329
    format types, 329
    general floating-point, 329
    online example, 329
    show leading zeros, 328
    string, 329
    writing text files, 328–329
`forName` method, `Class` class, 525
`Frame` class, 519
frames
    closing, default action, 467, 541
    customizing with inheritance, 469–470
    displaying, 466–467
    as event listeners, 478–479
    extending with `main` method, 470
    grouping components, 468
    menu bar, 541
    panels, 468
    size, setting, 469
    titling, 519
    user-interface components, 467–468, 541
fraud detection, video example, 352
free software, 402
function objects, 454

G

Game of Life (video example), 299

general floating-point, formatting, 329
General Public License (GPL), 402
genetic code (video example), 118
geometric shapes, drawing. *See* drawing
German characters, 66
get method
    ArrayList<E> class, 291, 532
    Calendar class, 533
    Map<K, V> class, 536
getFirst method, LinkedList<E> class, 535
getHeight method
    Component class, 518
    Rectangle class, 520
getLast method, LinkedList<E> class, 535
getMessage method, Throwable class, 341, 531
getProperty method, Properties class, 537
getSelectedFile method, JFileChooser
        class, 322, 541
getSelectedItem method, JComboBox class, 540
getSource method, EventObject class, 534
getter methods, instance variables
        for, 390–391
getText method, JTextComponent class,
        482–483, 545
getTimeInstance method, DateFormat
        class, 532
getValue method, JSlider class, 543
getWidth method, 492–496
    Component class, 518
    Rectangle class, 520
getX method
    MouseEvent class, 521
    Rectangle class, 520
getY method
    MouseEvent class, 521
    Rectangle class, 520
Gosling, James, 5–6
GPL (General Public License), 402
graphical shapes, drawing. *See* drawing
graphical user interface. *See also* drawing;
        user interface
    reaction to user actions, 470–471. *See also*
        event handling; events
    text processing. *See* text input
Graphics class, 180, 519–520
Graphics objects, drawing on user-interface
        components, 487–489
greater than, equal (>=), comparison
        operator, 88–89
greater than (>), comparison operator, 88–89
Greek characters, 66
Gregorian calendar, 535
GregorianCalendar class, 535. *See also* Calendar
        class

grep command, 330
grid layout, user-interface components, 520
GridLayout class, 520
grouping frame components, 468
grow method, Rectangle class, 520

H

hand-tracing. *See also* tracing code
    animation, 149
    loops, 147–150
    overview, 103–104
hard disks, illustration, 3
hardware, definition, 2
hash maps, creating, 535
hash sets, creating, 535
HashMap<K, V> class, 535
HashSet<E> class, 535
hasNext method
    Iterator<E> class, 535
    Scanner class, 538
hasNextDouble method, Scanner class,
        116–118, 538
hasNextInt method, Scanner class,
        116–118, 538
hasNextLine method, Scanner class,
        325–326, 538
hasPrevious method, ListIterator<E>
        class, 536
Hebrew characters, 66
"Hello, World!" sample program, 8–9,
        12–14
high-level programming languages, 5. *See
        also* Java programming language
Hoff, Marcian E., 232
horizontal sliders, 543, 545
household expense division, video
        example, 21
hyphen (-), indicating program options, 330

I

IBM Personal Computer, 232–233
if statements. *See also* switch statements
    ? (question mark), conditional
        operator, 87
    combining. *See* nesting, if statements
    dangling else problem, 104
    flowchart, 83
    implementing, How To, 93–95
    input validation, 116–118
    nesting, 96–102, 104
    overview, 82
    sample program, 84–85
    syntax, 84

if statements, branching
    animation, 96, 100
    code duplication, 88
    multiple alternatives, 96–99
    nesting branches, 100–102, 104
IllegalArgumentException class, 338, 525
IllegalStateException class, 526
image icons, 540
image pixel manipulation, example, 175
ImageIcon class, 540
immutable variables, 35
implements reserved word, 450–451
implicit parameters
    dynamic method lookup, 433–434
    overview, 373–374
    this references, 397–399
importing classes from packages, 49
income tax
    calculating, sample program, 100–102
    federal tax rate schedule, 100t
incrementing/decrementing loop
        counters, 152
indenting nested statements with tabs, 87
indexes, arrays
    bounds errors, 252–253, 255, 275
    definition, 251
    starting number, 252
infinite loops, 145
inheritance. See also subclasses; superclasses
    animation, 425
    customizing frames, 469–470
    equals method, 447
    hierarchies, 416, 484
    overview, 416–417
    purpose of, 420
    sample programs, 418–419
    substitution principle, 416
    toString method, 446–447
inheritance hierarchies, developing
    How To, 436–441
    payroll processing example, 441
initializing
    instance variables. See constructors
    variables, 31, 34
initializing, arrays
    default values, 250–251
    uninitialized arrays, 255
    with zeros, 257–258
Initials.java class, 62–63
inner classes
    anonymous, 480–481
    declaring inside a method, 479–480
    definition, 474
    as event listeners, 473–475

local, 479–480
input. See also java.io package; text input
    definition, 4
    reading from arrays, 264–267
    redirecting, 161
input, reading. See also Scanner class
    closing a file, 319, 523
    from dialog boxes, 65, 321
    end of file, 522
    file not found, 348, 350, 523
    floating-point numbers, 50
    input error, 523
    integers, 49–50
    from the keyboard, 49, 530
    opening a file, 318, 522
    prompts, 49
    read operation, 523
    readers, constructing, 523
    strings, from the console, 50. See also next
        method
input dialog boxes, 65, 542
input errors, sample program, 347–351
input mismatch exception, 326, 535
input statements, syntax, 49
input validation
    with do loops, 156–157
    with if statements, 116–118
InputMismatchException class, 349, 535
InputStream class, 322–323, 523
InputStream in object, 530
InputStreamReader class, 523
inserting
    array elements, 261, 279
    array list elements, 290–291, 532
    primitive type values in array lists,
        293–294
instance methods, 64
instance variables. See also variables
    modifiers, 365
    accidental changes, 475
    declaring, 365
    definition, 365
    initializing. See constructors
    name, 365
    online example, 372
    overview, 365–367
    private, 366
    public vs. private, 374
    syntax, 365
    type, 365
    uninitialized, 378–379
instance variables, common patterns
    collecting values, 389–390
    counting events, 389

describing object position, 392–393
getter methods, 390–391
managing object properties, 390–391
modeling objects with distinct states, 391–392
running totals, 388–389
setter methods, 390–391
instance variables, in superclasses
protecting, 436
replicating, 423–424
instanceof operator, Object class, 444–445.
See also equals method
int type. *See also* integers
converting from double, 44–45
definition, 31–32
description, 40*t*
maximum value, 38
overflow, 38
Integer class, 294, 526
IntegerName.java class, 221–223
integers. *See also* int type
assigning floating-point numbers to, 44
converting from floating-point, 44–45.
See also cast operator
converting from strings, 526
definition, 31
formatting, 329
mixing with floating-point, 41
reading, 49–50
summing the digits of, 231–233
integers, division
% (percent sign), modulus, 42
/ (slash), division operator, 41, 42
accidental, 46
remainders, 42
video example, 47
integrated development environment, 8
interface types
vs. classes, 449
Comparable interface, 452
comparing two objects, 452
constants, 453
defining an interface, 448–450
definition, 449
final reserved word, omitting, 453
function objects, 454
implementing an interface, 450–451
online example, 454
public reserved word, omitting, 453
static reserved word, omitting, 453
syntax, 449
international alphabets, 66
InterruptedException class, 526

intersection method, Rectangle class, 520
intersections of rectangles, computing, 520
intValue method, Integer class, 526
inverting conditions, 112, 115–116
investment problems, examples
designing an algorithm for, 17–18
doubling your investment, 140–143
printing annual balances, 153–154
showing growth, 475–477, 482–483, 485–486, 492–496
InvestmentFrame.java class, 476–477
InvestmentFrame2.java class, 482–483
InvestmentFrame3.java class, 485–486
InvestmentFrame4.java class, 494–496
InvestmentTable.java class, 153–154
InvestmentViewer.java class, 477
IOException class, 321
isDigit method, Character class, 324*t*–325, 524
isEditable method
JComboBox class, 540
JTextComponent class, 545
isLetter method, Character class, 324*t*, 524
isLowerCase method, Character class, 324*t*, 525
isSelected method, AbstractButton class, 539
isUpperCase method, Character class, 324*t*, 525
isWhiteSpace method, 324*t*–325
iteration
end of list, testing for, 535
removing elements, 535
traversing a list, 535
iterator method, Collection<E> class, 534
Iterator<E> class, 535

J

Java library. *See also specific packages*
description, 6
inheritance hierarchy, 515–517
packages, 7
Java programming environment
class files, 9
compilation process (animation), 10
console window, 8
directories, 10
editors, 8
files, 10
folders, 10
integrated development environment, 8
organizing your work, 10
overview, 8–10
source code, 9

Java programming language. *See also* programming languages
  case sensitivity, 9
  creators of, 5–6
  "Hello, World!" sample program, 8–9, 12–14
  portability, 6
  safety features, 6
  versions, 7*t*
Java virtual machine (JVM), 6–7
java.awt package. *See also* user interface components
  BorderLayout class, 517
  Color class, 490, 518
  Component class, 518
  Container class, 518–519
  Dimension class, 519
  FlowLayout class, 519
  Font class, 519
  Frame class, 519
  Graphics class, 519–520
  GridLayout class, 520
  Rectangle class, 520–521
java.awt.event package. *See also* events
  ActionListener class, 472, 521
  KeyEvent class, 521
  KeyListener class, 521
  MouseEvent class, 521
  MouseListener class, 522
javadoc utility, 370–371
java.io package. *See also* input; output
  EOFException class, 522
  File class, 522
  FileInputStream class, 522
  FileNotFoundException class, 523
  InputStream class, 523
  InputStreamReader class, 523
  OutputStream class, 523
  PrintStream class, 523–524
  PrintWriter class, 524
java.lang package
  Boolean class, 524
  Character class, 524–525
  Class class, 525
  Comparable<T> class, 525
  Double class, 525
  Error class, 525
  IllegalArgumentException class, 525
  IllegalStateException class, 526
  Integer class, 526
  InterruptedException class, 526
  Math class, 526–528
  NullPointerException class, 528
  NumberFormatException class, 529

Object class, 529
  RuntimeException class, 529
  String class, 529–530
  System class, 530
  Throwable class, 530–531
java.math package
  BigDecimal class, 531
  BigInteger class, 531
java.text package, DateFormat class, 532
java.util package
  ArrayList<E> class, 532–533
  Arrays class, 533
  Calendar class, 533
  Collection<E> class, 533–534
  Collections class, 534
  Comparator<T> class, 534
  EventObject class, 534
  GregorianCalendar class, 535
  HashMap<K, V> class, 535
  HashSet<E> class, 535
  InputMismatchException class, 535
  Iterator<E> class, 535
  LinkedList<E> class, 535–536
  List<E> class, 536
  ListIterator<E> class, 536
  Map<K, V> class, 536–537
  NoSuchElementException class, 537
  PriorityQueue<E> class, 537
  Properties class, 537
  Queue<E> class, 537
  Random class, 537–538
  Scanner class, 538
  Set<E> class, 538
  TreeMap<K, V> class, 538
  TreeSet<E> class, 539
java.util.logging package, Level class, 539
javax.swing package. *See also* user-interface components
  AbstractButton class, 539
  ButtonGroup class, 540
  ImageIcon class, 540
  JButton class, 540
  JCheckBox class, 540
  JComboBox class, 540
  JComponent class, 541
  JFileChooser class, 541
  JFrame class, 541
  JLabel class, 542
  JMenu class, 542
  JMenuBar class, 542
  JMenuItem class, 542
  JOptionPane class, 542
  JPanel class, 543
  JRadioButton class, 543

JScrollPane class, 543
JSlider class, 543
JTextArea class, 543
JTextComponent class, 545
JTextField class, 544
KeyStroke class, 544
Timer class, 544
javax.swing.border package
EtchedBorder class, 544
TitledBorder class, 544
javax.swing.event package
ChangeEvent class, 545
ChangeListener class, 545
JButton class, 468, 540
JCheckBox class, 540
JComboBox class, 540
JComponent class, 487, 541
JFileChooser class, 321–322, 541
JFrame class, 466–467, 541
JLabel class, 481–483, 542
JMenu class, 542
JMenuBar class, 542
JMenuItem class, 542
JOptionPane class, 65, 542
JPanel class, 468, 543
JRadioButton class, 543
JScrollPane class, 543
JSlider class, 543
JTextArea class, 483–486, 543
JTextComponent class, 545
JTextField class, 481–483, 544
justifying text (video example), 233
JVM (Java virtual machine), 6–7

K

key words. *See* reserved words
keyboard, reading from, 49, 530
KeyEvent class, 521
KeyListener class, 521
keyPressed method, KeyListener class, 521
keyReleased method, KeyListener class, 521
keySet method, Map<K, V> class, 536
KeyStroke class, 544
keystrokes
    detecting. *See* events
    event listeners, 518, 521
keyTyped method, KeyListener class, 521
killing a hanging program, 145
Korean characters, 66

L

labels
    text fields, 481–483
    user-interface components, 542

languages, translating, 119
largest value, computing, 527. *See also*
    maximum/minimum value, finding
LargestInArray.java class, 265–266, 297–298
Latin/Latin-1 subsets of Unicode
    characters, 507–509
leading zeros, showing, 328
left paren ((), enclose negative numbers in
    parentheses, 328
Lenat, Douglas, 119
length method, String class, 59, 529
less than, equal (<=), comparison
    operator, 88–89
less than (<), comparison operator, 88–89
letters. *See also* characters; strings
    case. *See* lowercase; uppercase
    testing for, 324*t*
Level class, 539
lexicographic (dictionary) order of strings,
    92–93, 529
line breaks, strings, 60–61
linear search, arrays, 260
lines, drawing, 489–492, 519
lines of text, reading text files, 325–327
linked lists, elements
    adding, 535–536
    first, testing for, 536
    getting first/last, 535
    removing, 536
    replacing, 536
    traversing, 536
LinkedList<E> class, 535–536
List<E> class, 536
listIterator method, List<E> class, 536
ListIterator<E> class, 536
lists, elements
    adding, 535–536
    first, testing for, 536
    getting first/last, 535
    removing, 536
    replacing, 536
    traversing, 536
literals
    backslashes in file names, 321
    character, delimiting, 61
    numbers, 32–33
    reserved characters, 60–61
    string, 59–61
load method, Properties class, 537
loan, paying off (video example), 386
local inner classes, 479–480
local variables, 225
log method, Math class, 43*t*, 527
log10 method, Math class, 44*t*, 527

logarithms, 43*t*, 44*t*, 527
Logger class, 110
logging messages, 110, 539
logic errors. *See* run-time errors
Loma Prieta earthquake
   online example, 98
   photograph, 96
   printing descriptions of, sample
      program, 96–98
Long class, 294
long type, 40*t*
loop-and-a-half problem, 160–161
loops. *See also specific loops*
   asymmetric bounds, 155
   bounds, choosing, 155
   break statement, 160–161
   controlling with Boolean variables,
      159–160
   counting iterations, 156
   definition, 140
   do loop, 156–157
   enhanced for loop, 257–258, 292
   flowcharts, 157
   for loop, 150–152
   hand-tracing, 147–150
   How To write, 169–172
   indefinite. *See* while loops
   infinite, 145
   loop-and-a-half problem, 160–161
   nesting, 172–175
   off-by-one errors, 145–146
   post-test. *See* do loops
   pre-test. *See* for loops; while loops
   processing a sequence of values, 158–161
   sentinel values, 158–161
   symmetric bounds, 155
   terminating with a target value, 144
   traversing characters in a string, 154
   while loop, 140–143
loops, common algorithms
   averages, 165
   comparing adjacent values, 168–169
   counting matches, 165–166
   finding first match, 166
   maximum/minimum computations, 167
   online example, 168
   powers of *x*, calculating, 172–175
   printing a table, 172–175
   prompting for a match, 167
   running totals, 165
   summing numbers, 165
loops, counters
   counting loop iterations, 156

counting matches, 165–166
   declaring, 152–153
   incrementing/decrementing, 152
   infinite loops, 145
   off-by-one errors, 145–146
   updating inside a for loop, 155
   using outside the loop, 153
loops, terminating
   count-controlled. *See* for loops
   definite. *See* for loops
   event-controlled. *See* while loops
   with sentinel values, 158–161
lowercase letters, testing for, 324*t*. *See also*
      case sensitivity
lowercase strings, sorting, 93
luggage handling, Denver airport, 95

M

Macintosh computer, 233
magic numbers, 39
main method
   in classes, 380
   declaring, 12
   definition, 12
   extending frame classes, 470
   statements, 12
map keys, 536–537
Map<K, V> class, 536–537
math. *See* arithmetic; java.math package; Math
      class; numbers; *specific operations*
Math class, 526–528
matrices. *See* arrays, two-dimensional
Mauchly, John, 5
max method, Math class, 44*t*, 527
maximum/minimum value, finding
   algorithm for, 259
   in arrays, 295
   max method, Math class, 44*t*, 527
   MAX_VALUE constant, 526
   min method, Math class, 44*t*, 528
   MIN_VALUE constant, 526
MAX_VALUE constant, 526
MeasurableDemo.java class, 451
medal winners, example, 286–287
Medals.java class, 286–287
menu bars
   frames, 541
   user-interface components, 542
Menu class, online example, 385
menu items, 542
menus, 542
MenuTester class, online example, 385
messages, logging, 110

methods. *See also specific methods*
   abstract, 434–435
   API documentation, 53
   as black boxes, 202–203
   brevity, 223
   comments, 207
   definition, 202
   dot notation, 64
   duplicate names. *See* overloading
     methods
   execution flowchart, 202
   final, 435
   implementing, How To, 212–213
   inputs, 203
   instance, 64
   main. *See* main method
   mutator, 369
   outputs, 203
   overriding. *See* overriding methods
   passing values to. *See* methods,
     arguments; methods, parameter
     variables
   public *vs.* private, 374
   recursive, 228–232
   reusing, 215–217
   sample program, 206
   static, 64–65, 205, 400–402
   stepwise refinement, 218–219
   stubs, 224–225
   syntax, 205
   temporary placeholders for, 224–225
methods, accessor
   data representation, 371–372
   definition, 369
methods, arguments. *See also* methods,
   parameter variables
   array lists as, 293
   definition, 203
   modifying, 209–210
   passing, 207–209
methods, calling
   instance methods *vs.* static, 64–65
   on numbers, 64
   on objects, 64
   other methods, 13, 202
   recursively, 228–232
methods, instance
   description, 372
   example, 372–373
   explicit parameters, 374
   implicit parameters, 373–374
   syntax, 372

methods, parameter variables. *See also*
   methods, arguments; methods,
   variables
   animation, 208
   modifying, 209
   passing, 207–209
   passing with two-dimensional arrays,
     286–287
   variable number of, 272
methods, return values
   array lists as, 293
   definition, 203
   missing, 212
   multiple, 211
   omitting, 214–215
   online example, 211
   specifying, 210–211
methods, tracing
   animation, 220
   example, 223–224
methods, variables. *See also* methods,
   parameter variables
   duplicate names, 226–227
   local, 225
   scope, 225–228
microprocessors, history of, 232
min method, Math class, 44*t*, 528
minimum/maximum value, finding
   algorithm for, 259
   in arrays, 295
   max method, Math class, 44*t*, 527
   MAX_VALUE constant, 526
   min method, Math class, 44*t*, 528
   MIN_VALUE constant, 526
minus sign (-)
   left alignment, 328
   subtraction operator, 41
minus signs (--), decrement operator, 41
MIN_VALUE constant, 526
misspelling words, 16
mod method, BigInteger class, 531
modifiers, instance variables, 365
Monte Carlo method, 178–179
MonteCarlo.java class, 178–179
Morris, Robert, 256
mouse
   actions, event listeners, 518, 521–522
   clicks, detecting. *See* events
   position, event listeners, 521
mouseClicked method, MouseListener
     class, 522
mouseEntered method, MouseListener
     class, 522

MouseEvent class, 521
mouseExited method, MouseListener class, 522
MouseListener class, 522
mousePressed method, MouseListener class, 522
mouseReleased method, EOFException class, 522
mouseReleased method, MouseListener class, 522
multidimensional arrays, 289. *See also* arrays, two-dimensional
multiply method
    BigDecimal class, 40, 531
    BigInteger class, 40, 531
mutator methods, 369

N

\n (backslash n), newline character, 60–61
named constants, 35
naming
    classes, 33
    constants, 35
    constructors, 375
    instance variables, 365
    public classes, 12
    variables, 33, 38
Naughton, Patrick, 5
negating conditions, 112, 115–116
nested loops, tracing (animation), 285
nested statements, indenting, 87
nesting
    if statement branches, 100–102, 104
    if statements, 96–102, 104
    loops, 172–175
networks, definition, 4
next method
    consuming white space, 327
    Iterator<E> class, 535
    reading strings from the console, 60
    Scanner class, 538
nextDouble method
    consuming white space, 327
    Random class, 537
    reading floating-point numbers, 50
    Scanner class, 538
nextInt method
    consuming white space, 327
    Random class, 538
    reading integers, 49–50, 116–118
    Scanner class, 538
nextLine method, 325–326
Nicely, Thomas, 48
NoSuchElementException class, 340, 537
null pointer exception, 528

null reference
    default for objects, 379
    definition, 397
    testing for, 397
    uninitialized instance variables, 378–379
NullPointerException class, 528
number format exception, 529
number types, summary of, 40. *See also specific types*
NumberFormatException class, 340, 529
numbers. *See also* arithmetic
    comparisons, 88–92
    converting from strings, 326
    converting to words, 219–223
    as literals, 32–33
    overflow, 38
    range errors, 38
    reading text files, 327
    sorting, 93
    very large, 40
    whole, no fractions. *See* integers
    whole, with fractions. *See* floating-point numbers

O

Object class. *See also* superclasses
    available online, 441
    data type, testing, 444–446
    definition, 441
    description, 529
    object equality, testing for, 443–444, 447
    online example, 445
    string representation of objects, 442–443, 446
object references
    animation, 396
    copying, 396
    definition, 395
    null, 397
    shared, 395–397
    this, 397–399
objects
    belonging to same class, testing for, 447
    changing. *See* mutator methods
    clearing with constructors, 379
    comparisons, 525, 529, 534
    describing position, instance variables for, 392–393
    equality, testing for, 443–444
    examples of, 64
    managing properties, instance variables for, 390–391
    memory location. *See* object references

modeling with distinct states, instance variables for, 391–392
querying. *See* accessor methods
storing data. *See* instance variables
off-by-one errors, 145–146
OOP (object-oriented programming), 362. *See also* classes; methods; objects
Open File dialog boxes, 541
open source software, 402
operators. *See also specific operators*
   associativity, 511
   precedence, 511
   summary of, 511–512
output. *See also* `java.io` package
   definition, 4
   redirecting, 161
output, formatting. *See also* `printf` method
   currency, 50
   format specifiers, 50
output, writing
   closing a file, 319, 523
   closing the stream, 523
   to the console window, 530
   to dialog boxes, 65
   opening a file, 318, 523
   output error, 523
   write operation, 523
`OutputStream` class, 523
ovals
   drawing, 180, 489–492, 519
   filling, 180, 489–492, 519
overloading methods
   accidentally, 428
   overview, 380
overriding methods
   abstract methods, 434–435
   accidental overloading, 428
   forcing, 434–435
   overview, 424–428
   preventing, 435

P

packages. *See also specific packages*
   importing classes from, 49
   Java library, 7
`paintComponent` method, `JComponent` class, 487–489, 493–496, 541
painting user-interface components
   `paintComponent` method, 487–489, 493–496, 541
   `repaint` method, 493–496, 518
panels. *See also* frames
   definition, 468
   grouping frame components, 468

user-interface components, 543
parameter variables, methods. *See also* variables
   animation, 208
   explicit, 374
   implicit, 373–374
   modifying, 209
   passing, 207–209
parentheses (())
   enclosing arguments, 13
   in expressions, unbalanced, 46–47
`parseDouble` method, `Double` class, 326, 525
`parseInt` method, `Integer` class, 326, 526
partially filled arrays, 254–255
passing arguments to methods
   with arrays, 268–269, 286–287
   from the command line, 330–333
   syntax, 13
passing parameters to methods
   overview, 207–209
   parameter variables to methods, 207–209
   parameters to methods, 286–287
passwords, generating randomly, 213
patents, definition, 336
`pathSeparator` method, `File` class, 522
paying off a loan (video example), 386
payroll processing example, 441
PCs. *See* personal computers
`peek` method, `Queue<E>` class, 537
peeking at queues, 537
Pentium floating-point bug, 48
percent sign (%)
   in format specifiers, 329
   modulus operator, description, 42
   modulus operator, online example, 45
personal computers, history of, 232–233
PGP (Pretty Good Privacy), 337
PI constant, 45*t*, 528
pictures, drawing. *See* drawing
piracy, software, 182
pixel manipulation, example, 175
plural words, counting (video example), 105
plus sign (+)
   addition operator, 41
   concatenation operator, 59–60
   for positive numbers, 328
plus signs (++), increment operator, 41
polymorphism
   animation, 431
   dynamic method lookup, 431, 433–434
   overview, 430–431
   sample program, 432–433
portability, Java programming language, 6
post-test loops. *See* do loops

pow method, Math class, 43*t*, 528
PowerTable.java class, 173
pre-test loops. *See* for loops; while loops
previous method, ListIterator<E> class, 536
primary storage, 3
primitive data types, 64
print commands demonstration program
    (online example), 14
printf method
    formatting output, 50–51
    newline character, 61
    overview, 318–320
    printing multiple values, 51
    PrintStream class, 524
    PrintWriter class, 318, 524
printing
    numerical values, 13–14
    print method, 318–320
    printStack method, 531
    PrintStream class, 523–524
    PrintStream out object, 530
    with/without line breaks, 14
printing, printf method
    formatting output, 50–51
    newline character, 61
    overview, 318–320
    printing multiple values, 51
    PrintStream class, 524
    PrintWriter class, 524
printing, println method
    overview, 318–320
    printing with line breaks, 51–52
printing, PrintWriter class
    closing automatically, 346
    description, 523–524
    writing text files, 318–320
printStackTrace method, 340
PrintStream out object, 530
printTriangle method, online example, 230
priority queues, 537
PriorityQueue<E> class, 537
private class implementation, 367–369
private instance variables, 366, 374
private keys, 336
programmers
    application, 53
    system, 53
programming environment. *See* Java
    programming environment
programming languages. *See also* Java
    programming language
    compilers, 5
    high-level, 5

programs
    basic syntax, 13
    compiling. *See* compiling programs
    definition, 2
    "Hello, World!" sample program, 8–9,
        12–14
    running. *See* running programs
    terminating, 530
prompts, reading from, 49
properties, getting, 537
Properties class, 537
pseudocode
    algorithm design, 18, 20–21
    writing, How To exercise, 54–56
public classes, 12
public instance variables, 374
public keys, 336
public reserved word, omitting, 453
put method, Map<K, V> class, 536
pyramid volume calculation example,
    212–213

Q
question mark (?), conditional operator, 87.
    See also if statements
QuestionDemo1.java class, 419
QuestionDemo2.java class, 425–426
QuestionDemo3.java class, 432–433
Question.java class, 418–419
Queue<E> class, 537
queues
    peeking at first element, 537
    priority, 537
quiz scores, example, 275–278
quiz-taking program, 417–419, 424–427,
    432–433

R
radians, converting to degrees, 528
radio buttons, 543
Random class, 537–538
random number generators
    definition, 176
    finding approximate solutions, 178–179
    generating random numbers, 176–177,
        537–538
    generating random passwords, 213,
        249–253
    Monte Carlo method, 178–179
    sample program, 176
    simulating die tosses, 177
Raymond, Eric, 402
read method, InputStream class, 523

readability, computing (video example), 330
readInBetween method, 216–217
reading
    binary data, 322–323
    web pages, online example, 321
reading, text files. *See also* Scanner class
    abnormal input, 326–327
    characters, 324
    consuming white space, 323–324, 327
    converting strings to numbers, 326
    How To, 333–336
    input mismatch exceptions, 326–327
    lines, 325–327
    mixing numbers, words, and lines, 327
    no such element exceptions, 327
    numbers, 327
    overview, 318–320
    words, 323–324, 327
Rectangle class, 520–521
rectangles
    drawing, 519, 520
    filling, 180, 519
    height/width, getting, 520
    intersections, computing, 520
    moving, 520, 521
    size, adjusting, 520, 521
    union, computing, 521
    x - y coordinates, getting, 520
recursive methods, 228–232
regular expressions, 330
relational operators
    combining, 113–114
    overview, 88
    summary of, 89*t*. *See also specific*
        operators
remainders, 42
remove method
    ArrayList<E> class, 292, 295–296, 532
    Collection<E> class, 534
    Iterator<E> class, 535
    Map<K, V> class, 537
    PriorityQueue<E> class, 537
removeFirst method, LinkedList<E> class, 536
removeLast method, LinkedList<E> class, 536
removing
    array list elements, 292, 295–296, 532
    collection elements, 534
    elements from linked lists, 536
    elements from priority queues, 537
    keys from maps, 537
repaint method, Component class,
        493–496, 518
repainting user-interface components,
        493–496, 518

replace method, String class, 530
reserved characters, in string literals, 60–61
reserved words. *See also specific words*
    summary of, 513–514
    in variables, 33
return statement, 210–211
return values, constructors, 375
return values, methods
    definition, 203
    missing, 212
    multiple, 211
    omitting, 214–215
    online example, 211
    specifying, 210–211
reusing methods, 215–217
Reverse.java class, 270–271
Richter scale, 96*t*
Rivest, Ron, 336
robot escaping from a maze (video
        example), 393
robot travel time computation, example, 58
rocket explosion, 347
rolling dice, example, 278
round method, Math class, 44*t*, 528
rounding
    floating-point numbers, 45
    online example, 45
    Pentium floating-point bug, 48
    round method, 44*t*, 528
roundoff errors
    comparing floating-point numbers, 91
    overview, 38–39
RSA encryption, 336
running programs
    in an integrated development
        environment, 8
    video example, 11
running totals, instance variables for,
        388–389
run-time errors, definition, 15
run-time exception, 529
RuntimeException class, 341, 529
Russian characters, 66

S

safety features, Java programming language,
        6
sales tax computation, example, 387
Save File dialog boxes, 541
Scanner class. *See also* reading, text files
    closing automatically, 346
    constructing with a string, 321
    description, 538
    reading characters from a string, 326

Scanner class (continued)
    reading numeric values, 49–50
    reading text files, 318–320
    sample program, 51–52
scope, variables in methods, 225–228
Scores.java class
    with array lists (online example), 296
    with arrays, 277–278
    sample code, 277–278
scroll panes, 543
scrollbars, adding to text areas, 484–485
searching
    arrays, 260, 267–268, 533
    binary search, 267–268, 533
    binarySearch method, Arrays class, 533
    binarySearch method, Collections
        class, 534
    collections, 534
    linear search, 260
secondary storage, 3
security
    buffer overrun attacks, 256
    worms, 256
semicolon (;)
    after an if condition, 86–87
    ending Java statements, 12–13
    omitting, 14
    path separator, 522
sentinel values, 158–161
SentinelDemo.java class, 158–160
set method
    ArrayList<E> class, 291, 532
    ListIterator<E> class, 536
setBorder method, JComponent class, 541
setColor method, Graphics class, 180, 520
setDefaultCloseOperation method, JFrame
        class, 467, 541
Set<E> class, 538
setEditable method
    editing text fields, 484
    JComboBox class, 540
    JTextComponent class, 545
setFocusable method, Component class, 518
setFont method, JComponent class, 541
setJMenuBar method, JFrame class, 541
setLayout method, Container class, 519
setLocation method, Rectangle class, 520
setPreferredSize method, Component
        class, 494, 518
setSelected method, AbstractButton
        class, 539
setSelectedItem method, JComboBox class, 540

setSize method
    Component class, 518
    Rectangle class, 521
setter methods, instance variables
        for, 390–391
setText method, JTextComponent class, 545
setTimeZone method, DateFormat class, 532
setTitle method, Frame class, 519
setVisible method, Component class, 518
Shamir, Adi, 336
shapes, drawing. See drawing
shared object references, 395–397
shipping cost computations
    online example, 108
    sample flowchart, 106–108
shopping for cars, example, 20–21
Short class, 294
short type, 40t
short-circuit evaluation, 114–115
showInputDialog method, JOptionPane
        class, 65, 542
showMessageDialog method, JOptionPane
        class, 542
showOpenDialog method, JFileChooser
        class, 322, 541
showSaveDialog method, JFileChooser
        class, 322, 541
simulation programs, 176
sin method, Math class, 43t, 528
sine, computing, 43t, 528
single quote ('), character literal
        delimiter, 61
size, arrays
    getting, 291
    increasing, 263–264
    requirements, estimating, 267
size method
    ArrayList<E> class, 291, 533
    Collection<E> class, 534
slash (/), division operator, 41, 42
slash asterisk... (/*...*/), long comment
        delimiter, 36
slash asterisks... (/**...*/)
    explanatory comment delimiter, 36
    method comment delimiter, 207
slashes (//), short comment delimiter, 35–36
smallest value, computing, 527, 528. See also
        minimum/maximum value, finding
software. See also programs
    definition, 2
    development schedules, 109–110
    piracy, 182

sort method
    Arrays class, 533
    Collections class, 534
sorting
    collections, 534
    lexicographic (dictionary) order of
        strings, 92–93
    numbers and letters, 93
    space characters, 93
    uppercase *vs.* lowercase strings, 93
sorting, arrays
    with the Java library, 267
    by swapping elements, 262
source code
    compiling programs, 9
    definition, 9
space characters, sorting, 93
spaces. *See also* white space
    after method names, 47
    around operators, 47
    in expressions, 47
    vs. tabs, 87
    in variable names, 33
spaghetti code, 106
spirals, drawing (video example), 181
spreadsheets, VisiCalc, 232–233
sqrt method, Math class, 43*t*, 528
square roots, 43*t*, 528
squares, drawing, 180–181
squelching exceptions, 345
Stallman, Richard, 402
stamp cost computation, example, 56
start method, Timer class, 544
stateChanged event, 545
static methods, 64–65, 205, 400–402
static reserved word, 400–402, 453
static variables, 400–402
stealing software, 182
stepwise refinement, 218–223
stop method, Timer class, 544
storage, primary *vs.* secondary, 3
storage devices. *See specific devices*
storyboards, 162–164. *See also* flowcharts
String class, 529–530
string literals
    definition, 59
    escape sequences, 60–61
    including reserved characters, 60–61
string variables, definition, 59
strings. *See also* characters
    case conversion, 530
    comparisons, 88–92, 529
    concatenating, 59–60

converting from arrays, 533
converting to, 442–443. *See also* toString
    method
converting to numbers, 326, 526
definition, 13, 59
drawing, 520
empty, 59
enclosing in quotation marks ("..."), 13
formatting, 329, 529
length, computing, 59, 529
line breaks, 60–61
positions, counting, 61
printing in a box, 214–215
reading from the console, 50
replacing, 530
returning characters from, 61. *See also*
    substrings
traversing with loops, 154
stubs, 224–225
subclasses. *See also* inheritance
    accessing private instance variables,
        423–424
    definition, 416
    implementing, 420–424
    online example, 423
    substitution principle, 416
    vs. superclasses, 424
    syntax, 422
substitution principle, 416
substring method, String class, 61–62, 530
substrings. *See also* strings
    extracting from strings, 61–62, 95, 530
    length, computing, 62
    sample program, 62–63
subtract method
    BigDecimal class, 40, 531
    BigInteger class, 40, 531
summing array values, 259
super reserved word
    calling a superclass method, 425
    calling the superclass constructor, 429
    omitting, 429
superclasses. *See also* inheritance;
        Object class
    constructors, calling, 429–430
    definition, 416
    vs. subclasses, 424
    substitution principle, 416
superclasses, instance variables
    protecting, 436
    replicating, 423–424
swapping array elements, 262, 279–281

switch statements. *See also* if statements
    branch on floating-point values, 99
    break instructions, 99
    overview, 99
    terminating, 99
symmetric bounds, 155
syntax errors. *See* compile-time errors
System class, 530
system programmers, 53
System.out.print method, 14
System.out.println method, 14

T
tabs
    aligning text, 87
    indenting nested statements, 87
    vs. spaces, 87
tally counter, example, 364–367
tan method, Math class, 43*t*, 528
tangent, computing, 43*t*, 528
TaxCalculator.java class, 101–102
taxes. *See* income tax
terminating steps, 19
test cases
    boundary conditions, 108
    coverage, 108
    overview, 108–109
tester classes, 380–382
testing
    classes, 380–382
    collection elements, 534
    data types, 444–446
    digits, 324*t*
    letters, 324*t*
    lowercase letters, 324*t*
    null reference, 397
    strings for equality, 90
    unit testing, 380–382
    uppercase letters, 324*t*
    white space, 324*t*
text
    aligning with tabs, 87
    drawing on user-interface components, 489–492
    justifying (video example), 233
text areas
    appending text to, 543
    creating, 483–486, 543
    definition, 483–486
    scrollbars, 484–485
    setting to read-only, 484
text fields
    creating, 481–483, 544
    definition, 481

    labeling, 481–483
text files, reading. *See* reading, text files
text input
    multiple lines, 483–486
    single lines, 481–483
    text areas, 483–486
    text fields, 481–483
text strings, identifying to the compiler, 13
Thai characters, 66
this references, 397–399
threads, interrupting with exceptions, 526
throw statement, 338
Throwable class, 530–531
throwing exceptions, 338–339, 345, 530–531
throws clause, 342–343
Thrun, Sebastian, 119
tile layout, 57–58
time. *See* date and time
time zone, setting, 532
Timer class, 544
timers, 544
TitledBorder class, 544
titles, frames, 519
toDegrees method, Math class, 43*t*, 528
toLowerCase method, String class, 530
toRadians method, Math class, 43*t*, 528
toString method
    Arrays class, 259, 533
    Integer class, 526
    Object class, 442–443, 446–447, 529
toString method, Object class, 442–443
Total.java class, 319–320
toUpperCase method, String class, 530
tracing code. *See also* hand-tracing
    instance variables, 386–388
    logging messages, 110
    nested loops (animation), 285
    recursions (animation), 230
    tile layout, 57–58
tracing code, methods
    animation, 220
    examples, 223–224, 386–388
transistors, in computers, 3
translate method, Rectangle class, 521
translating languages, 119
travel time computation, example, 58
traversing
    array lists, 292
    arrays, 257–258
    collection elements, 534
    linked lists, 536
    lists, 535–536
tree maps, 538
tree sets, 539

TreeMap<K, V> class, 538
TreeSet<E> class, 539
triangle, printing, 229–232
TrianglePrinter program,
 online example, 230
truth tables, 111
two-dimensional arrays. *See* arrays, two-
 dimensional
TwoRowsOfSquares.java class, 181

U

unambiguous steps, 19
unchecked exceptions, 341–343
undeclared variables, 36–37
underscore (_), in variable names, 33
Unicode characters
 Latin/Latin-1 subsets, 507–509
 overview, 66
 testing for, 524–525
uninitialized
 constructors, 376
 instance variables, 378–379
 variables, 36–37
union method, Rectangle class, 521
union of rectangles, computing, 521
uppercase letters. *See also* case sensitivity
 camel case, 33
 constant names, 35
 in the middle of words, 33
 testing for, 324*t*
uppercase strings, sorting, 93
useDelimiter method, Scanner class,
 324, 330, 538
user events. *See* events
user interface, definition, 233. *See also*
 graphical user interface
user-interface components. *See also* java.awt
 package; javax.swing package
 adding to containers, 518
 borders, 517, 541, 544
 button groups, 540
 button labels, 540
 buttons, 467, 539
 check boxes, 540
 coloring, 490, 518, 520
 combo boxes, 540
 confirmation dialog boxes, 542
 detecting user actions. *See* event listeners
 file chooser, 541
 fonts, 541
 in frames, 467–468, 541
 grid layout, 520
 grouping, 468
 height, getting, 518

horizontal sliders, 543
image icons, 540
input dialog boxes, 65, 542
labels, 542
menu bars, 542
menu items, 542
menus, 542
painting, 541
panels, 543
preferred size, setting, 518
radio buttons, 543
receiving input focus, 518
repainting, 518
scroll panes, 543
showing/hiding, 518
size, setting, 518
width, getting, 518
user-interface components, text
 editable, 545
 returning, 545
 setting, 545
 text areas, 543
 text fields, 544

V

variable types
 numbers, 32–33. *See also* floating-point
  numbers; integers
 specifying, 31
variables. *See also* Boolean variables
 and operators; constants; instance
 variables; parameter variables
 assignment statements, 34
 case sensitivity, 33
 declaring, 30–32
 definition, 30
 distinguishing from constants, 35
 final, 35
 immutable, 35
 initializing, 31, 34
 limiting to a set of values. *See*
  enumeration types
 naming conventions, 33, 38
 reserved words, 33
 sample program, 36
 static, 400–402
 syntax, 31
 undeclared, 36–37
 uninitialized, 36–37
variables, methods
 duplicate names, 226–227
 local, 225
 scope, 225–228
vending machine example, 54–56

`VendingMachine.java` class, 56
versions, Java programming language, 7t
vertical lines (||), *or* operator
    definition, 111
    flowchart, 112
    negating, 115–116
    vs. and operator, 114
    short-circuit evaluation, 114–115
VisiCalc program, 232–233
void reserved word
    in methods without return values, 214
    in constructors, 379
`Volume1.java` class, 36
voting machines, 394

W

web pages, reading (online example), 321
`while` loops. *See also* loops
    body of, 141
    overview, 140–141
    sample program, 142–143
    syntax, 141
white space. *See also* spaces
    consuming, 323–324, 327
    testing for, 324t
Wilkes, Maurice, 146
words, reading text files, 323–324, 327
wrapper classes
    array lists, 293–294
    `Boolean`, 294

`Byte`, 294
`Character`, 294, 524–525
`Double`, 294, 525
`Float`, 294
`Integer`, 294, 526
`Long`, 294
    overview, 293–294. *See also specific classes*
`Short`, 294
`write` method, `OutputStream` class, 523
writing. *See also* output
    binary data, 322–323
    programs. *See* software, development schedules
writing, text files
    format flags, 328–329
    format specifiers, 328–329
    formatting output, 328–329
    How To, 333–336
    overview, 318–320

X

x - y coordinates for rectangles, getting, 520

Z

zeroes, leading, 328t

ILLUSTRATION CREDITS

Preface
Page vii: © Terraxplorer/iStockphoto.

Chapter 1
Page 1, 2: © JanPietruszka/iStockphoto.
Page 3, 22 (left): © Amorphis/iStockphoto.
Page 3 (right): PhotoDisc, Inc./Getty Images.
Page 5 (top): © UPPA/Photoshot.
Page 5 (bottom): James Sullivan/Getty Images.
Page 11, 22: © Tatiana Popova/iStockphoto.
Page 12, 22: © Amanda Rohde/iStockphoto
Page 15, 23: © CarlssonInc/iStockphoto.
Page 17: © mammamaart/iStockphoto.
Page 19, 23: © Claudiad/iStockphoto.
Page 20: © dlewis33/iStockphoto.
Page 21 (top): © rban/iStockphoto.
Page 21 (bottom): © YinYang/iStockphoto.

Chapter 2
Page 29, 30: © Eyeidea/iStockphoto.
Page 30 (middle): © blackred/iStockphoto; © travis manley/iStockphoto.
Page 30 (bottom), 66: Javier Larrea/Age Fotostock.
Page 31, 66: © Ingenui/iStockphoto.
Page 33, 66: © GlobalP/iStockphoto.
Page 37, 67: © jgroup/iStockphoto.
Page 39: © FinnBrandt/iStockphoto.
Page 41: © arakonyunus/iStockphoto.
Page 42, 67: © Michael Flippo/iStockphoto.
Page 46: © Croko/iStockphoto.
Page 47: © Maxfocus/iStockphoto.
Page 48: Courtesy of Larry Hoyle, Institute for Policy & Social Research, University of Kansas.
Page 49, 67: © Media Bakery.
Page 51, 67: © Koele/iStockphoto.
Page 55: Photos.com/Jupiter Images.
Page 58: Courtesy NASA/JPL-Caltech.
Page 59, 67: © essxboy/iStockphoto.
Page 61, 67: © slpix/iStockphoto.
Page 62, 67: © Rich Legg/iStockphoto.
Page 65: © janrysavy/iStockphoto.

Page 66 (left): © pvachier/iStockphoto.
Page 66 (center): © jcarillet/iStockphoto.
Page 66 (right): © Saipg/iStockphoto.
Page 70: © Media Bakery.
Page 72: © asiseeit/iStockphoto.
Page 74: © José Luis Gutiérrez/iStockphoto.
Page 75: © Captainflash/iStockphoto.
Page 77: © TebNad/iStockphoto.

Chapter 3
Page 81, 82: © zennie/iStockphoto.
Page 82: © DrGrounds/iStockphoto.
Page 83, 120: © Media Bakery.
Page 86: © TACrafts/iStockphoto.
Page 87: Photo by Vincent LaRussa/John Wiley & Sons, Inc.
Page 88, 120: © arturbo/iStockphoto.
Page 91: © caracterdesign/iStockphoto.
Page 92, 120: Corbis Digital Stock.
Page 93: © MikePanic/iStockphoto.
Page 95: Bob Daemmrich/Getty Images.
Page 96, 120: © kevinruss/iStockphoto.
Page 99: © travelpixpro/iStockphoto.
Page 100, 120: © ericsphotography/iStockphoto.
Page 103: © thomasd007/iStockphoto.
Page 105: © mikie11/iStockphoto.
Page 108: © Ekspansio/iStockphoto.
Page 110: Bananastock/Media Bakery.
Page 111, 121: Cusp/SuperStock.
Page 112: © toos/iStockphoto.
Page 115: © YouraPechkin/iStockphoto.
Page 116, 121: Tetra Images/Media Bakery.
Page 118 (top): © jeanma85/iStockphoto.
Page 118 (bottom): © bcnjaminalbiach/iStockphoto.
Page 119: Vaughn Youtz/Zuma Press.
Page 128 (top): © rotofrank/iStockphoto.
Page 1298 (bottom): © lillisphotography/iStockphoto.
Page 130: © Straitshooter/iStockphoto.
Page 131: © Mark Evans/iStockphoto.
Page 132: © drxy/iStockphoto.
Page 133 (top): © nano/iStockphoto

Page 133 (bottom): © Photobuff/
iStockphoto.

Page 134: © rotofrank/iStockphoto.

Page 135: Courtesy NASA/JPL-Caltech.

Chapter 4

Page 139, 140 (top): © photo75/
iStockphoto.

Page 140 (middle): © AlterYourReality/
iStockphoto.

Page 140 (bottom), 182: © mmac72/
iStockphoto.

Page 144: © MsSponge/iStockphoto.

Page 145: © ohiophoto/iStockphoto.

Page 146: Courtesy of the Naval Surface
Warfare Center, Dahlgren, VA., 1988.
NHHC Collection.

Pages 147–149 (paperclip): © Yvan Dubé/
iStockphoto.

Page 151, 183: © Enrico Fianchini/
iStockphoto.

Page 156: © akaplummer/iStockphoto.

Page 158, 183: © Rhoberazzi/iStockphoto.

Page 161: © Michal_edo/iStockphoto.

Page 162: Courtesy of Martin Hardee.

Page 166 (top): © Hiob/iStockphoto.

Page 166 (bottom): © drflet/iStockphoto.

Page 167: © CEFutcher/iStockphoto.

Page 168: © tingberg/iStockphoto.

Page 169: © Stevegeer/iStockphoto.

Page 172 (top): © MorePixels/iStockphoto.

Page 172 (bottom), 183: © davejkahn/
iStockphoto.

Page 175: Cay Horstmann.

Page 177, 183: © ktsimage/iStockphoto.

Page 178: © timstarkey/iStockphoto.

Page 181: © Rpsycho/iStockphoto.

Page 182 (top): © RapidEye/iStockphoto.

Page 182 (bottom): © thomasd007/
iStockphoto.

Page 189: © Anthony Rosenberg/
iStockphoto.

Page 191: © GlobalP/iStockphoto.

Page 194: © hatman12/iStockphoto.

Page 195 (top): © Charles Gibson/
iStockphoto.

Page 195 (bottom): © MOF/iStockphoto.

Page 196 (top): *Introduction to Engineering
Programming: Solving Problems with
Algorithms*, James P. Holloway (John
Wiley & Sons, Inc., 2004) Reprinted with
permission of John Wiley & Sons, Inc.

Page 196 (middle): © Snowleopard1/
iStockphoto.

Page 196 (bottom): © zig4photo/
iStockphoto.

Chapter 5

Page 201, 202: © attator/iStockphoto.

Page 203, 234: © yenwen/iStockphoto.

Page 204: © studioaraminta/iStockphoto.

Page 205, 234: © princessdlaf/iStockphoto.

Page 207 (collage), 234: © christine
balderas/iStockphoto (cherry pie);
© inhauscreative/iStockphoto (apple
pie); © RedHelga/iStockphoto (cherries);
© ZoneCreative/iStockphoto (apples).

Page 210, 234: © Tashka/iStockphoto.

Page 212: © holgs/iStockphoto.

Page 214, 234: © jgroup/iStockphoto.

Page 217: © Lawrence Sawyer/iStockphoto.

Page 218, 234: © AdShooter/iStockphoto.

Page 219: © YinYang/iStockphoto.

Page 224: © lillisphotography/iStockphoto.

Page 225: © pkline/iStockphoto.

Page 226 (collage): © jchamp/iStockphoto
(Railway and Main) (also 235);
© StevenCarrieJohnson/iStockphoto
(Main and N. Putnam); © jsmith/
iStockphoto (Main and South St.).

Page 228: © Janice Richard/iStockphoto.

Page 230, 235: © nicodemos/iStockphoto.

Page 233 (top): © Kenneth C. Zirkel/
iStockphoto.

Page 233 (bottom): Reprint Courtesy of
International Business Machine
Corporation, copyright © International
Business Machines Corporation.

Page 236: © stacey_newman/iStockphoto.

Page 240: © mbbirdy/iStockphoto.

Page 241: © Straitshooter/iStockphoto.

Page 243: © MichaelJay/iStockphoto.

Page 245: © alacatr/iStockphoto.

Chapter 6

Page 249, 250: © traveler1116/iStockphoto.

Page 252, 300: © Luckie8/iStockphoto.

Page 254, 300: © AlterYourReality/
iStockphoto.

Page 257: © nullplus/iStockphoto.

Page 259 (top): © CEFutcher/iStockphoto.

Chapter 15 ✚

Page 669, 670: © nicholas belton/ iStockphoto.

Page 671 (top left): © Filip Fuxa/ iStockphoto.

Page 671 (top center): © parema/ iStockphoto.

Page 671 (top right): © Vladimir Trenin/ iStockphoto.

Page 671 (bottom), 702: © david franklin/ iStockphoto.

Page 673, 701: © andrea laurita/ iStockphoto.

Page 678: © Denis Vorob'yev/iStockphoto.

Page 679, 702: © Alfredo Ragazzoni/ iStockphoto.

Page 680, 702: © Volkan Ersoy/ iStockphoto.

Page 686, 701: © Tom Hahn/iStockphoto.

Page 688, 702: © one clear vision/ iStockphoto.

Page 690 (top), 702: © John Madden/ iStockphoto.

Page 690 (bottom): © budgetstockphoto/ iStockphoto.

Page 691, 700, 702: Photodisc/Punchstock.

Page 692: © paul kline/iStockphoto.

Page 695, 702: © Jorge Delgado/ iStockphoto.

Page 698: © Skip ODonnell/iStockphoto.

Page 701 (top): Courtesy of Nigel Tout.

Page 701: © Ermin Gutenberger/ iStockphoto.

Page 706: © martin mcelligott/iStockphoto.

Page 708: © Luis Carlos Torres/ iStockphoto.